ORIGINS AND ORDEALS OF THE WESTERN
WORLD

ORIGINS AND ORDEALS
OF THE WESTERN WORLD

Lessons from
Our Heritage in History

by
W. G. HARDY
Professor Emeritus and Formerly
Head, Department of Classics
University of Alberta

SCHENKMAN PUBLISHING COMPANY

Cambridge   Massachusetts

Copyright © 1968
Schenkman Publishing Company, Inc.
Cambridge, Mass. 02138

Printed in the United States of America

Library of Congress Catalog Card Number

66-16760

Table of Contents

PART III. OUR HERITAGE FROM ROME

FOREWORD

In the 17th century A.D. an Anglican Archbishop, James Ussher, confidently fixed the year of creation as 4004 B.C., and until about 100 years ago few people would accept the view that mankind or any other form of life could have existed before that date. Today, it is estimated that the age of the earth is between four and a half and five billion years. Furthermore, although there are no final answers, it is thought that the earliest forms of life on this planet appeared about two billion years ago. Then as the long eras[1] went by amoebae (single-celled organisms) developed into trilobites, fishes, amphibians and reptiles, including the dinosaurs, until, about sixty-three million years ago, in the Mesozoic era, mammals came into existence. Among them were the first small and primitive primates, the order of animals to which mankind belongs; but it was not until close to two million years ago that the first "near-men" (hominids) came on the stage. As compared to the age of the earth or of some other still-existent life-forms, man's time-span is brief. It has been calculated that, if the time-span of the earth were to be compressed into a single year, man would not appear until about 10.45 p.m. of the very last day of that year and that the whole of recorded history would be crowded into its last minute, that is between 11.59 p.m. and 12 o'clock midnight of a mythical December 31st.

The brief time-span of the human race is, however, the material of history. Since the story of mankind is a unit, since, anatomically, man is an animal who came to life as a part of the development of all life, and since his history and fate, even as he reaches into interstellar space, is linked with the history of the earth, the historian of today must depend for much of his information on experts, such as the geologist, the paleontologist, the paleobotanist, the astronomer and the physicist, as well as on the archeologist, epigrapher, paleographer and anthropologist. For convenience, although the divisions are artificial, the story of man is divided into prehistory and recorded history; and recorded history is separated into modern, medieval and ancient.

7

Ancient history used to be regarded as the story of Greece and Rome. Today, it includes the early civilizations of Egypt and Mesopotamia as well as the slightly later urban complexes of the Indus Valley of India and the Hwang-Ho Valley of China and takes a fleeting glance at the findings of prehistory. Its scope, then, is so extensive that any specialized and authoritative study, as, indeed, is true in any field of history, must concentrate on a single age, or people, or phase, or individual. A survey of ancient history, on the other hand, such as this book is, depends heavily on borrowed material and is, necessarily, marred by omissions and over-simplifications. Furthermore, ancient history is not static. Instead, new discoveries are constantly adding to the available facts and altering or supplementing the interpretation of them. There is, therefore, no pretence that this volume offers a definitive or original picture of ancient life, but it is hoped that it will be an invitation to the student or the non-specialist to delve into what interests him.

Sources and Dating

In prehistory, the historian's sources are the material remains of early man as discovered by the archeologist and anthropologist, and the interpretation by experts of the significance of those remains, whether they be stone tools, campsites, fossilized skeletal remnants or the like. It seems obvious, for example, that if the bones or tools of primitive man are found in conjunction with the bones of extinct animals such as the mammoth or the sabre-tooth tiger, man existed in that same period. For recorded ancient history the primary sources are either archeological, such as the ruins of buildings or the remains of pottery, toys, weapons and other objects, or records and histories written during ancient times. To these are to be added the art and literature of the various periods.

Dating in prehistory cannot be precise and is often conjectural, although it is aided by modern techniques such as C14 dating[2] (which can also be used for dating recorded history) and potassium-argon 40 dating[3]. Even in recorded history dates from before 1000 B.C. frequently vary. In general, however, that sequence of events, which is so important to the student, can be established.

Savages, Barbarians and Civilized Man

Although hominids appear to have existed for close to two million years, the time-span of true men is uncertain but it seems that their existence for at least half a million years can be proved. For most of that 500,000 years early men were hunters and food-gatherers and their culture is classified as "savage". Then, in the Neolithic period, for close to 4000 years but varying in time in different areas, there were no cities but men were food-producers, living in villages or small towns. This stage of development is often called "barbarianism". It should be noted that savages and barbarians as well as civilized men possess "cultures". Culture in this sense of the word does not mean the "culture" of a bacteria or the right way to hold a fork or even a proper knowledge and appreciation of art and literature, but is the term applied to the whole way of life of a group, people or nation at a given time—their customs, costumes, political and social organization, religious beliefs and the like as well as their housing, arts, crafts and technical achievements. One should further remember that in considerable sections of the modern world, peoples are still living in a savage or barbarian stage of culture.

Eventually, between 5500 and 5000 years ago the first civilizations came into being in Mesopotamia and Egypt. Early civilizations are characterized by city life, the use of metals, complex political, social and religious systems, the keeping of written records, and the development of specialists in the arts and crafts as well as in trade, communications and property. As compared to mankind's time-span civilization is as yet only a short-lived phenomenon. It would not have become possible, either, without the slow development and the inventions, such as speech and the use of fire, of Stone Age men.

The Value of History

Most of our modern way of life is deeply rooted in the past. The study of ancient history, in particular, is essential for a comprehension of today's western civilization. Here are the origins of our political and religious systems, our artistic concepts, of many of our beliefs, prejudices and ideals and even of part of our technology. In the fields of human conduct and organization we can often recognize the same problems as those we face and analyze the attempts to solve them. He who can look deeply into our past is more likely to be able to understand our present and conjecture our future. Above all, the study of history satisfies the desire to know, which is, perhaps, one of the highest of human attributes.

Notes to the Foreword

1. Apart from the Azoic (without life) era of the earth, the geologist divides the time span since the first rocks were laid down into five eras according to the evidence in them of the kind of life in each era. These five eras are the Archeozoic, Proterozoic, Paleozoic, Mesozoic and Cenozoic. These adjectival names are derived from Greek, the Cenozoic era for instance, meaning "the era of recent life". Each era consists of periods, generally according to its rock formations, the periods in the Cenozoic being the Tertiary and the Quaternary. Each period is further subdivided into epochs. Thus, the Quaternary consists of the Pleistocene epoch (most forms of life, recent) and the Holocene (all forms of life, recent). In addition, some phases are called "Ages". The Cenozoic, for example, is designated as the "Age of Mammals" just as the Mesozoic is called the "Age of Reptiles".

2. C14 dating depends on the fact that radioactive carbon (C14 which is different from ordinary carbon, C12) is liberated in the earth's atmosphere by the interaction of cosmic rays with nitrogen. The C14, combined with oxygen, is absorbed as radioactive carbon dioxide in a fixed percentage into the structure of all living organisms. When the organism dies, the intake ceases and the C14 begins to disintegrate at a fixed rate. On January 10, 1961 as a correction to previous findings, it was announced that it takes 5760 years for one-half the C14 to disappear. Furthermore, after another 5760 years one-half of the remaining C14 has disintegrated. Consequently, by taking a fixed amount of material, such as bone, charcoal or wood, from an ancient site and measuring how much of the original C14 is left, the date of the material can be determined with a fair amount of accuracy. C14 dates can be used as far back as 40,000 or 50,000 years and, in one case, in attempting to fix the dates during the last glaciation of Europe, was used as far back as 70,000 years.

3. Potassium-argon dating is based on the breaking down of potassium 40 at a fixed rate into calcium 40 and argon 40. Argon 40 can be distinguished from other types of argon, and it takes roughly 1,300,000 years for half of the potassium 40 to be transformed into calcium 40 and argon 40. This dating method, therefore, requires a rock with a potassium-bearing mineral in it but can reach far backward into time. It is now being used to date rock strata in which bones of early men have been found.

PART I

Early Man and the Civilizations of the Near and Middle East

The foundations of our western civilization, except for the Hebrew contribution, were laid by the Greeks and Romans. A considerable part of Greek and Roman culture, however, was rooted in the early civilizations of the Near and Middle East and, furthermore, those areas continued to influence the classical world throughout its history. Yet the first cities of Egypt and Mesopotamia and, likewise, those of the Indus Valley in India and of the Hwang-Ho River in China, would not have been possible without the contributions of Paleolithic, Mesolithic and Neolithic men. The first savage hunter who picked up a stone to fashion it into a pebble chopper or a fist hatchet unwittingly started humanity on the long and stumbling road to civilization.

CHAPTER 1

Paleolithic or Old Stone Age Man

Paleolithic is an adjective derived from two Greek words, *palaios*—"old" and *lithos*—"stone". According to modern estimates the Paleolithic age reached backward from some 10,000 years ago to around 1,750,000 years ago. The evidence for the development of early man during this period is scanty, consisting chiefly of stone or bone implements and of a number of fossilized skeletons or, more properly, parts of skeletons. Inevitably, many of the conclusions which have been reached by archeologists and anthropologists are conjectural, and subject to revision. Yet, if we consider that the scientific study of this period is scarcely more than a century old, that large areas of the globe are unexplored from an archeological and anthropological point of view, and that there was strong opposition rooted in human prejudices, the advance in knowledge about early man, particularly in the last half a century, has been striking.

Near-Men and Men

The theory of the evolution of life from primitive forms to higher and more complex types is now generally accepted. Similarly the thesis of the evolution of man seems to fit what facts are known, although there is disagreement about his beginnings.

The primates existent at present include tarsiers, lemurs, monkeys, apes and mankind itself. All share a number of characteristics such as comparatively large and complex brains. Man's "Super-Family" (*Hominoidae*) consists of monkeys, apes and men, all of whom, for example, possess stereoscopic vision. Man's "family", the *Hominidae*, is divided into hominids ("near-men") and *Homo*. Apart from a possible common ancestor for man's Super-Family, it is thought that the great apes and men may have both evolved from one original type but that, perhaps about twelve million years ago, the ancestors of mankind and the great apes began to diverge.

12

All the primates were less specialized than other animals. This fact is believed to account for their survival and development. Humanity's ancestral stock appears to have been the least specialized of the primates. Man's evolution was, in particular, toward an erect posture, the opposability of the thumb leading to manual dexterity and the handling of tools, and, above all, toward the expansion and complexity of the brain.

Today, despite differences in color and certain other physical characteristics, there is only one species of man, *Homo Sapiens* (Man Who Thinks) on this planet.[1] In earlier times, other genera and species existed, although there is often disagreement about how the scanty skeletal specimens of them are to be classified. The Australopithecines (*australis*—"south" and *pithecus*—"ape") were first discovered in South Africa in the 1930s. These beings, of whom there were several types, walked erect and seem to have used tools but their brain capacity was only 450–500 cc. (cubic centimeters) as compared to modern man's average of 1350 cc. Some of these Australopithecines were on this earth about a million or more years ago.

In 1959 and 1960 the British anthropologist, Dr. L. S. B. Leakey, uncovered in the Olduvai Gorge of Tanganyika in East Africa the bones and stone tools of creatures to whom he gave the name of *Homo Zinjanthropus boiseii*. The fossil remains of this "Zinj Man" were found in conjunction with the bones of a six-foot-tall sheep, a pig as big as a rhinoceros, a giant ostrich and a short-necked giraffe. By potassium-argon dating of the strata just below Zinj Man, he is placed at around 1,750,000 years ago. Although claimed at first to be an ancestor of man he is now classified as an Australopithecine.

Still more recently Dr. Leakey discovered in the same gorge the skeletal remains of even older man-like beings who although small-brained, apparently made and used tools, ate meat and vegetables and made rough shelters. To these creatures Leakey has assigned the name of *Homo habilis* (Man Having Ability). Some experts agree that they are a new species of man; others disagree.

In any case these various discoveries push the existence of man-like creatures back to close to two millions of years ago. Other finds of early men or near-men have been made at Kanam and Kanjera on the shores of Lake Victoria Nyanza in Kenya. Africa appears to have been an early home of hominids and, perhaps, of men. As for the Australopithecines, the distinguished anthropologist, Dr. Carleton Coon, believes that they extended from South Africa as far as China. Whether or not they were part of true man's ancestral line is a matter of debate.

Other skeletal remains of an early date are regarded as belonging to true man. Among these might be noted *Pithecanthropus* (Ape-Man) found

in Java in 1891 (brain capacity c. 900 cc.) and dated at 500,000 years ago
and *Sinanthropus* (brain capacity c. 1000–1225 cc.), first discovered in a
cave near Pekin in 1927, and dated at 360,000 years back. *Sinanthropus*
made and used tools, lived in caves, knew of fire, stored hackberries
and was, almost certainly, a cannibal. Some authorities think him to be
an ancestor of today's Mongoloids. Similarly, because of the discoveries
of intermediate forms of men in Java, it is believed by anthropologists
such as Professors Weidenrich and Coon that *Pithecanthropus* was the
ancestor of the Australoids.

In Europe, the oldest remnant of early man is the lower jaw found in
the village of Mauer six miles southeast of Heidelberg in Germany in
1907. Known as *Homo heidelbergensis*, this man was roughly contemporary with *Sinanthropus*. A number of other skulls and skeletal
remains of early men, such as the Ehringsdorf, Steinheim, Swanscombe
and Fontéchevade specimens, have also been unearthed in Western
Europe and Great Britain. Then, about 75,000 years ago, *Homo neander-
thalensis* came into Europe, possibly from the East. This type possessed
a definite culture but was replaced about 40,000 to 35,000 years ago by
men who definitely belonged to *Homo sapiens*.

Whether *Homo sapiens* developed alongside other species of men, as
the Swanscombe and Fontéchevade skulls might suggest, or whether he
evolved from the older species is still a matter of debate. All types of men,
however, made and used tools.

Man, the Tool-Maker

The first man-made implements were probably of wood, such as the
spear-point of yew found in a peat bog at Clacton-on-Sea in England, or
of bone. Quite early, however, primitive man began to fashion tools of
stone. The first of these were either pebble-choppers or pear-shaped
fist-hatchets, pointed at one end and fitted for grasping at the other. From
these crude implements Old Stone Age men, using both percussion and
pressure techniques, advanced to more specialized flake and, eventually,
blade tools for scrapers, knives, spear-points, awls, needles, chisels and
the like. Artifacts of this sort aid the specialist in estimating cultural
progress in the Paleolithic period; and it was the manufacture and use of
tools which set mankind's feet on the road to his mastery of the earth.

For the development of Paleolithic culture the most plentiful evidence
comes from Western Europe. One reason for this fact is that this part of
the globe has been more accessible to scholars. Furthermore; although the
Ice Age in Eurasia and North America provides a sort of gigantic time-
clock for both continents, the Americas were not inhabited by man until
at the earliest, according to present reckoning, 25,000 to 30,000 years ago.

The Ice Age in Europe

The Ice Age in Eurasia and North America began around 600,000 years ago during the Pleistocene epoch. One cause may have been the uplifting of the Himalayas, Alps and Rocky Mountains to new heights. There may also have been changes in the sun's radiation. Whatever the reasons, there were four glaciations, known in Europe as the Günz, Mindel, Riss and Würm glaciations. In North America at the maximum, ice, in places a thousand or more feet deep, covered most of Canada and reached into the United States as far as the Missouri and Ohio valleys. In Eurasia, although the Günz glaciation was more local, the other three were vast ice-caps which in their furthest advance blanketed the Scandinavian countries, Great Britain as far as the Thames Valley, North Germany and Northern Russia; while glaciers also flowed out from the Pyrenees, Alps and the Caucasus. So much water was locked up in the ice that Great Britain was joined to Europe and there was a land-bridge at Gibraltar and another between Italy, Sicily and North Africa. Early man could travel back and forth.

In between the glaciations, which are thought to have lasted only about 13 per cent of the time, there were warm periods, called interglacials. The second interglacial, for example, between the Mindel and Riss ice sheets, is estimated to have endured for 180,000 to 240,000 years. Furthermore, there were minor retreats of the ice, known as interstadials. Thus, the last or Würm glaciation, had two interstadials, dividing it into Würm I, II, and III. Würm III finally receded about 10,000 years ago to about where the glaciation is at present. The period since the withdrawal of Würm III is called post-glacial; but we may only be living in an interglacial period.

Climate, Fauna and Flora During the Ice Age

During the glaciations the climate in Europe was arctic or sub-arctic. On the ice-cap, as in Antarctica or Greenland of today, very little could live. South of the ice was barren tundra. Further south, France, Spain and Italy, though cold in winter, were more habitable. Arctic foxes, musk-oxen and the like eked out an existence on the tundra; while southward was the home of the woolly mammoth, the woolly rhinoceros, the rein-deer, the cave-bear and other animals.

Throughout the interglacials, however, Europe tended to be warmer and moister than it is now, and there were dense forests, swamps and jungles. Bones of straight-tusked elephants, rhinoceroses, camels and sabre-tooth tigers have been found, some as far north as the Thames Valley. Whenever the ice began to encase the land again, these animals moved south; but there were transitional periods when much of Europe was steppe-land and herds of bison and of wild cattle and horses abounded.

Meanwhile, during the glaciations what is now the Sahara desert, along with the whole of Near and Middle East, seems to have been well-watered grassland or swamp or jungle. Pictures, for example, of men swimming or hunting hippopotamuses are found on rocks in the Sahara desert. But, whenever the ice retreated, the whole area dried up.

Alternations of glacial cold and interglacial warmth and of arctic as contrasted to tropical or sub-tropical flora and fauna were important factors in early man's development in Western Europe. Furthermore, the land-bridges made interchange of peoples between North Africa and Europe possible while steppe-land or tundra south of the ice provided a migration route from the East.

The Development of Paleolithic Man in Europe

The glaciations undoubtedly destroyed much of the evidence for man's existence in Europe. The first proof of European habitation, apart from the "dawn-stones" (eoliths) which are disputed, come from stone tools found in river gravels. These tools (called Abbevillian-Chellean) are uniform in their style of manufacture from England to India and the Cape of Good Hope. No bones of Chellean man have as yet been found in Europe but in 1961 Dr. Leakey discovered the skull of a Chellean man along with his stone tools in the Olduvai gorge.

From the evidence of the stone tools it is certain that early man lived in Europe at the end of the first interglacial and the beginning of the second or Mindel glaciation. There were also "Europeans" during the second interglacial, as proved both by tools (the Acheulian type) and the skeletal remains of men such as Heidelberg, Swanscombe and Fonté-chevade Man. Presumably the men of this period used fire, speech and were organized into packs to hunt animals. Then, towards the end of the third interglacial, as already noted, Neanderthal man, so named from the Neander River near Düsseldorf in Germany where the first Neanderthal skeleton was found in 1856, appeared in Europe.

Some authorities think that Neanderthal Man may have been a descendant of Heidelberg Man; most scholars, however, believe that he came from the East. At any rate when the fourth or Würm glaciation began, the Neanderthals took to caves in Switzerland, France and elsewhere as protection against the cold. In these caves, in some cases previously inhabited, are found Neanderthaloid bones, stone tools and the bones of the animals he hunted. Neanderthal men and women may well be among our physical ancestors.

How Neanderthal Man Lived

To visualize the life of the Neanderthals, let us suppose that we can step back some 60,000 years in time. It is a winter night. We are about 300 miles south and west of where Paris now stands. The valley we are following is to be known 60,000 years later as the valley of the Vézère river. It is an area which today is a tumbled sea of rugged, tree-clad hills and deep and tortuous valleys, the region known as the Dordogne—and often called "the Museum of Primitive Man."

60,000 years ago a wind from the ice-cap beyond the barren tundra to the north is shrieking down the valley, driving the whirling snow before it. An arctic fox yaps. There is the howl of wolves. In a nook sheltered by an outcrop of rock, a clump of musk-oxen is massed, cows and yearlings in the centre, the shaggy-haired, massive-horned bulls facing outwards.

It looks like the land God is said to have given to Cain. Then, in the distance, we see a tiny spot of light flickering. If we come close and, ourselves unseen, look in, there in a cave a fire is burning. Around it is huddled a group of men, women and children. Bear pelts are pulled around them. A beetle-browed elder of about thirty-five (early man did not live beyond about 30 years as a rule) is cracking the bone of a reindeer to get at the marrow. A child is squalling until its mother stuffs a gob of half-cooked meat into its mouth. The howl of a wolf sounds close. A lad of fourteen gets up to drag a log from the side of the cave. He tosses it on the fire.

As the flames flare up, we get a clearer glimpse of these early humans. They are short, about five feet one inch, but they are stocky and powerfully muscled. Their heads are big. These men, in fact, average about 1450 cc. of brain capacity to our 1350 cc. But they have heavy ridges above their eyes, practically no forehead and no chin. A shock of coarse, thick hair completes the picture.

Yet these powerful though strange-looking brutes are true human beings. If we were to follow them winter and summer we might conceive an admiration for them. Armed only with crude stone axes and flint-tipped spears, we would see them face the mammoth, the cave bear and the cave lion. At other times they hunted the bison and met the charge of the woolly rhinoceros.

The skeletal remains of some eighty-two Neanderthaloids have been found in Europe, Palestine, Turkey, Iraq and Iran. The same type of man seems to have inhabited Central Asia and Africa. The skulls and bones of cave bears set up on stone shelves in Swiss caverns suggest a sort of totemistic worship; while the grave of an exceptionally big-brained (1650 cc.) Neanderthal man of advanced years was found in the La Chapelle aux Saints cave in France with tools, necklaces and the bones of animals arranged around the skeleton. The Neanderthals may have invented the burial of the dead. In any case this practice of theirs indicates a belief in some sort of a life after death.

And then came a minor recession of the Würm glaciation, known as the Gottweig Interstadial. It lasted from about 40,000 to 29,000 B.C. During this period modern types of men appeared in Europe and the Upper Paleolithic period began.

Upper Paleolithic Man in Europe

The varying types of the new immigrants all belonged to the *Homo sapiens* species. It is thought that some of them entered Europe en route from the Near East by way of the land-bridges at Gibraltar and Africa-Sicily-Italy; while other groups moved in along the windswept corridor in eastern Europe south of where the ice had been.

The men who occupied Western Europe had an average height of five feet eight inches with some six-footers among them. They were big-brained with broad foreheads, high cheekbones and strong chins. Although varying names are given to differing groups, they are usually called Cro-Magnons from the name of a cave in the Vézère Valley in which six skeletons of these Apollos of the Upper Paleolithic were found. When the Gottweig Interstadial ended and the Würm II glaciation advanced, the Cro-Magnons took to caves, particularly in France and northwestern Spain, often the same ones previously inhabited by the Neanderthals. They stayed in Western Europe during Würm II, the ensuing interstadial and Würm III, that is from about 30,000 to 8000 B.C. Their cultures have been named and approximately dated. First is found the Chatelperronian culture, which was mingled with the Mousterian culture of the Neanderthals, then the Aurignacian cultures, lasting until about 22,000 B.C. After this date, archeologists call the cultures Gravettian (22,000–18,000 B.C.) and Solutrean (18,000–15,000 B.C.). Finally, came the highly advanced Magdalenian culture from about 15,000 to 8000 B.C.

These cultures show in general a continuous advance. Blade tools of stone were fashioned into a variety of chisels, adzes, scrapers, graving-tools and the like. There was work in bone and ivory. In some cases tools were hafted and in others polished. Shelters to make "houses" out of the caves were built. Game and fish seem to have abounded. Most spectacular, perhaps, was the achievement in art.

Meanwhile in eastern Europe a shorter, stockier race, generally called Brünn man, made his home along the wind-swept loess (glacial dust) in Austria and Czecho-Slovakia. This people built rude homes partially sunk in the ground, and seem to have been excellent mammoth hunters. At Prědmost in Czecho-Slovakia a tomb made of the jaws and shoulder-blades of mammoths was found. In it were the skeletons of twelve men and women and eight children. It is estimated that parts of at least a thousand mammoths were uncovered at Prědmost. The successful hunting of such beasts indicates courage, skill and community co-operation. The

Solutrean period in western Europe is sometimes thought to have been a temporary extension of Brünn culture. What happened when the Cro-Magnons and the Brünn men met the Neanderthals? It used to be believed that the Neanderthals were all killed. Today the evidence seems to be that the stocks interbred.

Cro-Magnon Art

The peak of Upper Paleolithic art was achieved by the Cro-Magnons, particularly in the Magdalenian period, although the first cave paintings date back to Aurignacian times. Suppose that once more we step back, this time to about 15,000 years ago. It is a bright summer morning. Outside the sun is pouring down on the rugged hills and on the winding valley of the Vézère river. Deep in a cave near what is now Lascaux in France is a long gallery, hollowed out of the limestone by water. In that gallery flickers a little tongue of flame. It comes from the wick of a stone lamp, filled with animal fat. That lamp is held by a tall, narrow-hipped Cro-Magnon. By its light another man is drawing a proud-headed bull in bold, sweeping lines. Crouched beside him still another artist is blowing powdered red ochre through a bone tube on to the flanks of the bull.

All around, on the walls and on the arched ceiling, we glimpse a bewildering profusion of similarly drawn animals, one often superimposed on the other. As we lift our torches higher, we see, painted in browns, reds, yellows and blacks, shaggy horses in procession and a frieze of wild cattle, with one cow leaping over another.

There is another gallery at right angles to the first and from it, in turn, opens an apse-like dome. These walls and the ceilings, too, are covered with paintings. There are curious rectangular patches of color, arranged like escutcheons. In the apse there is a bison pictured with its entrails hanging down through a slit in its belly and its head lowered to charge, while behind it a rhinoceros walks away. In front is a man lying on the ground and nearby is a pole with a bird on it. The drawing of the man is crude, although this group of pictures may tell the world's first story. The fifteen-thousand-year-old paintings of the animals cannot be improved. Lascaux has been called "an ancient Louvre" and a French art critic has said of the paintings: "One cannot paint better; one can only paint differently."

The Lascaux galleries were discovered in 1940 by four schoolboys and their dog. They were hunting rabbits on the wooded hill when the dog disappeared down a hole made by an uprooted tree. The boys followed the dog. Suddenly, they were staring at paintings which no human being had seen for at least twelve thousand years.

The Lascaux cave is only one of some fifty similar caves. Undoubtedly there are more waiting to be found. These picture-caves, which were not meant to be lived in, stretch from the Vézère Valley in France to Altamira in northwest Spain. The paintings in them cover from 28,000 to 10,000 years ago. They show us the steppe horse, the cave-bear, the cave-lion, the ibex, wild cattle, the bison, the mammoth, and the woolly rhinoceros, all depicted with marvelous skill by men who had hunted these animals. One of the most striking pictures in the cave of Font-de-Gaume in the Vézère valley is of the head and shoulders of a snarling wolf emerging from the shadows, just as the artist must have seen it in the light of the campfire. Similarly, the magnificent bison and wild boars of Altamira in Spain take one's breath away by their vivid coloring and by the life and force which emanate from them.

Were there, in that far-off day, traveling schools of artists? At any rate, in one case, a drawing made on a piece of slate was clearly used as the rough sketch for a magnificent bull-bison painted in the Font-de-Gaume cave. That piece of slate was found 183 miles away from Font-de-Gaume.

Why were animals painted so vividly in these dark caves which are difficult to enter? It is generally supposed that Cro-Magnon man painted them to assure, as they believed, success in the hunt and the increase of game. It seems likely that they held ceremonies in the caves in which they pretended to hunt and kill the animals. In the cave of Trois Frères in southern France, there are long-ago footprints on the sand of the floor and the figure of a man in the skin and mask of a stag stares at the viewer with owl-like eyes. Such rites partake of what is called "sympathetic" or "imitative" magic. In this kind of magic it is believed that by imitating the desired event one can help it to happen. Some of Canada's Eskimos, for instance, will imitate all the stages of hunting and killing a seal, in the hope that this will give them good luck in the actual hunt.

The important thing is that in these paintings we have the birth of art. One of the major qualities which distinguishes man from the rest of the animal creation is his aesthetic sense, that is, his compelling impulse to add some sort of decoration to his functional objects, whether they be pots or swords or automobiles. The Cro-Magnon paintings go beyond the mere life-like reproduction of the animals. There is often an "impressionism" by which the artist sought to convey a feeling of the strength or speed or ferocity of the beast.

The same aesthetic sense is found in the shape and decoration of the excellent tools the Cro-Magnons made from flint, bone, and ivory. They fashioned artistic barbed harpoons like those the Eskimos use today. They made bone needles with eyes in them. They decorated their arrow-straighteners and their spear-throwers (used to increase the length of a cast) with beautiful carvings of partridges, horses' heads, and ibexes. They carved pictures of herds of reindeer, charging mammoths or salmon in a stream on slate, bone, and horn. They even modelled the human figure. Some of these, as for example the Venus of Willendorf, seem to us fat-laden grotesques. Yet the head of a girl in ivory with a plaited hair-do from Brassempouy, France, might have come from the pages of a fashion magazine.

Apart from their remarkable art, these early ancestors of ours seem to have had, like Neanderthal man, some notion of an existence after death. At any rate they buried tools, necklaces, and weapons with their dead. At times, too, they scarified the bones and painted them with red ochre. Was this to simulate the life-blood or was it merely a ceremonial observance?

Yet the Cro-Magnons were still savages in that they lived by hunting and fishing. Salmon was evidently a favorite food. The mammoth was hunted. According to the changes in climate, they chased the bison, or the reindeer, or the wild horse. At one time, for instance, there was a hunters' camp near Solutré in France. Here were found the remains of campfires and the charred, split, or broken bones of an estimated 100,000 horses. Apparently, as used to be done with the buffalo by our plains Indians, the wild horses were herded over the precipitous lip of a hill to destruction.

The Cro-Magnons were still the slaves of their environment. Between 10,000 and 8000 B.C. the ice was receding for the last time. As it disappeared, the reindeer retreated. Then, as the rains poured down on Europe and as the centuries went by, thick forest replaced the open steppe and tundra. The wild horse left Western Europe. The cave-bear, cave-lion, mammoth, and woolly rhinoceros had already become extinct. Under these circumstances, the Cro-Magnons appear to have followed the reindeer northward. New people seem to have moved up from Africa through Spain to France. To them, or to a mingling of them and the Cro-Magnons, are to be assigned the remarkable abstractionist paintings, which are found in rock-shelters in Spain. These paintings are alive with movement and drawn with economy of outline. They show us men fighting with bows and arrows or hunting deer, or dancing. In one picture, a man is climbing a tree after honey while the bees swarm around him. There are women, too, in the pictures, but they are no longer fat. Instead, they are lithe, active, Diana-like huntresses.

But it was the end of an era. With the retreat of the ice, the Paleolithic Age ends and the Mesolithic and, slightly later, the Neolithic Ages begin.

Summary: The Achievement of Old Stone Age Man

What had Old Stone Age man accomplished during his 500,000 years?

He had developed speech, learned to use fire, to clothe himself against the cold, and to seek shelter when necessary in caves. Drawings and a few remains indicate that the Cro-Magnons had begun to build summer shelters as well as additions to his cave-dwellings, while further east, as we have seen, there were roofed habitations which were partially sunk into the ground. In tool-making, man had progressed from crudely fashioned wooden implements, rough pebble-choppers, and fist-hatchets to finely wrought instruments of stone, ivory, and bone for digging, scraping, sewing, fishing, hunting, and carving. The spear was one of his first offensive weapons. At long last, the bow and arrow had been added. Thus, man had adapted himself to his environment and had gained some control over it. As compared to the lower animals, his progress was immense.

Old Stone Age Man had also learned to live and hunt in groups. It is probable that while the men hunted and fished, the women gathered nuts, berries, and seeds. Living in groups must have meant the growth of social customs and of religious beliefs. It seems likely that the Cro-Magnons thought that both animate and inanimate objects and phenomena such as rocks, lakes, or the thunder had a "force" or "spirit" in them. In this belief, if a rock crashed on you from a cliff, it was because the "force" in the rock *wanted* to injure you. Everything was sentient.

One or two paintings also suggest that there were Cro-Magnon "medicine men". These men were supposed to have the power and the spells to avert evil or even to influence the "spirits" to provide good hunting or the like. As noted, it appears probable that there was a belief in some sort of an existence after death. The rock-paintings also show activities such as music and dancing. In all this we perceive the crude beginnings of a more advanced way of life.

Apart from his progress in techniques of hunting and in living conditions, the most amazing achievement of Upper Palaeolithic man were his cave-paintings, his pictures on slate, horn, and his carvings of partridges, horses' heads, ibexes, and the like. One realizes that these long-dead ancestors were as gifted as any people, past or present. By this time, in fact, early man was poised for a great stride forward, the stride that is called the "Neolithic Revolution".

Note to Chapter 1

1. The usual non-technical division of existing human stocks is into Australoids (Browns), Caucasoids (Whites), Mongoloids (Yellow) and Negroids (Blacks). Color of skin, however, is not the only physical differentiation between these five stocks. Each of them, in turn, is subdivided into minor classifications. All modern stocks, as has been noted, belong to the *Homo sapiens* species. How *Homo sapiens* arose is a moot question. In a recent publication, *The Origin of Races*, Dr. Coon divides human stocks into five classifications and argues that primitive stocks of men "crossed the threshold" to become *Homo sapiens* five times, e.g. that the Australoids are descended from early men in Java and the surrounding area and that the Mongoloids are derived from"Pekin Man".

Anthropologists, in general, agree that primitive stocks intermingled with each other, as did the varying types of *Homo sapiens*, an intermingling which has continued throughout recorded history. Consequently, there is no "pure" race, nor is any modern stock potentially superior to any other except that the Australoids and some sub-stocks may be more "primitive" in structure and intellectual development. In general, however, there are no "superior" races but, no matter what the color of the skin, only "superior" individuals.

The story of Western Civilization involves chiefly the Caucasoids. A popular division of them is into Alpines, Mediterraneans and Nordics. In general the ideal Alpines are supposed to be short, stocky, swarthy, brown or hazel-eyed and broad-headed; the Mediterraneans, short, slight, olive-complexioned, black-eyed and long-headed; the Nordics tall, fair-complexioned, blue-eyed and long-headed. All these break into further classifications. It should be noted that Alpines and Mediterraneans were responsible for the first change to a food-producing culture and for the two earliest civilizations.

CHAPTER 2

Mesolithic and Neolithic Man and the Food Producing Revolution

The Middle Stone or Mesolithic Age (mesolithic from two Greek words, *mesos*—"middle," and *lithos*—"stone") was an era of transition. By the New Stone or Neolithic (*neos*—"new" and *lithos*—"stone") Age men had learned to polish and grind their stone tools to a fine edge by rubbing them with sandstone, but the most important achievements of the Neolithic period were the invention of farming and the taming of animals.

The Mesolithic Age in Europe

As the last glaciation melted, western Europe and the British Isles gradually assumed their present configuration. Meantime, the rain-belt shifted northward, and in central and northern Europe, lakes and dense forests replaced the steppe and the tundra. Bison, wild cattle and horses gave way to deer, wild boars, bears, lynxes, foxes, beavers, rabbits and water-rats and to flights of swans, geese, ducks and partridges. As a result, the descendants of the Upper Paleolithic peoples were forced to become woodsmen, fishermen and fowlers. Some Mesolithic groups left behind them huge banks, called kitchen middens, along the shores of the North Sea. These middens, made up of oyster shells and the like, are at times twenty feet high and over a thousand feet long. On the campsites are found the remnants of cod, herrings and eels. These people, evidently, depended heavily on sea products and must have used nets and boats.

Campsites have also been discovered around a huge peat bog at Maglemose in Denmark. The Maglemosian culture used blade tools, tanged arrow points and gravers of flint. There are many microliths (Greek *mikros*—"small"), tiny geometrically-shaped blades of flint. Microliths used, apparently, either as arrow-heads to bring down small game, or as "teeth" in wooden implements, such as knives, are first found in Europe during the Solutrean period of the Upper Paleolithic. But, besides the older types of tools, there were hafted stone axes for cutting down trees and some tools were ground and polished as in the later Neolithic period. Bone and antler were fashioned into fish hooks, fish spears and handles and hafts for stone tools such as adzes. The peat bog fortunately preserved a great many wooden articles, such as paddles, sled-runners, handles, and bark floats for fish-nets. There is even part of a fish net and obviously canoes or dugouts were in common use. Dogs, which may have been tamed in the last phase of the Upper Paleolithic, were now men's constant companions. There is no evidence for the domestication of other animals. Further south two important Mesolithic cultures at, presumably, about the same stage of development as the Maglemosian, were the Azilian and the Tardenoisian. There were, however, no further cave paintings; although dots and geometric designs were, for some unknown reason, painted on pebbles. An intriguing discovery at Ofnet, South Germany, in a stratum in which are the bones of modern types of forest animals, were two groups of heads arranged in each case like eggs in a nest. The neck bones in some cases show the marks of stone tools. One nest contained twenty-seven skulls, the other six. Nineteen of the skulls belonged to young children, four were of adult males and ten of young women. Was this an ancient sacrifice?

The Mesolithic peoples of Europe, did not advance beyond food-gathering until, about 3500 B.C., farmers began to move in from North Africa and the Near East. For the decisive leap from food-gathering to food-producing we must turn to the Near and Middle East.

The Mesolithic Age in the Near and Middle East.

While Europe was being reforested, the whole area from Morocco to the Caspian Sea began to dry up. The Sahara and Arabian deserts began to re-appear. The plateaux on either side of the Nile valley became stretches of sand. Game and water were increasingly scarce, and the hunters of the Middle Stone Age were forced to search for new sources of food. The Natufians of Palestine, for instance, a Mesolithic people of Mediterranean type existent about 8000 B.C., still depended on hunting and fishing for their livelihood; but sickles of grooved bones fitted with flint "teeth" are found in their burial sites. These were used, probably by the women, to reap the wild grasses from which barley and wheat developed. The Natufians also built stone-walled enclosures, possibly for domesticated animals. In these two respects they seem to have been pointing the way to the so-called "Neolithic Revolution," the period when men became *food-producers* instead of *food-gatherers*.

The Food-Producing Revolution of the Near and Middle East

The word "Neolithic" properly refers to an improved way of preparing stone tools. Instead of flaking or chipping flints, men now rubbed and polished their stone weapons and implements with sandstone. This technique meant that, in addition to flint, other stones could be used. There were also new types of tools with better cutting edges. These New Stone Age tools, such as flint knives from Egypt or stone axes and adzes found in Denmark, were remarkably efficient. In a modern experiment a Danish carpenter using a *stone* axe, was able in ten hours to fell twenty-six pine trees averaging eight inches in diameter, and shape them into logs.

The two most important changes in the Neolithic Age were the taming of animals and the development of farming. Both were gradual processes. By the Mesolithic Age the dog, as we have seen, had become man's companion. Other animals were probably corralled at first as a reserve of "meat on the hoof". Men and women, however, came to realize the advantages of breeding stock. Pigs, sheep, and goats were tamed, and later, cattle and donkeys. Men learned the uses of wool, goat's hair, milk, and cheese. They discovered that donkeys and oxen could be used for "animal-power".

The development of farming was equally gradual. To judge, for example, from early Neolithic settlements in Egypt, it seems certain that at first the men continued to hunt and fish, while the women cultivated garden patches of barley, millet, flax, and wheat with sticks and stone hoes. Then the men began to give up their bows and arrows, spears, nets, and fish hooks and to turn to farming. Late in the Neolithic period some genius invented the plow. The first plow was made of three sticks, one with a pointed end to scratch the ground, another at an angle to the first to serve as a handle, and the third for pulling the plow along. Later, the one handle became two and a stone was fitted to the pointed tip. (Plows of this sort are still used in Egypt today.) When another genius hitched oxen to the plow, true agriculture was born.

Where the Food-Producing Revolution Took Place

The Fertile Crescent in the Near and Middle East is a fringe of cultivable land between the mountains to the north and the desert to the south. Beginning at the Persian Gulf, it curves like a giant sickle-blade through Iraq and Iran and Syria and Palestine. The Nile valley can be regarded as an extension of it. It was in this Fertile Crescent that farming seems to have begun. The earliest Neolithic site so far discovered is at Jericho in the Jordan valley, just north of the Dead Sea. The Jordan valley is part of the "Great Rift" valley which runs for 4000 miles south into

Africa and Jericho itself is 900 feet below sea-level. Most of the Jordan Valley is semi-desert. But at Jericho there is a perennial spring and oasis. As the country dried up, the Natufians occupied this oasis, and on top of their occupation level the distinguished archeologist, Miss Kathleen Kenyon, found "The Oldest Town in the World".

She actually discovered two Neolithic towns. The third level from the bottom of the first town is C14 dated at 6800 B.C.; so, the town apparently reaches back at least to 7000 B.C. The second town lasted from around 6200 to 5000 B.C. Both towns occupied an area of from eight to ten acres. Their population is estimated at 3000. Agriculture was practised, and there may even have been irrigation of the fields. Both towns were surrounded by defensive walls: even at that early date there were, apparently, raids and wars. Neither people, however, had invented pottery.

Other Neolithic Sites

Jericho was a surprisingly early town. Other Neolithic sites began as villages. For example, at Jarmo in Iraq there is a "tell", or mound, made up of the ruins of village after village, one on top of the other. The oldest settlement at the bottom of the mound has been C14 dated at 7000 B.C. It was a mud-brick, pre-pottery village of about 200 people.

Other early Neolithic settlements are found in south-west Asia, in Iran, Iraq, Cilicia, Syria, Palestine, Egypt and, recently, at Hacilar in Turkey. By 4500 B.C. a string of farming villages stretched from Turkestan to the valley of the Nile. In this area, men had stopped being *food-gatherers* and had become *food-producers*. In so doing they had begun to gain a greater control over their environment.

You should note that on the fringes of this farming area, for instance, in the Arabian desert or on the Iranian plateau and in Central Asia, there were nomads who did not farm or hunt but depended, as similar peoples do today, on flocks and herds for their livelihood. From time to time these "barbarians" erupted into the settled areas.

Pottery and Weaving

With food-producing went the discovery of new techniques such as how to weave and to make pots, at first by hand and then on the potter's wheel. The first pots were reed baskets daubed over with clay to hold liquids. Then it was discovered that the reed framework could be omitted and that clay pots could be dried in the sun. The final step was to bake clay vessels either in an open fire or in a rude oven. Such pots were invaluable for holding liquids and for boiling food, instead of roasting it, and could be used for rat-proof storage of grain.

Similarly, weaving began when it was discovered that threads could be twisted out of wool or the fibers of flax. Looms were soon invented, and linen and woollen clothes replaced skin garments. Farming, tame animals, pottery, woven clothes, mud-brick villages—all these developments were characteristics of the new way of life.

The New Way of Life

Suppose we were Neolithic farmers. If we were hunters we would have to follow the game, and our homes would be temporary shelters. Now that we are farmers we are tied to the land and our houses are grouped for protection in a village. From that village we go out each morning to work the fields. But our homes, even if they are of mud-brick, are permanent dwellings. It makes sense, therefore, to improve them.

There is a group of hunters in the hills near us. There is another group of nomads in the nearby desert who have flocks and herds but no farming land so that they must wander from oasis to oasis. Both groups are envious of our herds, crops, possessions, and reserves of food. There is another difference between us. Membership in the nomad group is based on blood-relationship. Most of us are blood-relatives, too. But we do have some outsiders; and we have learned that good neighbors are more important than cousins. As an ancient Greek poet later expressed it: "When there is trouble neighbors come post-haste but kinsfolk stop to put clothes on". The village rather than a clan is our unit.

Similarly, our leader is now a headman. He and his council of elders have problems to settle which never arise among the hunters, such as the boundaries of fields and the rights to water. Also, some of us are beginning to accumulate our own private property, whereas among the hunters everything goes into the common pot. Furthermore, with plenty of food, some of us can spend our time in making pots, clothes and sandals. Our village is a busy hive with everyone, men, women, and children, doing something all the time. There are more of us, too, on less land than it takes to support the hunting or desert-dwelling groups. Each hunter needs one square mile of territory. We can feed a small village off that space.

Accelerated Change

The above are some of the observations which we, if we were Neolithic farmers, might make. Yet even these differences between food-gatherers and food-producers are only part of the pattern of change. As with the technological advances of this present century, one discovery begot another. Oats and rye were not cultivated until later but lentils, fruit trees, and the olive and the vine were added to wheat, barley, flax and millet. It is interesting to note that Neolithic man soon learned to make beer and wine. Meanwhile improved axes and adzes led to skilled carpentry. Sleds were made and beasts trained to pull them. Somewhere in the Middle East, possibly on the Iranian plateau, the wheel, on the variations of which the modern world depends for machines and transportation, was invented. Likewise, rude dugouts progressed to boats. Neolithic surpluses of food, improvements in means of travel and specialization also made a wider trade possible. The hunters had developed a rudimentary trade as, for example, in salt. In the New Stone Age regular trade routes were established. One of these brought to the early villages along the Nile sea-shells for adornment and malachite to be ground on slate-palettes into eye-shadow for long-ago Neolithic belles.

New Stone Age Religion

Along with changes in the materialistic field went changes in humanity's religious life. The nature-spirits of the hunter's religion were kept but were retailored to suit the needs of farmers' communities, and new deities were added. Quite clearly, New Stone Age man, like his Upper Paleolithic forebears, believed that without the aid or, at least, the appeasement of supernatural powers, human efforts could not succeed.

He worshipped, then, the sun, moon, storm, and other natural forces and phenomena; and he still believed that "spirits" resided in springs, trees, rocks and the like. But the most characteristic religion of the agriculturist was the worship of an Earth-Mother deity.

To the earth-mother there was usually added a male consort to personify the spirit of the grain. Their union was supposed to ensure the germination of the seed grain when it was placed in the earth. There seems often to have been some sort of human sacrifice. For example, the evidence suggests that in pre-dynastic Egypt a man who represented the grain-spirit was sacrificed each year and pieces of his body planted in the fields. Then, another man would be picked for the next year. The Neolithic peoples believed that by ceremonies of this sort they could make certain the annual rebirth of vegetation.

Meanwhile, shrines were built in the villages and the medicine-men of the hunters developed into priests who, in return for their supposed ability to propitiate and influence the deities, were given a good living and leisure time to meditate and inquire. The priests became the first scholars. Village life, too, meant a village cemetery. With the graves of the dead constantly in view, more definite ideas about life after death were likely to develop.

If you will pause again for a moment to pretend that you are a hunter who has become a farmer, you will realize that the change from a wandering food-gathering life to a settled food-producing economy affected the very psychology of humanity. The hunter's life had been one of daring and of periods of intense activity alternating with stretches of laziness. Time meant little to him and the hunter did not need to plan for very far ahead. He was, moreover, constantly on the move. But the farmer must work steadily and with foresight. Thrift and hard, stubborn work became virtues and recklessness, carelessness and "take no thought for the morrow" vices. A new type of man was bred.

Few changes in mankind's pattern of living have been more important than the shift from a hunting, food-gathering economy to a food-producing one. In this "revolution" were the seeds of civilization.

The New Stone Age in Europe

It ought to be emphasized that the food-producing revolution took place first in the Near and Middle East. Thence, gradually, between 4000 and 2500 B.C. it spread over the whole of Europe and Great Britain. By this time, however, the Age of Metals (copper by about 4500 B.C. and bronze by 2500 B.C.) had begun in the Near and Middle East. Likewise, by about 3500 B.C., while Europe was still "barbarian", the first cities were burgeoning in the valleys of the Nile and the Tigris-Euphrates rivers.

CHAPTER 3

The First Civilizations—Mesopotamia

Rivers and the first Civilizations

It was not by accident that the two earliest civilizations were born in the valleys of the Nile and of the Tigris and Euphrates rivers. Both Egypt and Lower Mesopotamia are almost rainless, but in both valleys the rivers bring down each year a rich deposit of silt. Here for the Neolithic farmers of the Fertile Crescent was soil and water to make the crops grow thick and tall, provided that there was irrigation and flood control. Civilization in both areas began because flood control and irrigation required community effort on a large scale, and, therefore, a centralized government and these factors, when combined with the increase in population because of soil-productivity, led to the first cities. Cities, as has been stated, seem inseparable from what is called civilization, and the period when the first cities burgeoned is sometimes called "The Urban Revolution". Whether this revolution took place first in Mesopotamia or Egypt is still being debated but a number of scholars believe that Mesopotamian civilization is the older.

The Geography of Lower Mesopotamia and its Influence

Mesopotamia is a Greek word meaning "the land between the rivers". These rivers, the thousand-mile-long Tigris and the Euphrates, rise in Armenia. After a sweep southward which, in the case of the Euphrates, forms a bridge between northern Syria and Upper Mesopotamia, the two rivers flow southeast, parallel to each other, to pour into the Persian Gulf. The silt which the rivers bring down each year after the snows melt in Armenia built, and is still building, the rich delta of Lower Mesopotamia. In the fourth millenium B.C. the Tigris and Euphrates, which now join, issued into the Gulf by separate mouths. Furthermore, the Gulf reached

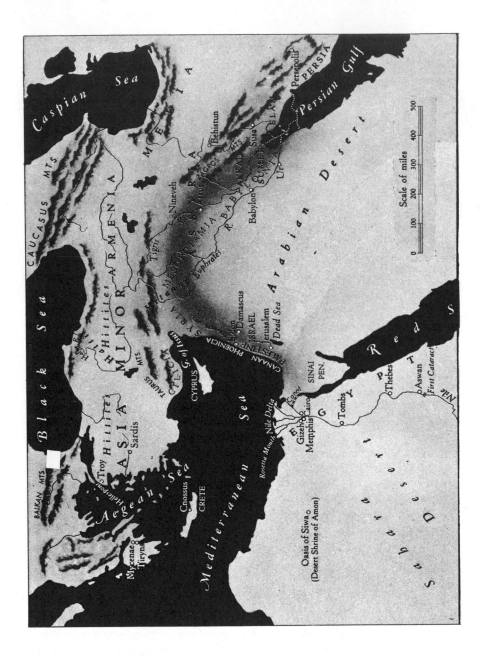

The Ancient Near East

well over 100 miles further inland than it does today. Consequently Lower Mesopotamia was a plain of about 10,000 square miles.

Lower Mesopotamia, generally called Babylonia, though small in area, was a tremendously fertile country. It lacked stone and timber. Its inhabitants had to use bricks for building, although there was asphalt for mortar. Clay tablets had to serve as their writing material. Unlike Egypt, the land had no natural defenses and therefore invaders from the desert of the highlands could pour in easily.

The Beginnings of Civilization in Lower Mesopotamia

During the early Neolithic period, Lower Mesopotamia was a stretch of swamps. Later an alluvial plain gradually emerged. As it became habitable, beginning before or early in the fourth millenium B.C., settlers moved in from the desert to the south, from the highlands to the north and northeast, and from Upper Mesopotamia. The result was a mixture of long-headed Semites and broad-headed Alpines. Since there was only about seven inches of rainfall annually and since flash floods were frequent, these settlers soon had to co-operate in irrigation and flood control.

Archeologists distinguish three main phases—Ubaid, Uruk, and Jemdet Nasr—in the fourth millenium B.C. development. The people of the Ubaid culture were villagers but already possessed artifacts of copper, although most of their implements were of stone or baked clay. During the Uruk period (dated at from 3400–3100 B.C.) new immigrants, probably Sumerians, appear to have arrived. Villages became towns. Sculpture began and copper was in use, although stone implements were still employed (a phase of culture called Chalcolithic). At Uruk a mound thirty-five feet high was built and on it a temple with foundation blocks of limestone brought from the hills was erected. Marks on clay tablets show that the beginning of writing, and trade had developed.

In the Jemdet Nasr era (beginning between 3100–3000 B.C.), copper tools were in common use, wheeled carts had been improved, the pictographic script had been expanded to express abstract ideas, cities dotted the plain, and an elaborate irrigation and flood control system had been devised. Though there is no recorded history, civilization had begun.

This development was in the southern part of Lower Mesopotamia, called Sumer after the Sumerians. Meanwhile, a Semitic people had infiltrated the northern section. They are named Akkadians. Under the influence of their neighbors they, too, developed cities. The whole of Lower Mesopotamia came to be known as plain of Sumer and Akkad.

The Sumerians

The Sumerians are a mystery people. As had been mentioned, they are believed to have arrived in Lower Mesopotamia in the Uruk period and to have dominated the country in the Jemdet Naṣr phase. The location of their original home is not known. Because they put their temples on artificial mounds called ziggurats, and because ziggurat means "House of the Mountain", it is thought that they must at some time have lived in a mountainous country. Their own legends said that they swam up the Persian Gulf "like a fish". Scholars are inclined to think, however, that they came originally from Central Asia.

Whatever their provenance, their own representations of themselves show a short, stocky people with beak noses, bulging eyes and shaven skulls, though some statuettes present bearded, flowing-tressed men. They spoke a language which has no affiliations with any known speech and was agglutinative.* Sumerian king-lists assign impossible lengths to their early dynasties. A rule of more than twenty-five thousand years, for example, is attributed to the twenty-three kings of the Kish Dynasty.

It seems clear that the Sumerians were the people who in the latter part of the fourth millenium B.C. developed an advanced civilization in Lower Mesopotamia. Their dykes and irrigation canals criss-crossed the plain. They reaped rich harvests of wheat and barley. They bred cattle, sheep, pigs, goats, and poultry. Gold, silver and copper were plentiful. Their priests kept records of the possessions of the gods in a pictographic script written on tablets of clay. The temples to those gods glittered on brick ziggurats in the cities planted in Lower Sumer and Akkad. Traders streamed from their city-states through the plain, into the highlands and upstream into Upper Mesopotamia and beyond.

The Sumerian city-states were small in territory and were ruled by priest-kings, called ensis. In Sumer, religion dominated life. There was, however, a class of nobles who led the warriors. War was endemic. There were wars for land and water and for dominion over the plain. One side of the First Dynasty Royal Standard of Ur, for instance, a beautiful mosaic of mother-of-pearl and blue lapis lazuli set in bitumen, shows us a Sumerian army. First come the nobles in four-wheeled chariots, each drawn by four asses. Each chariot has a driver while the warrior is armed with an axe and four javelins. Next march the skirmishers carrying axes, swords, spears, and daggers. Last of all advances the phalanx of heavy-armed infantry,

---

*That is, a language in which sentences are made up of monosyllables, each monosyllable expressing an idea, which are combined together like beads on a string, to body forth a thought. For instance, part of a Sumerian sentence which translates as: In the palace of Urgur, the King of Ur, the builder of Eanna, forms one word and is translated literally as: Palace-Urgur-King-Ur-man-Eanna-he built-(genitive particle)-in. (From Van Sickle, "A Political and Cultural History of the Ancient World", Vol. I, Houghton Mifflin Co., New York, 1947). Turkish and Eskimo are examples of agglutinative languages.

each citizen-soldier having a shield, a spear, a heavy cloak, and a conical copper helmet. Arrow-points found on forgotten battle-fields prove that archers formed a part of the army. On the other side of the Royal Standard is a victory banquet.

The Sumerians made great strides in the development of the art of war. Whenever an ensi subjected another city he called himself a *lugal*, or king. The tendency was for the lugal to become a temporal ruler, who either claimed to be the vice regent of a god or to be himself divine.

Such were the people who toward the end of the fourth millenium B.C. developed a rich, city-state, riverine civilization in the plain of Sumer and Akkad. For centuries dominion over that plain shifted from city to city, from Kish to Uruk to Lagash. Finally, the First Dynasty of the Sumerian city of Ur, the city in which Abraham of the Bible was later to be born, won hegemony over Sumer. This dynasty is generally dated at about 2500 B.C. With its advent recorded history begins, since from its Royal Graves come the written names of kings, queens and princes, such as Mes-kalam-dug, whose golden helmet has been found, and Queen Shub-ad, with whom were buried necklaces, golden earrings, vanity-cases, and a "Spanish" comb.

Some of these Royal Graves were death-pits. With the help of a little imagination we can recreate one of those scenes of long ago. The tomb vaulted with brick, is already dug. A ramp leads down to it. Along that sloping ramp, to the sound of music, the body of the dead ruler of Ur is borne. Precious objects are laid in the tomb such as harps decorated with bulls-heads of gold and bearded with blue lapis lazuli, gaming-boards of ivory and shell-mosaic, tumblers and goblets of gold and a ram caught in a thicket, the whole made of gold, lapis lazuli and silver.* Ranks of garlanded waiting-women and spear-bearing soldiers (often the spear points are of gold or silver) move, as in a daze, into the tomb. Priests lead the way. The soldiers and waiting-women line up around the body of the ruler. They drink, it is assumed, a potion. They crumple to the ground where they stand. The priests emerge. The tomb is filled in. The dead ruler has his attendants for the next world. Close to 5000 years later, when the archeologist enters, he will find the skeletons in these death-pits, the cups from which they drank beside them. There will be no sign of violence or of compulsion. It would seem that these attendants went to their death voluntarily, in the belief, perhaps, that thus they would share immortality with the dead ruler. In the death-pit of Queen Shub-ad, in addition to the skeletons of her waiting-women, there was found the remains of a wheeled wagon and the bones of the asses which had pulled it.

---

* These treasures can be seen in the British Museum or in the University of Pennsylvania Museum.

The yoke-pole was decorated with an amazingly life-like sculpture, in electrum (an alloy of silver and gold), of a mischievous donkey foal.

As time went on, the line of a Sumerian hymn, "I offer a lamb for a human" suggests that the sacrifice of animals was substituted for that of human beings.

Sargon, the Semite, and the First Empire in History

The First Dynasty of Ur finally lost its power. Umma, another Sumerian city, came to the fore under Lugal-Zaggisi who conquered Uruk, Ur, and Nippur, destroyed Lagash and, apparently, mastered the greater part of the plain of Sumer and Akkad. His inscriptions assert that his god, Enlil, had invested him with the "dominion of the world" and that he had subdued peoples from "the Lower Sea (the Persian Gulf) . . . to the Upper Sea (the Mediterranean)." His raids seem to have followed the Sumerian trade routes which by this time had permeated Assyria and had reached to Syria and Asia Minor.

About 2350 B.C. Lugal-Zaggisi was defeated and captured by Sargon of Agade. Sargon, a Semite, went on to subdue Elam and Assyria and to march upstream to Syria and Cilicia. He may even have reached Cyprus. Legends accumulated around this conqueror. It was said, for instance, that as an infant (like Moses of a later period) he was entrusted in a basket of reeds to the broad Euphrates by his mother and rescued not by a princess but by a gardener. His grandson, Naram-Sin, styled himself "king of the four quarters of the earth". A victory stele of his, now in the Louvre in Paris, shows him striding up a mountain to defeat a tribe called the Lulubu.

Under Sargon and Naram-Sin the first empire in history was established. What motivated its formation? Partially, no doubt, a lust for power. Yet we ought not to forget that one way to prevent raids of the highlanders into the plain was to conquer them; nor must we forget that from early in the third millenium B.C. traders had already made their way into Elam, Assyria, Syria, Cilicia, and even into the depths of Asia Minor. In those days, as in later periods, there was a tendency for armies to follow the traders.

This first empire did not last too long. From the Zagros mountains, which Naram-Sin had penetrated, a horde of barbarians called the Guti swarmed over the plain. When they were expelled, the Third Dynasty of Ur arose (about 2125 B.C.). Here was the final brilliant resurgence of the Sumerians. Under Ur-Nammu and his successors, until about 2000 B.C., Ur ruled Sumer, Akkad, Elam, and Assyria. Trade prospered. There was peace and plenty.

Life in Third Dynasty Ur

Woolley's excavations have told us a good deal about Ur of the Third Dynasty. Let us try to visualize a few of the dominant features of Sumerian life.

Let us suppose that we are making our way down the great stone road on the south bank of the Euphrates toward Ur. There will be pack-saddle donkeys driven by pedlars starting out for a season's business. There will be other donkeys carrying people, although most of the travelers will be on foot. On our left the Euphrates will swarm with boats and rafts bringing cedar from Lebanon, stone from Syria, silver from Cilicia, and copper ore from Asia Minor. Those rafts, when they reach Ur, will be broken up and the wood sold. The river is fringed with date-palms. If we look between and beyond them, as far as we can see stretch the fields, thick with barley, wheat, gourds, sesame, lentils, beans, and vines, so closely tilled and rich that they look like gardens. Among them are the silver lines of the intricate network of the canals.

Agriculture

In Akkad and Sumer, agriculture is the life-blood of the economy. A farmer is fined if he does not keep in repair his share of the irrigation system or even if he does not make proper use of his land. Contrariwise, if a man brings new land into cultivation, he is exempted from taxes for a period; and there is a provision that farmers' debts cannot be collected until after the harvest. There are fat cattle, grunting pigs, bleating sheep and goats, and braying donkeys. It is a full-fed farmers' country.

The City of Ur

But now we are approaching Ur. There are villas and orchards by the side of the road. In front is the great wall of the city, built of bricks; this wall is a mile in circumference, 25 feet high, and 77 feet thick at the base. The Euphrates runs along its northern side. From it a canal in a huge loop surrounds the city like a moat. There is a western harbor for river traffic and a sea harbor at the northeast corner for trade down to the Persian Gulf. A canal from this harbor runs through the city to come out under the wall to join the other canal. The city is shaped like an open-mouthed sack facing north and a little west. Over the wall, in the north-west section, the temple of Nannar, god of the moon, gleams on its ziggurat.

The Temple of Nannar

Nannar is the protector of Ur. More than that, Ur is *his* city, for the cities of Sumer and Akkad, like Jerusalem later, are holy cities. Nannar, then, *is* Ur. In theory it is he who makes war, declares peace, and signs treaties. His temple dominates the city. When we enter Ur it will be the first place we visit.

There is a wall around the temple precincts. The area is roughly 600 by 1200 feet. Three great gateways in the eastern wall admit us. We are immediately in the midst of bawling cattle, bleating sheep, donkeys laden with sacks of grain, men and women carrying geese, ducks, and the like. Nannar owns broad temple-lands and rents are paid in kind. There are tithes to be paid, too—a custom which the Sumerians introduced. It is all very business-like. The receiving priests stand at triple gates leading to an inner precinct. Clay receipts are given for each item, a copy to the person paying and a copy for the temple. Around the walls of the outer precinct are storehouses to which temple servants take the grain and the animals.

In front of us now is still another wall. If we pass through the gate and ascend the brick steps, we are in front of the great ziggurat. It is in the northwest corner and faces east to the sunrise. In the pavement before us is the ring where bulls are tied for the morning sacrifice.

The huge mass of brick inspires awe in the visitor. It is 200 feet long by 150 wide. Three great stairways, two from the side, one directly in front, meet at the top of the first step of the 70-foot-high ziggurat. These stairways and the first step still stand today. In the angles between them are the day-temples and kitchens of Nannar and his consort, Nin-gal, goddess of the moon. Two more steps with stairways rise above the first great step. On the top sits the blue and gold temple of Nannar. It will occur to us that, as in Jerusalem later on, this area is the last center of defense.

Nannar, like all the great gods of Sumer, is conceived of in anthropomorphic terms; that is, he is thought of as having all the characteristics of a human being. In his temple is a golden bedstead on which, each night, a wife or concubine sleeps. Each morning his image is brought down the stairways to his day-temple. Meals are cooked for him in great copper caldrons. Each spring he is taken in procession to his country temple so as to insure the fertility of his crops. In addition to temple lands, he owns ships (we have the bill of lading from one ship which was away for three years and brought back teak, cinnabar, and ivory), warehouses and factories for making cloth, and the like. Strangest of all, he has his own Minister of War, Treasurer and Minister of Justice. A few days in Ur would convince us of the power and influence of the priesthood of Nannar.

The Priests

There are many priests, both men and women. The most powerful are

the high priest of Nannar and the high priestess of Nin-gal. The latter
is the chief wife of Nannar. As a special taboo, she cannot enter a tavern
under pain of being burnt to death.* High among the other priests are the
musicians and the anointers. At the bottom are the temple-sweepers.
Incidentally, nothing can be got from the stores, whether it be a bull for the
sacrifice or a pot of ointment without a signed requisition. Woolley found
hundreds of receipts and requisitions, all on tablets of baked clay.

The priestesses are all "brides of Nannar". They are supposed to bring
a dowry. Though the lower class of them are temple prostitutes, to be a
bride of Nannar is regarded as a great honor.

Education in Ur

If we roam through the outer precinct of the temple we will come upon
the temple school. If we step in as school is beginning, the first thing
we will note is that each pupil stops by a box to dig out a handful of clay
and pat it into a tablet. Around the wall are hung maxims on baked clay
tablets. If we could read them, we would find the equivalents of "Honesty
is the best policy" and "Honor thy father and mother".

The pupils sit on the floor, each with his clay tablet and his bronze or
reed stylus in his hands. The teacher, a shaven-skulled priest, begins the
lesson. Learning to read and write is the first laborious task. Sumerian
writing began as picture writing in which pictograms represented a fish, a
bird, an ox-head, and so on. By this time, however, the pictograms,
because of the cuneiform writing (Latin, *cuneus*—"wedge") which developed from pressing a wedge-shaped stylus into damp clay, have lost all
resemblance to the original pictures. Moreover, most of the signs or letters
now represent either ideas such as "flying" (*ideograms*) or the sounds of
syllables (syllabic *phonograms*); and there are at least 600 of them. As
we look at these youngsters we see that they have in front of them long
lists of all the syllables beginning with T.

The students are taught grammar, and mathematics, as well. There is
no sign for zero but there is both a decimal and a sexagesimal (units of 60)
system. Our division of the circle into 360 degrees and of the hour into 60
minutes and 60 seconds comes from these Sumerians of over 4000 years
ago.

If we ask about advanced education we will find that surveying and
engineering are taught and that there are crude maps in baked clay of the
world as the Sumerians know it. We will discover, too, that to become
doctors, architects, or sculptors we have to become apprentices. Or we
can study astronomy, a field in which the Sumerians are well advanced.

*We can speculate that this taboo existed because the chief wife of Nannar had to comport
herself with dignity, particularly in sexual matters, and the taverns were "low class".

They know the planets and the length of the solar year. But they have a clumsy calendar of 12 moon months, totalling 354 days. Every three or four years the priests have to add a number of days to bring the calendar into line with the solar year of $365\frac{1}{4}$ days.

The City Streets

As we leave the school and the temple we will realize that, although the average Sumerian can calculate, comparatively few can read and write. Hence, in the streets we will find letter-writers and story tellers.

Unless we have a guide, it will be easy for us to lose our way in Ur. The streets are narrow and twisting, as behooves a city jammed within protecting walls. If we wander to the north-east corner of Ur, we will find the harbor filled with boats of every description. These are the ships which go out to the Persian Gulf and thence to the Arabian coast and, quite possibly, to the Red Sea, India, and Ceylon. If we turn back from the harbor into the city, we will find the lanes and squares crowded with bald-headed Sumerian men, clad in a single garment, and women in long robes. Women of the upper class wear jingling jewelry, cosmetics and elaborate coiffures. We will note taverns jammed with singing, arguing men and women. In the squares people haggle around the goods exposed for sale. There are hotels and restaurants, the smell of bakers' shops, the hammering of coppersmiths and goldsmiths, the monotonous fingers of women busy at looms. Children dash here and there. Dogs bark. Through an open door we see a traveler making an offering to Pa-sag, the deity of travelers. In the shrine of this goddess, Woolley found the list of the temple properties and the roll of the priests with their tours of duty.

A Home in Ur

Suppose that we have been invited into the home of a middle-class merchant. As we enter a lobby, we find a jar of water to wash the dust off our feet, since if we are wearing Sumerian dress we will be in sandals. From the lobby there is an entrance to a central patio, open to the sky. It is tiled, and in the center is a pipe thrust down 50 feet to a cess-pool. At Eshnunna, above Babylon, there is a public sewerage system, but in Ur each citizen looks after his own sewage. Around the patio, at the front and to the right, are the slaves' bedrooms with brick bedsteads, the workroom, and the kitchen. At the back is the staircase to the second story. Under it is the lavatory.

To our left is a long, narrow guest room. It has its own chapel and lavatory. If we go out through the back door, we will see a narrow lean-to, roofed for one-third of its length. This is the family chapel. In it on a display table are the household gods, and here, each day, prayers for the whole household are held. Underneath this chapel is the burial vault for the family dead. Upstairs are the sleeping-rooms for the family. The furnishings of the house, which is about 40 to 50 feet in area, are simple—chests, low tables, stools, rugs, and tapestries. But graceful arches are prevalent and pillars are decorated with shell mosaic.

Many citizens of Ur, of course, live in tenements or in one-room lodgings. Yet the whole atmosphere of this ancient city is not too different from sections of modern Cairo or Baghdad, if we omit the intrusion into the Near and Middle East of motor-cars, new apartment blocks and the like.

Attitude toward the Gods

It is time to summarize a few major aspects of Sumerian civilization. A striking feature is the Sumerian attitude toward their gods. To them the great gods, who were the personified forces of nature, ruled the universe, and in the sight of the gods, man was nothing. Whatever he received came as a favor from them. Hence, the Sumerian abased himself before the gods. It is no accident that the statues of Sumerians show them with their hands clasped in the attitude of prayer, or that each city was the holy city of one of these gods. Below these great gods were the smaller gods, such as Pa-sag, to whom an ordinary man could pray and hope to be heard. And then, as we have seen, each family had its own household gods. There were also hosts of demons, waiting to seize the unwary. Fear was a strong component of Sumerian religion.

Perhaps we should note that, unlike the Egyptians, the Sumerians, and the Semites after them (including the Hebrews) never developed a Paradise for the average man. In their belief a few favored people were taken by the gods to themselves before death. For everyone else, death meant a shadowy, miserable existence for a shadowy spirit, though the lot of the spirit could be mitigated by proper offerings and prayers made by the living.

Sumerian Social Divisions

By the time of the Third dynasty of Ur, the king was the apex of the social structure. Although in theory the god Nannar ruled Ur, the king seems to have been regarded as divine. Grouped round him were the nobles who were the core of his army and his administrators. Another important group were the priests, headed in Ur by the high priest of Nannar. Both these groups possessed great wealth, and formed a separate class, called the Amelu. The rest of the freemen—minor officials, shop-keepers, artisans and farmers—were the *burghers*. Below the freemen were the slaves, who were kindly treated. There was no difference in color, for one thing, and besides, slavery could happen to anyone. Prisoners taken in battle became slaves. Furthermore, a man could, upon occasion, sell his wife and children into slavery for three years. A slave could buy his freedom, run a business, and keep part of the profit and ask to be sold to another master. Likewise, in marriage or concubinage involving slaves and freemen or free women, the children were born free and on the death of a master his concubine was set free.

The Status of Woman

Sumerian women were remarkably free. They could own and bequeath property, appear in a court of law, and run businesses. Marriage was arranged by the parents. A betrothal gift was given by the prospective bridegroom. If he changed his mind, he forfeited that gift. If the bride-to-be changed her mind, she had to pay back *double* the amount of the gift. In this respect Sumerian law protected men against women.

The Legal System

Law was based upon codes which tried to provide for every possible kind of civil or criminal action. We have fragments of a Third Dynasty of Ur law code. Trial was before three judges, not a jury. Evidence was taken on oath, there were constables to carry out the sentences, and the sentences were recorded on baked clay tablets. Sumerian law accorded a primitive justice, in that an offense against an amelu was punished more severely than one against a burgher. But, similarly if an amelu sinned, he suffered a more severe penalty than a burgher.

Sumerian Art and Literature

The Sumerians produced nothing in stone comparable to the Egyptian achievement. To a large degree this was because stone had to be imported. Similarly, their brick-built ziggurats lack the majesty of the pyramids, obelisks and temples of Egypt.

On the other hand their work in what we may call "jewellers' craftsmanship" was superb. The ram in the thicket which has been mentioned, the miniature bulls' heads, the mosaics of shell and lapis lazuli, and their carved seals are second to none. In these arts they passed on their techniques to their successors.

Although there are many Sumerian fragments, much Sumerian literature has come down to us in later Semitic adaptations. Most of it was religious. There are hymns, prayers and penitential psalms. One begins: "Lord, my sins are many and my faults are grave." The Sumerians also composed the famous Gilgamesh Epic. It relates the mythical adventures of a creature, two-thirds human and one-third divine, who seems to be the prototype of the Biblical Samson and the Greek Hercules. There are interesting legends of creation, including the story of Ut-Napishtim who built an ark and saved his family from a great flood. He is sometimes called the Sumerian Noah.

There was, probably, a secular literature—popular songs, fables told by the story-tellers and the like. A love letter in the period of Hammurabi from one Gimil-Marduk to a certain Bibiya is in sentiment universal and modern.

Business Life

The Sumerians were the ancestors of modern business-men. The priests administered the broad temple lands and the manifold business interests of the gods with careful attention to records, profits, and interest rates. Private merchants, traders and shopkeepers followed suit, and used double-entry bookkeeping. Credit was advanced: for example, pedlars were granted a season's credit for goods to be sold throughout the plain, with the provision that if the pedlar could prove he had been robbed, he would not have to pay for the goods. The normal interest rate was 20% on loans to be repaid in metal, but $33\frac{1}{3}$% if repayment was to be in barley. There was no proper coinage but metal was valued by weight. Sixty shekels made a mina, and sixty minas a talent, which weighed about 68 pounds. By Hammurabi's time the weight was stamped on the talent. At first four pounds of silver equalled one of gold but by Hammurabi's reign the ratio was eight of silver to one of gold.

The Sumerians were already using bills of lading as we do. Their trade was far-flung. Seals from the Indus valley civilization in India are found in Sumer. On land, Sumerian donkey caravans made their way into Elam, Assyria, Cilicia, and Anatolia. Sumerian imports included copper, silver, gold, pearls, ivory, lead, wood, and stone: they exported textiles, jewelry, weapons, copper pots, and the like. Contacts with Egypt probably date back to 3000 B.C. or earlier and are definite by the time of Egypt's Sixth Dynasty.

The traders also exported Sumerian civilization. One of the important features of this, and of Hammurabi's age, was the spread of Mesopotamian goods, ideas (religious and otherwise), and the cuneiform script. Cuneiform was used in Assyria, Syria, and Anatolia and became finally the script of diplomacy.

A Planned Economy

We must not forget that the whole economy rested on agriculture. Each year the fields were re-surveyed, and the crops to be sown and the amount

of seed to be used (less than three pecks of barley per acre, for instance)
were dictated. Furthermore, an estimate of the crop was made, and a
budget was drawn up based on that estimate. Renters paid two-thirds of
the crop to the landlord (usually the temple or the king) and kept one-third
for themselves.

The Fall of Sumer

The Third Dynasty of Ur was the last great period of Sumerian culture.
In the reign of its fifth king, Ibi-Sin, Semitic Amorites from the desert
and Elamites from the hills combined to sack and burn the great city.
Other Amorites established themselves at Babylon (which means in the
original form, Bab-Elim, the Gate of God). After over a century of chaos,
the sixth king of Babylon, Hammurabi, whose date is about 1750 B.C.,
took over Sumer and Akkad, added Elam, Assyria, and parts of Syria to
his kingdom, and established the First Babylonian Empire. It is possible
that he invaded Palestine.

In this way the Sumerians, after about two thousand years, ceased to
be independent. The Semitic Amorites, however, founded their civilization on Sumerian culture. Under Hammurabi, Sumerians were secretaries
and advisers. The Sumerian speech gradually died out as a spoken
language. It continued to be used in religious ceremonies, just as Latin
is used in some of our church services today, and Sumerian cuneiform
characters were used for Semitic writing.

The Babylonians: Hammurabi's Empire

Hammurabi's chief fame rests on his code of laws. A copy of this
code, written on a pillar of black basalt, was found at Susa, the capital
of Elam, by the French scholar de Morgan in 1901. The pillar, now in
the Louvre in Paris, is eight feet high. On it, in bas-relief, is carved
a picture of Hammurabi standing before the seated sun-god, Shamash,
and receiving laws from him. The laws, therefore, purport to be of divine
origin. A section of them was erased in ancient times, but two hundred
and eighty-two laws remain. Like the Sumerian codes, on which these laws
are based, they attempt to cover the whole field of human conduct, civil
and criminal. The basic principle is an "eye for an eye" justice. It is
written, for example, that if a builder builds a house and it collapses and
kills the son of the householder, then the son of the builder is to be put to
death. Similarly, if a surgeon is responsible for the loss of a patient's eye,
then the surgeon will lose his own eye.

Hammurabi was both a law-maker and an excellent administrator. His
empire was divided into provinces under governors, and the power of the
priests was curbed. As a result, private enterprise flourished and trade

increased. Hammurabi also built a great ziggurat to the god of Babylon, Marduk, who, by a rewriting of Sumerian theology, now became the supreme god in the hierarchy of deities. This ziggurat may be the Tower of Babel of the Bible.

Considerable cultural growth took place during the First Babylonian Empire. The Babylonians worked out the value of π to six places, solved quadratic equations, and, apparently, used tables of logarithms. In literature, the Sumerian epics were recast in Semitic versions. Great roads were built and a postal service introduced. In this period of peace and prosperity, trade reached out through Palestine to Egypt, into Anatolia and across the sea to Cyprus and, perhaps, to Crete.

Mesopotamia prospered, but the usual fate was awaiting the civilization of the plain. The Amorites themselves had swept in from the desert. Now it was the turn of the mountain peoples: Indo-Europeans[1] had arrived in the Near and Middle East. About 1600 B.C., a group of these, the Hittites, who had occupied Anatolia, raided the plain as far as Babylon. The city was captured and sacked. The Hittites returned home loaded with captives and loot. Behind them they had left a monument of their victory, to be rediscovered many centuries later—the massive sculpture of a Hittite lion trampling on a Babylonian warrior. Afterward, a weakened Babylon fell to another mountain people, the Kassites. They seem also to have been led by Indo-Europeans. Then, for centuries, Mesopotamia ceased to have political importance. But its trade, wealth, and civilization continued.

Summary

We have seen how the Sumerians developed a riverine civilization in Lower Mesopotamia while Europe was still in the Neolithic Age. In the use of metals, in irrigation and flood control, in the keeping of records, in law, in literature and the arts, in knowledge, in the ease and comfort and even luxury of daily life, Sumerian achievement was considerable. Man had begun to exercise a definite control over his environment. Government, however, was despotic, and religion seems to have dominated life.

One great weakness of the Sumerian civilization was its frequent lapse into civil war. This may well have been the cause of their defeat by the Semites, whom they had civilized. Sumerian influence, however, was passed on through the Babylonian Semites. The use of 60 as a basic unit is one example. Sumerian astronomy found its way to Greece and Rome. The business practices of the Sumerians spread far afield. Their religious attitudes influenced the Hebrews; there are parallels between the Sumerian versions of the Creation and the Flood and the early chapters of Genesis. The Sumerio-Semitic civilization of Mesopotamia was one of the ancestors of our own. The other was Egypt. Before we turn to Egypt, however, two other early riverine civilizations, both of them later in origin than those of Mesopotamia and Egypt, ought to be mentioned.

The Indus Valley Civilization, c. 2500–1500 B.C.

In 1921 A.D. a forgotten civilization was discovered in the Indus Valley of what is now West Pakistan. The Indus River flows into the Arabian Sea. Along with its tributaries it drains northwestern India as far as the Simla hills. In those hills and stretching out from them were Neolithic farming villages. As with the rivers of Egypt and Mesopotamia, the lower reaches of the Indus offered rich rewards to agriculturalists if flood control and irrigation could be achieved. By 2500 B.C. civilization had begun. The Indus Valley civilization was later to develop than Mesopotamia and Egypt, but it antedates the one other early civilization we know, that of the Hwang-Ho or Yellow River in China.

Sixty of the Indus Valley sites have been identified. Only three have been excavated to any considerable degree, Mohenjo-Daro, two hundred miles northeast of Karachi, the capital of Pakistan, Harappa, four hundred miles upstream, and Chanhu-Daro, which is downstream.

The people of this civilization appear to have been, in general, small and dark-skinned and, apparently, native to the country. They left writing which cannot, as yet, be read, and seem to have lived a communal life of controlled activity. The same weights and measures are found at Mohenjo-Daro and Harappa, though the two cities, each of which was about three miles in circumference, are four hundred miles apart. Both cities were dominated by massively fortified citadels on which are the remnants of large buildings. Below the citadels were the lower towns, in each case extending to the river. Those towns were laid out in a grid pattern; that is, broad streets up to thirty feet in width divided the whole area into rectangular and regular blocks, four hundred yards by two hundred to three hundred yards. Each block was then criss-crossed in the same rectangular pattern by lanes, which were "dog-legged" against the winds. This pattern suggests cities planned by a governing class.

The houses were of brick and two stories in height. What is remarkable is that these ancient cities had public sewerage systems, with manholes at regular intervals to enable the sewers to be cleaned, as well as public garbage collection bins. There were big granaries at Harappa and kilns for brick-making at Mohenjo-Daro. Both cities had separate quarters for workmen and arrangements at the riverbank for unloading grain.

Agriculture was, as in Sumer and Egypt, the basis of the economy. There was irrigation, and dykes were built along the river brink to prevent flooding. Excavations have proved that wheat, barley, sesame, peas, melons, and dates were grown. The bones of cattle, sheep, goats, and water buffaloes have been found. There is evidence, too, that the elephant may have been tamed. Arts and crafts flourished. There are fragments of cotton cloth. Metal-working in silver, electrum, and copper was common, and bronze was in use for saws, adzes, swords, spears, arrow-heads, knife-blades, and razors. There was sculpture in stone and bronze.

Trade was wide-ranging, chiefly along the river and to the north. But, just as Indus Valley seals are found in the Sumer of about 2300 B.C., so Sumerian seals, gold disc-heads, and socketed axes have turned up in the Indus Valley. In religion, an earth-mother deity was among the objects of worship.

The women of this civilization wore skirts only, the men kilts and shawls. Buttons, beads, bracelets, rings, combs, earplugs, and the same sort of nose-rings that are used in modern India have been unearthed. Children played with miniature carts and toy animals on wheels. A toy monkey which jumped when a string was pulled must have been a special plaything. Marbles, jacks, dice, and board games add a modern touch. So does a brick which shows the paw-marks of a cat followed by those of a dog (both printed in the clay before the brick was fired). One wonders if the cat escaped.

The whole picture is of a productive but highly regimented way of life. Then, about 1500 B.C., disaster struck. Most archeologists believe that the culprits were the hordes of Indo-Europeans who, about this time, overran northern India. Driving chariots drawn by galloping ponies and led, according to their belief, by their god Indra, who at times was called the "Fort-Destroyer", these invaders, who called themselves Aryans and described their heroes as blond and blue-eyed, seem to have swept over the Indus Valley civilizations. The cities and towns were stormed and the inhabitants massacred. At Mohenjo-Daro the excavators found heaps of skeletons of men, women, and children who had been cut down in the streets and lanes. Yet the Indus Valley civilization may have passed on to succeeding generations in India certain elements such as the worship of the sacred fig-tree, of snakes, and of Siva the Destroyer.

Aryan India: 1500–500 B.C.

By about 1500 B.C. the Aryans had seized the whole of northern India. The following thousand-year period, which in British history would take us back to before the Norman Conquest (1066 A.D.), is divided into the Vedic era (1500–1000 B.C.) titled after the Vedic hymns of the Aryans, and the Epic period (1000–500 B.C.), named after the two great Hindu epics. During the Vedic era, the Aryans were settled in villages as herdsmen and farmers in a tribal and aristocratic society. Their "rajahs" or kings were at first elected but tended to become hereditary. There were tribal councils and assemblies of freemen.

Like other early Indo-Europeans, the Aryans worshipped the forces of nature such as Indra, the storm, and Agni, the fire (cf. Latin *ignis*—fire). They were warlike and loved dancing, music, charioteering and fermented drinks. Unlike later Hindus they ate beef and horseflesh and had animal sacrifices. There was a scorn of outsiders and a desire to keep the bloodstream pure. From this feeling came four classes, the *Kshatriyas* or warriors, the *Brahmans* or priestly order, the *Vaisyas* or traders and agriculturalists, and the *Sudras*, slaves or non-Aryans. Although the Kshatriyas were dominant at first, the Brahmans supplanted them. In these four orders were the beginnings of the caste system.

In the Epic period sixteen or more small kingdoms were gradually formed in North India, each with its own capital city and rajah and each at war with its neighbors. Metal-working, weaving, leather-working and other crafts developed, agriculture was improved, coinage replaced a clumsy barter method in which the cow was used as the unit of trade, and wealthy merchants were common. Meanwhile, a number of castes came into existence. *Varna*, the word for caste, originally meant color, which suggests that one source of caste was the attempt to keep the Aryan blood-strain pure. But occupations, place of origin and other factors also helped determine caste. Finally there were some 3000 castes, each with its own niche in Hindu life. Although modern Hindu leaders are reforming the system, particularly with reference to the "Untouchables," caste is still an important factor in India.

Hinduism

The growth of the caste system was tied in with the birth of Hinduism. By the middle of the Epic period the Aryan gods, except for Indra, had been replaced by many of the deities which are still worshipped in India. Foremost among these are four-faced Brahma, the Creator, Vishnu, the Preserver, and Siva, the Destroyer, the anthropomorphic (in the shape of man) trinity which is believed to keep the universe operating. There are a multitude of other deities, including anthropomorphic and animal gods and nature spirits. Each of these manifold objects of worship was and is regarded as a manifestation of some part of the universal spirit. Meanwhile the notion of a god being incarnated as a man came into being. Thus Hinduism is able to shelter animistic, anthropomorphic and higher types of worship under the one roof.

It was in the Epic period, too, that in philosophical treatises known as the *Upanishads* the basic beliefs of Hinduism were expressed. Put briefly and, therefore, inadequately, Hinduism believes in a Cosmic Self, known as *Brahman*, which is the Supreme Reality, the "Unity ... behind all multiplicity." Of this Brahman the psychic self (*Atman*) of each individual is a part. The goal of each Atman is reunion with Brahman; but this reunion can only be achieved after proper behavior in a succession of lives.

The rebirth of the psychic self is, therefore, a fundamental concept in Hinduism; but whether the individual psychic self is reborn into a higher or lower caste or in an animal is determined by the law of *Karma*. Karma (which originally meant "deed" or "action") is the doctrine that each act, good or bad, reaps its consequences either in this life or in the next rebirth. Since the individual's acts in his previous life or lives have determined his caste in his present life and since each caste has its own moral duty, the doctrine of Karma gives a religious sanction to the caste system. Furthermore, the belief in rebirth into animals gives Hinduism a strong trend toward vegetarianism, has abolished animal sacrifices, and in part led to veneration of the cow. The desire for proper behavior has also fostered asceticism and "holy men." Meanwhile, the belief that the supreme Reality is one and eternal has made Hindu thinking emphasize the unreality of the visible world as a mere illusion of the senses. We ought to note that the concepts of rebirth and of the unreality of the visible world will reappear when we study the thinking of Greek philosophers such as Pythagoras (6th century B.C.) and Plato (4th century B.C.).

Hinduism, like other great religions, ranges from popular beliefs and superstitions to the concepts of an intellectual class. Today, in one form or another, it is the way of life for over two-thirds of the people of India.

Buddhism

From Hinduism Buddhism was born. Its founder, Gautama (traditional dates, 567–487 B.C.), was a noble who through his meditations became the Buddha (Enlightened One). He accepted the doctrines of Karma and rebirth but rebelled against the caste system, the Brahmanical spells and rituals, and Hinduism's multiplicity of deities. His basic teaching, simplified, was that life is inseparable from suffering and sorrow; suffering and sorrow are caused by desires begotten by the illusory world; to be rid of suffering and sorrow one must escape desires which cause rebirth and tie one to the "Wheel of Life"; to escape desires and rebirth one must either renounce the world for meditation (and hence Buddhist monasteries) or follow the "Noble Eightfold Path." This path is defined as Right Outlook, Right Aims, Right Speech, Right Action, Right Living, Right Effort, Right Mindfulness and Right Meditation. "Rightness" was defined as not killing any living being (and hence, vegetarianism), not taking what is not given freely; not speaking falsely; not drinking intoxicating liquors and not being unchaste. The goal of the path is *Nirvana*, a state of peaceful bliss, involving the abolition of desire and therefore of pain, release from rebirth and absorption into the *All*. Compassion for all living beings and serene meditation were attributed to Buddha and these qualities have a strong part in Buddhism.

In the first five centuries after his death there were no statues of Buddha. Then, two differing views of him developed. In the "Lesser Vehicle" Buddha was regarded as a teacher; in the "Greater Vehicle" he was looked upon as an incarnation of the godhead. Meanwhile, Buddhism was a rival of Hinduism in India and spread over southeastern Asia. In the 3rd century B.C. Buddhist missionaries even found their way to Syria, Egypt, Cyrene, and Epirus in northwestern Greece. Then, about the time of the birth of Christ, Buddhism spread into Central Asia and thence to China, Tibet, Korea and Japan. In these countries as well as in south-eastern Asia it is a vital force today; but in India itself, by the eleventh century A.D., it had succumbed to Hinduism, partly because of a "counter-reformation" in Hinduism during which Buddhism was incorporated into the Hindu pantheon as the ninth incarnation of the god Vishnu.

The literature of Aryan India

Our cursory survey of Buddhism has led us far beyond the Vedic and Epic periods of Aryan India. The four Vedas were hymns to the gods and are the most sacred of the Hindu scriptures. Although composed between 1500 and 1000 B.C. they were not written down until centuries later. Of the four, the *Rigveda* ("rich knowledge"), 1017 hymns in ten books, is the most important. Apart from their religious content, the Vedas give us a picture of the life of their period. In the Epic era, the *Upanishads*, which have been already mentioned, were added. These along with the Vedas and other religious and philosophical works, form what we may call the "Old Testament" of Hinduism, while the *"Discourses"* of the Buddha became the principal sacred book of Buddhism.

The most striking literature of the Epic period were the two epics, the *Mahabharata* and the *Ramayana*, both of which were passed along orally before being written down. The *Mahabharata*, of which the hero is Krishna, describes a civil war in North India. Thought to have had originally 8800 couplets, it grew to more than 100,000 and is a composite of Hindu ideas from a succession of Brahman editors. In its sixth book is the mystical "Song of the Lord" which decrees that action is inevitable in existence but that one's duty should be performed without passion or desire.

The *Ramayana* (24,000 couplets) is more interesting to western readers. It relates the expulsion of Prince Rama and his wife Sita, from their city, their adventures in the forest, the abduction of Sita by a demon king, the war for her recovery and the triumphant return of the reunited couple to their home. Today Rama and Krishna are both regarded as incarnations of the god Vishnu.

The Vedas, the epics and the other works of Aryan India were the early productions of a vigorous Hindu literature which, later on, included a great drama, the *Shakantula* and the *Jakatas* or *Tales of Buddha*. All these works were written down in classical Sanskrit, a language developed from the original Indo-European speech of the Aryans. Sanskrit ("the refined language") became a sacred tongue and ceased to be spoken. But important Hindu languages of today, such as Hindi and Bengali, are derived from it. The early period of India, down to 500 B.C., to a considerable degree set the basic patterns of Hindu life and thought.

India from the Persians to the Roman Empire (ca. 520 B.C. – 180 A.D.)

We will learn later that Cyrus the Great founded a wide-ranging Persian Empire between 550 and 529 B.C. It was his second successor, Darius the Great, (521–485 B.C.) who added the northwestern part of India to the Persian realm. In consequence there was a two-way traffic in goods and ideas between northern India and Persia. Then, in 326 B.C. Alexander the Great of Macedonia, after his conquest of Persia, marched into India, defeated a Hindu king (Porus) and took over northwest India. After Alexander's death in 323 B.C., Chandragupta Maurya built the first Hindu empire. From a Greek who was an envoy to Chandragupta's court in 302 B.C. we learn that the Hindu capital on the Ganges River was nine and a half miles in length and a mile in width, was surrounded by a huge wall, governed by a strict bureaucracy, abounded in the arts and wealth, and that its rich citizens were dressed in "flowered muslins embroidered with jewels."

Asoka (269–236 B.C.) Chandragupta's grandson, extended the empire further; then, renouncing conquest, he promulgated Buddhism. The Mauryan dynasty ended in 287 B.C. But Alexander the Great had left Greek colonies behind him, both in India and to the northwest of India, and particularly in a country called Bactria to the east of the Caspian Sea. From Bactria in the 2nd century B.C., Greek rulers invaded northern India and set up kingdoms which lasted for about a century and a half or until about the time of the birth of Christ. One result was the spread of a somewhat garbled form of Greek culture. In sculpture and painting, for instance, Greek influence is evident and was carried by Buddhists to China. More important, perhaps, was the two-way commerce which from the time of the death of Alexander the Great flowed for some centuries between what, as we shall see later on, was called the Hellenistic Greek world and India.

In this commerce a caravan road ran from Babylon through the northwest passes into India while there were two sea-routes, the one along the Persian Gulf to the Indus Valley, the other from Hellenistic Egypt along the Red Sea and across the southern India. It is said that 120 ships a year sailed from Egypt to India. Later on the Romans took over these trade routes. From India the chief exports were cottons, gems, scented woods, drugs, pepper and other spices and, in Hellenistic times, war-elephants; the Graeco-Romans on their side sent wines, lead, tin, coral, arms, glass, pottery and coins. It is reasonable to suppose that there was some interchange of ideas as well as of goods.

India in post-Roman times

From the beginning of the Christian era to the coming of the Europeans, there were a score of invasions of India, though there was also a second native Hindu empire, that of the Guptas (ca. 320–535 A.D.). One result of these invasions was the coming of Mohammedanism into India. Finally, India was conquered by the Mongols in 1525 A.D. The Mogul (Persian name of Mongol) empire which they established lasted until the British overturned it. In modern times, India, divided into India and Pakistan, is independent.

Throughout their long history the people of India have shown a remarkable ability to assimilate foreign invaders, customs and religions and to blend them all into a way of life which is peculiarly their own. Even in ancient times, apart from a two-way flow of goods, they seem to have contributed to the West something of their philosophical and religious ideas, while in the Middle Ages their invention of the decimal system and the all-important sign for zero was transmitted via the Arabs to Europe. In modern days, to a western world which tends to exalt force, power and the reality of the visible world, the Hindu point of view presents an emphasis on spirituality and a belief in the unity of the Real and the unsubstantiality of the visible world. This attitude toward life reaches back to close to 1000 years before Christ. Meanwhile, during somewhat the same period, the Chinese people were developing their own characteristic civilization.

China: The Middle Kingdom

China (the name is supposed to have been derived by Malay seafarers from the Ch'in dynasty of 255–206 B.C.) was until recent times pretty well isolated. On the east and south are sea and jungle, to the west and north mountainous plateaus and arid wastes. The Chinese themselves often called their land "The Middle Kingdom", believing it to be the centre of the world and the only civilized country, and regarding it as supplying everything humanity needs.

Isolation also meant that China was left freer than India to develop its own specific way of life. Yet, at times, China extended its power and influence beyond China proper into the "Outer Provinces", such as Tibet, Manchuria and Mongolia, and likewise into Korea and Japan. Today its 700 millions of people make it by far the most populous nation of the world.

China proper is about the size of India. Although there is a uniform system of writing, its people speak a multiplicity of dialects and differ greatly in stature and appearance. Apart from considerable variations in terrain and climate, the country divides into North and South China. It was in the north, along the southward loop of the Yellow River (Hwang-Ho) that China's first civilization developed.

Paleolithic and Neolithic China

As you have learned, forty-five skeletons of a near-man (*Sinanthropus*), dating back to 300,000 B.C. or earlier, were found in caves at Choukoutien near Pekin. This type of man knew fire, stored berries, hunted animals and was probably a cannibal. Evidence of other Old Stone Age men of a much later date has been discovered at various places in North China. Then, as elsewhere in the neolithic period, farming villages developed. It was out of these along the Yellow River where flood-control and irrigation were essential that the first urban civilization grew.

Chinese legends tell of a H'sia dynasty (traditional dates 2207–1766 B.C.) and a Shang or Yin dynasty (1766–1122 B.C.). No evidence for the H'sias has been found, but the Shang or Yin dynasty has been proved by "oracle-bones" and the "Mounds of Yin."

The Mounds of Yin

The Mounds of Yin are near today's town of Anfang north of the Yellow River. From these mounds and from the surrounding area for many years bones with writing on them were sold by the peasants to Chinese pharmacists to be made into medicine as "dragon bones". In modern times these bones were discovered to be the shoulder-blades of oxen or deer which had been used to divine the future by scapulimancy (Latin, *scapulae*, "shoulder-blades" and Greek *manteia*, "prophecy"). The method was to ask a question of a seer such as: Will next year be a good year for millet? The seer then took the shoulder-blade of an animal or the bottom shell of a tortoise and applied a hot point to a part weakened by incisions. From the cracks which appeared, the seer "divined" the answer to the question.

Both the question and the answer were often written on the shell or bone which was then buried. The some 2500 pictograms used (also found on bronze vessels of the period) turned out to be the ancestors of today's Chinese characters. Furthermore, the names of about three-fourths of the legendary Shang rulers were found and this dynasty was proved to be historical. Then, when the Mounds of Yin were excavated, it was discovered that they were the tombs of Shang kings.

Their sepulchres are in the shape of an inverted pyramid. In each case steps of pounded earth on the north, east and west and a ramp on the south lead down to a grave in the shape of a cross. Round about, as in the royal tombs of Ur or of the first and second dynasties of Egypt, are the skeletons of the mass slaughter of men, women and animals. Bronze vessels and the remains of chariots and musical instruments have been unearthed. Further excavations nearby uncovered the remnants of a capital city of the Shangs.

Shang culture

The Shang civilization was well advanced. There were towns and cities (the legends tell of 1800 city-states) and a fairly large realm. In warfare, cavalry, infantry and chariots were used. Government was by a bureaucracy under a despotic ruler. There was sculpture in stone, a well-developed script, a calendar and bronze vessels and implements of a quality not surpassed elsewhere.

Farming was the basic occupation. Millet and wheat were grown. Pork and dogmeat were popular foods and horses, cattle, chickens and pheasants had also been domesticated. As in today's China, as well as in Japan, Korea, Indo-China and Malaya, dairy products were not used. The secret of making silk seems to have been known. Tigers, bears and wolves were hunted and there is one reference to an elephant.

The poor lived in hovels dug out of the earth and roofed with mud-covered timber. The upper classes dwelt in houses with the same plan of courtyards and rooms as is used today. A pictogram shows a gabled roof.

In religion the king seems to have ruled by the "Mandate of Heaven." There was a worship of nature-spirits and animal and human sacrifices; and ancestor-worship was already present. All in all the picture is of a civilization which was already setting the patterns of the Chinese way of life.

The Chou Dynasty: 1122 or 1027 to 256 B.C.

The Shangs were overthrown by the Chous who came from the western frontier. After a succession of strong men who extended the realm and gained a footing in the Yangtze valley, their power decayed. In the middle and late periods of the Chou dynasty (776–256 B.C.) China was a group of warring states with the Chou kings (known as *Wangs*) as nominal rulers.

Yet during this period of confusion there were important developments. The ox-drawn plough was introduced, rice was grown, the silk industry was promoted, fermented rice and millet liquors became popular, irrigation was extended and fertilizers used. Meanwhile, metal coinage supplanted cowry shells as money, commerce prospered and wealthy merchants appeared. Iron and the seven-day week came in along trade routes from the West.

Art and architecture flourished, and the lacquering of wood became common. In the same period the five Chinese Classics took shape. These were three historical works: the *Classic of History*, the *Spring and Autumn Annals*, the *Bamboo Annals* (originally written on slips of bamboo) and the *Classic of Change* (divination, but including principles of government and philosophy), and the *Classic of Poetry*. These works, along with various compilations of rituals and ceremonies, were studied by successive generations of scholars and were fundamental in shaping Chinese customs and institutions.

Politically the king was the sole ruler, but in the middle and late periods his chief functions were in religion and in conferring investiture on the various feudal leaders. A host of officials governed. The chief feature of Chou society was the patriarchal family, with as many members and relatives as possible under one roof. The state itself was conceived of as a great family with the king as the father, but there was a sharp distinction between the lower class families and the aristocratic clans which traced their descent from a god, hero, or monarch.

In religion ancestor-worship was firmly established but a host of terrestrial and heavenly spirits were also venerated with ritual and sacrifices by the state, the family and the individual. From the Chinese point of view the objective of worship was to secure the co-operation of the spirits for human well-being.

Chou philosophers: Confucius, Lao-Tzu and the Legalists

The same common-sense attitude is found in the Chinese philosophers. Their interest lay not in abstruse speculation, but in how to produce the best society. The most influential of them was K'ung-Tzu (551–479 B.C.), known to us as Confucius.

Confucius was a dignified, upright and somewhat humourless man. Believing that an ideal society could be best achieved by a return to the methods of the sage-rulers of Chinese legend, he stressed ceremonial and ritual and conduct in accordance with each person's position in life. Rulers, for example, were to act as rulers and subjects as subjects. Inferiors were to behave properly to superiors and vice versa. Inside the family sons were to respect fathers, and younger brothers elder brothers and so on. Furthermore, the correct ceremonial for each and every occasion was specified, whether it was a meeting between equals or between superior and inferior or was a ritual or a sacrifice. From these regulations was derived the formalism of Chinese society.

To achieve good government, Confucius held that the ruler and the governing class must cultivate virtue in themselves, and thus act as an example to which the subjects would automatically respond. His ideal ruler was an educated man of high moral quality but possessed of an aristocratic polish. Among his many ethical concepts was the saying: "What you do not like when done to yourself, do not do unto others."

Confucius left a book of precepts, known as "Analects" and many disciples. After a brief period of persecution under the succeeding Ch'in dynasty, Confucianism became the dominant philosophy in China for century after century. It was one of the chief forces to give continuity to Chinese civilization and to make it static.

Opposed to Confucianism was Taoism. Its founder was Lao-Tzu, an older contemporary of Confucius. By the *Tao* Lao-Tzu seems to have meant the Unknown and Unknowable conceived of as underlying, permeating and controlling the universe, and man, in his view, would find his fullest life by conforming to the *Tao*, thought of as a sort of idealized nature. The "way of the Tao" was defined as "doing everything by doing nothing." As translated into practice, this paradox meant spontaneous and natural actions with a minimum of social organization and regulations. In Taoism, which is a sort of "return to nature" idea, there would be no commerce, trade, wealth, laws, ceremonies, higher government or codes of ethics. In the Taoist society, if two villages were side by side, the people of neither village would even *want* to visit or see the other.

Another strain in Taoism was mystical. It was believed that the Unknowable might be comprehended, not by reason, but, as in Buddhism, by contemplation and revelation. There was a search also to achieve the continuation of one's personal existence by magic and the discovery of the "elixir of life."

In its various aspects, Taoism became an important Chinese religion. A third philosophical school of the Chou period were the Legalists. Where Confucius seems to have held that there was a force for good in the universe, the Legalists believed that man's nature was evil. Put briefly, they taught that society could only be saved by enforcing codes of laws under a totalitarian regime; while simplicity and ignorance was the proper state of the common people. The Legalists were the guiding philosophers of the next Chinese dynasty, the Ch'in.

The Ch'in Empire: 221–207 B.C.

Out of the warring states of the later Chou period, the Ch'ins, a people of northwestern China, emerged as victors and built the first Chinese empire. Following the Legalists, a single code of laws was enforced, a stern bureaucracy was installed, the realm was divided into thirty-six (later forty) provinces, and a single system of weights and measures and of writing was made compulsory.

This last measure was important. The Chinese language is monosyllabic and, furthermore, in the official Mandarin (a Portuguese word) uses four "tones". The monosyllable *ma*, for example, according to the pitch or tone in which it is pronounced can mean "mother," "horse," "flax," or an interrogative particle somewhat akin to "huh?" Similarly, there is the story of an American who bought a coat but received a caged tiger instead because he had used the wrong "tone" for the word for coat. But there are many mutually incomprehensible dialects in China so that an inland Chinese cannot, for instance, understand a man from the coast. Yet thanks to the Ch'ins, educated Chinese can read and write the same script, no matter what their pronunciation of the words is.

The Chinese script, however, is difficult, since it is ideographic-pictographic and not alphabetic. Today there are 40,000 characters, although only from 4000 to 8000 are in general use. Of these characters 214 are basic symbols which are used in various combinations to represent other objects or ideas. Thus the pictogram for a woman plus the one for a broom means "housewife," similarly two pictograms for "woman" side by side mean "quarrel" and three mean "gossip." Nevertheless, the difficulty of learning the Chinese script has tended to restrict the number of educated people. In the Ch'in period, to stifle discussion there was also a great burning of books.

Another achievement of the Ch'ins was the building of the Great Wall of China. Starting at the sea north of Pekin this wall curved inland in a great arc for 1500 miles to protect the northern and northwestern parts of China. Its average height is twenty feet, the roadway on top is fifteen feet wide and at every hundred to two hundred yards there are towers. Thousands of criminals, peasants, merchants and even Confucian scholars were drafted to build the wall; and thousands died. So oppressive was the rule of the Ch'ins that they were overthrown.

The Han Dynasty: 206 B.C.–221 A.D.

Except for a break from 9 to 23 A.D., the Hans ruled for over 400 years.

The Ch'in laws were repealed, taxes lightened and Confucianism adopted as the basis of government. To ensure that the best people would become officials, elaborate civil service examinations were instituted; examinations which came to be tests of one's knowledge of the classics revered by Confucius.

It was during the Han rule that Chinese armies marched southward, and also into Korea and Central Asia. As one result, Chinese culture now had a strong impact upon Japan, giving that country, for example, its system of writing. For another, Chinese silks, furs and iron reached India and the Hellenistic Greek world and, later on, Rome. We can visualize the slow-moving caravans plodding league after league along the Silk Road either through the Khyber Pass into India or to Ctesiphon on the Tigris. From India Chinese goods went to the West by boat; from Ctesiphon either by boat or by caravan to Palmyra or Antioch. The Romans called the Chinese the "Silk People" (*Seres*) and in the time of the Roman Emperor Marcus Aurelius (161–180 A.D.) Graeco-Roman traders are said to have reached the Chinese court. There must in those days have been many an exciting saga of travel.

It was along the Silk Road that, about the time of the birth of Christ, Buddhism reached China to become one of its most important religions. It was a modified Buddhism which, in addition to the pursuit of meditation and tranquillity, gave the Chinese hells or purgatories and heavens and the hope of immortality. From China, as has been mentioned, it was exported to Tibet, Korea and Japan.

Life in the Han period was static in government but, elsewhere, showed many advances. Architecture was elaborate, jewellers' craftmanship exquisite, music developed further and falconry, juggling, dancing, bull and cock fighting, archery, foot-races, board games and gambling were among the popular amusements. Among inventions we might note the sun dial, the water-clock and the discovery of paper (105 A.D.). In general, by the end of the Han period, the main patterns of Chinese society were set and static. Change was sacrificed to uniformity and stability.

From the Han Dynasty to the present

More than three and a half centuries of confusion and invasions followed the fall of the Hans, until first the Sui dynasty (589–618 A.D.) and then the T'angs (618–907 A.D.) re-united the country. Under the T'angs the Chinese empire reached its greatest extent, stretching southward into Indo-China and westward to the Aral and Caspian Seas. The Sung dynasty (960–1279 A.D.) ended another period of anarchy but it was overthrown by the Mongols (1279–1368 A.D.). Their most famous monarch was Kublai Khan to whose court the Venetian Marco Polo found his way. The expulsion of the Mongols was followed by the Ming dynasty (1368–1644 A.D.). Then, China was conquered by the Manchus from the north, who introduced the pigtail and held the throne until the Empire was replaced by the Republic in 1912 A.D.

Meanwhile, Europeans had finally forced their way into China. Their impact on Chinese institutions was somewhat shattering. Yet, in spite of the Europeans and in spite of today's Communist regime, it is probably still true that each Chinese "is born at least thirty-five hundred years old" in the sense that the institutions and customs which shape him reach back that far into antiquity. Both China and India have the faculty of absorbing the influences that reach them and transmuting them into something which conforms to their long and continuing way of life.

Notes to Chapter 3

1. Indo-European is a linguistic term denoting a language-group, which includes the Sanskrit spoken in early India and its derivatives, ancient and modern Persian, Hittite, ancient and modern Greek, Latin and its derivatives (Italian, French, Spanish, Portuguese and Rumanian), and the Celtic, Teutonic, Scandinavian and Slavic tongues. The speakers of the original language may have been "Nordics", but by the time the Indo-European speaking peoples appear in history they were already composed of mingled stocks; and it must be remembered that language and race are not identical, since, otherwise, the negroes, Finns, Norwegians, Irish, Italians and other peoples in the United States would have the same racial origin. Very often, then, the term Indo-European refers to a congeries of people who spoke the same general type of language and had the same type of social and political organization. One or two examples of the similarity of Indo-European languages may be given, as follows:

Sanskrit	Greek	Latin	German	English
pitr	pater	pater	vater	father
matr	meter	mater	mutter	mother
dva	duo	duo	zwei	two
tri	treis	tres	drei	three

2. Alexander the Great established cities of Greeks and Macedonians in Bactria. Originally part of the Hellenistic kingdom of Syria, Bactria finally became practically independent and Graeco-Macedonian adventurers raided into India.

Readings from Sources of the Period

(a) A passage from the Akkadian version of the Sumerian Epic of the Deluge, describes how Utnapishtim built a ship to avoid the Flood.

With the first glow of dawn,
The land was gathered about me....
The little ones carried bitumen,
While the grown ones brought all else that was needful.
On the fifth day I laid her framework.
One whole acre was her floor space,
    Ten dozen cubits the height of each of her walls,
Ten dozen cubits each edge of the square deck.
I laid out the shape of her sides and joined her together.
I provided her with six decks,
Dividing her thus into seven parts.
Her floor plan I divided into nine parts.
I hammered water-plugs into her.
I saw to the punting-poles and laid in supplies.
Six 'sar' (measures) of bitumen I poured into the furnace,
Three sar of asphalt I also poured inside.
Three sar of oil the basket-bearers transferred,
Aside from the one sar of oil which the calking consumed,
And the two sar of oil which the boatman stowed away.
Bullocks I slaughtered for the people,
And I killed sheep every day.
Must, red wine, oil, and white wine
I gave the workmen to drink, as though river water,
That they might feast as on New Year's Day.
I opened ... ointment, applying it to my hand.
On the seventh day the ship was completed.
The launching was very difficult,
So that they had to shift the floor planks above and below,
Until two-thirds of the structure had gone into the water.

Whatever I had I laded upon her;
Whatever I had of silver I laded upon her;
Whatever I had of gold I laded upon her;
Whatever I had of all the living beings I laded upon her.
All my family and kin I made go aboard the ship.
The beasts of the field, the wild creatures of the field,
    All the craftsmen I made go aboard.

(McDermott and Caldwell, *Readings in the History of the Ancient World*, p. 39, New York: Rinehart, 1951.)

(b) After the Empire of 3rd Dynasty Ur was destroyed and Ur itself was sacked an unknown Sumerian wrote a lament about the fate of his city.

O thou city of high walls, thy land has perished.
O my city, like an innocent ewe thy lamb has been torn away from thee;
O Ur, like an innocent goat thy kid has perished....
Thy lament which is bitter—how long will it grieve thy weeping lord?

Its walls were breached; the people mourn. . . .
In its lofty gates, where they were wont to promenade, dead bodies lay
about.
In its spacious streets, where feasts were celebrated, scattered they lay. . . .
Its corpses, like fat placed in the sun, melted away. . . .
The old men and women who could not leave their homes were overcome
by fire.
The babes lying on their mothers' laps like fish were carried off by the
waters. . . .
The judgment of the land perished. The people mourn. . . .

(Translated by S. N. Kramer, *Sumerian Mythology*, American Philosophical
Society, Philadelphia, 1944.)

(c) In the time of Hammurabi (1728–1686 B.C.) a young man in Babylon, Gimil-
Marduk sent a love letter to his sweetheart, Bibiya, in the city of Sippar, where
almost four thousand years later, it was unearthed.

"To Bibiya say: thus Gimil-Marduk. May Shamash (the sun-god) and Marduk
(the supreme god of Babylon) give you health forever for my sake. I have sent
(to ask) after your health; let me know how you are. I have arrived in Babylon
and do not see you; I am very sad. Send news of your coming that I may be
cheered; in the month of Markheswan you shall come. May you live forever for
my sake."

(The Cambridge Ancient History, edited by J. B. Bury, S. A. Cook and F. E.
Adcock. Vol. I, Chapter XIV, written by R. Campbell-Thompson. Cambridge,
2nd edn., reprinted 1928, hereinafter called C. A. H. I have changed—thee, thy
and thou,—to you and your, shalt to shall and mayst to may.)

(d) During his reign Hammurabi had a code of laws carved on a shaft of black
diorite almost eight feet high. In 1901 a French archaeologist discovered this
shaft at Susa in what is now Iran whither it had presumably been carried by an
Elamite conqueror. It is now in the Louvre Museum in Paris. At the top of the
shaft is a bas-relief showing Hammurabi receiving the code of laws from the
seated sun-god, Shamash. Below are a few excerpts from the code. They illustrate
both how Hammurabi tried to set down laws for all contingencies and the "eye
for an eye" principle.

25.   If a fire has broken out in a man's house and one who has come to put it out
has coveted the property of the householder and appropriated any of it, that man
shall be cast into the self-same fire.
42.   If a man has hired a field to cultivate and has caused no corn to grow on
the field, he shall be held responsible for not doing the work on the field and
shall pay an average rent.
48.   If a man has incurred a debt and a storm has flooded his field or carried away
the crop, or the corn has not grown because of drought, in that year he shall not
pay his creditor. Further, he shall post-date his bond and shall not pay interest
for that year.
53,54.   If a man has neglected to strengthen his dike and has not kept his dike
strong, and a breach has broken out in his dike, and the waters have flooded the

meadow, the man in whose dike the breach has broken out shall restore the corn he has caused to be lost. [54.] If he be not able to restore the corn, he and his goods shall be sold, and the owners of the meadow whose corn the water has carried away shall share the money.

110.   If a votary, who is not living in the convent, open a beer-shop, or enter a beer-shop for drink, that woman shall be put to death.

122.   If a man has given another gold, silver, or any goods whatever, on deposit, all that he gives shall he show to witnesses, and take a bond and so give on deposit.

128.   If a man has taken a wife and has not executed a marriage-contract, that woman is not a wife.

141.   If a man's wife, living in her husband's house, has persisted in going out, has acted the fool, has wasted her house, has belittled her husband, he shall prosecute her. If her husband has said, "I divorce her," she shall go her way; he shall give her nothing as her price of divorce. If her husband has said, "I will not divorce her," he may take another woman to wife; the wife shall live as a slave in her husband's house.

159.   If a man, who has presented a gift to the house of his prospective father-in-law and has given the bride-price, has afterward looked upon another woman and has said to his father-in-law, "I will not marry your daughter"; the father of the girl shall keep whatever he has brought as a present.

160.   If a man has presented a gift to the house of his prospective father-in-law, and has given the bride-price, but the father of the girl has said, "I will not give you my daughter," the father shall return double all that was presented him.

195.   If a son has struck his father, his hands shall be cut off.

196.   If a man has knocked out the eye of a patrician, his eye shall be knocked out.

200.   If a patrician has knocked out the tooth of a plebeian, he shall pay one-third of a mina of silver.

206.   If a man has struck another in a quarrel, and caused him a permanent injury, that man shall swear, "I struck him without malice," and shall pay the doctor.

218.   If a surgeon has operated with the bronze lancet on a patrician for a serious injury, and has caused his death, or has removed a cataract for a patrician, with the bronze lancet, and has made him lose his eye, his hands shall be cut off.

229.   If a builder has built a house for a man, and has not made his work sound, and the house he built has fallen and caused the death of its owner, that builder shall be put to death.

(G. H. Knoles and R. F. Snyder, *Readings in Western Civilization*, Vol. I 3rd ed. New York: Lippincott, 1951.)

CHAPTER 4

Early Civilizations:
Egypt to the end of the Middle Kingdom

While Mesopotamia was developing its riverine civilization, the same process was in motion in Egypt. Even more than in Sumer and Akkad, a river goaded Egypt's growth.

The Nile

The 4000-mile-long Nile makes Egypt. Its source is a chain of fresh-water lakes in equatorial Africa. About 1350 miles from the Mediter-ranean, the White Nile is joined by a tributary, the Blue Nile, which begins in Abyssinia. After the two streams merge, the river slithers northward, like a huge snake, through uplands, deserts, and granitic rocks until it tumbles over the First Cataract. Here the granite on either side of the river changes to limestone. For over 500 miles through this softer rock the Nile has carved a canyon between ten to thirty miles wide, bounded by flat-topped hills. Beyond them the desert begins.

About 100 miles from the Mediterranean, near modern Cairo and ancient Memphis, the Nile emerges from the canyon to flow in seven channels through the delta it has built. Seen from the air, most of Egypt is desert. Through the center runs a narrow, twisting ribbon of green which expands into the Delta. Cultivable ancient Egypt, like lower Mesopotamia, consisted of about 10,000 square miles of land.

The Geography of Egypt

This, then, was the setting for early Egyptian civilization—the strip of green on both flanks of the river in the canyon and the swamps and prairie-like flat lands of the Delta. Hence Egypt was divided by nature into Upper Egypt (the canyon) and Lower Egypt (the Delta). The Nile united the whole country, and unlike Lower Mesopotamia, ancient Egypt was protected and isolated. The first cataract and the unproductive region beyond formed a defense to the south. To the north was the Mediterranean. To east and west were deserts. There was a route along the west to Libya and a narrow land-bridge to Asia in the east. But in general, ancient Egypt, once it attained a strong government, was left free to develop its own civilization.

We might note that there was little timber in Egypt but plenty of rock. From an early period, the Egyptians learned to work in stone. The climate was (and is) dry: there is little rain in the Delta and practically none in Upper Egypt. This aridity is the reason why so many objects, including ancient linen and paper, have been preserved for thousands of years. It also explains the value of the inundation.

The Inundation

The inundation is still Egypt's annual miracle. In the spring of the year, as the equatorial rains pour down into the sources of the Nile, a huge surge of water rolls downstream. Toward the end of June it reaches the first cataract. It covers the canyon floor and floods the Delta. From July to October Egypt is either a shallow sea or stinking mud flats.

That flood, like the waters of the Tigris-Euphrates rivers, is loaded with silt. Once again, to harvest rich crops the Neolithic Egyptian villagers had to learn to co-operate in irrigation and flood-control and to submit to a powerful centralized government.

Pre-Dynastic Egypt

The record of pre-dynastic Egypt reaches back into the Paleolithic Age. Since the Nile gorge was uninhabitable in those days and the Delta had not yet emerged, early man hunted on what were then grasslands to the east and west. During the Mesolithic era, as North Africa began to dry up, hunters of a culture called *Sebilian* began to follow game into the gorge, which was by this time covered with rich silt, and into the emerging Delta. These people seem to have corralled animals and to have collected the seeds of the wild grasses. During the fifth millenium B.C. Neolithic farming began at sites such as those found at Tasa and Badari in the canyon, and at Merimde on the southwestern rim of the Delta. Earlier villages may be buried deep under the mud of the Delta.

In the Tasian culture the men still hunted and fished but pottery was made and cereals cultivated, probably by the women. At Merimde there was a village street and storage-bins for grain, and there is evidence that goats and pigs were kept. The Badarian sites show dependence on farming, the domestication of animals, and the manufacture of linen. A few copper beads have also been found in their burial sites. Shells from the Red Sea are present as well as turquoise from Sinai.

The people in these villages were a short, lithe race of Mediterranean stock with distinct traces of Negroid blood. In the fourth millenium B.C. Hamites from Libya (a sub-stock formed by a fusion of Mediterraneans and Negroids), and Semites from Asia migrated into the land. Later, there were successive infiltrations of broadheads, also from somewhere in Asia, while from time to time Negroid tribesmen made their way down the Nile. Out of this mingling of stocks came the ancient Egyptians. Their language was Hamitic but it had a strong infusion of Semitic words.

Archeologists divide the pre-history of the fourth millenium into three main phases—Amratian, Gerzean, and Semainean. During the first of these periods, as in Lower Mesopotamia, the Neolithic villagers learned co-operation in order to control the inundation and to store water between the annual overflows. This first irrigation was basin irrigation; that is, the water was impounded in broad and deep excavations. As a result the first little kingdoms were formed, each with its own town, priest-king, temple and totem god, such as the jackal, the cat, the hawk, and even the harpoon. The priest-kings were thought to be the living incarnations of these gods.

These first little kingdoms were named after their totem gods. Ultimately, there were 42 of them, 22 in Upper Egypt and 20 in the Delta. The Greeks later called them *nomes*. Meanwhile, the Libyans had introduced the ass and the olive, boats made of bundles of papyrus reeds floated on the Nile, marks of ownership appeared on vases, and trade reached to Sinai, to Syria, and, perhaps, to Crete.

In the next period, the Gerzean (about 3500 B.C.), intruders from Asia brought in the vine. At this time the first great irrigation canals were built, and there was artificial drainage of the swamps of the Delta. Boats had sails added to them. An early hieroglyphic script began to develop. The potter's wheel was introduced, again from Asia. Finally, after countless little wars, the two kingdoms of Lower and Upper Egypt were formed. These two are the earliest nations. The names of six of the kings are known.

It is thought that about 3300 B.C. the kings of Lower Egypt conquered Upper Egypt. If so, this first union did not last too long. The union fell apart into two kingdoms again at the beginning of the Semainean period when new intruders from Asia arrived.

By this time there were cities and civilization along the Nile. In each kingdom the king or Pharaoh (although this name came into use later) was regarded as a living god. In each kingdom, too, there was an elaborate court and a complex bureaucracy. Gold and silver were in common use and so were copper tools and weapons. Beautiful stone vases were being fashioned. Expeditions were sent to Sinai for copper and turquoises, cedar was being brought from Lebanon, and there appears to have been communication with Crete and Mesopotamia. Writing (about which more will be said later) had begun, and a solar calendar of 365 days had been invented long before this time. It might be noted that eventually a calendar which provided for a leap year was introduced. It was this calendar which under Julius Caesar was brought to Rome to form the basis for the Julian calendar which in turn with slight changes is the one we use today.

By the end of the fourth millenium, Egypt, like Lower Mesopotamia, was the home of a highly developed, metal-using, riverine civilization. At this point, about 3100 B.C., the Pharaohs of Upper Egypt conquered Lower Egypt and began the Old Kingdom.

The Old Kingdom: The First Two Dynasties

Egyptian legend attributed this second union of the Two Lands to Menes. Archeological discoveries, which include the finding of tombs of the First Dynasty Pharaohs, prove that it was the work of several kings of Upper Egypt. For instance, the ceremonial mace-head and slate palette of Narmer, one of these Pharaohs, records his conquests in the Delta in primitive hieroglyphics.

These Pharaohs were Horus-kings; that is, they were believed to be the incarnation of the falcon-god, Horus. In the Narmer palette, the king, wearing the tall white crown of Upper Egypt, clubs a defeated enemy, while the Horus-falcon holds a rope thrust through the nose of a man, close to whom is a sign for the Delta. On the other side of the palette, Narmer, this time wearing the red crown of Lower Egypt, proudly views a battlefield littered with dead. But it was not until the reign of Khasekemui, the last Pharaoh of the Second Dynasty, that Egypt was finally united.

In this way, through war, the whole of Egypt became one nation. The Pharaohs of the first two Dynasties ruled the Two Lands from Thinis in Upper Egypt, although they also had a center at Memphis, near modern Cairo, at the junction of the Delta and Upper Egypt. They were buried in huge rectangular pits lined with brick or stone possessing a super-structure above ground level, called *mastabas*. Those of the First Dynasty show the same mass-slaughter of attendants as in the death-pits of the First Dynasty of Ur. The court and the bureaucracy were elaborate. Copper had almost completely replaced stone for tool-making, the irrigation and flood control systems were carefully handled, the art objects were excellent and trade was widely extended. A fleet of sea-going vessels, for instance, was sent to bring cedar from Lebanon.

The Pyramid Age: The Third and Fourth Dynasties

The Old Kingdom reached its peak in the Third and Fourth Dynasties. Under Zoser, the first Pharaoh of the Third Dynasty, the oldest freestone building in the world, the step pyramid at Sakkara, was erected. It was said to have been designed by the famous architect and physician, Imhotep.

This step pyramid is a series of six mastabas, progressively diminishing in size, like a huge wedding-cake. It was 204 feet high. Around it Imhotep created a complex of beautiful buildings with fluted columns and arches of the finest limestone. By this time the Egyptians, though only possessing copper tools, had mastered the handling of stone.

Zoser also led a military force to Sinai and his fleet had in it several vessels over 170 feet long. The last Pharaoh of the Third Dynasty, Snefru, built a large pyramid at Medum. The most famous pyramid is the Great Pyramid put up by Khufu (Cheops in Greek history), Snefru's son. This mass of stone on the west bank of the Nile covers roughly 13 acres. It was sheathed at that time with a casing that glittered in the sun and was 481 feet (now 479 feet) high or about half the height of the Empire State Building in New York. In it are approximately 2,300,000 blocks of stone, which average two and one half tons apiece in weight. Some weigh much more. Although the sides of the pyramid measure 755 feet 8 inches, there is in each side not more than a deviation of one inch from a straight line. The joints of the casing stones fit to one-fiftieth of an inch. If we walk into the entrance, we will find that the interior of the pyramid is honeycombed with galleries and rooms. The original entrance is in the north face from which a passage slopes down to an underground room, intended, probably, as the burial chamber for the Pharaoh but never finished. From this passage, about 63 feet from the entrance, another shaft leads upward. This ascending shaft opens abruptly into the Grand Gallery, 158 feet long and 28 feet high. From it a short horizontal tunnel leads into the King's Chamber in the very heart of the pyramid, though not in its center. Above the King's Chamber are five little chambers, intended probably, to relieve the weight of the mass of stone overhead. In the King's Chamber is the sarcophagus; it was carved from a solid block of granite, 7 feet 6 inches long, 3 feet 3 inches wide and 3 feet 4 inches high, but it was empty when found.

If the visitor, instead of entering the Grand Gallery, moves into a horizontal passage which joins the ascending one he will shortly find himself in another room, called the Queen's Chamber. It has a pointed roof while that of the King's Chamber is flat. Two channels leading to the outer surface, the north one 245 feet long, the southern 173 feet long, made the air breathable in both chambers for the workmen of Khufu's reign. The casing then covered the outer apertures. In spite of the tremendous weight of stone above and around them, the passages, Grand Gallery, and King's and Queen's Chambers have kept their shape.

The Great Pyramid stands today as a magnificent memorial to the power and material achievements of the Old Kingdom. It took first-class architects and engineers to plan and supervise the construction. According to Herodotus, 100,000 slaves labored for twenty years to build it. Furthermore, it is believed that it was reared by sheer manpower with the help of nothing more than earthen ramps, sledges, rollers, levers, and ropes.

The guardian Sphinx was carved out of natural rock by the craftsmen of either Khufu or Khafra. It is located to the right of the causeway to Khafra's pyramid. The Sphinx is 66 feet high and 187 feet long. Its mouth is $7\frac{1}{2}$ feet wide; between its great paws it holds a temple. Its face is thought to be a portrait of Khafra. Milleniums later, invading soldiers bounced cannon-balls off the face, but the battered countenance still looks toward the rising sun.

The other two of the great pyramids were built by Khufu's successors, Khafra and Menkaura. For each pyramid there was a temple at the bank of the Nile and a causeway from it to the pyramid. Around the pyramids were clustered in rows the mastaba tombs of the Pharaoh's women and of the nobles. All of them hoped in this way to share in the immortality of the Pharaoh. The Egyptians of the Old Kingdom believed that a happy life in the hereafter was reserved for the Pharaohs and for those whom they favored. The mass of the people, it was thought, lived a shadowy existence after death in caverns along an "underground Nile."

To the subterranean chambers beneath the flat-topped, rectangular mastabas were carried the mummified bodies of their dead owners. Weapons, jewelry, cosmetics and the like were buried with them. Periodically, materials for the dead to eat were brought to the tombs—beef, fowls, vegetables, fruits, bread, beer, wine, and even flowers for decoration. There was regularly, too, a funerary statue of the dead person (the Ka-statue; see below), while carved and colored pictures of the life of the Old Kingdom decorated the walls. The Egyptians believed that the soul could reanimate the mummy, and then the dead person would enjoy again the scenes depicted on the walls.

Those pictures show us Old Kingdom peasants sowing, reaping, and threshing grain. Herdsmen drive cattle across a ford. Coppersmiths, jewelers, goldsmiths, and men drilling stone vases work at their trades. In the market a carpenter's wife offers an inlaid box for a bangle. The men wear kilts or, often, if peasants, nothing at all; the women, a sort of half-slip which leaves the upper part of the body bare.

Other evidence of the life of the day comes to us from the contents of the tombs. In February of 1927 a Boston-Harvard expedition found the tomb of Hetepheres, the mother of Khufu, builder of the Great Pyramid. In it was her gold-mounted carrying chair, her beautiful anklets and armlets, decorated with inset dragon-flies, her bed with its wooden uprights sheathed with gold, her alabaster head-rest, and her armchair.

The great pyramids and the Sphinx make vivid the power of the Pharaohs of the Fourth Dynasty. Many other lesser pyramids were built up to about the time of the Twelfth Dynasty, until there was a "pyramid field" which reached for 60 miles along the west bank of the Nile.

The Fall of the Old Kingdom

Why are there only three really big pyramids? It seems likely that some sort of upheaval, caused, perhaps, by the building of those pyramids, put an end to the Fourth Dynasty. The Fifth Dynasty was initiated by the priests of Re, the sun-god. Although its Pharaohs and those of the Sixth Dynasty sent out far-reaching trading expeditions, they seem not to have had as much power as their predecessors. Instead, the governors of the nomes rose in authority. They passed on their office to their sons. Finally they became almost independent, probably about 2250 B.C.

At the same time Negroes from the Sudan forced their way into Upper Egypt. There may also have been an internal revolt. At any rate, after about 900 years, the Old Kingdom fell. Egypt, once again chaotic, was broken into several units. In the writing of a remarkable man of this period, Ipuwer, we read:

> All is ruin . . . the plunderer is everywhere . . . the poor have become the rich . . . Nile overflows but no man works for him.

Society and Government in the Old Kingdom

We have made a few references to what life was like under the Old Kingdom. To understand it more clearly, we must remember that society was shaped like the Great Pyramid, with the Pharaohs at the top and the peasants and slaves at the base.

The Power of the Pharaoh

The name Pharaoh means "He of the Great House." Like the earlier priest-kings of Upper and Lower Egypt, the Pharaoh was believed by his people to be a living god. All Egypt was Pharaoh's and on his well-being depended the fate of the country. He was the final voice in war, in economics, in religion, in law, in everything. His name could not be spoken. He had to be approached by salaaming. In his magnificent palace at Memphis were scores of wives and concubines; his queen-wife was often his sister. It is possible that his priests did not allow him to die a natural death, but killed him by a snake-bite, since the cobra was a sacred power with which the Pharaoh was identified.

The Nobles

The nobility of Egypt was comprised of the highest of the royal officials. Their offices were usually hereditary, although a man of ability could occasionally rise to a prominent position. The Biblical story of Joseph is an example.

Next to the Pharaoh sat his *vizier*. His job was to supervise the administration of the two kingdoms. Beneath him were the governors of the 42 nomes, who were appointed by the Pharaoh. In addition there were hosts of royal officials. In the Old Kingdom, as in modern states, every detail of administration was departmentalized. The resulting vast bureaucracy (we would call it a civil service) reached its fingers down to the humblest hovel and the poorest peasant. The freedom of the hunter and the farmer had given way to the slavery of a highly centralized control. This was the price ancient Egypt paid for its splendor.

Many of the nobles were also priests. There was, however, a separate class of priests, the more important of whom ranked with the nobles. The life of the nobles and priests, as we learn from the tomb-pictures, was one of ease and refinement. Their roomy homes were made of brick. Their furnishings were luxurious, their wine-spiced meals large and varied. We have a menu which featured "ten kinds of meat, five kinds of poultry, sixteen kinds of bread and cakes, six kinds of wine, four kinds of beer, and seven kinds of fruit."

The nobles were carried about in chairs, or litters. The men wore linen loincloths and shaved their heads and faces. The women clothed themselves in diaphanous gowns. Both men and women decked themselves with wigs and jewelry and made up their faces with cosmetics. Around their homes were beautiful gardens, fitted out with lily ponds and fish ponds. Boating, swimming, listening to story-tellers with musicians, and fishing and hunting in the marshes or the desert were their diversions. Birds were brought down by boomerangs and lions and hippopotamuses with spears.

The Middle Class

In the middle class were lumped the minor officials and the city-dwellers. These last were made up of the professional classes, such as scribes, doctors, architects, and the like; the artisans, who included bakers, jewellers, coppersmiths, sandal-makers, and a score of other occupations; and the shopkeepers. All of these lived reasonably comfortable lives.

The Peasants

Since there were, as yet, only a few slaves, the broad base of the pyramid of society was formed of the peasants. In theory, as has been mentioned, the Pharaoh owned all the land of Egypt. In practice large grants were made to the nobles and to the priests and temples.

On these lands the peasants lived, in effect, as share-croppers. They worked from dawn to dusk. Their homes were miserable mud hovels, grouped in stinking, unsanitary villages. They paid taxes and rent in kind; that is, the tax-collectors took their cattle and sheep and pigs and collected their grain. Hence the government came to need huge store-houses and corrals, and masses of records.

The peasants could be beaten for failing to do enough work, for not paying enough taxes or for any fault, real or imaginary. They were subject to forced labor in the mines, in the quarries, on irrigation projects, or on the building of the pyramids. Their pay was their maintenance only.

Since they could not remember as far back as the comparative freedom of their New Stone Age ancestors, the peasants were doubtless more or less content. The land was rich in crops of wheat, barley, flax, sesame, beans, lentils, and other cereals and vegetables. They bred swine, goats, sheep, cattle and donkeys. They had the date palm and wine and beer on days of festival. There were fish to be caught and flights of wild fowl in the swamps and marshes. There were simple toys for the children, a doll made out of a bit of wood or leather balls stuffed with barley husks. More expensive toys for the upper-class youngsters are to be seen in the museums, such as a crocodile which opens and shuts its mouth as you pull it along with a string, or dwarfs that whirl around on a rim, again when a string is pulled.

Egyptian Crafts

Agriculture continued to use age-old, primitive methods, although the fields were manured each year. In the crafts, however, Egypt of the Old Kingdom was already well advanced.

Egyptian craftsmen of the Old Kingdom produced articles of the highest quality, primarily because of the luxury demands of the households of the Pharaoh and the nobles, and the service of the gods. Linen was woven as fine as silk; the hardest stone could be shaped into vases so thin that the light shone through; coppersmiths could produce chisels and saws to cut through granite (saw-cuts through stone of a yard in length have been found); cabinet-makers, using imported wood, turned out furniture which equals ours in design and excellence. At an early date, too, the secret of making glass was discovered. Similarly, from an early date military forces and caravans of donkeys pressed south beyond the first cataract. One objective of these expeditions was to stop raids by Negro tribes, and political control was achieved as far as the second cataract. The peasants formed the body of the army, and the nobility and the middle class supplied the officers. That army was armed with shields, spears, bows and arrows, and hatchets or knives.

The traders sought gold, ivory, ebony, ostrich feathers, and slaves. As early as the Fourth Dynasty a fleet was sent for the same articles down the east coast of Africa to the "Land of Punt", which is thought to have been modern Eritrea and Somaliland. Another expedition to Punt by boat up the Nile and by land was made in the Sixth Dynasty. When the twelve-year old Pharaoh, Pepi II, learned that the leader of the expedition, Harkhuf, was bringing back a dwarf with him, he wrote a charming letter to Harkhuf giving him detailed instructions about the care of the dwarf. Dwarfs were the court jesters of the Pharaohs.

In the other direction, to the north, Egyptians had long been active. Even in pre-dynastic times Palestine and Syria had been linked with both the Nile and Mesopotamia by trade routes. As early as the Second Dynasty cedars from Lebanon had been brought to Egypt by sea. In the time of Snefru of the Third Dynasty, there is a record of forty ships bringing back timber from the same source. The chief port used was Byblos in Syria, which became practically an Egyptian dependency. Furthermore, by the time of the Fourth Dynasty and probably as far back as pre-dynastic times, Egyptian traders were sailing to Crete.

Thus, from pre-dynastic times onward, rivulets of Egyptian influences were flowing into Palestine and Syria. There is no doubt, either, that in Syria Egyptian traders were contacting their Sumerian and Semitic counterparts from Lower Mesopotamia. The two streams of early civilization were meeting and Palestine and Syria were fertilized in the process. Meanwhile, in their contact with Crete, the Egyptians of the Old Kingdom were planting the seeds of the first European civilization.

Egyptian Knowledge

Estimates of the knowledge possessed by the ancient Egyptians vary from the attribution of almost supernatural powers to an attempt to denigrate what they knew. Their achievements, viewed soberly, were quite considerable. The pyramids make clear a high standard in architecture and engineering, particularly when we consider the copper tools they used, even though the copper ore they mined seems to have been a natural alloy which was tougher than pure copper. They worked the hardest stone and drilled stone vases to translucence. Their linen was so finely woven that it was like silk. They were experts in handling gold, silver, and jewels. Their carpentry was superb and plywood was in common use. They also invented glass.

Apart from these few examples of their technical skill, they were fairly well versed in mathematics and medicine and were far advanced in astronomy. It is thought that their priests knew that the earth was a globe and it is possible that some of them tended toward monotheism. But advanced knowledge was clearly restricted to a comparatively small class and this was one of the weaknesses of ancient Egypt.

Mathematics

The pyramids show that the Egyptians of the Old Kingdom had a considerable knowledge of mathematics. In arithmetic they used a decimal notation but without a sign for zero. They could add, multiply, subtract, use fractions and knew the value of π. Simple algebraic problems were solved, as we know from a document, the "Rhind Papyrus", the original of which is believed to date back to the Old Kingdom. Surveying was essential in a land in which each year after year the inundation fields had to have boundaries defined anew. The Egyptians could measure the area of a triangle, a trapezium, a circle, and a hemisphere. They could calculate the volume of a cylinder or a pyramid.

Education

Egyptian boys learned surveying, medicine, and other trades and professions by apprenticeship. There were, however, temple schools in which they were taught how to read and write.

Not much is left of Old Kingdom literature. There are triumph-songs and "Wisdom Literature" in which, for example, advice is given on how to keep a wife happy by giving her fine clothes and jewelry. There are also the "Pyramid Texts", a collection of hymns, records, and magic spells.

Medicine

In Egyptian medicine it was believed that disease was caused by evil spirits. Hence there was a mixture of sound practice and magic spells. Surgery, however, was excellent. Egyptian doctors could remove a piece of the skull so skilfully that the patient lived, and for such a delicate operation to have been successful they must have used some sort of an anaesthetic.

Sculpture

The sculpture of the Old Kingdom was surpassed only by that of the Greeks. This art was developed in the service of the Pharaohs and the gods. The Egyptians worked chiefly in stone. Three conventions limited their sculpture: frontality, in which statues are sculptured so as to be viewed from the front; centrality, in which each statue tends to fall into two equal halves; and stiffness of the hands and feet. The application of these conventions to bas-relief, in which the background is cut away so that the figures stand out in relief, produced not only stiffness and centrality but also the full eye and shoulders in profile.

These conventions aimed at achieving majesty and dignity, and the Egyptians succeeded magnificently. Consider, for example, the portrait statue of Khafra, builder of the second pyramid, which conveys to us a sense of eternity. The same timelessness looks at us from the portrait of an unknown scribe. He sits cross-legged, pen in hand, his roll of papyrus open on his knees, alert for dictation. A woman kneading bread or Prince Ranefer striding forward proudly—the Old Kingdom statues breathe the spirit of a civilization that was dignified and confident. The same artistry and sureness of technical skill informs the sculpture of the Middle Kingdom.

The Egyptians also incorporated sculpture into their buildings. They passed on to the Greeks the use of stone columns. The arch was known as early as the Third Dynasty. The "clerestory," or high central nave bordered by two lower side-aisles, appears in the mortuary temple of Khafra. This clerestory was to reappear in the Great Hall of Karnak in the time of the Egyptian empire and again in the work of the Romanesque and Gothic architects of medieval Europe.

The Middle Kingdom: 2160–1788 B.C.

We have seen that the Old Kingdom dissolved into chaos. The governor of the nomes became feudal barons. There were concurrent dynasties in the land. Finally, far to the south at Thebes, where the valley of the Nile opens briefly to a greater width, new Pharaohs of the Eleventh Dynasty began to re-unify Egypt.

The process was completed by the Theban rulers of the Twelfth Dynasty. Under a series of powerful Pharaohs the rule of the nobles was restricted. The Pharaoh now had a standing army. To the south Egypt was extended to the second cataract. In the north there were successful military expeditions into Libya and Palestine.

At home the land was divided into lots among the peasants, who became free hereditary tenants. Similarly, the artisans, on payment of a tax or license fee, were left alone to work as they wished. Under Amenhemet III, the "Good God of Peace", the nobles were replaced as governors of the nomes by officials appointed by the Pharaoh. During his reign Amenhemet also built a dam and locks in the gorge leading to the Fayum so as to impound water from the inundation for the dry season, just as the dam at Aswan does today. In the Fayum itself he reclaimed 27,000 acres of fertile land.

Under this sort of administration the Twelfth Dynasty ushered in a period of great prosperity and economic activity. There was a lively trade with Syria, Palestine, Cyprus, and Crete. Cretan pottery (called Minoan) is found in the Twelfth Dynasty cliff-cut tombs. Egyptian influence and civilization spread widely to Syria and Palestine. Meanwhile a canal was dug from the easternmost branch of the Nile to the north end of the Red Sea, thus anticipating the Suez canal by about 3800 years. The Pharaoh's Mediterranean ships could now sail into the Red Sea and along it to Arabia or down to Punt. Gold, spices, ebony, incense, Minoan pottery, copper ores, silver—these and other goods flowed into Egypt. The cliff-cut tombs of the period have yielded magnificent treasures in jewelry, golden diadems, inlaid pectorals (elaborate ornaments for the chest), obsidian jars banded with gold, and the like.

These tombs are a pictorial treasury of the life of the Middle Kingdom. They contain vivid paintings which show scenes of hunting, fowling, feasting, reaping, and also miniature wooden models of the butchering of cattle, the brewing of beer and the like. The Metropolitan Museum in New York has some of these beautifully finished models. A miniature boat, for example, has its sailors, sails, rudders, and cabin furniture even to two tiny "steamer" trunks, and a toy villa and its garden is a complete picture of a luxurious life, even to its lotus pool.

In this period sculpture and architecture flourished. There was a burst of literature, much of it found in papyrus rolls in the tombs. Before the Middle Kingdom, as noted, Ipuwer had described the chaos in Egypt and had also predicted the coming of a "good shepherd" to bring justice and happiness. From that same era of helplessness comes the "Dialogue of a Man Weary of Life with his own Soul" and the "Song of the Harper." In the Middle Kingdom itself we find simple songs of shepherds and farmers, religious poems, hymns to gods, and songs of love. The tale of the sailor who was shipwrecked on a voyage to Punt, and the "Romance of Sinuhe", who fled Egypt to become the chieftain of a tribe of nomads in Syria, are our first examples of adventure stories. The "coffin texts" present us with the "Book of the Dead", giving instructions on how to get to Paradise. Hence, too, comes our first drama, the drama of the death and resurrection of the god Osiris. By this time immortality had been, as it were, "democratized".

The Gods of Egypt

The Greek, Herodotus, called the Egyptians "the most religious of peoples." In the pre-dynastic period there were already over 2000 deities. To these, in the dynastic era, more were added and throughout Egyptian history there was a great deal of syncretism, that is, a merging of the ritual and attributes of various gods. A creation myth and a hierarchy of the important gods were worked out by the priests, but in general no one worried about inconsistencies. Egyptian religion was, in fact, a mixture of mana, animism, and anthropomorphism.

At the bottom of the scale were the little gods whom the peasants worshipped, the power immanent in a certain cave, for instance, or in some deep pool in the marshes, or in charge of the fertile fields. We may put next the totemistic gods of the nomes, which go back to pre-dynastic times, remembering at the same time that the Egyptians believed that gods, men, and animals were of the same substance but that the gods excelled in power.

The totemistic gods explain the mummification of cats and crocodiles, the worship of the sacred bull, Apis, though a fertility cult is probably present here as well, and the prevalence of bird and animal-headed gods in Egyptian representations of their deities. Horus, originally a falcon-god, could, for example, be sculptured as a falcon, a falcon-headed human, or, because of anthropomorphism, as a young man.

National Deities

The nome gods, in general, and the peasant deities were not believed to have power outside of their districts. But certain gods in one way or another came to be worshipped throughout the length of Egypt. Some deities achieved this importance through conquest. Horus, as the god of the conquering Pharaohs of Upper Egypt, became a national deity. During the Middle Kingdom, Amen, the goose or ram god of the Theban Pharaohs, achieved the same status.

Other deities became national because of the prevalence of a craft or industry as, for example, Thoth, the ibis-headed god of scribes. The universality of a phenomenon promoted others, such as Taurt, the goddess of childbirth. To these deities are to be added the worship of universal natural forces such as the sun (Re) and the moon (Hathor); while the Pharaoh was god on earth.

The Pharaoh as God

The concept of the ruler as a living god is found among several peoples.

The Inca rulers of Peru, for example, were regarded as divine, and so is the Mikado in Japan. In Egypt the supposed divinity of the Pharaoh dates back to pre-dynastic times. In the developed form of the Pharaoh-worship, partly because of the syncretism of cults, the Pharaoh was in one aspect regarded as the incarnation of Horus, the falcon-god. When sun-worship became dominant the Pharaoh was said to be the son of Re by a mortal mother, and Horus was equated with Re (Re was often represented as a disc with a falcon's wings). Then, when the Isis-Osiris cult came to prominence, Horus was made the son of Isis and Osiris, and the Pharaoh was declared to be Horus on earth and Osiris after death. The contradictions in these concepts did not seem to trouble the Egyptians. As Horus, the falcon, the Pharaoh smote the enemies of Egypt. As Osiris, and dressed as a mummy, he presided each year over the Sed festival, which was the festival of the dead. In still another aspect he opened the first irrigation channel after the inundation, since, again as Osiris, he was regarded as the force which made the grain grow. A picture of one Pharaoh, for example, shows grain growing through his burial wrappings and the inscription reads: "I am Osiris; I am barley."

Strange as these tangled concepts may seem to us, they explain why the power of the Pharaoh was so absolute. From the supposed divinity of the Pharaoh comes, in fact, by a somewhat circuitous route, Caesar-worship during the Roman Empire. Moreover, during the Old Kingdom, as has been mentioned, only the Pharaoh and those he favored could attain immortality. But, as the Isis-Osiris cult became "democratized," from the Twelfth Dynasty onward, anyone—artisan, physician, or peasant—could hope for immortality if he could afford some sort of mummification and funeral rites.

The Isis-Osiris Immortality Cult

According to tradition, this cult was originally introduced from Byblos to the Delta. In the beginning Osiris seems to have been a vegetation-god; that is, the force immanent in the wheat or barley which made it grow, while his consort, Isis, was the Earth-Mother. It is possible that in pre-dynastic Egypt a couple was chosen each year to represent these deities, treated as gods for a year, and then, in the case of the man representing Osiris, killed and the body cut up and pieces of it buried in the different fields. In any case Osiris, like vegetation, was supposed to die and be revived each year.

As time went on, however, as happened to other vegetation gods (such as Cybele), Osiris was transformed into a deity who promised immortality to those who worshipped him. The myth of his death and resurrection was that Osiris was attacked and killed by his evil brother, Set. Set dismembered

Osiris' body and scattered the pieces throughout Egypt. Isis, Osiris' wife, mourned her husband's death and searched for and collected the fragments of his body. By her magic he rose from the dead and became the ruler of the Osirian Paradise. Horus, now adopted into the cult as the son of Isis and Osiris, then led his followers into a battle with Set and the evil spirits and defeated them.

This myth, as has been noted, was written into a "Passion-Play" which was performed each year from at least 2000 B.C. onward and which Herodotus, the Greek, saw in the fifth century B.C.

The Soul and Mummification

The Egyptians believed that the body must be preserved if true immortality was to be enjoyed. Hence they preserved the bodies of their dead by mummification. The practice probably began in pre-dynastic times when the body was mummified naturally by the dry climate and the dry sand in which it was buried. In the British Museum, there is the body of such a naturally mummified pre-dynastic Egyptian. The body is dated at around 4000 B.C. It is lying curled on its side. There are still red curls on the head, and the stomach contained the last meal this ancient man had eaten.

But when corpses began to be buried in brick or stone-lined tombs, they rotted. The Egyptians, therefore, thought that some vital principle had left the body. They called this the *ka*. Ultimately, they thought of three major souls, the *ka*, *ba*, and *ikh*. The attributes of the three souls are not clearly distinguished, but it was believed that the *ka* and the *ba* could reanimate the body. Then the body could relive the life pictured on the walls of the tomb, or represented in the models of ships, the butchering of cattle, hunting, and so on, while the attendants could come to life to serve the dead man or woman. The average Egyptian, apparently, could think of no life more pleasant than Egyptian life on this earth.

Hence arose the importance of mummification. In this process the brains were drawn out through the nose; the vital organs were removed and placed in stone jars, called "canopic jars". Then the body was filled with various kinds of spices and embalming fluids and wrapped in specially treated linen. There were elaborate spells and ceremonies to ensure that when the *ka* or *ba* (often represented as a human-headed bird) reanimated the body, it would live again. Such was the ceremony of the "Opening of the Mouth". A "Ka-statue", which could be re-inhabited, was also set up.

The Osirian Paradise

These concepts of immortality were primitive and crude. There were, however, more sophisticated beliefs. In these the soul traveled a perilous journey to the "Land of Osiris" in the west. Here it was judged for deeds done in the flesh. The heart of the dead person was weighed against the "feather of truth" in the presence of Osiris and the forty-two gods of the forty-two nomes. At the same time the dead person had to make what is called "the Negative Confession." In this confession he had to declare that he had not harmed widows or orphans, had not robbed anyone, had not treated anyone badly; the heart was supposed to cry out if the dead person told a lie.

If the dead person passed the tests, he was admitted to Paradise; if not, his soul was cast outside to be devoured by waiting demons. The ethical content of Egyptian religion is reflected in the texts of the time. A ruler of a nome declares: "There was no artisan's daughter that I misused, no widow whom I oppressed, no peasant whom I turned away."

Influence of Isis-Osiris Worship

The Egyptian concept of immortality was the most developed of its period. It had a great influence in the Greek and Roman world, especially since the worship of Isis-Osiris was exported to Greece and Italy. It also influenced Christianity. Juvenal, a Roman satirist of the 1st Century A.D., writes about the penances required of Roman women by the priests of Isis. In Pompeii, the Roman town buried by the eruption of Vesuvius in 79 A.D., a temple of Isis was found; and in the Easter celebration of the resurrection of Christ we can see a modern parallel to the ancient belief in Osiris' re-birth.

The Fall of the Middle Kingdom

The fatal weakness of Egypt, as of any absolute government, was that its prosperity and success depended upon the character of its rulers. After the strong Pharaohs of the Twelfth Dynasty, a succession of weak Pharaohs followed. The land again fell into chaos. About 1750 B.C. a horde of barbarian peoples descended upon Egypt from the north. They brought with them the horse and chariot. The Delta was overrun, and Upper Egypt was forced to pay tribute. For about 200 years these foreigners, called the Hyksos, ruled Egypt.

The Hyksos were part of a world movement of peoples, about which more will be said later on. Their coming put an end to the first great phase of Egyptian development.

The Hieroglyphs

The Greeks, gazing in wonder at the beautifully carved writings which they saw on Egyptian temples and monuments, named them *hieroglyphs*, which means "sacred writings." As in Sumer, Egyptian writing sprang from the compulsion of civilized man to keep records and began at an early period as picture writing.

Picture writing has obvious limitations. A new set of pictures has to be made to express each thought or event. The first step in developing true writing is to agree that a picture such as ☼ will *always* mean "sun" and not "circle" or "pond."

Such conventionalized pictures are called *pictograms*. But there are ideas which are difficult to put into pictograms. So ideograms were invented. ～○～ can mean "sun-rise." For instance, too, the Sumerians took their pictogram for sun ◇ and made it into an ideogram to mean "month" by putting in three ticks, each tick standing for ten days: ◈

The real breakthrough came when *phonograms* were invented. In a phonogram a sign means not an object or an idea but a *sound*. In Sumer the sign for "arrow" (Sumerian *ti*) was used to mean not "arrow" but the sound, *ti*. Similarly, in Egypt, the symbol for mouth (Egyptian *ro* ⊜) could signify not mouth but the sound *r*, and the symbol for a flying goose, the sound *tha*. But "determinatives" also had to be used to tell the reader, for example, whether the sign ⊖ meant "mouth" or the sound *r*.

This breakthrough meant that the sounds of spoken speech could now be represented by pictures or by signs developed from these pictures. To give a commonly used example to suit our English language, the picture of a bee, 🐝 and of a leaf, 🍃 would now mean not "bee" and "leaf" but the word, "belief." Writing was tied to the *spoken* language.

The first use of this discovery was to make the signs represent syllables. But any language has in it a great many syllables. In consequence, Egyptian children, like Sumerian youngsters, had to learn about 600 signs, or letters as we would call them, before they could begin to read and write. We only have to learn 26 letters. Why? Because, as we shall see later, some unknown genius in Syria invented the alphabet. In an alphabetic script, the spoken language is broken down into signs, not for syllables but for the basic sounds, such as "a" for "ah" or "b" for the sound "b."

By the time of the First Dynasty the Egyptians had invented an alphabet of 24 *consonantal* signs. The vowels were not written. This fact explains some of the uncertainty about the spelling of Egyptian names. Thus, the sign for mouth could mean either "mouth" or the sound "r" plus a vowel. The failure to write vowels, if applied to our language, would mean that we would write in a sort of shorthand: "yr" for *year* and "bldg" for *building*. We could understand these abbreviated words but a non-English-speaking person might find it difficult. If the Egyptians had now abandoned their pictograms, ideograms, syllabic signs and determinatives, they would have had an alphabetic script. But they kept them all, making much more difficult our attempt to learn about them from their writings.

The Sumerians, as we have seen, wrote on clay tablets so that their cuneiform script soon lost all resemblance to the original pictograms. But Egyptian hieroglyphic writing which was on stone and on papyrus, retained many of the original pictures. Quite early, however, for writing on papyrus (paper) the Egyptians invented a *hieratic* ("holy") script which abandoned pictures and could therefore be written faster. Then, in the 7th century B.C., a still more simplified script, *demotic* ("the people's script") came into use.

The Invention of Paper

The Egyptians took the stalks of a bamboo-like reed, which the Greeks called *papyrus* (hence our word "paper"), cut the pith into flat strips, put a layer horizontally over a longitudinal one, and fused the two into one by moistening and beating them. This process produced a tough, serviceable paper. On it the Egyptian scribes wrote with ink made from soot, water, and vegetable gum, and with reed pens, frayed at the ends into tiny brushes. This paper was exported. Until the 4th century A.D., it was the usual writing material of the Greek and Roman world. Then, parchment and vellum made from the skins of animals, which had already been employed for expensive books, replaced it. Later, the Moors of Spain and the Arabs of Sicily brought to Europe paper made from rags or hemp. This kind of paper, as noted, was invented by the Chinese early in the 2nd century A.D.

The Rediscovery of How to Read Hieroglyphic and Cuneiform

Cuneiform, as we have seen, was taken over by the Semites and Assyrians as well as by the Hittites of Anatolia. Then, when the Persians came to power, they took some 40 cuneiform signs to use for their writing. But, by about the beginning of the Christian era, because of the invention of alphabetic writing cuneiform and hieroglyphic writing fell into disuse and, ultimately, knowledge of how to read them was forgotten.

The story of how cuneiform and hieroglyphic writing were deciphered is a monument to human ingenuity and persistence. In the case of the hieroglyphs, war provided the key. When Napoleon invaded Egypt in 1799, soldiers digging fortifications found a slab of black basalt at Rosetta, at the mouth of the Nile. After the British conquest of Egypt in 1801, the Rosetta Stone fell into their hands. The Rosetta Stone has on it a decree of 196 B.C. in honor of a Graeco-Macedonian Pharaoh Ptolemy V, Epiphanes. This decree was written in Greek as well as in hieroglyphic and demotic Egyptian. Using the Greek as the key a number of savants solved the hieroglyphs. They used the name of Ptolemy as the first clue and assumed that hieroglyphic characters surrounded by a heavy line (called a cartouche, the French word for *cartridge*, from its shape) represented his name. As a result of the decipherment, ancient Egyptian records and literature were made available to scholars.

For cuneiform there was no Rosetta Stone. But there were inscriptions. The most important of these was on the face of a cliff, 100 feet above the road at Behistun in Iran. The man to whom is due the chief credit for solving cuneiform was Sir Henry Rawlinson, an Englishman. Using the known names of ancient Persian Kings (Hystaspes, Cyrus, Xerxes, and Darius) he deciphered at Behistun what proved to be a Persian cuneiform inscription set up by Darius in 316 B.C.

In addition to ancient Persian cuneiform, the record had also been carved on the cliff-face in cuneiform in two other languages. Using the Persian, these were deciphered. One language turned out to be Elamite. The other was discovered to be Babylonian Semitic. It was easy, as a result, to decipher Assyrian records.

Although Sumerian had died out as a spoken language in ancient times, it had still been used in religious ceremonies. Consequently, there were ancient cuneiform dictionaries on clay tablets giving the Sumerian equivalents for Semitic words. In this way Sumerian was learned. Once again, a tremendous volume of ancient records and literature—Sumerian, Babylonian, Assyrian, Persian—was made available to the historian. Modern knowledge of the ancient history of the Near and Middle East dates from the deciphering of the ancient scripts and from the relatively recent discoveries of archeology.

Summary

We have followed the story of Egypt from about 3000 B.C. to 1750 B.C.—a period of some 1200 years. During that time, except for the break between the Old and Middle Kingdoms, the valley of the Nile was subject to an absolute monarchy. The material achievement was impressive. And, in spite of superstitions and of deities and religious beliefs which may seem crude and peculiar to us, the Egyptians had developed an idea of life after death which, to a certain extent, rested upon a code of ethics.

The way of life for the upper classes was luxurious. The main mass lived in poverty and ignorance, though the Middle Kingdom did ameliorate the condition of the peasants and artisans. An important point to note is that, because of trade, by the end of this period Egyptian civilization had crossed the sea to Crete and Cyprus and had found its way to Palestine and Syria. In the latter country, in particular, it met and mingled with civilizing influences coming from Lower Mesopotamia. Then, as in Mesopotamia, the development of this civilization was arrested by an influx of barbarians.

Readings from Sources of the Period

(a) The "Pyramid Texts" of the Old Kingdom consist chiefly of hymns, spells and triumph songs. There is, however, a human touch in the letter which Pepi II of the 6th dynasty, as a child of six, sent to a Commander, Harkhuf, who had sent word to Pepi that he was bringing back a dwarf for him as a court jester. Harkhuf was so proud of the letter that he had it inscribed on a stone outside his tomb which was found at Aswan. Below is part of this long-ago letter.

Letter of Pepi II

I have noted the matter of this thy letter, which thou hast sent to the king, to the palace, in order that one might know that thou hast descended in safety from Yam with the army which was with thee. Thou hast said in this thy letter, that thou hast brought all great and beautiful gifts, which Hathor, mistress of Imu hath given to the ka of the king of Upper and Lower Egypt Neferkere, who liveth forever and ever. Thou hast said in this thy letter, that thou hast brought a dancing dwarf of the god from the land of spirits, like the dwarf which the treasurer of the god Burded brought from Punt in the time of Isesi. Thou hast said to my majesty: "Never before has one like him been brought by any other who has visited Yam."

Each year . . . thee doing that which thy lord desires and praises; thou spendest day and night with the caravan in doing that which thy lord desires, praises and commands. His majesty will make thy many excellent honors to be an ornament for the son of thy son forever, so that all people will say when they hear what my majesty doeth for thee: "Is there anything like this which was done for the sole companion, Harkhuf, when he descended from Yam, because of the vigilance which he showed, to do that which his lord desired, praised and commanded!"

Come northwards to the court immediately; thou shalt bring this dwarf with thee, which thou bringest living, prosperous and healthy from the land of spirits, for the dances of the god, to rejoice and gladden the heart of the king of Upper and Lower Egypt, Neferkere, who lives forever. When he goes down with thee into the vessel, appoint excellent people, who shall be beside him on each side of the vessel; take care lest he fall into the water. When he sleeps at night appoint excellent people, who shall sleep beside him in his tent; inspect ten times a night. My majesty desires to see this dwarf more than the gifts of Sinai and of Punt. If thou arrivest to court this dwarf being with thee alive, prosperous and healthy, my majesty will do for thee a greater thing than that which was done for the treasurer of the god, Burded in the time of Isesi, according to the heart's desire of my majesty to see this dwarf.

(McDermott and Caldwell, *op. cit.* p. 81.)

(b) During the Fifth Dynasty, a vizier, Ptahotep, wrote instructions to his son on how to be successful, although the copy we have belongs to the Middle Kingdom period. Below are two extracts.

How to Manage a Wife.

"Give her food in abundance and raiment for her back, anoint her with unguents . . . . Be not harsh in thy house, for she will be more easily moved by persuasion than by violence."

Evil Destroys—"Great is right and endureth and prevaileth, it has not been brought to nought since the days of Osiris . . . It is vice that maketh away with wealth; never has evil brought its venture safe to land!

(C.A.H., p. 289, Chapter VII, and p. 347, Chapter VIII.)

(c) During the period of anarchy between the Old Kingdom and the Middle Kingdom, a vivid picture of the confusion was written by a wise man, named Ipuwer. Here are extracts from his works:

"The desert is throughout the land. The nomes are laid waste. A foreign tribe from abroad has come to Egypt . . . . The wrongdoer is everywhere. The plague is throughout the land. Blood is everywhere. Gates, columns and walls are consumed by fire. No craftsmen work. Nile overflows but no one ploughs for him. Every man says: 'We know not what has happened throughout the land'. Men are few, women are lacking . . . cattle are left to stay as there is none to gather them. All is ruin."

(*Ibid.* p. 341.)

(d) The Eleventh Dynasty began to reunite Egypt but there was still confusion. From this period comes the *Song of the Harper*.

> All hail to the prince, the good man,
> Whose body must pass away,
> While his children remain for aye.
>
> The gods of old rest in their tombs,
> And the mummies of men long dead;
> The same for both rich and poor.
>
> The words of Imhotep I hear,
> The words of Hordedef, which say: -
> "What is prosperity? Tell!"
> Their fences and walls are destroyed,
> Their houses exist no more;
> And no man cometh again from the tomb
> To tell what passeth below.
>
> Ye go to the place of the mourners,
> To the bourne whence none return;
> Strengthen your hearts to forget your joys,
> Yet fulfil your desires while ye live.
>
> Anoint yourselves, clothe yourselves well,
> Use the gifts which the gods bestow,
> Fulfil your desires upon earth.
>
> For the day will come to you all
> When ye hear not the voices of friends,
> When weeping avails you no more.
>
> So feast in tranquillity now,
> For none taketh his goods below to the tomb,
> And none cometh thence back again.

(*Ibid.* pp. 324–325.)

(e) Equally eloquent and strangely modern is the Dialogue of the Man-weary-of life with his soul. Part of it is translated as follows:

"Death is before me to-day like the convalescence of a sick man, like going forth after an illness (?). Death is before me to-day like the smell of myrrh, like sitting beneath the sail of a boat on a breezy day. Death is before me to-day like the longing of a man to see his home when he has spent many years in captivity."

(*Ibid.*, p. 345.)

CHAPTER 5

Indo-Europeans and the New
Kingdom of Egypt
1580–1200 B.C.

To understand why Egypt and Mesopotamia were overrun, we must think ourselves back to a period when there were neither frontiers nor international law and when, except for the Indus and Hwang-Ho Valleys, civilization was limited to Egypt and Mesopotamia and the areas they influenced; that is, to Assyria, Phoenicia, Syria and Palestine, the island of Crete and parts of mainland Greece, and Asia Minor. In such a period the only bar to folk movements anywhere was superior force, while the very luxuries and wealth of civilization invited inroads.

These inroads came from three great reservoirs of peoples. One was the Arabian desert. It had already sent forth the Akkadians and those Amorites who established the First Babylonian Empire. These same Amorites had also flooded over Syria and Phoenicia; while to the south, starting about 3000 B.C., other Semites, called Canaanites, had occupied Palestine. (Another wave of Semites, the Arameans, was to swell out of the desert between 1400–1200 B.C., and in the 6th century A.D. Mohammedan Arabs swept over the Near East, northern Africa and Spain.) Another source from which invasions came were the mountains and highlands to the north and northeast of the Fertile Crescent, as, for example, the eruptions southward of the Elamites and the Kassites. Behind this area were the almost limitless reaches of southwestern and Central Asia. Time after time, great hordes, such as the Parthians, the Huns, the hosts of Tamurlane and Genghiz Khan, and the Seljuk Turks have appeared out of Asia to terrorize either the Near and Middle East or Europe.

The Indo-Europeans

Still other breeding-grounds of invaders were the forests of Germany and the steppes north of the Black Sea. Across this area in Neolithic times a "battle-axe" people, whose original home is thought to have been south of modern Moscow, seem to have found their way. The core of this battle-axe people is supposed to have been blond Nordics. As they expanded their territory they mingled with the folk they subdued. Shortly before the second millenium, bands of this people, of varying racial origins, were spread all the way from Denmark to the steppes of the Ukraine and as far as the Caspian Sea. Whatever their origin, as we have seen, all the bands spoke some variant of the same tongue, and to the language-group ultimately formed from these dialects the name *Indo-European* is generally given, a term also applied to the peoples of the language-group.

By the Second Millenium B.C. these Indo-Europeans had tamed the horse. Among their religious observances was the worship of a sky-god and of the goddess of the hearth and her undying fire. Cremation was often practised. They seem to have had a compulsion to seek the southern sun. We shall find their folk-movements recurring. The Germanic invasions which overthrew the Roman Empire, and, later, the Viking raids and settlements, are part of their folk-wanderings.

The First Indo-European Invasions in the Near and Middle East

Early in the second millenium B.C., Indo-Europeans began to infiltrate Greece and Italy. Later in the same millenium, as we have noticed, their war-bands, bringing the horse with them, poured into northern India. Meanwhile, others forced their way into the highlands north of Mesopotamia and some of the leaders of the Kassites who overthrew the Babylonian Empire had Indo-European names. Further west, about 1500 B.C., a surge of Indo-Europeans mixed with Hurrians (a people who lived around Lake Van in Armenia) established the horse-breeding kingdom of the Mitanni in the great bend of the Euphrates. Here Carchemish became their principal city. Other Hurrians pushed into Palestine.

Meanwhile, about 1900 B.C., Indo-European bands entered Asia Minor. This people, the Hittites, with the help of the horse and the war-chariot, subdued Anatolia and established themselves along the Halys river. The story of the Hittites is still being uncovered. It was in the period of their so-called "First Empire" that they raided and sacked Babylon. Then their power declined; their "Second Empire" was to fight Egypt.

The Hyksos

It was probably as a result of all the turmoil caused by these influxes that the Hyksos swept into Egypt. One view is that they were a horde of displaced peoples, many of them Semitic, led by Hurrians. It was possibly during the Hyksos regime that a group of Hebrews, who were Semites, entered Egypt. From their capital city of Avaris the Hyksos ruled the Delta and their own possessions in Palestine, and forced Upper Egypt to pay tribute.

But the time came when the Seventeenth Dynasty Pharaohs of Thebes revolted. According to legend, the final war began when the Hyksos king, Apophis, complained that the bellowing of the hippopotamuses in a pool at Thebes, 500 miles away, disturbed his royal slumber. Finally, about 1580 B.C. Ahmose, the first Pharaoh of the Eighteenth Dynasty, captured Avaris and drove the Hyksos from Egypt.

The New Kingdom (Egyptian Empire)

First Phase: 1580–1375 B.C.

The Hyksos had taught the Egyptians the use of the horse and the war-chariot. Now, in pursuit of their hated enemies, the Egyptians pushed into Palestine. Soon Egyptian power reached to the Upper Euphrates. This expansion was halted for a brief period by a woman Pharaoh, Hatshepsut, the first great queen known to history. She dominated her husband, Thuthmose II, and on his death, she relegated her step-son, Thuthmose III, to obscurity, and put on the false beard of a Pharaoh. Set against the western cliffs across from Thebes is her beautiful temple at Deir-el-Bahri. In it are pictures of the five ships she sent to Punt. On the wall is carved a Negro chief coming to meet the Egyptians. Behind him is a very fat woman, labeled as his wife, with a small donkey to carry her. There are also pictures of Egyptians loading their ships with ivory, apes, slaves, panther-skins, eye-cosmetics, and gold dust.

Hatshepsut died in 1482 B.C. Her step-son, Thuthmose III, chiseled her name off her monuments. Then he set out to war.

The "Napoleon of Egypt"

We need a brief glance at the world situation which Thuthmose III faced. Europe was still backward, almost a *terra incognita*. In Crete, however, the Minoan civilization had been flourishing for centuries, while to the north, in Greece, the first Greeks were already firmly established. Soon, around 1400 B.C., the Achaean Greeks were to overthrow the Minoans and to establish what is loosely called the "Mycenean Empire."

Meanwhile the Phoenicians had long been sailing out from their seaports. In Syria and Palestine the Hyksos had disappeared. These countries were divided amongst a host of kinglets, though South Palestine was more or less controlled by Egypt. The people of the whole area were a mixed lot—Hurrians, Hittites, and Semites, with the Semites predominating. Over the centuries they had been civilized by Egyptians and Mesopotamian influences. When, for example, Thuthmose III captured Megiddo in northern Palestine, included in the spoil were 924 chariots, over 2000 horses, 200 suits of armor, 500 bows, thousands of head of cattle, and huge quantities of gold and silver. Further north the Mitanni were a powerful people who from time to time controlled Assyria. Downstream, Babylonia was sunk in lethargy under its Kassite kings. In Anatolia, however, the Hittites were recovering from the disunion which had shattered their first empire.

It was into this welter that Thuthmose III marched. In a series of brilliant campaigns he subdued Palestine and Syria. (In one campaign he transported his army by a fleet to Syria to out-flank his enemies.) He also defeated the Mitanni. Among his records is the story of an elephant hunt on the Upper Euphrates, something which makes us realise that at that time these great beasts were common as far west as Syria.

By the time of Thuthmose III's death (1450 B.C.) the Egyptian Empire stretched in a long, narrow band for 3000 miles from the Upper Euphrates in Syria to the fourth cataract of the Nile. It was well governed and garrisoned. This phase of its history lasted for close to 100 years.

During this period the situation in the north changed. By 1400 B.C., at about the same time that the Achaean Greeks ended the hegemony of Crete over the Aegean Sea, the Hittites had established their "New Empire." At about this time, too, they had learned how to smelt and work iron. This discovery was to revolutionize the Age of Metals. Once iron, and, later, steel, were available for weapons and implements, both industry and the art of war forged ahead.

The Hittite Civilization

It was not until the early years of this century that excavations in Anatolia (such as those near Boghaz-Kheuoi on the Halys river where lay Hattusa, the capital of the Hittites) began to reveal the lost story of the Hittites. The Hittite language—or rather languages—began to be deciphered in 1917 A.D.

The Hittites, called "Kheta" by the Egyptians, were a remarkable people. Their "empire" appears to have been a loose federation, arranged somewhat like the later feudal system of mediaeval Europe. At the top was the "Great King," who gradually assumed many of the attributes of the Egyptian Pharaohs. Beneath him was a group of petty kings who owed him troops and support. The council of these kings decided important matters, but there was also an assembly (pankus) of the warriors, similar to that of Homeric Greece. Each petty king in turn appears to have had as vassals the equivalents of barons and knights.

The Hittite cities were stone-walled. Hattusas, for example, covered 300 acres and was crowned by a huge citadel on top of a hill. Hittite architecture was massive and crude. So was the sculpture. They worshipped a bewildering profusion of gods. Prominent among these was an Indo-European sky-god, Teshub, and an Anatolian Earth-Mother deity. They wrote chiefly in cuneiform script, and borrowed much of their civilization from Mesopotamia, but their laws were comparatively humane and sought to secure justice for all from the highest to the lowest. From their codes of law we also learn that the Hittites branded cattle, kept bees, grew vines, paid great attention to the breeding and care of horses, and sometimes bit off one another's noses. From the monuments we observe that they wore trousers and neat pigtails.

Such were the people who around 1400 B.C. began to press upon both the Mitanni and the Egyptians. As a result an Egyptian-Mitanni alliance was formed, and blonde Mitanni princesses married swarthy Egyptian Pharaohs. Later, when Ikhnaten came to the throne, the Hittites, under a monarch named Shubbuliamas, overran both the Mitanni and Syria. Meanwhile, from 1450 to 1375 B.C., the Egyptian Empire flourished.

The Peak of the Empire

What were the effects of this empire? For one thing, it shattered the isolationism of Egypt and spread Egyptian gods and ways of life over Palestine, Syria, and Phoenicia. It also made Egypt the richest country in the ancient world. Thousands of pounds of gold and silver, hundreds of thousands of cattle, sheep, and goats, and tens of thousands of prisoners poured into the Two Lands. In the ninth year of his reign, for example, the son of Thuthmose III brought back no less than 90,000 captives.

This first phase of the Egyptian Empire reached its peak in the reign of Amenhotep III (1412–1375 B.C.). The Nile was alive with trading craft. Egyptian ships sailed out daily to Phoenicia, and to Cyprus, Crete, and, later to Greece. They went down the Red Sea to Punt and perhaps further. Caravans of donkeys plodded back and forth between Egypt and Asia. Traders found their way far up into Nubia.

"Gold" it was said, was "as common as dust in Egypt." If we could be transported back to this Egypt, we would see cities teeming with goldsmiths, weavers, sandal-makers, cabinet-makers, shop-keepers, merchants. At Memphis and at Thebes ships would be disembarking visitors from every known land—pig-tailed Hittites, keen-eyed Phoenicians, swarthy and bearded Semites from Palestine and Syria, black Nubians, blond "Myceneans" from Greece, bearded Babylonians, and blue-eyed Mitanni. We would observe the palaces of the nobles where the lords of the empire ate the finest of foods from gold and silver plates. They dressed in the sheerest of linen. They bedecked themselves and their wives with elaborate jewelry. Every whim was anticipated by hosts of slaves.

We would learn that the Pharaoh himself had a hundred wives and concubines, among them one Mitanni and two Babylonian princesses, but that his principal wife, Tiy, was a commoner's daughter. We would note hosts of priests, and we would hear it whispered that even the Pharaoh dared not oppose the high priest of Amen-Re. We would stare at huge obelisks, weighing as much as 338 tons in one tapering shaft, and wonder how they were quarried and brought 200 miles to Thebes without being broken. We would be certain to gape at the two newly-erected and gigantic portrait-statues of the Pharaoh, Amenhotep III. Each of these, we would learn, weighs 700 tons in one solid block, and we would know that the two statues would still be standing some 3350 years later.

Underneath this seeming magnificence we would, if we observed carefully, detect signs of trouble. The priests of Amen-Re, for one thing, became too powerful and too rich. From mines in Nubia alone they received in one year 700 Troy pounds of gold. For another, the Egyptians grew accustomed to ease and abundance. Their army, of which they were so proud, was now filled with mercenary troops. Furthermore, there were rumours that up to the north the Hittites and rebellious Amorites were taking over Syria, and that desert raiders, among whom were a people called the Habiru, were dashing into Palestine.

The Religious Revolution

When Amenhotep III died, his son, Ikhnaten, came to the throne. Ikhnaten (1375-1366 B.C.) and his beautiful wife, Nefertiti, had only one idea in mind, namely, to replace all the gods of Egypt by the worship of one god who should be the god of all peoples, Egyptian and non-Egyptian. The symbol of this deity was the Aten, the shining disc of the sun, reaching down beneficent hands to all mankind.

In pursuit of this objective Ikhnaten outlawed the other Egyptian gods, including Amen-Re, and built a new "Aten-city" at Tel-el-Amarna 200 miles downstream from Thebes. A new and realistic art was introduced, in which Ikhnaten is shown as a man with spindly legs, a protruding abdomen, and the long face of a visionary.

Noble though Ikhnaten's attempt was, the priests of Amen-Re were too strong for it to succeed. In the meantime, the Hittites under

Shubbiluliamas occupied Syria and pushed further south while the Habiru occupied parts of Canaan. The Egyptian empire was lost.

Among the ephemeral successors of Ikhnaten was Tutankamen (1355–1357 B.C.). Forty-one years ago, in 1922 A.D., there was great excitement when his almost untouched tomb was discovered by Sir Howard Carter. Although Tutankamen was only a minor Pharaoh, his tomb held unbelievable wealth: a coffin of solid gold an eighth of an inch thick is one example of its treasure.

The Egyptian Empire

Second Phase: 1350–1192 B.C.

After the religious revolution had sputtered out, the Egyptians tried to reconquer their empire. They were only partially successful, since the Mitanni, who had been allies of Egypt, had by now been overcome by the Hittites with their iron weapons. At last, in 1278 B.C. Ramses the Great (1299–1235 B.C.) signed a treaty of peace with the Hittites. By this treaty, which was written on silver tablets, the Egyptians held Palestine and South Syria. North Syria was kept by the Hittites. Later, in the style of European royal alliances of a later date, Ramses took the daughter of the Hittite king as one of his wives.

Ramses the Great ruled for 64 years. He had a hundred sons and at least fifty daughters. His building ventures were tremendous. In the great temple at Amen-Re at Karnak, on the outskirts of Thebes, is the great hall Ramses built. Its pillars are 79 feet high. A hundred men can stand on top of each of them.

The reign of Ramses the Great marked the end of an era. In the north another great movement of Indo-Europeans was in progress. In the Aegean area it destroyed the Greek Mycenean Empire. In Asia Minor it rolled over the Hittites. About 1192 B.C. the surge caused by the disturbances poured down on Egypt. Another Ramses, Rameses III, turned back that attack. Egypt was saved, but the empire was gone.

The remaining story of ancient Egypt can be told briefly. There were nine more Ramses, and then the priests of Amen-Re took over. Next, a Libyan dynasty mastered Egypt. After the Libyans came the Nubians, and finally the country was conquered, first by the Assyrians and then by the Persians. Alexander of Macedon took it from the Persians, and at Alexander's death, one of his generals, Ptolemy, set up a Macedonian dynasty. The last Pharaoh of this dynasty, the fascinating Cleopatra, committed suicide in 30 B.C., when the Romans seized the valley of the Nile.

Yet we must remember that from about 3100 B.C. until about 1000 B.C., or for over 2000 years, Egypt, except for the short period of the Hyksos, was an independent and civilized nation. Even when she was conquered, she retained her own distinctive way of life. We ourselves owe to Egypt our calendar, the first paper, and possibly the partial ancestry of the alphabet we use. Over and beyond these contributions, Egypt made a great impact on the Hebrews, and she exerted an even greater influence on the Greeks. The Greeks came to Egypt to stare and wonder. They went away with new religious and philosophical ideas. As we shall see, Egyptian ideas influenced the Greek philosophers, and, through them, us. In a certain sense, something of ancient Egypt still lives on in our civilization.

Readings from Sources of the Period

(a) Egyptian hymns to the gods often breathe deep religious feeling. Below is Ikhnaten's Hymn to the Aten.

Thou risest beautifully in the horizon of heaven,
O living Aten who creates Life!
When thou risest in the eastern horizon
Thou fillest every land with thy beauty.
Thou art beautiful, great, gleaming and high over every land.
Thy rays, they embrace the lands to the limits of all thou hast made.
Thou art Re and bringest them all,
Thou bindest them (for) thy beloved son.
Thou art afar off, yet thy rays are on the earth;
Thou art in the faces (of men), yet thy ways are not known.

When thou settest in the western horizon
The earth is in darkness after the manner of the dead;
They sleep in their rooms,
Their heads are covered
And the eye sees not its fellow.
All their possessions are stolen from under their heads, and they know it not.
Every lion cometh forth from its lair,
All snakes bite, for darkness is a danger (?)
The earth is silent, for he who created it rests in his horizon.

Day dawns when thou risest in the horizon.
Thou shinest as Aten in the sky and drivest away darkness.
When thou sendest forth thy rays the Two Lands are in festivity,
The people awake and stand on their feet, for thou hast raised them,
Their limbs are washed and they take their clothing,
Their arms are (raised) in adoration at thy appearance.
The whole earth does its work,
All cattle rest in their pastures,
The trees and herbage grow green,
The birds fly up from their nests,
Their wings are (raised) in praise of thy *Ka*,
All goats jump on their feet,

All flying and fluttering things live when thou hast shone upon them.
The boats sail up-stream and downstream likewise,
And all ways are open because thou hast appeared.
The fish in the river leap before thee,
Thy rays are in the midst of the Sea.
Creator of germ in woman, who makest seed in men,
Who givest life to a son in his mother's womb,
Who pacifiest him so that he may not cry,
A nurse (even) in the womb,
Who givest breath to vivify all that he has made.
When he comes forth from the womb . . . on the day of his birth,
Thou openest his mouth duly (?) and suppliest his needs,
The chick in the egg that chirps while in the shell,
Thou givest him breath therein to let him live.
Thou makest for him his appointed time that he may break it in the egg.
He comes forth from the egg at the appointed moment to chirp,
And he runs on his feet as soon as he comes from it.

How manifold are thy works!
They are hidden from the face of men, O sole god,
Like unto whom there is none other.
Thou madest the earth at thy will when thou wast alone:
Men, cattle, all animals, everything on earth that goes on its feet,
Everything that is on high that flies with its wings,
The foreign lands, Syria, Kush, and the land of Egypt.
Thou settest every man in his place, and suppliest their needs.
Each one has his food, and their days are numbered.
Their tongues are diverse in speech, and their forms likewise,
For thou has differentiated the peoples,
Thou makest the Nile in the Underworld;
Thou bringest it at thy will to cause the people of Egypt to live,
For thou hast made them for thyself, O Lord of them all,
Who growest tired through them,
O Lord of every land who shinest for them,
Thou Disk of the Day, great of dignity.
All the distant lands, thou makest their life.
Thou settest a Nile in heaven that it may descend for them
And make floods on the mountain like the sea,
In order to water their fields in their towns.
How excellent are thy plans, thou Lord of Eternity!
The Nile in heaven is thy gift (?) to the foreign peoples
And all herds that go on their feet,
But the (real) Nile comes from the Underworld for Egypt.

Thy rays nourish every field.
When thou risest, they live and flourish for thee,
Thou makest the seasons in order to create all that thou hast made;
Winter to cool them, and the heat (of summer)
That they may taste thee.
Thou hast made heaven afar off in order to shine therein

And to see all thou hast made, thou alone, rising in thy form as the living
  Aten,
Appearing and shining, afar off and yet close at hand (?)
All eyes see thee before them, for thou art the Aten of the day over (the
  earth) . . .

Thou art in my heart,
There is none that knoweth thee but thy son
Nefer-kheperu-Re, Wa-en-Re,
And thou hast made him wise in thy plans and in thy might.
The earth exists in thy hand, just as thou hast made them;
When thou risest they live; when thou settest they die.
Thou thyself art length of days, by thee do men live.
Eyes see beauty until thou settest,
But when thou settest on the right hand
All work is laid aside;
When thou riseth thou makest . . . to grow for the king;
Movement (?) is in every leg since thou hast founded the earth.
Thou hast raised them up for thy son, who came forth from thy flesh,
The king of Upper and Lower Egypt, who lives on truth,
The Lord of the Two Lands,
Nefer-kheperu-Re; Wa-en-Re; son of Re, who lives on truth,
Lord of Diadems, Akhnaten, whose life is long:

(Cottrell, *The Lost Pharaohs*, pp. 180–183, translated by H. W. Fairman, Pan
Books, London.)

(b) The Egyptian "Book of the Dead", includes what is known as the
"Negative Confession" which the soul of the dead person had to make before
the god, Osiris, in the "Hall of the Double Truth" as a prerequisite to entering
the Egyptian Paradise. Below are extracts from it:

1. I have not acted sinfully towards men.
2. I have not oppressed the members of my family.
3. I have not done wrong instead of what is right.
4. I have known no worthless folk.
5. I have not committed abominable acts.
8. I have not domineered over servants.
9. I have not belittled god [or the God].
10. I have not filched the property of the lowly man.
13. I have not inflicted pain (or caused suffering).
14. I have not permitted any man to suffer hunger.
16. I have not committed murder (or slaughter).
17. I have not given an order to cause murder.
26. I have not encroached upon the fields [of others].
27. I have not added to the weights of the scales [to cheat the seller].
29. I have not snatched away milk from the mouth[s] of children.
36. I have not neglected the times for the chosen offerings.

(Knoles and Snyder, *op. cit.*)

(c) Besides hymns, admonitions, records, triumph-songs and the like, the
Egyptians also wrote romances, dramas and love-songs. Here are four
examples of their love-poetry.

  I. Come through the garden, Love, to me.
        My love is like each flower that blows;
     Tall and straight as a young palm-tree,
        And in each cheek a sweet blush-rose.

 II. When in the house I lie all day
     In pain that will not pass away,
        The neighbours come and go.
     Ah, if my darling to me came,
     The doctors she would put to shame,
        She understands my woe.

III.   *Sweet of love is the daughter of the King!*
     Black are her tresses as the blackness of the night,
        Black as the wine-grape are the clusters of her hair.
     The hearts of the women turn towards her with delight,
        Gazing on her beauty with which none can compare.

        Sweet of love is the daughter of the King!
     Fair are her arms in the softly swaying dance,
        Fairer by far is her bosom's rounded swell!
     The hearts of the men are as water at her glance,
        Fairer is her beauty than mortal tongue can tell.

        Sweet of love is the daughter of the King!
     Rosy are her cheeks as the jasper's ruddy hue,
        Rosy as the henna which stains her slender hands!
     The heart of the King is filled with love anew,
        When in all her beauty before his throne she stands.

 IV. Lost! Lost! Lost! O lost my love to me!
        He passes by my house, nor turns his head,
     I deck myself with care; he does not see.
        He loves me not. Would God that I were dead!

     God! God! God! O Amon, great of might!
        My sacrifice and prayers, are they in vain?
     I offer to thee all that can delight,
        Hear thou my cry and bring my love again.

     Sweet, sweet, sweet as honey in the mouth,
        His kisses on my lips, my breast, my hair;
     But now my heart is as the sun-scorched South,
        Where lie the fields deserted, grey and bare.

     Come! Come! Come! And kiss me when I die,
        For Life—compelling Life—is in thy breath;
     And at that kiss, though in the tomb I lie,
        I will arise and break the bands of Death.

(Margaret Murray: *The Splendour That Was Egypt*: New York, Philosophical
Library, 2nd impression, 1949.)

CHAPTER 6

From the Fall of the New Kingdom to the Persian Empire: 1200–500 B.C.

The time is about 1150 B.C. Iron is just beginning to come into use. Among the results will be better and cheaper weapons, as well as iron plowshares, and increases in population because of improvement in agriculture. Meanwhile, Egypt, except for brief forays, is locked up in the valley of the Nile. Throughout the Aegean Sea area the ships of the Myceneans have disappeared. The Phrygians, part of a new Indo-European inroad, have replaced the Hittites in Asia Minor. Further south, where the Mitanni used to dwell, are Syro-Hittites. In Mesopotamia the Kassites have vanished, but desert Semites, the Chaldeans, have occupied Lower Mesopotamia and are creeping upstream to Babylon. Northwest of them, the Assyrian lion is beginning to stir; the Assyrians sacked Babylon in 1247 B.C.

This is only part of the changing world. Along the Mediterranean coast the Amorite Phoenicians have managed to repel another wave of desert Semites, the Arameans. But the Arameans have occupied most of Syria. Their chief city is to be Damascus, and by the use of camel caravans instead of donkeys they are to become the principal traders throughout the Fertile Crescent. Meanwhile, in Palestine the Hebrews have gained a stubborn foothold, but the Canaanites, who are more civilized, still hold cities such as Shechem, Bethshan and Jerusalem (called Jebus at this time). Along the coast a new people, the Philistines, are established. Thenceforth, the country is to be called Palestine instead of Canaan.

The Philistines are a product of the migrations which brought about the fall of the empire. Among them are Pulesti (probably from Crete), peoples from Asia Minor, and, very likely, a few Achaean Greeks. Their civilization shows Minoan-Mycenean characteristics, such as the table-leg pillar and theatrical areas. They are organized into a loose federation of five cities, each ruled over by a king-like leader, called a Seren.

This is the new world which has emerged from the shattered empires. For four centuries, until Assyria sweeps forward, there is a chance for small independent states. To us it is primarily the period of the Phoenicians and the Hebrews.

The Phoenicians

Geography destined the Phoenicians to be sea-farers. Their home country is a narrow strip, about a hundred and fifty miles long, but in width scarcely more than twenty miles. What land there is rises in terraces from the Mediterranean Sea to the Lebanon mountains. But there were good harbors at, from south to north, Tyre, Sidon, Berytus, Byblos and Aradus and great cedars for shipbuilding on the Lebanon range.

As we have seen, the Egyptians had sailed to Phoenicia early, eager for those cedars. Their chief port of entry was Gebal, called Byblos by the Greeks. Mesopotamia, however, had, from an early period, sent armies and caravans into Phoenicia. Consequently, the culture was a mingling of Egyptian and Mesopotamian influences with the native New Stone Age and Amorite customs and beliefs.

From 1100 B.C. onward, although the Phoenicians sent far-ranging caravans inland, their chief expansion was seaward, especially since the disappearance of the Minoan-Myceneans had left the Mediterranean trade open to the first-comer. The shrewd, black-bearded Phoenicians seized opportunity by the throat. With restless energy they established colonies and trading posts in Cyprus, Sicily, Sardinia, North Africa, and Spain. Modern Cadiz was originally a Phoenician settlement and Carthage, fated to become the rival of Rome, was founded by the Phoenicians in 814 B.C.

Following in the tracks of the Minoans, the Phoenicians ventured into the rough Atlantic. Southward they probably reached the Azores. Later, about 600 B.C., they may well have circumnavigated Africa. Northward, they gathered the tin of the Scilly Isles and of Cornwall in England. Nearer home, as time went by, their sailors traded with the emerging Greek world. A number of Phoenician words, such as *sesame*, *mina*, and *shekel*, are found in Greek. The Greek alphabet came from the Phoenicians. In a word, the Phoenicians helped to civilize the Greeks. The Greeks repaid them by becoming their commercial rivals.

How did the Phoenicians do business? Trade was by barter and profits were huge. The Phoenicians were after food and raw materials, such as

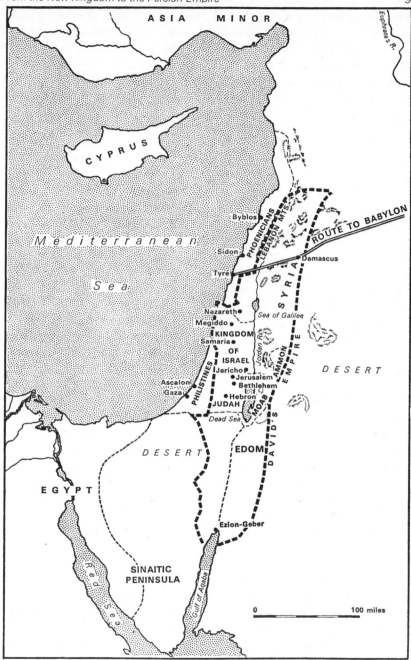

Phoenicia, Syria, Israel, and Judah

iron, copper and tin ores, gold, hides, grain, olive oil, and wine. In return
they proffered gums, spices, tools, weapons and household implements of
copper, bronze, and iron, gaudy jewels and trinkets, cheap pottery, and
textiles dyed with the famous Tyrian purple (obtained from a shell-fish,
the *murex*). They also manufactured glass. Less admirable was their traffic
in slaves, which they either took in trade or kidnapped.

Tyre, which was built on a rocky island half a mile from shore, Sidon
and the other Phoenician seaports must have buzzed with activity in these
centuries. We can imagine the noise and bustle. There would be hammering and shouting as new ships rose bit by bit at the water's edge. There
would be other ships rowing out to sea, laden to the gunwales with goods
for a year's trading in distant and exciting lands. There would be the
smell of tar, pitch, freshly cut planks, and dead fish. There would be still
other vessels, slipping into harbor, equally heavily loaded with tin or
copper or iron ores or hides and cheeses and slaves, the black-bearded
sailors cheering as they beheld their home city again. Behind the docks,
in the hundreds of shops in the narrow, twisting streets, men and women,
chiefly slaves, would be busy at the looms or sweating at the forges,
furnaces and bellows, or whirling clay on the spinning potters' wheels or
hammering out swords or ploughshares or spear points, or perhaps
fashioning gauds and trinkets. Noise and people would be everywhere.
Further up the hill would be the temples and the palaces of the merchant-
princes and the King. It was Hiram of Tyre (ca. 970–940 B.C.) who sent
timber and craftsmen for King Solomon's temple in return for grain,
olive-oil and wine.

The Phoenicians on the whole were culture carriers, not culture-
makers. There was no great literature or art and their religion was
primitive and blood-thirsty. In times of national emergency, they
placed their babes on the red-hot palms of the god, Moloch, to roll down
into the fiery furnace of his belly. Yet they did make a considerable
contribution through their wide-ranging trade whereby they knitted the
Near East, southern Europe, and North Africa into one commercial unit
and thus prepared the way for the Greeks and Romans.

The Alphabet

The most important Phoenician legacy to our civilization was the
invention of an alphabet and its transmission to the Greeks. As we have
seen the Sumerian and Egyptian systems of writing were awkward to use
because some 600 signs or letters had to be learned. As a result reading
and writing were limited to a comparatively small educated class. Quite
early, however, some Syrian genius or geniuses began to experiment with
an alphabetic script, one in which the signs or letters would express the

basic sounds of their language. The earliest inscription in such an alphabetic script is found on the sarcophagus of a king of Byblos who is dated in the 17th century B.C., and before 1000 B.C. there were North and South Semitic alphabets in use. It is possible that clues for these alphabets came from cuneiform and hieroglyphics, but it is thought that the invention was basically a Semitic one. From these early alphabets are derived the alphabets we know, such as those used in Sanskrit, Hebrew, Aramaic, Arabic, Ethiopian and, via the Greeks and Romans, the one current among the peoples of western civilization.

The Phoenician alphabet was a North Semitic one. It used 22 letters, each of which represented a consonantal sound, and was written from right to left. The Greeks seem to have adopted it shortly after 800 B.C. They called it "alphabet" from the Semitic names for the first two letters, aleph (ox) and beth (house), which the Greeks renamed alpha and beta. At first the Greeks, too, wrote from right to left, then wrote "boustrophedon" (as the ox turns while plowing) that is, the first line was written from right to left, the second left to right and so on, but they finally adopted the left to right method.

The Greeks made one important change. The Semitic alphabet had letters for consonants only, but the Greeks used some of the letters to represent vowels and thus achieved a true alphabet. The Greek alphabet reached the Etruscans, the "mystery" people of Italy about whom more will be said when we come to the Greeks and Romans. From the Etruscans it was passed on to the Romans. The Romans invented the letter *G* and made certain changes in the shapes of the letters. Then they handed on the alphabet to medieval Europe. Since Roman times three letters, *J*, *V*, and *W* have been added.

The invention of the alphabet was a tremendous stride forward in the field of communications. With only 22 to 26 letters to be learned for reading and writing instead of about 600, literacy was no longer limited to the learned scribes but could be extended to the ordinary man and woman. There was now a chance for a certain degree of education for everyone, and for inherited knowledge to become universal. For this gift the world owes a considerable debt to the swarthy Phoenician traders.

From the 8th century B.C. onward, Phoenician dominance of the Mediterranean trade-routes began to decline. They now had two trade rivals in the Mediterranean, the Greeks and the Etruscans of Italy. To embarrass them further, Assyria began to march. Time after time the Phoenicians bought off these "Tigers of the East." In the seventh century B.C., however, their cities were occupied, except for Tyre which stood a siege of five years. It was at this time that Carthage assumed independence.

Palestine

No people has made a deeper imprint on our western civilization than the Hebrews. Yet they lived in a small, poor country. Palestine is about 140 miles long and from 65 to 80 miles wide. It is divided into four zones, the coastal plain, the central hill country, the rift valley of the Jordan, including the Dead Sea (1300 feet below sea-level), and the narrow strip of cultivable land between the Jordan and the desert. Modern Israel has done much through irrigation and the latest farming methods to increase the agricultural capacities of their part of Palestine, but in ancient times much of the country was wasteland. There are stone and potters' clay but few other natural resources. In those days only a desert-dweller could call it a land flowing "with milk and honey".

Sources for Hebrew History

The chief source for the history of the Hebrew people and for the development of Judaism to the period after the return from the exile in Babylon is the Hebrew Old Testament, a collection of historical, legal, ritualistic, prophetic and poetic writings. The oldest manuscript in Hebrew dates from about 940 A.D., or over a thousand years later than the writing of the last passages of the Old Testament, but there are 5th century A.D. manuscripts of the "Septuagint" (Greek *septuaginta*—"seventy"), a translation into Greek made, according to legend, by seventy Jewish scholars in Alexandria in the time of Ptolemy II (285–246 B.C.). To the late 4th century A.D. too, belongs the Vulgate, a version translated into Latin by St. Jerome. In 1947 the first of the "Dead Sea" scrolls were found. These scrolls include Isaiah and parts of other books as well as writings attributed to an ascetic sect, the Essenes, and are dated as belonging to the 1st and 2nd centuries B.C. As has happened in the transmission of other manuscripts, there are a number of variants in the readings of different manuscripts of the Old Testament.

The first five books of the Old Testament (the Pentateuch from the Greek *pente*—"five" and *teuchos*—"tool" or "book") along with the books of Joshua, Judges, Chronicles, Kings and references in other books, contain the Hebrew account of their own origin and history. But the Old Testament was not written down in its present form until comparatively late, and the whole of it was composed primarily for religious purposes. Furthermore, although parts of it were passed down orally from early times, such as the Song of Deborah, and although the account of David's reign suggests an eyewitness account, and elsewhere there are factual details, yet it is generally accepted by scholars that most of the Old Testament was reworked time after time to drive home moral lessons and to give sanction to ritualistic practices. The Pentateuch,[1] in particular,

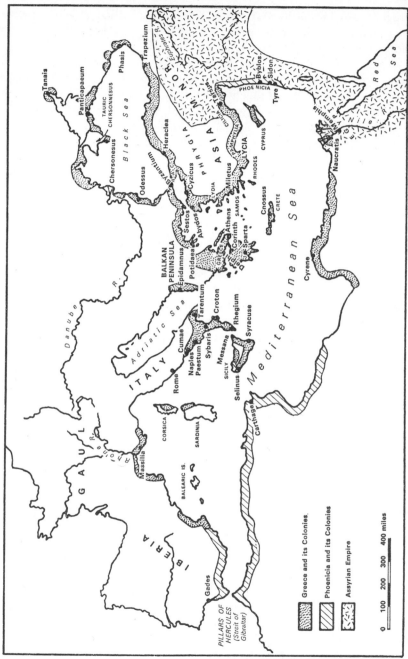

Colonial Settlements of the Greeks and Phoenicians

is regarded as exhibiting four main strata of composition; hence, there are a number of inconsistencies and contradictions. As a historical source the Old Testament must be used with caution.

Because the Hebrews were, in terms of political power, a relatively unimportant people, references to them in Egyptian, Babylonian and Assyrian records are infrequent. Babylonian documents of the time of Hammurabi (c. 1750 B.C.) mention the "Habiru" as desert Semites wandering into Babylonia. Similarly, the Tel-el-Amarna letters of the time of Amenhotep III and Ikhnaten (14th century B.C.) refer more than once to the "Hapiru" as among the peoples raiding into Palestine, and in the days of Ramses the Great (1299–1235 B.C.) the "Hapiru" are listed as laborers in Egypt. If the "Habiru" and "Hapiru" are to be identified with the Hebrews, as some authorities suggest, there would be backing for the view of the Hebrews as a wandering Semitic people organized in patriarchal tribes, who migrated from Mesopotamia and finally moved from the desert into Palestine, part of them, in the meantime, having been in Egypt. In any case, the triumph song of Merenptah, the son and successor of Ramses the Great, in listing his successes during a raid into Palestine, exults that: "Israel is desolate: her seed is not."

This solid reference is the first appearance of the word "Israel" in history and shows that toward the end of the 13th century B.C. part of the Hebrews, at least, were established in Palestine. But there is no mention of an "Exodus" in Egyptian records.

The Assyrian annals, which are fairly trustworthy, contain a number of references to the two kingdoms of Israel and Judah; and bas-reliefs show their kings paying tribute. In these annals, respect is shown for the "house of Omri", to which Ahab belonged, and it is recorded that Ahab himself contributed 10,000 infantry and 200 chariots to the forces which in 854 B.C. temporarily stopped the Assyrians at the battle of QarQar. Similarly, a letter of Mesha, king of Moab (c. 830 B.C.) makes clear the power of Omri. In the Old Testament Omri and Ahab are both vilified as men who "wrought evil in the eyes of the Lord", whereas they seem to have been capable monarchs. The Assyrian accounts also record the subjugation of Israel and Judah and Babylonian accounts tell of the capture of Jerusalem.

Another source for Hebrew life and history are archeological discoveries in Palestine. There are comparatively few inscriptions or documents but the royal stables of Solomon at Megiddo have been unearthed and also his copper-smelting complex at Ezion-Geber on the Gulf of Akaba. Other finds, such as those at Jericho and Shechem, tend to confirm features of the Biblical account. Elsewhere, excavations make clear the extent of Canaanitish and other pagan cults among the Hebrews, such as the worship of Baal and Astarte.

Early History of the Hebrews

The descriptions in Genesis of the Creation and the Flood seem to depend heavily on previous Mesopotamian accounts. Likewise, although Abraham and Moses were probably actual persons,[2] many legends appear to have accumulated around them. A number of scholars, however, are inclined to accept the view that the ancestors of the Hebrews migrated from Mesopotamia to become part of the desert tribes roaming along the borders of Palestine. It seems possible, or even probable, that one group of tribes began to infiltrate Palestine in the fourteenth century B.C., and that later on another group, which had suffered oppression in Egypt and had undergone a spiritual regeneration in the desert, entered the country from the south. It is, perhaps, germane to this view that in the Biblical account there was a division, which was never really healed, between the tribes in the north and those in the south.

Some scholars believe that it was that southern group which emphasized the worship of Yahweh. He may at first have been conceived of as a God of the storm-clouds and lightning.[3] Jehovah, by the way, is the mistaken transliteration by a medieval monk of the letters *YHWH*. The Hebrews of the early period wrote consonants only.

In any case, by 1150 B.C. the Hebrews were settled in the hill-country of Palestine. They were small farmers, shepherds and herdsmen, tough but comparatively uncivilized. The Canaanites, who were a civilized people, were not willing to give up their homes without a struggle. They held the northern part of the coastal plain and a group of strongholds which, as noted, included Shechem, Bethshan, and Jerusalem. On the southern coastal plain the Philistines were firmly established in their five cities. Meanwhile, cousins of the Hebrews, such as the Edomites, and Moabites, were pressing into the land.

The earlier centuries of the Hebrews in Palestine were years of confusion and fierce fighting against the Edomites and the other desert tribes, against the Canaanites and against the Philistines. When other enemies failed, the Hebrew tribes sometimes fought each other. Well on in the 11th century B.C., a coalition of the northern Hebrew tribes defeated the Canaanites in the Valley of Megiddo and took the plain of Esdraelon from them. Then, about 1050 B.C., the Philistines, who had excellent chariots and archers, conquered the Hebrews west of the Jordan and forbade them the use of iron.

These troubled centuries are related in the Bible in the Book of Judges. About 1020 B.C. the Hebrews revolted under their first king, Saul. He was defeated and committed suicide.

David

About 1000 B.C. the great hero of the Hebrews, David, who had been a Philistine vassal first at Ziklag and then at Hebron, was anointed king. Under him, in a series of achievements as thrilling as those of any nation, Jerusalem was captured and the yoke of the Philistines shattered. It should be noted, though, that three centuries later, the Philistines still appear in Assyrian records. Next, David built for himself what may be termed a little empire which stretched from Damascus to the Gulf of Akaba, and from the Mediterranean to the desert.

Solomon

His son, Solomon, (ca. 970 to 935 B.C.) is renowned for his wisdom, his thousand wives and concubines, the visit of the Queen of Sheba, and the building of the temple. This temple was 90 by 30 feet as compared to the great hall in the temple of Amen-Re at Karnak, which was 338 by 170 feet. But it had no image of a god in it, only the Ark of the Covenant and the invisible presence of Yahweh. To build this temple, as we have seen, Solomon imported timber and craftsmen from Hiram of Tyre.

Solomon may have been a partner of Hiram in other business ventures. At any rate, as already noted, archeology has discovered his ancient smelting plant at Ezion-Geber on the Gulf of Akaba. From that Gulf, Solomon's trading ships sailed down the Red Sea. His stables at Megiddo had stalls for 120 horses.

Israel and Judah

Solomon was an Oriental despot. His luxuries exhausted the country, and during his reign Damascus was lost. Five years after his death, the Libyan Pharaoh, Shishak, raided Palestine to capture and sack Jerusalem. About the same time the Hebrews split into two kingdoms. The tribes of Israel had their capital, finally, at Samaria; the tribes to the south held Jerusalem. Meantime, the Moabites, Edomites, and Ammonites recovered their freedom, while Hiram of Tyre seized most of Galilee. The Arameans took the rest of it.

The Hebrew day of glory had been brief. The two kingdoms now fought a long series of petty wars with each other, with the Moabites, and with Damascus. Many kings were assassinated. Others died in battle.

The Old Testament gives a melancholy picture of this period, although Ahab, the king of Israel who married Jezebel, the daughter of King Itto-baal of Tyre, did, as has been mentioned, contribute 10,000 infantry and 2000 chariots to the forces which stopped the Assyrians at the battle of QarQar. But in 722 B.C. the Assyrians captured Samaria and deported 27,290 Israelites (the "ten lost tribes").

This was the end of the northern kingdom. Judah survived by paying tribute to Assyria. Unfortunately, after the fall of the Assyrian Empire in 612 B.C., Judah's king sided with Egypt in the ensuing power struggle between Egypt and the Second Babylonian Empire. In 586 B.C. Jerusalem was captured by Nechuchadrezzar, (Biblical Nebuchadnezzar) of Babylon. Its last king, Zedekiah, in the style of that day, saw his sons killed in front of him; then his eyes were put out. About a third of the Jews (as the people of Judah may rightly be called) were carried off to Babylon.

When Cyrus the Persian captured Babylon, he allowed those Jews who wished it to return to Judah. This was in 538 B.C. In the fourth century B.C., a scribe, Ezra, brought from Babylon the Pentateuch, known as the "Torah" or "Law". From this time forward the Jews were ruled by high priests. Yet, except for a brief period under the Maccabees, the Jewish people were never again independent until modern Israel was established.

This swift sketch of their national history makes it clear that the Hebrew contribution to our civilization was not in the political field. Nor was it in sculpture and architecture. Instead, it was in the concept of Yahweh as a God of "righteousness" and finally as the one true God of all mankind.

The Spiritual Growth of the Hebrews

The concept took a long time to develop. Archeology and the Bible both make it evident that the Hebrews, after they entered Palestine, frequently worshipped Canaanite gods. They also, as was natural, sometimes added Canaanite religious practices to the worship of Yahweh. Solomon himself built shrines and temples to foreign deities such as those of Tyre and Egypt.

But the priesthood which served Yahweh continued to insist on His uniqueness. He alone was not represented by any "graven image." And He was a "jealous God" who would not tolerate the worship of any "false gods" by His followers. The priesthood also built up an elaborate ritual and the "Law."

We must remember that the nomad Hebrews were civilized in the first instance by the Canaanites. Consequently, their religious concepts and practices were strongly influenced by Mesopotamian, Egyptian, and Canaanite customs. The Passover and the Sabbath occurred in Canaanite religion. The "eye for an eye" Mosaic law shows certain similarities to the Code of Hammurabi, although it also incorporates desert customs. Jerusalem as the sacred city of Yahweh is prefigured in the sacred cities of Sumer and Akkad. The borrowings are far less significant than the repudiations of Canaanite, Egyptian, and Tyrian gods. However often the kings and the people might "backslide" into the worship of these gods, the priests and above all the prophets always reproached the backsliders strongly.

The Influence of the Prophets

Even though Yahweh was accepted as the God of the Hebrews, He was at first, in the style of the peoples around them, thought of merely as their own special God, and other gods were believed to exist, a stage of religion known as "monolatry". But the long roll of the great Hebrew prophets gradually emphasized the concept of Yahweh as the *only* God, not merely as a special Hebrew one. During the drastic economic changes of the 9th and 8th centuries B.C., prophets such as Amos and Micah presented Yahweh as the God of social justice. Others, such as Isaiah and Jeremiah, preached that He was the God of the Covenant between Him and the Hebrews, namely, that they should worship Him and Him only and obey His will as laid down in the Law. If the Hebrews kept the Covenant, said the prophets, they would prosper, if not, they would be punished. Much of the Old Testament is devoted to proving this argument.

Under the Law all Hebrews were equal. Thus, the worth of the individual was recognized. Yet before this awful God, all men, in the spirit of the much older Sumerian religion, were as nothing. Man in the Hebrew concept must abase himself before the will of God, whether he understands it or not. Such is the lesson of the Book of Job. Nevertheless, this god was a God who loved "Righteousness."

The Hebrews needed their belief in their one special God during the Babylonian captivity. It was during and after the return from captivity that, at last, prophets such as Ezekiel and "the Second Isaiah" (Isaiah, Chapters 40–55) arrived clearly at the concept of Yahweh as the One and Only God for all mankind, and the Hebrews became the first nation of monotheists.

The Impact of Hebrew Monotheism

The influence of the Hebrew concept of a universal God of Righteousness and of their Old Testament on western civilization can scarcely be over-estimated, although it must be remembered that Greek and Roman ideas also had their impact on early Christianity. The Old Testament, a name invented by Christians of the 3rd century A.D., is, throughout most of it, also great literature. In passing it might be noted that the word Bible is simply the Greek word, *biblia*, for "books." The Greek word in turn arose from the Phoenician seaport, Byblos, because through it papyrus was imported from Egypt.

The Assyrian Empire: 745–612 B.C.

In the British Museum there is a room of which the walls are covered with sculptured reliefs from Assyrian palaces. If you study those reliefs you will see soldiers assaulting cities with battering-rams and movable towers from which archers shoot. Look more closely and you will observe men being impaled and skinned alive. "I flayed the chief men of the rebel and I covered the walls with their skins," relates the Annals of the Assyrian monarch, Ashurnazirpal (about 885–858 B.C.). "Some of them were enclosed alive within the bricks of the wall, some were crucified with stakes along the wall . . . ", and again, "From some of them I cut off their hands and fingers, from others their noses and ears, of many I put out their eyes." The Assyrians made cruelty a calculated part of warfare and boasted of it. And the Assyrians were, from the point of view of the Hebrew prophets, the whip and sword with which Yahweh punished His erring people.

Who were these Assyrians? Their homeland was on the Upper Tigris. Here at an early date non-Semites from the Armenian mountains and Semites met and mingled. By 3000 B.C. the area was under Sumerian influence. Henceforward for centuries, the country was dominated by Sumerians, Akkadians and Babylonians. Later, the Mitanni and then the Hittites overran the Assyrians. Foreign domination bit deep. In their fierce resistance, the Assyrians were forged into tough fighting men. When the Hittite empire crumbled, they were ready to march.

For various reasons their first two attempts at empire failed. In the 8th century B.C. they tried again. They overran Mesopotamia. Then they turned westward. Damascus fell in 732 B.C. Ten years later it was the turn of Samaria. Judah and the cities of Phoenicia became tributaries. Northward, their armies took over part of Asia Minor.

The Assyrian Style of Fighting

If we were to accompany an Assyrian army we would perceive the reasons for their swift success. Their bearded troops were the first army to be equipped throughout with iron weapons. Their chariotry was superb. The arrows of their massed archery darkened the sky. Their soldiers lived off the land. Where there were no bridges they swam rivers on inflated skins. When they attacked a city, there was no faltering. Before the time of the Assyrians, walled cities had to be carried by a surprise assault or else starved out, but we would see the Assyrians in business-like fashion bringing against the mud-brick walls the battering-ram and the movable tower. Before these inventions the walled towns and cities crumpled. In 701 B.C., for instance, Sennacharib boasted of capturing 46 cities and villages of Judah. He failed to take Jerusalem, but the Jews had to pay tribute.

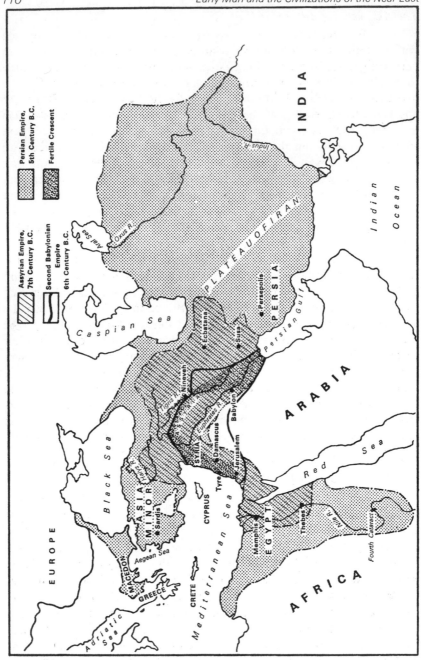

The Assyrian, Second Babylonian, and Persian Empires

Whenever a people seemed particularly troublesome the Assyrians deported a large number of them to another section of their empire and brought in other inhabitants. Thus, they forcibly made their empire a melting-pot of peoples. In the next century, in 671 B.C., the Assyrians subdued Egypt. As a result, for the first time in history, the whole of the civilized Near and Middle East, except for Lydia, was under one ruler.

The Collapse of Assyria

The Assyrian empire was to dissolve as quickly as it was formed. By 650 B.C. Egypt had freed itself. Furthermore, at about the same time the Assyrians were faced by a savage inroad into Asia Minor of wild invaders from the north, the Cimmerians. The Assyrian armies overcame the onslaught but their resources were strained as a result. One other effect of this invasion was the replacing of Phrygia as a power by Lydia. Meanwhile, there was rebellion in Babylonia and from the north the Medes were advancing.

The Medes, of whom the Persians were a subsidiary people, were among the new groups of Indo-Europeans who, in the 10th and 9th centuries B.C., had moved southward from east of the Caspian Sea. The Medes and Persians gradually occupied the Iranian plateau until their boundaries extended from the frontiers of India to the Halys river in Asia Minor. They were a semi-nomadic people and successful breeders of cattle and horses. Men were divided into three classes—warriors, priests, and farmers. The warriors out-ranked the other two.

In 612 B.C. a combined force of Chaldeans from Babylonia and Indo-European Medes captured Nineveh, which under Sennacherib had become the capital of Assyria. The looting was savage. The Babylonian records say that "they burnt the city into ruined mounds." A shout of joy went up from the liberated peoples. "Woe to the bloody city," cried the Hebrew prophet, Nahum, "all that hear the report of thee clap their hands over thee." Six years later the last Assyrian army was shattered at Carchemish.

Assyria is a striking illustration of a people who triumphed by the sword and perished by the sword. Today their huge winged bulls, weighing up to 450 tons, stare out vacuously at the visitor in museums. Somehow, when one looks at them, they seem to body forth the emptiness of an empire built on cruelty and the sword. (The Assyrians gave their lions and bulls a false fifth leg, so that these monsters always appeared to have four legs, whether viewed from the front or the side.)

The Achievement of Assyria

The culture of the Assyrians was largely derivative, although they tended to add their own touch to whatever they borrowed. Their writing was in Babylonian cuneiform, although later they used the Aramaic script. In literature and science they contributed little but they did establish royal libraries, such as the 22,000 tablets in the library of Assurbanipal, which have preserved for us Babylonian literature, science and law-codes. They also made considerable revisions in the Babylonian legends. Their religion, too, was largely Babylonian, although they did have their own supreme national god, Assur; the priests never became as powerful as in Sumer, Akkad, or Babylonia. In architecture, once again they imitated the Babylonians, while their massive human-headed and winged bulls were adopted from the Hittite palaces. Yet they erected huge, well-planned cities which were to influence Nebuchadrezzar's Babylon and the Persian cities of a later date. In sculpture their human figures are lifeless but their animal figures are superbly realistic, such as the bas-relief of a wounded lioness dragging herself along in anguish.

Their great contribution to the future development of civilization, however, lay in their forcible political and economic unification of the Fertile Crescent. By the suppression or destruction of local and national opposition and customs, and by their mass deportations they helped the evolution of a uniform culture throughout their empire. In economics, for example, the Arameans became the carriers of trade to such an extent that their weights and measures were used everywhere, and their language was the one common language. The Jews of the time of Christ, for instance, spoke not Hebrew but Aramaic. The blotting out of boundaries and the intermingling of peoples tended to introduce the idea of universalism, that is, that all peoples are akin to each other; and this in turn was to lead ultimately to the ideas of the brotherhood of man and the fatherhood of God.

Another continuing feature of the Assyrian Empire was its efficient organization and administration, which included a postal service, and a close surveillance over governors and subject kings. The Persian Empire was, later on, to borrow much from the Assyrian. Yet these contributions were marred by the personal despotism of hereditary kings, by the policy of calculated terror, and by a militant imperialism. The Persians were to prove themselves kinder masters than the Assyrians.

The Chaldeans and the Medes

The inheritors of the Assyrian Empire were the Chaldeans of Babylonia and the Medes.

The Chaldeans built themselves a short-lived but glittering empire. It included Mesopotamia, the southern part of Assyria, Syria, Phoenicia, and Palestine. The most able monarch was Nebuchadrezzar (604–562 B.C.)

who captured Jerusalem. During his reign, Babylon became a magnificent city. Its fortified area had a perimeter of 13 miles. Its huge walls were 85 feet thick. Through it from north to south ran a great sacred way. It was paved with red and white limestone slabs, and along the flanking walls marched, rounded out in brilliantly-colored glazed tiles, a frieze of bulls, dragons, and lions. We can see a section of these walls in the Louvre in Paris.

There was also a great palace for the king; his audience room measured 56 by 171 feet. Nearby, or as part of the palace itself, were the famous Hanging Gardens. These were huge terraces, one on top of the other, brilliant with the leaves and flowers of every known tree and shrub. They were built, we are told, to alleviate the homesickness for her native mountains of the Median princess who was Nebuchadrezzar's queen. Not too far away was the mighty ziggurat of Marduk, the chief god of Babylon. It was 300 feet square at the base and towered up 250 feet. Herodotus says of it that:

> On the summit of the topmost tower stands a great temple with a fine large couch on it, richly covered and a golden table beside it. The shrine contains no image and no one spends the night there except . . . one Assyrian woman, all alone, whomever . . . the god has chosen.

Such were a few of the marvels of the new Babylon. We can imagine Herodotus gaping this way and that as he strolled through the mighty city. We can also conceive of the wonder and loneliness of the Jewish exiles. Most of them, however, were soon assimilated into the life of this busy metropolis, and from this time forward there was a large Jewish community in Mesopotamia. We might note, too, that the capture of Jerusalem in 586 B.C. caused a number of Jews to take refuge in Egypt. Thus, the dispersion of the Jews had already begun.

But the priests of Marduk were the evil geniuses of the new Babylon. After the assassination of two kings, Nabonidus, whose son was the Belshazzar of the Bible, came to the throne. Nabonidus devoted himself to archeology and to the rebuilding of temples. The priests intrigued with Cyrus the Persian who conquered Babylon in 539 B.C. Today, among the ruined mounds, only the great Ishtar Gate gives any hint of the long-dead magnificence of Babylon.

The Persian Empire: 550–331 B.C.

The story of Cyrus the Great is a success saga of the Hollywood type. In 559 B.C. he was the vassal king of the Persians, a small people in one corner of the huge territories of their cousins, the Medes. Nine years later he was king of the Medes and the Persians.

The western frontier of the Median empire was the Halys river in Asia

Minor. West of that river the wealthy Croesus ruled the Lydians. By this time he had conquered all the Greek cities on the coast of Asia Minor, except Miletus. With it, he had formed an alliance. Croesus was a brother-in-law of Astyages, the king of the Medes, whom Cyrus had deposed. This fact may have influenced him. More probably, he was afraid of the ambitions of the new king. According to Herodotus, he sent to the Greek oracle at Delphi for advice. He received the answer: "If you cross the Halys river, you will destroy a great empire." That empire was his own. The war began and ended in 546 B.C. Lydia was added to the Persian empire, which now ruled a number of Greek cities. Next, Cyrus turned against Babylon. By 538 B.C. the whole of Mesopotamia and the rest of the Fertile Crescent was in his hands as far as the frontiers of Egypt.

Cyrus was killed in 529 B.C. while fighting against the Scythians. His son, Cambyses (529–522 B.C.), overwhelmed Egypt. When Cambyses died, the son-in-law of Cyrus, Darius the Great, (521–486 B.C.), took the throne. Under him the Persians crossed into Europe and sent two expeditions against the Greeks.

Darius the Great

The chief achievement of Darius was to organize the huge Persian Empire into 20 provinces or *satrapies*. That empire stretched from the Aral Sea in south-west Asia and the Indus river of India to the Danube in Europe and to the first cataract of the Nile in Africa. It was close to the size of the United States. The capital was first at Susa and then at Persepolis. Like the empires which preceded it, the Persian empire was a despotism. Under the king, the Persians and Medes were the ruling caste. They supplied the governors of the 20 provinces. Each satrap, or governor, had a court, treasury and army of his own, and could even wage war without the permission of the Great King. Yet the commander of the Persian corps in the province was appointed by the king, and inspectors, called "the King's Eyes", came periodically to take a close look at what was being done. The Greeks were amazed at the royal couriers. For, like the Romans in a later day, the Persians built great roads to link their realms to their capital. Along these roads, night and day, with changes of horses ready, sped the King's messengers.

In this type of organization, the Persians copied from the Assyrians. But their rule was, on the whole, humane and just. There were no deportations. Subject nations, such as the Jews, were allowed to keep their own customs and religions, although all paid tribute and sent contingents of troops to the Persian army. We are told by Xenophon, the Greek general and author who had fought with and against the Persian nobles, that they were taught to ride hard, to shoot straight, and to tell the truth. Until luxury and power corrupted them, the Persians were good rulers.

Persian Religion

The religion of the Persians as reformed by Zoroaster was, in essence, dualistic. On one side was the great sky-god of good and light, Ahura-Mazda and his "angels" (angel is from a Greek word, *angelos*, meaning "a messenger"). On the other was the god of darkness and evil, Ahriman (the prototype of our Satan) aided by his "demons." Life to the Persians was a constant struggle between evil and good. The part of every good man was to enlist himself on the side of Ahura-Mazda. To Zoroaster the struggle was to end in the triumph of good in a renovated world, but each man was to be judged after death for his deeds done in the flesh. *Paradise*, by the way, is a Persian word, meaning "a park."

The early Persians, like many other Indo-Europeans, also worshipped the undying fire. The Magi, from whom our word "magic" comes, were their priestly caste. Later, a deity called Mithras was thought to have been sent down by Ahura-Mazda to be his intermediary to men. The worship of this god reached Rome and hence found its way to the German frontier and to London where, a few years ago, a "Mithraeum" (church of Mithras) was found.

The Persian empire lasted until Alexander the Great of Macedon destroyed it in 331 B.C. at the battle of Gaugamela or Arbela. But with Darius the Great we have reached a meeting point of East and West. It is time to turn to the people who began western civilization as something distinct from every other civilization. These people were the Greeks.

Summary

We have seen how the first civilizations sprouted about five thousand years ago from the seeds sown in the Neolithic Age. Apart from early developments in India and China which had little influence on the beginnings of our own civilization, we have watched cities grow along the Nile, the Tigris, and the Euphrates. We have had a glimpse of how those civilizations influenced Anatolia, Syria, Phoenicia, and Palestine. We have noted how, like lions drawn to herds of deer drinking, the peoples of the desert and the mountains, time after time, sprang upon the centers of civilization.

Out of the reaction to these invasions came the development of empires, first in Mesopotamia and later in Egypt, while the Indo-European Hittites framed an empire of their own. The smashing of the empires provided a period of four centuries in which the Phoenicians carried elements of civilization over the Mediterranean and beyond as they followed routes already pioneered by the Minoan-Myceneans. Meanwhile, the Hebrews were gradually developing their own peculiar gift to western civilization, the concept of one God of Righteousness for all mankind.

But the wheel of empire had been set in motion, a fascination for the ambition and greed of men. With the Assyrian and Persian empires we come to huge units which leaped over the frontiers of geography, races, nations and creeds. The seed-bed of "universalism" was being prepared— and "universalism" suggests not only one world, but one God and all humanity as brothers.

Viewed in perspective, then, there was a continuing development in the 2500 years at which we have glanced. Human knowledge had increased and control over mankind's environment was now considerable. Man's horizons had widened. And from these ancient civilizations have come contributions to our own. Some of these are easy to recognize, such as the alphabet, the use of 60 as a basic number, the calendar, the concept of private property, the development of business practices, and in the spiritual field, the Old Testament and Hebrew monotheism.

Other influences are not so easy to assess except to say that, in general, the Greeks and the Romans borrowed much from the Near and Middle East. Yet it is clear that some of the roots of our civilization of today are buried far back in the valleys of the Nile and the Tigris and Euphrates, and in the hills of Judea.

Notes to Chapter 6

1.   Biblical scholars in general agree that one stratum in the Pentateuch is the "J document" in which the deity is called Yahweh (Jehovah), composed originally about 850 B.C. The "E document", in which Elohim, a plural Semitic word for God is used, is thought to have been composed at about the same time. The "D document", the source for Deuteronomy is believed to have come into existence about 625 B.C. P, the "Priests' Code", apparently composed after the Exile, used J, E and D as a basis. It is thought that finally, about the time of Ezra (400 B.C.) all the above were woven together into the present Pentateuch. Other reworkings of parts of the Pentateuch are also thought to have occurred.

2.   It seems likely that the strong emotional impact on the Hebrews of the Exodus and of the experiences at the Mount of Sinai enshrines actual occurrences and an actual person. Similarly, the story of Abraham's migration from Ur to Haran and thence to Palestine may retain memories of an actual folk movement.

3.   A tablet found in Ras Shamra (ancient Ugarit) in Syria mentions a deity

known as "YW" who was worshipped there; the Hebrew spelling of their deity is YHWH.

Readings from Sources of the Period

(a) Chapter 5 of 1 Kings of the Old Testament describes the alliance between King Solomon and King Hiram of Tyre.

When Hiram king of Tyre heard that it was Solomon who had been consecrated king instead of his father, he sent his officers to Solomon; for Hiram had always been friendly to David. Then Solomon sent this message to Hiram: "You know how my father David could not build a temple in honour of the Eternal his God, until the Eternal had crushed under him the warlike foes who surrounded him. The Eternal my God has now given me rest on every side; I have neither foe nor misfortune, and I propose to build a temple in honour of the Eternal, my God, as the Eternal told my father David that 'your son, whom I place on your throne, shall build the temple in my honour.' Now give orders that cedars be felled for me on Lebânon; my servants will join your servants, and I will pay you any wage you fix for your servants; for you know we have no one fit to fell timber like the Phoenicians." When Hiram heard what Solomon said, he was overjoyed. "Blessed be the Eternal the God of Israel this day," he cried, "for granting David a wise son to rule this great people!" Hiram sent this message to Solomon: "I have heard your message; I will do all you desire in the matter of cedars and firs; my servants shall bring the timber down from Lebânon to the sea, and I will make the logs into floats to reach any spot you decide upon; then I will have them broken up for you to take away. You will meet my wishes by providing the food for my servants." So Hiram gave Solomon all the cedar and fir-wood that he desired, while Solomon gave Hiram two hundred and twenty thousand bushels of wheat and a hundred and eighty gallons of beaten oil as food for his servants— such was Solomon's annual gift to Hiram. Solomon and Hiram were at peace; the two men made an alliance with each other. Solomon raised a labour-force from all Israel, a levy of thirty thousand men, whom he sent to Lebânon in relays, ten thousand a month; one month they were at Lebânon and two months at home. Adoniram was in charge of this forced levy. Solomon also had seventy thousand carriers and eighty thousand stone-masons in the hills, as well as three thousand three hundred foremen, who controlled the workmen. By order of the king, they quarried huge, expensive blocks of stone, to have the foundation of the temple laid with dressed stone.

(Moffatt *The Moffatt Translation of the Bible*, p. 386 Old Testament, London: Hodder and Stoughton).

(b) The prophets opposed the greed of the rich and invoked a God of Righteousness. An example of their preaching is found in Amos, chapter 5, vv. 7–24.

Ye who turn judgment to wormwood, and leave off righteousness in the earth. *Seek him* that maketh the seven stars and O-rî'on, and turneth the shadow of death into the morning, and maketh the day dark with night: that calleth for the waters of the sea, and poureth them out upon the face of the earth: The LORD *is* his name:
That strengtheneth the spoiled against the strong, so that the spoiled shall come against the fortress.

They hate him that rebuketh in the gate, and they abhor him that speaketh uprightly.

Forasmuch, therefore, as your treading *is* upon the poor, and ye take from him burdens of wheat; ye have built houses of hewn stone, but ye shall not dwell in them; ye have planted pleasant vineyards, but ye shall not drink wine of them. For I know your manifold transgressions and your mighty sins: they afflict the just, they take a bribe, and they turn aside the poor in the gate *from their right*. Therefore the prudent shall keep silence in that time; for it *is* an evil time.

Seek good, and not evil, that ye may live; and so the LORD, the God of hosts, shall be with you, as ye have spoken.

Hate the evil, and love the good, and establish judgment in the gate: it may be that the LORD God of hosts will be gracious unto the remnant of Jō'seph.

Therefore the LORD, the God of hosts, the Lord, saith thus. Wailing *shall be* in all streets; and they shall say in all the highways, Alas! alas! and they shall call the husbandman to mourning, and such as are skilful of lamentation to wailing.

And in all vineyards *shall be* wailing: for I will pass through thee, saith the LORD. Woe unto you that desire the day of the LORD! to what end *is* it for you? the day of the LORD *is* darkness, and not light.

As if a man did flee from a lion, and a bear met him; or went into the house, and leaned his hand on the wall, and a serpent bit him.

Shall not the day of the LORD be darkness, and not light? even very dark, and no brightness in it?

I hate, I despise your feast days, and I will not smell in your solemn assemblies. Though ye offer me burnt offerings and your meat offerings, I will not accept *them*: neither will I regard the peace offerings of your fat beasts.

Take thou away from me the noise of thy songs; for I will not hear the melody of thy viols.

But let judgment run down as waters, and righteousness as a mighty stream.

(c) Sennacherib, an Assyrian monarch describes his attack on Jerusalem in 701 B.C.

As to Hezekiah, the Jew, he did not submit to my yoke, I laid siege to 46 of his strong cities, walled forts and to the countless small villages in their vicinity, and conquered them by means of well-stamped earth-ramps, and battering-rams brought thus near to the walls combined with the attack by foot soldiers, using mines, breaches as well as sapper work. I drove out of them 200,150 people, young and old, male and female, horses, mules, donkeys, camels, big and small cattle beyond counting, and considered them booty. Himself I made a prisoner in Jerusalem, his royal residence, like a bird in a cage. I surrounded him with earthwork in order to molest those who were leaving his city's gate. His towns which I had plundered, I took away from his country. . . . Hezekiah himself, whom the terror-inspiring splendour of my lordship had overwhelmed and whose irregular and elite troops which he had brought into Jerusalem, his royal residence, in order to strengthen it, had deserted him, did send me, later, to Nineveh, my lordly city, together with 30 talents of gold, 800 talents of silver, precious stones, antimony, large cuts of red stone, couches inlaid with ivory, chairs inlaid with ivory, elephant-hides, ebony-wood, box-wood and all kinds of valuable treasures, his own daughters. . . . In order to deliver the tribute and to do obeisance as a slave he sent his personal messenger.

(W. C. McDermott and W. E. Caldwell, *op. cit.* pp. 53–54.)

(d) Darius the Great, King of Persia (521–486 B.C.) carved on a great rock at Behistun near Ecbatana in Iran a record of some of his achievements. Note that Ahura Mazda was the supreme god of the Medes and Persians.

6.   Saith Darius the King: These are the countries which came unto me; by the favour of Ahuramazda I was king of them: Persia, Elam, Babylonia, Assyria, Arabia, Egypt, those who are beside the sea, Sardis, Ionia, Media, Armenia, Cappadocia, Parthia, Drangiana, Aria, Chorasmia, Bactria, Sogdiana, Gandara, Scythia, Sattagydia, Arachosia, Maka: in all, XXIII provinces.
7.   Saith Darius the King: These are the countries which came unto me; by the favour of Ahuramazda they were my subjects; they bore tribute to me; what was said unto them by me either by night or by day, that was done.
8.   Saith Darius the King: Within these countries, the man who was excellent, him I rewarded well; him who was evil, him I punished well; by the favour of Ahuramazda these countries showed respect toward my law; what was said to them by me, thus was it done.
58.   Saith Darius the King: By the favour of Ahuramazda and of me much else was done; that has not been inscribed in this inscription; for this reason it has not been inscribed, lest whoso shall hereafter read this inscription, to him what has been done by me seem excessive, and it not convince him, but he think it false.
67.   Saith Darius the King: If thou shalt behold this inscription or these sculptures, and shalt destroy them and shalt not protect them as long as unto thee there is strength, Ahuramazda be a smiter unto thee, and may family not be unto thee, and what thou shalt do, that for thee may Ahuramazda utterly destroy!
70.   Saith Darius the King: By the favour of Ahuramazda this inscription in other ways I made. In addition, it was in Aryan, and has been made on leather. In addition, this inscription as a whole has been confirmed by the impression of a seal. And it was written, and the written document was read off to me. Afterwards this inscription was sent by me everywhere among the provinces; the people universally were pleased.

(*Ibid.,* pp. 58–64.)

(e) Ezekiel, a Hebrew prophet who wrote in Babylon during the first thirty years of the 6th century B.C., describes the commerce of Tyre.

This word from the Eternal came to me: "Son of man, raise a dirge also for Tyre, and say to Tyre that sits at the door of the sea, trading with many a coast-land for the nations—'The Lord the Eternal declares:
O Tyre, you deemed your beauty perfect; your moorings were deep—a perfect beauty had your builders made you, with cypress trees from Senir for your planks, with cedars from Lebânon for your masts, with oaks from Bashan for your oars, with ivory inlaid in larch from Cyprus for your deck; fine linen with Egyptian embroidery made your canvas, serving as your pennon; purple and blue from the coasts of Elishah furnished your awnings; men from Sidon and Arvad were your rowers, your own experts, O Tyre, they were your pilots, the sheikhs and councillors of Gebal were your caulkers. All ships and their sailors were in your harbour to handle your trade; Persia, Lud, and Put served in your army

as your soldiers, they hung their shields and helmets within you, and lent you splendour.

Men of Arvad and of Cilicia manned your walls, men of Gammad were in your towers, hanging their shields all round your walls and making your beauty perfect. Tartessus brought you merchandise for your great wealth of every kind, fetching you wares of silver, iron, tin, and lead. Ionians, Tubal, and Meshek brought you merchandise, supplies of slaves and copper ware. Armenians fetched you wares of horses and mules. Men from Rhodes brought you merchandise, and many a seaport at your service brought you traffic, with ivory tusks and ebony as their tribute. Edom brought you merchandise for your rich wealth, fetching you wares of garnets, coral, and agates, of purple dyes, embroidery, and fine linen. Judah and the land of Israel brought you merchandise, fetching you wares of wheat from Minnith, wax, honey, oil, and balsam. Damascus brought you merchandise for your rich wealth, supplies of wine from Chalbûn, and white wool. From Uzal you received wrought iron, cassia, and sweet cane; Dedan brought you wares of saddle-cloths for riding; Arabia and all the chiefs of Kedar were at your service, bringing you merchandise of lambs and rams and goats; Shĕba and Raamah brought you merchandise, supplying you with the pick of all spices, with jewels and with gold. Harran and Kalneh and Eden, Assyria and all the Medes, brought you merchandise, supplying you with choice fabrics, mantles blue and embroidered, stuffs of all colours, and strong, twisted cords. Ships of Tartessus carried your trade.

(Moffatt, *op. cit.* p. 931.)

PART II

The Greek Contribution

The ancient Greeks borrowed much from the Near and Middle East, as well as from the people who preceded them in the Aegean area, but transformed everything they received as if there was some magic in their fingers. It was they who, along with the Hebrews and the Romans, implanted in western civilization those qualities which distinguish it, for example, from Chinese or Hindu civilization. But the Greeks began the process. They laid our foundations in art, literature, science and philosophy, and exercised a quite considerable influence on the development of Christianity. As a result our language is permeated with words derived from ancient Greek such as "theology," "music," "politics," "physics," "athletics," "democracy"; and, what is more important, the ideas which infuse those words are also Greek in origin. Wherever modern man moves in the arts, the letters, or in the field of thought he is likely to discover that some ancient Greek has blazed the beginnings of the trails he follows. The story of Greece is the story of the youth of our own civilization.

Dates B.C.

800	Rule of Aristocracy		Homer	
750	First colonies sent out New Nobility.			
700			Rise of Sparta	
600	*Formative Years* — Age of Tyrants	End of era of colonization	Rise of	
550			Athens	
500	Oligarchy or Democracy			
	The Persian Wars Rise of the Athenian Empire Periclean Athens Peloponnesian War	*Historians* Herodotus Thucydides Xenophon	*Poets* Aeschylus Sophocles Euripides Aristophanes	*Sculptors* Myron Phidias Polyclitus
400	Spartan Supremacy to 371 Theban Supremacy 371–362 Conquest by Macedonia 338 Campaigns of Alexander the Great—336–323		*Philosophers* Plato Aristotle	*Sculptors* Scopas Praxiteles Lysippus
300	Hellenistic Kingdoms of Macedonia (to Rome 168 and 146) Syria (to Rome 63) Egypt (to Rome 31)	Age of Greek Science	Stoics Epicureans and Cynics	Hellenistic Sculpture and Literature
200				
146 133	Greece—a Roman Province Roman Province of Asia			
100				
Birth of Christ				

CHAPTER I

Minoans, Myceneans, and Homer

Only a century ago, the story of Greece began with the Greek poet, Homer, who is supposed to have lived about 800 B.C. Now we know that long before Homer there was an advanced culture in Crete and mainland Greece: this was the culture of the Minoans of Crete and of the Achaean Greeks of the Mycenean era.

The Rediscovery of the Minoan-Mycenean Civilization.

Homer's epics, the Iliad and the Odyssey, tell of a ten years' war between "the bronze-armored Achaeans" and the Trojans for the sake of that Helen whose face "launched a thousand ships." Troy, according to Greek legend, was captured in 1184 B.C. Scholars used to dismiss Helen of Troy, the war, and Troy itself as poetic fancies. But Heinrich Schliemann, a wealthy German businessman, believed in Homer. In 1870 A.D., on the hill of Hissarlik in the northwest corner of Asia Minor, he uncovered not one but nine Troys. Of these, *VII A* is thought to be the one sacked by the Achaean Greeks.

The leader of the Greeks, Homer sang, had been "wide-ruling Agamemnon" from "golden Mycenae." In southern Greece, on the reputed site of Mycenae, were massive walls. In 1876, inside those walls, Schliemann discovered five untouched rock-cut tombs. Later a sixth was found. In those vaults were nineteen skeletons and a great treasure which included jewelry, bronze daggers, gold cups, ostrich eggs banded with gold, and golden death-masks. With these discoveries the Trojan war ceased to be legend. It became clear, too, that long before the 8th century B.C. there had been an advanced civilization in mainland Greece. To it the name Mycenean, after Mycenae, was given.

Greek legends also suggested an early civilization on the long, narrow island of Crete. In Homer, a monarch, "the Minos", was said to have

ruled in Crete for "nine seasons." There was likewise a description of
"wide-wayed Cnossus" in which there was "a dancing floor for Ariadne
of the lovely tresses," and a Greek myth told of an annual Athenian tribute
of seven maidens and seven youths to the Minos to be devoured in the
"Labyrinth" by the Minotaur. The Minotaur was described as half-man,
half-bull. But, according to the story, the hero Theseus volunteered to
be one of the youths. In Crete, with the help of Ariadne, a daughter of the
Minos, Theseus killed the Minotaur, escaped from the Labyrinth, and got
back to Athens.

These references and other clues led the English archeologist, Sir
Arthur Evans, to buy a hillock four miles from the sea near Herakleion,
the capital of modern Crete. In 1900 A.D. he sank a shaft and struck
stone. In the midst of what are now grain-fields and olive orchards, he
had hit upon the six-acre palace of the Minos at Cnossus. There was even
a "dancing floor," although it is usually thought to have been some sort
of theater. Today, we can wander through that palace. We can sit on "the
oldest throne in the world." We can walk down five flights of stone stairs
to the "Queen's Rooms" in the southeast quarter of the palace. Because
these rooms were filled with hardened mud before they could collapse,
Evans was able to restore them pretty much as they were. In one of them
was found a beautiful painting of blue dolphins on a silver sea. Behind it,
in the "Queen's bathroom," the original bathtub still sits. The Cretans
of that day had excellent plumbing.

Evans called this rediscovered civilization, "Minoan," after Homer's
Minos. Minos is thought to have been a title like Pharaoh or Czar. From
this palace and other finds, such as the unearthing of another great
palace at Phaestus[1] on the south coast of Crete, it was realized that this
Minoan civilization was the parent of Schliemann's Mycenean culture.

The exploration of the Minoan-Mycenean civilization is still proceeding.
In southwestern Greece, for instance, Professor Blegen has brought to light
a palace at Pylos. In Homer, King Nestor is said to have ruled over "sandy
Pylos", so that this discovery is called "the Palace of Nestor." Likewise,
at Mycenae another grave-circle outside the walls has been found. In one
of the graves was the skeleton of an infant, wrapped in gold foil and with a
gold rattle beside it. Rich Minoan finds, too, have been made in Crete. The
latest of these was the discovery in 1961 of an unplundered palace, covering one and three-quarters acres, at Kato Zakro on the east coast. Since
1961 to the moment of writing, 50 of some 180 rooms have been excavated.
From these rooms beautiful vases, a bull's head in steatite (soapstone)
and other art objects along with a wine press and four Syrian elephant
tusks have been recovered. It can be confidently expected that, as time
goes by, still more about this forgotten civilization will come to light.

How Minoan Civilization Began

Neolithic men lived in Crete.[2] Later on, there were immigrations from Asia Minor, Libya, and, possibly, predynastic Egypt. Gold, copper, and silver came into use. The potter's wheel was introduced. Sea-going ships were built. And then, about 2500 B.C., bronze was invented.

Bronze is an alloy of 90% copper and 10% tin. Minoan[3] ships brought tin from the West and copper from Cyprus (the name, Cyprus, became the Latin *cuprum*, meaning "copper"). Soon the Minoans were exporting bronze articles and a beautiful polychromatic eggshell-thin pottery. This pottery is found in the tombs of Middle Kingdom Egypt (2000–1750 B.C.). Minoan trade reached not only to Egypt but also to Greece and Asia Minor, while westward Minoan vessels established posts in Sicily, Sardinia, North Africa, Spain, and, possibly, Cornwall.

The Minoan Golden Age: 2000–1400 B.C.

Wealth poured into Crete. The first great palaces were completed by 1800 B.C. Although these were destroyed about one hundred years later, new and bigger palaces arose, and from about 1600 B.C. the Minos of Cnossus is thought to have ruled the whole island.

In this period the Minoan navy seems to have controlled the Aegean Sea. In Crete there were a hundred unwalled towns and cities. Cnossus itself is estimated to have housed 100,000 people. In the countryside there was herding, farming, and lumbering, and copper crosscut saws of a yard in length have been found. In the cities, there were goldsmiths, potters, and jewelers. From Phaestus on the south coast a great road led to Cnossus. Up that road, thirty-five hundred years ago, plodded donkey caravans and travelers on foot. At its northern terminus, just where a gorge opens to give a view of the palace of Cnossus, Evans found an inn. In the mangers of its stables were discovered carbonized oats and barley. From its dining-room came an exquisitely colored frieze of partridges, looking as natural as if they had just settled in an American wheatfield.

Minoan Life

The evidence of archeology suggests a gay and easy life. Paintings of the people, done by the Minoans themselves in murals on wet plaster which, when it dried, preserved the colors, depict a lithe, Mediterranean type of people. The men, painted red-brown, wear kilts. There is a copper band around their slim waists. The women, with faces and bodies colored white, are dressed in elaborately flounced skirts and open bodices. Boxing, with the athletes clad in helmets and loin-cloths, is shown on the "Boxer's Vase". But the favorite entertainment, which may have been connected with a Minoan worship of a bull-god, was bull-grappling. Here, male and female toreadors faced charging bulls and, catching the bull's horns, used the upward thrust of the bull's toss to somersault over its back. An impaled toreador, carved on a vase of steatite, shows what happened if an athlete missed. In this sport may lie part of the explanation of the legend of the Minotaur.

Minoan Government and Religion

It seems likely that the government was a despotism with the Minos as a priest-king. Religion included a mother-goddess. Doves, animals, and snakes were among her cult objects. In the Boston Museum of Fine Arts, for instance, there is a figurine, only seven inches high, in ivory and gold, of a charming girl with snakes coiled around her outstretched arms.

The bull appears to have been worshipped as the principle of fertility under the symbol of a double-axe (used, perhaps, to kill a sacred bull on certain ritual occasions). It is possible that, just as the Pharaoh was regarded as a living god, the Minos was thought to be the incarnation of the bull-god. Furthermore, Labyrinth means "Place of the Double Axe", and part of the basement of the Palace of Cnossus has a double-axe carved on its pillars. Did, then, every so often, the Minos, wearing a bull's-head mask, wait in the Labyrinth, double-axe in hand, to kill unarmed captives, and, afterward, his potency once more proved, emerge to be greeted with shouts of joy? If so, this might help to explain the story of Theseus killing the Minotaur in the Labyrinth. The mother-goddess and the so-called "Cretan Zeus", survived in Greek religion. As for death, the Minoans looked upon it as a sea-voyage.

Minoan Art

In their art, in particular, these long-dead Minoans come alive for us. In processional figures, as in the mural of the Cup-Bearer, there is Egyptian influence in the stiff shoulders and in the full eye in profile. But there is none of Egyptian rigidity in most Minoan artistic expression. The reeds and flowers in their fresco paintings and on their exquisite pottery seem to wave in the wind. Their bulls charge in long, fluid lines. In the Harvester Vase, the reapers march along in gay procession, singing lustily. The "gaming-board of Minos" and a beautiful bull's-head rhyton (a type of libation vase) are marvels of workmanship. We can say that here is the first "European" art, different from anything produced in the Near East. Everywhere in the paintings is a blue wavy line for the sea. Taste is excellent, colors are vivid, and the designs are light and graceful.

The Decline of Minoan Power

The Minoans seem to have been overthrown by the Achaean Greeks. About 1450 B.C., according to the latest evidence, a dynasty of bearded Achaeans appears to have seized Cnossus. The evidence for this conclusion is based largely on writing. The Minoans had used hieroglyphic writing, but later invented what is called a "Linear A" script, which at this writing has not been deciphered, but is presumed to be in the unknown Minoan language. Still later, a second script, "Linear B" was developed from Linear A.

Linear A is found principally in Crete, although, fairly recently, Professor Caskey, when excavating on the island of Ceos near Attica, dug up a fragment of a wine jar with Linear A characters incised on it. Tablets in Linear B, discovered by Evans at Cnossus, have turned up at several sites in Greece, notably in the "Palace of Nestor" at Pylos, at Mycenae and in 1964 at Thebes. For years scholars attempted to decipher Linear B. Finally, in 1953, two English archeologists, Michael Ventris and John Chadwick, published a generally accepted interpretation of it as *archaic Greek*.

The tablets chiefly turned out to be brief records of chariots, vases and occupations. Yet they do shed light on life in Mycenean Greece. Furthermore, since Linear B tablets occur at several places in Greece but only at Cnossus in Crete, and since they seem to be in archaic Greek, weight is given to a view that this script was developed out of Linear A by Achaean Greeks and that, about 1450 B.C., a dynasty of Achaeans ruled in Cnossus. If they did, their rule did not last long. About 1400 B.C., according to the generally accepted belief, the palace of Crete was destroyed and the power passed from Cnossus to Mycenae in Greece.

The Achaean Greeks and the Mycenean Empire

The first dwellers in Greece were, like the Minoans, a dark-haired, swarthy-skinned Mediterranean people. Later, Anatolian round-heads and other stocks came in. About 2400 B.C. Minoan traders began to arrive. They may have planted settlements.

By 1900 B.C., however, the first Greek-speaking bands had reached northern Greece. As time went on, other Greek-speaking tribes pressed into the peninsula. By about 1650 B.C. varying groups of them had occupied Thessaly and east-central and southern Greece, the Peloponnesus (island of Pelops) as the Greeks called it.

These intruders are called in general, Achaeans. Yet they came to be divided by differences in dialects and cultural habits into three major groups. Those in Thessaly spoke Aeolic; the inhabitants of Boeotia and Attica spoke the Ionic dialect, while the Achaeans of southern Greece spoke Arcadian. At about the same time, other Greek-speaking bands, the Dorians, occupied Epirus.

The Achaeans subdued the Mediterraneans. They built fortress cities. But they accepted Minoan culture. Then, when Cnossus fell, the so-called Mycenean "Empire" was established (ca. 1400–1150 B.C.). In this "empire" there was a group of fortified cities, such as those at Athens, Mycenae, Tiryns and Pylos. The king of Mycenae was the over-lord king. The society seems to have been a feudal one with the equivalent of barons and knights as vassals of the minor kings, and with the minor kings owing troops and service to the king of Mycenae.

Meanwhile, the Achaeans took over the Minoan trade routes. Colonies were planted in Rhodes, Cyprus, and at Miletus in Asia Minor. Ware-houses of the Achaean merchants have even turned up at Ras Shamra in Syria. There seem, also, to have been piratical raids, and Hittite documents tell of trouble with a land which may have been Achaea.

Even today when you visit Mycenae, there is an aura of age-old power and splendor. The ruins of its walls and palace sit on a hill about ten miles north of the blue waters of the gulf of Argos. From Mycenae, its rulers could watch the ships which unloaded at water's edge, and check the caravans moving through the plain to and from Corinth. The walls of the long-dead city are still tremendous. Inside the entrance-gate is the grave-circle Schliemann discovered. Across the valley in front of the hill of Mycenae is the so-called "Tomb of Agamemnon."

A walled roadway or dromos 117 feet long leads to its doorway. Inside, hollowed out of the hill, is a stone vault 50 feet in diameter and 48 feet high. The masonry is beautifully fitted together. The inner lintel stone in one solid block is estimated at a weight of 121 tons. To the right, as one enters, is a small doorway to the actual burial-place.

There are other beehive tombs in the hill but none as large as this one. The king who built it must have been powerful and wealthy. But his palace on top of the hill of Mycenae is only a ruin, although its outlines can be traced. When one sits there, looking down over the modern plain with its scattered villages, it is tempting to recreate something of Mycenae's ancient splendor. The palace would glitter with bronze and with gold. The walls of the fortress and of the houses inside the walls would be strong and newly-built. Other houses would cluster close under the walls (a few have been uncovered), where there are now fields about the size of tennis-courts. There would be the buzz of people and the sound of hammers and the clang of armored men.

Down at the gulf of Argos ships would be loading and unloading. Donkeys would be plodding across the plain. There might also be Hittite envoys riding up past the Tomb of Agamemnon, or the King of Mycenae might be leading his chariots and his infantry out for war. Where we are sitting, Helen of Troy, if she ever existed, may once have stood staring out over the busy city. According to Greek legend, Helen of Troy was the sister of Clytemnestra, the wife of Agamemnon, the great king of Mycenae.

The Mycenean society of the Achaeans is now regarded as the first stirring of the Greek spirit. Besides Minoan craftsmen and artists, it is thought that there were bards to sing, as Homer did later, of the great deeds of the Achaeans.

The expedition against Troy, of which Homer sang, seems to have been the last tremendous effort of the Achaeans. Many scholars believe that it was fought to break Troy's stranglehold on the trade of northwest Asia Minor and Thrace, and on the passage through the Dardanelles to the Black Sea. Even so, the abduction of a princess, such as Helen of Troy, may have been the incident that set off the war.

Troy fell about 1184 B.C. In the meantime, the Dorian Greeks were pressing upon the Achaeans.

The Dorians, as noted, had long been settled in northwestern Greece. About 1200 B.C. or earlier, however, new bands, apparently from Illyria, began to press into Northern Greece. In the resulting confusion, groups of dislodged Dorians moved into Thessaly and mingled with the Aeolians; although some of the Aeolians fled across the Aegean Sea to the island of Lesbos and Chios and eventually to the northwestern coast of Asia Minor, henceforward known as Aeolis. Other Dorian groups occupied central Greece and thence crossed to the Peloponnesus, the heartland of the Achaeans.

It should be noted that Ionian Attica escaped the invasion. In the Peloponnesus, the uncivilized Dorians sacked and destroyed the Mycenean fortress-cities, although Arcadia, the most backward part of southern Greece, was unconquered. Some of the Achaeans fled to Attica, others to the northwestern tip of the Peloponnesus which in classical times was called Achaea. Still others, mingled with Ionians from Boeotia and Attica, migrated to the central coastline of Asia Minor, thenceforward named Ionia, and to the central islands of the Aegean. Meanwhile, the Dorians occupied the islands of Crete and Rhodes, and the mainland opposite Rhodes, which was then called Doris. From this time forward the four principal dialects of the Greek world were Aeolic, spoken in northwestern Asia Minor, and the islands off it, Thessaly and west central Greece, Ionic used on the islands and coastline of Ionic and in Attica, Arcadian the language in Arcadia, and Doric the dialect for all Dorian countries. Doric and Ionic, the two most important dialects differed considerably and there was an ancient and deep-seated hostility between the two stocks who spoke them. Incidentally, Aeolis and Ionia, both in Asia Minor, are usually referred to as Ionia.

Meanwhile the Mycenean civilization had fallen. It must be remembered, however, that the Dorian invasions were part of a wide movement of peoples. It was in this epoch that the Phrygians overthrew the Hittite empire, that the "Sea-Peoples", among whom was a folk identified with the Achaeans, swept down on Egypt; that the Philistines settled in Palestine, and that the period of small states in the Near East began.

When the invasions were over the "Dark Age" began, although it is possible that this age was an era of transition rather than of a complete breakdown. Out of the welter was to emerge the beginning of Classical Greek culture, which, possibly, owed more to the Mycenean civilization than is known as yet. At any rate the first European poet, Homer, has given us vivid recollections of the Minoan-Mycenean world, recollections which probably had been carried to Aeolis and Ionia by refugees from the Dorian inroads.

Homer and His World: 1100–800 B.C.

"All things," the ancient Greeks used to say, "begin with Homer." Today, it is believed that Homer came at the end of a long line of epic poets, reaching back into the Mycenean period.

Who was Homer? That a real person named Homer ever existed has been doubted. Today it is generally agreed that an actual Homer lived around 800 B.C., somewhere along or just off the coast of Asia Minor, and that he composed the *Iliad* and, less certainly, the *Odyssey* out of sagas which were already in existence, and which dated back to Mycenean days. There is a genius shining through these two epics which does suggest a single great author for each or both of them.

If Homer existed he was a "rhapsode." The word "rhapsode" means a "stitcher-together of song." In the period from 1100 to 800 B.C., and possibly before that time, rhapsodes used to travel like the Anglo-Saxon bards around the courts of the nobles to sing, or rather chant, sagas to them. Homer's great contribution was that he "invented the spacious epic on a single theme."

His epics were not written down until much later. They were passed on orally, and certainly there were additions made. The *Iliad* told of the *Wrath of Achilles* during the ten years' war against Troy. The *Odyssey* relates the wanderings of the crafty Odysseus and his homecoming from Troy. Neither epic is primitive poetry. Instead, there is richness of imagery, nobility of motivation, vividness of characterization, speed of action, wealth of plot-structure, tears for the human suffering behind the panoply of war, and a meter which flows or thunders as the mood demands.

The epics purport to be about the bronze-armored Achaeans and their war against Troy at the beginning of the 12th century B.C. Yet, for instance. the iron of Homer's age is mentioned. From both poems, we get glimpses of the world of Homer's own day of the late 9th or early 8th century B.C.

It is a somewhat primitive world. There are a multitude of small states. The basic units are the family, the clan and the tribe. A Zeus-born king rules, assisted by a council of nobles or clan-heads. The assembly of fighting-men can express approval or disapproval. Farming and herding are the primary occupations, but piracy is honorable. In the Odyssey, a traveler is asked: "Are you a pirate or have you come to trade?" Trade is by barter. The Aegean is well-known but the western Mediterranean is a world of one-eyed giants, sirens, and the like. The habitable world, it is thought, is like a plate and is surrounded by a fast-flowing river called *Okeanos*.

Ethics and the gods are equally primitive. Hospitality and the keeping of oaths are the prime virtues. The gods are simply Greeks, endowed with supernatural power and immortality. In the *Iliad,* Zeus, the supreme god, is tricked by his wife, Hera and Ares, the god of war, is wounded by a Greek hero, Diomede, and bellows like ten thousand bulls. Yet behind the gods we catch glimpses of an immutable fate or Destiny, which even the gods cannot change. As for death, in the Homeric epic most people when they die go to Hades (a pit on the western rim of the world) as "strengthless shades." A few heroes, however, go without dying to a garden of the sungod, also in the west, called the Elysian Fields. Even in Homer's world, there already is directness, nobility, and an aura of freedom. In the next three centuries the Greeks were to swarm out over the Mediterranean and Black Sea areas and to develop further their own special characteristics.

Notes to Chapter 1

1. Other important finds were a summer palace at Haghia Triadha near Phaestus, a big palace at Mallia on the northern coast-line and, further along, a town and a small provincial palace at Gournia. Around the palace of Cnossus, a number of interesting buildings have been unearthed, such as the "Royal Villa" and the "Priest's House".

2. The Neolithic Age in Crete, which is dated at prior to 3000 B.C.. when

copper began to be used, has lately been extended a thousand years into the past through C14 dating. After the Neolithic came a Chalcolithic period with copper and stone tools used alongside each other.

3. Evans' dating scheme for Minoan history, as revised by R. W. Hutchinson in 1947, is as follows:

Early Minoan	I	2500–2400 B.C.
	II	2400–2100
	III	2100–1950
Middle Minoan	I	1950–1840 B.C.
	II	1840–1750
	III	1750–1550
Late Minoan	I	1550–1450 B.C.
	II	1450–1400
	III	1400–1050

This dating scheme, which was based on Homer's Minos ruling for "nine seasons", is artificial and does not apply to the whole island.

4. Professor Palmer of Oxford has questioned the accuracy of Evans' date for the destruction of Cnossus, arguing that it was 200 years later, and that hence the whole problem of the relationships between Crete and mainland Greece must be re-examined.

Readings from Sources of the Period

(a) Four examples of the contents of the numerous tablets found in the "Palace of Nestor" at Pylos, as translated by Messrs. Ventris and Chadwick are given.

10. At Pylos: twenty-two sons of the bath-attendants, eleven boys.
30. Philaios, the goat-herd (who is acting as) *seizer has seized the cattle of Dunios.*
53. Rowers to go to Pleuron: eight from Ro-o-wa, five from Rhion, four from Po-ra-, six from *Te-ta-ra-ne,* seven from a-po-ne-we.
240. (first of three lines).
    One *stone* table with strutting of *ebony* and ivory, of *encircled* type, a nine-*footer,* carved with a running spiral.

(Michael Ventris and John Chadwick, *Documents in Mycenean Greek*, Cambridge: University Press, 1956).

(b) From Homer's *Iliad*.

I. In the sixth book of the Iliad, Homer tells of the meeting of the Trojan hero, Hector, with his wife, Andromache and his son, Astyanax. Andromache begs Hector not to return to the battle outside the walls and Hector replies.

    Then great Hector of the glancing helmet said to her: "I, too, take thought of these things, dear wife. But I feel great shame before the Trojans and their long-robed wives if like a coward I skulk from war. Nor does my own heart permit it; for I have learned to be valiant always and to fight among the foremost Trojans, striving greatly for my father's glory and my own. For well I know this in my heart and soul: there will come a day when holy Ilium shall fall, and Priam and the people of Priam of the good ashen spear. But not so much does the anguish of the Trojans of aftertime move me, nor Hecuba's own nor King Priam's nor that of my brothers, many and brave, who may fall in the dust at the hands of their foemen, as your anguish, when some bronze-clad Achaean shall lead you forth weeping and rob you of your day of freedom. And then, perhaps, dwelling in Argos, you shall weave at another's loom or carry water from Messeïs or Hypereia, much against your will, and harsh necessity shall lie upon you. Then some man shall say as he sees you weeping, 'This was Hector's wife, he who was the best in battle of the horse-taming Trojans when they fought around Ilium.' So someone will say. And upon you then shall come fresh grief for want of such a man to ward off the day of bondage. But may the heaped earth cover me in death before I hear your cry or the sound of your captivity."

So spoke glorious Hector, and reached out for his son, but the child shrank back with a cry into the arms of his fair-girdled nurse, frightened at the sight of his dear father, afraid of the bronze and the horsehair crest as he saw it nodding dreadfully from the helmet's peak. His dear father and queenly mother laughed, and glorious Hector quickly took his helmet from his head and laid it all gleaming on the ground. Then, when he had kissed his dear son and dandled him in his arms, he spoke in prayer to Zeus and the other gods: "Zeus, and ye other gods, grant that this child of mine also may become, even as I am, pre-eminent among the Trojans, as great in strength, and that he may rule with might over Ilium. And may someone say of him one day, as he returns from war, 'This man is much better than his father.' May he slay his enemy and bear away the bloodstained spoils, and may his mother's heart rejoice."

(MacKendrick and Howe: *Classics in Translation,* Vol. 1. *Greek Literature,* p. 28, Madison: University of Wisconsin Press, 1952, translated by Alton B. Chase and William C. Perry, Jr.)

II. In the eighteenth book of the *Iliad,* Homer describes the scenes hammered out on the shield of Achilles by the lame god, Hephaestus (in Roman mythology, Vulcan). One of these scenes describes Cnossus (Knossos) of the Minoans.

On it the renowned lame god placed a dancing floor like that which once in broad Cnossus Daedalus made for Ariadne of the lovely tresses. There youths and dearly courted maidens danced, holding each other's wrists. The maids wore robes of fine linen and the lads well-woven shirts, just touched with olive oil. The maidens wore fair garlands and the lads bore golden daggers, hanging from silver belts. Sometimes they ran most easily on skillful feet, as when a potter sits and fits his hand about his wheel and tries it, if it run; sometimes they ran in lines toward one another. A great throng stood in delight about the charming dance, and among them a divine bard played on his lyre, and two tumblers, beginning their sport, spun through their midst.

(*Ibid.,* p. 41.)

(c) From Homer's *Odyssey.*

In the ninth book of the Odyssey, Odysseus tells how the one-eyed giant, Polyphemus, shut himself and his comrades in a cave and proceeded to devour them, two at a time. When four had been eaten and Polyphemus, after closing the mouth of the cave with a huge rock, was out feeding his sheep, Odysseus had his comrades prepare and sharpen a drill of olive-wood, which they hid. That night, after Polyphemus had eaten two more Greeks, Odysseus gets him drunk, and tells him that his name is "Noman." Then, Polyphemus falls asleep and Odysseus thrusts the drill under a heap of glowing coals. Below is what happened next.

"As soon as the olive-wood club was about to burst into flame, though it was quite green, and when it was giving off a fearful glow, I brought it from the fire and came up close to the giant, with my helpers standing around me. They lifted the sharp-pointed club and pressed it into his eye, while I pushed down on it and turned it around, just as a man bores through a ship's timber with a drill. (His helpers below whirl it around with a strap that they pull from either side, and so the drill keeps steadily turning all the while.) That's how we kept turning the fiery pointed club in the Cyclops' eye. The blood flowed out around the hot wood, and the blast from the burning eyeball singed his lids and eyebrows, and the roots of his eye burst in the heat. As when a smith with marvellous art dips a great ax or adze in cold water, and it send out a loud cry and a hiss—that is how iron gets its strength—so the giant's eye sizzled about the olive-wood club. He roared and bellowed in agony while the rocks about him resounded with his cries. We all ran from him in terror.

"Then he pulled the blood-soaked club from his eye, and mad with pain, flung it from him. In a tremendous voice he called to the Cyclopes who lived far above, in the caves on the windy heights. Hearing his cries, they came running from all sides, and standing outside around his cave, they asked him what was wrong. 'Polyphemus, why are you so desperate, and why do you shout so in the celestial night-time and keep us all from sleep? Is any man driving your flocks off against your will? Is any man taking your life by trickery or violence?' From his cave mighty Polyphemus answered, 'My friends, Noman is killing me by trickery and not by violence.'

"Their words came flying in reply, 'If no man is mistreating you and you are alone and in pain—well, there is of course no way of escaping sickness sent by mighty Zeus. You can only pray for help from your father, Lord Poseidon.'

"With those words they went off, and my heart laughed because thanks to my cleverness the false name had fooled him. The Cyclops, groaning and suffering sharp pangs of pain, groped about with his hands and took the stone from the entrance. Then he sat down in the opening and stretched out his hands to see if he could catch anyone walking out among the sheep. That's how simple minded he thought I was!

"All the while I was trying to find out the best way of saving my companions and myself. I was weaving all sorts of tricky schemes and plans, because I knew that this was a case of life or death and I felt that a real calamity was unpleasantly near. Here is the plan that struck me as best. The rams in the flock were well fed, big handsome fellows, with thick coats of dark-violet wool. Taking three at a time, I quietly tied them firmly together with some of the willow twigs on which the monster usually slept. The ram in the middle carried one of my men tied beneath him, while the two on the outside went along for protection. Thus there were three sheep carrying each one of my comrades. For myself, I chose a ram that was by far the best of the whole flock. Taking hold of him I doubled myself up under his shaggy belly; then with my face upwards I boldly clung tight to his marvellous wool. So we stayed there, unhappily waiting for morning to come.

"When Eos, the early born, the rosy-fingered goddess, appeared, the males ran out to pasture, but the females stood bleating about the pens, as they had not been milked, and their udders were almost bursting. Their master, though tortured by cruel pains, ran his hands over the back of every sheep as it came and stood beside him on its way out. Poor fool, he did not understand that my men were tied under the bellies of his thick-fleeced sheep! Last of all, the prize ram of the flock came walking toward the entrance. He had been slowed down by his thick fleece and by the weight of his tricky passenger.

"As he ran his hands over him, mighty Polyphemus said, 'Good old fellow, what does this mean? Why are you the last of the flock to leave the cave? You were never left behind before, but you always went striding ahead and were always the first to be grazing on the lush flowers of the grass, the first to reach the flowing streams, and the first to want to return to the fold at evening. But today you are the last of all! I think you feel the loss of your master's eye, which was put out by that bad man and his cruel comrades. Noman it was who drugged me with wine, but he is not safe yet, I swear! Oh, if you only could share my thoughts and had a voice to tell me where that man is hiding from me! Then I would scatter his brains through the cave in every direction, as I dashed him to the ground, and my heart would have some relief from the troubles that no-account Noman brought me.'

"With these words he let the ram go out the door. When we had gone a little way from the cave and the yard, I first let myself down and next untied my comrades. We quickly drove off the fat slender-legged flocks, often turning to look back until we finally reached the ship. Our good comrades were more than glad to see all of us that had escaped, and they began to sob and cry for the rest. But I would not let them weep and gave each man a stern look as I told him to stop.

"I ordered them to quickly throw plenty of the fleecy animals on the ship and then to sail the salt sea. Soon the men were going on board and taking their seats, and once in their places they struck the grey water with their oars and were off. When we were as far from shore as a loud cry can be heard, I began to shout insults at the Cyclops. 'Cyclops,' I said, 'you see I was not so helpless, and you see it was not meant for you to gulp down my men with all your might and main! But it was meant that your wicked deeds would find you out, because you were shameless enough to eat strangers who were staying in your own house. So Zeus and the other gods have punished you well.'"

(*Ibid.*, pp. 66–67, translated by Reuben A. Brower.)

CHAPTER 2

The Formative Centuries: 800–500 B.C.

During these centuries the Greeks swarmed out over the Black Seas to plant settlements on the lands around them. A "New Poetry" replaced Epic poetry, and the first prose writing began. Philosophical thinking burst into bloom. Architecture and sculpture had their beginnings. Meanwhile, in this new and restless world, there were political, economic, and social upheavals. Out of these disturbances the *polis*, or city-state was developed. In these city-states, finally there was either the "Rule of the Few" (Oligarchy) or the "Rule of the Demos" (Democracy). To achieve an insight into some of the reasons for this burgeoning of the Greek spirit, we need to understand their environment.

The Greeks, believing that they had a common ancestor, Hellen, called themselves Hellenes and their homeland, Hellas. To them Hellas was the Greek peninsula, but *not* Macedonia and Thrace, the coast of Asia Minor, the islands of the Aegean Sea, and that sea itself. It was a small country. The ancient Greek peninsula had an area of 25,000 square miles and the northern and west-central parts of it played a very minor role in Greek history. (For the sake of comparison, ancient Greece was about the size of present-day West Virginia, the area of which is 24,181 square miles.) Even with the addition of the coast of Asia Minor and the Aegean islands, the land area is only about 50,000 square miles.

The Influence of Geography on Greek Development

Spain, Italy, and Greece all project into the Mediterranean Sea. Inevitably, all three trap migrations from the north so that each is a mixing-bowl of peoples; and each of them is part of the Mediterranean world. This second fact means, for one thing, that Greece, like southern Spain and southern Italy, is a sub-tropical country. As a result the summers are hot and dry, while in winter, although it is wet and chilly,

136

the temperature seldom drops below the freezing-point. The Greeks could, and did, live an outdoor life. Their business, social, and political gatherings took place, not in blocks of sky-scrapers or in auditoriums, but under the open sky.

Greece is, however, the *easternmost* of the three projections. Its best harbors face east, and the Aegean islands are stepping-stones to Asia Minor. In consequence, the Greeks, after the Minoans, were the first people to be civilized by the Near East.

Seen from the air or from the sea, Greece is a tumbled mass of mountains. Among them, dropped as if by accident, are plains. Sixty-four percent of mainland Greece is bare rock. Only 18 percent could be put under the plough. Furthermore, the soil grew grapes, olives, and barley better than wheat. Except for potter's clay and building stone, there were few other natural resources. It was the Greek Herodotus who said: "Hellas and Poverty have always been foster-sisters." The mountains did more than make ancient Greece poor. They fostered the growth of the Greek city-states, each on its own isolated plain and each fiercely independent. This is why ancient Greece never developed into a nation-state.

And then there is the sea. No part of ancient Greece was more than fifty miles from it, and the coastline is deeply indented with coves and harbors. Moreover, the Aegean is practically tideless, so that boats can be drawn up anywhere. In such an environment the Greeks were bound to become mariners and traders.

Mountains and sea, then, shaped the Greek way of life. They also helped fashion the beauty of the Greek landscape. The sea is a deep, almost indigo blue, with a violet haze shimmering over it. The mountains are smitten by the sun into russet, golden-brown, violet, and purple. The whole is bathed in a peculiarly lucent light which makes every color and every outline stand out sharply. Here, some people suggest, is part of the explanation for the clarity of Greek art and thought. Few people have been more influenced by their environment than the ancient Greeks.

Greek Unity and Lack of Union

After the Dark Ages we find the Greeks scattered in small communities along the coast of Asia Minor over the Aegean islands, and the Greek peninsula. The fierce individualism of each community was accentuated by the age-old hostility between Ionians and Dorians. Moreover, Ionians found difficulty in understanding Dorians, and vice versa. There were also, as has been noted, a number of other Greek dialects.

Geography, Greek individualism, racial and linguistic differences— these factors prevented unity. At the same time, other influences fostered it.

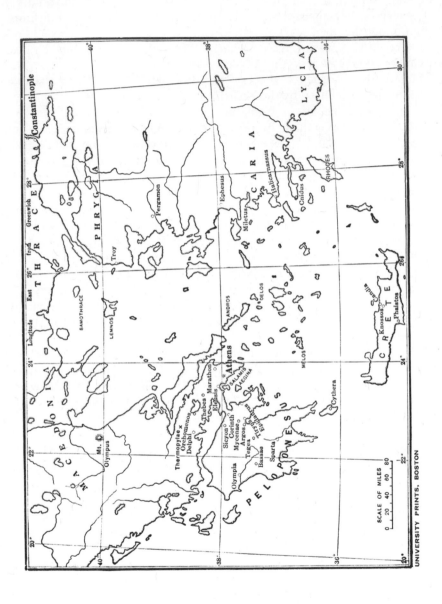

Map of Greece

The Greeks, in spite of local divergences, worshipped the same gods and consulted the same oracles. Of these oracles, the most famous was the oracle of Apollo, the god of prophecy, in central Greece. Delphi is set half-way down Mount Parnassus on a sloping ledge which overlooks a plain to the south and a deep gorge amid mountains to the east. Here in ancient times was a temple of Apollo. In it sat a round stone to mark what was believed to be the exact center of the world. At first the oracles were given through the interpretation of words supposed to be whispered by the wind soughing through the leaves of a laurel tree in the sacred enclosure. Later, a priestess, called the Delphic Sibyl, sitting on a tripod over a chasm from which fumes were said to rise, entered a real or a pretended trance, and her mutterings were translated by the priests into Homeric hexameters as prophecies of Apollo. It is difficult for us to realize how completely Greeks and non-Greeks believed in the validity of these prophecies. The oracle at Delphi was consulted on matters of state, such as the time when Croesus, the Lydian king, asked whether he should make war on Cyrus the Persian or not, and was told that if he did he would "destroy a great empire." (The empire turned out to be his own.) But the oracle was also asked to determine trivial matters such as where to go for a good catch of fish.

As a result, thank-offerings poured into Delphi. Statues were erected. At Delphi, too, were the treasuries of Greek cities including the treasury of the Athenians, and on the walls of Apollo's temple were precepts such as "Know Thyself" and "Nothing to excess." The priests likewise selected the "Seven Sages" of Greece, concentrating their wisdom in pithy sayings, and issued parables to suggest how to worship the gods "with a pure heart." Inevitably they became a political force and the causes they favored usually won. As we shall see later, they were consulted about colonies. In this way they aided in the expansion of the Greeks. Almost equal status was attached to the oracle of Apollo at Cumae, north of Naples. Here the Cumaean Sibyl prophesied for the western Greeks and for the Romans.

Connected with religion, too, were the Great Games. The foremost of these were the Olympic Games, begun in 776 B.C. Three other national athletic festivals followed, the Pythian at Delphi, the Isthmian at Corinth, and the Nemean at Nemea south of Corinth. In these games only Hellenes could compete.

As Hellenes, the Greeks were also conscious of a common ancestor, a common literature, and a common language. A man who did not speak Greek was a "barbaros." By "barbaros" the Greeks meant at first a man whose speech sounded to them like a stammering of "bar-bar-bar." Later, "barbaros" came to imply that anyone who did not speak Greek was not a civilized being.

A common religion, a common participation in the Great Games, the use of the same oracles and language, and the belief in descent from the same ancestor—these features gave the Greeks an overall sense of unity.

The Classical Greeks Begin to Become Civilized

Classical Greek civilization began in Ionia, because the Ionian Greeks, through the Phrygians of Asia Minor, (and later through the Lydians), came into contact with Mesopotamian influences. In addition, something of Mycenean civilization seems to have lived on along the coast of Asia Minor. It is no accident that it was in this area that Homer sang, or that here the "new Poetry" of the 7th century B.C. began, or that it was in Ionia that philosophy and history had their beginnings. Meanwhile, Phoenician traders were bringing goods and civilizing influences to the maritime communities of Ionia, the islands, and mainland Greece. It seems to have been early in the 8th century B.C. that the Greeks adapted the Phoenician alphabet to their own use.

In this early Greek world the Greeks were settled on the land in villages. West-central, northern Greece, and Arcadia, with a few exceptions never got beyond the village stage. Elsewhere the villagers of each plain chose a center for defense, as, for instance, the flat-topped hill of the Acropolis (*akros*—"high" and *polis*—"city") in the Attic plain. Such centers often went back to Mycenean days. On them the king dwelt, and around them clusters of dwellings for artisans and the like huddled, with an open space (the *agora*) for a market. They were, naturally, centers for justice, religion, trade, and social gatherings as well as for defense. You might note that the Athenian Acropolis was four miles from the sea as a protection against pirates. From centers such as these, in the 8th and succeeding centuries, the Greek *poleis* or city-states developed; and geography, as we have seen, favored their development.

The Greek City-State

The ideal Greek city-state was ultimately a defensible town or city, in the center of a plain, surrounded by farming villages, a ring of pasture-land and a barrier of mountains with, however, one flank open to the sea, and a good harbor. Politically, the ancient Greeks never got beyond the city-state. In each city-state there was an intense loyalty of the citizens to their own city; and yet, because politics in a small community are certain to be extremely local and personal, there were often equally fierce inter-factional disputes. But to be *apolis*, a man without a city, was an evil fate. To a Greek, exile from his city was almost worse than death. We should also note that, while each city-state had its patron deity, none was dominated by religion, as were the Sumerian city-states. For one thing, except for the priests of Apollo at Delphi, there was no separate class of priests. Instead, laymen performed priestly duties as part of ordinary life. For another, Greek communities were so small and personal contact so frequent that no king came to be regarded as either a god or the incarnation of a god, as in Egypt. A third reason was that, as we shall see later, there was a basic difference between the attitude of the Greeks and that of the Near and Middle Eastern peoples towards the gods. As a result, the loyalty of Greek citizens was a *secular* loyalty.

City-state rivalries caused war after war among the Greeks, culminating in the great war between Athens and Sparta in 431–404 B.C. Those same rivalries produced great achievements. In athletics, for instance, if an Athenian or a Rhodian won at the Olympic Games, his victory was a victory for his city and he was welcomed home as a conquering hero. At Athens, in addition to a gift of money he was given free living for the rest of his life. Similarly, the city-states competed in rearing temples and statues to their patron gods or goddesses; and hence the rapid development of architecture and sculpture. The intense individualism of the Greeks mirrors the individualism of each of their separate communities.

To understand the Greek world we must think of it, in spite of the overall unity which has been noted, as divided into a multitude of city-states of varying sizes and types. The island of Crete, about 130 miles long and 30 miles across at its widest point, contained no less than 43 city-states. Early Attica within an area of 886 square miles, was, at first, parcelled out among twelve separate communities. Corinth, a powerful maritime city-state, possessed only 376 square miles of territory.

The Rule of the Aristocracy

While the city-state was developing, settlement on the land was bringing other problems to the 8th century Greeks. It seems likely that originally all land had belonged to the clans in which the Indo-European Greeks were organized. But now the idea of private property appeared, and the clan-heads, or nobles, seized the best fields. Their followers became either peasant-farmers or landless men. The natural increase of population, plus erosion (because of the cutting down of the trees) had, in fact, brought about a scarcity of land. Finally, in the 8th century B.C. the landed aristocrats, as we may now call them, did away with the kings, except in Sparta and Thessaly.

The aristocrats called themselves the "beautiful and good" and the rest of the people "the mean." They made and administered the laws. This rule of the aristocrats was the first great political and economic change in Greece. The Greek poet, Hesiod, writing in the 7th century B.C., presents a vivid picture of an "iron age" in which the farmer works from before daylight to dark and even then can hardly make ends meet. He calls upon his brother, Perses, to stand up with him against the injustice of the nobles.

Causes of the Expansion of Greek Trade and Colonization

Meanwhile masons, carpenters, potters, smiths, weavers, and the like had become specialized laborers to provide for the home markets and also to produce articles for export. Some farmers, too, as recommended by Hesiod, had gone on brief trading trips with their products. There were disgruntled younger sons of the nobility who learned the tricks of trade from the Phoenicians. And the Phoenicians, thanks to Assyrian expansion, were in difficulties. The Greeks seized the chance.

Around 750 B.C. numerous factors turned the Greeks to colonization. They were motivated by over-population, lack of land, Phoenician influence, discontent, opportunity, and a natural spirit of adventure. The first colonies developed to answer the need for land, but opportunities for trade were an additional spur. The poor, led usually by dissatisfied aristocrats, surged out in search of land, new homes, and wealth. The nobles were glad to see them go. This was the first outpouring. Later on, factional struggles and the coming of tyrants kept up the flow.

Greek Colonization: 750–600 B.C.

For a century and a half the Greeks from the maritime states of both mainland Greece and Ionia swarmed outward. Colonies from Chalcis and Eretria, in the island of Euboea off Attica, and from Corinth occupied the three-pronged peninsula, known as Chalcidice, jutting out from Macedonia. Here, the prizes were farmland, ship-timber, hides, and metal ores. The Greeks also put settlements along the coast of Thrace and along the Dardanelles, the Sea of Marmora, and the Bosphorus. One of those colonies, Byzantium, planted by Megara, just north of Corinth, became Constantinople and is now Istanbul.

Greek sailors burst into the Black Sea. In an attempt to propitiate its storms, they called it the "Euxeinos," which means "hospitable to strangers." Land, the wheat of southern Russia, fish, slaves, iron, and silver were their objectives. Miletus, the principal Ionian city of Asia Minor, is said to have planted 90 colonies around the Black Sea. Miletus made and exported excellent textiles, and the profits from trade in this area were enormous. The Milesians also developed a port at Naucratis on one of the mouths of the Nile. Egyptian paper, linen, and the cat found their way to the Greek cities, and Greeks began to study in Egypt. Meanwhile, the little island of Thera founded a colony at Cyrene in Libya. The Greeks, too, contested Cyprus with Phoenicia.

In general, however, just as Lydia and Syria blocked the expansion of the Greeks of Asia Minor into the hinterland, so Phoenicia and the Philistines shut Greek traders off from the eastern Mediterranean south of Rhodes. The great Greek swarming was westward.

Here they faced difficulties. Carthage, the former Phoenician colony, kept a stranglehold on the north shore of Africa and on the southern coasts of Spain. They sank every ship which tried to move into the Atlantic. They fought with the Greeks for Sicily. Meanwhile, the Etruscans blocked off the Greek traders from much of Italy and clung to Elba, Corsica, and Sardinia. The Greeks were defeated off Alalia in Corsica in 535 B.C. by a combined Carthaginian and Etruscan fleet.

The Greeks were not to be denied. They dotted the heel, toe, and instep of southern Italy with colonies. Cumae, just north of Naples, and Naples itself, (Greek *Neapolis,* "new city") were founded by Chalcis. Other Greeks took over the eastern part of Sicily. Syracuse, Messina (called Zanclé at first), Agrigento, Taranto, Brindisi—these are only a few of today's cities which owe their origin to the colonies established by the Greeks. The Romans later were to call these settlements *Magna Graecia,* that is, "Greater Greece." Further west, about 600 B.C., settlers from Phocaea, in Asia Minor, founded Massalia (Roman Massilia and modern Marseilles) at the mouth of the Rhône river. In this way they tapped the Rhône-Seine route to Britain.

These examples illustrate how flocks of Greeks, like birds seeking nesting places, occupied the coasts of the Black Sea and the Mediterranean. All the important Greek states participated except Athens and Sparta. Sparta, except for colonists sent to Taras (modern Taranto) on the instep of Italy, won new land by conquering her neighbor, Messenia. Athens was overshadowed by Chalcis, by Aegina, and by Corinth.

How a Greek Colony was Founded

The planting of a Greek colony was, in general, a private enterprise, although the colonists often received help from the mother city. It was usually decided upon by a meeting of those interested. A common practice was to send to the oracle of Apollo at Delphi for information. The priests of the oracle must have had considerable knowledge of the ancient world. At any rate, their advice about where to go was often excellent. Incidentally, we know from the Greek philosophers, Plato and Aristotle, what the Greeks looked for in a site for a colony: first, tame natives, then good land, spring water, a harbor, a city-site not too near the sea for fear of pirates, and timber for ships. Meanwhile, in the home city, an *oecist* or founder was appointed. When all was ready he took on board ship with him fire and a bit of soil from home. The rest of the emigrants—men,

women, children, and animals—followed. We can see and hear the frantic
farewells, the looking back, and, perhaps, at the last moment, a man
jumping to shore or a girl leaping on board. Then the tiny ship, or ships,
set out. When it reached the new home the *oecist* divided the land. He
picked a place for a citadel. He apportioned the jobs in the new, strange
country. He established the religious rites.

From the moment the ship set sail the new colony was on its own. It
had religious, commercial, and sentimental ties with its mother-city, but
politically it was independent—not a colony at all in our sense of the term
but a new slice of Greece. The word 'colony' is Latin and the Roman
colonia remained under the control of its mother-city, Rome, but there
are cases of Greek colonies fighting against their home-cities. Thus, in
435 B.C., Corcyra, now Corfu, defeated its mother-city, Corinth, in a
great naval battle.

Effects of Greek Trade and Colonization

In these years from 750 to 600 B.C., the Greeks spread themselves
around the shores of the Black Sea and the western Mediterranean. The
effects were profound. For one thing, in the colonies birth and class did not
matter as much as ability. For another, the varying strains of Greeks were,
to a certain degree, mingled, although the distinction between Ionians and
Dorians remained. For a third, the Greeks in the colonies had a wider view
of the world and of the differing peoples and cultures in it. The western
Greek, in particular, was likely to be more open-minded.

Even more important was the effect on western civilization. Each new
colony radiated the Greek way of life as a stove sends out heat. Above all,
the Greeks were the chief civilizing influence on the Romans. To give one
example only, it was from the Greek colony of Cumae that the Romans, via
the Etruscans, received the alphabet which they, in turn, passed on to us. It
was the Chalcidic version of the alphabet, which differed from the Attic.
This fact helps explain why our alphabet diverges somewhat from that of
modern Greek.

The Class Struggle

Colonization revolutionized the life of the home cities. The products
and wealth of the known world flowed into cities such as Miletus or
Corinth. Industry tripled and quadrupled to meet the growing demands.
The nascent city-state developed rapidly from a town to a full-fledged *polis*.
New techniques were imported along with luxuries from foreign lands.
The cost of living rose and the middleman came into being. Merchant
princes, with a new wealth based on trade, began to compete for political
power with the landowning aristocrats. There were faction fights.

Sometimes the aristocrats compromised by marrying rich merchants' daughters, or by exporting wine and olive-oil from newly-planted orchards and vineyards. At the same time, a new technique of warfare forced them to give ground to the "mean." For, with the development of the city-state, there was now a citizen army. Victory depended, not on the duels of single champions as in Homeric days, but on well-drilled "hoplites" (heavy-armed infantry) advancing in a phalanx.

Hoplites are first mentioned in a war about 700 B.C. between Eretria and Chalcis, both, as we have seen, on the island of Euboea. The nobles became an élite cavalry, but anyone who could afford the armor was in the ranks of the hoplites. Distinctions began to be made according to property and not according to birth.

A Greek poet, Theognis of Megara, as late as the mid-sixth century B.C., cried out against this intermingling of the "mean" and the "good." Of the merchants he exclaimed: "Let me drink their blood."

One class, however, suffered during this economic revolution, the small farmers. They did not have the capital for trade, and the high cost of living crippled them. To make matters worse, about 650 B.C. coined money was introduced from Lydia. The middlemen and the high cost of living both squeezed the peasant, and the farmer did not understand metal money in place of actual barter. He seemed to get less for his produce, so he was forced to borrow at interest rates ranging from 12 to 20 per cent or more. First, he mortgaged his farm. When he lost this, he mortgaged his wife and children, and finally himself. The Greek world became filled with debt-slaves. Out of the muddle came the tyrants.

The Age of the Tyrants: 650–500 B.C.

The tyrants were usually nobles who "took the people into partnership" and drove out the landed aristocrats. As such they represented a triumph of the commercial and industrial classes, although they were also supported by the peasant farmers. Pheidon of Argos (ca. 675–650 B.C.) was the first tyrant. Then Corinth, Sicyon, Megara, Miletus, Mitylene, and almost every maritime state acquired a tyrant. Those at Sicyon (just west of Corinth) ruled for a hundred years. About 657 B.C. Cypselus took over Corinth. His son, Periander, (ca. 625–585 B.C.) was one of the most famous of the Greek tyrants. According to Aristotle, the philosopher, it was Periander who, when asked by an envoy from Thrasybulus, tyrant of Samos, how he prevented revolts, took the envoy into a field of wheat. Periander did not say a word, but as he walked along with his stick, he lopped off the tallest heads.

"Tyrant" to the Greeks meant originally a man who seized and held power by unconstitutional means. They were not, on the whole, bad rulers. They broke the power of the landed aristocrats (Periander exiled or exterminated the old Corinthian nobility), developed trade and commerce, founded colonies, encouraged art and literature, and improved the lot of the average man. But absolute power tends to corrupt. The second generation of tyrants often became bloodthirsty and arrogant. When they were driven out, the new government was usually a "timocracy;" that is, office-holding and voting power depended not on birth but on the amount of property a man had.

Tyrants lasted longer in Asia Minor than on the Greek mainland, because first the Lydians and later the Persians supported them. In Sicily, there were great tyrants in the 5th and 4th centuries B.C. In one case, however, in Athens, when the tyrants were expelled, not timocracy but *democracy*, the rule of the people, was instituted.

Literature, Thought, and the Graphic Arts During the Formative Years

Homer had composed epics about nobles for nobles. The new and restless age of trade, colonization, and widening horizons required a new poetry to express it. This new poetry sprang essentially from religious hymns such as dirges, marriage songs, triumph songs, and the like, and from popular songs of work and play. Where Homeric poetry was stately, long, and objective, and dealt with the past, the new poetry consisted of short pieces which expressed a vivid, personal and present emotion. It was, in some aspects, quite modern.

Again, while the epic was always chanted in one special meter (the dactylic hexameter) to the harp, the new poetry was composed in varying meters and was *sung* to either the flute or the lyre. One should note that Greek poetry was normally sung or chanted to music and that the *kind* of poetry was determined by the meter, or rhythm.

Among the most famous of the earliest poets of the 7th and 6th centuries B.C. were Archilochus of Paros, who is said to have written such savage invective that both the sweetheart who had spurned him and her father hanged themselves; Alcaeus of Mytilene, who wrote passionate verse on politics and wine; and Sappho of Lesbos, who composed such frank and direct love verses that the Byzantine churchmen of the Christian period burned her books. Yet the fragments we have left rank her as perhaps the greatest woman poet of all time. Semonides, of the island of Amorgos, wrote of women, comparing them to an ape, a dog, and the like. The only type of which he approved was the "bee-woman" who was virtuous and industrious. Similarly, Hipponax of Ephesus (Asia Minor) wrote that "A woman gives a man two days of pleasure, the day he marries her and the day he carries her out for burial." The theme of the briefness of life was sung by Mimnermus of Colophon.

You will observe that all these poets lived in or around Asia Minor. On the Greek mainland, Alcman of Sparta wrote songs of war and "maiden-songs" for Spartan girls. At Corinth, Arion, under the tyrant Periander, made the initial beginning of Greek tragedy. In Megara, Theognis, and in Athens, Solon, composed gnomic, or aphoristic, poetry. However, the king of lyric poets, Pindar (525–450 B.C.), was born at Thebes in Boeotia. His victory songs in honor of athletes who won at the Olympic and Pythian games are still in existence.

Meanwhile, around 600 B.C., the first writing in prose began, again in Ionia. Some of the first prose writers composed travelogues (*periodoi*, journeys by land and *periploi*, journeys by sea) and chronicles of cities. All of these accounts were spiced with legends, anecdotes, and tales of marvels. As such they were the fore-runners of the prevalence of this sort of thing in the 5th century B.C. historian, Herodotus. Other early prose writers were the philosophers, who in Ionia in the 6th century B.C. initiated unfettered thought and speculation.

At about the same time Greek sculptors began to carve their first statues of the gods in stone. Previous statues had been in wood and the sculptures in stone not only imitated wooden figures but also followed the Egyptian conventions of frontality, centrality, and rigidity. Similarly, architecture in the service of the gods advanced from temples in wood to buildings in stone. But the supreme Greek expression in both sculpture and architecture was to wait until the 5th century B.C.

From this brief sketch of the graphic arts and of literature, you will realize that the years from 800–500 B.C. were burgeoning, restless years in which the Greek genius was being shaped into readiness for the great era which was to come. But before we turn to the 5th Century B.C. we need to outline the growth of the two states which in revulsion against each other were to determine the course of Greek history. These two states were Sparta and Athens.

Sparta—The Warrior State

Few peoples are more fascinating to the student than the Spartans. Their home was Laconia (from which, because of Spartan brevity of speech, comes our word "laconic"). Laconia is the south-eastern quarter of Southern Greece. Here, between mountains to the east and the tall range of Taygetus to the west runs the broad plain of the Eurotas river. It boasts some of the richest land in Greece.

At first, after their conquest of the previous Achaean owners, the Dorian Spartans developed like the rest of Greece. For a time, particularly in the 8th century B.C. and the first half of the 7th, Sparta was a center of growing culture. It had trade, archaic sculpture and architecture. Meanwhile, two kings instead of one were instituted. But the land problem became acute, and about 730 B.C. the Spartans reached across Mt. Taygetus to conquer their Dorian neighbors in Messenia, and thus doubled their land.

About 630 B.C. the Messenians revolted. They were helped by the Argives, the Arcadians, and the people of Pisa near Olympia. For almost twenty years the Spartans fought for their lives. When at last they won, they organized their state for one purpose only, to maintain their supremacy by force of arms. In so doing they sacrificed the individual to the state. There were periodic expulsions of foreigners and foreign trade was practically eliminated. The only money officially permitted was iron bars. Similarly, the arts were abandoned. The Spartan boy was trained for only one thing—war. The Spartan girl had only one purpose, to become the mother of fighting-men.

Social Classes

The population was divided into three classes, the Spartiates, the Perioeci, and the Helots. The Helots were serfs tied to the land, which they worked on shares for their Spartan masters. Each year war was formally proclaimed against them so that any dangerous ones might be put to death. For this purpose a secret police, called the Crypteia, ranged among them. In time of war some of the Helots were used as light-armed troops, but the Spartans were always afraid of a Helot revolt. As a result Spartan foreign policy was cautious.

Around the Helots were the Perioeci, which means "Dwellers-round-about." The Perioeci were individually free and had local self-government. They carried on what trade there was and served in the Spartan army as hoplites. They had no share in the government, and they could not marry Spartan women.

The highest class, the Spartiates, were never very numerous. At the beginning of the 5th century B.C. they are thought to have numbered from four to five thousand fighting-men. It is estimated that, including women and children, there were 25,000 Spartiates, 100,000 Perioeci and 250,000 Helots.

Education of the Spartiates

At birth all sickly or deformed children were exposed on Mt. Taygetus. How many able men this practice cost the Spartans will never be known. We do know that the lame king, Agesilaus, who was hidden by his mother, grew up to be one of Sparta's best leaders.

At the age of seven boys were taken from their mothers. They were put under the leadership of an older boy. They made their own beds from reeds from the Eurotas river, had only one garment in winter and summer, and had to steal and forage their food. They were taught a few warlike passages from the *Iliad*, a few war songs and moral verses, and military marches to the flute. The rest of their education was military and athletic.

At twenty the Spartan young man joined a club mess of fifteen mess-brothers (*syssition*, "eating together"). From his plot of Spartan land, his helots provided him with barley-flour, wine, and cheese for the mess. With these mess-brothers he marched, trained, and fought. At thirty he was eligible to vote in the Assembly of Spartiates. From twenty to sixty years of age he lived in barracks. Marriage was "by stealth", that is, a Spartan tried to conceal his marriage and his visits to his wife as long as possible; but it was compulsory. Meanwhile, girls were trained not only in household duties but also in athletics, which made them the finest-looking women in Greece. Because their husbands lived in barracks, they were the freest women in the Greek world. Many an Ionian matron envied her Dorian cousin.

The Spartan System of Government

The Spartan constitution was conservative. The two kings acted as checks on each other. The kings were assisted by a council of 28 elders, (men over sixty) called the *Gerousia* (body of elders). The Assembly (*Apella*) elected the members of the Gerousia and voted on questions brought before it. The voting was viva voce, and the side with the loudest shout won.

The Apella also elected a board of 5 ephors ("watchers"), which had been instituted after the First Messenian War to protect the Spartiates from the kings and the council. Their powers were extensive. They handled the Assembly and the Secret Police. For a period two of them accompanied the army to war. Later, one king, chosen by the ephors, led the army, while the other stayed at home.

Such was the Spartan system which the Athenian philosopher, Plato, admired. It did not encourage restless, inquiring minds or great artists and writers. But it did produce disciplined soldiers who put Sparta first and themselves second. All Greece admired them for their willingness to die rather than yield ground. With such troops, by the beginning of the 5th century B.C., Sparta owned one-third of southern Greece, and through the Peloponnesian League they controlled almost all the rest of it except Argos and Achaea. The league was for defensive purposes. In it each state, big or small, had one vote. This league could put 40,000 to 50,000 heavy-armed infantry into the field. When the Persian Wars came, this army helped save Greece. Its core were the scarlet-cloaked, long-haired, plumed-helmeted Spartan soldiers marching steadily into battle to the sound of the flute. At that time Sparta was the leading state in the Greek world.

There was one flaw in the Spartan system. His training gave the Spartan citizen a "plaster-of-Paris" virtue. When, as time went on, some Spartans got away from home and were exposed to the temptation of luxuries they had never known, their virtue was liable to collapse.

Athens: The Founder of Democracy

A glance at the map will remind you that Attica thrusts out like a wedge from central Greece into the Aegean. The word *Attica* means promontory. It is favored by geography. To the northeast the long island of Euboea keeps off the chill winds from Thrace. To the west the range of Cithaeron tempers its climate and protects it from invasion. Hence, the country escaped the Dorian inroads. Its other flank faces on the island of Salamis and the Saronic gulf of the Aegean sea. From the Peloponnesus the only attacking route is through the difficult passes of Megara. Not only is Attica more or less difficult to invade, it also has the clearest air and best climate in Greece. It is Pindar of Thebes who sings of "violet-crowned Athens." Four miles from Athens is the excellent harbor of the Piraeus.

Attica is not a big country. Its whole area, if one includes the island of Salamis, is 886 square miles, and 386 square miles are covered by mountains. In the plains the soil is thin, but there was plenty of stone for building, good potter's clay and silver at Laureium on the very tip of Attica.

The biggest plain is the Attic plain. When one stands today on the flat-topped Acropolis of Athens, one can see it in its entirety. To the southwest, four miles away, is the sea. From the sea, like a giant fishhook four miles wide, the plain sweeps around the Acropolis. Mountains hem it in. To the east is the Aegaleos range. To the northeast sits Mt. Lycabettus, like a bald-headed eagle. To east and southeast is the long ridge of Hymettus. Yet this small, poor, but beautiful country was the founder of the world's first working democracy. It was also in the 5th century B.C. the center of achievements in art and literature which have rarely, if ever, been equalled.

Early History

In early times Athens was an important Mycenean center. The palace of those days has been found on the Acropolis. Later, as has been noted, Athens escaped the Dorian invasion and remained Ionian. The population was a blend of dark-haired Mediterraneans and Indo-Europeans. During the Dark Age there were many independent communities throughout Attica. To that legendary Theseus who slew the Minotaur is attributed the bringing together of these communities under the aegis of Athens. This was bound to happen. The Attic plain was the biggest plain, the Acropolis, rising 300 feet above the plain, was a natural center of defense, and Piraeus, four miles away, was the best harbor in Greece, although until Themistocles (see later) the Athenians used instead the nearby roadstead of Phalerum.

At first, Athens was governed by a king helped by the Council of the Areopagus. This Council was made up of *Eupatrids* ("the well-born"). There were four Ionian tribes in the country, to one of which each citizen belonged. Each tribe was divided into three phratries or brotherhoods. There were also aristocratic clans ("clan"—Greek *genos*, Latin, *gens*).

Athens did not share in the outburst of colonization and trade. Otherwise she went through the normal development of a Greek city-state. The kings were replaced by three *archons* (rulers) who were elected by the Areopagus. One of them was still called the king-Archon. Later six junior archons (*Thesmothetae*) were added to help as judges. At the end of their term of offices, which was finally one year, the ex-archons joined the Areopagus.

Only Eupatrids could be archons. They had the best land and dominated the army. When, however, the phalanx was introduced, men had to be recruited from all those rich enough to afford armor. In consequence, the people were divided into three classes according to their property.

There began to be, also, a gradual but slow development of trade and industry. Coinage was not introduced until around 600 B.C. Before this time the stage was already set for trouble. The peasants were deeply in debt and ready to follow anyone. There were many landless men. In 635 B.C. a noble named Cylon tried to establish a tyranny but failed.

Draco and the Codification of the Laws

Cylon's attempt frightened the nobles into appointing Draco (621 B.C.) to write down the laws. It is difficult for us to realize a period when laws were not written down. In Athens the nobles alone knew the laws and also administered them. They could, as it were, change the rules while the game was on. Written laws prevented this sort of thing. But the economic situation became worse and worse. Many Athenians had either become serfs at home, or, as debt-slaves, had been sold into slavery abroad. At this point, when bloodshed seemed inevitable, all parties agreed to appoint a Eupatrid as sole archon with power to reform the state (594 B.C.).

The Reforms of Solon

This man was Solon, one of the Seven Wise Men of Greece, who had inspired the Athenians to capture the island of Salamis from Megara. Solon modified the constitution, so as to make wealth instead of birth the basis for holding office. This was, then, a timocracy. But even the lowest class could now vote in the Assembly. He may also have instituted the *heliaea* (sun-courts) and may have allowed appeals from legal sentences to the Assembly. In these three measures he is credited as taking the first steps towards democracy.

His economic reforms, called the *seisachtheia* ("shaking off of burdens"), were drastic. First of all, he cancelled all debts made on the security of the land or person of the debtor. One can imagine the uproar today if the first of these measures were put into effect, since it would mean the cancellation of all farm mortgages. Secondly, he forbade slavery in the future and bought back as many as he could of those Athenians who had been sold into slavery abroad.

There were other economic measures. Attic coinage was changed from the Aeginetan standard to the Euboic. This meant that Athens could have a broader trading range, since Euboic currency, if you recall the colonies of Chalcis of Euboea in Macedonia and Italy, was widely accepted. This change likewise meant inflation because it took 100 of the lighter Euboic coins to equal 70 of the Aeginetan, and yet the Euboic coin was made equal in value to the Aeginetan one. This move was to encourage trade. Solon also prohibited the export of any farm products except olive oil (to force Attic farmers to grow olives), and forbade the importing of figs (to compel the farmers to put in fig-trees). From this last bit of legislation comes our word, "sycophant". In Greek it meant "fig-shower", that is, the man who reported anyone importing figs and thereby got a reward.

Among other interesting measures was one which ordered every citizen, in case of a faction-fight, to declare which side he was on within twenty-four hours. Still another was one which instructed every father to teach his son a trade. If he did not do so, the son was not responsible for maintaining his father in his old age. Citizenship was also offered to foreign artisans and Solon opened up the silver mines at Laureium.

By these various measures, Solon started Athens on the road to commercialism. The first important industry to develop was the making of pottery.

When Solon had finished his reforms, he is said to have gone traveling and to have visited Egypt where, according to Plato, he heard from the Egyptian priests the story of lost Atlantis.

The Tyranny of the Peisistratids: 546–510 B.C.

The reforms, though they had alleviated the economic distress, had not solved it. By 560 B.C. three factions were fighting each other—the Plain (the rich aristocrats) the Shore (the merchants and craftsmen) and the Hill (the peasants). The situation was made to order for a tyrant. An ambitious noble, Peisistratus (who had led in the recapture of Salamis in 570 B.C. after the Megarians had taken it back), became the leader of the people of the Hill. His first two attempts at tyranny did not last long.

Finally (546 B.C.), after making a fortune in silver mines in Thrace and hiring mercenary troops, he returned and, driving out the Alcmaeonids, (the most powerful group of nobles) made himself tyrant. Upon Peisistratus' death in 527 B.C., his sons, Hippias and Hipparchus, succeeded him.

The tyranny of Peisistratus was beneficial to Athens in several ways. Peisistratus solved the land problem by breaking the power of the nobles and distributing much of their land among the peasants. We are told by the unknown author of the *Hellenica Oxyrhynchia* (a history written on papyrus and discovered in Egypt), that, until the great war with Sparta, the Attic farms were "the best equipped in Greece." Furthermore, under Peisistratus trade and colonial expansion were encouraged. Thus Miltiades, later the great hero of Marathon, was set up as a tyrant in what is now Gallipoli in order to help Athens participate in the trade to the Black Sea Area. For the same reason, Sigeum on the southern shore of the Hellespont was occupied and placed under the rule of one of Peisistratus' illegitimate sons. Another son was set up as ruler of Lesbos, and a friend was made tyrant of Naxos. Meanwhile, the export of Attic olive oil, pottery, wine, and honey was encouraged, while wheat was brought in from southern Russia. Under Peisistratus, Athens began to flower into an industrial and commercial city.

At home there was a great program of public works. This measure, as with similar modern programs, was intended to prevent unemployment as well as to beautify and improve the city. A great drain was put through the Agora (the market-place of the Athenians). Fountains were improved, an aqueduct built, and a network of roads constructed throughout Attica. Peisistratus also built a huge new temple to Athens' patron goddess, Athena, on the Acropolis. It was called "The Hundred-Foot-House." On the principle of "feed the people and amuse them," he enlarged the public festivals such as the *Panathenaea* (in honor of Athena) and the *City Dionysia* (in honor of the god Dionysus). At this second festival, the first true European drama was presented in 535 B.C. by Thespis; we still call actors "thespians." Peisistratus was a patron of the arts and of letters. Architects were imported and sculptors from the island of Chios brought in. Poets flocked to Athens. It is said that the first edition of Homer's poems was issued, although this statement is now doubted.

Peisistratus found Athens a backward town and left it a flourishing city, adorned with buildings, fountains, and statues and reaching out into the world of trade. Meanwhile, by purifying Delos, the supposed birthplace of the Ionian god Apollo, and by building a strong fleet and army, he established Athens as a leader of the Ionians. It was he who laid the foundations for the 5th century B.C. Athenian political and commercial empire, and the period of his rule is rightly referred to as a "golden age."

After his death in 527 B.C. his sons, Hippias and Hipparchus, at first ruled well. But in 514 B.C. Hipparchus was assassinated in a personal quarrel. Hippias became suspicious and tyrannical. In 510 B.C. the exiled Alcmaeonids, led by Cleisthenes and helped by a Spartan army, drove him out. Hippias fled to the court of Darius, the Persian king, and urged him to invade Greece.

Cleisthenes and Democracy

For two years after the expulsion of Hippias, the future of Athens hung in the balance. The nobles, led by one Isagoras, and backed by a Spartan garrison, tried to set up an *oligarchy* (rule of the few). But the Athenians, led by Cleisthenes, expelled the Spartans and put to death the leading oligarchs. Later, the Spartans in alliance with Thebes and Chalcis prepared to invade Attica but one of their kings opposed the move and the Spartan army returned home. Cleisthenes then defeated Thebes and Chalcis and, in addition, established an Athenian *cleruchy* (a colony in which the men retained their Athenian citizenship) in Euboea. Cleisthenes could now have made himself tyrant. Instead, in 508 B.C., by a series of drastic reforms he gave the government to the people, that is, to all Athenian male citizens over twenty whether they held land or property or not. In this year, therefore, democracy, the rule of the *Demos* (people) was born.

Readings From Sources of the Period

(a) Greek lyric poetry during the formative years is often surprisingly modern in its individualism and in the sentiments it expresses.

From Sappho (born about 612 B.C.)

A BRIDE

Like the sweet apple which reddens upon the topmost bough,
A-top on the topmost twig,—which the pluckers forgot somehow,—
Forgot it not, nay, but got it not, for none could get it till now.

Like the wild hyacinth flower which on the hills is found,
Which the passing feet of the shepherds forever tear and wound,
Until the purple blossom is trodden in the ground.

(Robert Warnock and George E. Anderson, *The Ancient Foundations*, Vol. I, New York: Scott-Foresman, 1950, p. 302.)

From Simonides (ca. 556–468 B.C.)

For the Athenians who died at the battle of Plataea in 479 B.C.

> If to die nobly is the chief part of valour,
> Then to us beyond all others Fortune has given this meed;
> For, hastening to cast a cloak of freedom around Greece
> We lie here, possessed of a glory that never grows old.

From Hipponax (ca. 540 B.C.)

> A woman gives a man two days of pleasure,
> The day he marries her and the day he carries her out for burial.

(b) Pindar, (522–475 B.C.) the "King of Lyric Poets" is difficult to translate in such a way as to establish the music and grandeur of his verse. A few lines from his first ode to a victor at the Pythian Games in honor of Apollo at Delphi, may give some idea of the vividness of his imagery.

Music Hath Charms

(Pythian 1, *ll.* 1–12)

> O golden lyre, common treasure of Apollo
> And the violet-haired Muses, the footstep hears you and the gladness
>   begins;
> The singers obey your measures
> When, trembling with music, you strike up the choir-leading prelude.
> You quench the speared thunderbolt
> Of ever-flowing fire; and the eagle sleeps on the sceptre of Zeus,
>   Drooping his two swift wings,
>
> The Lord of birds, and over his bending head
> A dark mist you pour, sweet seal of the eyelids, and sleeping
> He ripples his soft back, caught
> In the tides of music. Even stern Ares, putting aside
> His rude spears, melts his heart in drowsiness.
> Your shafts enchant even the minds of the gods by grace of the skill
>   Of Leto's son and the deep-bosomed Muses.

(MacKendrick and Howe, *op. cit.*, p. 99, translated by Warren R. Castle and L. R. Lind.)

(c) A Greek, Plutarch, (46–127 A.D.) wrote *Parallel Lives* of famous Greeks and Romans. In his Life of Lycurgus, the Spartan law-giver, he describes the education of the Spartans.

[The] offspring was not reared at the will of the father, but was taken and carried by him to a place . . . where the elders of the tribes officially examined the infant, and if it was well-built and sturdy, they ordered the father to rear it . . .; but if it was ill-born and deformed, they sent it to . . . a chasm-like place at the foot of Mount Taÿgetus, in the conviction that the life of that which nature had not well equipped at the very beginning for health and strength, was of no advantage either to itself or the state. On the same principle, the women used to bathe their new-born babes not with water, but with wine, thus making a sort of test of their constitutions. For it is said that epileptic and sickly infants are thrown into convulsions by the strong wine and lose their senses, while the healthy ones are rather tempered by it, like steel, and given a firm habit of body. Their nurses, too, exercised great care and skill; they reared infants without swaddling-bands, and thus left their limbs and figures free to develop; besides, they taught them to be contented and happy, not dainty about their food, nor fearful of the dark, nor afraid to be left alone, nor given to contemptible peevishness and whimpering. . . .

. . . But Lycurgus would not put the sons of Spartans in charge of purchased or hired tutors, nor was it lawful for every father to rear or train his son as he pleased, but as soon as they were seven years old, Lycurgus ordered them all to be taken by the state and enrolled in companies, where they were put under the same discipline and nurture, and so became accustomed to share one another's sports and studies. . . .

Of reading and writing, they learned only enough to serve their turn; all the rest of their training was calculated to make them obey commands well, endure hardships, and conquer in battle. Therefore, as they grew in age, their bodily exercise was increased; their heads were close-clipped, and they were accustomed to going bare-foot, and to playing for the most part without clothes. When they were twelve years old, they no longer had tunics to wear, received one cloak a year, had hard, dry flesh, and knew little of baths and ointments; only on certain days of the year, and few at that, did they indulge in such amenities. They slept together, in troops and companies, on pallet-beds which they collected for themselves, breaking off with their hands—no knives allowed—the tops of the rushes which grew along the river Eurotas. . . .

. . . one of the noblest and best men of the city was appointed . . . inspector of the boys, and under his directions the boys, in their several companies, put themselves under the command of the most prudent and warlike . . . [youths of twenty years of age. Each such youth] commands his subordinates in their mimic battles, and indoors makes them serve him at his meals. He commissions the larger ones to fetch wood, and the smaller ones potherbs. And they steal what they fetch, some of them entering the gardens, and others creeping right slyly and cautiously into the public messes of the men; but if a boy is caught stealing, he is soundly flogged, as a careless and unskilful thief. They steal, too, whatever food they can, and learn to be adept in setting upon people when asleep or off their guard. But the boy who is caught gets a flogging and must go hungry. For the meals allowed them are scanty, in order that they may take into their own hands the fight against hunger, and so be forced into boldness and cunning.

. . . The boys make such a serious matter of their stealing, that one of them, as the story goes, who was carrying concealed under his cloak a young fox which he had stolen, suffered the animal to tear out his bowels with its teeth and claws, and died rather than have his theft detected.

(*Plutarch's Lives* translated by B. Perrin, Loeb Classical Library, Boston: Harvard University Press.)

CHAPTER 3

Fifth Century Greece: the Persian Wars and Athenian Democratic Imperialism

The high point of the Greek achievement was ushered in by the Persian Wars and brought to its close by the Peloponnesian War. The first was a struggle for freedom against a foreign foe; the second, a fratricidal strife of Greek against Greek. Herein lies the difference between the effects of the two wars on the Greek spirit.

The Background of the Persian Wars

During the mushroom-like expansion of the Persian Empire, in 546 B.C. Cyrus the Great, by conquering Lydia, had assumed the overlordship of the Ionian Greek cities. The Persian rule was not severe. The Ionian cities were governed by Greek tyrants who were subject to the Persian satrap at Sardis. Yet the democratic factions in the Ionian cities were never quite reconciled to their loss of freedom. Meanwhile, probably in 514 B.C., the Persian king, Darius the Great, crossed the Bosporus on a bridge of boats to raid as far north as the Danube. When he withdrew, the general whom he left behind occupied the whole Thracian coast and parts of Macedonia.

It is possible that Persian expansion might have led ultimately to an attack on mainland Greece. Before this could happen, the Ionian Greeks revolted (499 B.C.). Athens sent twenty ships to help, Eretria in Euboea two. The allied Greek forces captured and burnt Sardis, the capital of Lydia. Then the Athenians and Eretrians returned home.

The revolt was crushed at the battle of Ladé (494 B.C.). Meanwhile, according to the Greek Herodotus, who recorded the history of the Persian Wars, Darius had appointed a man who had only one task: to say to Darius once each day: "Remember the Athenians."

In 492 B.C. the Persians reconquered Thrace, which had expelled their garrisons during the Ionian revolt. But their fleet, which may have intended to attack Athens, was wrecked off Mount Athos. In the next year Darius sent envoys to the Greek states to demand earth and water as symbols of submission. Some states complied, but at Sparta the ambassadors were flung into a well and at Athens into a pit, and told to get their own earth and water. War was now inevitable.

The First Persian Expedition and Marathon: 490 B.C.

A Greek David now faced a Persian Goliath. If we put ourselves back into the period we can understand why to the Persians (who were, though they did not know it, far-off cousins of the Greeks) it seemed like a bear preparing to swat a mosquito. On the one side were the small and disunited Greek States; on the other the reputedly invincible Medes and Persians backed by a vast expanse of territory and unlimited resources of men and money.

In the summer of 490 B.C. a Persian fleet sailed across the Aegean. According to modern estimates it carried between 30,000 and 40,000 soldiers. On board was the deposed tyrant, Hippias, and it seems likely that the anti-democrats in Athens were prepared to welcome him.

The Persians sacked and burnt Eretria in Euboea, then landed on the coastal plain of Marathon, some 26 miles to the northeast of Athens. The Athenian army marched to the hills facing Marathon. Before they left the city they sent a runner to Sparta. In less than forty-eight hours that runner, Pheidippides, had covered the 140 miles of plain and mountain to Sparta. But the Spartans were celebrating a festival. They said they could not come until the festival was over. We can well imagine the tension in the Athenian camp. 1000 hoplites from Plataea, just over the border in Boeotia, had come to their aid. 10,000 men faced three or four times their number. Miltiades, who was one of the generals, persuaded the Athenians to leave the safety of the hills and attack. They moved into the plain and charged. The Athenian center was broken by the enemy. For here the Persians themselves fought and Miltiades had made the Athenian center weak and the flank heavy. Those flanks shattered the Persian right and left wings and then closed on the Persian center. The victory was complete. According to the Athenians, they killed 6400 Persians and captured seven ships, while only losing 192 of their own men. Those 192, except for two dug out in modern times, still sleep under a mound put up where the fighting was most fierce. Today one can climb that mound (called the *soros*) and look out over the ancient battlefield. According to Greek legend, as soon as the battle was won, the runner, Pheidippides, sped over the twenty-six miles from Marathon to Athens. On reaching the market-place he gasped to the waiting throng: "Victory" and fell dead. From this famous run comes the Marathon race in our modern Olympics.

The Persian fleet now sailed to Phalerum, hoping, no doubt, for help from the anti-democrats. But the shields of the victors of Marathon were by this time flashing on the heights. The Persians made for Asia. Later, after a three days' march, the Spartans arrived, when there was nothing for them to do but view the battlefield, congratulate the victors, and return home.

Such was the dramatic victory of Marathon. It sent a wave of confidence through Greece. It had shown that the Greek hoplite was better armed than the Persian. It proved that the Persians could be beaten. It also made democracy respectable.

The Ten-Year Interlude

It was ten years before the Persians returned. Darius died in 486 B.C., and it took his son, Xerxes, four years to put down a revolt in Egypt and to complete preparations.

Meanwhile, at Athens Miltiades, the hero of Marathon, had fallen into disgrace and died. A new man, Themistocles, had come to the fore. Themistocles was a democrat and a far-seeing statesman. The conservatives argued that Athens must build a big army to meet the Persian threat. This policy was urged by Aristides, known as the "Just." But Themistocles was convinced that Athens needed a navy. About 484 B.C. a new lode of silver, which produced annually an extra hundred talents, was discovered at Laureium. It was proposed that this windfall should be distributed equally among all citizens, giving each a "dividend" equal to about ten days' wages for an unskilled laborer. Themistocles urged that the whole amount be spent on a navy. Fortunately, the Athenians could see further than their own individual and immediate profit. Aristides, who opposed Themistocles, was "ostracized", and Athens built 200 warships. Those warships were to help save Greece.

Meanwhile, news of the Persian preparations dismayed the Greeks. Thebes, Thessaly, and a number of other Greek states were prepared to surrender. The Delphic oracle wavered in its patriotism, and Argos, because of hostility to Sparta, refused to join the resistance. Sparta and Athens organized the remaining states into a Hellenic League. This league sent for help to Gelon, the tyrant of Syracuse. But Carthage, possibly by arrangement with the Persians, was about to attack the Greeks of Sicily, and Gelon refused aid unless he was put in command of all Greek forces. The demand was refused.

The Second Persian Expedition—Thermopylae, Salamis, and Plataea.

In 480 B.C. the Persians set out by land and sea, following the route through Thrace and Macedonia. Vast preparations had been made. Two bridges of boats had been built across the Hellespont, supply depots of food had been established along the proposed route, and, to avoid the promontory of Mt. Athos where the 492 B.C. expedition had been wrecked, a huge canal, of which traces are still visible, had been dug across the neck of the peninsula which joined it to the mainland. It is clear that the Persians knew a good deal about the logistics of warfare. The size of their fleet and army can only be estimated. Herodotus states that their fleet numbered 3000 transports and 1207 warships and that the land army contained 1,700,000 foot-soldiers and 100,000 cavalry. Modern estimates suggest 1000 vessels in all, of which 600 were warships, and a land force of from 250,000 to 300,000 men. On the Greek side, the Hellenic League, led by Sparta, prepared to meet them.

We all know the story of the 300 Spartans who died at the pass of Thermopylae (the "hot gates") after blocking the whole Persian army for three days with the help of their allies (7000 men in all). Meanwhile, the Persian and Greek fleets fought an indecisive battle at Artemisium. Then the Persians occupied central Greece. Athens was captured and burned, while the Athenians moved themselves and their families to Salamis, Aegina and the Argolid. Meanwhile, the Greek fleet, totalling about 378 ships, of which 180 were Athenian, anchored in the Bay of Salamis (see map) while the Persian fleet of about twice their number, was moored in the roadstead of Phalerum and in the harbor of the Piraeus. The Greek army was at the Isthmus of Corinth.

The Spartans were determined to build a wall across the Isthmus and to have the fleet retire to the Saronic Gulf, a strategy which, undoubtedly, would have brought disaster. Themistocles argued vehemently against the plan, even threatening, in case of retreat, to use the Athenian ships to carry the Athenian people to a new home in Italy. Finally during the night, according to Herodotus, he sent a faithful slave to Xerxes, the Persian King, to warn him that the Greeks intended to flee from the Bay of Salamis and advising him to cut off their retreat.

Xerxes believed Themistocles. During the night he had his squadrons block both exits from the Bay of Salamis. The Greeks had to fight. On the morning of September 23rd the Greeks sailed against the eastern half of the Persian fleet while Xerxes watched from a throne set up on a promontory overlooking the straits. Warship clashed against warship. The sea was reddened with blood. As the battle swung in favor of the Greeks, Aristides, who had been recalled from his ostracism, led a band of hoplites to the little island of Psyttaleia, which had been filled with Persian troops, and slew them all. The Greeks could swim, so that from their wrecked warships many men were saved, but a large number of Persians drowned. When the day was over the Persian armada had been shattered. On the same day, according to Greek legend, the Greeks of the west slaughtered the Carthaginian host at Himera in Sicily and the Carthaginian general, Hanno, flung himself into the fires of his own sacrifices for victory. That battle brought peace to the Greek cities of Sicily.

Salamis was the battle which decided the war against the Persians. Xerxes fled to Asia. He left an army under Mardonius, a son-in-law of Darius, to continue the struggle. Next year that army was defeated at Plataea, and Mardonius was killed. In this battle, it was the Spartan contingent which won the fight. The general, Pausanias, became the hero of Greece. After the victory the Greeks put up a tripod with its three legs twisted together like the coils of a serpent. On it were inscribed the names of the Greek states whose troops fought at Plataea. That tripod is in Istanbul today.

In the same year, and again (according to the Greeks) on the same day, the Greek navy destroyed a Persian fleet and army at Mycale in Ionia. Later in the year, the Athenians captured Sestos on the Dardanelles. For the Greeks were now intent on liberating their brothers and also on reopening the trade route to the Black Sea.

Effects of the Persian Wars

It is true to human nature that the victory over the Persians sparked the Great Age of Greece. As with the Elizabethans after the defeat of the Spanish Armada, the Greeks now felt that there was nothing they could not attempt. In commerce and in arts and letters they reached great heights, and nowhere more so than at Athens. The Athenians by themselves had won Marathon. Their navy had been the backbone of the fleet which conquered at Salamis. They stood out as the leaders of the Ionian world and as a rival to Dorian Sparta so that the Persian wars led directly to the Athenian empire. Their empire, in turn, helped make possible the Parthenon, the sculptures of Phidias, and the plays of Aescyhlus, Sophocles, and Euripides. As we can see today, the empire likewise made inevitable the war between Sparta and Athens, the war which ultimately destroyed the "Great Age."

The Formation of the Delian Confederacy

As with the western allies after their victory over Germany and Japan in World War II, victory over the Persians soon shattered the Hellenic League. The Spartans, afraid of the growing power of Athens, made strong representations against the Athenians rebuilding the walls which the Persians had destroyed, alleging as a pretext that, if the Persians returned to Greece, they ought not to find any fortified place which they could occupy. In the winter of 479–8 B.C., Themistocles went to Sparta to argue the case, meanwhile leaving instructions to delay sending his fellow-ambassadors and to rebuild the walls as fast as possible. Today on the Acropolis of Athens, one can still observe the drums of the columns of temples and gravestones in the wall which was hurriedly built at that time. When the Spartans heard rumors that the walls were being rebuilt, Themistocles had them send envoys to find out what was being done, instructing the Athenians to keep those envoys in Athens until he and his fellow Athenian ambassadors, who had meanwhile arrived, had returned safely. Then he told the Spartans bluntly that Athens was an independent state which would act as it wished. In this way Themistocles rebuilt the walls of Athens. Later, he built walls around the Piraeus so as to make it Athens' harbor. He saw that the future of his city was on the sea. He likewise made changes in the constitution of Athens which moved the city to a more complete democracy.

The episode of the walls had strained Athenian-Spartan relations. The next spring Pausanias, the Spartan victor of Plataea, led a Greek fleet which liberated cities in Cyprus and captured Byzantium. Success went to Pausanias' head. He put on the manners of an Oriental despot and intrigued with Persia in order to get himself made tyrant of Greece. As a result the Spartan Ephors recalled him for trial. Though he was acquitted his prestige was gone. In consequence, when in 477 B.C. the Spartans sent out a new admiral, he found that he was not welcome and returned home. Sparta withdrew from the Hellenic League which was now dissolved.

In 477 B.C. Pausanias sailed to Byzantium as a private individual and occupied the city. When he was expelled by the Athenians in 476 B.C., he went to the Troad and continued his intrigues with the Persians for two years until he was again recalled by the Ephors and thrown into prison. He was released, but was still suspected of treason and of planning a revolt among the Helots. Finally in 471 B.C., a slave, whom he was sending to the Persian king with a letter, opened that letter to discover that its final paragraph was one instructing that the bearer be put to death. The slave went to the Ephors. Following their directions, he had a conversation with Pausanias which proved the latter's treason, while the Ephors listened in an adjoining room. The Ephors now decided to arrest Pausanias but he took sanctuary in a temple, the "Brazen House." The Ephors walled up the entrance and left Pausanias to starve, but just as he was about to expire, they brought him out so that his death would not pollute sacred ground.

The Spartans now sent men to Athens to accuse Themistocles of complicity in the intrigues of Pausanias. Themistocles in the meantime had fallen out of favor in Athens, and in 472–1 B.C. had been ostracized through the influence of Athens' new leaders, Cimon and Aristides, and was living in Argos. The Athenians sent envoys to arrest him. Themistocles escaped and, after an exciting chase across the Greek mainland and the Aegean, arrived safely in Asia Minor. Then he persuaded the Persian king to grant him the revenue of three cities for his support, one to furnish him with bread, another with wine, and a third with other provisions. On his death one of these cities, Magnesia, put up a monument in his honor.

Such was the fate of the two men responsible, respectively, for the victories of Salamis and Plataea. Meantime, in 477 B.C., after the withdrawal of Sparta, the Athenians organized the Confederacy of Delos. This Confederacy was composed of Ionian states. Its objectives were to liberate the Ionian Greeks and to continue the war against Persia. Its Council met on the island of Delos, the legendary birthplace of Apollo, the chief Ionian god. Each state had one vote and the Confederacy was to last until masses of iron, flung into the sea, floated again. Each state, too, was to contribute either men and ships or money, and the treasury was at Delos. But Athens had a predominant position. The treasurers of the Confederacy were Athenians, and most states finally preferred to make a money contribution. The generals, too, were Athenians. In the years to follow Athens turned this league into an empire.

Cimon, and the Beginning of the Athenian Empire: 477–461 B.C.

Aristides the Just had organized the league. Its first leader was Cimon the Athenian, son of Miltiades, the hero of Marathon. His policy was peace with Sparta and war with Persia. He won brilliant victories, notably in destroying the Phoenician fleet in 466 B.C. at the Eurymedon river in Asia Minor, established Athenian cleruchies at key points, such as at the Nine Roads in Thrace, and helped expand Athenian trade in Thrace, along the coast of Asia Minor through the Aegean islands, and into the Black Sea area.

Cimon was also responsible for beginning the Athenian political empire. By his subjugation of the island of Scyros, which had been a nest of pirates, he removed a hazard to trade; he planted an Athenian cleruchy there. Next he compelled Carystos on the southern tip of the island of Euboea to join the Confederacy. The Athenian argument here was that since the Confederacy of Delos assured safety for the Aegean world from the Persians and security for trade, all states who benefited therefrom ought to be members. The vital test, however, came when first Naxos (470 B.C.) and then Thasos (465 B.C.) tried to secede from the Confederacy on the ground that the danger from the Persians was over, although in the case of Thasos there was likewise a dispute over gold mines in Thrace. Athens replied by using the forces of the Confederacy to compel both states to stay in the Confederacy. But—and this is an important but—after tearing down the fortifications of Naxos and Thasos, Athens reduced both of them to the status of subject states paying a heavy annual tribute. In this way, the transformation of the Confederacy into an Athenian Empire was begun. From this time forward, there gradually came into being three types of states in the Confederacy—free naval allies, states which were nominally free but paid tribute, and states subject to Athens. The aim of Athens was to reduce all states to subject states. By 440 B.C., as we shall see, there were only two free states left.

The fall of Cimon came through his admiration for Sparta where, after an earthquake that left only five houses standing, a helot revolt had erupted. When the Spartans had no success in reducing the helot stronghold on Mt. Ithome in Messenia, they called on Athens for help. The radical democrats in Athens, led by Ephialtes and Pericles, argued against sending aid. Cimon used his war popularity to carry the day and led an Athenian army to attack the helots. But when the Athenians, who were supposed to be skilled in siege operations, achieved little or nothing, the Spartans, becoming suspicious, sent them home. Cimon was exiled and Ephialtes and Pericles came to power. Soon afterward the assassination of Ephialtes cleared the stage for Pericles. He was at the time a little more than thirty years old.

Pericles, Son of Xanthippus: 460–429 B.C.

Suppose we take a look at this remarkable Athenian. He was an aristocrat and yet he was a radical democrat. It was he who, in 450 B.C., introduced the two obols a day pay (about $1.20) for jurymen. He treated the Assembly with an Olympian detachment, and yet the people voted him back into power year after year. He drove Athens forward on the road to commercial imperialism and was backed by the merchants of the Piraeus, and yet around him were gathered the most brilliant minds and the greatest of artists and writers. His ambition seems to have been to make Athens the intellectual, commercial, and political leader of the Greek world.

The Empire Grows

There were never more than 43,000 to 44,000 adult Athenian male citizens. The country, as we have noted, was small. Yet under Periclean leadership the Athenians broke into a fever of achievement. By capturing the island of Aegina in the Saronic gulf, they blocked Athens' commercial rival Corinth from the Aegean and the Black Sea trade. By building the Long Walls (*see map*) from Athens to the Piraeus and adding a third wall running to Phalerum, they made their city into a sort of island protected by sea-power. By acquiring Megara and marching into Boeotia, they built a little land-empire in central Greece and got Thessaly as an ally. In one hectic year (459 B.C.) an inscription tells us that 168 citizens of the Erechtheid tribe of Athens lost their lives in battle in Cyprus, Egypt, Syria, Aegina, the Haleis (in southern Greece just across from Aegina), and in the Megarid. This was the year, too, in which, since all the fighting men were away, an Athenian army of the "old and the young," led by Myronides, defeated the Corinthians in the Megarid. In these years the Athenians fought, at one and the same time, the Persians, the Corinthians, and the Spartans.

By 456 B.C. the Athenian empire was at its height. There was even a post at Naupactus in the Corinthian gulf, and an alliance with Achaea. These moves were intended to hamper Corinth's trade with Sicily and Italy. But Pericles had reached too far. He had sent a fleet of 250 warships to aid an Egyptian revolt against Persia. In 454 B.C. that fleet was annihilated, and few of the men ever returned to Athena.

As a result of this disaster, Athens lost control of the Aegean Sea for a short time and used this fact as an excuse to transfer the treasury of the confederacy from Delos to Athens. In 451 B.C., Cimon, who had returned from exile, patched up a five years' truce with Sparta. In 449 B.C., he won a great naval victory in Cyprus but died shortly afterward. A peace was made with Persia the next year, after a war which had lasted for over forty years.

These were attempts to save what Athens had. But in 447 B.C. an Athenian army was defeated at Coronea in Boeotia. The next year Euboea, which was now part of the empire, revolted. Megara then massacred its Athenian garrison, and, the truce over, a Spartan army marched into Attica. To judge from the evidence we have, Pericles bribed the Spartan king to withdraw his army. Then, after reconquering Euboea, he relinquished Boeotia and the Megarid and signed a thirty years' truce with Sparta. From 445 to 431 B.C., a period of about fourteen years, Athens was more or less at peace. She used the time to consolidate her maritime empire and to erect the Parthenon and other glorious buildings on her Acropolis.

Periclean Democracy: The Empire

If a Greek from Corcyra in Sicily had been sent in those years to Athens to estimate her power, the first impression he would have received would have been that Athens was an imperial city. From her harbor trading vessels went out over the known world. The Aegean was an Athenian sea, and the Black Sea was her private preserve. The products of the world flowed to her harbor—papyrus and linen from Egypt, purple textiles and dates from Syria and Phoenicia, ship timber and ores from Macedonia, fish and wheat from the Black Sea, rugs and cushions from Carthage, hides from Gaul (modern France), tin and silver from Spain.

From the Piraeus went olive-oil, arms and armor, manufactured goods, and, above all, the famous Athenian pottery, which had by this time ousted Corinthian ware from the Mediterranean market. An Athenian 5th century B.C. *kylix* (drinking cup) was even found in London when excavations were being made for an extension to the Bank of England.

Our Greek from Corcyra, (suppose we call him Alcidas, and make the year 436 B.C.), would note delegates and visitors from the islands, from Asia Minor, and elsewhere finding their way from the Piraeus up to Athens. If he wandered to the law-courts, he would see cases from the empire being tried before Athenian jurymen. Enquiry would tell him that there are now only two free states, Lesbos and Chios, remaining in what used to be the Confederacy of Delos. The almost 200 other states, chiefly in the islands of the Aegean and along the coast of Asia Minor have been organized into five tribute districts. The money that comes in, 460 talents per year (a talent was worth probably more than $20,000 in today's purchasing power) can be used by Athens as it likes. The tribute is used to pay the jurymen, and to finance the officials and garrisons which administer the empire. The gleaming Parthenon on the Acropolis is, in part, a product of it. The empire, in fact, is the economic background for the great age of Athens.

If Alcidas investigates further he will discover that there are separate treaties between Athens and each of its subject states. Commercially, the states have to trade with Athens. In legal matters, many law-suits have to be judged in Athenian courts, and, in particular, all those involving Athenian citizens. Politically, the government of each subject-state must be loyal to Athens and is likely to be a democracy. After this, Athenian control varies. Many states have Athenian garrisons and the Athenian commander, as in Erythrae in Asia Minor, has as much power as the city government. Other cities are left to run their own local affairs. Foreign affairs are reserved for Athens. We are reminded of today's "satellite" states. As is more or less inevitable with any empire, Athens has become "a tyrant city." Yet without the empire her achievement could not have been so spectacular. Unlike other Greek states, her public treasury actually has a reserve. Before the expenditures on temples and public works, this reserve was 9700 talents, a tremendous sum for a small Greek city state.

How Athenian Democracy Operated

Alcidas, coming from a city which is ruled by an oligarchy, is certain to be interested in how Athenian democracy operates. He will learn that Cleisthenes established its basis, but that first Themistocles and then Pericles had put it more completely in the hands of the citizens. There are ten tribes, formed by Cleisthenes. Each tribe is divided into three "thirds", but the basic units of each tribe are the *demes*. The demes, about 100 in all, each have a *demarch* (mayor) and a town-hall. The demes keep the registers of citizens. They do what electing is done.

The actual machinery of government consists of the Council of Five Hundred, the executive officers (about 1400 in all), and the Assembly of all male citizens. The Council of Five Hundred is selected in a complicated way. Each year each of the ten tribes elects 500 candidates, a total of 5000 candidates. From each group of 500, 50 are picked by lot to sit on the Council. To select the 50 from each tribe, 50 white beans and 450 black beans are put in a jar and thoroughly mixed. When the man whose name is called comes forward, a bean is drawn from the jar. If it is a black bean, that citizen is rejected; if it is a white bean, he has been chosen to sit on the Council for one year. But, during his whole lifetime, a citizen can only sit on the Council twice.

This Council of Five Hundred supervises the executive officers, handles all routine business and prepares the business for the all-powerful Assembly. From it, each day, a new president of Athens is chosen, again by lot. This president serves for only one day and cannot be re-selected during the year.

Almost all the executive officers needed to run the city and the empire are also selected annually by lot, usually in boards of ten, one from each tribe. But, except for the council, a citizen cannot be re-selected for the same office; that is, if he has been a Market Commissioner in 442 B.C. he can never again hold that office, although he can be picked for another office, such as that of an Inspector of the Dockyards. The Athenians wanted to make sure that no official or councillor became too powerful, and, furthermore, that every citizen, at some time or other, took part in the actual government. The lot system, therefore, was truly democratic. A few executive officers, however, and notably the board of ten generals, were not picked by lot but were elected by popular vote. Such officers could be re-elected time after time. Pericles, for example, was elected as one of the generals year after year.

Alcidas, as an oligarch, will probably consider this method of choosing who will administer the state much too chancy. If he argues with an Athenian, it will be pointed out that each of the men selected by lot has to undergo a physical and mental examination before he takes office (*dokimasia*) and give an account of his actions afterward (*euthune*). Furthermore, the Athenian will say, how else can you assure that each citizen will take part in the government? Athenians, he will state proudly, administer themselves and the empire. They do *not* leave the job to a separate civil service.

In passing we might note that from 17,000 to 20,000 of the 43,000 Athenian citizens are on state duty each year and most of them are paid for it. This list includes councillors, 6000 jurymen, soldiers and sailors, and all the officials needed to administer Athens at home and the empire abroad. The pay is not high. The basic coin, the obol, is worth 3 cents but in purchasing power by our standards about 60 cents. The two obols' (later increased to three) a day pay for jurymen was enough, apparently, for room and board.

Alcidas will discover, however, that, although the Council and the executive officers perform the functions for which they have been selected, the Assembly of the adult (eighteen years of age and over) male citizens of Athens is the real governing body in Athens. It can, if it wishes, act as a court. It has the power to question and depose any councillor or executive officer. It is the sole body to pass laws and determine policies, domestic and foreign, and can, if it wishes, change the constitution. In a word it is Athens' Parliament, only in this parliament every adult male citizen casts his vote in person, not through elected representatives. It is a "town meeting" type of government.

It will not surprise the Corcyraean Alcidas that no woman has a vote. After all, it is not until the twentieth century A.D., 2500 years later, that women do get the vote. But Alcidas will probably find a meeting of the Athenian Assembly interesting. It comes together generally four times a month but more often if necessary. The regular meeting place is in the open air on a hill called the Pnyx, straight west of the great entrance to the Acropolis. Here in early morning the citizens assemble. The agenda has been posted five days in advance so that each man has the opportunity of knowing what business is to be handled. The councillors preside. In front of their seats, which face the audience, is a stone platform for speakers. A sacrifice to the gods opens the meeting. The first item on the agenda is read out, either with a recommendation from the Council or with alternative proposals or simply stated as a fact. Then, the herald asks "Who wishes to speak?"

There are no set political parties but there are well-known leaders (such as Pericles). One of them will mount the speaker's platform, with the gleaming temples of the Acropolis to his right, and to the left in the distance the blue sea. The business moves forward. The Assembly can accept, reject, or amend the Council's recommendations, can send the matter back for further study, or a speaker can propose an entirely new solution. All proposals have to be in writing. There is no doubt in anyone's mind that this Assembly can do anything it likes, vote new laws, depose magistrates or councillors, act as a court of law, or change the constitution, although there are procedures to make certain that this last cannot be done on the spur of the moment.

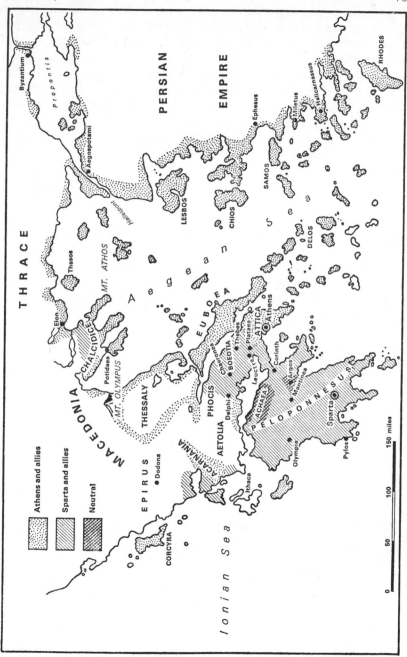

The Athenian Empire

This, then, is Athenian democracy. In general, the Assembly is likely to be dominated by the city workers. It takes a vital issue to make the farmers trudge in from the country. The aristocratic Alcidas will be disgusted to realize that in this Assembly a sausage-seller, a potter, or a metal-worker is equal to a landed noble or a wealthy merchant.

The Athenian law-courts will also interest him. They are called the Heliaea or "Sun-Courts," and are usually divided into ten "dicasteries" of from 201 to 1001 jurymen. These mass juries are picked each day by lot from 6000 jurymen, who are selected annually, again by lot. The courts are held in the open air, or, if it is wet, in the colonnades around the market-place. There is a dais for the presiding magistrate, seats for the jurymen, and benches for the prosecution and the defense. Each side has a set time to speak, determined by a water-clock. There are no lawyers, and hence the accused man and the prosecutor have to speak for themselves. When the jury votes, its decision is final. Here is where, normally, all criminal and civil cases are tried. The Athenians, however, put all men sixty years and over on a Board of Arbitrators. These, and the Forty (traveling judges) try to settle as many civil suits as they can. Alcidas will be pleased to learn that all cases of murder and manslaughter go before the courts of the Areopagus, composed of ex-archons. This is because the shedding of blood is thought to bring a religious pollution on the state.

If our Corcyraean is fortunate, he will observe a curious practice known as *ostracism*, which was instituted by Cleisthenes. Each year the Assembly is asked if it wants a day set aside for ostracism. If the Assembly votes in favor, on the set day, in the Agora, each citizen marks on an *ostrakon* (fragment of pottery) the name of a man he would like to see exiled. We have such an *ostrakon* marked with the name of Aristides. This reminds us of the story that Aristides was asked by a farmer who did not know him and could not write to put down "Aristides" on his ostrakon. Aristides asked why. "Oh," said the farmer, "I'm tired of hearing Aristides called 'the Just'."

If, to take the usual interpretation, the majority of 6000 votes is cast against any one man, he is exiled for ten years without loss of property or rights. Ostracism was a favorite way of getting rid of unpopular leaders. For example, Aristides, Themistocles, and Cimon were ostracized. We may pause to consider what would happen if the practice were introduced in modern political life. "Ostracism" has, of course, become a word in our language with a somewhat different connotation.

An Appraisal of Athenian Political Democracy

After his visit Alcidas will return to Corcyra, quite happy that his city is ruled by a sensible oligarchy and not by all the people. How are we of the present to assess the world's first democracy?

It had obvious defects. For one thing, a "town meeting" will work only in a small community. Even in Athens, only a comparatively small number of the citizens would attend. In war-time the fighting men would be away, and in peace-time 9000 would be a good attendance. Discussion would be difficult, mass emotion was common and a consistent foreign policy hard to attain. For instance, in 427 B.C. the Athenians voted to put all the rebel Mytileneans (on the island of Lesbos) to death, and the next day they changed their minds.

Wise leadership in any democracy is essential. As long as Pericles guided the Athenians, they did not make too many mistakes. Furthermore, we must remember that most of the citizens, unlike ourselves, had had experience in the actual administration of the state. Similarly, any criticism that government was run by "a rapid succession of amateurs," forgets that many of the councillors or other magistrates and officials would already be experienced in administration.

What were the virtues, again with an implicit comparison to our own system? In Athens the people actually did govern themselves. There was a constant interest in politics, not just during an election campaign every four years or so. In our system what the people vote for is often never carried out. In Athens, there was no "time-lag" between the will of the people and the carrying out of that will, and a politician who made a promise was expected to fulfill it. Another great difference was that economics did not dominate politics, partially because economics were not so complex, but also because Athenians were more concerned with living an interesting life than in piling up possessions.

The bell-like keynote of the world's first democracy was freedom. In Athens, very definitely, the state existed for the benefit of the individual. Citizens had duties such as being magistrates or serving in the army or navy which they performed as a matter of course because they themselves *were* the state. But there were no laws to make people "good." And there was no censorship. In the midst of the great war against Sparta (431–404 B.C.) the comic poet, Aristophanes, could write plays attacking the war. Instead of being put in prison, he sometimes won literary prizes. "We have no black or angry looks for our neighbor if he enjoys himself in his own way," said Pericles. In a word, Athenian democracy trusted humanity. It believed, rightly or wrongly, that, given free choice, men and women would on the whole choose the better instead of the worse.

This kind of democracy won and managed an empire. It produced an art and literature which the whole world since may have equaled but has not surpassed. For twenty-seven years it withstood the might of Sparta in the Peloponnesian War. It cannot, therefore, be dismissed lightly. If we wish to consider the basic principles of democracy we must study Athens.

A method of government, however, is only part of a people's way of life. To understand the Athenian we need to take a look, necessarily brief, at the classes of society, the state finances, the educational system, and the occupations available.

Periclean Athens: Social Divisions

The whole of ancient Attica had an estimated population of between 250,000 and 350,000. In modern terms, this would be the population of merely a fair-sized city. That population was divided into citizens, metics, and slaves.

After 451 B.C., to be an Athenian one had to have Athenian parentage on both sides. Citizenship and the vote were prized possessions. The estimates of the total number of Athenians, men and women and children, range from 120,000 to 170,000. Every adult male citizen as a matter of course was liable to service in the army or navy or both.

The metics were resident aliens who came in to be merchants, manufacturers, and artisans. Pericles encouraged them to settle. Their total population was between 45,000 and 65,000. They had to pay a special tax and serve in the army. In the lawcourts they were represented by an Athenian.

It has been said that the civilization of the Athenians rested on a slave base. This statement is not quite fair. It is true that Athenian slaves helped, but only helped, take the place of our modern machines. But slaves were a natural part of society in those days. Neither the slaves nor their masters saw anything extraordinary in the situation. For that matter it is only a century since slavery was abolished in the United States. As was said with regard to the Sumerians earlier, we must not think of Greek slavery in terms of Uncle Tom's Cabin. Athenian slaves often worked side by side with their masters. From the lists of payments for the building of the Erechtheum, a temple on the Acropolis, we know that slaves received the same wages as free men. They were allowed to keep part of their earnings and to buy their freedom. The law provided certain safeguards against cruel treatment. In law-suits, however, they could be offered for examination by torture to prove the truth of a statement. Since both sides regularly made this offer, it may be suspected that it was a legal manoeuvre. As a proof of the treatment of Athenian slaves we may present both the plays of Aristophanes and the words of a crusty old oligarch who was critical of Periclean democracy. "At Athens," he says, "the impudence of slaves is at its peak. To strike them is not permitted there, and yet a slave will not stand out of the way to let you pass.

For . . . if it were lawful for a slave to be struck by a freeman . . . you would often think an Athenian a slave and hit him."

As with the Sumerians, one reason for this kindly treatment of slaves was that any Greek might find himself a slave, particularly if he were captured in battle. Another reason, of course, is that, although most slaves were non-Greeks (the statuette of a 5th century B.C. negro bootblack has been found in Athens), there were many who were. These spoke the same language as their masters and had had the same education.

One group of slaves was badly treated. These were the slaves who worked in the hot, narrow galleries of the silver mines at Laureium, which were hired out to contractors by the state at a fixed price. To make profits the contractors worked the slaves hard.

A fair estimate of the total number of slaves in 5th century Athens is probably around 90,000. Their treatment, if we except Laureium, was as humane as slavery is ever likely to be.

Periclean Athens: State Finance

Athens was one of the richest of the Greek city-states. The public revenue came from the tribute, from the silver mines at Laureium, from harbor tolls, market dues (really a sales tax), customs dues (2% on all exports and imports), court fees, the tax on metics, and so on. From all sources, the annual revenue in peace-time is reckoned at about 1000 talents or roughly, $20,000,000 in terms of its purchasing power today. In war-time there was an additional war tax.

On the other hand Athens was not a welfare state. It did not have to pay for state education, state hospitalization, sewerage, and the like. There were no baby bonuses and no old age pensions. The biggest peace-time expenditure was the payment of the 17,000 who, as has been mentioned, ate "state bread". The surplus—for Athens had a surplus—was put, not into productive enterprises, but into the glorious buildings on the Acropolis. The Parthenon, for instance, took seven years to build. Yet it and the rest of the building program provided employment. There were few jobless in Athens.

Another heavy expenditure was on public festivals. Here, the state tapped the rich, both citizens and metics, by means of liturgies. These were of various kinds. In the *choregia*, for example, a rich man was picked to stand the cost of a chorus in the tragedies and comedies presented every year. This might take from $10,000 to $12,000. In the *trierarchia*, a rich man had to pay for the operation of a trireme (the regular Greek warship) for a year. This might cost him from $14,000 to $20,000. In this way, as the Old Oligarch complained, the rich were taxed to pay for the pleasures of the poor. This policy also meant that too big an inequality between the poor and the rich was not allowed to develop. There was a trend toward an economic democracy.

It was difficult, however, for the economy to stand the strain of war. For one thing, to keep her war-fleet of 300 triremes at sea, Athens had to hire rowers. Yet mastery of the sea was vital.

Periclean Athens: Education

We have glanced at the state finances, the classes of society, and the government of Periclean Athens. In the last, in particular, we have seen that the Athenians, quite literally, governed themselves. What sort of education prepared them for such a system?

In Sparta, the state determined whether a child should live or not. In Athens the choice was left to the father. If the father could not afford any more children, he had the right to expose the baby, and unless some stranger picked it up, the baby died. Here, undoubtedly, is an ugly practice of Greek society, though it may not be much uglier than certain of our own practices. In Athens in the 5th century, infanticide seems to have been rare.

If a child survived, whether boy or girl, it lived in the women's quarters until it was seven. The museums and the paintings on vases show us plenty of toys—rattles, balls, hoops, swings, toy carts, wagons, tops, and dolls with movable limbs. Small dogs, tortoises, and ducks were among the pets. Cats were not often seen. The family mouser was usually a weasel or a pet snake.

At seven, girls had to begin to learn household duties. Formal education was reserved for boys. A boy was regularly assigned a *paidagogos* and sent to school. The *paidagogos* was a slave whose job it was to attend the boy and supervise his manners and morals.

Athenian schools were private schools, with fees payable at the end of each month. The curriculum was not vocational. Writing and reading were taught. As soon as a Greek boy learned to read he began to memorize in whole or in part the *Iliad* and the *Odyssey*. Memorization was supposed to train the mind, while the nobility of the people in the Homeric epics was believed to shape and improve character. We read in Xenophon, a 4th century B.C. historian and educator, of a man who could recite from memory the almost 28,000 lines of the *Iliad* and *Odyssey*. Such a feat was not too uncommon. Arithmetic was difficult. The Greeks had no sign for zero, and letters of the alphabet were used as numerals. The difficulty was solved by the use of the abacus, borrowed from Egypt, operating on the same principle as the device used by the Chinese today.

The more advanced curriculum was divided into "music" and gymnastics. "Music" to the Greeks included poetry; so the student learned still more poetry, and also how to play the lyre and to sing to it. Athletics were regarded as of almost equal importance. Most Greek states had an athletic festival once a year. In Athens, there was the Panathenaea, which included track and field sports, swimming, and a beauty contest for young men.

The best athletes, when they were ready, could look forward to competition in one of the four great athletic festivals of Greece. At the top of these were the Olympic Games. Only a young man who was a Greek, who had had six months' training, and who was of good character could compete. If he won, he was, even as today, a hero.

When a boy was between fourteen and sixteen, he began to learn his vocation, whether as a potter, or a farmer, or a businessman. His education, however, continued. There were three gymnasia for athletics. There were dramatic and religious festivals. There were also, everywhere, philosophical and political discussions.

At eighteen, the Athenian young man entered the army for two years. His first year was spent in Attica. During the second year he went out over the empire. When he returned, it was with some idea of the greatness of his city.

This was the old-time education. After 450 B.C. those who could afford it could take a sort of university curriculum from the "Sophists". The word means "wise man". These men taught geometry, astronomy, ethics, politics, philosophy, grammar, literature, and, above all, public speaking. From the *Apology* of Socrates, we learn that the Sophist, Evenus, charged about $2000 a course.

Periclean Athens: Occupations

How did Athenians make a living? The basic occupation was farming, and many Athenians had property in the country. Under Pericles industry and trade were also major pursuits. In Athens and in the Piraeus, there were shoemakers, metal-workers, dyers, tanners, jewelers, stone-masons, and a host of other craftsmen. There was not much mass manufacturing. Generally Athenian shoes, pots, hoes, axes, and other articles were turned out by workers in small shops, which sometimes served as homes.

The workers of each craft lived side by side. The potters of Athens, for example, all lived in one district called the *Cerameicus*. Guilds set the prices and looked after such things as conditions of apprenticeship and quality of workmanship. Athenian pots, for instance, had to be good pots to compete well on the foreign market. Sales were made directly to exporters. For the home market there was direct bargaining with the consumer. There was also a host of retail shops in the city, and pedlars carried goods through the countryside.

The basic wage was a drachma a day (18 cents but worth about 20 times that amount in purchasing power). From various sources, we learn that it cost an Athenian single man about 120 drachmas a year to live, and a married man with two children double that amount. An Athenian artisan could and did take time off.

There was also a middle class which owned property and could live from it and their investments. Bankers, called "tablemen," were the exporters and importers. Each spring the merchant-skippers loaded their round-bellied ships and set out, like today's freighters, for a season's trading from port to port. Before they returned, they could have visited Massalia, Carthage, Syracuse, Naucratis in Egypt or Tyre in Phoenicia. One big item was wheat from southern Russia. By this time Athens had to import grain to feed her people.

Periclean Athens: The Status of Women

Athens was a man's city. Women, as we have seen, did not receive a formal education. Marriage, usually at about fifteen years of age, was arranged by the parents of the bride and bridegroom as is often the case today in France, Italy, Spain, and South American countries. The groom was generally twice the bride's age.

After marriage, the wife's main task was to look after the house and the children. Dorian women had great freedom. Athenian women were restricted to their own section of the house, called the women's quarters, whenever male guests came. They were not supposed to go out un-accompanied, while their husbands spent comparatively little of their time at home. In his Funeral Speech for the Athenians killed in the first year of the Peloponnesian War, Pericles advised the women present that "the best of you is she who is least spoken of for good or ill among men."

Other evidence indicates that the life of Athenian women was not as dreary as one might think. They went calling. They attended the public festivals, including the drama. Like women everywhere they were fond of clothes. Their dress was an inner tunic with a gown over it, and their favorite colors were golden brown or saffron. Hair dressing was elaborate and so were cosmetics. The vase-paintings show parasols. Their brace-lets and necklaces were expensive. We can also be pretty sure that many of them were highly respected by their husbands. The great statesman, Themistocles, is reported to have said: "I rule Athens and Athens rules Hellas and my wife rules me and the child rules my wife." Similarly, we read that Socrates, the famous Athenian philosopher, said to a friend: "Is there anybody to whom you entrust more serious matters than to your wife—and with whom you have fewer arguments?"

We can be fairly sure, then, that the Athenian wife was not downtrodden, even if she was not supposed to mix freely in male society. There was, however, one class of women in Athens who mingled freely with men. These were the *Hetaerae*, a word which means "companions." These women were educated in music, poetry, and dancing and their status was similar to that of today's Japanese Geishas. Aspasia, Pericles' common-law wife, was a *hetaera*. She had a brilliant salon, as did other *hetaerae*.

Periclean Democracy: A Man's Day

For some other details of daily life, suppose we follow an Athenian through an ordinary day in June. We will call him Aristippus. Aristippus is a middle-class Athenian with a property in the country and an interest in trading ventures.

On this morning, as on every morning, Aristippus gets up as soon as there is light, and for a good reason. There are no electric lights, only candles or rush-lights or tiny bronze or clay lamps. Therefore one uses as much daylight as one can. He washes, puts on a tunic, and has a bit of breakfast (bread dipped in wine). The women and children are up. Aristippus greets them, then dons his *himation* which is a wrap-around of wool, usually white. When Aristippus was a young bachelor he wore a bright-colored cloak—scarlet or frog-green or purple. When he is out in the country working on his farm he makes do with a tunic only, arranged so as to leave his right arm and shoulder bare. In the city he wears a himation and slips his feet into sandals. He does not bother with a hat. Like most Athenians his hair and beard are thick and curly. There is a signet-ring on his finger and he carries a walking-stick. He glances around the house. It is built around a central court and the room in which he is standing, the biggest one, is used for both dining and sleeping.

Greek houses face inwards and are flimsy, built chiefly of sundried brick. That is why the word for burglar is "a man who digs through walls." The furniture is equally simple—couches with three-legged tables packed under them, chests, a rug or two, a tapestry, perhaps, and armor on the walls. There is a stove of sorts in the kitchen. There is no heat in winter, except for smoking braziers. If any of us were put into Aristippus' place, we would find that we would have to do without a great many things we take for granted, not only television sets or automobiles, but also small articles such as soap, tea, coffee, sugar, and the like.

There is a porter in the vestibule of the house. Aristippus and he greet each other as old acquaintances. Two other slaves follow their master into the street. That street, like all the streets of Athens, is narrow and twisting. Projecting balconies make it still narrower. There is dust blowing and offal lying about. Ahead a pot is emptied from an upstairs window. There is no sewerage in Athens or garbage collection and in June it gets very hot. But Aristippus is used to this. A friend, Glaucon, joins him. As the street turns, there is a quick glimpse of the Acropolis. Both men glance at it. The Parthenon, just finished, gleams white. So do the pillars of the great entrance-gates (*Propylaea*). In the northwest corner, the bronze statue of Athena Promachos, fifty feet high, thrusts up a spear into the blue sky. Athenian houses may be flimsy but their public buildings are built of marble.

The goal of the two men is the Agora or market-place. There are public buildings here, too, notably the *Bouleuterion* in which the Council of 500 meets; Aristippus was a councillor in the previous year. Everywhere by this time, with the sun just nicely up, are temples, shrines, colonnades, and swarms of men. The Agora is where one hears all the news. Often, too, the snub-nosed Socrates will be there, arguing and discussing subjects such as "What is justice?" "Does any man *willingly* make another man bad?"

Aristippus makes his way to the market. In Athens men, not women, do the buying. In the market everything is carefully sectioned—flowers in one place, for example, fish in another and bread-women in another. There are market-commissioners to keep order. The market-police, like all the police, are Scythian slaves, armed with bows. Since Aristippus is giving a dinner for his brother that evening, he buys fish, bread, vegetables, fruits, and the like. He hires a chef, too. For any important dinner one's women-folk are not to be trusted. In another quarter of the market are dancing and flute-girls for hire. Aristippus arranges for a couple of flute-girls.

What with all the bargaining, and ancient Athenians loved to bargain, this takes until "full market" which is about ten o'clock. At this point Aristippus turns over his purchases to his slaves, and goes over to arrange a loan from his banker for a venture with his brother on a cargo of wheat from southern Russia. His banker has a table with piles of coins on it. Every city puts out its own coinage and one has to be sure the coins are sound. "Attic owls," as Athenian coinage is called because they have Athena's owl ("wisdom") on one side of them, are good anywhere.

When Aristippus is finished, he thinks of a walk to the metal-worker's quarters to see if he can pick up a new bronze ewer. There the smiths will be sweating in the heat of the forges with nothing on but leather aprons. He also needs a few new drinking-cups. For this he will have to visit the potters' quarter and look over the piles of vases outside the shop doors. Inside, the potters' wheels will be spinning as the potters draw clay into graceful forms. Others will be firing the pots and still others will be painting them with the vigor and skill which in succession has made Athenian black-figured and red-figured pottery the most popular in the world.

But the sun is hot. Aristippus gives up his notion. He goes instead to one of the barber shops which line the streets near the Agora. Here he meets friends. As he settles down for a beard-and-hair-trim, everyone gets into a discussion about what ought to be done about the threat of war from Corinth and Sparta.

At lunch-time Aristippus goes home. His lunch is substantial and is eaten with his wife, two sons, and a daughter. After lunch Aristippus takes a siesta. Then, like all his friends, he sets out for a walk outside the walls to his favorite gymnasium, the *Akademia*, which is one of three in Athens.

These gymnasia are men's clubs. There are terraces, rows of plane-trees, benches, and open spaces for exercises. The young men go in for running, jumping, boxing, wrestling, and throwing the javelin or the discus. Aristippus and his friends play catch. Everyone participates because everyone believes in keeping his body in good shape. There are also lecture and game rooms. After his exercise, Aristippus has a bath, talks with his friends, and goes home. The slaves have prepared the big room for dinner. The women have retired to the women's quarters. When Aristippus' brother and the other guests arrive, they recline on couches. The three-legged tables have been pulled out. There are no knives or forks. Fingers and occasionally a spoon are used.

The meal is simple—fish, vegetables drenched in honey, olive-oil, or sauces, and bread. Dessert is fruit, almonds, cakes, cheese, and salt. Salt is a luxury. At intervals the flute-girls play.

After the meal the *symposium* begins. This means "a drinking-together." The Athenian always mixes his wine with water. He is usually temperate, though not always so. Opinion is against drunkenness. "Drinking is bad," says Aristophanes, the comic poet, "for wine means banging at doors, hitting people and having to pay for it, and a headache into the bargain."

Symposiums vary. Sometimes, there is revelry. Quite often, the entertainment is conversation. When the symposium is over the slaves accompany their masters home through the unlit streets with torches or horn-lanterns. Aristippus goes to bed.

There are times, of course, when Aristippus is much busier than this. There is the Assembly to attend. He may easily be picked by the lot to be a magistrate. Quite often he has a law-suit on his hands. If war comes, he will have to put on his helmet, take up his shield, spear, and sword, and go out to fight.

Yet even the poor took more leisure time than we, although they worked hard when they worked. Their food was cheaper than ours: the staple dish was barley-porridge or barley-cakes with a bit of salt-fish or an onion as a relish. On festival days there might be a piece of kid or lamb. Blood-puddings, tripe, and sausages were popular. Aristophanes accused the butchers of making sausages of dog or donkey-meat.

The chief amusement seems to have been talking about politics, the latest sculpture, the latest play, and the latest news. The "egg-heads", of whom Pericles was literally one (he wore a helmet to disguise the shape of his head), went in for philosophical discussion. Herodotus, too, might give a reading of the history of the Persian War which he was writing, or there might be a lecture by a Sophist. Each year there were public festivals. These included, twice a year, the great dramatic festivals, which, like all the festivals, were religious. The Athenians were in a certain sense of the word, very religious. For the young men about town there were joint-contribution picnic dinners on the seashore, cock-fights, horse-racing or the maintenance of an expensive *hetaera*.

It was a simple way of life as compared to our own, but the Athenians seem to have been happy. There was more to do than could, seemingly, be done. There was a sense of achievement and a pride in their city. There was an interest, greater than our own, in intellectual and artistic achievements; and Athenians saw nothing peculiar in a man being a great poet and at the same time an athlete and a soldier. Aeschylus, the first great writer of tragedy, fought at Marathon. Sophocles, the second tragedian, was a general and also a treasurer of the Delian League.

A remarkable surge in arts and letters, which will be considered later, was an integral part of 5th Century Athenian life. But the Periclean Age met disaster in the Peloponnesian War.

The Peloponnesian War: 431–404 B.C.

It is not necessary to describe in detail the actual incidents which led to the war. There were the Potidaean affair (433–430 B.C.), in which Potidaea in Macedonia revolted and was helped by Corinth; the Corcyraean affair (433 B.C.), in which Athens aided Corcyra against her mother-city Corinth; and the Megarian decree (ca. 432 B.C.), which closed all Athenian-controlled ports to Megarian goods and brought that country to starvation.

The real reasons for the conflict seem quite modern. Sparta had been the leading state in Greece. Now Athens had challenged that position. Two first class powers, each the leader of a bloc of states, faced each other like two snarling dogs. Racial hostility was added. Athens led the Ionians and Sparta the Dorians. Then there was an ideological conflict, in that Sparta championed oligarchy, Athens democracy. But it was Corinth, fearful of a trade rival, who pressured slow-moving Sparta into the struggle. Corinth had been beaten in the battle for the trade of the

Aegean and the Black Sea. Athenian guard-ships, posted at the island of Aegina, prevented Corinthian ships from sailing out. Now Athens was moving to capture Corinth's trade with Italy and Sicily.

The Corcyraean affair was an example. Corcyra was the half-way house for ships on their way to Italy and Sicily by the long route, which is still followed today, up the coast of Greece, across to Brindisi in Italy and then along the instep and toe of that country to Sicily and the western coast-line. Athens had made an alliance with Corcyra and established a democracy there; Corcyra also had the biggest navy after Athens and Corinth. From Corinth's point of view, the situation was desperate.

Power-blocs, ideological and racial differences and a trade-war—in the words of the French maxim, "*plus ça change, plus c'est la même chose.*" Sparta even announced a "war of liberation."

In the first phase of the Peloponnesian War a plague, probably a bubonic plague, hit Athens (430–429 B.C.). It carried off at least one-fourth of the population of Attica. Pericles' legitimate sons died. So did Pericles.

His death weakened Athens as much as the plague did. Demagogues, such as Cleon the Tanner, took over the leadership. The war dragged on and the Spartans continued to invade Attica. The Athenians were safe as long as they stayed behind their walls and kept control of the sea and of the supply lines which brought in food. Finally, Cleon was killed in battle. The leader of the conservatives, Nicias, arranged a peace. This left both sides exactly as they had been.

Now Alcibiades, the brilliant nephew of Pericles, came to the fore. At his urging, Athens fought an undeclared war against Sparta but was beaten at the battle of Mantinea in southern Greece (418 B.C.). Later, the imperial city forced the island of Melos into her empire, with no excuse except her own desire. Athens was now, truly, a "tyrant-city" and ultimately this ruthless imperialism was to defeat her. Finally, in 415 B.C., Alcibiades promoted a great expedition to conquer Sicily and the West. The first objective was Syracuse.

This expedition was the ruin of Athens. Altogether, 134 triremes and 30,000 soldiers, of whom 5100 were hoplites, left for Sicily. Along with that armada went a mob of merchants in smaller craft. There were three generals, Alcibiades, Nicias (who had opposed the scheme), and Lamachus, a professional soldier. Later, reinforcements had to be sent.

But, with Alcibiades' supporters out of the city, his opponents had him recalled to stand trial for alleged sacrilege; when it came to conduct, Alcibiades had always been somewhat delinquent. Alcibiades escaped, went to Sparta, and persuaded the Spartans to send help to Syracuse. The result (413 B.C.) was the loss of 240 of Athens' warships and 40,000 of her own and her allies' men. For a state which by this time had about 30,000 fighting men, it was a shattering blow.

Also in 413 B.C., Sparta, again at the urging of Alcibiades, formally began the war anew. This war (413–404 B.C.) is called the Decelean War, because Sparta fortified a post in Attica at Decelea north of Athens and stayed there. Previous invasions had been for about 30 days each year. Now, the Athenians had to man their walls all year round. Likewise, the Spartans, by agreeing to abandon the Asiatic Greeks to the Persians, got Persian gold to build a fleet. The subject-allies of Athens were eager to revolt, and, now that there was a Spartan fleet, they seized the chance. The tyranny of Athenian imperialism was reaping the harvest it had sown.

Yet the Athenians fought on. They built a new fleet and, when it was destroyed, still another. The Assembly, except for a few brief months, continued to govern. In 406 B.C. that jewel of Ionic architecture, the Erechtheum, was completed. There were still tragedies and comedies presented in the great theater on the south slope of the Acropolis. Democracy showed that it could face adversity.

But in 405 B.C. Lysander, the Spartan admiral, after four days of skirmishing, attacked the last Athenian war-fleet at Aegospotamoi (the "goat-streams") in the Dardanelles as the Athenians were disembarking for their evening meal. One hundred and seventy ships and 4000 men were captured. The 4000 prisoners, except for a single traitor, were butchered like swine. Conon, the Athenian admiral, escaped with twenty ships to Cyprus. With the command of the Aegean lost, Lysander blockaded Athens by sea while the Spartan army from Decelea besieged it by land. After six months the city was starved into surrender.

By the terms of surrender Athens lost all her foreign possessions, her navy was limited to twelve ships, her Long Walls and the Piraeus fortifications were destroyed to the music of flutes, and she became a subject ally of Sparta. Meanwhile a Spartan garrison sat on the Acropolis, the democracy was dissolved, the rule of the "Thirty Tyrants" (men appointed by Lysander to "restore the ancient constitution") began, and all the rest of Hellas rejoiced at the downfall of the "tyrant city."

The fratricidal strife was over. In addition to the defeat of Athens, it left behind a legacy of confusion and destruction. By abandoning the Greek cities of Asia Minor in return for gold to build a fleet, Sparta had brought Persia back into Greek affairs. Meantime, Spartan supremacy soon proved harsher than Athenian rule and unrest and civil war resulted. The economic picture was even more disastrous. Practically the whole Greek world had been drawn into the struggle. Farm lands had been devastated. Tens of thousands of Greeks had been killed or uprooted. Trade had been disrupted. The story of the succeeding fourth century is

How Periclean Democracy Operated

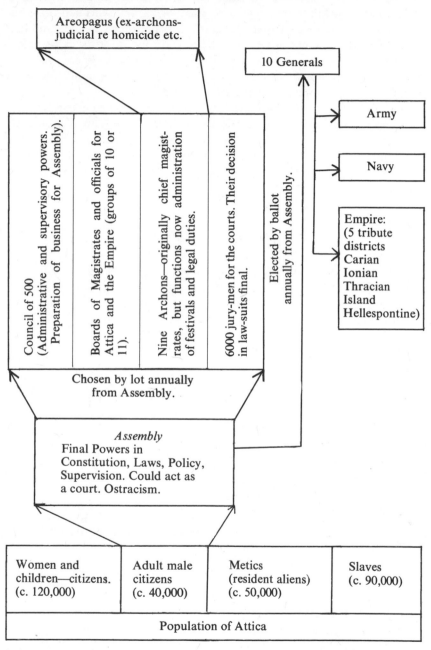

(After Jones, *Ancient Civilization*, Rand, McNally & Co., Chicago, 1960. p. 235)

of rising prices and the increase of debt, even though it is also the era of important bankers such as Pasion. Pasion, who had been his master's trusted slave, was freed, married his master's widow, and left a fortune of 50 talents of which 11 belonged to depositors in his bank. It is significant of 4th century economic unrest that it is the era of Greek mercenaries serving in foreign lands, because there was no future or apparent hope or interest for them in Hellas.

Though trade was re-established and there was again a certain amount of prosperity, the most serious effect of the Peloponnesian War was the destruction of the high confidence which had marked the 5th century. Arts and letters continued at a high level and with Plato and Aristotle Greek philosophy reached its peak. But more and more a feeling of futility brooded over the Greek world. The Great Age was over.

Readings from Sources of the Period

(a) Herodotus (ca. 484–425 B.C.) describes the battle of Marathon (490 B.C.) where 10,000 Athenians and Plataeans defeated a much larger force of Persians.

This was roughly the method of drawing up the Athenians at Marathon: their line was stretched out equal to the Persian line, but its center was only a few ranks deep, and here the line was weakest, whereas each wing was strong in numbers. *112* When the troops had been deployed and the sacrifices had turned out propitious, the Athenians were given the command to charge, and they made for the barbarians on the dead run. The distance between the armies, from spear point to spear point, was not less than a mile. The Persians, seeing them attacking at the double, prepared to receive them, thinking them the victims of a madness that would destroy them utterly, seeing that they were few, and yet coming on at a run without either cavalry or archers for cover. That is what the barbarians thought; but when the Athenians in a body came to grips with the barbarians, they fought a battle worthy of the name. For they were the first of all the Greeks we know of to use the charge against the enemy; they were the first to bear up against the sight of the Persian uniform and the men wearing it; up to then the very name of Mede had been a terror for the Greeks to hear. *113* While they fought at Marathon, a long time passed. And in the center of the line the barbarians were winning, where the Persians themselves and the Sacae had been drawn up. Victorious in this quarter, the barbarians had broken through and were chasing their foes into the interior, but on each wing the Athenians and the Plataeans were winning. In their victory they let the repulsed barbarians go, but linked their two wings and fought those of the enemy who had broken through, and the Athenians won. They followed the fleeing Persians, cutting them down, until they came to the sea; then they called for fire and seized hold of the ships. *114* And in this struggle the polemarch lost his life, having proved his mettle (and of the generals, Stesilaus the son of Thrasylaus). Also Cynegirus the son of Euphorion [brother of Aeschylus the tragic poet] fell there, his hand cut off with an axe as he was laying hold of a ship's stern, and many other famous Athenians were killed. *115* The Athenians overpowered seven of the ships in this way, but with the rest the barbarians backed off, and picking up the Eretrian slaves from the island where they had left them, they sailed round Cape Sunium, wanting to beat the Athenians to Athens. *116* So the barbarians sailed round Sunium, but the Athenians went to the relief of the city as fast as their legs would carry them, and they beat the barbarians to the city. They arrived from the precinct of Heracles in Marathon and encamped in another Heracleum in Athens, the one in Cynosarges. The barbarians with their fleet lay off Phalerum (which in those days was the port of Athens) a while at anchor, and then sailed back to Asia. *117* In this battle at Marathon there died of the barbarians about 6400 men, and of the Athenians 192. . . .

(MacKendrick and Howe, *op. cit.*, pp. 121–122, translated by Paul Mac-Kendrick.)

(b) In the first book of his history about the great war between Athens and Sparta, Thucydides (460–401 B.C.) digresses to describe the rise of the Athenian Empire. The energy of the Athenians was amazing. In 459 B.C. besides fighting in Egypt and Cyprus, they waged war against Aegina and Corinth, as described in the following passage:

An Athenian fleet made a descent upon Haliesis, where a battle took place against some Corinthian and Epidaurian troops; the Athenians gained the victory. Soon afterwards the Athenians fought at sea off Cecryphaleia with a Peloponnesian fleet, which they defeated. A war next broke out between the Aeginetans and the Athenians, and a great battle was fought off the coast of Aegina, in which the allies of both parties joined; the Athenians were victorious, and captured seventy of the enemy's ships; they then landed on Aegina and, under the command of Leocrates the son of Stroebus, besieged the town. Thereupon the Peloponnesians sent over to the assistance of the Aeginetans three hundred hoplites who had previously been assisting the Corinthians and Epidaurians. The Corinthians seized on the heights of Geraneia, and thence made a descent with their allies into the Megarian territory, thinking that the Athenians, who had so large a force absent in Aegina and in Egypt, would be unable to assist the Megarians; or, if they did, would be obliged to raise the seige of Aegina. But the Athenians, without moving their army from Aegina, sent to Megara under the command of Myronides a force consisting of their oldest and youngest men, who had remained at home. A battle was fought, which hung equally in the balance; and when the two armies separated they both thought that they had gained the victory. The Athenians, who did however get rather the better, on the departure of the Corinthians erected a trophy. And then the Corinthians, irritated by the reproaches of the aged men in the city, after twelve days' preparation came out again, and, claiming the victory, raised another trophy. Hereupon the Athenians sallied out of Megara, killed those who were erecting the trophy, and charged and defeated the rest of the army.

(G. Howe and G. A. Harrer, *Greek Literature in Translation*, revised by P. H. Epps, pp. 245–6, New York: Harper, 1948, translated by Benjamin Jowett, *Thucydides*, Oxford: Clarendon Press, 1900.)

(c) Fascinating glimpses into the daily life of the Athenians of the 5th Century B.C. are found in the plays of Aristophanes the comic poet. In the *Wasps*, in which he pokes fun at the Athenian courts, he has a juryman say, in part:

> To prove that no kinglier power than ours in any part of the world exists,
> Is there any creature on earth more blest, more feared and petted from day to day,
> Or that leads a happier, pleasanter life, than a Justice of Athens, though old and grey?
> For first when rising from bed in the morn, to the Criminal Court betimes I trudge,
> Great six-foot fellows are there at the rails, in anxious haste to salute their judge.
> And the delicate hand which has dipped so deep in the public purse, he claps into mine.
> And he bows before me and makes his prayer, and softens his voice to a pitiful whine;
> *O pity me, pity me, Sire,* he cries, *if you ever indulged your longing for pelf,*
> *When you managed the mess on a far campaign, or served some office of state yourself.* . . .

> So when they have begged and implored me enough, and my angry temper is wiped away,
> I enter in and take my seat, and then I do none of the things I say.
> I hear them utter all sorts of cries, designed expressly to win my grace,
> What won't they utter, what won't they urge, to coax a Justice who tries their case?
> Some vow they are needy and friendless men, and over their poverty wail and whine,
> And reckon up hardships, false and true, till he makes them out to be equal to mine.
> Some tell us a legend of days gone by, or a joke from Aesop, witty and sage,
> Or jest and banter to make me laugh, that so I may doff my terrible rage.
> And if all this fails, and I stand unmoved, he leads by the hand his little ones near,
> He brings his girls and he brings his boys; and I, the Judge, am composed to hear.
> They huddle together with piteous bleats; while trembling above them, he prays to me,
> Prays as to a God his accounts to pass, to give him a quittance and leave him free.
> *If thou lovest a bleating male of the flock, O lend thine ear to this boy of mine;*
> *Or pity the sweet little, delicate girl, if thy soul delights in the squeaking of swine.*
> So then we relax the pitch of our wrath, and screw it down to a peg more low.
> Is *this* not a fine dominion of mine, a derision of wealth with its pride and show? . . .

> But the nicest and pleasantest part of it all is this, which I'd wholly forgotten to say,

'Tis when with my fee in my wallet I come, returning home at the close
  of the day,
O then what a welcome I get for its sake; my daughter, the darling, is
  foremost of all,
And she washes my feet and anoints them with care, and above them she
  stoops, and a kiss lets fall,
Till at last by the pretty Papas of her tongue she angles withal my three-
  obol away.
Then my dear little wife, she sets on the board nice manchets of bread in
  a tempting array,
And cosily taking a seat by my side, with loving entreaty constrains me to
  feed;
I beseech you taste this, I implore you try that.

(Aristophanes, *Wasps*, 11. 548–614, translated by B. B. Rogers, for the Loeb
Classical Library, Harvard University Press.)

(d) The Funeral Speech of Pericles for the Athenians who were killed in the first
year of the Peloponnesian War is regarded as the finest expression of the ideals
of Periclean democracy. A few extracts from it are given below.

Our form of government does not enter into rivalry with the institutions of
others. We do not copy our neighbors, but are an example to them. It is true
that we are called a democracy, for the administration is in the hands of the
many and not of the few. But while the law secures equal justice to all alike in
their private disputes, the claim of excellence is also recognized; and when a
citizen is in any way distinguished, he is preferred to the public service, not as
a matter of privilege, but as the reward of merit. Neither is poverty a bar, but
a man may benefit his country whatever be the obscurity of his condition. There
is no exclusiveness in our public life, and in our private intercourse we are not
suspicious of one another, nor angry with our neighbor if he does what he likes;
we do not put on sour looks at him which, though harmless, are not pleasant.
While we are thus unconstrained in our private intercourse, a spirit of reverence
pervades our public acts; we are prevented from doing wrong by respect for the
authorities and for the laws, having an especial regard to those which are
ordained for the protection of the injured as well as to those unwritten laws which
bring upon the transgressor of them the reprobation of the general sentiment.

. . . and thus too our city is equally admirable in peace and in war. For we are
lovers of the beautiful, yet simple in our tastes, and we cultivate the mind
without loss of manliness. Wealth we employ, not for talk and ostentation, but
when there is a real use for it. To avow poverty with us is no disgrace; the true
disgrace is in doing nothing to avoid it. An Athenian citizen does not neglect the
state because he takes care of his own household; and even those of us who are
engaged in business have a very fair idea of politics. We alone regard a man who
takes no interest in public affairs, not as a harmless, but as a useless character;
and if few of us are originators, we are all sound judges of a policy. The great
impediment to action is, in our opinion, not discussion, but the want of that
knowledge which is gained by discussion preparatory to action.

To sum up: I say that Athens is the school of Hellas, and that the individual

Athenian in his own person seems to have the power of adapting himself to the most varied forms of action with the utmost versatility and grace. This is no passing and idle word, but truth and fact, and the assertion is verified by the position to which these qualities have raised the state. For in the hour of trial Athens alone among her contemporaries is superior to the report of her. No enemy who comes against her is indignant at the reverses which he sustains at the hands of such a city; no subject complains that his masters are unworthy of him. And we shall assuredly not be without witnesses; there are mighty monuments of our power which will make us the wonder of this and of succeeding ages; we shall not need the praises of Homer or of any other panegyrist whose poetry may please for the moment, although his representation of the facts will not bear the light of day. For we have compelled every land and every sea to open a path for our valor, and have everywhere planted eternal memorials of our friendship and of our enmity. Such is the city for whose sake these men nobly fought and died; they could not bear the thought that she might be taken from them; and every one of us who survive should gladly toil on her behalf.

Such was the end of these men; they were worthy of Athens, and the living need not desire to have a more heroic spirit, although they may pray for a less fatal issue. The value of such a spirit is not to be expressed in words. Anyone can discourse to you forever about the advantages of a brave defence, which you know already. But instead of listening to him I would have you day by day fix your eyes upon the greatness of Athens, until you become filled with the love of her; and when you are impressed by the spectacle of her glory, reflect that this empire has been acquired by men who knew their duty and had the courage to do it, who in the hour of conflict had the fear of dishonor always present to them, and who, if ever they failed in an enterprise, would not allow their virtues to be lost to their country, but freely gave their lives to her as the fairest offering which they could present at her feast. The sacrifice which they collectively made was individually repaid to them; for they received again each one for himself a praise which grows not old, and the noblest of all sepulchres—I speak not of that in which their remains are laid, but of that in which their glory survives, and is proclaimed always and on every fitting occasion both in word and deed. For the whole earth is the sepulchre of famous men; not only are they commemorated by columns and inscriptions in their own country, but in foreign lands there dwells also an unwritten memorial of them, graven not on stone but in the hearts of men. Make them your examples, and, esteeming courage to be freedom and freedom to be happiness, do not weigh too nicely the perils of war. The unfortunate who has no hope of a change for the better has less reason to throw away his life than the prosperous who, if he survive, is always liable to change for the worse, and to whom any accidental fall makes the most serious difference. To a man of spirit, cowardice and disaster coming together are far more bitter than death striking him unperceived at a time when he is full of courage and animated by the general hope.

(Translated by Benjamin Jowett, *Thucydides*, Clarendon Press, Oxford, 1900.)

(e) A different view of Periclean democracy was expressed by an unknown author, generally called the "Old Oligarch".

Introduction: The Athenian democracy is a good thing if you believe in democracy, which I do not.

1 As for the government of the Athenians, the form they chose I do not approve of, and for this reason, that in choosing it they chose that scoundrels should become better off than decent citizens. This, then, is the reason for my disapproval. But since this is the course that seemed satisfactory to them, I shall point out how well they preserve their form of government, and what their other practices are in which they *seem* to the rest of Greece to be in error.

The people, who fight for the state, argue that they should reap its profits without sharing its responsibilities.

2 In the first place, then, I say that it seems only right that the poor and the common people there should have more than the well born and well-to-do; for this reason, that it is the common people who row the ships and gird the city about with strength: helmsmen, coxswains, ship-captains, bow-lookouts, shipwrights— it is these who surround the city with power far more than the heavy-armed troops, the well born, and the decent citizens. This being the case, it seems just that all should share in ruling, both in election by lot and in voting by the show of hands, and that any one of the citizens who pleases should have the right to speak in the Assembly.

3 Then again, such offices as bring security to the whole state when they are well administered, but risk when they are not—these the common people want no part of. (For example, they do not think that they ought to share by lot in the responsibility of generalship or cavalry command.) The people know that there is more profit for them in not holding such offices personally, but in letting men of position hold them. But whatever offices there are which involve pay and making private profit, these are the ones which the common people seek to control.

The cornerstone of democracy is consideration for the working class.

4 Again, there are those who are surprised because in all cases they give a larger share to the rascals, the poor, and the popular party than to the decent citizens; but in this very case they are obviously safeguarding popular government. For when the poor, the common people, or the worse element are well off, and the number who become so is large, this increases the power of the democracy, whereas if the rich and the decent prosper, the popular party is then strengthening its own opposition. *5* Everywhere the best people are opposed to democracy, because among the best element there is least excess and injustice, and most self-discipline to useful ends. Among the people, on the other hand, ignorance is at its height, as well as disorder and vulgarity. For poverty, lack of education, and in some cases the ignorance which arises from lack of money lead them more to unseemly conduct.

Free speech may make for bad government, but bad government keeps the people masters.

6 Someone may say that they all ought not to be allowed to speak one after another, or to deliberate as senators, but only the shrewdest, and the aristocrats, but in this case too they take best counsel for themselves by letting the rascals speak too. For if the decent people were to do the speaking and the deliberating, for those who were like themselves it would be advantageous, but not so for the popular party. But as it is, any scoundrel who pleases can get up, say his say, and get what is good for him and his like. *7* It might well be asked, "What that is good for himself or for the state would such a man know?" But the people know that this man's ignorance, commonness, and good will profit them more than the virtue, wisdom, and disaffection of the conservative. *8* Perhaps it is not as a result of such practices that a state becomes perfect, but this is the way democracy would be best preserved. For what the people want is not that they should be enslaved in a well-ordered city, but that they should be free and that they should rule; and bad government concerns them but little. For what *you* think makes bad government makes the people strong and free. *9* But if you are looking for good government, first of all you will see to it that the shrewdest men impose the laws on the common people; next, the decent people will make the vulgar cads behave, the decent people will take counsel for the state, and they will not allow madmen to sit in the Senate, make speeches, or sit in the Assembly. But note that as a consequence of these reforms the people would very quickly be degraded to slavery.

(MacKendrick and Howe, *op. cit.,* pp. 224–225—translation by Paul Mac-Kendrick.)

CHAPTER 4

The Fourth Century and Pan-Hellenism to 336 B.C.

The 4th century saw the March of the 10,000, the break-up of the Spartan supremacy, the restoration of the Athenian Empire, the dissolution of Theban ascendancy, and the reduction of Hellas to a group of warring states. It was also marked by social and economic revolutions, and by the growth of a "Pan-Hellenism" which called upon the Greeks to cease civil war and to march, united, against Persia. But unity, when it came, was imposed by Philip of Macedon.

The Spartan Supremacy: 404–371 B.C.

For twenty-three years Sparta remained the dominant power in Hellas, but she was not fitted to rule. Her ideals were narrowly patriotic and brutal, and the Greeks soon became restless under her military governors (*harmosts*) and the *decarchies* (oligarchic supporters of Lysander) which were set up in the cities. Athens threw off the yoke, others followed, and war succeeded war.

Thrasybulus and the Restoration of Athenian Democracy: 403–401 B.C.

The Thirty Tyrants of Athens, under the leadership of Critias and in the pretence of restoring the ancient constitution, became a despotism of confiscations and executions. In all the victims totalled about 1500. A patriot, Thrasybulus, put himself at the head of the refugees who had fled across the border, seized Phyle on the northern frontier, captured the Piraeus, and expelled the tyrants. The Spartan garrison was withdrawn and the democracy restored. In a number of other cities Lysander's decarchies were overthrown, particularly since Lysander had fallen out of favor in his homeland. Sparta was already in difficulties.

191

The March of the Ten Thousand: 401–399 B.C.

An amazing episode of the period was the march of the ten thousand, as recounted by the Athenian historian, Xenophon, in his *Anabasis*. The march began when Cyrus, the younger brother of the Persian king, decided to revolt. In 401 B.C. with a large Persian force and some 13,000 Greek mercenaries he set out for the Persian capital. At the battle of Cunaxa near Babylon, thanks to his Greeks, Cyrus defeated his brother but was killed in the moment of victory. The leaders of the Greeks were then treacherously murdered during a parley. Instead of surrendering, the Hellenes elected ten new leaders, of whom Xenophon was one, and fought and marched through hostile forces, mountain passes, and snow-clad uplands to Trapezus (modern Trebizond) on the Black Sea.

This march of the ten thousand was a remarkable exhibition of the Hellenic spirit. Even more significant was the proof that a comparatively small Greek force could penetrate deep into the Persian Empire, win a victory over forces greatly superior in numbers, and fight and march its way back. Cyrus' expedition was a sort of preview of the conquests of Alexander the Great.

Agesilaus in Asia Minor

When the 10,000 returned early in 399 B.C., they found Sparta and the Persian satraps of Asia Minor at war. The conflict was precipitated when the Persians, in accordance with their treaty with Sparta, began to take over the Greek cities of Asia Minor. The cities appealed to Sparta, and Sparta, changing its mind, sent in an army, which Xenophon and others of the 10,000 joined.

The war lagged until the arrival of Agesilaus, the lame king of Sparta, in 396 B.C. He freed the Ionian cities and raided far inland until he dreamed of conquering the whole of Asia Minor. But in 394 B.C. events in Greece recalled him.

War in Greece: 395–387 B.C.

Dissatisfaction with Spartan rule had risen rapidly in Greece. It came to a head in 395 B.C. when Locris and Phocis quarreled. Thebes supported those opposing Sparta. Lysander, the victor of Aegospotamoi, was defeated and killed in the first battle of the ensuing war and Thebes was joined by Athens, Argos, and even Corinth, Sparta's old ally. Hence came the recall of Agesilaus. Though he won two engagements, his success was overshadowed by the achievements of Conon, the Athenian admiral who had escaped from Aegospotamoi and had entered the service of Persia. After inducing Rhodes to revolt from Sparta, he led a Persian fleet to a shattering victory (394 B.C.) over the Spartan navy off Cnidus, then sailed to Athens, which had secretly sent him rowers and money, and, with Persian gold, rebuilt the Long Walls and the fortifications of the Piraeus. Meanwhile, since Sparta no longer controlled the Aegean, Athens regained the Islands of Scyros, Imbros, and Lemnos and once more had access to the Hellespont and the Black Sea trade. Within a decade after their disastrous defeat, the Athenians were once more on the march.

There followed a barren conflict known as the Corinthian War. Iphicrates, an Athenian, won a victory over a Spartan force, using light-armed troops in rough terrain, and Athens, completing a new navy, began to spread over the Aegean area.

The Persians had helped finance the anti-Spartan uprising. Now Sparta appealed to the Persian king. The result was the so-called "Kings' Peace", or Peace of Antalcidas (387 B.C.). To hear its terms the envoys of the Greek states were summoned to Sardis, a humiliating reminder that Persia was now dictating Greek affairs. By the terms of the peace, the Asia Minor Greeks were given to the Persians, Athens was to be allowed to retain Lemnos, Imbros, and Scyros, and autonomy was to be assured for all other Greek cities.

Spartan Aggression: 386–371 B.C.

Left free to operate under the King's Peace, since it forced Thebes, Athens, and Corinth to dissolve their alliances but permitted Sparta to retain her Peloponnesian League, Sparta now dominated Greece with an eye solely to her own interests. The citizens of Mantinea in Arcadia were forced to raze their walls and return to habitation in four country villages. In the north, in Chalcidice, Sparta compelled the dissolution of the Olynthiac Confederacy. Nearer home, in 383 B.C. she seized the citadel of Thebes. She even formed an alliance with Syracuse in Sicily.

When Sparta seemed at her strongest, she fell. Destruction came from Thebes. Here, in 379 B.C., a band of patriots, led by Epaminondas and Pelopidas, disguising themselves as women so as to be admitted to the citadel, assassinated the oligarchic rulers and effected a democratic revolution, all in one night. War followed. Thebes was joined by Athens because the Spartans had attempted to seize Piraeus.

The New Athenian Confederacy: 377–338 B.C.

With war in progress the Athenians formed a new Athenian maritime league. Between 377–374 B.C. about seventy states in the Aegean and from the Hellespont to western Greece joined Athens. Tribute and cleruchies were forbidden and the association was for trade and war.

Its Congress sat at Athens but Athens did not have a vote. Instead the decisions made by the Congress were referred to the Athenian Assembly and, if approved there, became law. In this second Athenian Confederacy, Athens shared power equally with her allies.

Leuctra and the Theban Supremacy: 371–362 B.C.

A number of conferences failed to bring about peace and meanwhile Epaminondas built a well-trained Theban army headed by the Sacred Band of 300 young men who had sworn to win or die together. Athens, fearful of the growing power of her ally, changed sides. Finally a Spartan army marched against Thebes. The decisive battle was fought at Leuctra in Boeotia in 371 B.C. This battle marked a revolution in Greek tactics. Until this time two phalanxes of hoplites had crashed together all along the line and success had gone to the better trained or more numerous troops. The Spartans themselves, despite the destruction of a regiment by Iphicrates in the Corinthian War, had not met defeat in a pitched battle on a fair field for over two centuries. But Epaminondas, the Theban leader, massed on his left, facing the Spartan contingent of the Lacedaemonian army, a column of men fifty files deep instead of the usual eight, and echeloned the rest of his army (that is, drew them up line obliquely behind line) in such a way that, in military parlance, he "refused his flank." When battle was joined his column crashed through the Spartan right like a battering-ram. The rest of his infantry was hardly in the fight. Sparta lost one of its kings and 1000 hoplites of whom 400 were Spartiates. So sadly had Spartan man-power been depleted that scarcely 1000 Spartiates fit to bear arms remained.

Thebes, in its turn, was supreme in Greece. In a few short years Mantinea was rebuilt, a new city, Megalopolis, was erected in Arcadia to check Sparta, Messenia was re-established as a separate state, and the whole of Thessaly joined the Theban alliance. But the Theban power rested on two men, Pelopidas and Epaminondas. Pelopidas was killed in Thessaly. Then, in 362 B.C., Epaminondas won a victory at Mantinea but was mortally wounded. With his death the Theban hegemony vanished. Greece collapsed into groups of warring states with no group strong enough to impose its will on the others. The Athenian Confederacy was dissolved during a war between Athens and its allies (357–355 B.C.), a war which had been caused by a new Athenian imperialism. The Greek cities had autonomy but were too weak to do anything effective. Meanwhile there was inflation (prices doubled and trebled during the 4th Century), violent class-struggles, and social and economic revolutions. The way was being paved for Philip of Macedon.

The Greeks in the West: 404–338 B.C.

While the Greeks in the homeland were fighting each other, in the West there had been struggles against Carthage and the rule of two outstanding tyrants. After the Syracusans had repelled the Athenians in 413 B.C., they had been too exhausted to maintain their control over the other Greek cities in Sicily. As a result the Carthaginians, eager to avenge their defeat at Himera, attacked, and in 409 B.C. Selinus, Himera, and Acragas fell to them.

The terror inspired in the Greeks made it possible for Dionysius, the son of a mule-driver, who had been first a clerk and then a leader of mercenaries, to become tyrant of Syracuse in 405 B.C. Before his death in 367 B.C. he had established an empire in Sicily and southern Italy, driving the Carthaginians to the western tip of Sicily and occupying the whole toe of Italy. Later he founded colonies in Illyricum and on the eastern coast of Italy, seized Elba, and sent settlers to Corsica. Although a renewed war with Carthage was not concluded when he died, Dionysius left Syracuse the strongest Greek state in the west. During his lifetime he took a definite interest in the affairs of mainland Greece. Plato, the philosopher, visited his court but disagreed with the tyrant and was made a slave until ransomed.

Dionysius was succeeded by his son, Dionysius II. The empire soon fell apart and civil wars followed. Finally, in 344 B.C., a Corinthian, Timoleon, was invited to reform Syracuse. Timoleon established a moderate democracy, drove back the resurgent Carthaginians, and then retired to private life in 338 B.C. It was twenty years before a new Carthaginian threat set up another Syracusan dictator.

The New Pan-Hellenism

While Hellas had been occupied with its dreary round of wars, a growing group of people had been urging that the Greek states forget internal strife and unite against Persia. Back in the 5th Century B.C. the Sophist, Gorgias, had tried to emphasize the fundamental unity of all Greeks, and the historian, Thucydides, had looked upon the Peloponnesian War as a fratricidal struggle. Then, about 390 B.C., the orator, Isocrates, opened a school in Athens which became a center of propaganda for Pan-Hellenism. Isocrates himself was the most prominent voice. At the Olympic Games of 380 B.C., in his *Panegyric*, he spoke strongly for the idea that the Greeks should abandon their quarrels and unite in a war against Persia.

When propaganda failed to bring the Greeks together, Isocrates began to look for an outsider to lead them against Persia. In 368 B.C. he even sent a letter to Dionysius I of Syracuse inviting him to assume the rôle.

As a result of the propaganda of Isocrates and his converts by the time
the Theban supremacy ended, there was a strong movement throughout
the Greek world to end the strife among the Greek states by uniting in
an expedition against Persia. Once more the way was being paved for
Philip of Macedon, and when Philip ended Greek freedom at Chaeronea,
Isocrates, now ninety-eight years of age, sent him a letter of congratulation
in which he again advised immediate war against Persia.

Philip of Macedon

The Macedonians were composed of approximately the same racial
ingredients as the Greeks and spoke a dialect of Greek, but they were
regarded by the Hellenes as barbarians. During the 5th century B.C.
alliances with their kings were sought by both Athens and Sparta. But
not until Philip reached the throne in 359 B.C. did Macedonia become
a force in Greek politics.

Few kings have had stronger and more contradictory qualities than
Philip of Macedon. He admired and copied Greek culture, and in intellectual ability he was superior to most of his opponents. Machiavellian in
his statesmanship and policies, knowing when to seduce by bribery,
when to advance or retreat, and when to strike with violence, he was
more than a match for the Greeks. As a hostage in Thebes from fifteen
to eighteen years of age, he learned the military science and tactics of
Epaminondas and put them to good use in the invention of the
Macedonian phalanx. In that phalanx the men were in fewer ranks with
three feet between each man so that changes in formation and manoeuvres
were possible. The soldiers were armed, too, with the *sarissa*, a pike
sixteen feet long as compared to the usual eight-foot spear of the Greek
hoplite. When the Macedonian phalanx advanced, five pike-points projected beyond the first rank. Philip also introduced heavy cavalry, the
so-called Companions, as a striking force, while his more lightly armed
cavalry and infantry were trained to act in close conjunction with the
phalanx. In this way Philip produced the most efficient fighting-force of
his day, while at the same time he strove to Hellenize his people. One
of his ambitions seems to have been to be recognized as a Hellene by the
Hellenes. Yet, in spite of his subtlety and his intellectual abilities, there
was in him a strong streak of barbarism which showed itself in drunken
orgies and wild savageries. Wholesale treacheries were native to him,
and he boasted that he could capture any city if he could drive a mule
laden with gold inside its walls.

Such was the man who set as his goal the domination of Greece. The
road to success was tortuous. By intrigues, by treachery, by breaking his
word time after time, by bribery and the formation of pro-Macedonian

parties among his foes (Philip anticipated the "fifth-column" technique of modern times), by advances and retreats, he finally, through the Greek civil wars, got himself a strong footing in Hellas. His major opponent was the Athenian orator, Demosthenes. For thirteen years Demosthenes strove to awaken Athens and Hellas to the danger of Philip, but his efforts were fruitless. By 346 B.C. Philip had conquered Chalcidice, occupied Thessaly, and, by defeating the Phocians in the so-called Sacred War, had won for himself a place on the Amphictyonic Council, of which the function was to protect the revenues and neutrality of the oracle of Apollo at Delphi. Philip had now broken into the center of Greece. Athens under Demosthenes strove to check him. After a war in the Thracian Chersonnesus (Dardanelles) in which Athens was successful, Philip, by the invitation of the Amphictyonic Council, suddenly appeared once more in Central Greece. Thebes and Athens took the field against him.

The decisive battle was fought at Chaeronea in Boeotia. The two armies were of about equal size, 32,000 men each. But Macedonian generalship was superior. Alexander, Philip's son, commanding the Macedonian heavy cavalry, broke the Theban Sacred Band. The Athenians, among whom was Demosthenes, were deceived by a feigned flight, drawn into a trap, and routed. One thousand of them were killed and twice that number taken prisoner, while Alexander's cavalry and Philip's phalanx annihilated the Sacred Band. Where they fell a stone lion stands today.

In victory Philip was comparatively moderate. Thebes was treated with severity but Athens was offered liberal peace terms. Although she lost her possessions in the Thracian Chersonnesus, her prisoners were returned without ransom, and she was received into alliance. Demosthenes was not touched. The fact remained that Philip could now dictate to Hellas. Only Sparta refused to submit.

Philip and the Congress of Corinth: 338–337 B.C.

Philip now summoned all states south of Thermopylae to send delegates to a congress at Corinth, with the objective of organizing a Pan-Hellenic union and a war against Persia, a sure proof of the spread of the influence of those who had been arguing for Pan-Hellenism. All states conformed except Sparta.

At this congress the League of Corinth was established. By its terms each state retained its autonomy but there were to be no more wars between them, and violent social or economic revolutions were forbidden. Each state was to furnish supplies and troops, both to punish any state which violated the rules of the League and for the projected campaign against Persia. The affairs of the League were to be administered by a federal council. Collectively the League entered into an alliance with Macedonia, which was not a member of the League. The domination by Macedonia, however, was made clear by the fact that the forces of the League were to be commanded by Philip *and his descendants*.

In this way the peace and unity which the Greeks had not been able to achieve by themselves was forced upon them. Philip began preparations for his campaign against Persia. At this point his private life overtook him. He had had several wives, among them Olympias, a beautiful and strong-willed princess of Epirus, who was the mother of Alexander. Philip, however, decided to take another new wife. At the marriage banquet he asked his nobles to pray that this one would give him a "legitimate" heir. Alexander, who was present, hurled his wine-cup at the face of the bride's uncle and Philip made for his son with drawn sword but tripped and fell. Alexander and his mother fled from the court. It was probably not a coincidence that a year later, in 336 B.C., at a wedding feast just as he was about to leave for Asia, Philip was assassinated by one of his courtiers. Alexander, at twenty years of age, won over the army and succeeded to the throne of Macedonia.

Summary

In this period, from the end of the Peloponnesian War to the assassination of Philip, Sparta and Thebes in turn tried to weld Greece into unity and failed, while Athens, rising from the ashes of her defeat, once more established herself as a commercial and political force. Once Greece had dissolved into a coterie of warring states, the idea of a Pan-Hellenism to unite all Hellas against Persia gained strength, and there were attempts to draw Sicily and the west into the scheme. But Syracuse was too much occupied by her struggles with Carthage to look eastward for long, and it was finally Philip of Macedon who imposed a league to prevent war among the Greek states and then prepared to lead them against Persia.

In the meantime, strong social and economic changes marked by inflated prices, debts, and class struggles were preparing the Greek world for the Hellenistic era which was to follow. Culturally the Greek contribution to civilization did not lessen. Sculpture chose more sensuous and individualistic themes, 4th century tragedy was inferior to that of the 5th century and comedy took on a new form, but Greek philosophy reached its apex in Plato and Aristotle. The 5th century B.C. is often called the first classical period and the 4th century the second. As far as basic ideals and techniques are concerned, the two centuries should be considered not as separate periods but as a single, continuing expression of the Hellenic genius.

Readings from Sources of the Period

(a) Thucydides describes the demoralization caused by the struggles between democrats and oligarchs during the Peloponnesian War, but his description is also applicable to Fourth Century Greece.

Party strife, then, brought a host of troubles upon the Greek cities, troubles which of course have recurred and will always recur as long as human nature remains the same, but which, if anything, are likely to be less severe and take different forms according to the different way in which circumstances change at one period or another. By this I mean that in times of peace and prosperity states and individuals alike have kinder dispositions, because they are not forced into want and privation; whereas war, by stripping life of its ordinary margin of comfort, keeps a hard school and generally shapes men's feelings to match their present circumstances.

Not only were the cities racked by civil war but the latecomers, hearing what had already been done before them, carried the progressive radicalization of thought to even further extremes by refining on previous methods of attack and inventing unheard-of forms of reprisal. They also reversed the customary application of words to actions as they saw fit. Harebrained recklessness now became the courage of a true party member; prudent hesitation, cowardice under a nicer name; self-restraint, an excuse for lack of manly spirit; and intelligence in any respect, supineness in all respects. Impulsiveness and vehemence were taken as the mark of a man, and an attempt at caution in laying a plot was a specious pretext for desertion. An angry man was to be trusted every time; anyone who opposed him was under suspicion. To bring off an intrigue was a sign of intelligence, to suspect one, a sign of genius, while the man who planned things so as not to need all this was a wrecker of the party and browbeaten by the opposition. In general there were two ways to win respect and approval: to anticipate someone else in a crime, or to urge him to one before he thought of it himself.

(MacKendrick and Howe, *op. cit.,* pp. 246–7, translated by Paul Mac-Kendrick.)

(b) The chief antagonist in Greece of Philip of Macedon was the Athenian orator, Demosthenes (384–322 B.C.). The extract below comes from his *Third Philippic*, delivered before the Assembly of the Athenians in 341 B.C.

1 Men of Athens, many speeches are delivered in almost every session of the Assembly regarding the crimes Philip has been committing ever since he made the peace, not merely against you but against the others as well. All, I am sure, even if they refrain from doing so, might well say that our words and acts should aim to compel him to abandon his wanton insolence and make amends. Yet, I observe, our undertakings are so misdirected and neglected that, even if it be blasphemy to say so, I fear it is true that, were all who address you eager to propose, and you to adopt, measures bound to result in the most deplorable conditions, we could not be worse off than we are today.

First, let us ourselves take steps for our defense, let us equip ourselves—I mean with ships and funds and troops—for though all others consent to be slaves, we at least must fight for our freedom. *71* When we have provided ourselves with all these things and have made them matters of public knowledge, then let us issue a call to the others and send envoys everywhere to spread the news—to the Peloponnese, to Rhodes, to Chios, yes, to the Persian King, for it is not wholly unconnected with his interests that Philip be prevented from becoming master of the world.

(*Ibid.*, pp. 287-288, translated by H. Lamar Crosby.)

(c) Xenophon in his *Hellenica* relates how the women of Sparta received the news of the Spartan defeat at Leuctra, 367 B.C.

After these events, a messenger was despatched to Lacedaemon with news of the calamity. He reached his destination on the last day of the festival of the Naked Youths, just when the chorus of grown men had entered the theatre. The ephors heard the mournful tidings with grief and pain, as was inevitable; but for all that they did not dismiss the chorus, but allowed the contest to run out its natural course. What they did was to deliver the names of those who had fallen to their friends and families, with a word of warning to the women not to make any loud lamentation but to bear their sorrow in silence; and the next day it was a striking spectacle to see those who had relations among the slain moving to and fro in public with bright and radiant looks, while of those whose friends were reported to be living barely a man was to be seen, and these went about with lowered heads and scowling brows, as if in humiliation.

(McDermott and Caldwell, *op. cit.*, pp. 212–213.)

CHAPTER 5

The Greek Achievement in Literature, the Graphic Arts, Oratory and Rhetoric, and Philosophy

---

The great age of Greek literature ranges from Homer (800 B.C.) to Theocritus (c. 275 B.C.). Architecture and sculpture, however, did not find their supreme expression until the 5th and 4th centuries B.C.

Greek philosophy began as early as the end of the 7th century B.C. but did not reach its peak until Plato and Aristotle of the 4th century B.C. Similarly, although the Greeks had been eloquent speakers since the time of Homer, oratory and rhetoric as special subjects were not fully developed until the end of the 5th and the beginning of the 4th centuries, B.C. In all of these fields the Greeks put an indelible imprint on our western civilization.

The Achievement of Greek Literature

Literature is the eldest sister of the arts. One amazing feature of the Greek authors is that we can read them and feel that here are people who looked at life in much the same way as we do. This is by no means always true of Byzantine or Medieval writers, or, for that matter, of the authors of early Irish or Scandinavian legends. In a word, ancient Greece is the first thinking civilization before our own, and its literature inevitably reflects the culture which produced it. In the Homeric epic, even though it comes at the beginning of the Greek expression, the essential qualities of the Hellenic genius are already present—nobility, dignity, restraint of emotion, frankness, directness, excellent workmanship, and an emphasis on man. The poetry of the Formative Age of Greece maintained these qualities, even though it also bodied forth the passionate individualism of the new world around it. In the 5th century B.C. Greek literature reached its heights in drama and in history.

Fifth Century History

There had been chronicles of cities and "travelogues" written in Ionia in the 6th century B.C. The "father of history," however, was Herodotus (484–425 B.C.). Herodotus was born at Halicarnassus in Asia Minor. Probably because of a political dispute he was expelled from that city. Thereafter he roamed the ancient world, gifted with the mind of an adult and the fresh curiosity of a child. To him history (which is a Greek word) meant an "investigation" into everything and anything which attracted his interest. Therefore, he took notes on Egypt, on Babylon, on the strange customs of the Scythians, on everything he saw and heard. "I must record what was told me," he says, "but I am under no obligation to believe it all alike."

Finally he paused in Athens to write the story of the Persian Wars, although for a time he joined the Utopian colony of Thurii in Italy (443 B.C.). There is in his history a predilection for the Athenians; but on the whole his account is without bias, setting down the good and bad qualities of both Greeks and Persians. To him the defeat of the Persians proved that "free men fight better than slaves" and that the gods destroy the prosperous and the arrogant.

Because Herodotus concentrated on a single theme, the struggle between East and West, and because he possessed a theory of history and, to a certain degree, analyzed motives and effects with objectivity, he is regarded as the ancestor of the European school of the writing of history. His eight books on the Persian Wars (the division into books was made after 300 B.C. in the Hellenistic period), however, are not a modern type of history. In the first five, there is a travelogue around the Persian Empire, and throughout the whole of the history there is little attempt to sift material or to arrive at the truth. Furthermore, Herodotus seasons his narrative profusely with anecdotes, legends, oracular pronouncements, strange customs, vivid stories, and hearsay information. As he himself writes his purpose was to entertain as well as to instruct. As a result his history is fascinating. One learns how Danube islanders get drunk on smells, how big Babylon was, or why Egyptian men go to bed when their wives have babies. One can read how the clever thief came to marry the King of Egypt's daughter. When the Persian Wars are described, there is a highly personalized account of Marathon, Thermopylae, Salamis, and Plataea. Tales of strange happenings and adventures, books of anecdotes, and the short story all trace their ancestry to Herodotus. We ought to note, however, that his account is our best source for the events of the

Persian Wars, and that the credibility of many of Herodotus' odd bits of information is more highly regarded than it used to be.

With Thucydides, (471–401 B.C.) we enter a different world. Thucydides was an Athenian admiral in the Peloponnesian War until he was exiled for losing Amphipolis in Thrace (424 B.C.). With him the art of writing history in the modern sense was born. As he himself tells us, he went to great trouble to collect and sift facts so as to get at the truth in his *History of the Peloponnesian War*. He frankly admits that in the speeches he reports, he sometimes put down what the speaker might or ought to have said, while adhering as closely as possible to what was actually spoken. He analyzes the motives behind events. He also makes comments on human nature and political movements which are as true today as when he made them. His picture of civil and ideological strife in Corcyra is a horrifying preview of what has happened time after time in our own world. In a word, when we read Thucydides, we are amazed at how modern he is.

Fourth Century Historians

The historians of the 4th century B.C. attempted to emulate Thucydides and failed. The Athenian, Xenophon (434–354 B.C.), a follower of the philosopher Socrates, had joined in the March of the Ten Thousand and chronicled that march in his *Anabasis*. His service under Agesilaus, the lame king of Sparta, led to banishment from Athens and an estate at Scillus near Olympia in 387 B.C. Here Xenophon lived as a country gentleman until Scillus was destroyed by the Eleans in 371 B.C. The last years of his life were spent in Corinth.

Well-bred, educated, rich, conservative, a soldier and a sportsman, conventional in religion and morals, and a cosmopolitan, his writings were popular in his own day. In addition to the *Anabasis*, he wrote a eulogistic biography of Agesilaus. His recollections of Socrates were put down in his *Memorabilia*, a more down to earth picture of the philosopher than the portrait in the dialogues of Plato. His description of the education of the ideal prince, Cyrus the Great of Persia, in his *Cyropaedia* was really an historical romance, while at the same time it emphasized the degeneracy of the Persians of Xenophon's own day. He issued a spate of essays on agriculture, household economy (the *Oikonomika*), public finance, hunting, and the like. A more ambitious effort was his *Hellenica*, a history of Greece from 411 (where the history of Thucydides ended) to 362 B.C. In the days when every schoolboy learned Greek, the *Anabasis* and *Hellenica* initiated them into its mysteries. Though Xenophon's works lack the depth and insight of Thucydides' writing, the style is smooth and easy.

Among the many other historians of the 4th century the most famous was Theopompus, born about 378 B.C. on the island of Chios. His principal work was a history of Greece from its earliest times to 334 B.C., the year in which Alexander the Great invaded Asia.

Oratory and Rhetoric

To judge from Homer's epics the Greeks had always prized eloquence, and, except for the Spartans, they seem to have been inveterate orators and talkers. At Athens, in particular, once democracy was established, to be able to speak well and persuasively was of prime importance. Attic oratory as a conscious art, however, owed its development to the Sophists. On the one hand, Sophists such as Protagoras from Abdera taught dialectic or methods of argumentation, and, on the other, Sophists like Gorgias from Sicily, who visited Athens in 427 B.C., emphasized the devices of rhetoric, such as flowery diction, antithesis, and the correspondence of sound and form. From this time forward Athens became the center of the art of speaking.

The first Athenian to publish his speeches as literature was Antiphon, the teacher of the historian Thucydides (and hence the complex nature of the speeches in Thucydides' history). Antiphon's rhetoric is austere and forensic. Similarly the speeches of Lysias, which belong to the first two decades of the 4th century, were plain, vigorous, and free from over-elaboration. Lysias was a metic, who joined the Athenian exiles under Thrasybulus and as a result was granted Athenian citizenship. A number of his speeches were written for clients in the Athenian law-courts where, as you have learned, the prosecutor and defendant had to present their cases in person. As a result the profession of speech-writing had arisen from the problem of having to write a speech for a client to deliver which would fit his character, appearance, and education.

With Isocrates, the Pan-Hellenist, Attic oratory came to maturity. His orations followed the showy style of Gorgias and were works of art, characterized by balanced, periodic sentences, parallelism, eloquent diction, prose rhythms, and a wealth of adornment. Though Isocrates spoke in public, his orations were intended to be read. He was a stylist, publicist, and educator rather than a pleader before a court or Assembly. His school for orators and statesmen, established about 390 B.C., added to his influence on the politics of the day. In Roman times he was imitated by the orator Cicero.

The king of orators was Demosthenes, the Athenian, who led the opposition to Philip of Macedon. Everyone knows the stories of how, weak in voice and with a tendency to stammer, Demosthenes used to put pebbles in his mouth and declaim against the waves, or how he would run uphill repeating verses of the poets as he ran. Like Lysias he wrote speeches for clients. His most tremendous achievements were his public addresses, particularly those in which he attacked Philip (from which a word, *Philippic*, "biting invective", has come to us) or his *Olynthiacs* in which he urged Athens to oppose the aggressor. In these addresses his literary genius, flaming patriotism, and mastery of all the arts of persuasion reach their heights. He could use picturesque imagery and sudden surprises and range from scurrilous invective to the sublime.

Demosthenes' most vivid opponent, the leader of the peace party, Aeschines, was also a master of eloquence. But, when Aeschines attacked Demosthenes obliquely over a golden crown decreed to him in 337 B.C. by his fellow-citizens for his services to Athens, Demosthenes crushed his opponent in his memorable oration *On the Crown*. Demosthenes in Athens and Cicero in Rome were the two most famous orators of antiquity.

Biography

There had been sketches and analyses of people in Herodotus and Thucydides, such as the latter's estimate of Themistocles. Biography as a separate form of literature did not begin until Isocrates published his panegyric on Evagoras, the king of Cyprus. Isocrates also brought out an autobiography toward the end of his life. Xenophon, too, was writing biography when he produced his *Agesilaus*. This form of literature owes its genesis to the Greeks.

The Origin and Development of Greek Tragedy

The supreme expression of 5th century Athenian literature was in its drama, a Doric word which means, "a doing or acting." (Our word poetry comes from the Ionic word *poieo* which also means "I do" or "I make.") The Greek word *tragoedia* from which our word tragedy is derived, means "The Song of the Goats."

The obscure origins of Greek tragedy, therefore, appear to go back to choral song-dances in which people dressed as goat-men (Satyrs) sang and danced at community festivals in honor of the god Pan. The dancers probably mimed the reproductive process by which herds and flocks and all nature are increased, for Pan was a nature and fertility deity of the woodland wild. In Greek his name means "all" or "everything." From him, too, our word "panic" is derived since the Greeks attributed to him the inexplicable terror which, at times, seizes humanity in solitary places or leaps suddenly upon armies.

Yet the god of drama was not Pan but Dionysus. This deity seems to have begun his career in Asia Minor as a god who, like the Egyptian Osiris, personified the death and revival of vegetation. In consequence, again like Osiris, he became the god of an immortality cult. But, as in the case of other deities of a similar type, he was also a nature and fertility god. Wild animals and a retinue of Maenads, Satyrs, and Sileni (drunken old men) attended him. From Asia Minor his worship spread into Thrace whence it was imported into Greece early in the 6th Century B.C. To judge from the legend of Pentheus, King of Thebes, who was said to have been torn to pieces by his mother and the women of Thebes when he tried to stop their wild revels in the mountains, the Dionysiac worship at first produced disturbances. Finally, the cult, as we shall see later, was merged with the Eleusinian mysteries and immortality was promised to the worshippers of Dionysus. According to the myth, Dionysus was sent by Zeus to reclaim the Titans. But the Titans, after Dionysus had changed himself into a bull, killed him and ate his flesh. Next, Zeus consumed the Titans with his lightning and from the ashes created the present race of men. Thus, each man had a spark of the divine Dionysus enclosed within an earthly and sinful body. Those worshippers, however, who remained pure through three reincarnations were granted immortality in the Elysian fields while sinners went to Tartarus (the Greek Hell).

This aspect of Dionysiac worship is often called Orphism from Orpheus, the Thracian singer whom rocks, trees, and animals followed, and who had been incorporated into the cult of Dionysus. Its doctrine of a pure soul in an evil body, of judgment after death for deeds done in the flesh along with rewards and punishments, and of personal immortality produced a genuinely spiritual religion. Its orgiastic features remained. At sacramental feasts the Dionysiac worshippers believed that by eating the flesh of a bull and drinking wine to represent the blood of Dionysus, they became "one with the god" and revelled in processions such as the one described in the *Frogs* of Aristophanes. Dionysus was, therefore, the god of the grape and his worshippers are often depicted as Satyrs, Maenads, and Sileni, carrying the thyrsus (a branch of the vine with clusters of grapes on it) in scenes painted on Greek vases.

The cult of Dionysus, under the name of Bacchus, was carried across the sea to Italy. Its orgiastic rites, and its exaltation of the need for individual salvation over a citizen's duty to the state, offended the Roman authorities. As related by the Roman historian, Livy, in 186–180 B.C., they tried to stamp out the cult by a bitter persecution. But the Dionysiac cult survived as well as the more general worship of Bacchus as god of wine. In the Villa of the Mysteries near Pompeii (buried like the town by the 79 A.D. eruption from Vesuvius), there was found a magnificent mural which is believed to represent the Dionysiac mysteries of the First Century A.D.

The connection of Dionysus with drama came from the song-dances in his honor (dithyrambs) which were danced and sung by a chorus of fifty dressed as Maenads, Satyrs, and Sileni. The Greek philosopher, Aristotle, in his *Poetics*, tells us that Arion of Corinth fused the dithyramb to Dionysus with the goatsong (*tragoedia*) in honor of Pan. Arion was also said to have introduced in the intervals of the dithyramb interludes in which the leader of the chorus, putting on a different mask at each appearance so as to represent various characters, such as Dionysus or Zeus or a Titan, spoke in recitative to the chorus and audience. In this way a story apart from the song-dance could be told. Then, when in 535 B.C. Thespis produced the first European drama in Athens, he added to the dithyrambic chorus an actor (in Greek, *hypocrites*, "an answerer") to talk with the leader of the chorus. In this way dialogue began.

From this time forward, the development in the form of tragedy was rapid. Aeschylus (525–456 B.C.), the first great Attic tragedian, added a second actor so that the dialogue was independent of the chorus and reduced the chorus from fifty to twelve. In his time, too, each poet presented a *tetralogy* (four plays), consisting of a linked trilogy (three plays on a single theme, as in the *Oresteia*), and a satyr drama which retained the obscenity of the original worship. Aeschylus' younger contemporary, Sophocles, (c. 495–406 B.C.) introduced a third actor and raised the number of the chorus to fifteen. But, whereas in Aeschylus' plays the choral songs sometimes overshadowed the dialogue, Sophocles reduced the rôle of the chorus to that of an "ideal spectator," that is, it expressed the feelings the audience was supposed to have about the scenes unfolding before it on the stage. He likewise abandoned the linked trilogy so that each of his plays is a complete unit.

The third of the great Attic tragedians, Euripides (484–406 B.C.), found the form and subject matter of tragedy established. However, he made extensive use of prologues in his plays, introduced novel musical effects and moved toward a five-act structure with the choral songs as interludes.

Such, in outline, was the genesis and early development of the earliest European drama. There is another point to notice. Of the six men ranked as the supreme writers of tragic drama in western civilization, there is one Englishman, Shakespeare, and two Germans, Goethe and Schiller. The other three all lived in the same century in the tiny country of Attica.

The Attic Tragedians

Of the three supreme Attic dramatists Aeschylus, who had fought at Marathon, was the "Thunderer." His style is majestic and his choral songs strongly masculine. In his *Prometheus Bound* he presents a single dramatic situation in which Prometheus, the Titan, who brought fire to men against the will of Zeus, is still defiant, even though he is to be punished by being chained to a rock in the Caucasus while each day vultures peck at his eternally renewed liver. The theme is the classic one of authority versus the individual. In his proud defiance of Zeus Prometheus reminds one of Lucifer in Milton's *Paradise Lost*. His attitude is in sharp contrast to the submission of Job to God in the book of that name in the Bible and, in this respect illustrates one of the differences between Hebraism and Hellenism.

The *Prometheus Bound* is the middle play of a linked trilogy of which the other two are lost (*Prometheus, the Fire-Bringer* and *Prometheus Unbound*). But we know that in the *Prometheus Unbound* a compromise was effected between Zeus and Prometheus. We do, however, have a complete trilogy in the *Oresteia (Agamemnon, Choephoroe, Eumenides)*. From this trilogy, best of all, we get our impression of the tremendous power and majesty of Aeschylean drama. Disaster is piled on disaster. The question which Aeschylus poses is: Why do the innocent suffer along with the guilty? His solution, as seen in the *Oresteia* is that when a man becomes rich and powerful he comes to feel that he is above the law. In this frame of mind he commits an act of arrogance (Greek, *hubris*) and this offends the gods. They, therefore, let loose upon the man and his family an evil Fury (*Ate*, a personified Doom), which pursues not only the sinner but all his family until either the family is wiped out or expiation is made. Thus, in the *Agamemnon*, Agamemnon, who has sacrificed his daughter with his own hand, is murdered by his wife, Clytemnestra. In the next play the son, Orestes, murders his mother and in the *Eumenides* we find him driven mad and pursued by the Furies until in a trial held at Athens it is decided that expiation has been made. Sin, says Aeschylus, brings punishment not only to the sinner but to his family as well.

Few writers have surpassed Aeschylus' tremendous characterization of the "man-counselling" and unrepentant Clytemnestra in the *Agamemnon*. Yet during his lifetime he was bested by his younger rival, Sophocles, called by Jebb, "the mellow glory of the Attic stage." Handsome, rich, twice general of the Athenians, he won more first prizes in tragedy (twenty) than anyone else. Where Aeschylus was first and foremost a preacher Sophocles was, above all, an artist. The eternal problems of humanity, such as the suffering of the innocent, affected him but he was inclined to present them as they were and say simply: "That is the way things are." Above all, in his dramas he was the master of the *peripeteia* or reversal of fortune structure. In his *Oedipus, the King*, for example, he presents to us Oedipus, a king of Thebes, who is told that to save his people from a pestilence he must find the murderer of the king who preceded him. Oedipus does not know, however, that the gods have, long ago, decided what his own destiny is to be. In pride and in pity for his people he

promises to find the murderer, and overcomes obstacle after obstacle.
At one point, he scoffs at the oracles of the gods.

Oedipus finds the murderer. This is the high point of his success. But he
discovers at the same instant that he himself is the murderer, that the
murdered man is his father and, furthermore, that, unwittingly, he has
married his mother. Thus, he has, though unknowingly, offended the basic
morality of his own people and has, besides, scoffed at the gods. The high
moment of his success becomes the moment of his ruin.

This brings on the "reversal of fortune." His mother-wife commits
suicide and Oedipus, the powerful king of Thebes, blinds himself and
goes into exile. Count no man happy, concludes Sophocles, until he dies
and, furthermore, do not think that any man can escape the destiny laid
down for him by the gods. The tragedy of Oedipus is all the more poignant
in that he acts from noble motives. The seven plays of Sophocles, which
are all we have left of the more than one hundred which he wrote,
exemplify the objectives of Greek tragedy which, according to Aristotle,
were to excite pity and terror in the beholder and thus produce a catharsis
of those emotions.

The third of the three Attic tragedians, Euripides, was not popular with
the Athenians. Aristophanes, the comic poet, claimed that Euripides was
the son of a woman who sold vegetables and of a bankrupt Boeotian
merchant, although other sources stated that he was of aristocratic birth.
Unlike Aeschylus and Sophocles, who were men of action as well as
dramatists, Euripides was a "study-poet"; that is, like many modern
authors, he concentrated on writing. This offended Athenian concepts.
In addition, Euripides was a rationalist, or sceptic, and an iconoclast
who attacked the sacred cows of his day. One of his constant themes was
the inhumanity of man toward his fellow men. In the *Trojan Women*, for
example, he portrays the fate of the Trojan women and children after
the capture of Troy by the Greeks, and thus presents the glory of war in
terms of the suffering of the vanquished. Similarly, in his *Hecuba* he shows
that the so-called justice of the gods is injustice. Plays of this sort did not
please either Athenian imperialists or religionists. He was accused, too,
of bringing gods and heroes on stage dressed as beggars, of presenting
women in love and of corrupting Athenian morals by sophistic epigrams
such as one in the Hippolytus which translates: "Twas not my soul but
just my tongue that swore."

The *Hippolytus* illustrates many of his literary devices such as the
"mechanical prologue" (a prologue spoken by a character who does not
appear again in the play), the use of two choruses, a double plot tied
together by the "recognition theme," (Theseus, after his wife, Phaedra,
has committed suicide because her step-son, Hippolytus, has refused her

advances, reads tablets written by her accusing Hippolytus of assaulting her and, consequently, drives his son from him), the employment of the *deus ex machina* (the goddess, Artemis, speaks from a cloud to tell Theseus that Hippolytus is innocent), death on stage for tear-jerking purposes, and the prominence of Phaedra's nurse in the first part of the play. (A far-distant descendant of this nurse is the one in Shakespeare's *Romeo and Juliet*.) The *Hippolytus* itself has inspired many derivatives, including the Phèdre of Racine.

The most powerful of Euripides' extant dramas is his *Medea*. Although most of his literary devices are used, the play is dominated by the portrait of the barbaric and passionate Medea and her desire for revenge on her husband, Jason. As presented on Broadway in translation in 1948, with Judith Anderson playing Medea, this play held audiences captive. Yet, during his lifetime Euripides won only five first prizes. Later, his influence on Hellenistic and Roman tragedy was immense. As a result we still possess eighteen, and possibly nineteen, of the plays he wrote, while only seven each of those by Aeschylus and Sophocles have survived. All in all we possess thirty-two tragedies of the more than 300 which these three poets wrote.

Production of Drama in 5th Century B.C. Athens

There were many other tragedians in 5th Century B.C. Athens besides these three, although only titles and fragments of their works have come down to us. Tragedy was produced in the theater of Dionysus on the south slope of the Acropolis. There, stretching up the hill, is what is left of the great theater. What remains today belongs to a theater of 340 B.C. with later Roman additions. In 5th century Athens, the theater seated between 18,000 to 20,000 spectators under the open sky. We should pause to point out that almost all Greek theaters were built on hillsides and accommodated around 15,000 people. Yet the acoustics were perfect, as can be proved at Athens or at the theater in southern Greece at Epidaurus. The seats were arranged in a huge inverted U down the side of a hill. They were in rows and were sectioned as ours are. We have ancient theater tickets, showing the section, row, and number of the seats, just as our tickets do. Next came the orchestra, either a full circle, or a three-quarter circle as at Athens. *Orchestra* means "dancing-floor", and that is what this was in the Greek theater. Here the chorus danced and sang the choral songs which were part of every drama. Behind the orchestra was a long narrow stage, with two entrances called *paradoi* for the chorus, one at each wing. Probably one or two broad, shallow steps connected the stage with the orchestra.

All action in Greek drama took place out of doors in one fixed place.

Hence we can see the importance of the messenger rôle in Greek drama to tell what has happened inside or offstage. Likewise, no curtain could be lowered to indicate that a week or ten years had gone by. All action had to take place within twenty-four hours. The choral songs filled the intervals between the scenes, or acts.

If we could be transported back to the 5th century B.C., we would also note an altar to the god Dionysus in the center of the orchestra. The drama was a religious festival and began with a sacrifice to Dionysus. Nor was there, as with us, theater all the year round. True, there were rural dramatic and choral festivals. But there were only two great public occasions, the *Lenaea*, or *Lesser Dionysia*, at about the end of January, and the *Greater* or *City Dionysia* around the end of March. Both of these were competitions. Three tragic poets presenting four plays each, and probably four writers of comedy, were picked. Prizes were given. As has been mentioned, rich men were picked by the state to bear most of the cost.

If we were in Athens on a March morning of, say, 442 B.C., from before daybreak we would find almost everyone in Athens making his way to the great theater, for the days of the Dionysiac festival are public holidays and even prisoners are released from jail to attend. There is also a fund to buy places for the poorer citizens. If we follow these people we will find the theater filling rapidly. Many spectators will be carrying lunches, for the plays go on continuously all day, one after another. The priest of Dionysus will be down front, and a row of magistrates. There will be citizens and foreigners from the islands, from Asia Minor, from Syracuse, and even, perhaps, from Egypt. There will be women, gay in green, plum-purple, saffron, or golden-brown gowns and carrying parasols.

As the sun peeps over Mount Hymettus—for we are, remember, in the open air, looking south—the priest of Dionysus finishes the sacrifice and the prayer. Then two "women" (played by men) come out from the palace door in the set. There are no theater programs, and their first two speeches to each other tell us the women's names: they are Ismene and Antigone. The play which is starting is the *Antigone* by Sophocles. As scene follows scene we learn that Sophocles' tragedy suggests that the laws of God are superior to the ordinances of men. This theme develops in tense, compelling drama punctuated by beautiful choral songs. Even in modern times the *Antigone*, presented in translation, grips the audience. So does the *Agamemnon* of Aeschylus or the *Medea* of Euripides, or any of the other Greek tragedies, because they present universal themes and compelling characters in drama that is full of clash and movement, and because these Athenian authors wrote with directness, lucidity, and frankness. *Man* was what interested them, in his weaknesses and in his strengths. "Many wondrous things there be but naught more wonderful than man," sang the chorus in Sophocles' *Antigone*.

In all Greek literature and art, man was central. Greek realism did not close its eyes to the facts of life, but neither did it linger over sordid details. Greek literature is characterized by nobility and restraint. "Sow with the hand but not with the whole sack" was one of the proverbs.

Attic Old Comedy

The other face of Athenian drama, comedy, was bawdy, free-spoken, and personal. Like tragedy its distant origins were in community festivals, but these were of a more joyous and licentious nature than those which begot tragedy. It seems likely that early comedies were satires on the gods and heroes (mythological comedies) and perhaps satires on the life of the day. But early in the 5th Century B.C. there arose in Athens a form of comedy which is known as Old Attic or Aristophanic Comedy. Its ancestors seem to have been farcical sketches, performed by travelling troupes of actors in southern Greece, and a community song-dance in Attica. The word *comedy* means "the song of the revel-band" (*komos*) and from this element there survived in Old Attic Comedy certain technical elements such as the *parabasis* (stepping-aside) in which the chorus interrupted the play to sing directly to the audience, and the *agon* or contest. From the farcical skits in southern Greece came what plot there was as well as the use of Dorian words and forms.

In its fully developed form from, possibly, 486 B.C. to 404 B.C., Old Attic Comedy was characterized by an elaborate chorus of twenty-four, by lampooning of persons in the audience, by obscenity, by a sketchy plot, and by attacks on trends and policies of the day. It was, in a way, a mixture of Gilbert and Sullivan light opera and the skits of American burlesque.

Its most important writer was Aristophanes. In the midst of the Peloponnesian War he attacked the Athenian war-party and leaders such as Pericles, Lamachus, and, later, Cleon the Tanner. Instead of being thrown into prison, he actually won the first prize for his *Acharnians*. In the *Clouds*, he assailed the new education in the person of Socrates and in the *Wasps* made fun of the Athenian predilection for litigation. Euripides, too, was a favorite target. One of Aristophanes' funniest and bawdiest plays is his *Lysistrata* in which he represented Athenian women as refusing their favors to their husbands until peace was made. It, too, won the first prize.

The twenty-four plays of Aristophanes illustrate fully the lack of censorship in Athenian democracy. They also demonstrate that old Attic Comedy, like Attic tragedy, was in a way the pulpit of Athens.

The New Comedy

The defeat of Athens in the Peloponnesian War brought about the demise of Old Attic Comedy. For one thing the state could no longer afford the cost of the elaborate choruses. For another, the spirit of Athens was now too sensitive for free-spokeness. After a period of transition known as Middle Comedy, about 350 B.C. New Comedy came on the stage. Some of its plots satirized the gods, but most of them held a mirror up to the life of the day and were comedies of manners. Stock characters and stock plots were used; that is, the people in the plays, whether old men or young men or courtesans, were given the same characterizations even though their names differed, while one basic plot was the story of a young man in love with a girl who tricks money out of his father in order to secure his lady-love.

There were many writers of this New Comedy, but its most popular exponent was Menander, an Athenian. Of him it was said: "O Life, O Menander, which of you two imitated the other." Some five of Menander's plays have survived. But our chief knowledge of Greek New Comedy comes from the Latin adaptations of it in the twenty plays of the Roman author, Plautus, and the six plays of his successor, Terence. This Latin Comedy, based on the Greek New Comedy, became the ancestor of our comedy. To give one example only, two Greek plays were the sources for the *Menaechmi* by Plautus, a story of identical twins. The *Menaechmi* was put on in 1486 A.D. in Italian as *I Menecmi* at the court of Hercules I, Duke of Ferrara. Later, another version was produced in Venice. This version found its way to France and thence to England, where it became the basis for Shakespeare's *Comedy of Errors*. A more recent version was the musical, *The Boys From Syracuse*. In every case, in fact, we can trace Italian, French, and English derivatives from the Latin comedies of Plautus and Terence.

Summary

From what has been said about Greek literature, it becomes evident that, beginning with Homer, Greek authors have cast a long shadow down the ages. In epic and lyric poetry, in the writing of history and later of philosophy, biography, and rhetoric, and in comedy and tragedy, what they wrote is the beginning point for our own literature. Above all, in clarity, directness, freedom, sense of proportion, perfection of workmanship, and emphasis on man they set standards of excellence which have been an envy and an influence ever since.

Architecture

Greek architecture began with wooden structures but then advanced to the use of stone. It found its chief expression in building temples to the gods. Like Egyptian architects, the Greeks did not use the arch but instead put up long rows of stone pillars to support the roof. The beams on top of the pillars and the roof between the two rows of pillars at the front and back and over the side aisles were also of stone. Stone roofing, if there is too great a distance between the pillars, will break. Greek architects had to know the amount of stress each kind of stone could stand.

Some of the Greek temples were of limestone, but the best were of marble. Within the limitations imposed by stone and by the failure to use the arch, the Greeks developed three styles of architecture, called "orders," which still influence us. These three "orders" were the Doric, Ionic, and Corinthian.

The Doric order was the first to be developed. The Parthenon on the Acropolis of Athens is its supreme example. Massive pillars set on stone steps support the superstructure. The line of the steps rises about two inches from each corner to the center so as to preserve the illusion of a straight line. If the line were straight it would seem to dip in the center. For the same reason there is a bulge in the pillars one third of the way up. These pillars are "fluted" (which means grooved up and down), the flutes coming to a sharp edge. Their capitals, or tops, are plain. Above the architrave (a stone beam which runs all the way round the temple) another stone beam is decorated with alternating triglyphs (three upright grooves) and metopes (open spaces). The metopes are filled with sculpture and the whole was painted. At each end of the temple is a gable or pediment, also filled with painted sculpture. The sculptures from the pediments and metopes of the Parthenon, most of which are now in the British Museum, are regarded as among the best in the world.

Facing east, inside the Parthenon, today, are the remains of the cella or sacred room in which, in olden days, stood a statue of Athena the Maiden, which, with its base, was forty-nine feet, two and a half inches high. This statue was of gold and ivory and represented Athena holding a statue of Victory in her right hand. The British Museum contains the frieze of the Parthenon, a long continuous band of sculpture carved in bas-relief which used to run high up around the outside wall of the interior of the temple. This frieze shows young girls and young men with horses in procession. In addition to being magnificent sculpture, it is one of our best sources for the costumes of young men and women in Periclean Athens.

In a Doric temple, such as the Parthenon, the lines are sharp and pure and the whole structure can be comprehended with clarity by the viewer, while in the Gothic cathedrals of France and England the eyes are drawn upward into almost misty heights.

Two other temples on the Acropolis of Athens, the Erechtheum and the Temple of Wingless Victory, illustrates the Ionic order. In the Ionic order the pillars are set on a base. They are less massive and more graceful than the Doric pillars, and the fluting has a ribbon of stone between the grooves. The capitals are adorned with volutes, a sort of curl in stone, and on the beam of stone above the architrave there is often a continuous frieze. The Ionic order is lighter than the Doric and is decorated quite profusely.

The Corinthian order (in Athens exemplified by the temple of Olympian Zeus) features tremendously tall pillars with elaborately decorated capitals. The story is that a Greek architect saw acanthus leaves (a plant something like the rhubarb plant) growing through a tile and from this sight got his inspiration. Among the stone leaves on the capitals are tiny volutes. This was the order the Romans adopted. We can still see these three Greeks orders existing in our architecture.

Sculpture

Greek sculpture shares the qualities of Greek literature and architecture. Archaic Greek sculpture was influenced by Egyptian rigidity. In the 5th century B.C., however, the Greeks broke free to put life and motion into their creations. Myron's *Discobolus* (Discus-Thrower), for example, is an outstanding expression in fluid circular lines of the instant before the discus-thrower explodes into energetic movement. The greatest of the 5th century B.C. sculptors was Phidias. His Athena, the Maiden, as mentioned, was almost fifty feet high. His Olympian Zeus was a magnificent figure of the sky-god father. One can see most of the sculptures he executed for the Parthenon, in the British Museum where they are known as the "Elgin marbles" after Lord Elgin who took them to England. Another great 5th century B.C. sculptor was Polycleitus, famed for his statues of nude male athletes in which the weight of the figure rests on the right foot with the left leg in the motion of walking.

In the 4th century, although sculpture retained the dignity and restraint of emotion seen in the 5th century expression, the selection of subjects and treatment tended to be more sensuous and individualistic. The first great sculptor of this period, Scopas, invented a wide-open upward and outward-looking Scopasian eye (width one-half the length) to express intense emotion, as exemplified in his *Niobe*. A contemporary, Praxiteles, developed the "Praxitelean slump" and a narrow dreamy eye (width one-third the length). His most famous sculpture was the *Aphrodite of Cnidus*, while his *Hermes* with the infant Dionysus is the chief treasure in today's museum at Olympia. To his school is supposed to belong the *Venus di Milo*, found by a French consul in a stone fence on the island of Melos, and now one of the masterpieces of the Louvre in Paris.

The last renowned 4th century B.C. sculptor was Lysippus. In his statues of athletes (head to body as one is to eight, giving a slimmer figure than that favored by Polycleitus) and in his *Hermes Resting* he combined the dreaminess of Praxiteles with the wide-open Scopasian eye.

After Lysippus, the Hellenistic era, as we shall see, went in for realism, art for art's sake, violent and agonized emotion and motion (as exemplified by the *Laocoon* group). It is still great sculpture, but it does not equal that of the classical period.

Greek sculpture, like Greek literature, regarded humanity as central. The nude male athlete and the female nude are common because the Greeks were not ashamed of the body. But the mind and spirit, too, are shown. A light seems to flow out from these works of long ago to us. Greek sculpture has never been surpassed. It is chastening to remember that the sculptures on Greek gravestones, done by unknown men, are to us great art. To quote Livingstone: "The Greeks touched everything they did with beauty."

Painting

Greek painting has not survived, although we know that Romans paid high prices for works by Greek artists such as Polygnotus who lived in Athens in the 5th century B.C., Zeuxis and Parrhasius who belong to the period of the Peloponnesian War, and Apelles, the most renowned of all Greek masters, who was a 4th century B.C. painter and whose *Aphrodite Anadyomene* (Venus Rising from the Sea) was the most famous picture of antiquity. These men worked in fresco (painting on wet plaster), tempera (using as a rule the yolk of an egg to fix the oil), and encaustic (in which the colors are burnt in by heat). It was Zeuxis and Parrhasius who, according to legend, about 400 B.C. competed in Athens. Zeuxis painted grapes so realistically that the birds flew down to peck at them but when, exultant, he went to lift the curtain to see what Parrhasius had painted, the painting was the curtain. Realism was clearly one of the criteria of Greek art criticism.

Some idea of the quality of Greek painting can be derived from the wall-paintings found in houses and villas in and around buried Pompeii and Herculaneum. Most of these paintings, although by unknown workmen, display skill in composition and vividness of coloring and, in some cases, quite obviously are copies of the themes used by the Greek master artists. In a few instances, and notably in the murals of the Villa of the Mysteries and in the *Flora* from Stabiae, the paintings are masterpieces.

Vase-Painting

Pottery was both the fine dinner-ware and the casks and oil-drums of antiquity. But with the Greeks, the designs and paintings on their best vases are works of art. 8th century B.C. pottery featured geometric designs and, where the human figure is used, the drawing is primitive. In the next century Corinthian potters introduced what is known as the "Orientalizing Style," which crowded the surface of the vessels with plant, animal, and human motifs. In the 6th and 5th century B.C. Attic black-figured and red-figured vases captured the pottery market. In the black-figured style, the figures were painted in black on the natural reddish color of the clay, while in the red-figured technique the background was painted black and the figures left in the reddish clay color. Later, a white-figure style was introduced, chiefly for burial with the dead.

These three styles present us with the finest of the vase-paintings. There is excellent posing of the figures to suit the space, the subjects are drawn from mythology and legend but also from ordinary life, and the lines lead to a center of interest with enough variety to avoid a monotonous symmetry. Stories are told and the vases display some of the best freehand drawing in the history of art. A study of Greek vases shows once again that the Greeks infused everything they touched with beauty.

The Torch of Greek Thought

Western science and philosophy began with the Greeks. In the 6th century B.C., in Asia Minor, Thales of Miletus and his successors began to speculate about the *why* and *how* of the universe. Since they lacked scientific apparatus, their answers were futile. But they had begun free inquiry. Rejecting religious explanations of the universe, such as those current among the Egyptians, Babylonians, and Hebrews, they tried to solve the riddle by reason. Their attempt was to find a primary substance or "world-stuff" from which everything else was derived. For example, Thales, who had studied in Egypt and who is said to have predicted the eclipse of the sun of May 28, 585 B.C., thought that this first substance was water. His successors, Anaximander and Anaximines, chose "the boundless" and air, respectively.

Heracleitus of Ephesus, who flourished about 513 B.C., followed in the path blazed by Thales. He postulated that everything came out of and returned to fire. He stressed the idea that ceaseless change is a natural law and the only reality. "You cannot step into the same river twice," he said. But the *way* in which change took place was determined, he believed, by the *Logos*, which was more than the "natural law" of later thinkers. This *Logos* had an element of justice, order, reason, and "rightness" in it.

Meanwhile Pythagoras of Samos (c. 580–510 B.C.) was following another track. Pythagoras, under the influence of Orphism, believed in a pure soul enclosed in an evil body and in the transmigration of souls. Music was a passion with him, and he found a mystical quality in numbers and mathematics, being reputed to have discovered the "Pythagorean theorem" (that is, that the square of the hypotenuse of a right-angled triangle is equal to the sum of the squares of the other two sides). In philosophy his interest was in the metaphysical (the inquiry into the nature of reality). His conclusion was that the substratum of the universe was "the boundless", but that this was parcelled out into geometric number-forms which were the only reality. For example, ten dots in the shape of an equilateral triangle was the perfect number and oath of the Pythagoreans. Similarly the number seven represented justice. These number forms were linked with musical notes in a somewhat complicated way. Health which, too, was a number, was being in tune with the universe. Of these geometric number-forms, the visible world, declared Pythagoras, is merely a reflection. What we see, hear, feel, smell does not really exist, because it is only a shadow of true reality. (These ideas foreshadowed a good deal of Plato's thinking.) Pythagoras himself migrated to Croton in Italy around 530 B.C. and did most of his teaching there. Pythagorean "brotherhoods" were formed. The "brothers" lived a simple, austere life, abstaining from meat, beans, and certain other foods, wearing linen, living according to strict rules, and having only communal property. They achieved considerable power in southern Italy, and their system anticipated Christian monasticism. Later, in the 1st century A.D., a revival of Pythagorean philosophy, neo-pythagoreanism, had an influence on early Christianity.

Contemporary with Pythagoras was Xenophanes of Colophon in Asia Minor, who later migrated to Elea in Italy. Xenophanes ridiculed the Pythagorean belief in the transmigration of souls and regarded the gods as figments of men's imagination. "If oxen and lions had hands and were able to paint with them, and to form statues as men do," he declared, ". . . horses would fashion them like horses and . . . lions like lions." He pointed out that "Aethiopians conceive their gods as black and snub-nosed; Thracians assign to theirs blue eyes and red hairs." His own concept was that God was uncreated, immovable, and unchanged, "like to mortals neither in body or mind," but was the "totality of mind and thought" permeating the universe.

The philosophical ideas of the 6th century were developed further in the 5th. Parmenides of Elea (c. 513–445 B.C.) is thought to have derived his basic concept of the "One," which is uncreated, eternal, unchanging, motionless, and spherical, and which is the only reality, from Xenophanes. This reality is "Being" which fills everything and there is no empty space or "Not-Being." In his view, there could be no change or motion, since these were merely illusions foisted on man by his senses. With him and Pythagoras, metaphysics gained a firm footing in Greek thinking.

Parmenides' pupil, Zeno, who, along with his teacher, visited Athens in 448 B.C., designed logical absurdities to prove that neither change, motion, sound nor any of the "illusions" of the senses really existed. Of these the best-known is his problem of the race between Achilles and the tortoise. Suppose, he said, you give the tortoise a start over Achilles, then no matter how fast Achilles runs, when he arrives where the tortoise *was*, the tortoise, using the same amount of time, must be in a new position further on. Therefore Achilles can never overtake the tortoise.

Other contemporary thinkers were more akin to the Milesians. Empedocles of Agrigentum in Sicily (495–430 B.C.) was a man of contradictions. He was influenced by Orphism and mysticism, was a poet, prophet, champion of democracy, and a famous physician. Legends about him accumulated. He was said to have been able to stir and calm the winds at will and to raise people from the dead. One story was that he cast himself into Mt. Etna to become a god; another had it that he was carried to heaven in a blaze of glory. Yet he drew from fossils the assumption that what was now dry land had once been sea, and he tried to harmonize the conflict between change and the immovable unchanging "One" of the Eleatics by postulating four unchanging elements—earth, air, fire, and water—which are forever being united or driven apart by divine Love and Hate. In this way the unchangeable elements in varying combinations take on different forms which can be apprehended by the human senses. God himself became, by a typically Greek concept, Mind, "shooting swift thoughts all over the world," a remark which is reminiscent of Xenophanes. It seems possible that, like Anaximander before him, he thought of universes being continually in the process of formation and destruction. He did, at any rate, like Anaximander, conceive of a crude form of evolution (Anaximander had suggested that man came from a fish), and of the idea of the survival of the fittest.

Empedocles is often called a Pluralist, because he believed in the reality of the "Many" (that which our senses perceive). Four hundred lines of his poem on *Nature* survive. (Greek philosophers such as he, Parmenides, and Xenophanes put their speculations into poems.) A more realistic thinker was Anaxagoras of Clazomenae in Asia Minor (500–428 B.C.) who, migrating to Athens, became one of the brilliant circle around Pericles and Aspasia where his nickname was "Brains." His suggestions that the sun was not a god but blazing metal "as large as the Peloponnesus" and that the heavenly bodies were pieces torn from the earth and fiery because of rapid rotation caused some of the Athenians to accuse him of atheism. Saved by Pericles, he was finally exiled and retired to Lampsacus in Asia Minor, where, after his death, a statue in his honor was erected.

In his theory of the Universe he was influenced by Anaximenes who had been his teacher. Anaxagoras held that all things have always existed as "seeds." Each of these seeds, except mind (*nous*), has in it something of everything else. But mind, existing as particles of mind and nothing else, permeates everything and is without limit, all-knowing and all-powerful. This mind, which is Anaxagoras' God, imparts a whirl to the mass of seeds whereby like is separated from unlike, wholes are formed, and universes come into being. In his thinking we recognize a pre-figuration of the directing intelligence of Plato's *Nous*.

The 5th century Atomists went a step further. Leucippus, of uncertain date, was followed by Democritus of Abdera (c. 460–361 B.C.), who was known to his contemporaries as "The Laughing Philosopher." These two men were the first conscious materialists in philosophy. Reality, Democritus held, consisted solely of the "Void" and homogeneous matter divided into an infinite number of atoms (the Greek word, *atome*, means that which cannot be divided) of different sizes and weights. Perpetual motion, he said, was inherent in these atoms by force of necessity, that is by natural law. The atoms were uncreated, that is, had always existed. As a result of their constant motion they collided and the collisions formed everything which existed, again according to natural law. "Nothing happens by chance," asserted Democritus, "but everything is determined by Necessity." Birth, therefore, was simply a combining of atoms and decay and death their separation. Consequently, in his thinking, there was no soul or immortality and the gods themselves, if they existed, were combinations of atoms like mortals. This purely mechanistic view of the universe was, later on, adopted by the Epicureans.

Greek Religious Tolerance

In the 6th and 5th centuries the Greek world was bubbling with ideas, many of them very much in opposition to the received religious ideas of the day, and some of them anticipating modern thought. In the medieval world of Europe such freedom of speculation was impossible, or, if indulged in, meant charges of heresy and death. It was not possible, either, anywhere else in the ancient world at the time of the Greek philosophers. So why was it possible in Greece?

The answer lies partly in the intelligence and tolerance of the Greeks themselves and partly in the nature of Greek religion. The Greeks were very religious. Their temples, sculpture, and much of their literature were closely connected with religion. Religious observances took up a great deal of their time and were meticulously observed. Even during dinner there was a sacrifice and a prayer.

The worship of pre-Greek gods and goddesses often contained primitive practices. For example, in the Eleusinian Mysteries the deities were Demeter, the Earth-Mother, and her daughter, Persephone. According to the legend Pluto, the ruler of the underworld, abducted Persephone. But after a three years' mourning by her mother, during which no crops grew, it was arranged that Persephone should spend six months on earth and six months in the underworld. In this compromise we recognize the pervasive myth of dying and reviving vegetation. Associated with the mother and the daughter was a youth, Triptolemus, the spirit of the wheat. In his honor each year, an acre of ground was ploughed at Eleusis with a golden ploughshare and planted with spelt. It is suspected that in pre-Greek times (see a fictionalized account in Marie Renault's *The King Must Die*), as in other early cultures, a youth was chosen each year to represent the spirit of the wheat and was then sacrificed. As you have learned, Dionysus was incorporated into this cult which then emphasized the idea of immortality. After a sacred procession each year from Athens to Eleusis, the *mystics* (Greek word) were initiated into the cult. The final ritual was performed in the "Great Hall of the Mysteries", which has now been excavated. Among people initiated into this worship was the Roman orator, Cicero. It is probable that devoted worshippers of this cult and others similar to it were as fixed and enthusiastic in their beliefs as some medieval and modern people.

But the worship of the Olympian gods, the "state religion" of the Greeks, was tolerant. There were the twelve great gods, headed by Zeus and Hera. There were also many other gods and most of them were anthropomorphic. The Greeks, in fact believed that nymphs inhabited the trees, rivers, and mountains, while Pan roamed the woods and Poseidon the sea. Above all there was no Greek Bible to lay down fixed and fast ideas about the God-head; notions about the gods could be changed or modified. Furthermore, except for a few cases such as the priests of Apollo at the oracle of Delphi, there was no separate and organized priesthood. The father was the priest of the family. The state priesthoods were filled, often by annual lot, from the ordinary citizens. The archons, for example, had priestly duties. There was no division between church and state—but the state, not the church, dominated. Above all, perhaps, the Greek was too reasonable to be a successful persecutor. He preferred freedom of thought, no matter where the argument led. In all of Greek history there are only four prosecutions on religious grounds, of which one was the prosecution in 399 B.C. of Socrates. A comparison with the trials for heresy and the Inquisition of the European Middle Ages makes the difference obvious. Let us repeat that the Greeks were indeed very religious, but that they were too tolerant and had too much respect for the intellect to persecute or to prevent free inquiry.

The Sophists

Greek speculation had travelled far by the 5th century B.C. Alongside the philosophers, as part of the exciting intellectual ferment of the day, there were the Sophists. They were skeptical of the search for the why and the how of the universe and the more radical of them inclined toward the Atomists. "Nothing exists," argued Gorgias the rhetorician in order to prove the uselessness of philosophy, "if anything did exist, it could not be known; if a man should chance to apprehend it, it would still be a secret; he could not communicate it to his fellowmen." Along with this scepticism of philosophic thought went a searching criticism of traditional values, institutions and religions. The Sophists decided that the only thing that mattered in the universe was man, or, as Protagoras of Ceos (a small island in the Aegean) put it, "Man is the measure of all things; of what *is* that it *is* and of what *is not* that it *is not*." Truth became the winning opinion of the moment and the universe was only important insofar as it was of value to humanity. The Sophists became the first *conscious* humanists, but they tended to regard success in life as the final objective.

The Sophists, moreover, were accomplished debaters and the first professional educators. Because 5th century Athens had the money, they swarmed from Sicily, southern Italy, Ionia, and the Aegean islands into the imperial city. As we have learned, to win influence in Athens, a man had to be able to speak. The principal arts taught by the Sophists, therefore, were rhetoric and dialectic. Different styles of speaking to suit the occasion, logic and methods of argumentation, rhetorical devices, voice training, how to organize a speech—all these subjects were included. Other Sophists taught mathematics, astronomy, geography, and the like. Still others ventured into analyses of politics and ethics. Above all, perhaps, the Sophists, along with the philosophers, were responsible for subjecting all human institutions and values to the white light of criticism. With them, higher education in the western world begins.

Socrates

An Athenian, however, the flat-nosed Socrates (469–399 B.C.), outmatched the Sophists. If we had lived in Athens in the second half of the 5th century B.C., we would have seen this stocky, ugly stone-mason everywhere, stopping people in the streets, catching at the tunic of a man in a colonnade, sitting at a symposium of one of his rich friends, and always asking questions. He himself said that the god at Delphi had made him a gadfly to sting the noble horse of Athenian democracy into action. He like-wise believed it to be his mission to prove to those who thought they knew something that they knew nothing because "only the god is wise."

Socrates lived the life of a normal high-principled man. He saved Alcibiades' life at the battle of Delium (424 B.C.). He was a councillor. He made a living of sorts for his wife Xantippe and their children. But he could not stop his own enquiring mind. He differed from the Sophists in that he did not take pay for his teaching and because his only desire was to search out the truth. He asserted that if he were the wisest of all men, as the god at Delphi (Apollo) had told one of his disciples, it was because he alone knew that he knew nothing. Hence he is called the "Great Agnostic." This does not mean that he was an atheist. It is clear that he believed in the providential direction of the universe. But he did not believe, as did the Medieval church, that anyone should be *compelled* to believe in doctrines of any kind.

With Socrates nothing was sacred from inquiry. His method of teaching is known as the Socratic "elenchos" (*elencho*, "cross-examine"). He would first propose a general idea with which his hearers would agree (such as, All good men lead happy lives), and then, by question and answer, guide his listeners to disproving the statement and suggesting a modification of it, which would then be examined in the same way until finally a general concept which seemed valid was reached. His examination in the *Republic* of the question, What is Justice, is an example of his method.

Socrates was chiefly concerned with ethics, the ideals of human conduct, and such was his influence that from his time forward ethics became the principal concern of philosophy. He himself wrote nothing, but he left behind him a group of ardent disciples among whom were Plato and Xenophon. Xenophon's *Memorabilia* consists chiefly of anecdotes about Socrates but Plato made him his principal character in many of his *Dialogues*, particularly in his earlier ones. It is difficult to decide in these Dialogues which statements represent Socrates' own thinking, which are Socrates' ideas as filtered through Plato, and which are chiefly Platonic notions. The *Apology*, however, purporting to be the speech delivered by Socrates when on trial for his life, is probably pretty well Socrates' own thinking. From it we learn of the "mission" which he thought had been imposed on him by the god at Delphi, of the "daemon" which told him what *not* to do, of his belief that death was not an evil since it meant either a dreamless sleep or immortality, and of his famous saying that virtue is knowledge and vice ignorance, since no man if he knows the good would, in Socrates' opinion, willingly do the worse.

When Socrates reached the age of 70, his constant questioning became too irritating for the Athenians. They had lost the war against Sparta and there was abroad a spirit of defeat and bitterness. In addition, among Socrates' followers had been Alcibiades, whose actions had weakened Athens and, still more damning, Critias, the leader of the Thirty Tyrants. The murders perpetrated by Critias and the tyrants were still fresh in people's minds, even though Socrates had refused to join in the arrest of certain individuals when ordered to do so. There must be something wrong, people felt, with a man whose pupils turned out so badly and, as Socrates himself pointed out, Aristophanes' play, *The Clouds*, had long ago predisposed Athenians against him. As a result, in 399 B.C., Socrates was accused of impiety and of corrupting the youth of Athens, and was condemned to drink hemlock, the Athenian way of putting condemned people to death. Although arrangements were made for Socrates to escape he refused to break the laws. A memorable dialogue, the *Phaedo*, describes his last hours.

The Lesser Socratics

If the measure of a man is his influence, Socrates ranks high. The schools of philosophy known as the Megarians, Eleo-Eretrians, Cynics, and Cyrenaics or Hedonists, all derived their inspiration from him, and were all concerned with the problem of how to achieve happiness for the individual. The first two of these schools are of little importance in the story of Greek thought, but the Cynics left a lasting impression. Their founder was Antisthenes, a pupil of Socrates, who taught at the gymnasium of Cynosarges (Swift Dog). Hence came the name of the school, though later because of the unpleasant habits of some Cynics the dog (Greek *Kyōn, Kynos*) was regarded as their exemplar.

The teaching of Antisthenes was intensified by his successor, Diogenes, the man who lived in a tub and told Alexander the Great to stand out of the sun. He is also said to have gone about Athens with a lantern in broad daylight, searching for an honest man.

To the Cynics virtue meant happiness, and virtue, they thought, was best achieved by the man who had the least wants. It was Antisthenes who said, "I would rather die than feel pleasure." Therefore, the Cynics did without all but the simplest necessities. Luxuries were anathema, and we are told about a Cynic who threw away his cup when he saw a dog lapping from a stream. Theirs was a back to nature movement and they scorned not only the trappings but also all the political and social institutions of civilization. They judged slavery to be unnatural and claimed that they themselves were world citizens. Later, in the Hellenistic and Roman world, they became ardent missionaries.

The Cyrenaics or Hedonists were founded by Aristippus of Cyrene (435–356 B.C.) who was also a pupil of Socrates. Their goal, however, was not virtue but pleasure. Subjective sensations was their standard of value, and they held that all promising experiences and sensations should be tried. The "wise man" chose his pleasures and subjected them to reason and, like the Cynics, lived in accord with nature. Many Hedonists (*hedone*, "pleasure") felt that he who experienced the most instants of intense physical pleasure was the happiest, but the true Cyrenaics were close to the asceticism of the Cynics and, like them, wanted to be masters of themselves and free of all externals.

Plato, the Giant of Greek Philosophy

Socrates' most famous disciple was Plato (429–347 B.C.). *Plato* is a nickname meaning "broad"; his real name was Aristocles and he was of noble birth. The death of Socrates shocked him so that he took a dislike to democracy. After Socrates' execution he traveled widely in Egypt, Cyrene, and Sicily. In 387 B.C. he returned to Athens to set up his own school in the "grove of Academe." Over his lecture-room was written, "Let no one enter here who does not know geometry." This school lasted for 900 years until, in 529 A.D., the Byzantine emperor, Justinian, abolished all schools of philosophy.

Plato published his ideas in *Dialogues* which are of charming literary quality. His thought is so far-reaching that only one or two aspects of it can be mentioned. Like the Pythagoreans, he thought of everything in the world as being imperfect shadows of true realities. These realities he called "ideas." Thus, somewhere, there exists the Idea of a perfect triangle, even though no one of us, no matter how good our instruments, can draw a perfect one. Similarly, there exists the Idea of perfect justice, while attempts at justice in this world are imperfect shadows of this eternal justice. The creator of the eternal verities is, to Plato, Mind (*Nous*) in the absolute. God then is Mind and, probably, also the absolute Good.

The creation of our universe was, in Plato's thinking a very complicated process. To simplify his scheme greatly, Mind thought into existence eternal stars and the "ideas" of matter in the abstract, and then the stars thought into existence stars "enduring only through time", and the notions of the various species of which existing things are pale reflections. The myth of the Cave in *The Republic* gives a concept of how far, according to Plato, this visible world is removed from true reality.

The influence of Orphism is evident in Plato's other-worldly ideas. He believes that each man has a soul which comes from God and is imprisoned in the "dungeon-house" of the body. At birth, Plato thinks, we know the beautiful and the good because glimpses we have of these qualities through life are due to these fading recollections. Since his thinking is somewhat differently expressed in dialogues such as the

Phaedo, *Phaedrus*, and *Timaeus*, Plato's exact concepts about the fate of the soul are somewhat difficult to determine. It seems clear, however, that he anticipated Christian doctrine in his theories of a judgment after death for deeds done in the flesh, and in his dogma of rewards and punishments. His hell (*Tartarus*) was placed beneath the earth and his heaven in the sky. There even seems to be a sort of purgatory for some souls when waiting to be reborn.

Unlike Christian dogma, he thought that there was rebirth nine times for average souls with a thousand years of purification, including rewards and punishments, between each life on earth. In the *Phaedo*, however, "godly" souls go to "fair mansions in the sky" between rebirths and the "super-godly" to "still fairer mansions." Finally, incurable souls go to Tartarus forever, while good souls rejoin the star assigned them at birth. The ultimate objective of the soul, apparently, is to rejoin the World-Soul.

The grandeur of Plato's thinking has strongly influenced Western philosophy. In his ideal political system, however, his dislike of Athenian democracy and his admiration for Sparta led him to prefer a totalitarian state, as described in his *Republic*. Here the state is to be supreme and the individual exists only to serve it. There are to be three classes. The lowest, of laborers and artisans, is to work for the state, being specialized into various occupations, but is otherwise left comparatively free. The two higher classes, the "Philosopher-Kings" or Guardians, and the Auxiliaries or Warriors, are not allowed to own property because, in Plato's view, the ownership of possessions would detract from their all-absorbing loyalty to the state. For the same reason, and also because Plato believed in "uniting the best with the best as often as possible," these two classes are forbidden marriage and families. Instead, they are brought together at great festivals. The children thus produced, says Plato, are to be brought up in state nurseries and educated in state schools. Education is to be strictly censored, and even Homer is to experience the Greek equivalent of the blue pencil. In this way children would grow up knowing and believing only what Plato had decided was proper for them to believe and know. On the other hand Plato, in advance of his times, provided that women were to have equal education, rights, and *duties* with men. Another interesting idea was a "ladder of opportunity" so that if a child of the lowest class showed unexpected intelligence he could be moved up, though, conversely, a stupid child in the two upper classes could be demoted.

Plato was given two opportunities in Syracuse in Sicily to put his theories in practice but lasted only a year on each occasion. In his old age he wrote his ideas about his second-best state in the *Laws*. This state,

Plato observed dourly, could be best established "under a tyrant." The ownership of private property was to be permitted but was subject to strict regulations. Similarly, marriage and families were allowed but sexual intercourse was to be restricted to intercourse for the procreation of children. Foreign travel was forbidden for anyone under forty years of age, and such travellers when they returned must proclaim that the system at home was the best system. There was an even stricter censorship of plays, literature and morals. In education there were to be prescribed games for children, and any child who introduced innovations into these games was to be carefully watched for possible radicalism, and if he proved incorrigible in his originality, was to be removed. In this state, as in the Republic, conformism was essential. A "Nocturnal Council" was provided to judge and punish deviations from the norm.

It is not surprising that the Platonic ideal state was popular with the Nazis and the Fascists and was closely studied in Soviet Russia. Some of his ideas are disturbingly prescient of certain trends in the so-called "Free World." At almost every point the Platonic Utopia and Periclean democracy are sharply opposed.

Aristotle, The Realist and Encyclopaedist

Plato's most brilliant pupil was Aristotle (384–322 B.C.) from Stagira in Macedonia. We are told that he was somewhat of a dandy who lisped and carried a cane. For three years he was the tutor of Alexander the Great, but in 334 B.C. he founded his own school in Athens in the Lyceum Gymnasium. It was named the Peripatetic school because Aristotle lectured while walking around (*peripateo*, "I walk around").

Aristotle published popular works which have been lost. What we have are a number of his works (forty-seven treatises of which about fifteen are usually considered spurious) which were essentially his lectures to his students. These treatises were carried to Asia Minor in antiquity, hidden in a cellar, and lost for a century before being discovered. The *Ethics, Politics*, and *Poetics* are the works which best repay reading in translation.

Although greatly influenced by Plato, Aristotle, whose own attitude was realistic, reacted against many points in his master's teaching. Rejecting the theory of Ideas and accepting the reality of matter, he thought of the creative cause of the universe as the "Unmoved Mover," that is, as intelligence in the absolute existing apart and "energizing continually" in contemplation of itself. By his existence and energizing, Aristotle's "God" attracted the universe, though he had no interest in it, in somewhat the same way, though on a much lower plane and in a much more definite way, as a beautiful sunset attracts viewers. The "moving cause" which keeps the universe going was, in Aristotle's view, the continuance of the species. Yet in his *Metaphysics* Aristotle is often decidedly Platonic in his thinking.

In his Nichomachean *Ethics* (Nichomachus was the name of a son) Aristotle set down that the final "Good" and the goal of every action is Happiness. The highest happiness, Aristotle thought, must be connected with the rational part of man since to him this was the part which was distinctively human as compared with functions shared with the "vegetative" and "animal" creation, such as the faculties of growth or motion. Virtue in which reason rules desire was, therefore, the primary requisite for happiness, although as a realist Aristotle admitted that "external goods" such as wealth and health could add to happiness. No man who was absolutely ugly, he believed in a view that was Greek, could be entirely happy. But virtue to him was not equivalent to knowledge. A man, Aristotle pointed out, can know what is right and yet willingly do the wrong. Instead virtue was to be achieved by the "Doctrine of the Mean," which was really an extension of the old saying of the oracle at Delphi: Nothing to excess. In this doctrine the virtuous man steered a middle course between two extremes. For example, in the use of money, the proper course was the middle road between extravagance and miserliness, although naturally the standards for what would be extravagant or miserly for a poor man would not be the same for one who was rich. To illustrate this doctrine Aristotle in his Ethics gives examples of various characters such as *The Magnificent Man*, a sort of exercise which parallels the development of stock characters in the New Comedy. An interesting part of his doctrine is that, rejecting the absolute good of Plato, Aristotle held that no act was good or bad in itself but that the circumstances surrounding the act made it good or bad. For instance, killing another man in peace time is murder but in war an act of patriotism.

The same realism is evident in Aristotle's *Politics*. To Aristotle politics was ethics in action since man was a "political animal" and, like most Greeks, he could not conceive of a human being except as part of a society. He rejected the Platonic Utopia almost in its entirety, criticizing the lack of private property and the lack of family life. The latter, he believed, was necessary and a strength for the state; the former, in his opinion, provided a necessary incentive, although he was scornful of retail trading and completely opposed to usury. Moreover, he thought that property should, in a certain sense, be common, in that friends should allow each other the use of their possessions. Similarly, he opposed the idea of equal rights and duties for women since women in his opinion were by nature inferior to men. He likewise regarded slavery as natural since some men were born to be slaves and others masters. Democracy was in his opinion a perversion of a proper type of government, although better than tyranny, and his own ideal was a small, self-sufficient, agricultural and aristocratic city-state, although he lived in an era when the city-state had failed and Alexander the Great was conquering the world. His *Politics* does, however, illustrate the "Aristotelian Method," since it is based on the analysis of 158 constitutions of the ancient world. One of these, the *Athenaea Politeia*, was discovered in papyrus in Egypt, although its Aristotelian authorship is sometimes disputed.

The *Politics*, with its practical suggestions about how to distribute wealth properly, how to train citizens for the "best life" (the real objective of the state in Aristotle's view), and how to keep a government from degenerating into tyranny, an oligarchy of wealth, or a mass democracy, is valuable reading. So is the *Poetics* in which Aristotle presents an analysis of the best literary qualities and techniques particularly as seen in Greek drama.

Possibly Aristotle's greatest achievement was his method of collecting all possible data from which to derive his conclusions and his encyclopaedic knowledge. His passion for truth and his emphasis on the possible value for knowledge of the most insignificant fact of nature (he reported, for instance, on about 540 species of animals and personally dissected many of them) made him the true founder of western science. As an encyclopaedist he collected, classified, and systematized all knowledge up to his time. Metaphysics, physics, rhetoric, the history of animals, the soul (ethics) these are among the many subjects investigated by him. His works were translated into Syrian and Armenian and thence into Arabic to become the basis for Mohammedan science and philosophy. Future Greek and Roman scholarship was founded on his material and methods. In the Middle Ages he became an authority second only to the Bible, and Dante, the Italian poet, called him "The Master of those who know." Unfortunately, the Christian Church assumed that every word he wrote was gospel so that to challenge Aristotle's conclusions was to be heretical. Galileo was forced to recant his non-Aristotelian findings and Copernicus did not dare to publish his discoveries during his own lifetime. In this way, a man who was a dedicated searcher for truth became, ironically enough, a hamperer of free thought.

On Aristotle's death he was succeeded in his school by Theophrastus whose chief contribution to us is a book of stock characters such as the Unseasonable Man and The Boorish Man, which makes fascinating reading. But with Plato and Aristotle the great age of Greek thought ends. If we consider, however, even the cursory sketch which has been given, we will realize how widely these curious, restless Greek minds, unfettered by tradition or religion, ranged in almost every field of thought. That is why words such as politics, tyranny, physics, geology, democracy, music, philosophy, and the like, and the ideas behind those words, are Greek. The popular saying, The Greeks had a word for it, is often quite correct.

Readings from Sources of the Period

(a) To appreciate the force and artistic perfection of Greek tragedy one must read the plays. Both the brief extracts below are from Sophocles, the *Antigone*. The first passage, which comes after Antigone has been arrested while performing a ritual burial of her brother's body, whom the king of Thebes, Creon has ordered to be left unburied, gives the basic conflict of the play between the laws of God and the laws of man; the second is the first stanza of one of the beautiful choral songs of the play.

I.   CREON. You there, you, with head bent toward the ground,
    Do you acknowledge or deny this crime?
        ANTIGONE. I say I did it; I will not deny.
        CREON. (*To* WATCHMAN) Go where you will, clear of a serious charge.
                            WATCHMAN *leaves.*
        (*To* ANTIGONE) You tell me now, and not at length, but briefly,
    You knew the edict had forbidden this?
        ANTIGONE. I knew. How could I help it? It was plain.
        CREON. And you presumed to disobey these laws?
        ANTIGONE. Yes. For it was not Zeus who made this edict,
    And Justice, dwelling with the gods below,
    Had never set such laws as these among men.
    Nor did I think your edicts of such force,
    That you, being just a man, could override
    Unwritten and unchanging laws of gods.
    Their life is not of now or yesterday,
    But always. No man knows when they appeared.
    In view of them, I would not, through the fear
    Of human will, meet judgment from the gods.
    That I must die I knew. Why should I not?
    Though you had never even made an edict.
    And if I die before my time, I shall gain.
    For when one lives, as I, in many troubles,
    How can he help but find a gain in death?
    Meeting my death this way does not pain me.
    But when my mother's son had died, if I
    Had left his corpse unburied, I would have grieved.
    For this, I am not grieved. And if I seem
    To do some foolish things at present, perhaps
    The man who charges folly is the fool.

II.   CHORUS
    Many things are wonderful, but none more wonderful than man.
    Over the white of the sea he goes, driven by the stormy
        southwind of winter;

He wanders under the surges,
Engulfed by the waves around him.
And the most ancient of the gods, the Earth,
The everlasting, the unwearied, he wears away,
Rolling the plowshares, as years follow on years,
Turning the furrows with mules, the offspring of horses

(MacKendrick and Howe, *op. cit.*, pp. 161–162 and p. 160, translated by Louis MacNeice.)

(b) In his Apology *Plato* (427–348 B.C.) purports to give us Socrates' defence when on trial for his life in 399 B.C. In the course of his defence Socrates in the following extract, tells how during his search for truth which he believed was a "divine mission" he created many enemies.

From this inquiry many enmities have arisen against me, both violent and grievous, as well as many slanders and my reputation of being "wise." For those who are present on each occasion suppose that I have the wisdom that I find wanting in others; but the truth is that only God is wise, and that by that oracle he means to show that human wisdom is worth little or nothing. And by speaking of "Socrates" he appears to use me and my name merely as an example, just as if he were to say, "Mortals, he of you is wisest who, like Socrates, knows that in truth his wisdom is worth nothing." That is why I go about even now, questioning and examining in God's name any man, citizen or stranger, whom I suppose to be wise. And whenever I find that he is not wise, then in vindication of the divine oracle I show him that he is not wise. And by reason of this preoccupation I have no leisure to accomplish any public business worth mentioning or any private business, but I am in extreme poverty because of my service to the god.

(*Ibid.,* p. 322, translated by William C. Greene.)

(c) In the *Republic* Socrates is the chief speaker. In the following passage he discusses the "Idea of the Good."

SOCRATES. This [the sun], then, is what I meant when I spoke of "the child of the Good" which the Good has brought forth in the visible world to stand in the same relation to vision and to visible things that the Good itself bears in the intelligible world to intelligence and to intelligible objects. You know that when one turns his eyes toward objects whose colors are not illuminated by the light of day but only by the moon and stars, their vision is dimmed, almost blinded; but that when the sun shines forth on these objects these same eyes see clearly. Well, consider the experience of the soul: when it fixes its gaze on an object that is illuminated by truth and reality, it has understanding and knowledge and is manifestly possessed of intelligence; but when it looks at that twilight world of things that come into being and pass away, then its vision is dimmed, and it entertains shifting opinions and seems now like a creature without intelligence.

This, then, I would have you call "the Idea of the Good"; this is what imparts to the objects of knowledge their truth, and to the knower his power of knowing. It is the cause of knowledge and truth, both precious things; yet you will do well to esteem it as something still more precious than either. For just as in our analogy we found it right to think of light and vision as like the sun, but not as identical with it, so here it is right to think of knowledge and truth as like the Good, but not to identify either to them with it; we must find for the Good a still higher place of honor.

(*Ibid.*, p. 336, translated by William C. Greene.)

(d) The style of Aristotle (384–322 B.C.) is very different from that of Plato and so is his attitude toward life. In the following passage taken from the *Nichomachean Ethics*, after arguing that every art and inquiry aims at some end, he lays down what he believes to be the end of politics.

IV. HAPPINESS, THE END OF POLITICS

All agree that the end which politics pursues is happiness, but what does this mean? There are several different ideas current.

1 Now resuming our argument, since every investigation and choice aims at some good, let us say what it is that we affirm politics aims at and what is the highest of all the goods of action. *2* As far as the name is concerned there is almost universal agreement, for both the many and the refined call it happiness, and consider living well and doing well to be the same thing as being happy. But they disagree about the definition of happiness, and the many do not account for it in the same way as the wise. *3* Some regard happiness as something manifest and obvious, like pleasure or wealth or honor, others as something different—and frequently the same person will contradict himself, in sickness calling it health, in poverty wealth. Realizing their own ignorance, people admire those who say something grand and above their comprehension. Again, some used to suppose that alongside these many good things there is something else independent which is the cause of their being good. *4* It would doubtless be unprofitable to examine every opinion; it will be enough to consider those which are most prevalent or which seem to have some reason in them.

(*Ibid.*, p. 356, translated by Edwin L. Minar, Jr.)

CHAPTER 6

The Old Age of Greece: 323–30 B.C.

In this period, because of the conquests of Alexander the Great, Greek culture was spread throughout the Near East. The resulting fusion of Greek and Near Eastern cultures is called *Hellenistic* to distinguish it from the *Hellenic* culture which flourished from Homer to Aristotle. It was a new world and the spirit of the age was "modern." Hence, we have nation-states, universalism, mystery-religions, philosophic brotherhoods, the age of science, forms of capitalism and state socialism, and a new art and literature. Yet the art and literature, at least, is still touched with the Greek spirit.

Alexander the Great: 336–323 B.C.

Few individuals have done more to usher in a new phase of history than Alexander the Great. When his father was assassinated, Greece and Macedonia broke out into a rash of pretenders and revolts. But the twenty-year-old Alexander acted with speed and decision. After rapidly dominating Greece, he crushed rebellions in the Thracian and Illyrian parts of his kingdom. A rumor that he was dead led to an uprising in Thebes. While the rumor was still fresh, Alexander appeared before its walls. The city was captured and razed to the ground, except for the temples and the house of the poet Pindar. The rest of Greece bowed its head. In the spring of 334 B.C. Alexander was free to cross over into Asia Minor to begin the expedition against Persia which his father had planned.

The army with which he assailed the sprawling and mighty Persian Empire totalled about 30,000 infantry and 5000 cavalry. But that army was the superbly organized and efficient fighting machine which his father, Philip of Macedon, had fashioned, and Alexander himself was completely confident of his own military genius and destiny. Handsome and well-

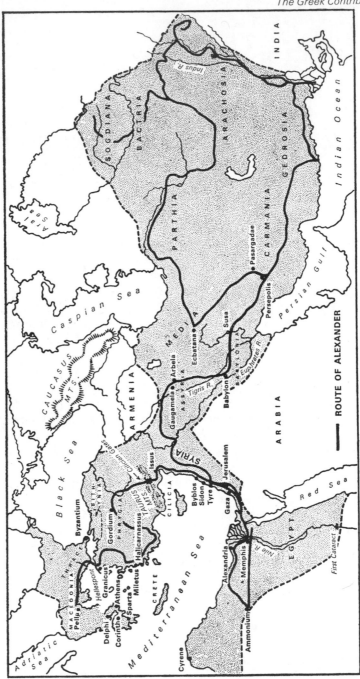

The Empire of Alexander the Great

proportioned, there clung to this young man an aura of inexhaustible energy and fiery ambition. Whether he really believed himself the son of a god as, apparently, his mother, Olympias, had told him, or not, he seemed quite convinced that he could never fail and his will was iron-armored. A masterful leader of men and a consummate tactician and far-ranging strategist, he was, however, subject to sudden and unpredictable fits of ungovernable rage, even although he was not as a rule prone to the uncivilized orgies of his father. He seems, moreover, to have developed a definite concept of a world unity of peoples.

In 334 B.C. all these features of his character were still to be proved. Thanks to his friend, Black Cleitus, he won a stiff engagement at the river Granicus in Asia Minor. The rest of the year was spent in taking over the cities of this area, and at Gordium Alexander, on being shown the knot of cornel bark and told of the prophecy that he who could untie it would rule Asia, cut it with his sword. In the next year he defeated a Persian host under the command of Darius III at Issus just south of the Cilician Gates. From this moment his ambition widened. He no longer thought of himself as the leader of the Hellenes against the Persians but as the successor of the Great King.

Issus had left Syria, Palestine, and Egypt open to conquest. The new Tyre of that time, situated on an island with a narrow arm of the sea intervening between it and the old city, held out for seven months while a mole was built to it from the mainland. In and after the assault 8000 Tyrians were killed and 30,000 were sold into slavery. Further along the coast Gaza resisted for two months. After it fell Alexander marched into Egypt, which received him as a liberator. During his stay in this ancient land, he founded the city of Alexandria, still one of the most important ports of the Near East, and visited the oracle of Zeus-Amen in the oasis of Siwah. Legend insists that the oracle addressed him as the "son of Amen," and from this visit dated the tendency of the easterners to deify Alexander, as indeed was their custom with all their rulers.

In 331 B.C., since the Near East was secure, Alexander plunged into the heart of the Persian Empire. Reinforcements had filled his depleted ranks but when he met the Persian forces at Gaugamela, north of Arbela, his army was still greatly inferior in numbers. Victory was soon won. Darius fled, Babylon, Susa, and Persepolis opened their gates, vast treasures (40,000 silver talents, 9000 gold darics along with gems at Susa, and 120,000 Persian talents at Persepolis) were seized and Alexander proclaimed himself lord of Asia. In the next few years he took over the far eastern provinces of the Persian Empire, built two new cities in Afghanistan and marched southward into the valley of the Indus river. At the Hydaspes river he met and defeated King Porus with whom he made friends. His intention now was, apparently, to cross India but his soldiers rebelled. His march back to Persia was through the desert while his fleet skirted the coast of the Persian Gulf.

The detailed story of Alexander's far eastern campaigns is one worth studying. Wherever he went he founded cities, some of which radiated Greek culture for centuries. Voluminous notes about new plants and animals, about curious customs, and about geography and peoples were made. At the same time Alexander took great strides in the scheme which now obsessed him, that of uniting East and West. His soldiers were encouraged to take Asiatic wives and he himself married Roxane, a princess of Sogdiana. On his return he celebrated at Susa a five-day marriage festival of Macedonians and Persians, he himself wedding the eldest daughter of Darius as a second wife.

Alexander seems to have had a genuine vision of a fusion of East and West. Beside the marriages, Persians were taken into his army with full rank and he himself assumed the dress and ceremonial of a Persian monarch. Embassies came to him from Libya, Carthage, South Italy, the Etruscans, and, possibly, the Romans. It is said that he planned to revisit India, to explore the Caspian Sea and to mount an expedition against Carthage, but all his schemes were cut short by his death at Babylon from a fever on June 13, 323 B.C. at the age of thirty-three. His body was finally interred at Alexandria. Legends inevitably clustered around him and, later, as the "Alexander Romance," influenced the literature of medieval Europe. In the story of civilization, his chief importance lies in the new world to which his conquests gave birth, a world in which Hellene and easterner were intermingled, and in which the idea of universalism took another stride forward. Alexander's career was the end of an epoch and his death the ushering in of a new era.

The Fate of Alexander's Empire

Alexander's death left his empire in confusion. It was finally decided to accept his unborn child by Roxane, if it were a son (which it was) and his feeble-minded brother, Philip, as monarchs with Antipater, the senior general whom Alexander had left behind in Macedonia, as regent. Meanwhile the empire, except for Macedonia under Antipater, was divided into satrapies to be ruled by his other generals, Antigonus "the One-eyed" in Phrygia, Ptolemy in Egypt, and Lysimachus in Thrace, while Persians governed in the eastern provinces.

Inevitably, Roxane, Philip, and Alexander's son were murdered while the generals strove between themselves for the supreme power. After a dreary succession of wars and intrigues, there finally emerged as the chief states, Egypt (including Cyprus) under Ptolemy and his descendants,

Macedonia, ruled by the Antigonids (descendants of Antigonus Gonatas, the grandson of the one-eyed Antigonus), and Syria, governed by the Seleucids (descendants of Seleucus, a general who had at first established himself in Babylon). These Hellenistic nation-states maintained an uneasy balance of power between themselves. There were also independent powers such as Athens, Sparta, Epirus, and the Achaean and Aetolian Leagues in Greece, Rhodes in the Aegean and Pontus, Bithynia, Cappadocia, Armenia, and Pergamum in Asia Minor. This latter kingdom owed its origin to a sudden sweep southward of a horde of Celts (Gauls) around 280 B.C. who, after ravaging Greece and Thrace, crossed into Asia Minor. Antiochus I, son of Seleucus defeated them, but they were driven back from the Greek cities of the coast by Attalus I of Pergamum. After their defeat they settled in Central Asia Minor in Galatia, a district named after them. During the 3rd century B.C. however, the Seleucids, who had been forced to cede Alexander's Indian conquests by 310 B.C. to a Hindu monarch, gradually lost all the eastern provinces of the empire. The ultimate blow was the occupation, about the middle of the 2nd century B.C., of Iran and Mesopotamia by the Parthians, hard-riding horsemen from Turkestan, who were later to become Rome's rivals in the East. In 168 B.C., too, the Seleucid, Antiochus IV, whose title was *Epiphanes* (God-Manifest) attempted to hellenize the Jews by force. The result was the heroic Maccabean revolt through which the Jews became independent until Pompey the Great occupied Jerusalem in 65 B.C.

The whole Near East was ultimately absorbed by Rome, Macedonia in 168 B.C., Syria in 65 B.C. and Egypt in 30 B.C. But it is worth noticing that it was not Hellenic culture which chiefly influenced the Romans but the Hellenistic culture of the post-Alexander world.

Chief Features of the Hellenistic Era

In the new era, although a few Greek city-states survived, their power and simple society was gone forever. Instead there was a world view. In Greece, Corinth, until its destruction by the Romans in 146 B.C., became the chief center of trade and Athens, although it remained a university city, was left to feed on its past glories. The Near East, however, formed with Greece, Sicily, and the Greek cities of South Italy a single cultural and trading unit. In the Near East itself, the Greeks were the ruling caste. A simple form of the Greek language, the *coene*, in which the New Testament was to be written, was the universal language. The monarchs of the three principal states were, naturally, Macedonian, and Macedonian princesses were the queens. The Ptolemies even adopted sister-brother marriages from the Egyptians.

The Hellenistic world was a world of big nation-states, of credit-capitalism, of universalism, of great luxury side by side with mass poverty, and, in Egypt, of state-socialism. It was also a busy world of big cities and flamboyant architecture. The city of Alexandria had nearly a million inhabitants, with one whole quarter reserved for the Jewish population. Alexandria's library had in it a copy of every known book. Its two main streets were a hundred feet wide and glittered with lights, according to the poet Theocritus, "like the sun in small change." The beams from its four-hundred-foot-high lighthouse, the Pharos, could be seen, we are told, 27 miles out at sea. Its amusement-center, Canopus, which had slot machines and tunnels for pleasure-boats, provided recreation for Mediterranean sailors.

There were many other big cities, such as Antioch, Pergamum, and Ephesus in Asia Minor, Rhodes in the Aegean and Syracuse in Sicily. The *Syracusa*, a ship built to run between Syracuse and Alexandria, was close to 4000 tons burden. It was furnished with luxury cabins, fountains and gardens; and the water in its hold could be pumped out by one man with the force-pump which Archimedes of Syracuse had invented.

The Age of Greek Science

It was an age of science and invention. Modern medicine was begun in the 4th century B.C. by Hippocrates who held that every disease had natural causes. Today's medical men still take the Hippocratic oath. Hippocrates himself died in 357 B.C., reputedly at the age of 104. In the 3rd century B.C., Herophilus of Chalcedon is said to have practised vivisection on condemned criminals. In any case he issued a detailed description of the brain, discovered the function of the nerves and their relation to the brain, wrote studies of the optic nerve and the eye, and found out that arteries were carriers of blood, not air, and used the pulse in diagnosis. His pupil, Erasistratus, founded physiology as a distinct science, made a distinction between motor and sensory nerves and emphasized hygiene. Later, in the 2nd century B.C., an empirical school of medicine stopped creative discoveries but did advance the knowledge of drugs. Finally, Galen of Pergamum (131–210 A.D.) published in twenty-two volumes the essentials of Greek surgery and medicine up to his day. Hellenistic Greeks, therefore, began modern medicine, in spite of the relapse during the Dark or Middle Ages of Europe. Faith cures, however, were in vogue, particularly at the temple of Aesculapius at Epidaurus. Here, *incubatio* was practised, in which the patients after examination by the priests, slept in the temple and, according to forty-two grateful inscriptions, were healed of deafness, blindness, lameness and the like.

In mathematics Euclid (323–285 B.C.) advanced geometry and his theorems are still used. Archimedes of Syracuse (287–212 B.C.), however, is the oustanding name in both mathematics and physics. He employed indeterminate equations, calculated square roots, anticipated integral calculus, and his proof of the ratio (3:2) between a cylinder and a sphere circumscribed by it was depicted on his tomb. Later, Apollonius of Perga wrote on conics, and Hipparchus of the 2nd century B.C. developed trigonometry. In physics the greatest achievement of Archimedes was his discovery of the principle of specific gravity, which is said to have happened while he was in his bath and noticed the amount of water displaced by his body. According to the story, he leaped from the bath and ran naked through the streets of Syracuse, shouting, "Eureka" (I've found it). Later, he used specific gravity to prove that a goldsmith, entrusted with the task of making a gold crown for the tyrant of Syracuse, had replaced some of the gold by silver. Equally famous was his enunciation of the principle of the lever. Among his inventions were cogged wheels, the compound pulley, the tubular screw for pumping water, and pneumatic machines. We are told that his machines destroyed a Roman fleet which was besieging Syracuse in 212 B.C. When the Romans captured the city, Archimedes was killed by a Roman soldier, apparently by accident. We might note, too, that the Hellenistic Greeks invented catapults and water-organs operated by compressed air, a fire-engine, and even a toy steam-engine.

In astronomy, the achievements were even more startling, and it is important to remember that these men had no telescopes or modern scientific apparatus to help them. As early as the 4th century B.C., Heracleides of Pontus had discovered that the earth revolved on its axis once in every 24 hours—and there was no nonsense, as in the later Middle Ages of Europe, about the earth being flat. In the 3rd century B.C., Aristarchus of Samos (310–230 B.C.) advanced the heliocentric theory. The Greeks held a scientific congress about the problem, but the theory that the earth was the center of the universe carried the day. The discovery of the name of Aristarchus in the margin of a Copernican manuscript, however, suggests that Aristarchus may have given the clue to Copernicus and Galileo for their re-discovery of the heliocentric theory. Meanwhile, Hipparchus measured with precision the length of the year, the size of the moon's disc and its distance from the earth. A 1st century B.C. Greek estimated the size of the sun and its distance from the earth, but arrived at only three-eighths and five-eighths, respectively, of the correct figures. Eratosthenes of Cyrene (272–192 B.C.) measured the earth's circumference and erred by only 195 miles. He also said that Europe, Asia, and Africa were really one big island so that if you sailed west far enough you would reach India. This statement filtered down to Columbus through Strabo, a Roman geographer. Although these Greek discoveries and inventions were known to the Romans, much was forgotten during the Dark Ages which followed the collapse of the Roman Empire.

The "Modernity" of the Hellenistic Era

But what of the spirit of the times? It was an age of skepticism and mysticism, of universalism and a sense of futility. The world was now so big that the average man felt lost in it. Some turned to the mystery religions, such as the Egyptian worship of Isis-Osiris, because such religions promised immortality. Others formed all sorts of clubs so as to feel important in a small group. Still others joined what are called the "philosophic brotherhoods." Three of these last had a definite impact on the Romans. These were the Epicureans, the later Cynics, and the Stoics. Instead of an objective search for the why and how of the universe, all three sought a way of living in it. The Hellenistic world had begun to turn its back on reason and to depend on faith.

Epicurus founded his philosophy in Athens about 306 B.C. He believed that pleasure was the road to happiness, but his highest pleasures were the pleasures of the mind. To remove fear of death and fear of the gods, he claimed that the gods took no interest in humanity and that birth and death were simply the coming together and dissolution of atoms as in the atomic theory of Democritus. The famous Roman poet, Horace, said that he was "a fat porker from Epicurus' herd." A generation before him, another Roman poet, Lucretius, also an Epicurean, made a slashing attack on religion and expounded the Atomic theory.

The Epicureans were lineal descendants of the 4th century B.C., Cyrenaics. The Hellenistic Cynics sometimes degenerated into tramp philosophers delivering what were called "diatribes" to the unlettered crowds. The best of them preached the "slave as good as his master," the brotherhood of man, and the fatherhood of God. In these tenets they were promulgating the same doctrines as the Stoics, but their appeal was to the lower classes while the Stoics were missionaries to the more educated.

Stoicism was begun about 300 B.C., when Zeno of Citium in Cyprus began to lecture in the *Stoa Poikile* or Painted Porch in Athens. From *Stoa* came the name Stoics. To the Stoics the way to reach happiness was through virtue, and virtue was to be attained by indifference to all emotions, particularly to pleasure and pain. From this tenet of theirs is derived our modern definition of the word "stoic." A true Stoic—that is, the *sapiens* or wise man—according to the Stoics was as happy in prison as on a throne. As the Roman Seneca was to write later, in Stoic belief God was to be found "within us."

The Stoics backed up their philosophy by the theory that a "Fire-Soul" permeated the universe. Each man had within him a spark of the Fire-Soul.

Those souls which yielded least to emotions and lived the purest lives would finally rejoin the world Fire-Soul.

The Arts and Literature

In the arts and literature the Hellenistic Greeks were closer to us than their predecessors. Painting tended to be "prettified", and sculpture shows a turning away from the dignified idealism of the classical period. Instead, Hellenistic sculptors present us with realism in portrait sculpture, and realism "of a type" such as the "Drunken Old Woman" or "The Aged Shepherdess", with interest in genre, with art for art's sake pieces, with antiquarianism, with charming statues of children (whom the classical sculptors did not handle well), and, most striking of all, with representations of violent motion and emotion. The *Laocöon Group* is only one example of this last trend. *The Dying Gaul* is another (based on the struggle between the Pergamenes and the invading Celts) and so is the *Gaul Killing his Wife*, which is possibly one of the best of Hellenistic groups, since the contrast of the limp figure of the already dead woman with the defiant and despairing vigor of the Gaul, as he starts to plunge the sword into himself, is rendered superbly.

Literature was as varied as sculpture. Among the features of the Hellenistic world was an interest in the writings of past generations and the founding of huge libraries, of which the most famous was the library at Alexandria. Here within a few years a half a million volumes (rolls) were collected, to which additions were made. The most eminent of the librarians of Alexandria was Callimachus, who was said to have made a catalogue of 120 volumes giving the authors in order along with short biographies of them. Other renowned libraries were established at Antioch and Pergamum. It was in Pergamum that parchment as a substitute for papyrus was invented. As in modern days legions of scholars classified the fields of knowledge, wrote histories of drama, poetry, philosophy, and biographies of famous authors, established canons of the best works in various branches of literature, compared and criticized texts of authors such as Homer, Sappho, Aeschylus, and many others, published critical editions with minute commentaries, and wrote voluminously on philology which included technical grammar. The libraries performed a considerable service in preserving some of the classical works for us. A great loss to knowledge was the burning of the library of Alexandria during Julius Caesar's struggles in that city in 48 B.C., and the later conflagration of it by the Arabs when they conquered Egypt.

From Hellenistic Scholasticism came a tribe of scholar-poets whose greatest desire was to win the epithet of "learned," a trend which is usually called Alexandrinism. The habit was to write didactic verse, in which there was a resurrection of interest. Aratus, for instance, described astronomy in a long epic, the *Phaenomina*, and the signs of weather in his *Diosemeia*. Callimachus, the librarian, wrote, according to tradition, 800 rolls, and was recognized as the supreme Alexandrine elegist. His *Aetia* or *Causes,* a series of short love stories from the more obscure myths in elegiac verse, was popular and his *Lock of Berenice's Hair*, a mock heroic poem on the supposed apotheosis into a constellation of Queen Berenice's hair when she had it bobbed, was translated by the Roman poet, Catullus, a translation which in turn inspired Pope's *Rape of the Lock*. Other scholar-poets carried the trend toward obscurity to absurdity on the principle that the fewer people there were who understood what they wrote, the better the poetry. In Latin literature, Cinna's the *Zmyrna*, a poem of 500 lines which took nine years to compose, was an illustration of this sort of thing. Within a few years a commentary to explain it was written, and then a commentary to explain the commentary. Callimachus had said, "A big book is a big nuisance," and had laid down the rule that no poem should be longer than what could be read in one sitting, that is, about 500 lines. Hence came the popularity of the *epyllium* or little Epic of which *The Lock of Berenice's Hair* was an example. Another poet, Apollonius of Rhodes, however, sought to revive the long epic. His *Argonautica* which is still extant, although clever, lacks the simplicity and directness of the Homeric poems. It is replete with pedantic erudition, decorated with pictorial description, and features struggles within the love-sick heroine's mind, the heroine being Medea, the barbaric princess of Euripides' *Medea*.

As has been noted, Hellenistic tragedy imitated Euripides, while the New Comedy displays the same realism as is seen in sculpture. In prose, there were a tremendous number of histories about contemporary events. The best of these, of which we have the first five books and extracts from forty books, was written by Polybius of Megalopolis who, in 167 B.C., was carried as a hostage to Rome. As a result he gives us an outsider's view of the Romans and their government. Biography, as was natural in such an age, was popular. So, as is true today, were digests and encyclopaedias. There was a considerable development in rhetoric, a development which was to influence the Romans. On the one side was the "Asian" school which carried the flowery or grand style to excess; on the other the "Attic" which was the "plain" style and employed humor and satire.

Because education was wide-spread, in addition to New Comedy, literature to interest the masses was prevalent. This vulgar type of production included travellers' tales of strange and wonderful lands and happenings, romances, gossipy scandal and anecdotes about famous people, popular preachments simplifying morality, miscellanies, parodies and mimes of low life cast in the coarsest realism. The mimes of Herondas exemplify something of this trend, and may have been composed originally for production in the cabarets of Alexandria.

In consonance with the spirit of that day, the literary epigram attained tremendous popularity. Collections of epigrams such as the Garland (Anthology) of Meleager were made. To the Greeks the epigram was basically a short poem, not longer than eight lines, in elegiac metre, and today we distinguish seven types. They have come down to us in two collections, the Palatine Anthology and the Planudean Anthology. Some of the epigrams are of surprising beauty. Taken as a whole they exhibit the gamut of Hellenistic literature. Sex is a recurrent motif and the love epigrams tend to be sensuous and, quite frequently, pornographic. Included in the amatory epigram are certain special themes such as *The Lover Locked Out* and the *Dawn Comes Too Soon*. In the *epideictic* or show epigram we find descriptions of strange events, realism, comedy, description for description's sake and, quite often, art for art's sake. The scoptic epigrams are amusing and biting, and the futility of life ("Dance of Death") theme is expressed. "We are all watched and fed for Death, like a herd of swine butchered wantonly", wrote Palladas. There was scarcely room in the epigram, however, for other features of Hellenistic literature, such as hysteria of emotion, the lack of action, and the emphasis on struggles within a person.

Of all the Hellenistic poets Theocritus is regarded by Jebb as the "last perfect voice of Hellas." Born in Syracuse he migrated to Alexandria and spent a period of time in the island of Cos. He wrote a panegyric on Ptolemy Philadelphus (283–246 B.C.) and an exquisite mime, *The Women at the Adonis Festival* which is both realistic and a charming picture of the life of the day. His great achievement lay in his *Idylls* (little pictures). The chief source for these were the country-songs which Theocritus had heard in Sicily. The *Idylls* are short pieces (75 to 100 lines long) in which the general scheme is a contest in responsive (amoebean) song between two shepherds. Some of them are realistic, using the sort of language and thoughts which would suit shepherds. Others are "artless art" in which, although the characters purport to be shepherds, the descriptions of scenery and the language are beyond them. One *Idyll* (VII) introduces the artificial pastoral or "pastoral convention." In it Theocritus and his friends masquerade as shepherds.

The poems of Theocritus are Hellenistic in their length, in their pictorial qualities, their realism and, occasionally, in their artificiality and "prettiness." But they still retain the Hellenic sense of proportion and do not agonize emotion. Their influence on Latin literature (as in Vergil's

Eclogues) and European pastoral poetry has been widespread. Arcadia, Corydon, Thyrsis, Meliboeus—these and other names come from Theocritus. The artificial pastoral, in particular, is to be found in Italian, French, and English literature, as for example, in Pope and Matthew Arnold. Marie Antoinette's charming *L'Hameau* at *Le Petit Trianon* is an expression in its artificiality of the influence of the pastoral conventions.

Such in outline, were some of the chief features of the Hellenistic era. Its culture was inferior to Hellenic yet it was the period in which that culture was widely disseminated throughout the Near East and the Mediterranean area. Likewise in many fields it made its own contribution and its way of life points toward that of the Roman Empire.

Summary

In this description of the Greek contribution we have seen that, behind classical Greek culture, there lay the long period of the Minoan-Myceneans. That period was ended by the Dorian invasions. The Dark Age which followed illustrates that an advance forward in civilization is not inevitable or continuous.

Out of the debris there emerged eventually Homer and the beginnings of the Formative Era of the Greeks. In that Formative Era the Greeks developed the city-state, spread themselves around the Black Sea and the Mediterranean and, after abolishing their kings, experienced the rule of the aristocracy and, later, of the tyrants. When they flung off the tyrants, in most cases government fell into the hands of a comparatively small group of the wealthy and the well-born. Meanwhile, two leading states had emerged. The one was Sparta, the Soldier-State. The other was Athens; and in Athens, by a series of unpredictable events, the world's first democracy was instituted.

All this had happened by 500 B.C. We then observed how the defeat of the Persians by the Greeks initiated the Great Age of the 5th century. In this century the history of the Athenian democracy is the central fact. In a burst of energy, the Athenians built themselves a commercial and political sea-empire. At the same time and almost as a by-product of their commerce and their political expansion, there was in Athens under the leadership of Pericles, the remarkable outburst of architecture, sculpture, literature and thought, which so greatly influenced our own civilization. But this democracy was born into too young a world and it made the mistake of adopting a policy of imperialism. The Peloponnesian War weakened it and destroyed the Great Age. Yet the 4th century did retain elements of greatness, particularly in the thinking of Plato and Aristotle.

We next saw how the conquests of Alexander the Great brought in the Hellenistic era, which is sometimes called "The old age of Greece." It was a different and more modern world; and this was the world which the Romans were to absorb. One value of the Romans is that they transmitted Greek culture to us. Yet they also made a great contribution in their own right. Our next task is to see how the Romans developed and what they achieved.

Readings from Sources of the Period

(a) Theophrastus (ca. 372–287 B.C.) succeeded Aristotle as head of the Peripatetic School of Philosophy. Of his three surviving books, the most interesting is the *Characters*.

THE GARRULOUS MAN

Garrulity is the discoursing of much and ill-considered talk.

The Garrulous man is one who will sit down beside a person whom he does not know, and first pronounce a panegyric on his wife; then relate his dream of last night; then go through in detail what he has had for dinner. Then, warming to the work, he will remark that the men of the present day are greatly inferior to the ancients; and how cheap wheat has become in the market; and what a number of foreigners are in town; and that the sea is navigable after the Dionysia; and that, if Zeus would send more rain, the crops would be better; and that he will work his land next year; and how hard it is to live; and that Damippus set up a very large torch at the Mysteries; and "How many columns has the Odeum?" and that yesterday he was unwell; and "What is the day of the month?" and that the Mysteries are in Boedromion, the Apaturia in Pyanepsion, the rural Dionysia in Poseidon. Nor, if he is tolerated, will he ever desist.

(Howe and Harrer, *op. cit.*, p. 744, translated by R. C. Jebb, *The Characters of Theophrastus*, London: Macmillan, 1870—revised edn. by J. E. Sandys, 1909.)

(b) The spirit of Stoicism is exemplified in the *Hymn to Zeus* by Cleanthes (331 ca. 233 B.C.), who succeeded Zeno of Citium as the leader of the Stoics. From this hymn, a brief extract is given.

> Most glorious of Immortals, many-named, all-powerful forever,
> Zeus, nature's ruler, guiding all through law, all hail!
> For right it is all mortals should invoke thee.
> We are thy off-spring; we alone of all mortality,
> That lives and creeps on earth, have been allotted
> The image of the One. Therefore, I'll always praise thee
> And always sing thy power. Thee all the whirling Cosmos
> In meekness follows ever where thou leadest, gladly ruled by thee.
> The undying, fiery, two-edged thunderbolt thou holdest
> Within thy hands invincible—a minister of power
> Beneath whose stroke all nature shudders.
> With this thou dost direct, great as thou art,

Supreme king over all, the universal reason, mingled with
The great and lesser lights, and moving ever through the universe.
No work is wrought apart from thee, O God; not in the sea,
Nor in the heavenly regions, nor on earth,
Except what wicked men do in their folly.
Thou knowest how to render smooth the rough
And how to create order from disorder.
Things unto us unlovely are lovely unto thee.
So into one has all been framed by thee, the evil with the good,
That, throughout all, eternal universal reason reigns!
The wicked, by not heeding this, fall on an evil lot.
And some, though ever yearning for the good, mark not
Nor ever heed God's universal law; which did they heed,
They would obtain and have a goodly life, one harmonized
With reason. But as they live, unheedful of the good,
They rush about, some to one thing, and others to another;
Some with contentious striving for renown;
And others recklessly intent on gain.
Still others, through impatience for indulgence
And bodily pleasures, win just the opposite.
But thou who givest all, enthroned in clouds, Zeus, lord of thunder.
Deign thou to save mankind from grievous ineptitude.
Disperse it far, O Father, from their souls; and grant to them
To obtain that knowledge which enables thee to govern all
With justice, so that we, thus honored, may be brought
To honor thee, hymning thy works always, as all men should;
Since neither for immortals nor for mortals
Is there a greater prize or honor than
Duly to hymn forever the universal law.

(Howe and Harrer, *op. cit.*, pp. 750–751, translated by P. H. Epps.)

(c) Theocritus (c. 315–250 B.C.) is famed for his pastoral poetry, known as *Idylls*.
The first brief extract below is the beginning of the first *Idyll*; the second comes
from a mime which gives a realistic picture of two Syracusan women.

THYRSIS

Sweet is the whispering of yonder pine
That sings beside the spring, and, goatherd, sweet
Your piping; after Pan, the prize is yours.
If he receives the horned ram, you win
The goat; if he the goat, to you will fall
The kid, whose unmilked flesh is best to eat.

GOATHERD

Your song is sweeter than the echoing water,
Shepherd, that tumbles from the rocks above.
If as their prize the Muses take the sheep,
Yours is the stall-fed lamb; but if they choose
The lamb, the sheep as second prize is yours.

(MacKendrick and Howe, *op. cit.*, p. 101, translated by Warren R. Castle and L. R. Lind.)

(d) The Syracusan Women (*Idyll* XV)

GORGO. Is Praxinoë at home?

PRAXINOE. Dear Gorgo, how long it is since you have been here! Yes she *is* at home. The wonder is that you have got here at last! Eunoë, see that she has a chair. Throw a cushion on it too.

GORGO. It does most charmingly as it is.

PRAXINOE. Do sit down.

GORGO. Oh, what a thing spirit is! I have scarcely got to you alive, Praxinoë! What a huge crowd, what hosts of four-in-hands! Everywhere cavalry boots, everywhere men in uniform! And the road is endless: yes, you really live *too* far away!

PRAXINOE. It is all the fault of that madman of mine. Here he came to the ends of the earth and took—a hole, not a house, and all that we might not be neighbors. The jealous wretch, always the same, anything for spite!

GORGO. Don't talk of your husband Dinon like that, my dear, before your little boy,—look how he is staring at you! Never mind, Zopyrion, sweet child, she is not speaking about papa.

PRAXINOE. Our Lady! The child does notice.

GORGO. Nice papa!

PRAXINOE. That papa of his the other day went to get soap and rouge at the shop, and came back to me with salt—the great big oaf!

GORGO. Mine is the same—a perfect spendthrift, Diocleides! Yesterday he got what he took for five fleeces, and paid seven drachmas a piece for—what do you suppose? —dog-skins, shreds of old leather wallets, mere trash. But come, take your coat and shawl. Let us be off to the palace of rich Ptolemy the King, to the Adonis. I hear the Queen has provided something splendid!

PRAXINOE. Yes, fine folks do everything finely.

GORGO. What a tale you will have to tell about the things you have seen, to anyone who has not seen them! It is nearly time to go.

PRAXINOE. It's always holiday for idlers. Eunoë, bring the water and put it down in the middle of the room, lazy creature that you are. You cats always like to sleep soft! Come, hurry, bring the water; quicker! I want water first; and how she carries it! Give it to me all the same; don't pour out so much, you extravagant thing. Stupid girl! Why are you wetting my dress? There, stop; I have washed my hands, as heaven would have it. Where is the key to the big chest? Bring it here.

GORGO. Praxinoë, that full dress becomes you wonderfully. Tell me, how much did the stuff cost you off the loom?

PRAXINOE. Don't speak of it, Gorgo! More than eight pounds in good silver money,—and the work on it! I nearly slaved my soul out over it!

GORGO. Well, it is *most* successful, I must say.

PRAXINOE. Thanks for the pretty speech! (*To Eunoë*) Bring my shawl, and set my hat on my head properly.—No, child, I'm not going to take you. Boo! Bogies! There's a horse that bites little boys! You may cry as much as you please, but I am not going to have you lamed.—Let us be moving. Phrygia, take the child, and keep him amused. Call in the dog, and shut the door. (*They go into the street.*) Ye gods, what a crowd! How on earth are we ever to get through this crush?

They are like numberless ants. Many a good deed have you done, Ptolemy! Since your father joined the immortals, there's never a thug to maul the pedestrian, creeping up on him in Egyptian fashion. Oh! the tricks those rascals used to play. Birds of a feather, rascals all!—Dear Gorgo, what will become of us? Here come the King's horses!—My dear man, don't trample on me. Look, the bay's rearing; see, what temper!—Eunoe, you foolhardy girl, will you never keep out of the way? The beast will be the death of the man that's leading him. What a good thing it is that I left my brat safe at home.

GORGO. Courage, Praxinoë. We are safe behind them now, and they have got in line.

PRAXINOE. There! I begin to be myself again. Ever since I was a child I have feared nothing so much as horses and slimy snakes. Come along; a huge mob is pouring after us.

GORGO (*to an old woman*). Are you from the court, Mother?

OLD WOMAN. I am, my child.

PRAXINOE. Is it easy to get there?

OLD WOMAN. The Achaeans got into Troy by trying, my pretty. Trying will do everything in the long run.

GORGO. The old wife had spoken her oracles, and off she goes.

(Warnock and Anderson, *op. cit.*, p. 309.)

(e) The epigrams of the Hellenistic Era range over the whole field of human life. Only three examples can be given.

I   HERACLITUS

> They told me, Heraclitus, they told me you were dead;
> They brought me bitter news to hear and bitter tears to shed.
> I wept as I remembered how often you and I
> Had tired the sun with talking and sent him down the sky.
> And now that thou art lying, my dear old Carian guest,
> A handful of gray ashes, long, long ago at rest,
> Still are thy pleasant voices, thy nightingales, awake;
> For Death, he taketh all away, but them he cannot take.
>
>   Callimachus.

(*Ibid.*, p. 311, translated by William Cory.)

II   MELEAGER
                                    (About 140–70 B.C.)
                                    To a Bee

> Flower-pastured bee,
>   Why dost thou cease to seek
> The buds of May and kissest
>   My Heliodora's cheek?
>
> Dost thou wish to signify
>   With thy caressing wing
> That there lurketh in her skin
>   Love's sweet and bitter sting?

> O friend of lovers, go,
>> If this be all thy lore,
> Back to the buds of May;
>> I knew it long before.

(MacKendrick and Howe, *op. cit.*, p. 103, translated by Warren R. Castle and L. R. Lind.)

III   DION OF TARSUS

> I, Dion of Tarsus, lie here at sixty.
> Having never married; and I would my father had not.

PART III

Our Heritage from Rome

The distinguished classicist, T. R. Glover, once said: "Rome is famed for its drains: Greece for its brains". By this he meant that the great Greek contribution to us is in art, literature, and ideas, while the Romans gave us practical things, such as engineering, roads, law, organization, and discipline. Their institutions have influenced us as massively as their roads once scored Europe. To study the story of how a small and insignificant collection of huts on the banks of the Tiber came to rule most of the known civilized world of its day is to marvel at what tough endurance and stern discipline can achieve, and then to realize the weaknesses inherent in the exercise of imperial power.

Rome—800 B.C. to 600 A.D.

Dates: (B.C. to Birth of Christ, A.D. thereafter)

800	
753	Legendary date of Founding of Rome.
700	
600	Rome under Etruscans.
509	Founding of Roman Republic.
500	Struggle for survival against Etruscans, hill-tribes, and Gauls.
400	Struggle between Patricians and Plebeians.
300	Conquest of Italy south of the Po River.
272	Capture of Tarentum. The 1st and 2nd Carthaginian Wars. Conquest of Western Mediterranean.
200	Conquest of Near East.
133	Destruction of Carthage and of Numantia in Spain.
102–101	Defeat of Teutones and Cimbri.

Principal authors
Naevius
Plautus
Terence
Ennius
Lucilius

Lucilius
Cato the Elder

Date	Events	Authors
100	Downfall of Republic — The Gracchi, Marius, Sulla 1st Triumvirate, Conquest of Gaul Civil War—Pompey vs. Caesar, Caesar's	Cicero Caesar Sallust Livy Lucretius Catullus Vergil Horace Ovid
31 Birth of Christ	Actium — Assassination—Defeat of Liberators Octavianus (Augustus) vs. Antony and Cleopatra	
14 68	Death of Augustus. Rule of Julio-Claudians.	Petronius Seneca Phaedrus Lucan
100	Flavian Caesars The Five Good Emperors — Period of Prosperity	Quintilian Tacitus Pliny Suetonius Apuleius Martial Juvenal
180 200	Military Monarchy and Chaos Persians in East.	
300 305 325	Barbarian Invasions in West. Diocletian and Empire re-established. Constantine the Great—Christianity the official Religion. Empire divided into Eastern and Western halves.	
400	Barbarian Invasions.	
476	Fall of Western Roman Empire.	
500	Germanic Kingdoms carved out of Western Roman Empire.	
600		

CHAPTER 1

Ancient Italy and its Peoples

Italy is a jackboot, 700 miles long, eternally poised to kick Sicily out of the Mediterranean. The arc of the Alps cuts it off from Europe and makes it part of the Mediterranean world. Yet, through the Alpine passes and along the coast on either side, from what is now France and Yugoslavia, invaders have made their way from time immemorial. Others have come by sea. Like Greece, Italy has always been a mixing bowl of peoples. Like Greece, too, the peninsula is segmented by mountains. The fertile valley of the Po, lying close under the Alps, and the highlands to the west and northeast of it spread over about one-half of its 91,000 square miles of territory (over three and a half times the size of continental Greece), but the ridges of the Apennines separate the Po valley from the rest of the peninsula so that to the Romans it was not part of their Italy but, until the middle of the 1st century B.C., was Cisalpine Gaul (Gaul this side of the Alps).

The Apennines do more than isolate the Po Valley. Curving southward, they form the spiny backbone of the rest of Italy. This part of the peninsula is never more than 125 miles wide, or roughly half the distance from Boston to New York. Because the mountains swing close to the eastern coast, on the Adriatic side of Italy there are few harbors and only narrow coastal plains. But among the Apennines are fertile valleys and, further west, the ridges open into the plains of what is now Tuscany and the bigger plains of Latium (around Rome) and Campania (around Naples). On the western coast are two navigable rivers, the Arno and the Tiber, and there are excellent harbors at Genoa and Naples. Just as Greece faces east, so Italy faces west, and the islands of Sicily, Elba and Sardinia are within its view. Geography, although it made civilization come to the peninsula later than to Greece, destined ancient Italy to control the Western Mediterranean.

The mountain ranges do tend to isolate some parts of Italy. In general they are not so much a bar to communications as are the Greek mountains. Moreover, because the plains and valleys are bigger, larger communities developed and it was much easier than in Greece for these communities to become united either in self-interest or as the result of force. As a result the Romans were able to forge Italy into a nation-state. Furthermore, as compared to Greece, Italy is a rich country. Its soil is fertile, its pasture-land lush. In ancient times the slopes of its mountains were thick with oaks and ash mingled with hazels, the arbute tree, and a dozen other varieties. Wheat and barley, melons, peas, beans, leeks, cabbages, green vineyards, apple and olive orchards, timber, herds of swine, sheep, goats and cattle (Italy means Cattleland)—in terms of ancient economy all these made the country wealthy. There was potter's clay, plenty of marble, and a good supply of water. To the Greeks Italy was an Eldorado.

Because of its length and because of the height of its mountains, Italy offers variety in climate. From Naples southward it is as hot in summer as Greece. From Rome to the north the temperature is more moderate and the Romans, like the Italians of today, used to escape from the heat to their villas among the hills. In winter, however, the snow can lie deep on the plains along the Po river and on and among the Apennines, though in Rome and Naples, as in Athens, the thermometer seldom drops below freezing. Like the Greeks, the Romans tended to live an outdoors life.

To Roman poets such as Vergil there was no land to compare to the countryside of Italy. Modern travellers often agree. There is the lushness of the Po valley and the turquoise of its alpine lakes. There are the bare and rugged colors of the hill-top towns and in the south the marvellous sweep of the Bay of Naples, with vegetation spilling over the cliffs to the blue below like waterfalls of vivid green. No land can offer a greater variety of natural beauty.

Such was the Italy which was to become the homeland of the Romans.

Early Peoples of Italy

Paleolithic men, including Neanderthal and Cro-Magnon types, lived in Italy. During the neolithic and early bronze ages varying stocks from North Africa, the Balkans, the Upper Danube Valley, Switzerland, and Spain infiltrated the peninsula. Among these peoples were the lake-dwellers of North Italy who, as in Switzerland, built their villages on platforms resting on piles driven into the Alpine lake-bottoms close to shore and, besides hunting and fishing, tilled nearby fields, kept cattle, sheep, and pigs, wove cloth from flax, hemp, and wool, made pottery, ate apples and pears, and brewed cider. A couple of centuries or so later, Indo-Europeans appeared at about the same time that they first intruded into Greece.

The developed bronze age from about 1700 to 1000 B.C. brought new stocks into the peninsula. Among them were the *Terramara* (Black-earth) people of North Italy. Terramara was the name given by North Italian peasants to huge mounds from which they took soil to fertilize their fields. In the 19th century A.D. it was discovered that these mounds, ranging from four to eighteen acres in extent and from ten to fourteen feet in height, were the refuse left by some seven centuries of village life. The huts of the successive villages had been built on posts and, in some cases like those of the lake-dwellers' villages, on platforms set on piles driven into damp ground. The Terramara folk are thought to have come from the north, possibly from western Hungary. They were superior farmers and excellent workers in bronze. Meanwhile Minoan-Mycenean influences were reaching Sicily and southern Italy.

The beginning of the Iron Age (around 1000 B.C.) saw an Illyrian stock settle in Venetia, Apulia, and the heel of Italy. As these migrants took over much of the eastern coast of Italy, new Indo-European tribes from the Balkans and the Danube valley appeared. The new-comers were divided into two major groups, speaking two distinct dialects of Indo-European. One group, the Umbro-Sabellians, of which the most important peoples were the Umbrians, the Sabines, and the Samnites, occupied central Italy from Florence and Rimini southward. They spoke Umbro-Oscan, of which the chief written survivals are the Iguvine tablets from Gubbio in Umbria and Oscan inscriptions found in Pompeii. The other group was composed of the Latins of Latium and their neighbors, the Faliscans, both of whom spoke Latin.

Meanwhile, the previous peoples of the peninsula were either assimilated by the invaders or pushed to the fringes of the country. The most important of these remnants were the Ligurians of northwestern Italy.

From this sketch of early Italy it is clear that by around 1000 B.C. the peninsula was already a conglomerate of peoples. All of them were in a fairly primitive state of culture. They lived in villages. Iron was scarce and bronze was still in common use. Both cremation and inhumation were practiced. But there were no cities and no developed civilization until the coming of the Greeks and the Etruscans.

The Greeks

The Minoan-Myceneans had established trading-posts in Sicily. When the Mycenean "empire" dissolved, the Phoenicians took over the trade routes. After the Assyrians occupied Phoenicia in the 8th century B.C., Carthage, formerly a Phoenician colony, established a commercial empire in the western Mediterranean and contended with the Greeks for Sicily.

Neither the Minoan-Myceneans nor the Phoenicians and Carthaginians left any important imprint on Italy. The Greek influence was to be pervasive. As early as the 8th century B.C. Greek traders were sailing up the Tiber and penetrating Etruria. But their massive impact was to come later from their colonies in southern Italy which reached up the western coast as far as Cumae, north of Naples, from their settlements in Sicily, and from the Roman conquest of the Greek world. Not the Greeks but the Etruscans were the first people to bring civilization to Rome.

The Etruscans

Paradoxically, we know most about the living Etruscans from their dead. Etruscan literature has disappeared. Of the almost 10,000 Etruscan inscriptions, which are written in the Greek alphabet, only ten contain more than thirty words. Scholars, by patient labor, can read many of the inscriptions, but they consist chiefly of proper names and repetitious religious formulas, dedications, epitaphs, and titles. Both the Greeks and the Romans wrote about the Etruscans but both were hostile witnesses. Most of our insight into the culture of this once powerful people comes from the ruins of their cities and, more especially, from their tombs. Like the Egyptians, the Etruscans regarded their final resting-places as "Houses for Eternity". As a result the upper class fashioned huge *tumuli* tombs (mounds on top of excavations into the tufa below) as at Cerveteri (ancient Caere), or dug out great vaults in hillsides as at Tarquinia, or made corridor tombs as at Orvieto. The rooms of the houses of the living were reproduced in stone to the last rafter. There were elaborate tomb furnishings of pottery, jewelry, gold cups, and the like. Sometimes the tomb-walls were painted with banqueting scenes accompanied by music and the dance. Greek legends also appear on the walls and, in the later days of Etruria, there are gloomy figures from the Etruscan underworld. It is from the wall-paintings, the tomb furnishings, the sculpture, and other art-objects that we can achieve a certain amount of understanding of the culture and thoughts of this enigmatic people who, suddenly, in the late 9th or early 8th century B.C. appear in Etruria among the primitive Italians as the possessors of an advanced civilization.

The origins of the Etruscans are still being debated. The Greek, Herodotus, who lived when the Etruscans were still a potent force, records in his history a legend that, because of a famine in Lydia in Asia Minor, the king's son, Tyrrhenus, led a migration to Italy. Although some scholars today argue for a development of the Etruscans in Italy, most authorities agree that they are of eastern origin and probably from Asia Minor. The Etruscans spoke a non-Indo-European language. Their religious practices were eastern not western, and many of their art forms seem to be connected with the East. To judge from their settlements, such as those at Caere and Tarquinii (modern Tarquinia), they landed on the grey-black beaches of Etruria, marched inland to the first spurs of the hills, and fortified them. With their superior civilization and military organization, they found it easy to subdue the natives and to set them to work, with themselves as a ruling caste. During the 8th century B.C. they established a group of powerful city-states in Etruria, such as those centering at Caere, Tarquinii, Vulci, Populonia, and Volaterrae. In the next century they reached into Umbria. Perugia, Assisi, Cortona, Arezzo, Fiesole near Florence, Orvieto, and Chiusi (ancient Clusium) are modern Italian centers which owe their origins to the Etruscans.

During the same 7th century and the 6th, the Etruscans seized Rome, overran Latium, and broke into Campania where they founded Capua and even reached the gulf of Salerno. Further expansion in this area was checked by the Greek cities. In the 6th century B.C. after building a base at Felsina (near Bologna) they thrust into the valley of the Po. Modena, Parma, Verona, and Mantua are among the places they founded. On the eastern seaboard they built Rimini, Ravenna, Spina, the port of Felsina which was a sort of ancient Venice, and Adria which gave its name to the Adriatic Sea. Further west they put down a post at Melpum near Milan. Meanwhile, they had seized the island of Elba and, in 535 B.C., joined with the Carthaginians to thrust the Greeks out of Sardinia at the battle of Alalia. At the height of their power, they ruled from the Alps southward through Umbria, Etruria, Latium, and Campania to the Gulf of Salerno. So potent was their fleet that the Greeks called the area between Sicily, Sardinia, and the west coast of Italy the "Tyrrhenian Sea" (today Mare Tirenno) from their name for the Etruscans. "The power of Etruria was so great," writes Livy, the Roman historian, "that the glory of its name filled not only the earth but even the sea, throughout the length of Italy from the Alps to the Straits of Messina".

Etruscan Economy

Etruscan prosperity was based on agriculture, lumbering, the exploitation of the iron mines of Elba and the deposits of copper and tin in northern Etruria, manufacturing, and trade and commerce. By land their goods went to France, Germany, the Upper Danube Valley, and even to Britain. On sea their ships controlled the Tyrrhenian Sea and sailed to the eastern Mediterranean. Their chief exports were metal work, leather goods, jewelry and pottery; their imports amber, tin, lead, Greek vases, and luxury goods such as ivory, glass, tapestries, gold, silver, and perfumes. The upper classes lived a life of ease and refinement.

Religion

The Greeks and Romans distinguished between secular and religious life. With the Etruscans religion was dominant. Every public act was governed by the taking of omens and once a year a "high priest" for all the Etruscans was chosen at a great festival. Their gods, who at first were impersonal forces, became personalized under Greek influence and were arranged in triads. Ritual (the so-called *disciplina*), especially in the art of divination, was all important. Triads of gods, triple-celled temples, and the art of divination were among the features of Etruscan religion which the Romans took over. Particularly important were preparations for the after life. At Cerveteri the "City of the Dead", with streets between the rows of tombs, sits on a spur of the hills to the north of what was the city of the living. Like the Egyptians the Etruscans seem to have believed that the dead could relive the scenes painted on the walls of the tombs. At the height of their power, the paintings show men and women reclining at feasts while flautists play and dancers whirl. In a recently discovered tomb there is a cheerful scene of hunting and fishing. But when Etruscan power declined there was an obsession with demons from the underworld.

Government

The Etruscans had a loose federal league of twelve cities, but, as with the Philistines, each city was independent. As a result no enemy ever met the combined might of the Etruscans, and, on occasion, an Etruscan city might even aid the foe of another Etruscan city, as when the people of Caere helped Rome in her struggle against Veii. The cities were at first governed by kings but later by oligarchies of powerful families. Later, in some of the cities there appear to have been revolutions by the lower classes. Many of the insignia of the Etruscan magistrates, such as lictors, magistrates' robes, and curule chairs, were adopted by the Romans. So was the Etruscan triumph. The cities were, individually, magnificent, and in some cases had more than 100,000 inhabitants, a large population for those days. Excavations also show at times a grid pattern based on two intersecting main streets, like the pattern of the later Roman military camps. But the lack of a central and cohesive government for all the cities proved to be a political and military weakness.

The Arts and Daily Life

At an early date Greek influences reached the Etruscans, as is shown by their pottery, their sculpture, their alphabet, and the use of Greek legends in some of their tomb-paintings. Greek artists undoubtedly settled in Etruscan cities, but whatever the Etruscans borrowed they made their own. The striding "Apollo of Veii" possesses a sheer physical power absent in similar Greek statues, and the Winged Horses in terracotta from a temple at Tarquinia are stylistically perfect. Terracotta was a medium in which the Etruscans were particularly successful. Their elaborate jewelry is eastern in motifs but is magnificently done. In architecture their use of the arch and their enduring masonry was adopted by the Romans. Though their tomb-paintings vary in quality, they have a definite Etruscan touch.

Daily life for the upper classes at least was luxurious and materialistic. Women seem to have been regarded as the equals of men. Hunting and fishing were popular sports. Gladiatorial combats of various sorts were in vogue. Music and the dance were passions. Their flautists, trumpeters, and lyre players were renowned. According to Aristotle, the Etruscans fought, kneaded dough, and beat their slaves to the sound of flutes. In their tomb-paintings, the dancers move in an almost orgiastic exuberance. The Romans accused the Etruscans of luxury and licentiousness. The evidence we have seems to suggest that at the apex of their power there was in them an over-powering vitality and love of life.

The Decline of the Etruscans

In 524 B.C. the Etruscans were repulsed in an attempt to seize Cumae. Then in 474 B.C., in a great sea fight, the Western Greeks under the command of Hiero, tyrant of Syracuse, defeated them. In the British Museum there is a helmet from this battle. On it is inscribed: "Hiero, son of Deinomenes, and the Syracusans—Etruscan spoils from Cumae for Zeus." Next, in 438 B.C., Samnites from the hills took Capua. The Etruscan possessions in Campania were lost and, in the meantime, the Romans and Latins had expelled them from Latium.

Disaster also struck in the north. At the beginning of the 4th century B.C. hordes of yellow-haired Celtic tribes (known as Gauls by the Greeks and Romans) poured into the valley of the Po, seized Felsina, defeated the Etruscans in a great battle near Milan and raided into Etruria. From this time forward the Etruscans were limited to their home country. As Roman power increased, their cities were captured one by one until all of them were subjugated.

Etruscan Influence on Rome

The Etruscans civilized the Romans. Apart from their political control they transplanted their institutions, industries and fine arts in Rome and Latium. Roman lictors, triumphs, augurs, the Roman alphabet, the key-stone arch, triads of gods, and the Etruscan temple—these were only a few of the borrowings. As late as 311 B.C. Roman young men of the upper class were sent to Etruria to learn Etruscan literature and the Etruscan art of divination. It was only when Greek cultural influence overwhelmed the Romans that the Etruscans began to be forgotten, although Maecenas, one of the chief ministers of Augustus, prided himself on being of Etruscan descent and Vergil, the Roman poet, wrote glowingly of "strong Etruria". Gradually the Etruscan language and literature died out. The emperor Claudius (41–54 A.D.), who wrote twenty books on the Etruscans, seems to have been one of the last persons to know the Etruscan tongue.

The discovery of the Etruscans is still proceeding. In recent years electronic devices are being used to locate tombs after which a hole is bored into each tomb. A metal tube is inserted in the hole and through it a small camera which can be turned to snap twelve different pictures of the interior of the vault is lowered. In this way tombs can be located and it can be decided from the pictures whether they will repay excavation or not.

In spite of the discoveries and in spite of modern interest in the Etruscans they still remain enigmatic. Their names such as Arnth or Vulca, the artist who is said to have done the Apollo of Veii and to have been brought to Rome to fashion the statues of the Capitoline triad of Jupiter, Juno and Minerva, seem alien to us. So do their titles, such as Lucumo. We have glimpses of long-lanced cavalry and of well-trained infantry, yet in battle these troops are said to have been preceded by priests brandishing torches and snakes. In the Villa Giulia in Rome the terra-cotta portrait statues of an Etruscan noble and his wife recline as if at an eternal banquet. Their narrow aristocratic faces smile ironically across the centuries at us. In these sophisticated faces is the mystery of the Etruscans. Yet for us the Etruscans are simply the prelude to Rome.

Readings from Sources of the Period

(a) In his *Georgics*, Vergil is lyrical in his praise of the land of Italy.

Here is perpetual spring and summer in months not her own; twice the cattle breed, twice the apple tree yields her service. But the raging tigress is not there or the fierce lion-brood, nor does monkshood deceive the wretched gatherer, nor the scaly serpent dart in huge coils over the ground or gather so long a train of spires. Add thereto all her illustrious cities and the labours wrought in her, all her towns piled high by men's hands on their sheer rocks, and her rivers that glide beneath immemorial walls. Or shall I tell of the seas that wash above her and below? or her great lakes, thee, lordly Larius, and thee, Benacus, heaving with billows and roar as of the sea? or tell of her harbours, of the barriers set upon the Lucrine and the thunder of the indignant sea where the Julian wave echoes afar in the tideway, and the Tyrrhene surge pours into the channels of Avernus? She it is likewise who unlocks from her veins streams of silver and ore of brass, and flows with abundant gold: she who rears a valiant race of men, the Marsian and the Sabellian stock, the Ligurian trained in hardship and the Volscian spearmen; she the Decii, the Marii, and the mighty Camilli, the seed of Scipio stern in war, and thee, princely Caesar, who even now victorious in Asia's utmost borders does keep aloof the unwarlike Indian from the towers of Rome. Hail, mighty mother of harvests, O land of Saturn, mighty of men: for thee I tread among the glories and arts of old, and dare to unseal these holy springs, making the song of Ascra echo through the Roman towns.

Now, for a space, of the tempers of the fields, the strength of each, and the colour, and the native power of fruit-bearing. First, stubborn soils and ungracious hills, fields of lean marl and pebbly brushwood, welcome the long-lived olive groves of Pallas; for sign thereof, in this same region the oleaster springs abundant, and strews the fields with her wild berries. But fat land glad with sweet moisture, and flats thick with herbage and bounteous in richness, such as many a time we may descry in the cup of a mountain valley (for hither streams trickle from the cliff-tops and draw down their rich mud), and the southern upland that feeds the fern, hateful to crooked ploughs; this one day will yield thee vines excelling in strength and flowing with wealth of wine, this is fertile of the grape, this of such juice as we pour in offering from cups of gold, when the sleek Etruscan blows his ivory flute by the altars and we offer the steaming entrails on bulged platters. But he whose desire is rather the keeping of cattle and calves, or the breed of sheep or she-goats that strip the plantations, let him seek the lawns and distances of rich Tarentum, or such a plain as unhappy Mantua lost, where snow-white swans feed in the weedy river: not clear springs nor grass will fail the flocks, and how much soever the cattle crop through the long days, as much the chilly dew of a brief night will restore. Land that is black and rich under the share's pressure, and crumbling-soiled (for this it is that we imitate by ploughing) is always the best for corn: from no other harvest floor shalt thou discern the slow oxen bring thy wagons oftener home: or where the angry plough-man has carted the forest-trees away, and levelled the copses that lay idle many a year, and rooted clean out the birds' ancient homes; they spring skyward from their abandoned nests, but the tangled field gleams behind the driven share. For in truth the starved gravel of the hill-country scarce serves the bees with dwarf spurge and rosemary; and scaling tufa and chalk tunnelled by black-scaled snakes call no other land their like to furnish dainty food and yield winding retreats for serpents. Such land as exhales thin mist and flitting smoke, and drinks in and drains away the wet at will, such as is evergreen in clothing of native grass, and mars not iron with a scurf of salt rust, this will garland thine elms with laughing vines, this is fruitful of oil, this wilt thou prove in tillage gracious to the flock and yielding under the crooked share. Such is the tilth of wealthy Capua and the coast that borders the Vesuvian ridge, and where Clanius encroaches on desolate Acerrae.

(McDermott and Caldwell, *op. cit.*, pp. 264–5.)

(b) In the passage below Livy relates the Roman version of how an Etruscan became king of Rome.

During the reign of Ancus Martius an Etruscan named Lucumo migrated to

Rome, a man of ability and wealth. The chief reason for his coming was ambition and the hope of winning honors, which he had no opportunity of achieving at Tarquinii because of his foreign birth. He was the son of Demaratus of Corinth, who had been exiled from his native city by a revolution and had happened to settle in Tarquinii. Having married an Etruscan wife, Demaratus had two sons, Lucumo and Arruns. He was survived by Lucumo, who fell heir to all his wealth, while Arruns died before his father, leaving a son still unborn. The father lived only a short time after Arruns' death and, not knowing that a child was to be born to his daughter-in-law, made no provision for it in his will. Thus the child was born to no share in the patrimony and was given the name Egerius, the needy one.

Lucumo on the contrary was fired to ambition not only by his inherited wealth but also by his marriage with Tanaquil, herself a woman of high station and not satisfied to marry beneath it. She could not endure the humiliation of the Etruscans' scorn for Lucumo, the son of an exile. Forgetting her natural attachment to her country in her determination to see honor accorded to her husband, she conceived the idea of moving away from Tarquinii. Rome seemed the most promising as a new home. In a new state where all distinctions were of recent origin and attainable by merit, there was likely to be a place for a strong and energetic man. At Rome Tatius the Sabine had been king, Numa had been called in from Cures to occupy the throne, and Ancus himself was half Sabine and had only one noble ancestor to display in his portrait gallery.

Accordingly they packed up their possessions and moved to Rome. They had travelled in their covered wagon as far as the Janiculum Hill at the edge of the city, when an eagle darted down and carried off Lucumo's cap, soared above the cart with great commotion and again, as if sent on this particular mission, replaced the cap on his head and flew away. The story is that Tanaquil, who like most Etruscans was skilled in reading signs from the heavens, interpreted this as a favorable omen. She bade her husband hope for great things. For an eagle appearing from that quarter of the sky was a messenger of Jove and had given a sign which concerned the highest point of a man's life. It had removed the adornment of his head only to replace it upon him as a crown. Bringing with them such dreams and hopes they entered the city, where they bought a house and established residence, Lucumo calling himself Lucius Tarquinius Priscus.

Tarquinius was at once conspicuous among the Romans because of the novelty of a new arrival in town and because of his wealth. This prominence he himself furthered by his graciousness of address, by his hospitality of entertaining in his home, and by doing kindnesses whenever opportunity offered, until his reputation became known even to the king. Before long that first favorable introduction to the king was transformed into close friendship by the generosity and capability of his services to the state. He became an active participant in public affairs and a trusted counsellor on all questions in peace and in war. At length, thoroughly tried and tested, he was designated in the king's will as guardian of the young princes.

Ancus reigned twenty-four years, unsurpassed by any of his predecessors in glory and in the arts of peace and war. At his death his sons were not far from the age of manhood. Tarquinius was therefore the more insistent that the election of the new king be held at the earliest possible moment, and as the time for the election drew near he sent the boys off on a hunting trip. He was the first man in our history to canvass for election to office or to make a campaign speech designed to win the votes of the populace. If he were the first foreigner to aspire to the sovereignty in Rome, he argued, men might justifiably look with surprise or disfavor upon his candidacy. But he was in no way departing from precedent. This would be the third time that the Roman throne had been occupied by a foreigner. Tatius had been made king, though he was not only a foreigner but an enemy. Numa, who was a stranger to the city, had been called in to accept the crown. He himself had lived in Rome from the time when he had come to manhood, and had made his home there with his wife and all his possessions. The years of his manhood—that part of life in which men contribute to the welfare of the state—had been spent more in Rome than in his native country. In military and civil life he had become conversant with Roman laws and institutions under tutelage at which no one could cavil, that of King Ancus himself. In loyalty and service to the king he could challenge anyone in the city. In service to the people of Rome he could match even the king.

Reminded of these many merits and recognizing the justice of his claims, the Roman people elected him by a huge majority.

(MacKendrick and Howe, *Classics in Translation*; Vol II, *Latin Literature*, pp. 286–7; Madison: University of Wisconsin Press, 1952.)

CHAPTER 2

Rome: Its Early History and Government

Eternal Rome owes its beginnings to a river, a ford, and seven hills. In early times a trade in salt ran from the evaporating pans at the mouth of the Tiber to Tibur (Tivoli) some 40 miles inland along a road bordering the river called the *Via Salaria*, the "Salt-Road." Some sixteen miles from the mouth of the Tiber, about where navigation ends, an island makes possible a ford, while on the left bank rise low hills, from two to three hundred feet above sea-level. Here is where Rome began. Of her seven hills, the nearest to the river are the Capitoline, Palatine, and Aventine with valleys between them. Behind, in a rough arc, are the Quirinal, Viminal, Esquiline, and Caelian. In later days, two hills across the river, the Janiculum and the Vatican, were added.

The Romans put the first year of their city (and dated events *Ab urbe condita*, "from the founding of the city") in the year we call 753 B.C., but excavations suggest that the first primitive settlements go back to before 1000 B.C. The first settlers may have seen that the hills could control the river-traffic, and navigable rivers, such as, for example, the Mississippi and Missouri rivers in the United States, are important in the early development of any country. They may also have perceived that north-south trade would flow across the ford. But they would not have comprehended that the site of Rome gave her a chance to master Italy.

If we look at the map we observe that Rome is favorably situated to control the plain of Latium. That plain is about 30 to 35 miles wide and around 60 miles long. It is not a prairie. There are rows of flat-topped pine-trees and much of it is broken into gullies and undulating folds of ground. Moreover, Latium was inhabited by people of the same stock and speaking the same language as the Romans. The plain of Latium is at about the center of Italy; from Latium, the Romans could strike outward and always have interior lines of communication.

265

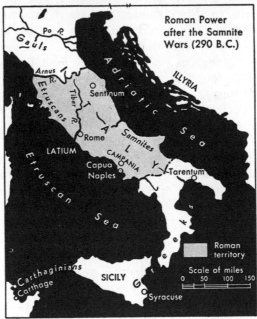

Growth of Rome

The Aeneas Legend

The early history of Rome is obscure. The Romans themselves in the 3rd century B.C. adopted a Greek legend that Aeneas, escaping from Troy, wandered about the Mediterranean and eventually founded Rome. According to their account, when Aeneas reached Latium there was a series of wars, after which he became King of Lavinium. His son, Ascanius or Iulus (the Julian *gens*, to which Julius Caesar belonged, held that Iulus was its ancestor and that, therefore, since Aeneas was the son of Venus, all its members were goddess-descended) was said to have founded Alba Longa (the Long White Ridge) which was at one time an important Latin center. Here a priestess, Rhea Silvia, bore twin sons, Romulus and Remus, to the god Mars. The twins were brought up by a she-wolf and, in young manhood, established Rome on the Palatine Hill. But Romulus, in anger at his brother jumping over the wall he had started to build, killed him.

In this way the Romans incorporated their own local legends into the Greek version, filled the gap between the traditional date of the fall of Troy in 1184 B.C. and their own year for the beginning of Rome in 753 B.C., and connected themselves romantically with the heroes of Homeric epic. Livy, Vergil, Horace, and other Roman authors popularized the story.

Early Rome

The findings of the archaeologists prove an early settlement, probably of Latins, on the Palatine Hill around 1000 B.C. This first village seems to have been laid out in *Terramara* fashion with two intersecting main streets. Later, a Sabine village was established on the Esquiline. The cemetery was in the Forum where excavators have found both cremation and inhumation burials to suggest two differing groups of people. The story of the Rape of the Sabine Women, according to which the Romans, in need of wives, invited the Sabines to a festival and then carried off their women, may be a reminiscence of the merging of Sabines and Latins.

As time went by, hamlets on other hills were added (not including the Aventine which was not taken into the city until the 4th century B.C.) and were drawn together into one community, an event celebrated by the festival of the Seven Mounts (*Septimontium*).

Early Roman Life and Religion

The early Romans were pastoralists and farmers. Their homes were one-roomed huts with openings in the thatched roofs to carry off the smoke. They grew chiefly beans and spelt, a form of wheat (hence the use of cakes of salt and spelt in religious and marriage ceremonies), and bred cattle, swine, and sheep. Daily life was one of harsh, unremitting toil in which all members of the family took part. Magic and taboos were part of their religion. Even in the Republican period water was poured through a hole in a sacred stone (the *Lapis manalis*) to bring about rain. In the *Lupercalia*, popularized by Shakespeare in his *Julius Caesar*, young men dressed in goat-skins raced around the Palatine, striking women with leather whips to banish sterility. Similarly, primitive taboos survived into civilized days, such as the taboos on the Vestal Virgins and on the priest of Jupiter who could not ride or touch a horse, she-goat, or dog, cut his nails or hair with an iron knife, eat wheat bread, raw meat, or beans, wear an unbroken ring, or have knots in his clothing. Among other taboos was the prohibition against women taking part in the worship of Hercules (a cult brought in early by Greek traders) and of men witnessing the rites of the Bona Dea (Good Goddess).

The native religion of the Romans and Latins is known as animism, in which non-personalized powers dwelling in certain sacred objects and places were supposed to possess a mysterious force. In Latin the word *numen* was used both for the force and the deity. Thus, Ceres, who like most of these powers was later personalized under Greek influence, was originally the spirit of grain crops, Robigus of the rust which attacked the wheat (two red dogs were sacrificed to him at the *Robigalia* to ward off the rust), and Flora of flowers. Each of these powers had its festival at the proper season of the year.

Festivals to promote the welfare of crops and herds were the most frequent. At the *Fordicidia* in April pregnant cows were sacrificed to the *numen* of the earth and their unborn calves were burnt and the ashes kept for the *Parilia* (see later). Toward the end of May at the *Ambarvalia* when the crops were ripening, the farmer and his family, dressed in white and carrying laurel branches, drove a pig, a sheep, and a bull three times around the circuit of the farm and then sacrificed them to the god Mars (later, according to Vergil in his *Georgics*, to Ceres). There was a similar state ceremony for the whole people. To Mars, as god both of agriculture and war, belongs the "October Horse", in which there was a two-horse chariot-race in the Campus Martius (Field of Mars). The left-hand horse of the winning pair was then sacrificed, its head fixed on the *Regia* (originally the king's residence) and the blood of its tail allowed to drip on the king's hearth, while the blood from its head was saved for the *Parilia*. The *Parilia* in April was a shepherds' festival to Pales, the spirit of the flocks. In the public ceremony as described by the poet Ovid of the Augustan Age, the congealed blood from the head of the October Horse was mixed with the ashes of the unborn calves burnt at the *Fordicidia* and the mixture flung on heaps of burning bean-straw over which men and women leaped as a purification rite. In the private ritual, the shepherds sprinkled and swept the folds, made fires of heaps of straw, olive branches, and laurel, drove the flocks through them, and made offerings and prayers to Pales. Because the Romans were a conservative people, these and other early festivals survived to the time of early empire.

Jupiter and Mars, however, though retaining animistic features, were personalized early. Jupiter was the sky and the spirit immanent in it, the power in the hurled lightning bolts and also the spirit of the vine. By the time Rome was founded he was the god of cities and towns and as Jupiter Latiaris (of the Latins) was worshipped at an annual festival at Alba Longa in which a white heifer was sacrificed and then eaten by the assembled leaders. In Rome he was the supreme deity, the symbol of the Roman state, the giver of victory and the spirit of law and justice. Similarly, Mars, at first the protector of the farmer's crops and herds, soon became the Roman god of war. At a later date Juno, a popular Italic goddess worshipped in Etruria as Uni, was added as Jupiter's consort, and either the Faliscans or the Etruscans seem to have brought in Minerva, the old Italian Goddess of arts and crafts.

In early Rome public and private worship, except for a deity such as Jupiter and except for degrees of ritual, were pretty much the same. The more intimate deities of the household were Janus, the spirit of the door, Vesta, the spirit of the hearth who in early times was not represented by a statue, the Penates, who guarded the stored food, and the Lares, who were deities of both the fields and the home. As spirits of the fields the Lares were worshipped at a Thanksgiving festival after the year's work was done, but, as household deities, they and the Penates were a synonym for home. Closely connected with the family, too, was the festival for the dead, the *Parentalia* in February, of which an important feature was a meal at the tombs of the dead, and the *Lemuria* in May, at which, according to Ovid, the householder, to expel inimical ghosts, patrolled the house at midnight nine times, spitting beans from his mouth, and finally called upon the spirits to depart.

The religious practices of the Romans of the early period lead us back into primitive beliefs and emotions when a multitude of spirits were to be appeased or to be made beneficent by sacrifices and prayers. As with the Greeks, the father was the priest for the household and the magistrates priests for the state. As time went by, the pastoral life was modified by the coming of Phoenician, Etruscan and Greek merchants, and later of Carthaginians, to the settlement by the Tiber. Outlanders began to put up habitations, trade developed, and some of the amenities of life were introduced. Yet Romans of the regal and early Republican periods were still basically farmers and landowners and their social structure reflects this fact.

Social Structure

The family. The basic unit of the Roman social order was the family, but the word *familia* included slaves, clients, and property and really meant "household." In the early period, as in other primitive societies, it was a joint and undivided household with grandparents, parents, children, and grandchildren and slaves all living under the same roof and sharing in the work and the meals. Plutarch in his biography of Aemilius Paullus, who defeated the king of Macedonia in 168 B.C., tells of a family of sixteen grown men who with their wives and families lived in one house and worked a small farm near Veii.

The whole family was under the authority of the *eldest* living male member, known as the *pater familias* (father of the household) whether married man, widower, or bachelor. His power (*patria potestas*) was absolute. He had complete control of the family property, and all property except for special personal possessions was family property, although later on sons could keep their own pay as a soldier or loot from a conquered city. He could mutilate, flog, sell into slavery, or put to death any of the family, including married sons and their wives. Normally his wife, the *matrona*, was his sober and serious partner but she was subject to his authority. Even the state could not interfere with the power of the *pater familias* within the family and this power lasted throughout the Republic, although by the 1st century B.C. public opinion and legal devices had modified its harshness. The *genius* of the *pater familias* (the other self which was supposed to accompany him through life) was worshipped. Although his sons and grandsons had to fulfil their duties as citizens, Roman law was essentially a law to settle disputes between families, not between individuals.

The Gens or Clan. Groups of families, believed in the case of each group to be descended from a common ancestor, were united into *gentes* (singular *gens*, translated as "clan" and with an adjective *gentilis* from which the word "Gentile" is derived). Each clan was originally a religious, social, and political organization, possessing lands and a large number of dependents, known as clients (from a Latin word meaning "I obey"). Each clan at first had its own fighting-force (cf. the Highland clans of Scotland). For example, according to Livy, when the Sabine, Atta Clausus, repelled the Etruscans, he, as Appius Claudius, along with 5000 dependents, was given land and Roman citizenship.

Under the Republic, by the middle of the 5th century B.C., the clan was reduced to a sentimental and religious union and clients now attached themselves to individual families. Yet the original importance of the clan was preserved in the male Roman name which at first was made up of a *praenomen* (given name such as Marcus or Gaius) and the *nomen* (name) which was the clan name such as Fabius or Tullius. Later a *cognomen* or *agnomen* (added name) designated the family within the clan. In Gaius Julius Caesar, for example, Gaius is the given name, Julius the clan name and Caesar the family name. Similarly, there were three important branches of the Claudian clan, known respectively as the Pulcher (beautiful), Caecus (blind), and Nero (brave) families. Girls were designated by the feminine form of the clan name. Caesar's daughter was Julia. If there were two girl babies the first was called Maior (Bigger), the second, Minor (Smaller), followed by the clan name, but if there were three or more, then they were called first, second, third, etc. (Prima, Secunda, Tertia etc.).

Patricians and Plebeians. Before the founding of the Republic the Romans were further divided into patricians and plebeians. Opinions about their origins differ. The patricians (*patricii*, "sons of the fathers") claimed to be the descendants of the founding fathers of Rome. It seems possible that, under the Etruscan kings in particular, the clan heads, along with other forceful individuals, took over lands and property as in early Greece to become the noble families, called patricians. Swarms of clients gave them power. The plebeians (multitude) were the mass of common freemen, including the landless men and the immigrants who had poured in. They were divided into the rich and the poor, but all plebeians were second-class citizens, possessing the right to trade, the right to defend themselves in the courts, and the right to vote, but not the right to hold office or to intermarry with the patricians. The division into patricians and plebeians was to lead to class-struggle during the early Republic.

The Rule of the Kings

There is no reason to doubt the Roman tradition that originally they were ruled by kings. Seven of these were listed by the Roman historians, the first four being given as the founder, Romulus, the Sabine Numa Pompilius, who was said to have established law and religion, Tullius Hostilius, supposed to have been a conqueror, and another Sabine, Ancus Martius. Governmental organization was simple. The king was elected for life from among the nobles and was commander-in-chief, high priest, and chief judge. To advise him there was a Senate (body of old men) from the nobles. If the people needed to be consulted, the male citizens were summoned by the braying of oxhorn trumpets to the *Comitia Curiata* (people meeting by *curiae* or wards). When the king died an *interrex* (king to rule in between) was appointed until a new king was elected. The *interrex* was retained during the Republic.

According to the Romans the next three kings were Etruscans: Tarquin the Elder, who was said to have seized Rome by guile, Servius Tullius, to whom was attributed a complete reorganization of the state, and Tarquin the Proud, whose despotic actions, including the legendary Rape of Lucretia, led to his expulsion. There seems to be some basis for the legend that it was the Tarquins who ruled Rome. Etruscan inscriptions prove that the Tarchna (Tarquins) were a noble family in Etruria and their tombs have been found at Caere. Furthermore, a 4th century B.C. wall-painting in the so-called François tomb near the Etruscan center of Vulci bears under one of the figures the name of Gneve Tarchu Rumach, which is translated as Gnaeus Tarquinius of Rome (Rome, from Ruma, is an Etruscan name). On the same painting is the name of Macstrna (Mastarna) and there is a possibility that Macstrna is to be identified with Servius Tullius, in part because the name of Tullius' legendary friend, Caelius Vibenna (written Caile Vipinas) also appears on the painting. At Vulci itself an inscription gives the name of Tanaquil who was said by the Romans to be the wife of Tarquin the Elder and the guardian of Servius Tullius.

Whatever elements of truth are preserved by the Roman tradition, archeology supports an occupation of Rome by the Etruscans in the 6th century B.C. Under their rule Rome seems to have become the dominant power in Latium. On the Capitoline a great temple was built to the triad of Jupiter, Minerva, and Juno, easily identifiable with the Etruscan triad of Tinia, Mnevre, and Uni, and Etruscan religious ritual and religious colleges (*collegium*, "a group of associates") were adopted. The Forum was drained by the *Cloaca Maxima* which still discharges into the Tiber. A street leading from the Forum kept the name of *Vicus Tuscus* (the Etruscan street) in the days of the Republic. Etruscan craftsmen and artists flocked to Rome, guilds of flautists, smiths, and potters were imported, trade with the Greeks and Carthaginians was encouraged, and a wharf for imported goods, according to tradition, was built under the Aventine by Servius Tullius. The Roman house with its *atrium* and surrounding rooms was now modeled after the Etruscan house. The purple bordered toga, ivory chair, and lictors of the Republican magistrates were insignia borrowed from the Etruscans. To this period, perhaps, belongs the marking of the sacred boundary (*pomoerium*) of Rome by plowing a sacred furrow around it with a bronze share drawn by a white bull and a white cow—an Etruscan rite—but wherever the gates were to be the share was lifted, carried across the space and the point set in the ground again. By this rite all the area inside the boundary was dedicated to the gods and thenceforward no dead body could be interred in it.

To Servius Tullius was also attributed the building of a wall about Rome, although the so-called Servian wall belongs to the 4th century B.C. He was said to have reorganized the army, and meetings of the army assembly, the *Comitia Centuriata* (people meeting by "centuries" or hundreds), were held outside the walls in the Campus Martius in the great bend of the Tiber which today forms part of the heart of Rome.

How much of Republican social and governmental institutions goes back to the Etruscan occupation is a matter of debate. It seems clear that the Etruscans made Rome a city and that their influence was pervasive.

The traditional year for the expulsion of the Etruscans is 509 B.C., though some scholars argue for a date after the defeat of the Etruscans by the Greeks off Cumae in 474 B.C. At about the same time they were thrust from Latium. But Rome lost her footing in Latium and her territory was reduced to a plot of country about ten miles by twenty-five.

The Early Republic

Once again we are in the land of legends such as that of Horatius at the Bridge or of the battle of Lake Regillus against the Latins, where the twin horsemen-gods, Castor and Pollux, were said to have brought victory to the Romans. It is clear that the Romans fought savagely for mere survival against the Etruscans, against their brothers, the Latins, and against the hill-tribes—Sabines, Hernici, Aequi, and Volscians—who raided into the plains.

The first great achievement was a treaty with the Latins in either 493 or 486 B.C. In this treaty Rome on the one side and the Latin League on the other became equal partners. Next, the Romans and Latins battled the hill tribes. By the end of the 5th century, Rome had conquered or incorporated them all.

The Romans were now ready to turn their attention to the Etruscan city of Veii, fifteen miles north of Rome. She defeated the Veians in battle and, according to legend, besieged the city for ten years. It was here that for the first time pay for Rome's citizen-soldiers was introduced. Fortunately, the Etruscan League did nothing and the Etruscan city of Caere, further north, aided Rome. At last, in 396 B.C., Veii was captured and looted, her citizens sold into slavery, and her territory annexed. Rome had made her first leap forward.

Immediately after success came disaster. In 390 B.C. a horde of Gauls moved from the Po valley against Etruscan Clusium and the Romans, we are told, were asked to mediate, but a Roman envoy struck a Gallic chieftain, and the Gauls swept on toward Rome. At the river Allia, eleven miles from Rome, the Roman phalanx of spearmen faced them. It was a black day in Roman annals. The gigantic yellow-haired Gauls, wielding huge broadswords and wearing nothing but shields and gold torques (twisted necklaces), charged in a yelling torrent. The Roman phalanx broke and its remnants swam the Tiber to Veii. The Gauls dashed on to Rome. Most of the inhabitants fled to Caere or to the country. A small detachment held out on the Capitoline Hill under Marcus Manlius. According to legend, the cackling of the sacred geese saved the Capitoline from capture. At last the Gauls, anxious to be gone, accepted a thousand pounds of gold (about a quarter of a million dollars), but at the last moment the Gallic leader, Brennus, tossed his sword in among the weights so that more gold had to be brought, with the saying *Vae Victis*, "Woe to the conquered." This was a maxim the Romans were never to forget.

The Romans returned and rebuilt their city. They now had to face uprisings from the Etruscans, the Latins, and the hill tribes, while other Gallic inroads were made. Rome was at war year after year. Gradually she won through. By 350 B.C. the Romans had reconquered the hill tribes, had become the masters of the Latin League, and had subdued the cities of southern Etruria. She was at last ready to move into central Italy.

The Early Roman Character

The Romans were basically farmers and landowners. This partially explains their character. The century and a half of constant war also shaped them. A people struggling for survival have little interest in philosophic speculation or in the search for beauty. Harsh, unbending discipline, dogged endurance, devotion to home, family, and state, bigotry, a willingness to kill or be killed, and no mercy toward the vanquished, adherence to the practical—these were the qualities which were needed in both men and women. Out of the conditions of their daily life came the virtues the Romans honored—simplicity, seriousness, chastity, dignity, and piety (by "piety" they meant doing one's proper duty to the gods, the state, and the family).

Such a people can fully understand only what they can grasp and hold. Furthermore, along with constant warfare went a bitter social and political struggle inside the state between the patricians and the plebeians.

The Early Republican Constitution

When the Etruscans were expelled from Rome, the patricians made the government their monopoly. The basic constitution was simple. The king was replaced by two annually elected magistrates, named praetors at first but later called consuls. The consuls possessed the King's insignia such as the purple-edged toga, the ivory chair, and twelve lictors. Outside the city each lictor carried a bundle of rods tied together with the head of an axe protruding, called the *fasces* (hence the *Fascisti* of Mussolini who adopted the Roman *fasces* as the symbol of his Blackshirts). In the field, therefore, the consuls were supreme with power of life and death but within the *pomoerium*, since by a law said to have passed in the first years of the Republic every Roman citizen accused of a capital charge had the right to appeal to the Assembly, the axe was removed. The *fasces* still symbolized the power of the consuls to scourge and arrest and to take action to preserve their own dignity and the safety of Rome.

In times of crisis, the consuls could be replaced by a dictator whose term was limited to a maximum of six months. The Roman hero, Cincinnatus, for example, when news was brought that the Aequi had trapped a Roman army, was said to have been summoned from his plow to the dictatorship, to have saved the army, and then to have laid down his office and gone back to his plowing. The dictator was accompanied by twenty-four lictors and the axe of the *fasces* was retained inside the city since a dictatorship was equivalent to martial law. Both consuls and dictators had to be patricians.

To advise the consuls there was, as under the king, a senate of 300 patricians. There were also the two Assemblies of regal days, the *Comitia Curiata* which was by this time limited pretty much to passing on wills and adoptions, and the army organization, the *Comitia Centuriata*. This second Assembly elected the consuls and could pass laws. The plebeians could vote in it but it was carefully arranged to give precedence to wealth and age. Of its 193 centuries, each casting one vote, the 18 centuries of Knights and 80 centuries of the first property class who voted first made a majority of 98 so that if those centuries voted in the same way, the matter was settled. The main mass of the people was crowded into the remaining centuries, yet, although a century of the lower classes would have in it many more members than a century of the first class, it still had only one vote. Similarly, centuries were divided into *seniores* (older men) and *iuniores* (younger men). In the first class, for example, there were 40 centuries of *seniores* and 40 of *iuniores*, although a century of the *iuniores* was likely to count more members than a century of *seniores*. Similarly, the 20 centuries of the second and third and fourth classes and the 3 of the fifth class were evenly divided into *seniores* and *iuniores* while into the remaining five supernumerary centuries were crowded the poorest groups. In this way the Romans made sure that the wealthy and the older men would dominate the *Comitia Centuriata*. Later, the number of centuries was increased to 373 but this assembly was still a stronghold of conservatism. Furthermore the patricians monopolized the religious offices.

Religious Offices

We have seen that, as with the Greeks, there was no separate class of priests. The magistrates, as priests, offered prayers and sacrifices. There were also priestly offices, filled in this period by the patricians who otherwise went on with their normal lives and duties. Among these offices, the *rex sacrorum* (king of the sacred rites) retained the name of king so that the gods would not be startled by a new title (cf. in Athens, the King-Archon). A very old group were the *Salii*, the leaping priests of Mars, who were supposed to guard the twelve golden shields of which one was said to have come from heaven. On occasion they paraded through Rome, beating the shields with spears, dancing, and singing a hymn which was in archaic Latin and of which a part has survived. They were famous for the luxuriousness of their banquets. Another ancient group were the *fetiales* whose duty it was to declare war by casting a spear into enemy territory. Later, a piece of ground in Rome was deconsecrated and declared hostile ground so that the spear could be tossed into it and war formally declared without a long journey. To certain deities, such as Jupiter, *flamens*, who are thought to have represented the sons of the ideal household, were attached. The daughters of the state household were the Vestal Virgins whose duty it was to keep the eternal fire of Rome burning in the round temple of Vesta in the Forum. They were vowed to chastity, lived in the house of the Vestal Virgins behind the temple, and were subject to various taboos such as wearing only woollen clothes and not being allowed to enter a house with more than one step up to the threshold. After thirty years of service they were given the choice of re-entering the world or renewing their vows of chastity for the rest of their lives.

The state mother of the Vestal Virgins was given the title *Mater*, "Mother." The *pater familias* of the ideal household seems at first to have been the *rex sacrorum* but he was replaced by the *Pontifex Maximus*, Chief Pontiff, who was the high priest of the Roman religion, and the head of the college of the *Pontifices* (bridge-makers), at first three, then six, and finally fifteen in number. Their original function is thought to have been the sacred welfare of the bridges over the Tiber and then of the Tiber itself which was regarded as possessing a *numen* or spirit, but their religious duties were widely extended as time went by. The *Pontifex Maximus* lived in the Regia, near the temple of Vesta, and he, along with the *Mater* of the Vestal Virgins had a strong influence in politics. Late in the Republic, Julius Caesar, politician, general, and religious cynic, was Pontifex Maximus. The state cult of Janus, the spirit of the door, was closely associated with that of Vesta but Janus also became the deity of all beginnings and endings (the month January is named after him) and of coinage because his double-head filled the first coins nicely. Further-more the doors of his temple were open in war-time and closed during days of peace.

There were three other important religious colleges. The *Augurs* (at first three, then five, then fifteen in number) interpreted the omens for the magistrates and, since the omens could decide, for example, whether elections could be held on a due date or not, the augurs were useful in politics. The *duoviri sacris faciundis* (two, later fifteen, in charge of carrying out the sacred rites) were almost equally important. They were in charge of the Sibylline Books of oracles which, according to legend, were sold to Tarquin the Elder. These oracles were consulted in times of crisis and it was through them that a number of Greek and eastern cults, such as the worship of Apollo and later of Cybele, were brought into Rome. The patricians claimed that, because of the religious element involved, they alone, as descendants of the original settlers, could fill all these offices. For the same reason, it was asserted that they alone could be magistrates and dispensers of the laws. The plebeians, as has been noted, although they could vote in the *Comitia Centuriata*, could trade, and could defend themselves in a court of law, could not hold any office or marry into a patrician family.

The Struggle Between the Orders

The plebeians, however, who formed the mass of the citizens, knew that Rome's wars could not be fought without them. In 494 B.C. (according to Livy, but 471 B.C. is usually accepted as the correct date) they seceded to set up a state of their own. As a result they won either two or four (later increased to ten) tribunes of the plebs. Their function at first was to protect the plebeians from physical harm at the hands of the patricians, and their persons were made "sacrosanct"; that is, if anyone laid violent hands on the tribunes or interfered with the perform-ance of their duties, that person was put under a curse and pain of death.

From physical veto (the Latin word *veto* means "I forbid") came the right to veto any law or action inimical to the plebeians. A bench was placed for them outside the doors of the Senate-House. From this they listened to the debate inside. If they disapproved of a proposal, one of them thrust his head inside the door and shouted *Veto*. In the later Republic they were allowed within the doors. Their powers, however, were effective only within Rome and a mile of the city limits, and they could not protect plebeians accused of serious crimes.

With the tribunes as leaders the plebeians now held meetings of an assembly organized by tribes. In the period of the kings there had been four city tribes to which were added sixteen rural tribes. By 241 B.C. the country tribes had been increased to thirty-one, so the final total was thirty-five tribes. Roman historians refer to two tribal assemblies, the *Concilium Plebis Tributum* (Tribal Council of the Plebs) and the *Comitia Tributa* (people meeting by tribes). If the two did exist separately, it may be inferred that the first comprised only the plebeians but the second all of the citizens. We may also infer that either of the two assemblies could pass resolutions, called *plebiscita* which, *if* passed by the *Comitia Centuriata* and given the sanction of the Senate, became law. Meanwhile, two plebeian aediles became assistants of the tribunes and later regular magistrates. Although two patrician curule aedileships were added, this office was soon thrown open to plebeians in alternate years.

The plebeians had gained a toe-hold. Other advances followed. After a bitter conflict, during which, according to tradition, there was another secession, the laws were finally written down in the Twelve Tables (451–450 B.C.). Shortly afterward by the Valerio-Horation Rogations of 448 B.C. resolutions of the *Comitia Tributa* (the *Concilium Plebis Tributum* seems to have disappeared) were given the force of law if the sanction of the senate were granted. In 445 B.C. by the *Lex Canuleia* intermarriage of plebeians and patricians was allowed.

Meanwhile the plebeians were striving for admission to the consulship. Between 444 or 436 B.C. and 367 or 362 B.C. (the dates are disputed) the patricians still kept the consulship for themselves by a law providing that in each year it would be decided whether two consuls or three to nine military tribunes with consular powers (for which office plebeians were to be eligible) were to be elected. Since the elections in either case were held in the *Comitia Centuriata* where the patricians tended to dominate, the concession was not too important. But in 367 or 362 B.C. the Licinian-Sextian laws abolished the military tribunate with consular powers (although military tribunes as army officers were continued) and provided that there should always be two consuls, of which, according to the Roman historians, one had to be a plebeian.

The economic provisions of these laws were important. By them interest already paid on a debt was to be deducted from the principal (a sure indication that debts were pressing on the Romans) and there was to be no more slavery for debt. Furthermore, since the patricians and wealthy plebeians had practically monopolized the land won in war (whenever the Romans conquered a people they annexed part of their land as *ager publicus*, "public land") it was laid down that no single person could occupy more than 500 *jugera* (310 acres) of the public land or pasture on it more than 100 cattle or 500 sheep. It was hoped that in this way the poorer plebeians would secure some of the public land. But the law proved impossible to enforce since the wealthy neither paid rent nor gave up the land but held it by "squatters' rights."

The Victory of the Plebeians

Meanwhile, over the years, in addition to the tribunes and aediles, new magistracies, open to patricians, had been created. Quaestors, at first two, then four, and finally twenty in number, had been appointed during the early Republic. In 421 B.C. this office was thrown open to the plebeians. Similarly they won admission to the praetorship, which had been established around 362 B.C., and the censorship (originating in 443 B.C.). By the *Lex Ogulnia* of 300 B.C. the colleges of the Augurs and Pontiffs were opened to them although the Chief Pontiff (*Pontifex Maximus*) was still to be a patrician. Finally, in 287 B.C., the *Lex Hortensia* provided that bills passed by the *Comitia Tributa* were to be binding on the whole people, whether or not the senate gave its consent. From this time forward, the *Comitia Tributa* became the principal law-making body.

The plebeians had won their battle for social, economic, and political equality. The victory did not benefit the main mass very much, since the patricians had already formed an alliance with the wealthy plebeians. From this partnership came a new nobility based on office-holding. Anyone who had held one or all of the higher magistracies, namely the curule aedileship, the praetorship, and the consulship, had the right to display wax death-masks of his ancestors in his home. Furthermore, the holders of such magistracies automatically became senators (later the plebeian aediles and the quaestors and finally the tribunes were eligible for the senatorship) so that the new nobility was in reality what was called the senatorial order. Throughout the Republic, by various devices, the senatorial order, except for a few notable exceptions, was able to restrict the holding of the higher magistracies to the members of about twenty noble families, plebeian and patrician. The struggle of the orders was followed by the "Rule of the Senate."

The Three Orders

By about the middle of the 3rd century B.C. Roman citizens were divided into three classes or orders. The main body consisted of the plebs, who were entitled to wear the white toga which only Roman citizens could wear. They were farmers, small shopkeepers, and laborers. Next in ascending rank were the Knights. Originally the cavalry, by the third century anyone who owned property worth 400,000 sesterces or about $20,000 (the usual valuation of the sesterce is at five cents but in terms of today's inflated prices it probably had considerably more purchasing power than five cents) automatically became a member of the Knights or equestrian order. They were entitled to wear two narrow purple stripes on their tunics (the normal official dress of a Roman citizen was a sleeveless tunic over which he wrapped his toga), special shoes, and a gold ring. This order became the capitalistic middle class of Rome. In the top rank were the Senators. They wore a tunic with a broad stripe, and red sandals. From 218 B.C. Senators were forbidden to own a sea-going ship capable of more than three hundred *amphorae* (jars) capacity (about $7\frac{1}{2}$ tons), a provision which debarred them from overseas trade. The business of the senatorial order was to govern.

Apart from the dress which distinguished the three orders, plebeian, equestrian, and senatorial, magistrates and priests were entitled to wear a toga with a purple edge (the *toga praetexta*) and a general in a triumph the elaborately embroidered *toga picta*. Rome, though a Republic, was conscious of class distinctions.

The Roman Constitution After 287 B.C.

The three component parts of the government of the Roman Republic from 287 B.C. onward were the Assemblies, the magistrates, and the Senate. In theory, the final power, as in Athens, lay in the hands of the Assemblies. They elected the magistrates and they alone could pass laws.

The Assemblies

Unlike the Athenian Assembly which had fixed times for meeting, the Roman Assemblies could only meet when called together by a magistrate. Furthermore, whereas the Athenian Assembly could bring in amendments to a proposal or introduce a new one, the Roman Comitia could only vote "yes" or "no". Again, as in Athens, a Roman citizen had to cast his vote in person. But where Attica was a tiny country and its citizen body comparatively small, by 350 B.C. Rome already had a considerable territory and a mass of citizens. Normally only the citizens living in Rome attended the Assemblies, but, as time went by, even these formed unwieldy mobs. For these reasons, the Roman Assemblies, unlike the Athenian Assembly, never succeeded in controlling the Republic. Instead the state was governed by the magistrates and the Senate.

The Ordinary Magistrates

Ultimately the ordinary magistrates were two consuls (to head the state and the army), eight praetors (to handle judicial matters), four aediles (to put down fires, care for the streets and handle certain public festivals), ten tribunes (to protect the plebeians and preside at meetings of the *Comitia Tributa*), and twenty quaestors (treasury officials). All these magistrates held office for one year only, the quaestors, aediles, and tribunes being elected by the *Comitia Tributa* and the praetors and consuls by the *Comitia Centuriata*.

The Machinery of Rome's Government
in the First Century B.C.

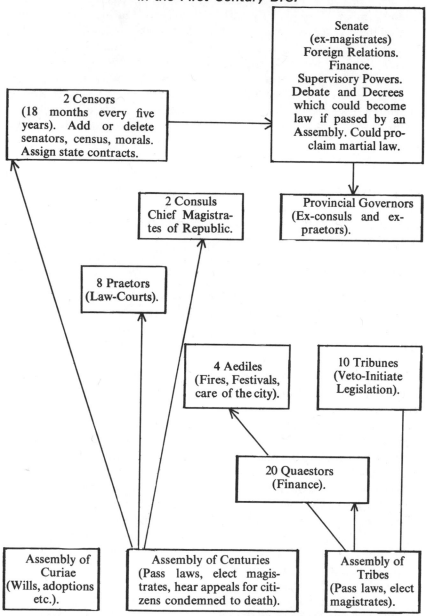

(Assemblies composed of all adult male citizens. All magistracies for one year only. Dictators could be appointed in time of emergency for six months.)

(After, Jones, *op. cit.*, p. 334)

Extraordinary Magistrates

Once every five years the *Comitia Centuriata* elected two censors. Their term of office was for eighteen months. During that time they revised the register of the tribes and the list of the senators. Because they could expel a senator for unseemly conduct, they soon acquired a general censorship over morals. In addition, the censors reviewed the finances of the Republic and let contracts for such things as the building of roads and bridges and, as time went by, the collection of taxes from the Roman provinces. Later, there were also proconsuls (in place of consuls) and propraetors (in place of praetors) to govern the provinces, and to hold extraordinary commands.

In times of crisis a dictator could be appointed but, as we have seen, it was carefully provided that his term of office could not exceed six months. In the later Republic, instead of a dictatorship the Senate claimed the right in moments of peril to proclaim martial law by instructing the consuls to "see to it that the Republic suffered no harm."

Limitations on the Powers of the Magistrates

The magistrates had considerable powers. The consuls in particular, as supreme officials, had almost unlimited powers outside Rome and considerable authority inside the city. Yet there were definite checks on their powers and on those of the other magistrates. One restraint was the right of any citizen, except when on a campaign, to appeal a death sentence to the Assemblies. Another was the fact that a magistrate only held power for a year and could not hold the same office again until ten years had elapsed. Furthermore, by the *Lex Villia Annalis* of 180 B.C., a man could not become consul until he had been in succession, quaestor, tribune or aedile, and praetor with an interval of two years between each office. The age for holding the quaestorship was set at 28, and later the dictator Sulla (82–78 B.C.) raised that age to 30. This provision, known as the *cursus honorum* ("sequence of offices"), meant that the consuls were men of wide experience; but, along with the year's tenure of office, it made any radical moves by any of the magistrates unlikely.

A third check was the power of the veto. Between magistrates of the same rank, "no" always won over "yes." In addition, any *one* of the ten tribunes, besides vetoing a proposal before the Senate or a bill before the Assemblies, could veto any of the magistrates, including his nine fellow tribunes. We ourselves have seen how a veto by any one member of the Security Council of the United Nations can block its proposals. In Rome the veto was still more far reaching.

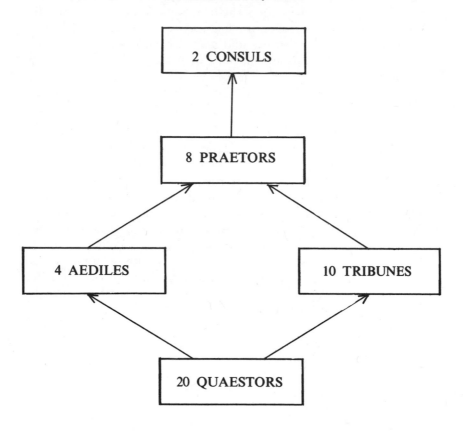

Sequence of Offices in the
Late Roman Republic

2 CONSULS

8 PRAETORS

4 AEDILES

10 TRIBUNES

20 QUAESTORS

NOTES

Constitutionally:

I.   A male citizen must be 30 years of age before he can be quaestor, 40 before he can be praetor, and 43 before he can be consul.

II.   Two years must intervene before the next succeeding magistracy can be held.

III.   Ten years must intervene before a man can be elected to a second consulship.

The Position of the Senate

In view of the weaknesses of the Assemblies and the checks on the powers of the magistrates, the Senate, as a rule, governed the Republic. For one thing, the Senate was a permanent body, its members sitting for life. For another, it controlled the finances of the state. For a third, it was composed of ex-magistrates and as a result had what the Romans called *auctoritas* which means an aura of prestige almost religious in character.

Why the Power of the Senate Grew

In theory the Senate only gave advice to the magistrates when consulted by them. But the consuls presided and they and the other higher magistrates would pass into the Senate when their year's term of office was over. Furthermore, since, as you have learned, the senatorial order usually succeeded in restricting the higher magistracies to about twenty noble families, the consuls and praetors were as a rule meeting with their fathers, brothers, uncles, or cousins. In later days, too, when consuls and praetors were appointed at the end of their year of office to govern provinces as proconsuls and propraetors, the Senate determined what province each man was to have. Consequently, it became the custom for the consuls to bring all questions before the Senate *first*; and in the Senate, unlike the Assemblies, debate was possible.

How a Proposal Became Law

If you and I were Romans and were anxious to have a law passed to ban Greek philosophers in Rome, as Cato the Elder did in the 2nd century B.C., we would first need to secure the approval of one of the consuls. The consul would then state the proposal and ask the senators their opinion, one by one, in order of seniority. Any one of the senators could move that the proposal be accepted or rejected or bring in an amendment or, by a peculiar habit of the Roman Senate, speak on something entirely different, such as: "We ought to make war on the Etruscans", and bring forward a resolution about that question. If our proposal won acceptance, the Senate would pass a resolution to that effect (*Senatus consultum*, "the Senate's advice") and the consul would be instructed to bring it before an Assembly (usually the *Comitia Tributa*) as a bill.

The *Comitia Tributa* met in the Forum. The bill would be read and a prominent person might speak, but there would be no discussion by the Assembly. Then, unless a tribune vetoed it (and this could also happen in the Senate), the tribes would be herded into the voting-pens. Each member of each tribe would be given two tablets, one to accept the bill, one to reject it. The votes of each tribe would be counted. If a *simple majority* of a tribe voted "yes", the single vote of that tribe would be cast for the bill. If the majority of the thirty-five tribes voted "yes" the bill would be carried and become law. But if our proposal was rejected in the Senate, in the normal course of events, it would never come before the Assembly. In this way, as in finances and other matters, the Senate was able to keep control of the government. Its rule was probably fortunate for Rome during the conquest of Italy and the first and second Carthaginian Wars. With conflict following conflict, the Senate was a steady rudder to steer the Roman ship of state.

Readings from Sources of the Period

(a) According to Roman legend, after the Romans had expelled Tarquin the Proud, Lars Porsena, the king of Etruscan Clusium (modern Chiusi), led a force against Rome to restore Tarquin, and the danger was great. Livy, the Roman historian, tells how Horatius Cocles saved Rome.

The most vulnerable point was the wooden bridge, and the Etruscans would have crossed it and forced an entrance into the city, had it not been for the courage of one man, Horatius Cocles—that great soldier whom the fortune of Rome gave to be her shield on that day of peril. Horatius was on guard at the bridge when the Janiculum was captured by a sudden attack. The enemy forces came pouring down the hill, while the Roman troops, throwing away their weapons, were behaving more like an undisciplined rabble than a fighting force. Horatius acted promptly: as his routed comrades approached the bridge, he stopped as many as he could catch and compelled them to listen to him. "By God," he cried, "can't you see that if you desert your post escape is hopeless? If you leave the bridge open in your rear, there will soon be more of them in the Palatine and the Capitol than on the Janiculum." Urging them with all the power at his command to destroy the bridge by fire or steel or any means they could muster, he offered to hold up the Etruscan advance, so far as was possible, alone. Proudly he took his stand at the outer end of the bridge; conspicuous amongst the rout of fugitives, sword and shield ready for action, he prepared himself for close combat, one man against an army. The advancing enemy paused in sheer astonishment at such reckless courage. Two other men, Spurius Lartius and Titus Herminius, both aristocrats with a fine military record, were ashamed to leave Horatius alone, and with their support he won through the first few minutes of desperate danger. Soon, however, he forced them to save themselves and leave him; for little was now left of the bridge, and the demolition squads were calling them back before it was too late. Once more Horatius stood alone; with defiance in his eyes he confronted the Etruscan chivalry, challenging one after another to single combat, and mocking them all as tyrants' slaves who, careless of their own liberty, were coming to destroy the liberty of others. For a while they hung back, each waiting for his neighbour to make the first move, until shame at the unequal battle drove them to action, and with a fierce cry they hurled their spears at the solitary figure which barred their way. Horatius caught the missiles on his shield and, resolute as ever, straddled the bridge and held his ground. The Etruscans moved forward, and would have thrust him aside by the sheer weight of numbers, but their advance was suddenly checked by the crash of the falling bridge and the simultaneous shout of triumph from the Roman soldiers who had done their work in time. The Etruscans could only stare in bewilderment as Horatius, with a prayer to Father Tiber to bless him and his sword, plunged fully armed into the water and swam, through the missiles which fell thick about him, safely to the other side where his friends were waiting to receive him. It was a noble piece of work—legendary, maybe, but destined to be celebrated in story through the years to come.

(Livy, *The Early History of Rome*, translated by Aubrey de Sélincourt, Harmondsworth: Penguin Books, 1960, pp. 99–100.)

(b) According to the Romans, when Rome was captured by the Gauls, a garrison which was holding out on the Capitoline Hill (the most of the Romans having fled to Veii or Caere) was saved by the cackling of geese, which were sacred to Juno. Livy tells the story in the fifth book of his history.

During these transactions in Veii the Citadel in Rome passed through a brief period of extreme danger from an attempted surprise. It may be that the messenger from Veii had left footprints, and the Gauls had noticed them, or possibly they had observed, in the ordinary course of their duties, that the rocky ascent near the shrine of Carmenta was easily practicable. In any case, one star-lit night, they made the attempt. Having first sent an unarmed man to reconnoitre the route, they began the climb. It was something of a scramble: at the awkward spots a man would get a purchase for his feet on a comrade below him, then haul him up in his turn—weapons were passed up from hand to hand as the lie of the rocks allowed—until by pushing and pulling one another they reached the top. What is more, they accomplished the climb so quietly that the Romans on guard never heard a sound, and even the dogs—who are normally aroused by the least noise in the night—noticed nothing. It was the geese that saved them—Juno's sacred geese, which in spite of the dearth of provisions had not been killed. The cackling of the birds and the clapping of their wings awoke Marcus Manlius—a distinguished officer who had been consul three years before—and he, seizing his sword and giving the alarm, hurried, without waiting for the support of his bewildered comrades, straight to the point of danger. One Gaul was already up, but Manlius with a blow from the boss of his shield toppled him headlong down the cliff. The falling body carried others with it; panic spread; many more who dropped their weapons to get a better grip of the rocks were killed by Manlius, and soon more Roman troops were on the scene, tumbling the climbers down with javelins and stones, until every man of them was dislodged and sent hurtling to the bottom of the cliff.

(*Ibid.*, pp. 376–377.)

(c) During the war against the Latins, in the crucial battle the consul, Decius Mus, "devoted himself" believing that in this way, he could assure the Romans of victory. The following extract from Livy describes his action.

The pontifex ordered him to don the toga of his office and, after veiling his head, to reach out from beneath his toga with one hand and touch his chin; then, standing upon a spear which was placed under his feet, he was to recite the following formula: "Janus, Jupiter, father Mars, Quirinus, Bellona, Lares, divine Novensiles, divine Indigetes, gods who have power over us and our enemies, and divine Manes, I pray to you and I implore, I beseech and I beg, that you may bestow upon the Roman people power and victory and afflict the enemies of the Roman people with fear, terror, and death. Even as I have uttered these words, thus on behalf of the republic of the Roman people, the army, the legions and the auxiliaries of the Roman people, I have devoted along with me the legions and auxiliaries of the enemy to divine Manes and to Earth."

Having completed this prayer he ordered the lictors to proceed at once to Titus Manlius and announce to his colleagues that he had devoted himself on behalf of the army. Then, donning his armor and girdling himself with the Gabinian cincture, he leaped upon his horse and rode headlong into the middle of the enemy. To both armies he appeared a striking figure, more magnificent than any human, as if sent from heaven to appease the anger of the gods and bear ruin away from his own people down upon their enemies. The panic and terror which accompanied him threw the first line of the Latins into disorder, then spread through all their ranks. Wherever he rode on his horse men quailed in terror as if stricken by a pestilential star; but when he fell under a barrage of spears the Latin cohorts openly panicked and fled. At the same time the Roman legions rose up and renewed the battle as if now the signal had been given for the first time.

(d) Cicero in his *The Republic* describes how Romulus came to choose the site of Rome.

10. Therefore how could Romulus more divinely embrace the uses of the sea and avoid its defects than by placing his city on the bank of a river that has water throughout the year, is calm, and whose broad stream flows into the sea? As a consequence, the city is able to receive from the sea what it needs and to send over it what it has in abundance, and by the same river it not only draws from the sea supplies that are most necessary for its provisioning and way of life but also receives provisions transported from the land. So Romulus seems to me to have divined even then that this city would at some time offer a center and a home for the greatest imperial power. For scarcely could a city placed in any other part of Italy hold such power so easily.

11. Who is so unobservant that he would not mark and understand the natural fortifications of the city itself? The length and course of its wall were marked out by the wisdom of Romulus and the rest of the kings. On every side there are abruptly sloping hills, so that the only approach is between the Esquiline and Quirinal hills, and there an exceedingly deep ditch is flanked by a very large rampart. Also, the fortified citadel relies upon a circle of steep cliffs almost like cut rock, which remained safe and untouched even in the fearful storm of the attack by the Gauls. He chose a place abundant in springs and healthful in an unhealthful area, for there are hills that lie open to the breeze and offer shade in their hollows.

(McDermott and Caldwell, *op. cit.,* pp. 267–8.)

CHAPTER 3

The Conquest of Italy South of the Po

By the middle of the 4th century B.C., at the time when Philip of Macedon was moving against the Greek states, the Romans dominated the Latin plain and the hill tribes bordering on it and controlled southern Etruria. The Etruscan League was more or less moribund and the Gauls of the Po Valley, though dangerous fighters, were disorganized and spasmodic in attempts to expand. The most powerful rivals of the Romans were the Samnites.

The Samnites, it will be remembered, were Indo-Europeans who spoke Oscan. An expanding population had led them from central Italy into Campania and Lucania. They controlled more territory than the Romans (8300 as compared to 2300 square miles) and had double the population. They were a pastoral people and stout fighting-men. On the other hand, where Rome was a closely-knit state, the Samnites were divided into four main tribes linked in a loose confederacy, and Rome, too, had the advantage of interior lines of communication. For a number of years the Romans and Samnites watched each other closely (a treaty of alliance was even made in about 354 B.C.) but it was probably clear to both that sooner or later there would be a struggle for supremacy.

The First Samnite War: 343–341 B.C.

Capua, it will be recalled, had been taken from the Etruscans by the Samnites in 438 B.C. This victory was followed by the occupation of a number of Campanian Greek cities. In the process the Campanian Samnites, now civilized and mingled with Greeks, were troubled by raids from their highland brothers (cf. the Lowland and Highland Scots in early times). In 343 B.C., according to the Roman historians, Capua appealed to Rome for aid because the highland Samnites were attacking the Sidicini, a small state south of Capua. Rome sent help but the ensuing war was a preliminary duel before the main event. When peace was made, the Roman alliance with Capua was recognized but the Sidicini were abandoned to the Samnites.

The Latin War: 340–338 B.C.

The Latins and some of the Campanians, not satisfied with the peace, continued the war. In addition, annoyed by the dominant position of Rome in the Latin League, the Latins demanded equal rights with the Romans, including a share in the magistracies and the Senate. There was a vicious struggle in which the Latins were aided by the Volscians and the dissatisfied among the Campanians. Rome won, and her control of coastal western Italy now reached to Naples. Because of her policy of annexing part of the conquered territory, she had expanded to 4250 square miles. She still had to decide what to do with the Latins.

Isolation and Incorporation

It was at this point that the Romans made a decision which was to influence their subsequent history. Other states of the ancient world regularly reduced the peoples they conquered to tribute-paying subjects who could never become the equals of their masters. The Romans devised a policy of *isolation* and *incorporation*, a policy to be followed centuries later by the British in India. First of all, the Latin League was dissolved except that it could hold meetings for religious purposes. Secondly, about half of Latium was annexed, but its people were made full Roman citizens. Furthermore, Roman colonies in which the people remained Roman citizens were sent to Antium and Terracina on the sea-coast.

The cities of Tibur and Praeneste, however, and the colonies planted by the Latin League before the war on previously conquered territory, were retained as "Latin Allies." These allies governed themselves, except that they had no control over foreign affairs. They were not permitted to trade or intermarry with each other, but only with Roman citizens. This was "isolation" along with a certain degree of "incorporation."

The remainder of the communities of Latium were bound to Rome, each by a separate and individual treaty, and were forbidden to trade or intermarry with any community except Rome. Their local rights varied. Some were governed directly by prefects sent out from Rome. Others retained their local governments. Their people were classed as citizens without the vote (*cives sine suffragio*), which meant that they could trade and intermarry with Romans but could not vote or hold office in Rome. Furthermore, any Latins who settled in Rome could become full Roman citizens. These communities were called *municipia* (hence our words "municipal" and "municipality") and their rights of local self-government were increased or decreased according to their behavior.

In this way Rome made the Latins her faithful allies. Further south, Capua and Cumae were classified as free allies and Latin colonies composed of both Romans and Latins were planted in Campania. All these communities had the same rights as Tibur and Praeneste. Later, as the Romans extended their conquests throughout Italy, they established both Roman and Latin colonies at strategic points.

By this political invention, which did not humiliate the conquered, the Romans were able to bind Latium and subsequently Italy to themselves.

The Second Samnite War: 327–304 B.C.

In the second Samnite war the Romans were successful at first but in 321 B.C. a Roman army of 40,000 men was trapped at the Caudine Forks, inland from Naples, forced to surrender, and sent under the yoke. In this ceremony, which symbolized unconditional surrender, two spears were driven into the ground and a third placed on top. Under this "yoke" the troops, stripped to a single garment, had to crawl. Hostages were given and the Romans agreed not to renew the war, a pledge they kept until 316 B.C.

The interval was used in devising a new type of military formation. Up to this time the Romans had used the Greek phalanx, which was excellent on level ground but which could be broken in mountain fighting. They now organized the legion so that the heavy infantry of each legion was divided into 45 maniples (a maniple means a handful from a bundle of straw tied to a pole to act as a flag) of 60 men each (later increased to 120). The maniples were drawn up in three lines with intervals between the maniples, the maniples of the second line covering the intervals between those of the first line and third those of the second. This arrangement meant that each maniple could manoeuver separately as a unit and hence there was flexibility on the plains and in rough terrain. For some of the troops the spear was replaced by a javelin, and, later, the javelin and the sword became the standard offensive weapons. Light infantry of about a thousand in number (archers and slingers) and 500 cavalry completed the legion.

When this type of army was trained the Romans found an excuse to renew the war. While it was still in progress in 312 B.C. a censor, Appius Claudius Caecus (the Blind) began the first of the great Roman roads, the Appian Way, driving it from Rome to Capua (it was later extended to the port of Brundisium on the east coast of Italy). Its original purpose was for the swift movement of troops but it soon became a carrier of trade. Today, we can still walk on stretches of the Roman paving. Later, the

Romans drove military roads throughout Italy and placed colonies at strategic points.

In spite of the Roman strategy of encircling the Samnites with fortified posts and driving deep into their territory the struggle was long and desperate, particularly since some of the Etruscans, fearful of Rome, joined the Samnites. When peace was made, although Rome had won, the Samnites still retained their independence and their original territory, but gave up any claim to Campania.

The Third Samnite War: 298–290 B.C.

The Samnites were not yet willing to concede the superiority of Rome and the rest of Italy was also alarmed. In 298 B.C. Sabines, Etruscans, Umbrians, and the Gauls joined the Samnites in a last desperate attempt to break the city by the Tiber. The Romans were victorious in both Etruria and Samnium where they captured the Samnite capital, Bovianum (Ox-town). But then, in 295 B.C., the Samnites broke through to the north and, with their allies, faced the legions at Sentinum in Umbria. The fighting was desperate. According to Roman legend, the hero, Decius Mus, won the day by devoting himself to the gods, rushing upon the enemy, gathering an armful of spears into his own breast, and opening the way for a break-through. Five years later, the Samnites, their lands ravaged again and again, surrendered and accepted the status of dependent Roman allies.

The fighting was not yet over. In 284 B.C. a combined force of Etruscans and Gauls cut a Roman army to pieces at Arretium, but in the next year the Romans shattered their enemies at Lake Vadimo. By 280 B.C. the Etruscan cities had surrendered and the Lucanians to the south of Naples had likewise submitted. Italy south of Cisalpine Gaul was Roman, except for Bruttium in the toe of Italy and the Greek city of Tarentum in the instep.

The War with Tarentum and Pyrrhus: 280–272 B.C.

Tarentum, a wealthy Greek city, had given lukewarm support to the Samnites in the third Samnite struggle. It had the largest navy in Italy and could field 15,000 soldiers. In 285 B.C. the Romans, answering an appeal for help from the Greek city of Thurii, not far from Tarentum, against the Lucanians, sent in troops. Thurii was an ally of Tarentum. Shortly thereafter when a Roman squadron of ten ships put in at Tarentum, the Tarentines, claiming a breach of a treaty by which the Romans were not to operate in the Tarentine gulf, sank four ships, killing the admiral, and then drove the Romans from Thurii. When the Romans asked for reparations, the Tarentines merely jeered at the bad Greek of the envoys.

For Tarentum in the meantime had asked Pyrrhus, king of Epirus, for aid.

Pyrrhus, a distant relative of Alexander the Great and married to a Ptolemaic princess, had visions of an empire in the West. In 280 B.C. he landed in Italy with an army which included elephants. His own generalship and his elephants won Pyrrhus two victories at Heraclea in the Gulf of Tarentum and at Asculum in Apulia, but he lost so many men that he is said to have exclaimed: "Another such victory and I am lost". Hence, we speak of a "Pyrrhic Victory". Between the two battles Pyrrhus tried a march to within 40 miles of Rome and offered peace through his eloquent envoy, Cineas. Appius Claudius Caecus, the builder of the Appian Way, persuaded the Romans not to listen, laying down a policy Rome was to follow: "Never treat with a victorious enemy."

After his two victories, in search of easier opponents, Pyrrhus crossed over to Sicily to help Syracuse against the Carthaginians. This led Carthage to offer help to Rome, and an old treaty of alliance dating back to 306 B.C. was renewed. In Sicily (278–275) Pyrrhus drove the Carthaginians from the island except for a fortress at the western end, Lilybaeum. But the Greek cities proved unreliable and Pyrrhus returned to Italy. There in a battle at Beneventum he was defeated (this place in southern Italy was called before this time Maleventum ("Ill-Come"), but after the Roman victory its name was changed to Beneventum ("Well-Come").) Pyrrhus went back to Greece where in 272 B.C. he was killed in street-fighting in Argos when a woman dropped a pot on his head from a second-storey window.

In the same year Tarentum surrendered. During the next few years Rome wiped out pockets of resistance among the Greeks, the native peoples, the Etruscans, and those Gauls who were south of the Po Valley. Her federation—for she had applied the policy of isolation and incorporation to the whole of her conquests—now covered 47,200 square miles. Through this territory she continued to drive her strategic roads.

If we glance back briefly we observe that it took Rome about a century and three-quarters (509–338 B.C.) to assure herself of survival. Then, in about another three-quarters of a century, she mastered peninsular Italy.

Organization of Italy

Rome's genius was evident in the way she organized Italy. Put briefly, the communities were divided into Roman citizens and Roman allies.

Full Roman citizens were the Roman citizens in Rome and Latium and in the Roman colonies, twenty-seven in all, planted at strategic points throughout Italy. Each of these colonies consisted of about three hundred Roman families. Citizens without the vote lived in municipalities in Latium, Etruria, and Campania. As you have learned, they had the right to trade and intermarry with the Romans.

Rome's allies were the Latin allies and the Italian allies. Each of these was tied to Rome by a separate treaty. The Latin allies included Tibur and Praeneste and the Latin colonies (thirty-five in all) in Italy. These allies had local self-government, the right to trade and intermarry with the Romans and, if they moved to Rome, could become full citizens. The remaining communities of Italy south of the Po were the Italian allies. Each of these was again bound to Rome by a separate treaty. Some, such as Capua and Naples, were independent allies with the same status as Tibur and Praeneste; others were governed by Roman prefects. The majority enjoyed local self-government. All Rome's allies had to furnish troops which they paid and equipped. These troops, whether land or sea forces, were kept in separate detachments. Only Roman citizens could serve in the Roman legions. By the time of the war against Hannibal Rome could put into the field 700,000 infantry and 70,000 cavalry, of which 400,000 infantry and 44,000 cavalry came from her Latin and Italian allies. She had come a long way from the small armies of farmers who had fought for survival. Even more important was the fact that she had devised a system whereby the Italians, though conquered, were made to feel that to a certain degree they were Rome's partners.

Effects of the Conquest of Italy

Rome was now a strong military power and her citizen-soldiers were war-hardened veterans. Her defeat of Pyrrhus made even the Hellenistic kingdoms realize that a new force had developed in the West. Her people remained basically agriculturalists, especially since in her Italian wars she had annexed large tracts of land throughout the peninsula. Yet the wars had meant a general increase in wealth and broader contacts, particularly with the Greeks. From them the Romans learned better methods of farming, including how to grow the vine and the olive, while the increase of slavery began to mean the development of large estates. A certain amount of rude luxury began to soften the harshness of Roman life.

Commerce was left to the Greek cities of Italy whose overseas interests were to lead Rome to a clash with Carthage. Meanwhile Greek contacts resulted in a better Roman coinage. The first Roman coinage of around 350 B.C. was the heavy copper *as*, weighing 12 ounces, which was gradually reduced to two ounces and made of bronze. After the defeat of Pyrrhus the two-ounce bronze *as* was standard but to it was added silver coinage, the *sestertius* (sesterce) valued at five cents and the *denarius* at twenty cents, but we can be certain that these coins would purchase in those days much more than a nickel or two dimes buy today.

Family life was still simple and so was the food. Wheat cakes, oatmeal porridge, beans, vegetables, and fruits, with meat only on festival days, was the basic fare. Olive oil served as butter and wine was diluted with water. The power of the *pater familias* was still untouched and the stern, disciplined standards of conduct were maintained.

Culturally, there were the beginnings of a change. The early Romans had been strongly affected by the Etruscans and the early Greek traders had made an impression but the struggle for survival had retained and emphasized the harsher features of the Roman character and disciplined way of life. The conquest of the Greek cities of Italy, however, started the stream of Hellenistic culture which was, ultimately, to permeate most aspects of Roman life. Up to this time, in particular, the education of Roman boys had been in the hands of the father and was narrow and vocational. The boys learned how to farm and how to fight and were strictly trained in the Roman virtues of order, obedience, self-control, reverence for their elders, devotion to the state, seriousness, and endurance. Only the elements of reading and writing were learned, and for material the Romans had merely the Twelve Tables of the law (which every boy was supposed to memorize), a few family eulogies, and a few political speeches. Girls were taught household duties. But now, after the capture of Tarentum, cultured Greek slaves, wherever they could be afforded, became tutors of Roman children. The result was an example of what control of education can accomplish. By 241 B.C. there were the beginnings of a Graeco-Roman literature and a Graeco-Roman education which was to help in transforming the old Roman character. "Captive Greece", to quote Vergil, "had begun to take her rude conquerors captive", although the complete revolution in manners and customs was to wait until the next century.

In religion, Greek influence had already been seen in the adoption of Greek gods such as the cults of Hercules, Apollo and Castor and Pollux. Now contacts with the Greek cities of Italy speeded up the process of anthropomorphizing the vague, animistic deities of the Roman religion and identifying them with Greek gods. Jupiter had become equivalent to Zeus, Juno to Hera, Diana to Artemis, and Ceres to Demeter. Venus, originally a goddess of gardens, was somewhat later equated with Aphrodite, the goddess of love. Other Greek deities were adopted early under different names, such as Fortuna for the Greek Tyche and Mercurius (Mercury), god of trade, for the Greek Hermes. Yet the old Roman festivals were retained and the formula "whether male or female" and "whether god or goddess", was frequent in the ritual for Roman deities to remind the worshipper of the earlier animistic concept of them. Nevertheless, Greek influence did lead to identification of Roman deities with the Greek gods. From the Greeks, too, came the *lectisternium*, first celebrated in 398 B.C. at which images of the gods, arranged in sex-pairs, reclined on couches before a table loaded with food and drink. In the 217 B.C. *lectisternium* the pairs were Jupiter and Juno, Neptunus and Minerva, Mars and Venus, Apollo and Diana, Vulcan and Vesta, and Ares and Mercury. Even more dramatic was the *supplicatio*, decreed either in times of crisis or as a thanksgiving (at one point in Caesar's Gallic Wars a *supplicatio* of fifteen days was voted), in which men and women with wreaths on their heads and laurel branches in their hands went from temple to temple to pray to the gods. Furthermore, Greek myths and legends accompanied the anthropomorphizing of Roman deities.

It was inevitable that Roman expansion over Italy should begin to transform the Roman character and way of life. That expansion also brought her into conflict with Carthage.

Readings from Sources of the Period

(a) A considerable portion of Livy's *History of Rome* is lost. Below is an extract from Book 10—303–292 B.C.

Colonies were planted at Sora, Alba, and Carseoli. The Marsi were received in surrender. The augural college was enlarged, so that there should be nine, whereas there had been four. A law on appeal was proposed to the people by the consul Murena, for the third time. Two tribes were added, the Aniensis and the Terentina. War was declared upon the Samnites, and many successful engagements were fought against them. When war was being waged against Etruscans, Umbrians, Samnites, and Gauls under the generals Publius Decius and Quintus Fabius and the Roman army was in grave danger, Publius Decius devoted himself on behalf of the army, following his father's example, and by his death gave victory in that battle to the Roman people. Papirius Cursor routed the army of the Samnites; that army had bound itself by an oath before going into battle, so that it might fight with greater fortitude and constancy. The census was taken and the lustrum closed. The count of citizens amounted to 272,320.

(Livy, *A History of Rome*, translated by Hadas and Poe, New York, Modern Library, 1962.)

(b) The extension of Rome's power in Italy led to the beginnings of Graeco-Roman literature. In Book VII, Livy, tells how Livius Andronicus, a Greek captured at Tarentum in 272 B.C., introduced Graeco-Roman comedy into Rome.

It was some time later than this that Livius Andronicus introduced regular comedies with a plot. He acted in his own plays, as was customary, and the story is told that he was so constantly in demand for performances that his voice grew hoarse, until finally with many apologies he brought in a slave to sing the parts which were set to music. He himself, being thus freed from the effort of using his voice, acted the *cantica* with more elaborate pantomime. In the course of time it became customary to have special singers to accompany the actors' mimic performance of the *cantica*, while the actors themselves spoke only in the dialogue parts.

As soon as real comedies were introduced, the older jesting dialogue without plot went out of fashion. But as drama was now gradually becoming an art, the young Romans resigned the performance of regular plays to professional actors, while they themselves revived the old fashion by putting on vaudeville skits in verse form. These eventually developed into the *exodia* which are often combined with the Atellan farces. That type of entertainment, which originated among the Oscans, the Roman youth kept in their own hands and refused to allow it to be taken over by professional actors. Hence it is that actors of Atellan farces do not lose their franchise and are eligible for army service just as if they had no connection with the theater.

I have thought it worth while to review the modest beginnings of theatrical entertainment in Rome, to show how this institution has grown from a comparatively simple and harmless origin to the present insane craze which the wealth of kings could hardly support.

(MacKendrick and Howe, *op. cit.*, p. 296.)

CHAPTER 4

Conflict With Carthage: 264–202 B.C.

Until Rome's conquest of the Greek cities of Italy, and particularly of Tarentum, there had been little or no clash of interests between Rome and Carthage but instead a treaty of alliance. After 272 B.C. a coolness began to develop. Rome was now conscious of its power and the commercial interests of her Greek possessions were in conflict with those of Carthage. Furthermore, Carthage was planted firmly in Sicily, and Sicily was an extension of Italy. It is possible that there were a few far-seeing Roman senators who perceived that either Rome or Carthage must dominate the western Mediterranean.

The Power of Carthage

Carthage was no easy antagonist. It will be remembered that it was a Phoenician colony which became independent and succeeded in building a commercial empire. In North Africa were rich wheatlands, divided into efficiently farmed plantation-estates worked by gangs of slaves. Into the excellent harbor of Carthage, a long narrow bay with a constricted entrance from the sea, her merchantmen brought silver, lead, zinc, copper, iron, mercury, and gold from Sardinia and Spain, tin from Britain and gold, ivory and precious stones from the interior of Africa. Expeditions even went down the western shore of Africa as far as the Gold Coast after gold, ivory, Negro slaves, and war elephants. Carthage also possessed a major share of the carrying trade between the Western Mediterranean and the Hellenistic East. Once the Etruscan cities had declined, her only commercial and naval rivals were the Greeks of Italy, Sicily, and Massilia, and it was her policy to sink any ship trying to pass through the Straits of Gibraltar or appearing in the Western Mediterranean between Sardinia, Spain, Sicily, and North Africa. This area, which was controlled by her navy, was her private lake. She held Malta and continually strove to occupy Sicily, the halfway house between the eastern and western Mediterranean. Meanwhile, profits from trade, returns from agriculture and mining, and the tribute-money from her dependencies had made her enormously wealthy and, perhaps, somewhat complacent. At the moment of her first conflict with Rome, for example, her powerful navy had been allowed to fall into a state of disrepair.

Although the basic culture and religion of Carthage was Semitic, there was a Hellenistic overlay. Greek methods of manufacturing, warfare, farming, and Greek styles of dress, architecture, and the like were copied. The government, as described by Aristotle, was republican in form but in reality an oligarchy of wealthy merchants and rich landowners. It tended to be corrupt and there were usually two factions, one of landowners who wanted peace and expansion in Africa, the other of sea-going merchants who strove to extend her empire overseas. Carthaginian policy and government lacked the steadfastness and stubborness which Rome exhibited. In fighting strength Rome had nothing to compare with the Carthaginian navy, the mistress of the sea, but where the Roman army was a disciplined force of citizen-soldiers, the Carthaginian was made up chiefly of conscripted natives from her possessions or hired mercenaries, such as Numidian cavalry or the famed slingers from the Balearic Islands (the principal ones are now named Majorca and Minorca). Her admirals and generals, however, tended to be long-term appointments as compared to the annual change in the consuls commanding the Roman troops, although a Carthaginian commander could face crucifixion if he failed. Essentially, the first war was between a sea-power and a land-power.

The First Carthaginian, or Punic, War: 264–241 B.C.

The incident which sparked the first war arose in Sicily. In 265 B.C. the tyrant of Syracuse, Hiero II, attacked a group of mercenaries belonging to an earlier tyrant of Syracuse, Agathocles, who in 289 B.C. had seized Messana on the northwest tip of Sicily, and were ruling it as Mamertines (children of Mars). The Mamertines called in Carthaginian help. The Carthaginians drove off Hiero but did not leave. The Mamertines then appealed to Rome for aid against the Carthaginians. The Senate refused the appeal but the assembly was persuaded by the consuls to vote for an alliance with the Mamertines, since it was clear that a Carthaginian post just across the Strait of Messina was a danger to Italy. Two legions, sent to occupy Messana, succeeded, and the Carthaginian admiral who had not prevented them from crossing the Strait was crucified.

Carthage now made an alliance with Hiero II and sent an army to win back Messana. The Roman commander defeated both the Syracusans and the Carthaginians. In this way the two nations sidled into war. In 263 B.C.

Hiero changed sides to become Rome's faithful ally and in 262 B.C. the Romans captured Agrigentum, where they enslaved the population and alienated many of the Sicilians.

They now had visions of taking over the whole of Sicily. The lack of a first-class fleet hampered them, since the Carthaginian warships, by this time refitted, could see to it that their own troops were reinforced and the Roman forces cut off from supplies. According to the colorful legend, the Romans found a wrecked Carthaginian quinquereme (thought to be a vessel of about sixty oars with five men to an oar which could overmaster the Greek trireme which probably had three men to an oar) and, using it as a model, built 100 quinqueremes and twenty triremes in 60 days, meanwhile training crews on wooden frames on land how to row. Actually the Romans had built 20 triremes back in 311 B.C. and at this time they had the service of the warships of the Greek cities including Syracuse, as well as of Greek ship-builders, so that their construction of a fleet, though energetic, was no marvel. But some genius added the *corvus* (raven) to the Roman quinqueremes. The Carthaginians, like the Greeks, regularly attacked by ramming their opponents' vessels with the bronze beaks on the prows of their warships. The corvus was a bridge or gangway, hinged so that it could be tied to the mast with a rope through a pulley and at the proper moment be let fall with a crash on the enemy's deck. At its end was a heavy curved spike to bite into the planks. From its beak-like appearance came the name of "raven." Over this gangplank Roman soldiers could rush to make the sea-fight a land-battle.

The raven worked. When in 260 B.C., with this new fleet, the consul, C. Duilius, met the Carthaginian navy off Mylae near Messana, he sank 14 ships and captured 31. In honor of the victory the *columna rostrata* was raised in the Forum, decorated with the bronze rams of the captured ships (*rostrum*, "a ship's beak or ram").

The Romans won another naval engagement off Sardinia in 258 B.C. and seized Corsica and Sardinia, the Carthaginian admiral as usual being crucified by his countrymen. Then, in a burst of enthusiasm, in 256 B.C. the Romans decided to invade Africa. The two consuls set out with 250 warships and 80 transports, won a great naval battle off Ecnomus on the south coast of Sicily, and landed near Carthage. Success went to the heads of the Romans. Confident of an easy victory they withdrew most of their forces, leaving one consul, Regulus, with a comparatively small army to finish the war. The Carthaginians brought in a Spartan general, Xanthippus. Under his command Regulus was defeated and captured. In 255 B.C. a Roman fleet of 250 ships, bearing the 2000 men left from his army, won a naval victory but was wrecked by a storm so that all but 80 vessels were lost. Although the Romans succeeded in taking all of Sicily

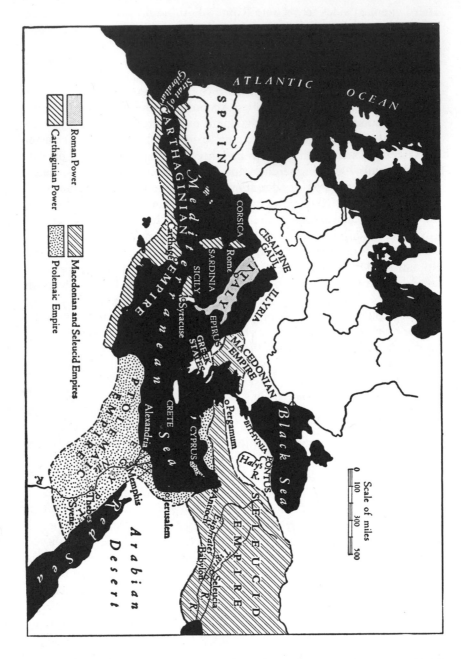

Roman Power at the Beginning of the Wars with Carthage (264 B.C.)

except Lilybaeum and Drepana on the western tip, they lost still another fleet in a storm.

The Romans rebuilt their fleet, but the Roman admiral, Claudius Pulcher, lost a naval battle off Drepana. Before the battle, we are told, when, according to Roman religious practice, grain was put down before chickens carried for the purpose (if they ate, it was a good omen) and the chickens refused to eat, Claudius had them flung into the sea, saying; "Well, they'll drink anyway." A second fleet was lost soon afterwards partly in battle and partly because of a storm. Carthage once again had the command of the sea.

The war now dragged on in Sicily year after year. A new and brilliant general, Hamilcar Barca (the lightning) harassed the Romans by swift moves behind their lines from his stronghold on Mount Eryx and by his raids on the Italian coast. But at home the Carthaginian landowners, led by Hanno, were occupied in African expansion and gave Hamilcar (the father of Hannibal) scant support. Finally Rome, with the help of a forced loan from its richest citizens, built a new fleet of 200 warships. In 241 B.C. off the Aegates Islands this fleet defeated the Carthaginian navy. Carthage sued for peace.

The war had cost Rome 200,000 men and at least 500 warships. She demanded an indemnity of 3200 talents (a talent, as you have learned, was worth in today's purchasing power of money possibly about $20,000) and the cession of Sicily and the islands between Sicily and Italy. Soon afterwards the Carthaginian mercenary troops, not having been paid, revolted in the so-called Truceless War. It was won for Carthage by Hamilcar, but Rome took advantage of it to seize Corsica and Sardinia and to collect another indemnity of 1200 talents. It seems to have been this treachery which put into Hamilcar his personal hatred of Rome.

The First Roman Provinces

Rome now had to decide how to organize her first overseas possessions. In Sicily the provincial arrangement (the Roman word *provincia* originally meant the "sphere of action" of a magistrate) was a patchwork. Hiero was left an independent prince with the title of "friend" of the Roman people. Messana and two other cities were given the status of Italian allies and five other towns were rewarded for joining Rome by being left free and untaxed. The other communities of the island became subjects (a new category) of Rome. Part of their land was made public land and rented for one-third of the crop. On the rest the Sicilians paid one-tenth of the crops and one-fifth of all other produce as tax or tribute.

For the collection of the tribute the Romans adopted Hiero's method of "farming" the taxes, that is the right of collecting them each year was sold at auction to the highest bidder. The tax-gatherers (*publicani*) were

entitled to keep as their own whatever they could collect over the amount
they had bid. As a result there was extortion, although the Sicilians could
appeal to the Roman governor. Additional revenues came from customs
dues of 5 per cent on all imports and exports, a pasture tax on each head of
stock, and royalties on mines and quarries. The same system was applied
to Corsica and Sardinia.

The Roman governors at first were quaestors. From 227 B.C., when the
two provinces were formally organized, two praetors were appointed
annually. Still later, the Roman governors in all the provinces were
regularly ex-praetors or ex-consuls.

The governor of a province, when he arrived, published an edict,
proclaiming the rules and regulations he would follow. Usually the edict
would repeat the one of his predecessor but there might be changes to
suit new conditions. A body of international law began to be built up. It
should be noted that although "allies" had to supply the Romans with
troops and equipment in time of war, "subjects" were free from this
obligation. But they paid the cost of the governor's administration, his
living expenses and those of his staff, particularly since it was the custom
for young Romans to be taken to the province supposedly to learn about
administration. For example, in 57 B.C. the poets Catullus and Cinna went
to Bithynia as friends of the governor, Memmius, and both hoped to make
a fortune. During his term of office the governor was supreme. His
sentences in court, where he had the power of life and death, were final, he
commanded the armed forces, could conscript provincials, and could even
wage war without asking permission from Rome. After 149 B.C. provincials could, however, try to persuade some Roman to prosecute a
governor for maladministration *after* his term of office was over. The
Roman system of provincial government like Topsy in *Uncle Tom's Cabin*
"just growed" and was characterized by many evils and injustices.

Events Between the Wars: 241–218 B.C.

Apart from organizing her two provinces, Rome as ruler of Italy fought
two Illyrian wars. The first (229–228 B.C.) was a police action against
Queen Teuta who had extended her domain from the coast of what is now
Yugoslavia and Albania over Epirus to the Corinthian gulf and who
allowed her Illyrians to carry on piracy, including raids on South Italy,
as an honorable profession. With her now powerful navy Rome soon
compelled Queen Teuta to sue for peace. Later, a Greek, Demetrius of
Pharos, who had betrayed the island of Corfu to the Romans and who had
been granted a small kingdom, pushed his power into Illyria and made
piratical raids in his turn. In 220–219 B.C. the Romans crushed him.
In both wars the Romans retained the towns and harbors she seized

so that she now had a footing on the east coast of the Adriatic.

More serious was a conflict with the Gauls of North Italy. In 238 B.C., in a protest against Roman colonization on their frontier, they had raided as far south as Ariminium but withdrew. In 225 B.C., new hordes of Gauls reached North Italy and an army of 70,000 crossed the Apennines into Etruria. As laden with loot they retreated northward, the Romans trapped them between two armies at Cape Telamon and almost annihilated them. The Romans now decided to end the Gallic menace. By 220 B.C. the Gauls of North Italy had submitted. Except for Liguria and a few Alpine tribes the Romans now ruled from the Alps to Sicily. In this same year the censor, Flaminius, arranged for the *Via Flaminia* to run to Ariminium as a military road and planted Roman colonies at Placentia, Mutina, and Cremona. Yet, when Hannibal arrived in the 2nd Punic War, the Gauls were eager to join him.

It was during these same years, possibly in 220 B.C., that the *Comitia Centuriata* was increased from 193 centuries to 373. Yet, as has been noted, the weight of influence still remained with the wealthy and the older men.

On the Carthaginian side the period between the wars was illumined by the remarkable exploits of the Barca family in Spain where the Carthaginian holdings had been greatly reduced during the 1st Punic and the Truceless Wars. Hamilcar Barca (238–229 B.C.) subdued all of southern Spain by a mingling of diplomacy and force of arms. His son-in-law, Hasdrubal, was even more successful, bringing all the rich mining districts under his control and building Cartagena as the capital and naval and military base of the Carthaginian power in Spain. When the Romans, alarmed at his success and pressured by Massilia, which was their ally and had trading interests in Spain, approached him, Hasdrubal signed a treaty agreeing not to "cross the Ebro under arms", a treaty which left to him about seven-eighths of the peninsula. The Graeco-Spanish town of Saguntum, one hundred miles south of the Ebro, was not mentioned but later, for protection, it allied itself with Rome.

On Hasdrubal's assassination by a Spaniard in 221 B.C., Hannibal, the eldest son of Hamilcar, succeeded to what was practically an empire of the Barca family. The silver mines brought in from 2000 to 3000 talents of revenue each year and the ranks of the well-equipped and well-trained army boasted the best soldiers of Spain and North Africa. According to Livy, the Roman historian, Hannibal at nine years of age had sworn eternal hatred of Rome. Self-restrained, worshipped by his soldiers, possessed of tireless energy, courage, and endurance, he was to prove himself to be one of the greatest generals in military history. In 219 B.C., after two years of preparation, he attacked Saguntum. There was a desperate siege of eight months, which is vividly described by Livy, while the Saguntines looked vainly for help from Rome. After the city fell, the Romans sent envoys to Carthage demanding the evacuation of Saguntum and the surrender of Hannibal. The Carthaginians evaded the demands. The leader of the Roman delegation gathered up a fold of his toga, telling them that he had here peace and war and to choose which they wished. They replied: "Which you will" and the Roman said: "Then, I give you war."

The Second Punic War: 218–202 B.C.

Since Saguntum was south of the Ebro and had not been included in the treaty with Hasdrubal but became a Roman ally later, and further, since the Carthaginians claimed that they had never ratified the Hasdrubal treaty, there was a technical argument that Hannibal had not broken any compact. On the other hand, he knew that an attack on a Roman ally meant war. That war was inevitable from the moment that Rome seized Sardinia and Corsica. On the one side, the Barca faction of Carthage was determined to overthrow Rome; on the other, the Romans had been watching the growth of the Spanish empire with unease. It was clear that at some time it had to be decided whether Rome or Carthage was to rule the Western Mediterranean. Hannibal's attack on Saguntum was simply the striking of the flint on steel to set fire to the torch.

In resources, and especially in her control of the seas, Rome was superior. Expecting to win the conflict speedily, she prepared two armies, one to invade Spain via Massilia and the land route, the other to invade Africa from Sicily. Hannibal foiled their plans. Leaving his brother, Hasdrubal, to hold Spain, he began his famous overland march to North Italy with, according to Livy, 90,000 infantry, 12,000 cavalry, and 37 elephants, a force which he cut to 50,000 infantry and the cavalry and elephants before he set out from the Pyrenees for the Rhône.

The Romans, meantime, had been leisurely in their preparations. When, in the summer of 218 B.C. a force under Publius Cornelius Scipio (the first of the Scipionic family to stand out in history) landed at Massilia, it was to find that Hannibal had already crossed the Rhône and had rafted his elephants across. Sending his brother with the army on to Spain, Publius Scipio returned with a small force to North Italy and took command of two legions already there.

Hannibal's march to the Alps and through them has always stirred men's imagination. Attacked by hostile tribes, faced by the wintry terrors of the Alpine passes and the almost greater dangers of the steep descent from them, somehow in early November after a march of over five months, of which fifteen days were spent in crossing the Alps, he emerged in North Italy. Of his splendid army only about 20,000 infantry and 6000 cavalry remained and most of the elephants had perished. With this small force he made ready to attack a nation which could put almost 800,000 men under arms. Hannibal's hope was that the Gauls of North Italy, some of whom had recently revolted against Rome, would join him.

The Ticinus and the Trebia: 218 B.C.

The battle of the Ticinus was a skirmish in which Hannibal's cavalry defeated Scipio's horsemen, but it resulted in a number of Gauls joining the Carthaginians. In the meantime the consular army, which had been preparing to invade Africa, had been marched up from Sicily. The Romans now had over 40,000 men in the field in a strong position on the eastern bank of the Trebia river, a tributary of the Po. Early on a bitterly cold December morning Hannibal sent a cavalry detachment across the river which, seemingly defeated, fled back over the stream. The Roman generals, flushed with success, ordered their infantry to wade through the freezing water without their breakfast. On the other side Hannibal's forces rapidly encircled them. At least 20,000 Romans were slaughtered and Livy says that only 10,000 escaped. Other Gallic tribes joined Hannibal. He now held the Po Valley and his army swelled to 50,000 men. What had seemed in Roman eyes to be a mouse had suddenly become a lion.

Trasimene and Cannae: 217–216 B.C.

The next year Hannibal surprised the Romans by marching by an unexpected route into Etruria (a march during which he lost an eye) and appearing suddenly before the Roman camp at Arretium. Then he enticed the Roman general into a battle on the shores of Lake Trasimene north of Perugia. Once again the Roman army was encircled and practically annihilated. Hannibal hoped that the Italian allies would revolt, particularly in Etruria. But they stood firm in their allegiance.

At Rome, Quintus Fabius Maximus was elected dictator. His strategy was to harass Hannibal but not to risk a battle. As a result he won himself the nickname of the "Delayer" (*Cunctator*), and from him we have derived the word "Fabian" for dilatory and cautious tactics. But Hannibal ravaged Italy far and wide and in the next year the Romans sent an army of 80,000 men under the two consuls into Apulia to crush him.

The divided command (each consul commanded on alternate days) proved disastrous. One consul was cautious; the other, Varro, was eager for an immediate battle, particularly since the Carthaginian army was only about half the size of the Roman. On his day in command he brought on an engagement at Cannae. Hannibal's arrangement of his troops and his timing became a classic example of battle tactics. His front line of Gauls and Spaniards bulged forward in a crescent formation. On either side of it, in deep columns, were his African troops. On the right and left was placed his cavalry. Meanwhile, because the engagement was being fought in a loop of land formed by the river Aufidus and space was limited, the Roman infantry was arrayed in a more solid mass than usual with the cavalry on the wings. When the battle was joined the Roman infantry pressed back the Carthaginian crescent until it sagged into a concave front but did not break. As a result, the Romans were jammed even closer together and Hannibal's cavalry, having driven the Roman horsemen off the field, fell upon their rear at the same time that the columns of African troops poured in upon their flanks. Massed together under a blazing sun so tightly that they could not even wield their weapons, the Roman infantry was sliced down like weeds by a scythe. Traditionally, 70,000, including the consul who had not wanted the battle, were slain; and Mago, another of Hannibal's brothers, is said to have poured on the floor before the Carthaginian Senate a peck of gold rings from the Roman knights slain at Cannae. Hannibal lost only about 6000 men.

The Aftermath of Cannae

Hannibal, though urged to do so, did not try to capture Rome, possibly because he lacked siege machinery but possibly also because he expected the Roman alliance in Italy to fall apart until Rome was left isolated. Parts of Samnium, Apulia, Bruttium, along with Heraclea, Thurii, Tarentum (except the citadel), and Capua did go over to him. Likewise in Sicily, on the death of Hiero, Syracuse defected to Carthage and in 215 B.C. Philip of Macedon concluded an alliance with Hannibal against Rome. For the moment Hannibal could feel that he was on the road to success. Yet the mass of the Italian allies still stood firm.

In Rome the citizens rose to what Sir Winston Churchill would call "their finest hour." Although almost everyone had lost a relative in the battle, instead of lamentations, they prepared for defence. Every male citizen above sixteen was enrolled, and two legions of slaves were formed. When Hannibal did not march on the city the Romans prepared for a long haul. Never again did they risk a set battle in Italy against the brilliant Carthaginian. Instead, they set themselves to winning back the cities which had gone over to Hannibal, to prevent him from getting supplies and reinforcement from Carthage (where the Hanno family was opposed to Hannibal and left him, as far as they could, to fight the war by himself), and to attacking Hannibal's bastion in Spain, whither Publius Scipio had gone after his defeat in North Italy in 218 B.C. Meanwhile, Philip of Macedon was kept in check by a Roman-inspired coalition of the Aetolian League, Athens, Sparta, Pergamum, and Rhodes, until Philip made peace in 205 B.C.

The Roman policy was successful. In Sicily, Syracuse was captured in 212 B.C. after a siege of three years, looted, and made tributary to Rome. In Italy city after city was recaptured and in 211 B.C. Capua fell to Roman arms in spite of Hannibal's desperate attempts, including a march on Rome, to save it. Two years later Tarentum was re-occupied. Hannibal could march and counter-march throughout Italy but his teeth were drawn.

The War in Spain and the Battle of the Metaurus River

Meanwhile in Spain the tide of battle had ebbed and flowed. In 215 B.C. Publius Scipio and his brother defeated Hasdrubal and in 212 B.C. recaptured Saguntum; but in the following year Hasdrubal won and both the Scipios were slain. The next year (210 B.C.) the young Publius Scipio, son of Publius, although he had never held any office beyond that of curule aedile, was sent as a proconsul to Spain. His capture of New Carthage was a brilliant achievement. He then defeated Hasdrubal but the Carthaginian was able to extricate his army. Abandoning Spain Hasdrubal led his army through France and over the Alpine passes into Italy (208–207 B.C.).

Rome's allies were by this time exhausted and her farms had been so ravaged that she had to import wheat from Egypt. She put two armies into the field, one to watch Hannibal in Apulia, the other to wait in North Italy for Hasdrubal. The tension was high. Both sides knew that if the two Carthaginian brothers could unite their armies, Hannibal might win.

The Romans got word of Hasdrubal's arrival first. The Roman consul in Apulia, Claudius Nero, leaving a small force with fires burning to deceive Hannibal, slipped away north with his army. The two Roman forces caught Hasdrubal among the rocky gorges of the Metaurus river. There was a grim day of slaughter along the slippery crags. The Carthaginians were annihilated. Claudius Nero hurried back to Apulia. The first news Hannibal had of his brother was when Hasdrubal's severed head was thrown over the ramparts into his camp.

The Metaurus battle was the real end of the war in Italy, although in 205 B.C. Hannibal's other brother, Mago, landed at Genoa, was defeated, and wounded, ordered by Carthage to return, and died on the way home. Hannibal retired to south Italy where no one dared attack him. Meanwhile in Spain the young Scipio completed the conquest of the peninsula. In 205 B.C. he returned to Rome in triumph and, contrary to the constitution, was elected consul.

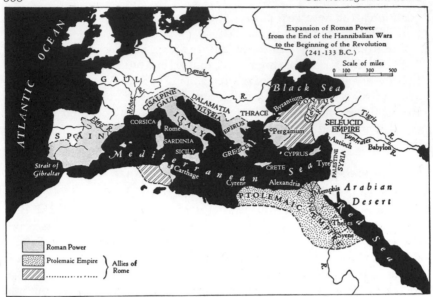

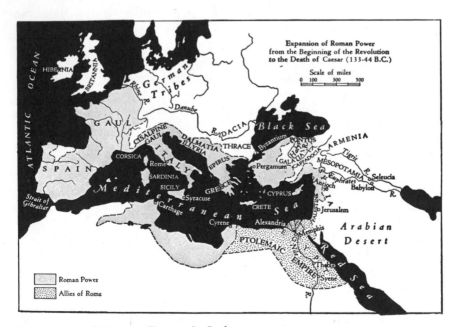

Expansion of Roman Power in Italy

The End of the Struggle

Scipio was convinced that the way to end the war was to invade Africa. Fabius, the Delayer, opposed the venture. But the people supported Scipio and in 204 B.C. he landed in Africa with about 30,000 men of whom 7000 were volunteer veterans. For some months his situation was critical but he won an ally in a Numidian, Massinissa, and then an unexpected victory as a result of which Massinissa became king of Numidia and sent Scipio cavalry. Negotiations for peace were started. During the talks the Carthaginians, who had done little to help Hannibal, recalled him. The veteran commander loaded his troops on to ships and we can well imagine how sadly he watched the shores of Italy recede. On his arrival in Africa the war was renewed. In 202 B.C. Scipio and Hannibal faced each other three days' march west of Zama. Hannibal's battle-plan was ingenious, involving the "hedgehog" type of defence used in World War II—that is, the maintenance of islands of resistance if the main line was overrun, and a fighting reserve to fling in at the critical moment. But Scipio, who had developed in Spain flexible legionary units, managed to turn the elephants back upon the African lines and used a sort of football "end-run" to get around Hannibal's wings. Scipio won the battle and on Hannibal's advice Carthage sued for peace. The terms were harsh. Carthage had to give up all her possessions outside of Africa, and even in Africa Rome established Massinissa as king of a Numidia which was to be a watchdog over Carthage. She was to pay an indemnity of 200 talents annually for 50 years, surrender all her war elephants and all of her navy except ten triremes, and she was forbidden to wage any war in or outside of Africa without Rome's consent. Rome herself kept Spain and the adjacent islands. Spain was organized into two provinces, Hither and Further Spain. Henceforward Rome was mistress of the Western Mediterranean. She kept a close eye on Carthage. When, under Hannibal's administration, Carthage prospered so that she offered to pay the forty remaining instalments of her indemnity in a lump sum, Rome demanded the surrender of Hannibal as a war criminal. He escaped to the east, there to be adviser of Antiochus the Great. On the defeat of Antiochus by the Romans he took refuge in Bithynia but when Roman envoys were sent there to arrest him, he committed suicide.

The long duel was over. It had been decided that a Graeco-Roman and not a basically Semitic culture would finally become the basis of medieval Europe. There was a huge sigh of relief in Rome. For years she had had to maintain some 25 legions in the field and at least 200 warships on the sea. Hundreds of thousands of Romans and Italians had been killed and many more wounded. When Scipio returned from Africa he was hailed as a hero. To his name of Publius Cornelius Scipio was added the honorary name of *Africanus* to which later, because of another Scipionic hero, was appended *Maior* (the Elder). Yet after the Second Punic or Hannibalic War, Rome and Italy were irretrievably changed.

Effects of the War on Rome and Italy

If any one of us were able to see Italy before and after the sixteen years of war, he would realize how drastically the conflict had affected the economy of Italy. The farms had been ravaged time after time—buildings burnt, crops trampled, and the stock butchered. The peasants of central and southern Italy were ruined. Many holdings were deserted both because of the lack of security and plundering and because the men who should have worked them were away fighting in Italy, Spain, Sicily, and Africa. Those that returned often had no desire to resettle on their ruined fields and crowded into Rome as an out-of-work mob. The state had to take over two million acres and lease them at a nominal rental to the wealthy, who worked them by slaves captured in the war. By a paradox seen in our wars of today, while the 2nd Punic War ruined many, it made profiteers and speculators enormously rich from war contracts, loot from captured cities, and the purchase of plunder, including slaves. The Hannibalic War produced Roman millionaires.

Apart from these obvious effects we would observe that the character of the Roman federation in Italy had altered. Those communities which had remained loyal were rewarded and those which had defected were punished. Syracuse, for example, was now a Roman dependency, and all the Senate of Capua was executed. The most important change was that the policy of incorporation of the Italians was stopped.

In government, the war had solidified the power of the Senate. "A democracy," the Greek historian, Thucydides, had had Cleon the Tanner say during the Peloponnesian War, "cannot make war." The Roman Assemblies had, on occasion (as for instance, in the appointment of the young Scipio) taken the bit in their teeth. In general, the Senate had managed the war. Yet there was one ominous foreshadowing of the future. The young Scipio's appointments had been contrary to the constitution and were, in effect, extraordinary commands. Fabius and Marcellus are further examples. Each held the consulship five times and were repeatedly proconsuls in alternate years. The way was being made ready for the military dictatorships which were to destroy the Republic. Meantime, Rome had to organize her foreign possessions, try to change a system which had ruled a city-state to manage an empire, and attempt to reconstitute the economics of Italy. But, immediately after the victory over Carthage, she was pitchforked into the conquest of the Hellenistic East.

Readings from Sources of the Period

(a) In the war against Hannibal (218–202 B.C.) the most serious Roman defeat was suffered at the battle of Cannae (216 B.C.). Below are extracts from Livy's description of the battle.

Hannibal, at break of day, having sent before him the Baliares and other light-armed troops, crossed the river, and placed his troops in line of battle, as he had conveyed them across the river. The Gallic and Spanish cavalry he placed in the left wing, opposite the Roman cavalry: the right wing was assigned to the Numidian cavalry, the centre of the line being strongly formed by the infantry, so that both extremities of it were composed of Africans, between which Gauls and Spaniards were placed. One would suppose the Africans were for the most part Romans, they were so equipped with arms captured at the Trebia, and for the greater part at the Trasimenus: The shields of the Gauls and Spaniards were of the same shape; their swords unequal and dissimilar. The Gauls had very long ones, without points. The Spaniards, who were accustomed to stab more than to cut their enemy, had swords convenient from their shortness, and with points. The aspect of these nations in other respects was terrific, both as to the appearance they exhibited and the size of their persons. The Gauls were naked above the navel: the Spaniards stood arrayed in linen vests resplendent with surprising whiteness, and bordered with purple. The whole amount of infantry standing in battle-array was forty thousand, of cavalry ten.

The battle, however, was more violent than lasting; and the Roman cavalry being repulsed, turned their backs. About the conclusion of the contest between the cavalry, the battle between the infantry commenced. At first the Gauls and Spaniards preserved their ranks unbroken, not inferior in strength or courage: but at length the Romans, after long and repeated efforts, drove in with their even front and closely compacted line, that part of the enemy's line in the form of a wedge, which projected beyond the rest, which was too thin, and therefore deficient in strength. These men, thus driven back and hastily retreating, they closely pursued; and as they urged their course without interruption through this terrified band, as it fled with precipitation, were borne first upon the centre line of the enemy; and lastly, no one opposing them, they reached the African reserved troops. These were posted at the two extremites of the line, where it was depressed; while the centre, where the Gauls and Spaniards were placed, projected a little. When the wedge thus formed being driven in, at first rendered the line level, but afterwards, by the pressure, made a curvature in the centre, the Africans, who had now formed wings on each side of them, surrounded the Romans on both sides, who incautiously rushed into the intermediate space; and presently extending their wings, enclosed the enemy on the rear also. After this the Romans, who had in vain finished one battle, leaving the Gauls and Spaniards, whose rear they had slaughtered, in addition commence a fresh encounter with the Africans, not only disadvantageous, because being hemmed in they had to fight against troops who surrounded them, but also because, fatigued, they fought with those who were fresh and vigorous.

CHAPTER 5

The Conquest of the Hellenistic East: 200–133 B.C.

It took Rome forty-two years to vanquish Carthage. In about thirty-two years of the next century (to the battle of Pydna, 168 B.C.) she made herself supreme in the Hellenistic East, although it was not until 133 B.C. that her dominion over the Mediterranean was unquestioned.

The Hellenistic East

Toward the end of the 3rd century B.C., the Hellenistic East was a patchwork of states. The three principal kingdoms were still Ptolemaic Egypt, Seleucid Syria, and Antigonid Macedonia. The Ptolemies ruled Egypt, Cyrene, Cyrus, Phoenicia, part of south Syria, several coastal cities and islands in the Aegean, and fought the Seleucids for the control of Palestine. The Seleucids governed theoretically from the Aegean to the Indus river but the Indian province had been lost, the eastern satrapies of Iran and Bactria had become practically independent, and so had Armenia. Likewise, in Asia Minor, Cappadocia, Bithynia, Pontus, Galatia, and Pergamum had become separate states. The Antigonids owned Macedonia and maintained a footing in Greece through an alliance with the Achaean League against Sparta. Of the smaller states, the most important were the Aetolian (central Greece) and Achaean (part of the Peloponnesus, including Corinth) Leagues, Pergamum, and Rhodes which had built a trade empire and was famous for the colossal fifty-feet-high statue of Apollo (one of the seven wonders of the ancient world) at the entrance to its harbor, until it was overthrown by an earthquake in 227/226 B.C. Rhodes was also a cultural center where, later, Cicero and Caesar studied oratory. Athens, although not influential politically, was still important as the home of art and philosophy.

During the 3rd century B.C. the three great Hellenistic states maintained an uneasy balance of power between themselves, but paid little attention to Rome, except for the expedition of Pyrrhus and the first Macedonian War of 215–205 B.C. In general, their leaders felt themselves superior to the crude Romans in culture and military science and, in spite of the defeat of Carthage, had no appreciation of the fighting qualities of the legions.

This scornful attitude helped in setting the stage for Roman intervention. The actual raising of the curtain came because of an upset in the balance of power. In 217 B.C. Antiochus III of Syria had been beaten by the Ptolemy of Egypt in a struggle for southern Syria and Palestine at the battle of Raphia. Later, after restoring his possessions in Asia Minor by a seven-years' march (212–205 B.C.) into the East as far as the Indus Valley, Antiochus reconstituted briefly the vast Seleucid Empire. On his return he was hailed as a second Alexander the Great and assumed the title of "the Great". Moreover, shortly after this, the king of Egypt died (205/4) and a weak Egypt was being ruled by a child. Antiochus fixed his eyes on this possible plum. (He later defeated the Egyptians in North Palestine and arranged a marriage between his daughter, Cleopatra, and the young Egyptian king.)

Antiochus' successes and ambitions stirred Philip V of Macedon to action. By attacks in Thessaly and against Greek cities in the Aegean he involved himself in a war with Rhodes and Pergamum and was accused of forming a plan with Antiochus to partition Egypt, which had been Rome's ally since 273 B.C. In 202 B.C. the Aetolian League appealed to Rome for aid but was rebuffed. The next year more urgent embassies from Rhodes and Pergamum approached the Senate, with charges of aggression by Philip against Pergamum, which, it will be recalled, had been Rome's ally in the First Macedonian War, and with a repetition of the charge that Philip had arranged with Antiochus to take over Egypt.

The Roman people, with the Hannibalic struggle just ended, were sick of war, and the *Comitia Centuriata* voted against a conflict with Macedonia. The senate, however, blandly sent an ultimatum to Philip to cease aggression against the Greek cities and Egypt and to pay reparations to Pergamum. Philip refused and then war was voted.

The Senate's high-handed action is difficult to explain except in terms of a chance for commercial exploitation in the Near East and a genuine fear that Philip and Antiochus, whose exploits made him seem a great conqueror, might combine against Rome. Moreover, Philip had been allied with Hannibal and the Senate may have thought it wise to crush him while Antiochus was occupied with his Egyptian designs. At any rate, a Roman army moved into Greece.

The Second Macedonian War: 200–196 B.C.

Rome's allies were Rhodes, Athens, Pergamum, and the Aetolian
League. Little was done until in 198 B.C. Titus Quinctius Flamininus,
a man who spoke faultless Greek and had a sincere appreciation of Greek
culture, took command. He won over the Achaean League and
manoeuvred Philip out of nearly all Greece except Thessaly. Here in 197
B.C. at Cynoscephalae (the "Dog's Heads", a ridge of hills), the Macedonian phalanx met the Roman legions. The phalanx broke through but it was
then destroyed by an attack on its flanks by the more manoeuvrable
legions. Philip sued for peace. The Senate specified that he must surrender
to Rome all his strongholds outside Macedonia, agree to the autonomy
of all Greek states, reduce his army to 5000 men, give up all his warships
except six, pay an indemnity of 1000 talents, and become an ally of Rome.
Philip was forced to accept and the power of Macedon was shattered.

Rome did not as yet want more territory. In 196 B.C. at Corinth during
the Isthmian games, Flamininus proclaimed the freedom of the Greek
states. There was an hysterical outburst of joy and, according to the
Greek historian, Polybius, who was present, the cheering mobs almost
tore Flamininus to pieces. In some cities he was worshipped as a god,
the first but not the last Roman to receive divine honors.

The War with Antiochus the Great: 192–186 B.C.

In the meantime Antiochus III had taken southern Syria from Egypt
and proceeded to capture Ephesus, Abydos, and other Greek cities in Asia
Minor. Then, in 196 B.C. he crossed into Thrace on the pretext that it
had once belonged to the Seleucids. In the same year Hannibal came to
his court as a refugee. The Romans warned Antiochus to withdraw from
Europe and to evacuate the Greek cities of Asia Minor. Antiochus paid
no attention. Meanwhile, the Aetolian League, disgruntled with the
Romans both because they had expected more territory than they had
received for their help against Philip and because they were no longer
allowed to plunder their neighbors, invited Antiochus into Greece. In
192 B.C. he invaded the peninsula. Rome, who had withdrawn her legions
from Greece, sent over an army which routed Antiochus and the Aetolians
at Thermopylae. A truce was made with the Aetolians (Philip V, the
Achaean League, Rhodes, and Pergamum had remained loyal to Rome),
and the Romans elected the great Scipio's younger brother, Lucius, to
command a force to invade Asia Minor. Lucius wisely took along his
brother Africanus. In 190 B.C. at Magnesia, Antiochus' huge army was
shattered by the legions. In the peace treaty, he was forced to give up all
his possessions in Asia Minor north of the Taurus Mountains and west
of the Halys river, all his war elephants, all his warships except ten,

promise to wage no war against Roman allies except in self-defence, and pay a huge indemnity of 15,000 talents. Hannibal, who was also demanded, escaped, as has been mentioned, to Bithynia but was later forced by the arrival of Roman envoys to take his own life.

In two brief wars, Rome had destroyed the power of Macedonia and Syria, and Egypt was so weak that it was not a danger. Though supreme, she again did not annex any territory. Rhodes and Pergamum were rewarded for their help with large tracts of Antiochus' former possessions, but Philip V, though he had been equally loyal, received only a few talents and the promise of some towns in Thessaly. He set to work quietly to increase the resources of his kingdom. Rome now turned on the Aetolians who were forced into the status of subject allies. Then the legions went home. Rome, having reduced the Near East to a welter of impotent states under the name of freedom, sat back like a benevolent grandfather who hopes that the children will behave but doesn't care too much if they don't.

This policy may in part have been due to war weariness and in part to the influence of Scipio Africanus who was a Philhellene.

Cato the Elder: 234–149 B.C.

Scipio Africanus and his pro-Hellenic group, and the later Philhellenic coterie (headed by Scipio the Younger and the younger Laelius), met a strong antagonist in Cato the Elder, a man who to the Romans seemed the embodiment of all the virtues of early Republican days. Although a "new man" (*novus homo*), which meant that none of his ancestors had held office, this red-headed, gray-eyed farmer pushed his way into the Senate and held all the offices from quaestorship to the censorship. As a soldier he fought in his first battle in 217 B.C. and in his last in 191 B.C. at Thermopylae against Antiochus. In his home life he was close-fisted in a bargain, cruel to his slaves, who in his view were animals to be worked until they were useless and then got rid of, and never kissed his wife except when it thundered. Yet he worked and ate on his farm with his family and his slaves, as in the early Roman household, never struck his wife or son, and tutored the boy himself, writing the *Origines* for him. He also composed a highly practical book on farming, the *De Agricultura*.

In public life Cato was incorruptible, although he evaded the Roman law of 218 B.C. against senators engaging in trade by using a dummy. But he never filled his own purse through his offices or his military victories and brought prosecution after prosecution against corrupt or dishonest fellow-countrymen. As censor in 184 B.C. he demoted senators and knights because of their morals, cut the pipes by which public water was being supplied to private homes, and, with an eagle eye, let out state contracts for the lowest prices, collected the highest possible fees from the tax farmers, and passed his Sumptuary Law against luxury, placing a 30 percent tax on all apparel, jewelry, furniture, and plate worth over 1500 denarii ($300 in actual coinage though worth from ten to twenty times that amount in terms of today's inflated prices and debased currency). Later, through his influence, other sumptuary laws (181 and 161 B.C.) limited the amount to be spent on banquets and funerals (25 sesterces or 75 cents on a banquet for nine persons which in itself tells us what 25 sesterces would buy in those days, but 1500 denarii for the silver plate which could be used).

Cato's dislike of Scipio the Elder went back to 204 B.C., when, as quaestor, he had tried to check Scipio's expenditures in Africa and failed. He was finally able to force Scipio out of public life not too long after the battle of Magnesia. Equally passionate was his hatred of Greek culture as the poison destroying the old sturdy Republican morals and religion, and he urged measures to ban Greek philosophers from Rome. Puritan, farmer, patriot, and conservative, he conceived himself to be the conscience of the Republic, as stern in his censure of those of his countrymen who fell short of his ideals as he was scornful of all who were not Romans.

His attempts to prevent the wave of Greek influence were futile, but he became the principal author of a new and agressive Roman imperialism in which all foreigners were despised, what was advantageous for Rome was always right, and any means, including deception, were legitimate to attain Rome's ends. It was ironical that this one hundred per cent Roman policy was used by Rome's businessmen to crush commercial rivals and win huge fortunes. The new "hard line" became evident during the Third Macedonian War.

The Third Macedonian War: 171–167 B.C.

On the death of Philip V, his son, Perseus, succeeded him. His father had left him an army of 43,000 men and a treasury of 16,000 gold talents. Meanwhile there was chaotic discontent in Greece. The Romans had placed the "haves" in control and the "have-nots" were revolting. Furthermore, the Greeks had discovered that "independence" under Rome meant doing only what Rome wanted. Philip first and his son after him began to form alliances with the Greek states and to make overtures to Syria, Egypt, Rhodes, and even Pergamum. But the king of Pergamum was Rome's subservient spy. Acting on information from him, in 172 B.C. the Senate presented Perseus with impossible demands and war broke out.

For the first two years there was little headway because of the incompetence of the Roman generals. Then, in 168 B.C., Aemilius Paullus, who belonged to the Scipionic circle, took command. Perseus was brought to battle at Pydna and defeated. The kingdom of Macedonia was ended. On his return to Rome, Aemilius Paullus celebrated a three days' triumph.

A Roman Triumph

A Roman triumph went up the Sacred Way through the Forum toward the Capitoline Hill. On the left was the Palatine Hill, on the right the Caelian and the Esquiline. At the triumph of Aemilius Paullus every column in the Forum would be wreathed with flowers, every shop decorated, and every vantage point would be jammed with men, women and children, looking eagerly for the procession to appear.

That procession began with the city magistrates, followed by trumpeters. Then came the wagons bearing the spoils. In Aemilius Paullus' triumph there were 250 wagons to carry the art, arms, silver, furniture, tableaux of the battle scenes, and other spoils of war, along with 300 golden crowns from the Greek States. So much booty was captured that the war-tax on the property of Roman citizens, levied constantly during the Hannibalic war, was not called for again until 43 B.C.—over a hundred years later. (We must remember, however, the tribute from the Roman provinces which continued to be levied.)

We can almost hear the cheering as each new wagon appeared. Behind the spoils came priests and oxen for the sacrifice, and then the captives. Among these walked the sons and daughters of Perseus and Perseus himself, clad in black. Finally, Aemilius Paullus appeared. He rode on a gilded chariot drawn by four white horses, robed in purple, and with a laurel crown on his head. Over that head a slave held an oak-leaf crown of gold while another, in a typical Roman touch, whispered in his ear from time to time to remind him that he was a mortal.

There must have been a tremendous and continuous roar of cheering as the victor rode along the Sacred Way. His soldiers, their javelins wreathed in laurel, followed, singing bawdy songs about their general and bandying jokes with the close-packed crowd. The procession ended at the Temple of Jupiter on the Capitoline Hill. Then the oxen were sacrificed and the general laid his wreath on the knees of the god. At night there was a state banquet given for the Senate, while throughout the city soldiers and citizens feasted and celebrated.

Aemilius Paullus' triumph was among the first of the elaborate and barbaric triumphs of which Rome was to see many. They pleased the city mob and whetted the appetite of Roman public men for similar honors. It is interesting to note that Aemilius Paullus also brought the library of King Perseus to Rome.

The Aftermath of Pydna

The new imperialism found expression after Pydna. Macedonia was divided into four autonomous republics (an interesting anticipation of a modern idea that a republican form of government solves all ills), but these republics were kept so completely separate that their people could not trade or intermarry with each other, the mines and royal domains were Roman property, and an annual tribute of 100 talents was exacted. Rhodes and Pergamum, although ostensibly allies of Rome, were stripped of much of their territory, the excuse being that they were suspected of dealings with Perseus. When the subservient king of Pergamum tried to put his case before the Senate, since Rome had no more use for him he was not even allowed to land in Italy (early winter 167–166 B.C.). As for Rhodes, which was a commercial rival of the Roman businessmen, its trade was destroyed by making the nearby island of Delos into a "free port" where no customs dues were paid.

Syria likewise felt Rome's heavy hand. Antiochus IV, the son of Antiochus the Great who had been assassinated in 187 B.C. while robbing a temple in Susa, had prospered so greatly that he had invaded Egypt in 168 B.C. and was about to attack Alexandria. A Roman envoy, Popilius, arrived, bearing a decree of the Senate that he must stop the war. When Antiochus played for time, Popilius took a stick, drew a circle around the king, and commanded him to decide yes or no before he stepped out of the circle. Antiochus withdrew from Egypt. Shortly afterward, when, as has been mentioned, the Jews revolted against Antiochus' attempts to hellenize them, Rome (161 B.C.) made a treaty with them and in 129 B.C. they became completely independent. With Antiochus' death late in 164 B.C. the Seleucid empire fell apart and shortly afterward the Parthian horsemen rode in to occupy Iran and Mesopotamia.

In Greece the Romans were harsh and arrogant. The leaders of the anti-Roman faction were put to death or exiled. Although no fault could be found with the Achaean League, 1000 of its principal citizens, including Polybius the historian, were taken to Rome as hostages, kept there for 17 years, and not released until some 700 of them had died. A much more drastic brutality was inflicted on Epirus. Its 70 towns were sacked and 150,000 of its people were sold into slavery. The aftermath of Pydna was a revolting imperialism and the guiding genius seems to have been Cato.

Macedonia a Province and the Destruction of Corinth: 148–146 B.C.

Rome had left a patchwork of weakened states in the Hellenistic East but still accepted no real responsibility for keeping order. The result was chaos. In the Aegean piracy was rampant, in Asia Minor and in Macedonia there were attacks by Celts, Thracians and Illyrians, and in Greece there was party-strife between a pro-Roman aristocracy and the masses. Finally, in Macedonia a pretender, claiming to be the son of Perseus, appeared and united the country against Rome. When he was crushed in 148 B.C. Macedonia was organized into a Roman province.

The next year, in despairing exasperation at Rome's interference in its affairs, the Achaean League revolted. The consul for 146 B.C., Lucius Mummius, ended the rebellion. Then, in part because Corinth was a commercial rival of the Roman business-men and in part as a lesson to the Greeks, he sacked the city, massacred many of its inhabitants, sold the rest as slaves, shipped its art treasures to Rome, and razed the place to the ground. Polybius, who had accompanied Mummius, tells of seeing Roman soldiers playing checkers with priceless pictures as the boards. The Achaean League was dissolved and each city-state, except for Athens and Sparta which had helped Rome, was made subject to Rome. The whole of Greece was administered by the governor of Macedonia until, over a century later, the emperor Augustus made it a separate province. Yet the cities were left a certain amount of autonomy.

The Roman actions in Macedonia and Greece made it clear that Rome was now concerned only with its own interests and despised the conquered. The same attitude was responsible for the third war against Carthage.

The Third Punic War: 149–146 B.C.

For half a century after its defeat in the Second Punic War, Carthage abode by the peace, sending troops and grain to aid Rome when called upon, and not taking any action against the continual aggressions of Massinissa, the king of Numidia, except to appeal fruitlessly to Rome. In spite of her difficulties, Carthage prospered. Then in 153 B.C., when by a further advance Massinissa had shaved Carthage down to about one-sixth of its previous area in North Africa, Cato the Elder appeared as head of a boundary commission. The commission, as usual, did not settle anything but the aged Cato (81 years) during a tour of Carthage was impressed by its prosperity. Returning to Rome, thenceforward he ended every speech in the Senate, no matter what the topic, with the words; "Furthermore, I think that Carthage must be destroyed."

Meanwhile, Carthaginian resentment against Massinissa led to the murder of some of his envoys and his declaration of war. Carthage was defeated, but by defending herself, she had broken the terms of the treaty made after Zama. Hearing that Rome was preparing an army, she sent ambassadors to the Senate to admit her fault and to seek peace terms.

There followed an outstanding example of Roman duplicity. The envoys were told that Carthage would retain her freedom and her territory if she would send 300 noble hostages to Rome and "obey the future orders of the consuls." When the consuls arrived they demanded the surrender of all arms and engines of war. The Carthaginians complied. Then, at last, they were ordered to abandon their city and to settle elsewhere at least ten miles from the sea, thus ending their commerce forever. One wonders if in this trickery one sees the final advice of Cato, who died in 149 B.C.

Enraged at the deception, the Carthaginians closed their gates, built new engines of war (the Carthaginian women were said to have given their hair to be braided into ropes for the catapults) and prepared to defend themselves. The siege lasted three years. Finally, young Scipio, the son of Aemilius Paullus and the adopted grandson of Scipio the Elder, was, like his adoptive grandfather, elected consul contrary to the constitution (he was about thirty and had not even been curule aedile) and put in command. He took Carthage by assault in the spring of 146 B.C. The 50,000 surviving Carthaginians were sold as slaves, the city looted and, like Corinth, razed to the ground. Rome formed a new province, Africa, with Numidia, its ally, controlling the hinterland. Once again a commercial rival of Rome had been eliminated.

Cisalpine Gaul, Liguria, and Southern Gaul

While Rome was conquering the Hellenistic East, she re-subdued Cisalpine Gaul and established a number of new colonies in the area. She also put a Latin colony at Aquileia at the head of the Adriatic, from which, shortly afterward, she completed the conquest of Illyricum where she had had posts since the days of Queen Teuta. Then she turned to the difficult task of subjugating the mountain fastnesses of the Ligurians. By 172 B.C. the Romans controlled what is now the Italian and French Riviera as far as the borders of Massilia, which was her ally. None of these campaigns gave them as much trouble as the wars in Spain.

The Spanish Wars: 154–133 B.C.

During the Second Punic War the Romans had been welcomed by the Spaniards as deliverers, and in 197 B.C. she had organized the two provinces of Hither and Further Spain. In that same year war erupted because of Roman tyranny and rapacity. It was not stamped out until the consul of 195 B.C., Cato, arrived with an army of 50,000 men. Cato, though stern, was just. His economic arrangements did something to keep the Spaniards quiet. A second governor, Tiberius Sempronius Gracchus, the son-in-law of Scipio the Elder (and father of the revolutionaries, Tiberius and Gaius Gracchus), who ruled from 180–178 B.C., inspired such confidence by his fairness and reforms that there was peace for a quarter of a century.

But the new imperialism of Rome after Pydna was reflected in the brutality and rapacity of the governors of Spain. In spite of appeals to the Senate and in spite of the championship of Cato, the Spaniards received no redress. In Further Spain the Lusitanians staged a formidable revolt in 154 B.C. under the leadership of the heroic Viriathus. The war was marked by Roman treachery in accordance with the idea that any means were legitimate to achieve Roman ends. On one occasion 7000 Lusitanians were persuaded by false promises to lay down their arms and then they were butchered. The perpetrator of this crime was prosecuted in Rome by Cato but used the money he had extorted from the Spaniards and the tears of his little children to escape punishment. At another time, in 141 B.C., Viriathus forced a Roman army of 50,000 to surrender and spared them in return for a treaty with the Roman general promising the freedom of his people. The treaty was ratified and broken the next year. Finally in 138 B.C. the Romans bribed two traitors to slit Viriathus' throat and the war in Further Spain ended.

In Hither Spain the Celtiberians had rebelled in 153 B.C. Here the war centered around Numantia, a strong fortress on a hill at the junction of two rivers. Once again there was Roman duplicity. In 137 B.C. the consul Mancinus surrendered an army of 20,000 men to a force of less than one-third that number. The consul then made a treaty by which the Romans were allowed to escape with their lives under a promise not to fight again. But the treaty was broken. At last, Scipio the Younger, the destroyer of Carthage, was given the command. He led 20,000 Roman legionaries and 40,000 Spanish auxiliaries against 4000 Numantines. Even so the siege took fifteen months and the defenders were not beaten but were starved into submission. Scipio set the town on fire and its flames marked the "pacification" of Spain. In Rome the next year Scipio Africanus Minor celebrated a splendid triumph. Yet it might be noted that Spain was the first overseas country to have Roman colonies planted in it.

The End of Pergamum: 133 B.C.

From the time of the Second Macedonian War Pergamum had been the jackal of Rome. The role had not saved her from the new Roman imperialism after Pydna, but she had continued to lick the sandals of her master and had recovered a good deal of her territory. Her last king, Attalus III, was childless. With amazing insouciance he bequeathed his kingdom and his people to Rome. The Senate gave portions of the kingdom to Pontus and to inland tribes and in 129 B.C. organized the remainder into the Roman province of Asia.

Effects of the Conquests

Rome was now the colossus of the Mediterranean world. Her provinces

were Sicily (227 B.C.), Sardinia and Corsica (227 B.C.), Hither and
Further Spain (197 B.C.), Macedonia (148 B.C.), Africa (146 B.C.), and
Asia (129 B.C.). In addition she controlled Greece, Illyricum (the coast
of Yugoslavia and Albania), and the whole of North Italy. A little later,
in 121 B.C., she organized a corridor to Spain along the southern shore
of Gaul into the province of Gallia Narbonensis with Massilia as a free
ally, and drove through it a road, the *Via Domitia*, as far as Numantia
in Spain. Although she had refrained from annexing more territory,
neither Numidia nor Egypt nor the kinglets, cities, and tribes of Asia
Minor dared make a move without a cautious glance at Rome. In these
areas, because Rome dominated without governing, disorder flourished,
and in the Aegean piracy was rampant.

Wherever the eagles went the Roman and Italian business-men
followed. The provinces were in general organized after the fashion of
Sicily. There were a few federated cities (except in Africa), Roman public
lands rented out to their former owners, Roman ownership of mines,
fisheries, and the like, and a mass of subjects paying tribute. As a result,
the farming out of taxes and of mining and fishing concessions and the like
made fortunes for joint-stock corporations of Roman Knights. Every
form of extortion was practised. The governors, theoretically supposed
to mete out justice, were usually "sleeping partners" of the Knights. As
Verres, governor of Sicily at a later date, was to boast, their objective
was to make three fortunes, one to pay off debts, one with which to bribe
the jurors in Rome, and one to keep. Injustice and plundering were
permissible and the only redress for the provincials was, as we have seen,
to persuade some Roman to prosecute the governor for extortion *after*
his term of office was over. A court for this purpose (*de repetundis*) had
been made permanent in 149 B.C. but few governors were convicted,
especially since the jurors were their fellow senators who had either
done the same sort of thing or hoped to. One result of the atrocious treatment of the provincials were the slave-revolts in Sicily; another, later,
the massacre of 80,000 Italians in the province of Asia. Roads and
bridges were bought by the provincials at a heavy price. Meantime, the
conquests had changed the fabric of the Roman way of life.

Economic Effects in Italy

In the second century B.C. Rome was becoming, to quote the historian
Mommsen, "a society of beggars and millionaires." The looted wealth
in gold, silver, works of art, and slaves which had poured into Italy
benefited the office-holding senatorial clique and the Knights. The
Knights were also the bankers of the new economy and, as noted, formed
the joint-stock companies to squeeze the last sesterce from the

provincials and from the natural resources of the provinces. They likewise amassed huge profits from contracts for public works in Italy and overseas, such as roads, bridges, and food and supplies for the troops, although overseas trade was, in general, left to the Greeks of South Italy. The senatorial class, although forbidden trade, often either, like Cato, used dummy figures or became unnamed partners of the Knights. Extortion in the provinces and plunder from the wars added to their wealth

A common form of investment was in huge plantation-farms in Italy, worked by gangs of slaves, a practice imported from Carthage. The First Carthaginian War had flung 75,000 slaves on the market, the Second twice as many, and the wars of the 2nd century B.C. hundreds of thousands more. As we have seen, the sack of Epirus alone had yielded 150,000. Slavery had become an integral part of Roman life. One estimate of the population of Italy at this time suggests 1,000,000 Roman citizens, 4,000,000 Italians, and 1,000,000 slaves. Although the lot of the house-slaves depended entirely on the whim of the master, their treatment, as a rule, was better than that of the slaves on the plantation-farms who were worked, fed, flogged, and stabled like animals. But the plantation-farms were profitable and spread over large areas, especially in Apulia and southern Italy.

Slave labor tended to complete the ruin of free labor. The plantation-farms in their turn aided in the wreckage of the peasant farms. The constant warfare had taken the Italian peasants into far fields where many of them had been killed or wounded, especially in the Spanish wars in which the Spaniards proved themselves more deadly fighters than the Romans. Those soldiers who returned had comparatively little loot and equally little desire to settle down to a farming life; and, besides, it was difficult for the small farms to compete with the plantation-farms or with the tribute wheat and other products from the provinces. Only in North Italy, where hundred-acre farms were the rule and the land rich, was farming prosperous. By 133 B.C. large tracts of Italy were desolate and Rome was crowded with a mob of unemployed, dissatisfied people. There was a middle-class of shopkeepers, artisans, and small businessmen. But in general a comparatively few families possessed the wealth, including the use of the state lands, and the masses were homeless and poverty-stricken. In 133 B.C., the tribune, Tiberius Gracchus, said:

> The wild beasts of Italy have their dens and holes . . . . while the men who fight and die in defence of Italy . . . homeless and without a spot of ground on which to rest, wander about with their wives and children . . . . and they die with the name of the lords of the world without possessing a single clod to call their own.

Out of this glaring inequality between the very rich and the very poor was to come the Gracchan attempt at revolution.

Government

The constant wars had put the Senate still more firmly in the saddle. Except for a Cato, a new man could not break into the office-holding clique of the some twenty families, such as the Metelli, Claudii, and Cornelii, who had made the magistracies their perquisite. It was in the 2nd century B.C. that a Roman poet, Naevius, wrote: "Unhappy Rome, with a Metellus always as consul." The Metelli, we are told, had the poet put in jail.

Wealth and success had corrupted the senatorial clique. They had been fortunate in moments of crisis in finding a Flamininus or an Aemilius Paullus or a Scipio the Younger to save them from their mistakes. But they misgoverned the provinces, failed to keep order in the Near East, paid no heed to the economic distress in Italy, and turned a deaf ear to the demands of the Latin and Italian allies for Roman citizenship, a problem made more acute by the abandonment after the Hannibalic War of the policy of gradual incorporation of the allies into the Roman state. To the Senate, however, the allies and the ordinary Roman citizens were only valuable as fighting-men to expend in their wars of expansion or subjugation. Complacent and arrogant, like the Bourbons of a later date, "they had forgotten nothing and learned nothing."

Culture

In spite of Cato's opposition and in spite of the contempt of most Romans for the Greeks, by 133 B.C. Greek, or rather Hellenistic, culture had captured their conquerors. Although they still maintained early practices and festivals, Roman gods had become more and more Graecized. Oriental cults, such as that of Cybele, the "Great Mother of the Gods," had been introduced. Her worship was orgiastic, promising personal immortality to believers, and her priests were self-made eunuchs. When the cult was introduced during the Hannibalic War because of a Sibylline oracle, a law was passed that no Roman citizen could be a priest of Cybele. Yet in a half-century the high-priest was a Roman.

The ruins of the temple of Cybele can still be seen on the Palatine Hill. The Romans, however, early in the 2nd century B.C., did attempt to stamp out the Bacchic cult in Italy and, according to Livy, thousands were put to death. But the worship of Isis was brought in from Alexandria and in the next century there was a spate of Oriental religions into Italy. Quite clearly, for the masses the Roman state religion was losing its appeal.

Similarly, Hellenistic philosophies spread among the upper classes, particularly Stoicism and Epicureanism, although Cato, on two occasions, had Greek philosophers banned from Rome. Furthermore, Greeks, starting, as we have seen, with the capture of Tarentum in 272 B.C., had become tutors of the Roman children and by this time many of them were running private schools. As a result, Roman boys now learned Greek literature as a major subject, and Roman literature had become Graeco-Roman.

There had been a nascent Italian literature. The "Fescennine verses", bawdy songs at weddings and triumphs, appear to have been a genuine native production. Later the Roman had imported from Etruria the *Saturae* which appear to have been vaudeville sketches. In prose the Romans had only the Twelve Tables, a few public speeches, and some family eulogies.

These comparatively simple forms of literary expression were soon overshadowed by works modeled on Greek literature. In 241 B.C. Livius Andronicus, a Greek slave from Tarentum who had been freed by his master, produced a Latin translation of the Odyssey which became a schoolbook. Five years later a Campanian, Naevius, brought out an epic on the First Punic War, and was famous, too, for his Latin adaptations of Greek tragedies and comedies. To the Romans, the father of Roman poetry was Ennius (239–169 B.C.), a half-Greek who was brought by Cato from Calabria to Rome. He was proud of his "three hearts", Latin, Greek, and Oscan, and was a Pythagorean who said that his soul had once been in Homer and then in a lion and next in a peacock so that he himself, there-fore, was boastful, courageous, and a great poet. His great work was his *Annales*, an epic in Latin hexameter (modeled on the Greek hexameter) relating the story of Rome from the migration of Aeneas from Troy to his own times. Some 600 lines are left. He was also renowned for his adap-tations of Greek plays, particularly tragedies. Two other writers of tragedy followed him, Pacuvius of Brundisium and Accius of Umbria.

It will be noted that none of these writers were Roman. Similarly the two great writers of comedy—or rather of Latin adaptations of Greek plays—were Plautus of Umbria (254–184 B.C.) and Terence, an emancipa-ted slave from Africa. Although the Plautine plays, of which we have twenty, were adaptations from Greek New Comedy, they are charac-terized by broad humor, an exuberant vigor, and many passages and allusions which are Roman. Terence (185–159 B.C.), a protégé of the Scipionic circle, wrote more refined Latin but was not as popular as Plautus. However, as we have seen, the twenty-six plays of these two authors led to the genesis of European comedy.

The Roman general public had not too much taste for any but the broad-est comedy and scarcely any for tragedy. They preferred the Atellan Farce, crude plays with stock plots and the same five characters in all of them, which had been imported from Campania, and the mime, brought in from south Italy, in which women did the strip-tease. Such entertainment made no demands on intelligence but could give many a "belly-laugh."

The one form of literature which the Romans claimed as their own was satire. Its founder was a Knight, Lucilius (ca. 180–103 B.C.), a member of the Scipionic circle. The one important prose writer of the period was Cato whose *De Agricultura* and *Origines* have been noted. Cato also published a collection of about 150 of his speeches. In spite of his anti-Greek attitude, he is said to have learned Greek at 80, the better to combat Greek influence.

The rise of Graeco-Roman literature illustrates how thoroughly Greek culture overwhelmed the Romans. In many other ways they imitated the Greeks. Roman aristocrats now reclined at banquets, although the women still had to sit upright. Greek statues and paintings adorned public buildings and the palaces of the wealthy. To the Roman *atrium* house was often added the Greek peristyle, a garden enclosed by a colonnade of pillars with rooms opening off it. The Romans, having no real culture of their own, aped the Greeks and often, like *nouveaux riches*, did a somewhat poor job of it.

Meanwhile, Rome itself had changed from a sort of overgrown country town to a great city with temples in the Greek style replacing the earlier Etruscan architecture, palaces on the hills, and jerry-built tenements for the poor in the hollows. Public works were extended, such as a new stone bridge across the Tiber, two aqueducts to bring in water, and the decoration of the Forum with triumphal columns, temples, and other buildings. To Rome, as the dominant city, all peoples bordering the Mediterranean flocked—Gauls, Spaniards, Africans, Greeks, Egyptians, and the rest. In spite of Cato, Rome became cosmopolitan.

Manners and Morals

By 133 B.C. the old Roman character had been pretty well dissolved by the acids of wealth and power. Bigger and better villas and palaces, more and more possessions, along with Oriental vices and luxuries, were the preoccupation of the rich. The hosts of slaves, forced to satisfy every whim of their masters, speeded the breakdown. The old authority of the father was eaten away, women had more independence, and the ruling clique was a law to itself. Money had become the ruling power. Meanwhile, in Rome the poor were hangers-on, avid for the free food and entertainment of the festival days, and willing to vote for whichever candidate gave or promised the most, while throughout Italy plantation-slaves toiled under the lash and the peasant-farmer and the broken-down veterans of Rome's wars strove to eke out a living. Out of economic inequalities and the corruption of senatorial government came the Gracchan attempt at reforms.

Readings from Sources of the Period

(a) Graeco-Roman literature began in 241 B.C. Plautus (ca. 254–184 B.C.) composed comedies in Latin based on Greek originals. Upon his *The Braggart Soldier* (Miles Gloriosus) is based a play of today, titled *A Funny Thing Happened on the Way to the Forum.* The opening scene is between the braggart soldier, (the prototype of Shakespeare's Falstaff) and his slave.

SCENE: *A street in Ephesus before the adjoining houses of* PYRGOPOLYNICES *and* PERIPLECTOMENUS.

PYRGOPOLYNICES.   See to it that my shield shines brighter than the rays of the sun on a clear day so that when I need it in the thick of the fight it may dazzle the eyes of the enemy in the line. I would like to console this sword of mine so that it won't become despondent at so long a vacation, when all it's dying for is to make hash of the enemy. But where is Artotrogus?

ARTOTROGUS.   Why he's standing right beside a brave and lucky man—a man as handsome as a king. As to being a fighter, even Mars wouldn't dare boast he's as good a fighter as you.

PYR.   And didn't I save the life of that fellow of Mars on Weevil Field where Bombasto Furioso, son of Clutomistaridysarchus was commander—a direct descendant of Neptune?

ART.   I remember. He's the one in golden armor, whose men you scattered just by blowing on them—like leaves in the wind.

PYR.   Oh, that was nothing.

ART.   Nothing's right compared to other things I could mention . . . *(aside)* which you haven't done either. If anybody ever saw a bigger liar than this man, he can have me—I'll be his slave. But there's one thing—he sets a good table.

PYR.   Where are you?

ART.   Right here. (*To* PYRGOPOLYNICES.) Or that time in India when you smashed an elephant's arm with your bare fist?

PYR.   What do you mean, arm?

ART.   I meant to say thigh.

PYR.   Oh, that was just a slight tap.

ART.   If you had really been trying, it would have been too bad for the elephant's shin and guts and neck as well.

PYR.   Enough of that now.

ART.   There's no need to tell of all your exploits since I know them all well. *(Aside.)* My stomach causes me all these troubles. I have to use my ears to give my teeth a bite. I have to back up any lie he tells.

PYR.   What was I talking about?

ART.   Oh yes, I know what you meant to say. It's an absolute fact. I was there when it happened.

PYR.   When what happened?

ART.   Whatever it was.

PYR.   Have you got . . . ?

ART.   You want writing tablets? I have them and a pen, too.

PYR.   You always know what I am thinking.

ART.   It's my job to know you well enough to smell out what you want before you say anything.

PYR.   And what was it you remembered?

ART.   This: 150 in Cilicia—100 in Scytholatronia, 30 Sardians—60 Macedonians—that is, just the ones you killed in one day.

PYR.   How many is that altogether?

ART.   7000.

PYR.   That's about right. Your addition is good.

ART.   I don't have it written down, but that's what I remember.

PYR.   By Pollux, you have a fine memory!

ART.   Food helps it.

PYR.   If you do as well as you've done up to now, you'll never have to worry
about eating; you can eat with me.

ART.   What about the time in Cappadocia when you would have killed 500 at
one stroke if your sword hadn't been dull?

PYR.   I let them live because they were just poor foot-soldiers.

ART.   Why should I tell you what everybody knows, that you are the one and
only Pyrgopolynices . . . incomparable in bravery, looks and accomplishments.
Every woman loves you . . . and no wonder . . . since you are so handsome. Those
two who actually grabbed me by the shirt yesterday . . .

PYR.   What did they say to you?

ART.   They kept asking about you. "Is that Achilles?" asked one of them.
"No," I said, "that's his brother." The other one says, "By Castor, that explains
why he is so good-looking. Look at his hair. The girls who get him are certainly
lucky!"

PYR.   And what was the upshot?

ART.   Why both of them begged me to parade you by them today.

PYR.   It's awful to be so handsome.

ART.   You're right there. Those two are a nuisance; they keep coming to me,
begging and pleading just to be given a glimpse of you. They bother me so that
I can't even attend to your affairs.

PYR.   Well, it's about time to go to the Forum and pay the soldiers I recruited
yesterday. King Seleucus asked me to do my best to get him men. I have decided
to work on that today.

ART.   Come on, let's go.

PYR.   Follow me, orderlies.

(Howe and Harrer, *Roman Literature in Translation*, edition revised by Albert
Suskin, New York: Harpers, 1952. Translated by Albert Suskin.)

(b) Cato (235–149 B.C.) the Roman Puritan and opponent of Greek culture, wrote
the earliest extant piece of Latin prose sometime before 152 B.C. on agriculture.
Below are a few extracts:

For our ancestors considered, and so ordained in their laws, that, while the
thief should be cast in double damages, the usurer should make four-fold restitu-
tion. From this we may judge how much less desirable a citizen they esteemed
the banker than the thief. When they sought to commend an honest man, they
termed him good husbandman, good farmer.

On feast days the old ditches should be mended, the public roads worked, briers
cut down, the garden dug, the meadow cleaned, the hedges trimmed and the
clippings collected and burned, the fish pond cleaned out. On such days,

furthermore, the slaves' rations should be cut down as compared with what is allowed when they are working in the fields in fine weather.

You should go over the cattle and determine what is to be sold. You should sell the oil, if you can get your price, the surplus wine and corn, the old cattle, the worn out oxen, and the cull sheep, the wool and the hides, the old and sick slaves, and if anything else is superfluous you should sell that.

The appetite of the good farmer is to sell, not to buy.

Be a good neighbour. Do not roughly give offense to your own people. If the neighbourhood regards you kindly, you will find a readier market for what you have to sell, you will more easily get your work done, either on the place or by contract. If you build, your neighbours will aid you with their services, their cattle and their materials. If any misfortune should overtake you (which God forbid!) they will protect you with kindly interest.

The overseer should be responsible for the duties of the housekeeper. If the master has given her to you for a wife, you should be satisfied with her, and she should respect you. Require that she be not given to wasteful habits; that she does not gossip with the neighbours and other women. She should not receive visitors either in the kitchen or in her own quarters. She should not go out to parties, nor should she gad about. She should not practise religious observances, nor should she ask others to do so for her without the permission of the master or the mistress. Remember that the master practises religion for the entire household. She should be neat in appearance and should keep the house swept and garnished. Every night before she goes to bed she should see that the hearth is swept and clean. On the Kalends, the Ides, the Nones, and on all feast days, she should hang a garland over the hearth. On those days also she should pray fervently to the household gods. She should take care that she has food cooked for you and for the hands. She should have plenty of chickens and an abundance of eggs. She should diligently put up all kinds of preserves every year.

The sum of the wine allowed for each hand per annum is eight quadrantals, or amphora, but add in the proportion as they do work. Ten quadrantals per annum is not too much to allow them to drink.

Save the wind fall olives as much as possible as relishes for the hands. Later set aside such of the ripe olives as will make the least oil. Be careful to make them go as far as possible. When the olives are all eaten, give them fish pickles and vinegar. One peck of salt per annum is enough for each hand.

(*Ibid.*, pp. 79–82, translated by Fairfax Harrison.)

CHAPTER 6

The Class-Struggle: From the Gracchi to Sulla: 133–78 B.C.

During these years the rule of the Senate was attacked and weakened. Except for the Cimbri and Teutones in the West and Mithradates of Pontus in the East, there was no challenge to the external power of Rome. The chief danger to the Republic was from within. Greed, materialism, slavery, economic distress, the resentment of the Latin and Italian allies at the denial of Roman citizenship, the complacency and corruption of the senatorial clique, and the failure to change a city-state system of government to one fitted to administer an empire—all these factors led to class-struggle and civil war and gave opportunities to ambitious men to seize power. As is often the case, the first attempts at reform came from two aristocrats, Tiberius and Gaius Gracchi.

The Gracchi: 133–121 B.C.

The father of the Gracchi was the Tiberius Sempronius Gracchus who had been an estimable governor of Spain, and their mother was Cornelia, the daughter of Scipio the Elder, the woman who is said to have presented her infant sons as her "jewels" and who was herself one of the best-educated women of her day. The boys were given excellent tutors, especially in rhetoric and Stoic philosophy, and grew up with an admiration for Greek culture and a knowledge of Greek history. It is tempting to think that the story of Pericles, the man who ruled the Athenian Assembly by his eloquence and personality, may have influenced the Gracchi. Of the two, Tiberius was the sincere and somewhat humorless crusader; and Gaius, though passionate in his convictions, the more polished politician.

Tiberius, who was the older, had been the first to scale the walls of besieged Carthage and later served with distinction in Spain as a quaestor.

It was on his journey to Spain that he was impressed with the unhappy lot of the Italian peasants. On his return, he married the daughter of Appius Claudius Pulcher. The Claudians were one of the most patrician families in Rome but had always done exactly as they pleased. Though the leader of the Senate, Appius Claudius supported his son-in-law in his reforms.

In 133 B.C. Tiberius, at the age of twenty, was elected tribune (his family, though noble, was plebeian). His solution for the ills of the un-employed in Rome and the peasant-farmers of Italy was to re-enact the Licinian-Sextian laws of 367 B.C., which had not been enforced, in a modi-fied form. In addition to any one person being allowed to hold 500 jugera (310 acres) of the public land, a man's two sons could each possess 250 jugera and the holders of estates between 500 and 1000 jugera were to be given clear title. The rest of the public lands were to be repossessed by the state but with reimbursement for improvements, and assigned to landless Roman citizens in lots of not more than 30 jugera per person in hereditary possession. To execute the law there was to be a commission of three.

The bill was moderate, especially since certain rich sections of the public lands, such as those in Campania, were excluded. But there were howls of anguished rage from the wealthy families who had squatted on these lands for generations and regarded them as their own. Moreover, Tiberius did not follow custom and bring the bill before the Senate first. Instead, he presented it directly to the Tribal Assembly as was constitu-tionally feasible. This action might strengthen a suspicion that Tiberius had Periclean Athens and its all-powerful Assembly in mind. The Senate persuaded another tribune, Octavius, to veto the bill. Tiberius had the Assembly depose Octavius. This act was probably illegal in Rome, though it would have been within the powers of the Athenian Assembly.

The bill was passed and a commission of three—Tiberius himself, his brother Gaius, and his father-in-law, Appius Claudius—was appointed with full power to act. But the Senate was in control of the treasury. It allotted about thirty cents a day for the operating expenses of the commission. Tiberius countered by having the personal treasure of Attalus, the king of Pergamum, who had just died and willed it along with his kingdom to Rome, assigned to the commission. Then, contrary to the law and custom, he stood for re-election to the tribunate. The Senate was in a frenzy. On the day of the voting, when the consul refused to act, led by Scipio Nasica, a mob of senators and their retainers, armed with clubs, staves, and chair-legs, rushed through the crowd, clubbed Tiberius and 300 of his followers to death and flung their bodies into the Tiber. Then a special court was set up which executed some of the Gracchan partisans and exiled others. The class-struggle had begun with the senatorial clique being the first to unsheathe the sword of violence.

The Tribunate of Gaius Gracchus: 123–121 B.C.

In the years between the death of Tiberius and the election of Gaius Gracchus, Tiberius' commission with two new members on it put over 75,000 new settlers on the land. Meanwhile, in 129 B.C., Scipio the Younger, who had been championing the cause of the Latin and Italian allies was found dead in his bed, not without a suspicion of foul play. Shortly afterward, Fregellae, a Latin ally, revolted. The town was crushed but its rebellion was a warning that the allies could not be denied Roman citizenship without danger. Then, in 123 B.C., Gaius Gracchus became tribune in spite of the opposition of the Senate.

Gaius was more magnetic in personality than his brother and a subtler politician. Like Tiberius he brought his laws directly before the Tribal Assembly. His first measure exiled the man who had presided at the special court to execute or exile his brother's chief supporters; his second arranged for a distribution of a fixed amount of wheat per month per person (5 *modii* or 5.5 pecks) at about half the regular price to any Roman citizen who claimed it in person. Granaries to store the wheat, which came almost altogether from the provinces, along with wharves on which to unload it, were built under the Aventine Hill, traditionally the stronghold of the plebs. The dole system for the unemployed had been begun.

This measure confirmed the support of the city plebs, and in the middle of 123 B.C. Gaius was re-elected tribune for a second term. With a sure eighteen months of power in front of him he next detached the Knights from their support of the senatorial clique by giving them special seats in the theater, turning over the province of Asia to the tax-farmers, and replacing the senatorial jurors on the court for extortion (*de repetundis*) by Knights. These last two actions turned out to be vicious ones. In Asia the Knights considered that they had purchased the right to exploit the provincials unmercifully and in their wake followed a horde of loan sharks (to loan the provincials money to meet the exactions of the tax-farmers) and speculators. Meanwhile, the equestrian jurors on the court for extortion used their power to *condemn* any senatorial governor who refused to countenance the extortions of the Knights. But those laws won Gaius the support of the equestrian order, and he now seemed as powerful as Pericles had been in Athens. To him flocked provincials, laborers, magistrates, would-be contractors, and foreign envoys, all recognizing him as the ruler. Meanwhile, he set the land commission to work again and built roads and bridges for the farmers of Italy.

His next project was to establish commercial and agricultural colonies for the artisans, traders, and small business-men among the unemployed of Rome. The sites were to be at Capua and Tarentum in Italy and overseas at Carthage. He also proposed a bill to extend Roman citizenship to the Latin allies and Latin rights to the rest of the Italians. But the senatorial clique was able to defeat the bill by pointing out to the city plebs that new citizens would crowd them out "at the games and festivals". Then, while Gaius was in Africa for seventy days supervising the settlement at Carthage, another tribune, Livius Drusus, was persuaded to make exaggerated promises to the electorate such as the founding of twelve colonies in Italy and the abolition of rent for those put on the land by Tiberius' commission.

These promises were not intended to be carried out, but they served their purpose. Gaius returned to find he had lost control of the city mob. He was defeated when in 122 B.C. he stood for re-election for a third term, although he was still technically safe from prosecution until the end of the year as tribune and beyond it as member of the commission to found the colony at Carthage. But his power was gone and the Senate was determined to be done with him. Early in 121 B.C. a proposal to repeal the law establishing the Carthaginian colony led to high tension. The Senate passed the "Ultimate Decree" instructing the consul, Lucius Opimius, to see to it "that the state received no harm". Opimius attacked Gaius and his followers on the Aventine Hill. About 250 of the Gracchans were slain and Gaius was either killed or had himself put to death by a slave. His severed head, crammed with molten lead, was brought to Opimius who paid for its weight in gold. Once again the final recourse of the senatorial faction was to unsheathe the sword—and later their power was to perish by it.

After Gaius' death a senatorial judicial commission put to death without trial some 3000 of his leading followers. The Carthaginian colony was annulled and in 118 B.C. the land commission was abolished. The Senate returned to power and, except that the proletariat soon recognized the Gracchi as heroes and martyrs, it might have seemed that they had died for nothing.

The Work of the Gracchi

Much of the actual legislation of the Gracchi was repealed or forgotten, the most enduring feature of it being the provision of wheat for the city mob. But after them Rome and Italy were never the same, and the power of the Senate was constantly challenged. For one thing, the Gracchi had coalesced the masses into a political party, known as the *Populares* or "People's party" (sometimes called the "Democratic party") and this party seldom lacked leaders. In contradistinction, the senatorial clique and its supporters now called themselves the *Optimates*, or "The Best People." In between was the equestrian order, the Knights, who now felt themselves a political force and swung their power to either the

Populares or the Optimates, according to the deal offered them. The class-struggle initiated by the Gracchi was to lead to civil war on civil war and ultimately to the collapse of the Republic.

The Gracchi had also shown how to by-pass the Senate by bringing laws directly before the Tribal Assembly, a device to be used by Julius Caesar in 59 B.C. Beyond this discovery, they had proved that in Rome, unlike Periclean Athens, persuasive eloquence was not enough but that to rule one must have an army which would move against the state. That type of army was provided by the revolutionary, Marius.

The Rise of Marius

Marius was born near Arpinum (later Cicero's birthplace) not far from Rome. His family was middle-class but he won the favor of an Optimate, Metellus, and was elected tribune in 119 B.C. Later, though a "new man", he achieved a praetorship and was then propraetor in Spain. Since by this time he was a "noble" he married into the patrician Julian family, his wife later becoming the aunt of Julius Caesar. Marius' rough, shaggy appearance, bluntness, and bad grammar (all of which may have been deliberate) had made him popular with the city mob. However, he still retained the patronage of Metellus so that when in 109 B.C. Metellus went to Numidia as commander against Jugurtha, he took Marius with him as his chief-of-staff.

The Jugurthine War: 111–105 B.C.

The Jugurthine War was an outstanding example of Optimate corruption and inefficiency. When in 118 B.C. the king of Numidia died he left his kingdom to two sons and a nephew, Jugurtha, whom he had adopted as a son. Jugurtha killed one of the king's sons, drove out the other, and then bribed the Senate to give him the western and richer half of Numidia. Three years after this he conquered the eastern half, torturing the remaining son to death but making the mistake of massacring the Italian traders who had settled in Numidia.

This latter action made the equestrian order rise up in wrath. They wanted a Numidia made safe for business-men. Uniting with the Populares they forced a declaration of war in 111 B.C. But the Optimate commander allowed himself to be bribed into a disgraceful peace and Jugurtha was summoned to Rome to give evidence under a pledge of safe-conduct. Two tribunes were bribed by the Optimates to prevent him speaking. Jugurtha's visit was not all in vain. A possible rival for the throne of Numidia lived in Rome; Jugurtha had him assassinated.

This was somewhat scandalous even for Rome. Jugurtha returned home and the war was renewed. But the Optimate commanders allowed their army to be entrapped and sent under the yoke and then signed a peace confirming Jugurtha in his kingdom. The treaty was rejected.

It was at this stage of the war that Metellus went to Africa, taking Marius with him. Metellus soon reduced Jugurtha to a guerrilla but could not seem to capture him, much to the exasperation of the Knights. Marius saw his chance. Returning to Rome, he stood for the consulship and with the support of the Knights and the Populares was elected. Next against the will of the Senate he got the command against Jugurtha, thus replacing his patron. In 105 B.C., with the help of his quaestor, Sulla, an Optimate, he captured Jugurtha and ended the war. Jugurtha walked in Marius' triumph and later died in a Roman dungeon.

The Cimbri and Teutones

Marius was now the idol of Rome. Even before his return he had been elected consul for 104 B.C., for Rome was now terrified by the threat from two Germanic tribes, the Cimbri and Teutones.

The Cimbri and Teutones show us the sort of folk-wandering which must have convulsed Europe time after time beyond the reach of history. Forced to leave Denmark and Schleswig because of over-population and tidal inundations, they had loaded their wives, children, and possessions into ox-carts covered with leather hoods, and started out in search of new homes. Their wanderings had taken them into Bohemia (Czechoslovakia) and across the Danube, where in 113 B.C. they had defeated a Roman army. Then, a nation on the march, after a four years' trek around the northern Alps, they crossed the Rhine into Gaul, bringing with them a Swiss tribe, the Tigurini.

The Romans, as we have seen, had in 121 B.C. created the province of Gallia Narbonensis, after defeating two Gallic tribes who will reappear in Roman history, the Allobroges and the Arverni. The horde asked the Romans for lands in their province and when refused, crushed the army of the consul, Carbo, in 109 B.C. Two years later the Tigurini shattered still another Roman army, sending the remnants under the yoke.

The tribes once again asked for lands and, when refused in 105 B.C., annihilated two Roman armies at Arausio (Orange), slaughtering, according to the Roman account, 80,000 men. Rome was in a panic. Fortunately the tribes did not invade Italy but turned away. Nevertheless the terror inspired by the stories of these blond giants led to the re-election of Marius not only for 104 B.C. but to successive consulships in 103–100 B.C.

Marius and his New Army

Marius used the respite given him by the tribes to enlist a new type of army. Up until this time the Roman legionaries had been citizens, serving for short terms only, and supposed to own property. Marius enlisted volunteers with no property qualifications for long terms. The army was to be their career and at the end of their service they were promised bonuses and lands. In this way he created an army of *professional* soldiers. Moreover, these soldiers took an oath of personal allegiance to their *general*. In time to come such an army would march against the state, if its commander were popular and promised sufficient rewards. This type of army was Marius' contribution to the revolution.

Marius also reorganized the fighting structure of the legion. Put briefly, he emphasized the *cohort* as the chief tactical unit within the legion. There were ten of these cohorts in each legion, the strength of each cohort varying from 400 to 600 men. Each cohort was composed of three *maniples*, one from each of the three lines of the legion so that the legion was now divided vertically as well as horizontally. Each maniple had in it two *centuries*, each commanded by a centurion. The centurions were the "sergeants" of the army. With their help, Marius trained his men to fight as individual duellists and accustomed them to long marches, carrying about 100 pounds per man in weapons, rations, cooking-pot, stakes for palisades, and entrenching tool. These soldiers were well called "Marius' Mules." At the end of a twenty-mile march, before they could rest, they had to make an encampment and fortify it. These were the kind of soldiers needed to meet the Germanic tribes.

Aquae Sextiae and Vercellae: 102–101 B.C.

In 102 B.C. the Germans prepared to invade Italy, the Teutones by way of southern Gaul, the Cimbri by crossing the Alps through the Brenner pass, the Tigurini by an encircling route through Venetia. Marius, who was in Gaul, let the Teutones pass by him, then attacked and annihilated them at Aquae Sextiae (today Aix-les-Bains). 100,000 are said to have been killed and an equal number, including women and children, captured. Next he led his army back into North Italy. Here his colleague, Catulus, a man better known for culture and the composition of literary trifles of the Hellenistic style than as a general, had retreated south of the Po while the Cimbri wintered in the Po valley. In 101 B.C. the two Roman armies attacked them near Vercellae (probably close to Turin). Marius had chosen a broad plain and had managed to get wind and sun in his favor. The Cimbri, their front line chained together, smashed the Roman center but were then assaulted on the flanks and destroyed, though there was a second fierce battle at the wagon line in which the Cimbric women joined. Italy was saved and blond Germanic captives flooded the slave-markets. The Tigurini turned back to reoccupy their former homes.

The Shadow Triumvirate: 100 B.C.

Marius had already been consul five times. Capitalizing on his victories, he allied himself with two Populares leaders and had himself elected consul for the sixth time. Colonies in the provinces and a grain dole at one-sixth the price set by Gaius Gracchus were part of the Popularis program. A new feature was a provision to compel senators to take an oath to obey all the proposed laws. Tribunician vetoes were brushed aside and the laws passed. But the Knights were by now alienated and Marius wanted to stand in well with the Senate as well as to maintain his connections with the Populares. The Optimates seized the opportunity to pass the Ultimate Decree (martial law) and called on Marius as consul to enforce it. To save his Populares friends, Marius locked them in the Senate-house. An Optimate mob climbed to the roof, ripped off the heavy tiles and pelted the refugees to death. As a politician Marius' career was over. Scorned by the proletariat and sneered at by the Knights and Senators, he retired to private life, a discredited and embittered man. The Optimates returned to power.

Slave Wars and Pirates

Meanwhile Roman misrule had been stirring up trouble. Near Capua a bankrupt Roman Knight organized 3500 slaves into a revolt which was soon crushed. But in Sicily a slave uprising under a man calling himself "King Tryphon" devastated the island (104–99 B.C.) and was only suppressed when a division of Marius' new army was sent against it. In the Near East the ravages of the pirates finally forced the Senate in 102 B.C. to commission Marcus Antonius (grandfather of the famous Mark Antony) to attack them. He captured their principal bases in Cilicia (southern bulge of Asia Minor) and formed a new Roman province there but did not eliminate the pirates.

Livius Drusus: 91 B.C.

In Italy the forces of reaction were in control. But in 93 B.C. the alliance between the Knights and the Senate was injured by the prosecution and condemnation by a jury of Knights of a thoroughly honest official who had protected the provincials of Asia against the extortions of the tax-farmers. In 91 B.C. this action led a noble, the tribune, Livius Drusus (son of the man who had outbid Gaius Gracchus), to put half Knights and half Senators on the juries but at the same time to double the number of the Senate by adding to it the wealthiest of the equestrian order. Consequently, he achieved the opposition to him of both orders. Turning, therefore, to the Populares he proposed new low prices for the grain dole and the founding of new colonies. Included in these bills was one to debase the coinage (inflation). The bills were passed but the Senate declared them null and void. Drusus then attempted to put through a law to give full citizenship to the Latin and Italian allies, but was assassinated. Abruptly, their last hope of citizenship gone, the allies revolted.

The Social* War: 90–88 B.C.

The allies were not content with mere revolt. With the Marsi and the Samnites as the focal points they set up a new confederacy which, with the exception of Umbria, Etruria, Campania, and the Greek cities, stretched from the Po to Messina. Corfinium in the central Apennines was chosen as the capital and renamed Italia. There was a Senate of 500, two consuls, and twelve praetors. A new coinage was issued with a female head, *Italia*, on one side and on the other an Italian bull goring a Roman wolf.

Never had Roman supremacy in Italy been in more danger. In the first year of the war the confederacy overran Campania and in the north, except for Marius who had been recalled to command, the Romans fared badly. When defeated, by three separate laws the Romans conferred on the Latins and Italians the citizenship they had so often refused. Many of the allies accepted the offers of citizenship and the confederacy began to collapse. In 89 B.C. Pompeius Strabo (father of Pompey the Great) won a signal victory at Asculum while in Campania Sulla, Marius' former lieutenant, achieved brilliant successes and advanced into Samnium. In 88 B.C. the death of the Samnite leader ended the war.

Aftermath of the War

Though brief the war had been bitter. There had been massacres and ravaging so that the losses in man-power and property were almost equal to the Hannibalic destruction. Food was scarce and prices high, and rich and poor were overwhelmed by debts, the only people profiting being the Roman bankers.

On the other hand, although the new citizens were restricted to 8 of the 31 rural tribes, all freemen south of the Po were now Roman citizens and local self-government was permitted in the communities and municipalities. North of the Po only Latin rights were granted. But, on the whole, the step to weld Italy into a unity had been taken, although nothing had been done to alleviate the vicious struggle between the haves and the have-nots. One reason for the granting of citizenship had been the danger in the East from Mithradates VI (the Great) of Pontus.

*"Social" from Socius-Ally.

Mithradates the Great

To the Romans, Mithradates was second only to Hannibal as their most dangerous opponent. His rise to power was the outgrowth of the Roman policy in Asia Minor of client kingdoms under her suzerainship. About 120 B.C., however, when Mithradates became king of Pontus, there were three states outside the control of Rome. These were Pontus, which had extended itself along the south shore of the Black Sea, Armenia in the highlands south and east of the Caucasian mountains, and the Parthians who around 140 B.C. had, as noted, overrun the eastern provinces of the former Seleucid empire, including Iran and Mesopotamia.

Legends accumulated around Mithradates. He was said to be a mighty athlete, hunter, soldier, and lover, and to have made himself immune to poisons by taking first small doses of each poison, then greater ones until no poison had any effect on him. As a ruler he was despotic and ambitious. By about 100 B.C., while Rome was thoroughly occupied with Jugurtha and the Cimbri and Teutones, he had managed to encircle the Black Sea as far as the mouth of the Danube and to have made that sea a Pontic lake. Hence came enormous armies and a fleet of 300 ships. He then turned his eyes upon the Roman client kingdoms of Cappodocia, Galatia, Paphlagonia, and Bithynia, all of which were resentful of Rome's domination. By varying intrigues he secured Galatia and Paphlagonia and finally in 90 B.C. seized Cappodocia and Bithynia. The Romans drove him out. But when the Social War erupted in Italy Mithradates seized opportunity by the throat. In the Roman province of Asia the provincials were looking for a deliverer from Roman rapacity. In 88 B.C. Mithradates swept across Bithynia and Cappodocia and into Roman Asia where at a given signal the provincials in a single day slaughtered 80,000 Italians, chiefly tax-gatherers, money-lenders, and merchants.

The massacre tells us how many Italians had flocked to the province and how bitterly Roman rule was hated. The rapacious Roman governor, Manius Aquilius, was captured, brought before Mithradates, and killed by pouring molten gold down his throat.

In one sweep Mithradates had conquered Asia Minor and his fleet now sailed into the Aegean. When Delos was captured, 20,000 more Italian merchants and slave-dealers were massacred. Next Mithradates' general, Archelaus, occupied the Piraeus, the port of Athens, and overran most of Greece. Suddenly, Rome's domination of the Hellenistic East had been overthrown. She prepared to send an army to reconquer her losses. But two generals wanted the command against Mithradates, Marius and Sulla, Marius' former lieutenant.

Marius versus Sulla: 88–87 B.C.

Sulla, an Optimate and the consul for 88 B.C., had been given the command by the Senate but with his army he was busy besieging Nola, south of Capua, which was a hold-out in the Social War. Meanwhile in Rome a combination of the Knights and Populares passed a law putting the aged Marius in charge of the war against Mithradates. Sulla's army was loyal to its commander. He led it to Rome and captured the city. For the first time in Roman history an army had followed its general against the state. Somewhat more ironically, the professional type of army which Marius had forged was used against him. From this time forward, it was clear that whoever controlled the legions ruled Rome.

Sulla, now in the driver's seat, killed the principal leader of the Marian party, a tribune, Sulpicius, outlawed Marius (who, however, escaped to Africa) and certain other Populares leaders, restored the Senate to power, and then, early in 87 B.C., set sail for Greece.

Scarcely were his ships out of sight of land, when the Marian party, led by the consul, Cinna, recalled Marius. While Cinna marched on Rome with an army raised in Campania, Marius, enlisting a force of slaves in Etruria, joined him. Rome was captured. For five days and nights the stones of the Forum and the streets of Rome were slippery with the blood spilled in the Marian massacres, and leading senators were killed and their heads exposed on the Rostra. Cinna finally ended the terror by having his troops put the Marian slaves to death. Rome had had a terrifying example of what happened when the army was called into politics. Marius himself entered on the seventh consulship which had once been prophesied for him on January 1st, 86 B.C. but died a few days later. But the Populares under the leadership of Cinna (whose daughter Julius Caesar married) and Carbo continued to control Italy. Significant of the economic chaos was a measure cancelling 75% of the principal of all debts. From 85 B.C. on the chief preoccupation of the Populares, however, was to prepare for Sulla's return. But in 84 B.C. Cinna, when preparing to lead an army overseas to meet Sulla in Macedonia, was killed by mutinous troops, and Carbo and the younger Marius were left to face the Sullan onslaught.

Sulla and Mithradates: 87–85 B.C.

In Greece Sulla captured Athens after a siege of several months, during which a mound thrown up outside the walls for his siege engines preserved for us of today part of the cemetery of the Outer Cerameicus. Then, after looting the shrines of Delphi, Epidaurus, and Olympia, he defeated Archelaus, Mithradates' general, at Chaeronea. At this point the Optimate

Sulla was faced by a Marian consul, Flaccus, sent to replace him, but Flaccus, avoiding a conflict, marched to Bithynia via Thrace. There he was killed by his soldiers, but his successor, Fimbria, recaptured the whole coast as far as Pergamum. Meanwhile Sulla won another victory over Mithradates' forces at Orchomenus but needed control of the Aegean to reach Asia. In the spring of 85 B.C. his lieutenant, Lucius Lucullus, a name we shall meet again, defeated Mithradates' navy.

Mithradates now sued for peace. Sulla, anxious to get back to Italy, gave him easy terms by which the King surrendered all his conquests in Asia Minor and eighty of his warships and paid a small indemnity of 3000 talents. The province of Asia was harder hit. Sulla imposed on it an indemnity of 20,000 talents ($25,000,000 but probably worth much more than that in terms of purchasing power as compared to that sum today) and five years' back taxes. During the winter, too, the provincials had to pay for the living costs of Sulla's soldiers. To raise the money, they had to borrow from the Roman bankers at 4% interest per month or over 48% per year. Roman bankers knew how to make profits.

Meanwhile Sulla took over the army of Fimbria who committed suicide and left it behind under the command of Licinius Murena (whom Cicero later defended in court) to garrison Asia, and made ready to sail for Italy. Shortly after he left, Murena provoked what is known as the Second Mithradatic War but on orders from Sulla made peace.

Civil War in Italy: 83–82 B.C.

In the spring of 83 B.C. Sulla, at the head of 40,000 veterans ready to follow him against the state, came ashore at Brundisium. The Optimates hastened to join him. Among these were Crassus (later to be the Roman billionaire), with a small army from Spain, and Pompey, a young man of 23, who had raised three legions. A bitter civil war followed, often with brother against brother and father against son. In 83 B.C. Sulla crushed one Popularis army and a second deserted to him. The next year he defeated Marius the Younger and shut him up in Praeneste. Marius promptly sent orders to Rome to massacre the chief Optimates there. Carbo was then beaten in battle in Etruria and fled to Africa. But the Samnites now made their last attempt against Rome. Failing to relieve Praeneste they marched straight to Rome itself. A battle outside the Colline Gate lasted far into the night. The Samnites broke Sulla's left wing but Crassus with the right wing saved the day. The victorious Sulla entered Rome and called the Senate together. As he spoke to them the Senators heard from outside the death-shrieks and groans of 6000 captured Samnites being butchered. Shortly afterward, Marius the Younger was killed at Praeneste and Samnium ravaged. Resistance in

Italy was ended, though Carbo still held out in Africa and Spain was in the hands of the Popularis leader, Sertorius.

Sulla's Dictatorship: 82–78 B.C.

Rome now lay at the feet of the conquering general. Even before he entered Rome, Sulla had had himself appointed dictator for an indefinite period at a meeting of the *Comitia Centuriata*. His first move was to slaughter his opponents. Hence came the "Sullan proscriptions." Each day a list of outlawed victims was posted. These men were to be killed on sight. Rewards were given to the murderers and the property of the proscribed was confiscated by the state and sold to the highest bidder. If the bidder were a favorite of Sulla, no one opposed him. One of Sulla's freedmen, for example, bought an estate worth $300,000 for $100. Furthermore, with a cynical disregard for any pretence of justice, Sulla put in his lists the names not only of his own enemies but also those of men suggested to him by gangsters and informers. In all 4700 were killed among whom were 90 senators and 2600 Knights. Meanwhile, Marius' ashes were disinterred, monuments to him overthrown, and his adopted nephew cut to pieces. The Social War, the Marian massacres, and the Sullan proscriptions—between them these events showed to what depths of disorganization and anarchy the Roman Republic had now descended. The wounds left in Rome and Italy were not to be healed until the fall of the Republic and the rule of Augustus Caesar. Moreover, it had become even more abundantly evident that he who led an army could rule Rome and the empire.

Sulla's second task was to take care of his veterans whom he settled on lands expropriated throughout Italy, particularly in Etruria and Samnium. Next he sent Pompey, in spite of his youth, as propraetor to Sicily and Africa. It took Pompey three years to oust the Populares from these provinces. When he returned, he was granted a triumph, illegally, and hailed as the "Great" (Pompeius Magnus). Spain, however, still held out under Sertorius.

Although one of the most cynical and brutal dictators the world has seen, except perhaps for those of Renaissance Italy and modern days, Sulla was a builder as well as a destroyer. His aim was to make the Senate, which he increased to 500, supreme, while the number of quaestors was raised from twelve to twenty and the praetors from six to eight. The minimum age for the quaestorship was set at 30, for the praetorship at 39, and for the consulship at 42. To cripple the tribunate, a tribune was disqualified from holding any higher office, his veto was limited to its old function of preventing physical violence, and his right to propose laws to the Tribal Assembly was abolished. Moreover no bill could now be brought before the Assembly without the previous approval of the senate. The control of the jury-courts was also returned to the senators.

In most of this legislation Sulla was simply turning back the clock, as many reactionaries would like to do. But his reform of the courts was lasting. He established seven permanent courts, each presided over by a praetor, to try cases of extortion, treason, bribery in elections, forgery, murder, assault, and embezzlement of public property. In this way he laid the true foundations of Roman criminal law. It was he, too, who made Cisalpine Gaul into a province.

In 79 B.C. when he was satisfied that the Senate was in control, Sulla abdicated his dictatorship to enjoy life in his villa in Campania. The next year "mulberry-faced" (he had reddish blotches on his skin) Sulla died. On his tomb was an epitaph composed by himself: "Here lies Sulla the Fortunate. He never forgave an enemy or forgot a friend."

Summary

In these years from 133 to 78 B.C. the Republic stumbled along the road leading to disaster like a blind man travelling at night along a path he doesn't know. The Gracchan reforms, well-intentioned, might have saved the state if the senatorial clique had not been jealous of its powers and possessions. Henceforth, instead of unity there was class-struggle; on the one side a comparatively small group who had amassed the loot of the Mediterranean and looked upon the empire as an oyster grown for their special benefit, on the other a mob of unemployed and a mass of poverty-stricken peasants. The Optimates were the first to use the sword in this struggle. The Populares were quick to learn the lesson. The denial of citizenship to the Italians added fuel to the conflict. When civil war blazed it was the inevitable outcome.

Meanwhile, the successive consulships of Marius, like the extraordinary appointments of the Scipios in previous times, were an indication that the ordinary machinery of a system designed to govern a small state could not manage the problems of a far-flung empire; and Marius unwittingly welded the professional army which could be led against the state. The dictatorship of Sulla was the culmination in this period of both the class-struggle and the break-down of government, but also proved that he who could command an army could dominate Rome.

More ominous for the future of the Republic was the collapse of morals and economics. Italy had been devastated again and again. A burden of debt and interest lay heavy on the land. The bankers prospered. Feuds and hatreds from the civil wars festered. The contrast between the few in their palaces and villas, attended by hordes of slaves who of necessity pandered to every vice or luxurious whim of their masters, and the hovels

of the peasants and the tenement-blocks of the unemployed was sharp-
ened. In such an atmosphere to get money by any and every means became
one of the paramount goals. But, except for the bankers and business-men,
the only way to gain money was to secure political office in the hope of
eventually being given a rich province to plunder. Partly for this purpose
and partly to maintain their social position, young nobles borrowed their
way into debt.

All these factors—the class-struggle, the feuds, the debt-situation, the
example of Sulla, the pervasive materialism—added up to an opportunity
for greedy and ambitious men to seize power. The only question was who
would win the prize—and the prize was Rome and the empire.

Readings from Sources of the Period

(a) The war against Jugurtha of Numidia (111–106 B.C.) was so badly mismanaged
by the Optimates that it brought about the election to the consulship of Marius.
The war was described by Sallust (86–34 B.C.) who was a friend of Julius Caesar.
In the extract given below, Jugurtha, after murdering one adoptive brother,
Hiempsal, and driving the other into exile, began to worry about possible reprisals
by Rome.

A few days afterwards, therefore, he despatched ambassadors to Rome, with a
profusion of gold and silver, whom he directed, in the first place, to make
abundance of presents to his old friends, and then to procure him new ones; and
not to hesitate, in short, to effect whatever could be done by bribery.

When these deputies had arrived at Rome, and had sent large presents, according to the prince's direction, to his intimate friends, and to others whose
influence was at that time powerful, so remarkable a change ensued, that Jugurtha,
from being an object of the greatest odium, grew into great regard and favour with
the nobility; who, partly allured with hope, and partly with actual largesses,
endeavoured, by soliciting the members of the senate individually, to prevent any
severe measures from being adopted against him. When the ambassadors, accordingly, felt sure of success, the senate, on a fixed day, gave audience to both parties.

(Howe and Harrer, *op. cit.*, translated by J. S. Watson.)

(b) Plutarch tells how Marius, fleeing after Sulla's first march on Rome, deserted
by everyone, was put under arrest in a house at Minturnae on the west coast of
Italy, and it was decided to put him to death. The extract tells how Marius
escaped death. He finally found refuge in Africa.

Meanwhile the magistrates and town council of Minturnae had been discussing
the situation and had decided to put Marius to death without any further delay.
No citizen of the town would take on the job of executioner, so a cavalryman,
either a Gaul or a Cimbrian (both versions of the story are current) took a sword
and went to Marius's room. There was not much light in the part of the room
where Marius happened to be lying; in fact it was almost dark and we are told that

it seemed to the soldier that the eyes of Marius were darting flames at him and out of the darkness came a great voice: "My man, do you dare to make an end of Caius Marius?"

At this the foreigner threw down his sword and rushed straight out of the room. He ran out of doors crying out simply: "I cannot kill Caius Marius."

(Plutarch, *Fall of the Roman Republic, Six Lives*, p. 47, translated by Rex Warner, Harmondsworth. Penguin Books, published 1958, reprinted, 1962.)

(c) In his life of Crassus, Plutarch describes how Spartacus, escaping from Capua, led a revolt of the slaves of Italy and became formidable. The extract below tells of his success before he was finally defeated.

Next Spartacus defeated the praetor himself in a number of engagements and finally captured his lictors and the very horse that he rode. By this time Spartacus had grown to be a great and formidable power, but he showed no signs of losing his head. He could not expect to prove superior to the whole power of Rome, and so he began to lead his army towards the Alps. His view was that they should cross the mountains and then disperse to their own homes, some to Thrace and some to Gaul. His men, however, would not listen to him. They were strong in numbers and full of confidence, and they went about Italy ravaging everything in their way.

There was now more to disturb the senate than just the shame and the disgrace of the revolt. The situation had become dangerous enough to inspire real fear, and as a result both consuls were sent out to deal with what was considered a major war and a most difficult one to fight. One of the consuls, Gellius, fell suddenly upon and entirely destroyed the German contingent of Spartacus's troops, who in their insolent self-confidence had marched off on their own and lost contact with the rest; but when Lentulus, the other consul, had surrounded the enemy with large forces, Spartacus turned to the attack, joined battle, defeated the generals of Lentulus and captured all their equipment. He then pushed on towards the Alps and was confronted by Cassius, the governor of Cisalpine Gaul, with an army of 10,000 men. In the battle that followed Cassius was defeated and, after losing many of his men, only just managed to escape with his own life.

This news roused the senate to anger. The consuls were told to return to civilian life, and Crassus was appointed to the supreme command of the war.
(*Ibid.*, p. 108.)

CHAPTER 7

The Collapse of the Roman Republic

In the three decades after the death of Sulla three men strove for the control of the Roman Empire. These three were Pompey, Crassus, and Caesar. Two others tried to keep the creaking machinery of the Republic working, Cicero, the great Roman orator, and Cato the Younger, who modelled himself on his great-grandfather, Cato the Elder, and fulminated against the decay of Roman morals. Although there were many other actors on stage, the actions and inter-relationships of these five men determined the fate of the Republic.

The Men

In 78 B.C. Cicero was twenty-eight years old. He did not belong to the nobles. His family was a middle-class one in Arpinum, the town near Rome from which Marius had come. Cicero himself, after a "university" education in Athens and Rhodes, had returned to Rome to become a lawyer. By this time he already had a reputation as an orator, and had shown courage in defending the son of one of the victims of the Sullan proscriptions.

When Sulla died, Cato was a precocious seventeen. A young man of unyielding temperament with grey-green eyes, he had as yet no weight in politics but he was already commented upon as the great-grandson of Cato the Elder.

The third of the five, Julius Caesar, was either twenty-four or twenty-two in 78 B.C., since his birthdate is either 102 or 100 B.C., although the former seems the more likely. He, too, was precocious. At fifteen, he had been made the priest of Jupiter, and at nineteen he had married Cornelia, the daughter of Cinna, the Popularis leader. This marriage linked him with the Popularis party, especially since his Aunt Julia was the widow of Marius. Yet he belonged to one of the oldest patrician families of Rome, and he claimed that through the Trojan Aeneas he was descended from the goddess Venus.

When Sulla triumphed, he ordered Caesar, at that time twenty years of age, to divorce Cornelia. Caesar refused and tried to escape from Italy, but was captured. The intercession of Caesar's uncle, Aurelius Cotta, induced Sulla to spare the young man's life, although he lost his wife's dowry and the priesthood of Jupiter. Caesar then went into voluntary exile and served at the siege of Mitylene, a rebel city which had joined Mithradates. Here, he won the civic crown for saving the life of a fellow-soldier and was sent to get ships from the king of Bithynia. His visits to the king's court gave rise to sniggering stories, according to which Caesar had plunged into all the vices. Later, Caesar joined in a campaign against the pirates.

On Sulla's death, the young man returned to Rome where he gave lavish entertainments to the mob, evidently in an attempt to become a Popularis leader, but did not join in the revolt of Lepidus. However, he did prosecute two members of the Sulla clique. When the prosecutions failed, Caesar set out for Rhodes to study under Molo, who had been one of Cicero's teachers. It was during this journey that, according to the story, he was captured by pirates and was ransomed but then collected a fleet, took the pirates prisoner, and had them crucified as he had promised during his confinement. When once more, he returned to Rome, it was to re-commence his attempts to woo the Roman mob. No one, except, perhaps, his strong-minded mother, Aurelia, took him seriously. Instead he was regarded as a gilded adulterer who was spending himself into debt. In spite of his precocity, Caesar was a slow starter in the field of Roman politics.

Of the other two men, Crassus was eight years older than Cicero. He had fought for Sulla. But he had a nose for money. He began by buying at bargain rates the property of some of the men proscribed by Sulla. Later, he went into a number of ventures. One of his successful projects is said to have been the organization of a fire-fighting squad. Rome had no fire-fighting system, but fires were always breaking out among the jerry-built tenements of the city and, once started, it was almost impossible to stop them until they had burnt a whole section. Now, however, when a fire erupted, Crassus first bought the burning buildings and those around them for practically nothing. Then he put in his fire-fighting squad and stopped the blaze. In this way, he came to own a good deal of Rome. As a result of such ventures and by making loans at a high rate of interest, before long Crassus was the richest of the Roman millionaires. This money gave him a good deal of power. He had political and military aspirations and disliked and was jealous of Pompey.

In 78 B.C. Pompey was Fortune's favorite. He had been only twenty-three when he had raised three legions to aid Sulla, and twenty-seven when, contrary to the constitution, he was granted a triumph for wresting Sicily and Africa from the Populares. Incidentally, unlike Caesar, Pompey at Sulla's command had divorced his wife and married a new one, selected by Sulla. At twenty-eight, the same age as Cicero, Pompey, handsome and successful, was already a power in Rome, although he was not popular with the Optimates. His weakness in politics was that he expected whatever he wanted to be offered without any exertion by himself.

These were the men who were to decide the future of Rome. Pompey at first overshadowed the others.

Pompey and the Revolt of Lepidus: 78 B.C.

The ashes of Sulla's funeral pyre were scarcely cold when Lepidus, one of the consuls for 78 B.C., began a revolt in Etruria and marched on Rome. The Senate put Pompey in command, although he was not a magistrate, along with the other consul. Pompey first defeated Marcus Junius Brutus (the father of the Brutus who was later one of the assassins of Caesar) in North Italy and, breaking a promise of safe conduct, put him to death. Then he crushed Lepidus who fled to Sardinia where he died. The remnants of his army were taken by his lieutenant, Perpena, to Spain to join Sertorius. The significance of the revolt was that already an attempt was being made to overthrow the Sullan constitution.

Pompey in Spain: 76–71 B.C.

It will be recalled that after Sulla's victory in Italy, the Popularis leader, Sertorius, still held out in Spain. Here he had won the devotion of the Spaniards, had organized a separate government with a Senate, and had defeated Sulla's general, Metellus Pius, time after time. By the close of 77 B.C. he controlled most of the peninsula.

Pompey, who had refused to disband the army used against Lepidus, demanded the command of the war in Spain, and the Senate, reluctantly, gave it to him, along with proconsular power. When he reached Spain it took five years, reinforcements, and the assassination of Sertorius by Perpena before Pompey won the war. However, in victory, he dealt justly with the Spanish people and was remembered gratefully by them.

Spartacus and the Slave-War: 73–71 B.C.

While Pompey was in Spain two wars flared. One, which will be described later, broke out in the East against Rome's inveterate antagonist, Mithradates. The other was in Italy itself. Here a Thracian gladiator, Spartacus, led a band of his fellows out of a training-school at

Capua, occupied the then quiescent crater of Vesuvius (it had never erupted within human memory and the crater was a grassy plain), defeated a Roman force, and called all slaves to the banner of freedom. Soon, with a following of 70,000 men, Spartacus vanquished the armies of four praetors and two consuls in battle after battle and overran Campania and the whole of South Italy. Most of his soldiers came from the brutal plantation-farms where floggings, torture, and starvation had been their lot. In victory, they inflicted what they had suffered on their former owners.

The Romans were desperate. They were fighting one war in Spain and another in the East, and Mithradates had established communications with both Sertorius and Spartacus. At this point Crassus, who was jealous of Pompey and eager for military glory to offset the reputation of a man whom he regarded as his rival, let it be known that he was available. The Senate gave him, like Pompey, an extraordinary command with the authority to raise six legions to add to the remnants of the defeated armies. Crassus took time to train his troops and then, aided by a division in the slave-army, defeated both sections of it. Spartacus was killed.

This victory ended the slave-war but Pompey on his return march from Spain met some 5000 of the slaves in Etruria as they were fleeing northward, annihilated them and promptly advertised that he had finished both the Spanish war and the slave-war. Then Pompey and Crassus went on a slave-hunt. By the time it was over, 6000 slaves hung on crosses along the Appian Way, a stench to prove the greatness of Rome.

Overthrow of the Sullan Constitution: 70 B.C.

Pompey and Crassus now demanded the consulship, unconstitutionally. The Senate refused but the two men made an alliance with the Populares and encamped their armies near Rome. The Senate was forced to yield. As consuls for 70 B.C., Pompey and Crassus overturned the Sullan constitution. For example, the juries, instead of being made up of Senators, now consisted one-third of Senators, one-third Knights, and one-third *tribuni aerarii* (probably from the lower middle-class). The functions of the censors, which Sulla had limited, were restored, and the powers of the tribunes were returned to them. From this time forward, however, the tribunes tended to become henchmen of people like Pompey, Crassus, and Caesar, since on the one hand the tribunes had the power of veto and on the other could propose laws to the *Comitia Tributa*.

Meanwhile Cicero, who by this time was a devoted admirer of Pompey, had undertaken the prosecution of a prominent Optimate, Verres. Verres had been for three years the rapacious propraetor of Sicily. He sold justice, priesthoods, and municipal offices to the highest bidder. He brought in false accusations against wealthy people, had them found guilty, and then confiscated their property for himself. He formed partnerships with the tax collectors to squeeze the last possible copper from the tax-payers. He stripped temples and homes of priceless statues and paintings. By these and similar measures he brought back to Rome 40,000,000 sesterces, but Verres was a noble, and the Optimates closed ranks behind him. Hortensius, the foremost orator of the moment and consul-elect for 69 B.C., defended him against the accusation of maladministration. Cicero, however, had been in Sicily (where he had been quaestor in 75 B.C.) to collect evidence. So scathing was his indictment (which we can still read for a picture of what it was like to be a provincial under the rule of the Roman Republic) that Verres did not wait for the end of the trial. Instead he went into exile to Massilia (Marseilles) where, as he wrote to his friends, the climate was lovely and the mullets delicious. Cicero's exposé (he had his speeches against Verres published) made the middle-class man from Arpinum the leader of the Roman bar and a political force.

At the close of 70 B.C. the Sullan constitution was dead, although the Optimates through the Senate still tried to rule Rome and the empire. Crassus retired from politics into making money. Pompey looked around restlessly for another extraordinary command. His first opportunity came through the pirates.

Pompey Against the Pirates: 67 B.C.

The rise of the pirates, like the slave-war, proved the incapacity of the Optimates. Although in 102 B.C., as we have seen, Mark Antony's grand-father had destroyed pirate bases in Cilicia and had made it into a province, the Romans had done nothing or little since that date to prevent the founding of a pirate empire in the eastern Mediterranean with a major base in Crete and bastions in Cilicia. Then, in 74 B.C., as part of the war against Mithradates, the father of Mark Antony was given an ex-traordinary command against them, as if wars against pirates were a prerogative of the Antonius family, and sailed away boastfully, carrying chains to bind captured pirates. He was defeated, however, and forced to sign a disgraceful peace. Next, in 68 B.C., when a Metellus (later surnamed Creticus) conquered Crete and made it into a province, he in turn failed to crush the pirates. Organized like the British pirates of the Caribbean in a later day into a sort of a confederacy, and with a thousand or more swift ships, they terrorized the Mediterranean, captured more than 400 towns and cities, carrying off plunder and selling the inhabitants as slaves, made attacks on cities in Italy including Ostia, the port of Rome, seized merchant-ships so that overseas trade was seriously damaged, and even snatched a Roman praetor from Italy. The pirates, not Rome, controlled the Mediterranean.

This chaos had arisen from the failure of the Roman government to police the sea. But when the pirates cut off the fleets bringing wheat to Rome, thus interfering with the grain dole, and bread rose to starvation prices, the city mob screamed for action. Pompey saw the opportunity. A henchman tribune, Gabinius, proposed a law to appoint a supreme commander of consular rank against the pirates with extraordinary power for three years over the Mediterranean and all its coasts for 50 miles inland and with superior authority in that whole area over all provincial governors. This man (not named, but everyone knew it was to be Pompey) was to be empowered to draw 6000 talents from the public treasury, to raise a fleet of 500 ships, an army of 120,000 infantry and 5000 cavalry, and to appoint 24 lieutenants with praetorian rank and two quaestors. In other words the unnamed man was to be king of the Mediterranean for three years.

The Senate, recognizing both the abdication of ordinary government and the tremendous power to be given one man, opposed the bill strenuously. The Populares and the Knights supported it, and Cicero, as a representative of the middle-class Knights and an admirer of Pompey, spoke strongly in its favor. The bill was passed. Pompey was appointed. His ability to organize was superb, and within forty days he swept the pirates from the seas and became the most popular and powerful man in Rome.

The Third Mithradatic War—First Phase: 75–66 B.C.

The Third Mithradatic War, which was being waged while Rome was fighting Sertorius, the slaves, and the pirates, had been in preparation since the end of the first one. Mithradates was allied with Tigranes, king of Armenia, who was his son-in-law and who in a few years had become a mighty monarch. Taking advantage of Rome's civil war and other preoccupations, he had occupied several provinces of Parthia and Mesopotamia and had attacked the remains of the Seleucid kingdom. He had also built a new capital at Tigranocerta, in the uplands near the sources of the Tigris river (the former capital was further back in the hills at Artaxtata), and had transferred some 300,000 people there. Finally, he had overrun Cappadocia.

Mithradates, meanwhile, had strengthened his control over the coasts of the Black Sea and had organized a powerful army and navy. When in 75 B.C. the king of Bithynia willed his kingdom to Rome, Mithradates occupied the country.

It took the Romans a year to move, and there is a suspicion that a

Roman woman, Praecia, the mistress of the then leader of the Optimates, Cethegus, was responsible, since we are told that three men were suing her for the command, Marcus Antonius (already mentioned), Cotta, and Lucius Lucullus, the lieutenant of Sulla in the First Mithradatic War. According to the historian, Ferrero, the result was a "triumph of salon diplomacy". Marcus Antonius, as we have seen, was given the command against the pirates, Cotta, one of the two consuls of 74 B.C. was appointed to Bithynia and the command of the Roman fleet, while Lucullus, the other consul, received a Roman army and the provinces of Asia and Cilicia.

The results of the division of authority were not so happy. While Antonius was getting himself mauled by the pirates, who had an understanding with Mithradates, Cotta lost almost seventy ships and 3000 of his army to Mithradates and was shut up in Chalcedon on the Hellespont, on the shore opposite to Byzantium. Lucullus, however, was a military genius. With a small force he raised the siege of Chalcedon, thus saving Cotta, and then managed to trap Mithradates and to destroy most of his army. During the same year he destroyed a Pontic fleet in the Aegean. In the next two years Lucullus, now in sole command, drove Mithradates from Pontus, reconquered Asia Minor, and forced Mithradates to take refuge with his son-in-law, the king of Armenia.

Lucullus spent the winter of 71–70 B.C. in regulating the finances of the Roman province of Asia. It will be recalled that in 84 B.C. Sulla had collected an indemnity of 20,000 talents from the people of this province, an indemnity which they had had to borrow from the Roman capitalists at 4% per month interest. By this time the debt, with interest, amounted to 120,000 talents, a good example of the workings of Roman capitalism. Lucullus cancelled two-thirds of this debt and set the future interest rate at 12% per annum. By these and other measures he saved the provincials but brought upon himself the bitter hatred of the Roman capitalists. Then, in 69 B.C., in pursuit of Mithradates he invaded Armenia, making for its capital, Tigranocerta.

His campaign was an amazing achievement. He had only about 18,000 battle-scarred veterans. When he reached Tigranocerta, Tigranes, who faced him with some 200,000 men, is said to have remarked that the Roman force was "too small for an army, too big for an embassy." In the ensuing battle, Lucullus won a tremendous victory. His report to the Senate read: "Five Romans, a hundred thousand Orientals slain". Then he captured Tigranocerta. The loot from this one city paid all the expenses of the war and gave the equivalent of $165 to each Roman soldier.

Lucullus now drove forward toward Tigranes' second capital city, which was high in the mountains. At this point his luck failed. His soldiers mutinied and Lucullus was compelled to withdraw to Mesopotamia where he captured Nisibis and spent the winter.

But there was another mutiny—and here we may suspect the machinations of the capitalists and, perhaps, too, agents of Pompey, who was slavering for the command of this war. In the spring of 67 B.C. Mithradates invaded his old kingdom of Pontus, and defeated Lucullus' commander there; while Tigranes, after recovering Armenia, moved into Cappadocia. Meanwhile, the Senate had appointed new governors in Asia, Bithynia and Cilicia. When Lucullus tried to march against Mithradates, his troops once again mutinied. Lucullus had to retreat to the coast, having lost in a short space of time all that had been gained in years of campaigning.

This was a situation made to order for Pompey. In 66 B.C. another henchman tribune, Manilius, proposed an extraordinary command for Pompey in the East. Once again the Senate was in opposition but the proletariat and the knights were in favor, and Cicero, as praetor, supported the appointment in a highly rhetorical oration which we still have. The law was passed. Shortly afterward Lucullus returned to Rome to find consolation in his gardens, the cherry trees which he had brought back from Asia, and in his famous "Lucullan" banquets.

Third Mithradatic War, Second Phase, and Pompey in the East: 66–62 B.C.

Pompey was still Fortune's favorite. Lucullus' campaigns had smashed the core of any resistance in Asia Minor, and Mithradates was easily defeated. He fled to the Crimea where he ultimately took his own life. Tigranes was forced to surrender and to become an ally of Rome. Then Pompey subdued the whole of the Near East except Egypt. His conquests included Judea.

It will be remembered that as a result of the struggles of the heroic Maccabees, Judea had been independent for a century under the rule of hereditary high priests of Yahweh. At this time there was a dynastic dispute between two brothers. Pompey espoused the cause of one of them and forced his way into Jerusalem. There was a three month's siege of the temple. When it was captured and its defendants massacred, Pompey entered the Holy of Holies to find nothing there except the Ark of the Covenant.

Pompey now reorganized the Near East. Bithynia with part of Pontus, and Syria with Judea annexed to it, were added as Roman provinces to Asia and Cilicia. The rest of Asia Minor, including Armenia, consisted of client kingdoms whose rulers had to be satisfactory to Rome and could do nothing important without Rome's consent. Even Egypt had to accept Roman supervision.

For five years Pompey ruled as a king in the Near East and was worshipped with divine honors by the provincials. By accepting bribes for favors and arranging for payments from kings and cities to himself, he became enormously wealthy. His soldiers were kept loyal by the loot they won. Meanwhile, in Rome, Crassus strove for power and there was the famous Conspiracy of Catiline.

Politics in Rome: 66–63 B.C.

When Pompey left for the East, Crassus saw an opportunity to dominate Rome. Because of his wealth he led Rome's capitalists. A number of senators who were in debt to him also had to vote for him. In addition to these supporters he wanted control of the Populares. Consequently, he formed an alliance with Julius Caesar.

Caesar had been quaestor in Spain in 68 B.C. On his return, at the age of thirty-five, he needed money to strengthen his position among the Populares. Crassus provided the money. As a result, in 65 B.C. Caesar was aedile while Crassus was one of the two censors.

Crassus' first objective was Egypt. It was said that in 81 B.C. the last legitimate ruler of Egypt had left it and Cyprus to the Romans in his will. Meanwhile Egypt was being ruled by Ptolemy Auletes (the Flute Player), the father of Cleopatra, and Cyprus was held by his brother. An extraordinary command to take over Egypt appealed to Crassus. The country was wealthy, a prospect which made his mouth water. Furthermore, such a command would give him an army with which to face Pompey; and Crassus was still jealous and fearful of Pompey. In the spring of 65 B.C. therefore, Caesar as aedile put on magnificent games with Crassus' money. The statues and trophies of his uncle Marius, the revolutionary, which had been torn down by Sulla, were re-erected. The temples and the Forum were decorated and hung with pictures. As a climax Caesar put silver armor on the criminals who fought the lions in the arena, and also exhibited three hundred pairs of gladiators. All this splendor won the support of the city mob. But when a law was proposed that Crassus as censor, or Caesar as his agent, raise an army to take over Egypt the Optimates blocked the law.

The next move of Crassus and Caesar was to back Catiline and a colleague of his, Antonius Hybrida, for the consulship of 63 B.C., for which the elections were held in midsummer, 64 B.C. Catiline was an extraordinary man. Like Caesar he was a patrician. He was said to have been one of Sulla's butchers during the Sullan proscriptions. Later in 68 B.C., he was praetor and the next year propraetor of Africa. On his return he stood for the consulship, but was made ineligible to run by being prosecuted for maladministration by Publius Clodius, although the case was settled out of court, probably through bribery. There followed a mysterious occurrence (the so-called First Catilinarian Conspiracy), of which differing accounts are given, in which Catiline, along with others, is said to have plotted to assassinate the incoming consuls on January 1st 65 B.C., and to establish Crassus as dictator with Caesar as his Master-of-Horse. Whatever the truth, no action was taken, but Catiline was known to be heavily in debt. Being cold-shouldered by the Optimates he turned to those young nobles who, like himself, were debt-ridden, to the out-of-works in Rome, to the veterans of Marius and Sulla, who, placed on farms they did not know how to work, were also in debt, to the sons of those proscribed by Sulla whose ancestral property had been confiscated, and to the peasants of Etruria.

By the accounts given of him by his enemy, Cicero, and by the Roman historian, Sallust, Catiline was a man of remarkable charm and tremendous physical endurance. Soon he was the leader of what we would call today the "Left Wing" or "radicals" of the Populares.

Cicero, too, was a candidate for the consulship of 63 B.C. He had the support of the middle-class, but, because he was a "new man", his chances were doubtful. The Optimates, however, were afraid that Catiline would win, and they flung their influence behind Cicero. In midsummer he was elected consul for 63 B.C., the first "new man" to gain that post since Marius. The other consul-elect was Catiline's colleague, Antonius Hybrida. But Cicero, by promising Antonius the proconsulship of Macedonia when his term as consul was over, detached him from Catiline.

All these manoeuvres, if we look at them closely, prove the modernity of Roman politics. They likewise set the stage for the conspiracy of Catiline.

The Conspiracy of Catiline, 63 B.C.

63 B.C. was the high point of Cicero's political career. On the first day of his consulship he faced a second attempt by Crassus and Caesar to get hold of Egypt, this time through a land bill to put veterans and unemployed citizens on farms by repossessing all the remaining public lands in Italy and by purchasing private estates. The "jokers" in the bill were that the scheme was to be financed by the sale of the Roman domains outside Italy acquired since Sulla's first consulship, a phrasing vague enough to include Egypt, and that the ten land commissioners to be appointed, in addition to other extensive powers, were to have the right to raise and maintain an army. Cicero spoke so strongly against the measure in both the Senate and the Assembly that it was defeated.

Caesar's next attempt to embarrass Cicero was to have a henchman tribune, Labienus (later one of Caesar's principal generals), carry a bill to prosecute an old man, Rabirius, for the murder of one of Marius' associates (the tribune Saturninus) in 100 B.C., thirty-seven years before. One objective of the trial was to prove the invalidity of the Ultimate Decree under the aegis of which Rabirius had killed Saturninus. When convicted in a court trial, Rabirius appealed to the *Comitia Centuriata* where the Optimates had power. Just before the voting was to begin, Caesar, using a political trick, had a red flag raised on the Janiculum Hill. Originally, this red flag was hoisted to warn of the approach of armed enemies and by law the Assembly had to be dissolved.

These rather circuitous political manoeuvres were followed by a victory for Caesar. In March, the election of priests having been restored to a special Tribal Assembly of 17 tribes selected by lot, proposed by the same Labienus, Caesar was chosen *Pontifex Maximus*, which made his person sacrosanct, although the rival candidate was Lutatius Catulus, leader of the Optimates. From this time forward, however, all attention was fixed on the elections for the consulship for 62 B.C. because Catiline was again a candidate, along with Murena, the man who had provoked the Second Mithradatic War, and Silanus, the husband of Servilia, Caesar's long-term mistress. Servilia, who was a half-sister to Cato and who had been married to the Brutus whom Pompey had killed during the revolt of Lepidus, was both the mother of Marcus Brutus and the center of a brilliant salon in Rome.

Catiline's election program this time was simple. It was "New Accounts" (*Novae Tabulae*) which meant "Cancel or scale down all debts." This sort of slogan did not suit Crassus. He and Caesar withdrew their support. It still looked as if Catiline might win. In the hot days of July, just before the election, Rome saw Marian and Sullan veterans and peasants from Etruria tramping into the city, ready to cast their votes for their champion. Cicero, using a technicality, had the elections postponed for a month. Many of Catiline's supporters had to trudge home again, and most did not return. In the delayed elections in August, at which Cicero appeared in armor, Catiline was once again defeated, although we might note that Caesar was elected as one of the praetors for 62 B.C.

Catiline still had another spear to throw. Shortly before the elections he had begun to prepare for an armed revolt of the poor against the rich. Rumors of this plan had reached Cicero so that he had surrounded himself with a bodyguard of Knights and had organized a network of spies. One of these, Fulvia, was the mistress of Curio, a supporter of Catiline. The whole city was on edge. And then on October 21st Cicero reported to a skeptical Senate that on October 27th a veteran, Manlius, would raise the silver eagle of the dead Marius at Faesulae, (modern Fiesole) just north of Florence, and that on the 28th senators and Knights were to be massacred in Rome.

As it turned out, Manlius did lift up the eagle of revolt at Faesulae on the 27th of October. Meanwhile, on the 22nd the Senate had passed the Ultimate Decree which instructed Cicero to take all necessary measures to prevent harm to the Republic. Two armies were set in motion against the rebels.

Catiline was still in Rome. We may well ask why Cicero did not have him arrested. For one thing Catiline was a noble and so were the Senators. They could not really believe the word of a "new man", Cicero, that one of their own ranks would plan a revolt and massacre—and besides the reported massacre had not been attempted. The second reason was that Cicero had as yet no firm evidence against the conspirators. But in the darkness of the early morning of November 7th the spy, Fulvia, came to Cicero to tell him that during the night just past, at a meeting held at the house of Laeca in "The Street of the Scythe-Makers", Catiline had approved a plan to massacre and loot in Rome, including the use of slaves, but first of all, to assassinate Cicero when he held his reception that same morning.

We can easily visualize the confusion and the hurried planning. Cicero got witnesses ready. When the assassins, who were two Knights, arrived, they were arrested and were found to have daggers concealed in their togas. Cicero now had his evidence. On November 8th he called the Senate together, not in the Senate-House but in the temple of Jupiter Stator (the Establisher) beside the ramp which led up from the Forum to the center of the Palatine Hill. The doors of the temple were guarded by armed men. Even at this distance in time we can almost feel the tension as the senators filed in, on edge with the rumors they had heard but not knowing what was to happen. It added to the confusion that Catiline (as a propraetor he was a senator) was in his place, darkly handsome and sneeringly confident. Cicero may not have expected him to put in an appearance. At any rate when, as consul, he rose to speak, he burst out with: "How long, Catiline will you abuse our patience!" Then in telling phrases, which we can still read in Latin, he disclosed Catiline's attempt at assassination and his plans for fire and massacre throughout Rome. Those nearest Catiline shrank away from him. Then, in words which seem an anti-climax, Cicero invited Catiline to leave Rome and join the rebels in the field. To us it seems as if Cicero still did not dare to arrest and execute a noble. He preferred him out in the open. That night Catiline rode north toward Faesulae, leaving behind him a note to the principal leader of the Optimates, asking him to look after his wife. The nobles of Rome, like the British aristocracy, stuck together.

Catiline was gone. But he left conspirators behind him in Rome. Among the leaders were Lentulus, a praetor and the step-father of Mark Antony (at this time a young man deeply in debt), and Sempronia of the family of the Gracchi, who, according to Sallust, "could dance better than any honest woman should."

The conspirators, however, had a juvenile idea of how to conduct a plot. They planned to strike in Rome during the *Saturnalia* (commencing on December 17th) when slaves and everyone had a period of license. In the meantime, it was hoped that Catiline's army would appear before the walls of the city. But they made the error of proffering overtures to envoys of the Gallic tribe of the Allobroges (north of the eastern part of Gallia Narbonensis), who had come to Rome to protest to the Senate about debts owed in their country to Roman money-lenders, and had been rebuffed. The plan of the conspirators was to stir up the Allobroges to support Catiline.

The envoys listened and reported to their patron (a Roman, Fabius Sanga) who in turn took them to Cicero. The consul instructed them to get written and sealed agreements. The conspirators stupidly gave letters in their own handwriting to the Allobroges, making large promises to that tribe, and instructed the envoys to visit Catiline en route home and to present him with a sealed letter from one of the conspirators.

On the night of December 2nd the Gallic envoys, accompanied by one of the conspirators, started home. In the best cloak and dagger tradition, Cicero by prearrangement had an ambush waiting at the Mulvian bridge about two miles from Rome. The ambush waited until the envoys were crossing the bridge, then occupied both ends of it, captured the envoys and the letters, and brought them to Cicero at about daybreak of December 3rd. Cicero promptly arrested the five principal conspirators, convoked the Senate, and had the conspirators acknowledge their handwriting and their seals.

There followed a tense three day's trial before the Senate in the Temple of Concord below the Capitoline Hill, while all Rome waited. Crassus, in fear, since he had once supported Catiline, stayed home. But Caesar came, although he was almost killed by the armed men at the door of the temple. The first motion was for the "extreme penalty", interpreted as death. Caesar then proposed that the five conspirators be imprisoned for the rest of their lives and their property confiscated. Everyone swung to this proposal until Cato, who was a tribune, rose to his feet. He glanced around, his high-bridged nose sneering. Then in acid words, as reported by the Roman historian, Sallust (86–34 B.C. and therefore twenty-three years old at the time), he reminded the Senators that, with Catiline still in arms, they were now fighting not for their fishponds or villas but for their lives. His motion was for death.

Cato's motion carried. Cicero, as consul, hurried immediately to the prison nearby (we can still visit this prison, in which St. Paul is said to have been immured), and had the five conspirators brought there and strangled. He came out. There was a huge crowd, waiting silently. Cicero raised his hand. "They have lived," he said.

That night, December fifth, there was cheering for Cicero and a torch-light parade. A month later, among the hills north of Florence, Catiline and what was left of his army died fighting. Sallust says that all their wounds were in front.

Such was the Conspiracy of Catiline. One result was that Caesar now became the acknowledged leader of the Populares; while Cato emerged as the most influential man among the Optimates. Meantime, Cicero was hailed as the "Father of his Country." Success went to his head. For the rest of his life he talked about how he, single-handed, had crushed Catiline until everyone was sick of the topic. Behind his back he was called "Old Know-it-all" (because he kept saying *omnia comperuisse* which means "to have found out everything"). A greater danger to him was the fact that he was accused by the Populares of having put Roman citizens to death by a decree of the Senate without giving them their constitutional right of an appeal to the Assembly, although Cicero's claim was that he had acted under the "Ultimate Decree", which in his interpretation meant martial law. Without realizing it, too, he had offended the man he admired, Pompey. Pompey had hoped to have a constitutional reason for bringing his army back to Italy, namely to crush Catiline.

Cicero was blind to criticisms. In his vanity he bought a house on the Palatine Hill on the most fashionable street in Rome for the equivalent of $175,000, borrowing the money, as he tells us in a letter, from Crassus at 6 per cent, half the usual rate of interest. From this time forward he worked for what he called "The Harmony of the Orders," by which he meant an alliance between the nobles and the Knights, with the city-mob kept in its proper place and, as he hoped, Pompey at the head. But the nobles never really accepted Cicero: his family was middle-class.

The Return of Pompey and the First Triumvirate: 62–60 B.C.

In December of 62 B.C. Pompey landed at Brundisium on the heel of Italy. In his years in the East he had increased Roman revenues from 240,000,000 sesterces to 340,000,000 and had given 384,000,000 sesterces to his soldiers. He brought back to Rome's treasury another 480,000,000 sesterces in a lump sum. His claim—for Pompey was never modest—was that he had conquered 1,538 cities and 12,178,000 people.

Everyone waited for him to march on Rome and make himself dictator. Crassus, worried about his machinations in Rome, his wealth, and the dislike between him and Pompey, had his furniture packed and a ship ready in which to flee to Africa. But Pompey disbanded his army. It seems likely that he shrank from doing anything unconstitutional, and further that he believed that his exploits alone would make him master of Rome. Once fear of him was gone, the Optimates snubbed him. They turned instead to the trial of Publius Clodius.

Clodius belonged to the Pulcher branch of the patrician Claudians. An elder brother was Appius Claudius, a dull but respectable noble. His three sisters had all made good marriages, one of them having been wedded to Lucius Lucullus, who divorced her on his return from Asia Minor and married a sister of Servilia and a half-sister to Cato. The most beautiful of the three sisters and the closest in spirit to Clodius was Clodia, who was married to the praetor of 63 B.C., Metellus Celer. She was almost certainly the Lesbia to whom the lyricist Catullus wrote poems of love and hate and, through her salon and her brother, had a considerable political influence in Rome.

Clodius himself had already had a stormy career. Besides prosecuting Catiline in 66 B.C., he had been one of the agents who had helped stir mutiny in the camp of his then brother-in-law, Lucullus. Brilliant, unstable, popular with the mob through his reckless high spirits, in December of 62 B.C., in pursuit of an intrigue with Caesar's second wife (Caesar's first wife had died leaving him a daughter, Julia), he had dressed himself as a woman to attend the ancient and holy festival of the Bona Dea from which, it will be remembered, all males were excluded. That festival was being held in Caesar's house since Caesar was Chief Pontiff. But Clodius had been caught and had had difficulty in escaping. At first it seemed that the affair would blow over. Caesar divorced his wife with the haughty remark, "Caesar's wife must be above suspicion," but he did nothing further, since at this time Clodius was one of his supporters. The stern Cato, however, picked up the scandal, particularly because it was a weapon to use against Caesar, whom he despised. He insisted that Clodius be brought to trial for sacrilege. Pompey found himself forgotten.

The trial was held in the early spring of 61 B.C. Clodius claimed an alibi, namely that he had been forty miles away on the night of the festival. But Cicero, although apparently he had promised Clodia that he would not testify against her brother, gave evidence that he had seen Clodius in Rome shortly before the alleged offence. Clodius was acquitted, however, because, according to a letter of Cicero, the jury was bribed, almost certainly by Crassus. Then Caesar, who had had to wait until the trial was over, left as propraetor for Spain, but only after Crassus had given security for his debts which totalled $1,200,000. Thus, both Clodius and Caesar were tied to Crassus.

There was one other long range result. Clodius and Clodia never forgave Cicero, and three years later Clodius had him exiled.

The First Triumvirate: 60 B.C.

While Caesar was in Spain, the Senate, led by Cato, succeeded in alienating both Crassus and Pompey. Pompey had requested lands for his soldiers and ratification of his arrangements in the East. Both requests were blocked. Meanwhile, the capitalists of Rome asked for relief from the price they had contracted to pay for the right of collecting the taxes in Asia because of poor harvests in that province. Once again Cato saw to it that this request was refused. Then, in the late May or early June of 60 B.C., Caesar returned from Spain where he had made money and conducted a successful military campaign. He wanted to stand for the consulship and at the same time celebrate a triumph. Therefore, since by law a general could not enter Rome before his triumph and since by another law to stand for the consulship a candidate must present himself before the Assembly, Caesar asked for the right to stand for the consulship *in absentia*.

Cato saw to it that this appeal was refused. Caesar, foregoing the triumph, entered Rome. Without Rome knowing it until later, he reconciled Pompey and Crassus and made a deal with them. In this way the First Triumvirate was formed. The terms of the agreement suited the cynical materialism of the day. Caesar was to be elected consul for 59 B.C. In return Caesar, when consul, was to get Pompey and Crassus what they wanted. There was a rider to the deal. At the end of his consulship Caesar was to receive an extraordinary command and an army. Caesar knew that an army was the weapon with which to win power.

Caesar's Consulship: 59 B.C.

Everything went according to plan. Caesar was elected consul, along with an Optimate named Bibulus. In the first weeks of 59 B.C. Caesar attempted to put his measures through the Senate in the regular way. When he found himself obstructed, particularly by Cato, taking a leaf out of the book of the Gracchi, he brought his bills directly to the Assembly. Here Pompey's veterans, swarming into the city, gave him control. When Caesar's colleague Bibulus tried to interpose his veto, he was chased from the Forum and a basket of filth was dumped over his head.

Bibulus shut himself up in his palace on the Palatine Hill; and Roman wits began to call the year "The consulship of Julius and Caesar." Pompey got lands for his veterans and ratification for his acts in the East. Crassus' friends, the capitalists, had one-third of the contract price for the collection of the taxes in Asia knocked off. Meanwhile, a henchman tribune, Vatinius, put through a bill giving Caesar a five-years' command, starting *on March 1st. 59 B.C.*, over Cisalpine Gaul and Illyricum (the Adriatic coast of modern Yugoslavia), with the right to raise three legions. This bill was made possible because Clodia's husband, Metellus Celer, consul for 60 B.C., to whom these provinces had been assigned, died suddenly in February. One rumor in Rome was that Clodia had poisoned him. Later, Gallia Narbonensis was added to these provinces.

Caesar was now in effect both consul and proconsul. He began at once to levy troops, stationing them outside Rome so as to over-awe any opposition in the city. In this same month of March, since Egypt was no longer needed as a possible arena, Caesar sold to Ptolemy Auletes the legitimate right to the throne he had occupied so long. The price was the enormous one of 6000 talents. We might note here that in the next year Ptolemy was expelled by his subjects, and came to Rome to ask to be restored to his kingdom. In 55 B.C. a Roman army, led by Gabinius, at that time governor of Syria, took him back, with Mark Antony leading the cavalry. Meanwhile, in Rome, late in March of 59 B.C., Cicero attacked the Triumvirs in a bitter speech. This oration was the beginning of Cicero's downfall. On the afternoon of the day he delivered it, his enemy, the patrician Clodius, in a meeting of the *Comitia Centuriata*, was adopted into a plebeian family so that he could stand for the tribunate. Caesar, as consul, presided at the meeting and Pompey officiated as augur. Cicero recognized that the move was directed against him, and he retired to a villa in the country.

Then, in the spring of the year, to cement his alliance with Pompey, Caesar married his daughter Julia to him. Pompey was four years older than Caesar so that the bride was half the bridegroom's age. To make the marriage still more of a political one, on his return from the East Pompey had divorced his then wife because of rumors of misconduct between her and Caesar. At about the same time Caesar married Calpurnia, who belonged to a powerful Roman family. Next, at the elections for consuls for 58 B.C., Caesar's new father-in-law, Calpurnius, was put in as one consul-elect. The other was Gabinius, who as tribune had proposed the law giving Pompey the command over the pirates. At the same time Clodius was elected as one of the tribunes.

These machinations present to us one of the most cynical periods in history. When 58 B.C. began, Caesar did not hurry to his province. Cato was an enemy to whom no overtures could be made, but Caesar had presented various offers to Cicero, whose eloquence he feared, the last being an honorary commission outside of Italy. Cicero, however, relying on Pompey, had refused them all. Clodius, therefore, who by Roman procedure had become tribune on the 10th of December (the other magistrates took office on the 1st of January), was let loose. Among other measures, he abolished any payment for the wheat distribution, thus winning the support of the city mob, and made political clubs legal. These clubs were used to form street-gangs controlled by Clodius through ward leaders so that he could at any moment dominate the Tribal Assembly. When this "Tammany Hall" type of organization was completed he brought in a bill that anyone who had had Roman citizens put to death without a trial should be outlawed. Cicero knew that the measure was aimed at him for his execution of the Catilinarian conspirators by a decree of the Senate. He appealed desperately to Pompey. Pompey refused to listen, and in tears Cicero left Rome.

Clodius next had Cato appointed to take over Cyprus for Rome (the Ptolemy of Cyprus had not, like his brother of Egypt, purchased immunity). Cato was away for two years and, incidentally, was efficient. Now, at last, with the two worst trouble-makers out of the way, Caesar hurried north to join his legions; and he was just in time.

Caesar in Gaul: 58–56 B.C.

The immediate crisis in Gaul had been caused by the Helvetii, a tribe which lived in Switzerland near Geneva. That tribe had decided to migrate to new homes in southwestern Gaul. Permission was asked to cross the Upper Rhone and move through the Roman province in the south of France. Caesar refused consent and fortified the Upper Rhone. The Helvetii set out by another route which took them through the country of the Sequani into the territory of the Aedui, north of the Roman province. The Aedui were allied to Rome and they asked Caesar for help. Thus, with a legitimate excuse, he moved into unconquered Gaul (called *Gallia Comata*, "Long-haired Gaul"), and defeated the Helvetii, forcing most of them to return home. Next the Aedui and the Sequani, north of them, requested aid against a German chieftain, Ariovistus, who had been invited across the Rhine to assist the Sequani and had refused to leave. Caesar marched against him in some embarrassment because during his consulship Ariovistus had visited Rome and had been decreed to be "A Friend of Rome." Many of his men were terrified at the sight of the huge Germans. According to Caesar himself, some of the young Roman nobles who had come with him either found excuses to leave or spent the night before the battle in making their wills. But Caesar won a great battle near Strasbourg and Ariovistus fled back across the Rhine.

This campaign of 58 B.C. was the entering wedge for the conquest of Gaul. Caesar was motivated in part, undoubtedly, by the desire to accomplish great exploits, and in part by the knowledge that Gaul would be an excellent training-ground for his legions. The Gauls, moreover, though civilized to a very considerable degree, invited their own destruction. They were divided into warring tribes. In addition, there were factions inside each tribe, so that, during Caesar's campaigns in Gaul, Gauls were constantly fighting on his side.

Caesar spent the winter of 58–57 B.C. in Cisalpine Gaul, which was an excellent recruiting-ground for soldiers and his base for supplies. During the next year Central Gaul was overrun and Caesar overcame the tribes who lived in what is now Belgium. When the news of his victories reached Rome, a fifteen days' thanksgiving was decreed.

Meanwhile, the political sea was in turmoil. Clodius, the agent of Caesar and Crassus, developed delusions of grandeur. He attacked Pompey and even turned on Crassus. In disgust, in 57 B.C. Pompey secured the tribune, Milo, to recruit gladiators to fight the street gangs of Clodius. The main issue was the recall of Cicero from exile. It was like civil war. After one battle in the Forum the dead bodies had to be pitched into the Tiber and the stones of the Forum swabbed to remove the blood. In August of 57 B.C. Cicero returned, but not before he had given an undertaking through his brother not to make attacks on the Triumvirs.

Cicero, however, saw a chance to detach a disgusted Pompey from Caesar and Crassus and to unite him with the Optimates. His intrigues seemed to be moving along successfully. Suddenly in the spring of 56 B.C., Caesar summoned a conference at Lucca, the southernmost point in his province, which by law he could not leave.

The Conference of Lucca: 56 B.C.

At this conference the three masters of the Roman world were reconciled. Caesar had his command in Gaul extended for another five years—that is, until the first of March 49 B.C., Crassus and Pompey were to be consuls for 55 B.C. Then Crassus was to have an army and a five-year's command in Syria; while Pompey was given a five-year's control of Spain and Africa, again with an army but without the necessity of leaving Italy. Clodius was told to behave himself. Cicero was ordered to show repentance by making speeches in favor of Caesar and of the henchmen of the Triumvirs, while his brother joined Caesar's army as what we would call a lieutenant-general. It was a bitter pill for the orator, but he swallowed it.

Caesar in Gaul: 56–49 B.C.

We still have Caesar's own account of his Gallic Wars (*Bellum Gallicum*). Quite clearly he was a consummate general. In 56 B.C. he conquered the

Veneti, who lived in the northwestern bulge of today's France. In 55 B.C. he crossed into Germany by a bridge over the Rhine, and in 55 and 54 B.C. he made two forays into Britain and another into Germany. These expeditions left no permanent impression except that Britain was brought into the ken of the Romans. In 52 B.C., however, under the gallant Vercingetorix, the Gauls revolted, and Caesar was defeated at Gergovia. Finally, after a bitter struggle, he shut Vercingetorix and his army in Alesia, where traces of Caesar's siege works can still be seen, and starved them into surrender. Vercingetorix was sent to a dungeon in Rome. There he waited until he was put to death during Caesar's triumph in 46 B.C.

We must not be misled by the glamor of Caesar's victories. He could, and was, clement when policy made it wise. He could be equally ruthless. When Avaricum (modern Bourges) was stormed, its 40,000 people, men, women, and children were massacred. Thousands of Gauls were killed. Thousands of them were sold into slavery. Caesar personally is said to have made $20,000,000 from the conquest of Gaul. He spent part of the money to beautify Rome, with Cicero, now reconciled to him, and Oppius as his agents. From this time dates the *Basilica Julia* (Julian law-courts), of which we can see the foundations and the bases of the pillars today, on the northwest side of the Forum. Not to be outdone, Pompey built Rome's first permanent stone theater (55 B.C.) and voting pens of marble, walks, and porticoes in the Campus Martius.

Caesar's officers and the contractors who supplied him likewise made fortunes—and so did the slave-traders. Just as the money from Pompey's conquest of the East had lifted Rome out of depression in 62 B.C., so now Caesar's war brought a bloom of prosperity to Italy.

Meanwhile, Roman traders and merchants flocked into Gaul. Roads were built. Latin replaced the Celtic language and the country was thoroughly Romanized. As a result, when the Roman Empire of the West fell, Gaul, as France (the country of the Franks, a Germanic tribe), became one of the bastions of mediaeval and Western civilization.

Events in Rome: 56–49 B.C.

The Conference of Lucca had re-established the First Triumvirate. Its patched structure soon began to disintegrate. Pompey and Crassus were consuls in 55 B.C. But in 54 B.C. Julia, Pompey's wife and Caesar's daughter, died suddenly. In the next year, 53 B.C. Crassus, who had gone as proconsul to Syria with the idea of conquering as far as India, was slain by the Parthians at the battle of Carrhae, and most of his army was slaughtered or taken prisoner.

The Triumvirate had now become a Duovirate, and the death of Julia had removed the one person who could keep Pompey and Caesar on good terms with each other. Caesar suggested one of his own relatives as a new wife for Pompey, but Pompey was attracted to and married the young widow of the son of Crassus who, like his father, had been killed at Carrhae. Her family was an Optimate one. Meanwhile the gangster war between Clodius and Milo had erupted again to such an extent that in 53 B.C. no elections could be held and 52 B.C. began with no consuls in office. Then on the wintry evening of January 17th, 52 B.C., in a brawl on the Appian Way outside Rome, Clodius was killed by Milo. Clodius' followers in Rome rioted. During his funeral in the Forum the Senate House was burned. In desperation, with even Cato agreeing, the Senate appointed Pompey sole consul. He restored order.

Pompey was now sole consul, proconsul of the two Spains and Africa and curator of Rome's grain supply (a position voted to him by the Senate soon after Cicero's return from exile.) His only real rival was Caesar and the Optimates argued that Caesar, as leader of the Populares, must be crushed. Caesar, on the other hand, realized that if he gave up his province on March 1st, 49 B.C. (the due date), and came to Rome as a private individual he would be prosecuted by the Optimates. Therefore he had made arrangements to retain his provinces until the 1st of January 48 B.C., and asked to be allowed to stand for the consulship for 48 B.C. *in absentia*. In this way he could move directly from his proconsulship into the consulship, and thence into another proconsulship, and the Optimates could not attack him, since magistrates while in office could not be prosecuted.

Intrigue and counter intrigue followed. Finally, after a heated debate on January 7th, 49 B.C., the Senate, after ordering that Caesar give up his army and provinces by a fixed date (perhaps March 1st, 40 B.C.), passed that same "Ultimate Decree" under which, in 63 B.C., Cicero had put the Catilinarian conspirators to death. Two of Caesar's men were tribunes in Rome, of whom one was Mark Antony. They fled to Caesar's camp, claiming that their lives were in danger. On January 10th Caesar crossed the Rubicon, a little stream on the Adriatic coast separating Cisalpine Gaul from Italy. The act meant civil war.

The Civil War and Caesar's Dictatorship: 49–44 B.C.

Pompey had told the Senate that he had only to stamp his foot and legions would spring out of the ground in Italy. When the test came he had to evacuate Italy and leave for Epirus in Greece.

Caesar occupied Italy and moved on to crush Pompey's legions in Spain. Then, he turned against Pompey. Pompey's fleet held the Adriatic, but Caesar somehow got his troops across. He was beaten at Dyrrachium (modern Durazzo), but, in 48 B.C. at Pharsalus in Thessaly, Caesar's trained legions were victorious. Pompey fled to Alexandria in Egypt. Caesar arrived in time to receive his rival's head, which had been chopped off by the Egyptians.

Caesar had brought only a few soldiers with him. For a time he was besieged by the Egyptians, who were engaged in a dynastic dispute between Cleopatra and her brother, who were supposed to be sharing the throne. It was during this period that Cleopatra, at the time only twenty-two, had herself smuggled into Caesar's presence. Caesar, now a man in his fifties, was enthralled. After Cleopatra's brother was killed and Caesar was in control of Egypt, he put Cleopatra on the throne again, along with a younger brother of hers whom she put to death in 43 B.C. Meanwhile, Cleopatra called her son by Caesar, Caesarion (little Caesar).

Caesar now reconquered the Near East, where Pharnaces, a son of Mithradates, had stirred up trouble. It was from his victory over Pharnaces at Zela in Asia Minor that he sent his famous message, "I came, I saw, I conquered" (*veni, vidi, vici*). Then he returned to an Italy which during his absence had been mismanaged by his lieutenant, Mark Antony. Next, he crossed to Africa. Here there was a Republican army with the indomitable Cato as its inspiring spirit. When Caesar defeated it at Thapsus (46 B.C.), Cato, as a good Stoic, committed suicide (the Stoics held it to be a man's own choice whether he continued to live or not).

It was after this battle that Caesar returned to Rome to celebrate his triumph, one day each for Gaul, Egypt, Pontus, and Africa. Among the captives in front of his triumphal chariot was the gallant Vercingetorix who, after the triumph, was strangled in the temple of Jupiter. There was an endless train of wagons jammed with costly furniture, 2822 golden diadems, sacks of gold, and the like. Five thousand denarii (the denarius was worth at least twenty cents and probably twice or thrice that in purchasing power in terms of today's prices) was given to each legionary. Each centurion received ten thousand and every spectator one hundred. On the night of July 28, 46 B.C., the people of Rome were fed at 22,000 tables throughout the city. In a wooden amphitheater in the Forum there were gladiatorial fights, animal hunts, plays, and mock battles. It is not strange that Rome cheered Caesar, the dictator.

The Republicans were not yet completely crushed. Next year (45 B.C.) at Munda in Spain, Caesar fought their last army and was victorious in one of his bitterest battles. He returned to Rome in September.

The Dictatorship of Caesar

In victory Caesar was magnanimous to Roman Republicans. Cicero, who after severe heart-searching had finally joined Pompey, was forgiven. So were many other Pompeians. Meanwhile, Caesar proceeded to push through reform after reform. The list of those on the dole was reduced from 320,000 to 150,000. A large public works' program was planned. Overseas colonies for the poor were begun. Cisalpine Gaul had already been given the citizenship. In the other provinces the evil taxation system was amended. Among minor changes, the calendar was reformed. The Roman calendar was by this time 80 days in advance of the actual seasons. The Egyptian solar year of 365 days, with a provision for leap year, was introduced. The year 46 B.C. was lengthened to 445 days to take up the slack, and the new calendar went into effect on January 1st, 45 B.C. Meanwhile, *Quintilis*, the fifth month of the oldest of Roman calendars, was renamed *Julius* (our July).

We still use this Julian calendar with slight corrections made by Pope Gregory XIII in the sixteenth century. England did not accept the Gregorian Calendar until 1732 A.D., and then there were riots because seventeen days were eliminated from the calendar and people thought they were losing seventeen days of their lives.

Caesar had many other reforms and projects in mind. But the fact that he seemed about to accept the title of king finally consolidated a conspiracy against him. Two of the principal leaders were Brutus and Cassius, both of whom he had pardoned. On the Ides of March (March 15th), 44 B.C., the sixty conspirators assassinated Caesar.

An Estimate of Caesar

How are we to evaluate Caesar? We know that physically he was tall and well-formed with a fair complexion and dark, piercing eyes. As a personality, few men have equalled his capacities. He was a consummate general, a first-class orator and writer, and a man who charmed most of those he met. His ability to work at top speed amazed his contemporaries. It was said that on his journeys in a coach to and from Gaul and Cisalpine Gaul he used to keep two secretaries busy. It is clear that he could be ruthless, even though he frequently showed clemency, particularly to Romans. As a statesman he was farsighted and most of his decisions were sound. In his ability to plan and organize he has had few equals in history.

Out of his assassination came not liberty but chaos. But Caesar's dictatorship marked the end of the Republic. It is, therefore, a good place to pause and assess what life in Rome was like in the years 78–44 B.C.

Readings from Sources of the Period

(a) Few authors wrote Latin with more clarity than Julius Caesar. Below is an extract from his description of his first invasion of Britain in 55 B.C. Neither this nor his second invasion in 56 B.C. subjugated the island. During his first invasion his men, while foraging, were attacked by the Britons and surrounded.

Their mode of fighting with their chariots is this: First, they drive about in all directions and throw their weapons and generally break the ranks of the enemy with the very dread of their horses and the noise of their wheels; and when they have worked themselves in between the troops of cavalry, they leap from their chariots and engage on foot. The charioteers in the meantime withdraw some little distance from the battle, and so place themselves with the chariots that, if their masters are overpowered by the number of the enemy, they may have a ready retreat to their own troops. Thus they display in battle the speed of cavalry together with the firmness of infantry, and by daily practice and exercise attain to such expertness that they are accustomed even on a sloping and steep place, to check their horses at full speed, and manage to turn them in an instant, run along the pole, and stand on the yoke, and from there return with the greatest speed to their chariots again.

Under these circumstances, while our men were dismayed by the novelty of this mode of battle, Caesar brought most opportune assistance, for upon his arrival the enemy paused, and our men recovered from their fear. Upon this, thinking the time unfavorable for provoking the enemy and coming to an action, he kept himself in his own quarters, and after a short interval, withdrew the legions to the camp.

(Guinagh and Dorjahn, *Latin Literature in Translation*, Longmans, Green, New York, 1948, pp. 205–206, from Eugene I. Burdock, *The Gallic War of Julius Caesar*, New York: Noble and Noble.)

(b) Below is the First Oration Against Catiline (63 B.C.) and a second extract about Catiline's meeting on the night when he planned the murder of Cicero. The extracts breathe the tension of those days.

THE FIRST ORATION AGAINST CATILINE

How far, I ask, will you try our patience, Catiline? How long will this madness of yours make sport of us? To what length will this unbridled insolence vaunt itself? Have you in no way been disturbed by the night guard on the Palatine, the city watch, the fear of the people, the gathering of all loyal citizens, the convening of the Senate in this highly fortified place, and the expression on the faces of these senators? Do you not perceive that your plans are manifest, do you not see that your conspiracy is already throttled by its being known to all these men? Who of us do you think does not know what you did last night, what the night before that, where you were, whom you called together, what plans you made? O the morals of these times! The Senate understands these facts, the consul sees, but this fellow lives. Lives? Why, indeed he even comes into the Senate, he becomes a participant in public deliberation, he marks and designates, as he looks about, each one of us for slaughter. But we, brave men, seem to do enough for the Republic if we avoid his madness and his weapons. Long ago, Catiline, you should have been led to death by order of the consul, long ago the destruction which you have been plotting for us all should have been visited upon you.

Review with me, then, that night before last; soon you will perceive that I am far more keenly on the alert for the safety of the Republic than you are for its ruin. I say that you on that night came to the street of the scythemakers (I will not speak vaguely) into the home of Marcus Laeca; that in that same place many companions of your mad crime had come together. Do you dare to deny it? Why are you silent? I shall prove it, if you deny it, for I see here in the Senate certain men who were there together with you. O ye immortal gods! Where in the world are we? In what kind of city do we live, what sort of Republic do we have? Here, here in our number, Senators, in this most sacred and most important council in the world, are those who plot the death of us all, who plot the ruin of this city and even of the whole world! I, the consul, see them and I call for their vote on matters of public concern, and I do not yet wound with my voice those whom it would have been fitting to put to the sword! You were, then, at Laeca's house that night, Catiline, you assigned where it suited you for each one to go, you named those whom you would leave at Rome, those whom you would take along with you, you marked off parts of the city for fires, you declared that you yourself would soon leave, you said that even now you were subject to a little delay because I was alive. Two Roman knights were found to free you of this annoyance, and they promised to kill me in my bed that very night a little before daylight. I discovered these facts before your meeting was hardly more than adjourned; I fortified and secured my home with a greater number of guards, and I kept out those whom you had sent in the morning to greet me when those very ones did come whose coming to me at that time I had already predicted to many very important men.

(Guinagh and Dorjahn, *op. cit.*, pp. 231–232 and 233–234 translated by Kevin Guinagh.)

(c) Cicero's letters and those of his friends to him present us with an intimate picture of the happenings of the day.

(i) Cicero in Exile, 58 B.C. to his wife, daughter and son.

Oh, how lost and afflicted I am! Why should I ask you to come now, you, a woman sick in body and broken in spirit? Shall I not ask you? Shall I, then, be without you? I think we had better do as follows: if there is any hope of my return, remain there and aid and abet my cause; but if, as I fear, it's all over with me, then come to me in any way you can. I want you to know that, if I have you, I shall not regard myself utterly lost. But what is happening to my dear daughter? You must look after her, for I have no suggestions. Surely, whatever may happen, we must safeguard that poor little girl's happy marriage and good name. And how is my son faring? I wish that he were always on my bosom and in my embrace. I can't write more now: weeping stays my hand.

(*Ibid.*, p. 224, translated by Alfred P. Dorjahn.)

(ii) Cicero, on his return from exile made friends with Caesar. Below is an extract in which he recommends a friend to Caesar, who was campaigning in Gaul.

Therefore I am sending Trebatius to you and I am doing so under circumstances which make it imperative that I send him, first, as a result of my own determination, and, second, as a result of your invitation. It is my wish, dear Caesar, that you receive him with all your affability and bestow upon him alone all the favors that you could possibly be induced by me to bestow upon my friends.

For him I do not request a tribune's or prefect's post nor any particular office, but I do ask for your goodwill and generosity; on the other hand, I do not object to your honoring him even with these distinguished offices, if such is your pleasure. In short, I am transferring him entirely from my power to yours, as the saying goes, since you are a man distinguished both by faith and honor. I may be a bit insistent, and yet there is no justification for it in a letter to you; but I know you will pardon me. Take care of your health and continue your affection toward me.

(*Ibid.*, pp. 227–228 translated by Alfred P. Dorjahn.)

(iii) An extract from a letter which Cicero's son, at University in Athens, where he has wasted time and money wrote to Tiro, his father's secretary.

The errors of my youth have brought me such grief and torment that my mind shrinks from the deeds and my ears abhor even the mention of them. It is known and clear to me that you bore your share of this worry and grief; nor is this strange, for while you wished me complete success for my own sake, you did so also for yours. It was always my wish that you should share my good fortune. Since, therefore, you formerly were worried about me, I shall promise that now you will derive twofold joy from me.

I want you to know that my very close connection with Cratippus is not that of a student, but of a son: not only do I gladly hear his lectures, but especially do I appreciate his gentle manner.

Why need I mention Bruttius, whom I never permit to get out of my sight? He leads a frugal and strict life, but he is also most delightful company; for in him mirth is not separated from our grammatical studies and our daily philosophical discussions. I've rented a place next door to him and as best I can I relieve his needs from my own slender allowance. Moreover, I have begun to declaim in Greek with Cassius, while in Latin I prefer to practise with Bruttius.

In the matter of financial help, I am as sorry as you are that I failed you. But never fear, dear Tiro, I shall come to your aid, if only fortune will come to mine, especially since I know that that farm has been purchased for both of us in common. As to my requests to which you are now giving your attention, I wish to thank you. But I beg of you that a secretary be sent me as soon as possible, especially a Greek, for much of my effort is lost in writing out lecture notes. I should wish above all that you take care of your health, so that we may have some learned discussions. I commend Anteros to you.

(*Ibid.*, pp. 229–230, translated by Alfred P. Dorjahn.)

(d) When the Civil War erupted, Cicero, although he finally joined Pompey, at first stayed in Italy and corresponded and even met with Caesar. On March 19th, 49 B.C. he wrote to Caesar from his villa at Formiae, on the west coast of Italy. Only the first paragraph of the letter is given.

FROM CICERO, GENERAL,   *Formiae, 19 March 49* B.C.
TO CAESAR, GENERAL

When I read your letter—passed to me by our friend Furnius—in which you
requested me to come near Rome, it did not surprise me that you wanted to
utilize my 'advice and position'. But I asked myself what you meant by also
referring to my 'influence' and 'support'. However, my hopes—and I based them
on your outstanding and admirable statesmanship—made me conclude that what
you aimed at was peace, and agreement and harmony among Romans: and for
that purpose I felt that both my character and my background suited me well.

(Michael Grant, *Cicero, Selected Works*, London: Penguin Books, 1960.)

(e) Caesar, on his way to Spain was anxious for Cicero not to join Pompey. The
whole letter is given.

FROM CAESAR, GENERAL,   *On the march, 16 April 49* B.C.
TO CICERO, GENERAL

Although I was convinced that you would take no rash or ill-judged
action, nevertheless my anxiety about what people are saying has impelled
me to write to you and urge, in the name of our friendship, that you should
not make any move, now that things have gone my way, which you did not
see fit to make while matters were undecided. For, everything having
manifestly turned out to our advantage and the disadvantage of the other
side, you will have seriously damaged the good relations between our two
selves—as well as acting against your own interests—if you display resistance to
the trend of events. It would then be evident that your action resulted not
from support of a cause, since the cause is the same as it was when you decided
to hold aloof, but from your objection to something that I have done. And that
would be the severest blow you could inflict on me.

Our friendship entitles me to ask you not to do it. Besides, what could be
more appropriate for a man of peace and integrity, and a good citizen, than to
keep out of civil disturbance? There were many who felt that to be so, but were
prevented from acting as they wished because of the dangers that would have been
involved. Weigh up the evidence provided by my career and by your own assess-
ment of our friendly relations, and you will find abstention from the quarrel the
safest and most honourable course.

(f) Caesar pardoned Cicero for joining Pompey. On his return from the East, he
visited Cicero in the latter's villa at Puteoli (modern Pozzuoli) north of Naples;
and Cicero described the visit to his friend and publisher, Atticus.

TO ATTICUS   *Puteoli, 19 December 45* B.C.

A formidable guest, yet no regrets! For everything went very pleasantly
indeed. However, when he reached Philippus on the evening of the 18th, the house
was so full of soldiers that there was hardly a room free for Caesar himself to have
dinner. Two thousand men! I was distinctly alarmed about what would happen
the next day, but Cassius Barba came to my rescue with a loan of some guards.
A camp was pitched on my land and the house was put under guard. On the 19th
he stayed with Philippus until one o'clock and let no one in—I believe he was
doing accounts with Balbus. Then he went for a walk on the shore. After two he

had a bath. Then he was told about Mamurra; but there was no change in his expression. He had an oil-massage and then sat down to dinner.

He was following a course of emetics, so he ate and drank without *arrière-pensèe* and at his ease. It was a sumptuous dinner and well-served, and more than that, *well-cooked and seasoned, with good talk; and in a word agreeable*. His entourage were very lavishly provided for in three other rooms. Even the lower-ranking ex-slaves and the slaves lacked for nothing; the more important ex-slaves I entertained in style.

In other words, we were human beings together. Still, he was not the sort of guest to whom you would say "do please come again on your way back." Once is enough! We talked no serious politics, but a good deal about literary matters. In short, he liked it and enjoyed himself. He said he was going to spend one day at Puteoli and the next in the neighbourhood of Baiae. There you have the story of how I entertained him—or had him billeted on me; I found it a bother, as I have said, but not disagreeable. Now I am going to stay on here for a little and then go to my place at Tusculum.

As Caesar passed Dolabella's house on horseback his whole guard paraded under arms to the right and left of him, which they did nowhere else, so I heard from Nicias.

(*Ibid.*, pp. 89–90.)

CHAPTER 8

Roman Life in the Last Century of the Republic

In the last century of the Republic Rome was a city of nearly three-quarters of a million people. Tenements huddled in its valleys, palaces glittered on its seven hills, villas and gardens lined the Tiber, and restless throngs surged through its streets and its Forum. The Forum (see the plan of Rome) was the heart of the city.

The Forum

Today the Forum is a melancholy remnant of the "grandeur that was Rome." If you and I were there, around 55 B.C., we would see a very different scene. The Forum faces northwest. In front of us would be the Capitoline Hill. On its twin peaks would gleam the temple of Jupiter-Juno-Minerva and the temple of Juno of the Mint. To our left and a bit behind us, would rise the palaces of the Palatine Hill.

The Forum itself, now that we are back in the past, is crowded with temples, statues, and columns, although the Arch of Septimius Severus is far in the future. To the right, as we face the Capitoline Hill, is the Senate-House. The open space before it is the place where the Assembly of the Tribes meets. At its head is the speakers' rostra. At one end of it is a column decorated with the gilded beaks of the warships taken from the Carthaginians in Rome's first naval victory (260 B.C.), a sort of Nelson's Trafalgar column. This, it will be remembered, is titled the *columna rostrata* (ships' beak column) and from it the rostra gets its name. Further back and still to our right, is a line of shops with balconies. Behind them is a basilica in which, as we look, lawsuits are being heard. To our left, across the Forum, are more shops and another basilica for lawsuits, the one built by Caesar from the loot of Gaul.

374

A Roman Law-Suit

While we are still looking at this part of the Forum, facing northwest, we are almost certain to see a case being tried in one of the basilicas. It will be remembered that Sulla established permanent courts to handle criminal suits. If we move up to look at one of these courts in action, we will note that a praetor, gorgeous in his magistrate's robe, presides, helped by two assessors who know the law. There are places for the prosecution and the defense. The jury have seats. These juries are not as large as the Athenian ones. In the trial of Clodius for sacrilege in 62 B.C., as we know from a letter of Cicero's, there were 56 jurymen.

As in ancient Athens, not the state but a private individual prosecutes, and both prosecutor and defendant are supposed to speak in person. In the Roman courts, unlike the Athenian, lawyers are permitted to orate. The fiction is that the lawyer is a friend of the accused or of the prosecutor. A defendant, for example, after pleading not guilty, may say a few words and add: "I am not very skilled in speaking but my friend, Marcus Tullius Cicero, has offered to speak in my defence." The prosecutor may be a person affected by the alleged crime (for instance, the brother or son of a man who is alleged to have been murdered), or he may be, as was the case when Cicero prosecuted Verres, someone who wishes to make a reputation for himself. In either case, there are often assistants to the prosecutor as well as to the defendants.

Lawyers, as in England, and as is often the case in actual practice in the United States, are divided into legal specialists (*iuris consulti*) and people who speak in court (*oratores*). Cicero was an *orator* not a *iuris consultus* but would have a legal expert to consult. By Roman law, a lawyer could not charge fees. Instead he received gifts or legacies. It is estimated that Cicero made $30,000 a year or more and was always in debt. The spectators had to stand; the more famous an orator, the larger the audience.

Evidence was on oath, precedents were quoted, and cross-examination was permitted. Much of our legal procedure of today comes from the Roman lawcourts. When the evidence was in and the final speeches made, the jurymen voted. They had three tablets. One was marked D for *damno*, "I condemn", one A for *absolvo*, "I acquit", and one N.L. for *non liquet,* "The case is not proved". In the trial of Clodius, 31 jurymen, bribed by Crassus, voted for acquittal, 25 for condemnation.

The View of the Forum, Looking Southeast

If we step into the Forum again and, mounting the *Rostra*, look, not at the Capitoline Hill but in the opposite direction, southeast, to our right will be the Palatine Hill with a ramp running up it to the magnificent palaces which overlook the Forum. At the foot of the hill, under its northwestern face, is the street of the Etruscans (*Vicus Tuscus*), lined with shops and taverns, which runs out to the Cattle-Market and the Tiber. In the Forum itself, as we gaze down the Sacred Way along which the Roman triumphal processions move, the Arch of Titus, which today stands on a slight rise of ground half way down, is not yet built. Neither is the Colosseum nor the Arch of Constantine. The most note-worthy sight is the round temple of Vesta. Near it is the *Regia*, the official residence of the Chief Pontiff, who at this moment is Julius Caesar, though he is far away in Gaul. Behind the temple of Vesta is the delightful house of the Vestal Virgins, with a garden and cubicles for the individual Vestals.

The Vestals, it will be recalled, whose task is to guard and keep burning the undying fire of Rome, are part of one of the earliest Roman cults. As is often the case in such cults, they are required to live as their ancestors lived when the worship of Vesta (goddess of the hearth) was first established. Ordinary Romans, if they are rich enough, can have water piped to their homes, but the Vestals must carry the water they need in earthenware pots from a special well, the *Fons Iuturnae*. Similarly, as has been noted, they cannot wear linen but only woollen clothes, because the first Romans wove wool but not linen (by a reverse process Egyptian priests could only wear linen and not woollen garments because, it is supposed, in Egypt linen was woven before wool), and they cannot enter a house with more than one step up from the threshold. Their clothes are girdled by a rope tied with a special knot called the *Knot of Hercules*, and their hair must be braided into six braids (both these last two features are also part of the attire of a Roman bride). Above all the six Vestals, who are chosen from noble families at between the ages of six to ten by the Chief Pontiff, must be chaste. If a Vestal is proved to have broken her vow of chastity she is immured in a stone tomb with a loaf of bread and a pitcher of water and left to die. It will be remembered, however, that after thirty years of service the Vestals have a choice between a lifetime vow of chastity and going out into the world. Most of them remained Vestals and the Vestals of Rome were respected and had a good deal of political influence.

The People in the Forum

Back in 55 B.C. the Forum is thronged. There are curly-haired Greeks, dark-skinned Africans, swarthy Spaniards, blond, big-limbed Gauls and Germans, black-eyed Syrians, Jews, and the like. There may well be a deputation of linen-robed Egyptians moving to the Senate-House.

Through the mob will stalk the Romans. The ordinary Roman citizen is entitled to a toga, which no foreigner can wear. The Knights have a gold ring and a white tunic with narrow purple stripes. A tunic with broad purple stripes and special shoes mark a Senator. The Romans are very class-conscious.

One sight will surprise us. Every important Roman has a group of slaves attending him. Even Cato, the champion of ancient simplicity, does not go down into the Forum with less than eight slaves. One of these slaves is the *nomenclator* ("name-caller"). His job is to remember the name of each person who is met, and to whisper it in his master's ear. The Roman politician knows that the way to keep popularity is to greet every Marcus, Publius or Lucius by name.

Beside the slaves, there is a swarm of clients, or hangers-on, around every important figure. If we see a man with a toga newly cleaned and chalked stopping to speak to everyone, we know that he is a "candidate" for some office. *Candidatus* means a man wearing a toga *candida*, or gleaming white toga, and this is the way Roman candidates for office dress. Candidates for the consulship usually start campaigning almost a year in advance.

We should not forget the women. Ordinary women stroll around the Forum and the streets at will. The highborn and wealthy ladies ride in litters and sedan-chairs. These are carried by eight slaves. We know that coal-black Nubians are the fashion. In those litters sits a Clodia or Servilia or a Sempronia, bejeweled and with an elaborate coiffure. The women of the upper class are by now completely emancipated. By a legal trick they can be freed of guardianship to own their own property. Clodia, whom Cicero accused in 56 B.C. of poisoning her husband, Metellus Celer, is immensely rich. She has a villa for swimming parties and the like on the right bank of the Tiber, and another villa at Baiae, which is the Miami Beach or the Riviera of ancient Rome. She also owns a palace on the *Nova Via* (New Street) on the Palatine Hill overlooking the Forum. Across from her home is the house of Cicero, her enemy. He paid, as has been mentioned, the equivalent of over $175,000 for it. Down the street, Clodia's brother, Clodius, has one valued at $740,000.

Great ladies such as Clodia, Servilia, the mistress of Caesar, and Fulvia, the wife of Clodius (and later of Mark Antony), hold elaborate salons and influence politics. The marriages of the upper classes are, very often, political alliances. Such was the marriage of Caesar to Calpurnia and of Julia, Caesar's daughter, to Pompey.

A Roman Marriage

A Roman girl was usually married at from 14 to 15 years of age, a man at 16 to 18. Marriage, as in Athens, was arranged by the parents. The ceremony took place at the home of the bride. At the end of it, there was a wedding-procession to her new home.

If we are fortunate while we are in Rome in 55 B.C., we will see such a procession. It takes place at dusk. A boy dressed as a cupid comes first, carrying a torch of whitethorn. Then we see the bride, her robes covered by a flame-colored veil, with two boys holding her by the hands. Behind follows the wedding party, laughing and joking with the bystanders who line the streets. There is a choir singing the wedding-song. Last comes the bridegroom, scattering nuts to the on-lookers.

At the bridegroom's home, the bride winds the doorposts with wool and smears the door with oil and fat (symbolic of prosperity and fertility.) In the big reception hall she is met by the bridegroom, who presents her with symbolic fire and water. Then the bride lights the hearth with the whitethorn torch and flings the torch, like the modern bouquet of flowers, to the guests. Finally, after she has been got ready for bed by the Matron of Honor, the balance of the wedding-song, the *epithalamium*, is sung outside the marriage-chamber.

After such an elaborate ceremony, it seems anti-climatic to mention that divorce is easy—easier than in the United States today. All the husband has to do is to say: "Go home" three times and he is divorced. By 55 B.C. divorce is almost as easy for a woman.

Homes, Tenements, and Palaces

And what of the homes? Those in the excavated city of Pompeii are middle-class houses in a small town of 20,000 people. Yet they are quite luxurious. In front is a reception room (atrium from *ater* "black" because in early days the cooking was done here), with a hole in the roof (*compluvium*) beneath which is an *impluvium*, or pool, to catch the rain-water. The floor is covered with patterned marble. At the sides are salons. At the back, separated by curtains and a step up from the *atrium* is a special reception-room which used to be the master's bed-room (*tablinum*). The ceiling of this part of the house is paneled with beams. Behind the *tablinum* is a garden surrounded by a pillared colonnade and by rooms. Furnishings are not too crowded—candelabra, chests, chairs, benches, rugs, tapestries, bedsteads, tables, sideboards, and statues. In one Pompeian house a set of silverware of 119 pieces was found. There is, by the way, excellent plumbing.

This is the Pompeian house of which a few examples were probably to be found in Rome. The mass of the people, however, as can be proved from literature and from the excavations at Ostia, the port of Rome, lived in huge apartment blocks. Some of these were four stories high, grouped like modern apartments around a central court. Most of them were tenements reaching as high as 70 feet. If we, in our 55 B.C. Roman excursion, walk down by the docks or in the poorer quarters around the Meat Market or off the Suburra, (a section near the Forum) we will find narrow, twisting alleys, stinking with garbage and offal, low taverns and dens, and whole families packed into single rooms or living in nooks and holes just off the street.

No sensible person goes into these unlit lanes after dark. There are "muggers", pickpockets, dozens of people who will murder you for the equivalent of a dollar. There is no proper police. The aediles are supposed to keep the streets clean but no one bothers. For here is where the city-mob huddles, the people on the dole. Cicero called them the "blood-suckers of the treasury." When Caesar counted them he found 320,000 people in Rome alone on the list for free grain. They have nothing to hope for, except a free feed or a big spectacle given by a magistrate who wants to buy their votes. The slums of New York or Chicago or London or any big modern city show us the same kind of problem.

But there is a contrast. Suppose we go up the ramp of the Palatine to the palaces on top of it. There are door-keepers here. If we get by one of them, we are in a lofty atrium with salons furnished so extravagantly that any one object is worth a small fortune. Cicero, a man of moderate means, spent $25,000 for one table of citrus-wood. Two ornamented gold cups were sold for $60,000. Behind are more rooms and spacious gardens with porticoes, arbors, summer-houses, fish-ponds, priceless statues, every luxury that money can buy. Caesar paid $100,000 for two paintings from Byzantium, and the brother of Lucullus $600,000 for one statue of Apollo.

The wealth of these Roman nobles is not to be out-matched until North America reaches its peak of luxury. Cicero, as we have noted, was not regarded as rich. Yet, in addition to his $175,000 house on the Palatine, he owned six villas, scattered from Tibur and Arpinum in the hills to the seashore at Formiae and Cumae. One letter tells of him having a special slave to put his library in order. Another refers to the purchase of Greek sculpture to decorate a library in his villa at Tibur.

Other Republican Romans far surpassed Cicero. Aemilius Scaurus, for example, had a villa at Tusculum valued at $1,500,000. We have mentioned the gardens of Lucullus on the Pincian Hill just to the north of ancient Rome. These and the gardens of the historian, Sallust, occupied part of the area over which the Borghese gardens now spread. Here were walks, race-courses, summer-houses, dining-rooms. Lucullus used to boast that he could provide a meal immediately for anyone, by simply telling a slave what room it was to be in.

Roman Food

What did the Romans eat? If we omit the banquets of the rich, the average Roman, like Cicero, began the day with a bit of bread and a glass of wine. For lunch he had bread, eggs or meat, a vegetable salad, and fruit.

At night there was the *cena* or dinner. First, there were hors-d'oeuvres (eggs, salt fish, lettuce, radishes) with wine, then the main meal of several courses—often a dish of mullet, then one of chicken or meat or wild boar, and one of vegetables. Dessert was a choice of pastries, apples, and other fruits, nuts, cheese and, as with the main course, wine. The average Roman ate better than the Greek. As for the poor people, they gobbled down whatever they could get. Sausages were a favorite food. Their wine was cheap and harsh. They often wolfed down what we regard as offal. And, of course, there was the free grain once a month from the state; hence there were varieties of foods made from flour. Porridge was a staple.

The Slaves

If in 55 B.C. we are lucky enough to get into a Roman palace, we will note slaves everywhere. There are so many that they are divided into classes, each with its own occupation. Thus, there is one class which does nothing but cook, another of which the sole task is to wait on table, another which is composed of litter-bearers, another of sweepers. Each class is broken up into *decuriones*, that is, into groups of ten.

On the whole the condition of these house slaves is not too bad. Any one of them, however, man or woman, may be flogged, tortured, sent to pull round the mill for crushing grain or put to death at the whim of the master or mistress. On the plantation-farms, as has been mentioned, they were treated like animals. The total number of slaves in Italy at this period is estimated at 4,000,000.

There is another side to this picture. Some slaves became the advisers of their masters. Many were freed. When freed they took the first two names of their former master. For example, Tiro, the confidential slave of Marcus Tullius Cicero was freed and became Marcus Tullius Tiro. The son of a freedman could become a Roman citizen. Greek freedmen in particular, were likely to become influential persons because of their education and ability.

Books

The name "Tiro" brings us to the question of books. Tiro had invented a shorthand, called *notae Tironianae*, to take down his master's speeches. One of Cicero's friends, Atticus, was a publisher as well as a business-man. His method was to have a slave read aloud a copy of one of Cicero's speeches or other works to a room of hundred trained copyists. If he had a dozen or a score of these rooms, an edition could be got out in a hurry. Cicero, for instance, in June of 60 B.C., wrote to Atticus about a work he had written in Greek about his own consulship. "If you like the book, see that it is to be had at Athens and the other cities of Greece", he said.

The copyists were all taught the same kind of writing, called a *bookhand*. The reading of the various bookhands used in Roman works is part of a study called *Paleography* (*palaios*—"old" and *graphe*—"writing"). The bookhands gave us the forms of our printed letters. Books were usually written on papyrus and sold in rolls, called *volumina*. Expensive editions were put on parchment (made from hides) which is said to have been invented in Pergamum. Because papyrus did not survive, except in Egypt and in the buried city of Herculaneum, although parchment did, only a small percentage of what the Greeks and Romans wrote has come down to us. We have only two Roman novels left, for instance—yet the Romans must have written and read many works of this kind.

In Rome the booksellers lived chiefly on the Argiletum, a street leading out of the Forum. In Horace's time, a quarter of a century after this, his publishers, the Sosii Brothers, used to put up banners when a new book was ready. If in 55 B.C. we walk along the Argiletum, we will see rolls stacked on shelves or in round receptacles called *capsae*. In either case, a rectangular tab with the name of the author and his work is attached by a string to the end of the roll, so that we can decide what book we want without opening the roll.

Roman Education in the Time of Cicero

At first, Roman education was at home, with tutors when necessary. When the Greeks took over education, private schools were established. In the primary school, the three R's were taught, with, as Horace tells us, much use of the cane. "A boy's ears are on his back," was an Egyptian, Greek, and Roman maxim.

In the secondary school, Greek language and literature was taught first and Latin language and literature second. The third school, as its name (*Ludus rhetoricus*) implies, was to teach people how to speak. One device was the *suasoria*, in which a student persuaded someone either to do or not to do something. In later days, whether or not Julius Caesar ought to cross the Rubicon became a favorite subject. Another method of teaching was a set debate, the *controversia*.

Comparatively few people went beyond this stage. Those who did studied either at Athens or at Rhodes where Molo was a famous professor of rhetoric. He taught both Caesar and Cicero. Philosophy was an integral part of the course because an orator was supposed to be "a good man skilled in speaking." Later, Cicero sent his son to Athens, with an allowance worth at least $4000 a year, and was worried because the young man did not study!

Except for the poverty-stricken and the unemployed, the average Roman usually received at least a primary education.

Occupations and Religions

We have not looked at the docks and granaries along the Tiber under the Aventine Hill, or at the boats and barges loading and unloading, or at the race-courses or at Pompey's new theater in the Field of Mars, outside the walls. Nor have we watched the brickmakers near the Janiculum Hill, or the young men swimming in the Tiber, or fencing and running and wrestling in the Field of Mars. We have not explored the streets of tiny shops, taverns, and small-shop industries. These last, as in Athens, are usually on the same street. There are the potters, scythe-makers, jewelers and the like, but much of the work is done by slaves. Incidentally, at this time mass-produced red-glazed ware was manufac-tured at Arretium in Etruria and glass-blowing had been introduced. There is no space, either, to do more than mention the temples and the varying rituals of Roman religion. The state religion is still the old Roman worship of Jupiter, Juno, and their attendant deities as modified by Greek influence. But by 55 B.C. almost every religion is beginning to get a footing in Rome. There is a synagogue for Jews. The temple of the Great Mother from Asia Minor stands on the Palatine Hill. Pompey's soldiers have brought back the worship of the Persian god, Mithras, from the East. The cult of Isis-Osiris from Egypt is already popular. Alongside the new religions the two Hellenistic philosophies of Stoicism and Epicureanism are strongly entrenched.

We ought, also, to have noted the host of scribes, accountants and officials required to handle the business of the empire. If, in spite of these omissions, you have received the impression that Rome of 55 B.C. was a lusty, teeming, cosmopolitan city, one in which almost unbelievable luxury rubbed shoulders with abject poverty, and one in which a host of slaves was the dark base to the public magnificence, then the excursion into 55 B.C. has given you some notion of the Rome of the last days of the Republic. Above all, we must always recall that at that time the Romans did not know what was going to happen, any more than we of today can predict next year—or ten years from now. Most Romans had no suspicion that the Republic was tottering to its fall.

Literature

No account of the period from 70 to 44 B.C. would be complete without a reference to its literature. In poetry the great names are Lucretius and Catullus. Lucretius (95–55 B.C.) wrote a long epic "On The Nature of Things" to expound Epicurean philosophy. He is the greatest of the philosophic poets.

Catullus (c. 84–54 B.C.) on the other hand, is the most passionate of

Roman lyricists. He was born at Verona in Cisalpine Gaul, the son of a prominent citizen who later entertained Caesar. He came to Rome probably in 62 B.C. Here he met "Lesbia". "Lesbia", as has been mentioned, is almost certainly Clodia, the beautiful patrician sister of the politician, Publius Clodius. His love affair with Lesbia and the agony which followed produced verses which show intense happiness and equally unrestrained jealousy and bitterness. He also wrote longer poems in the Hellenistic style. Along with these are a medley of short pieces which body forth Catullus' own feelings, and are often vivid vignettes of the life of Rome. The gay girls of "Pompey's portico", a purse "full of cobwebs", a rebuke to a friend who stole napkins at dinner, a tender poem on seeing his brother's grave in the Troad, a poem of delight at returning to his villa at Sirmio on turquoise-colored Lago di Garda (then called *Lacus Benacus*)—these are among the poems which influenced French and English poets. We should note, too, that he was the head of a literary circle which continued to write verses after his death. These were the men whom Cicero called the "men with little beards" (*barbatuli*) and the "new-fangled poets" (*neoterici*).

Prose, however, outstripped poetry. Caesar wrote his Gallic Commentaries and later his Civil War in beautifully phrased Latin. Sallust (86–35 B.C.) published historical monographs, notably on the Jugurthine War and the Catilinian Conspiracy. Biography was represented by Cornelius Nepos, to whom Catullus dedicated his book of verse. A man who ventured into almost every field of literature was Terentius Varro (116–27 B.C.).

The master of prose was Cicero. Whatever we may think of his politics, the fifty-seven orations of his which we have make him the most notable figure in Latin prose. His philosophical works are also important. Most interesting of all, perhaps, are his *Letters*.

Cicero was an inveterate letter-writer, particularly to his friend Atticus. He put down the news of the day and what he himself thought and felt without inhibition. As a result we have an intimate view of Cicero himself and likewise a sort of backstairs, day by day history of Rome. If we wish to achieve a thorough insight into the life of the Rome of that day, we read the *Letters of Cicero*.

The Death-Throes of the Republic: 44–31 B.C.

From the chaos after Caesar's death there finally emerged not the restoration of the Republic, as for a time Cicero hoped, but the Second Triumvirate. This was formed in November of 43 B.C. by Mark Antony, Octavianus, the great-nephew and adopted son of Caesar, who was not yet twenty years of age, and a nonentity, Lepidus.

The triumvirs took over on January 1st, 42 B.C. Then, emulating Sulla, they issued proscriptions. Three hundred senators and two thousand Knights were slaughtered and their estates confiscated to fill the treasury of the triumvirs. Among those sacrificed was Cicero. The old orator, now over sixty, had attacked Antony in a series of bitter speeches. He met death with fortitude. His severed hands and head were taken to Antony. It is said that Antony's wife thrust a golden bodkin through Cicero's tongue.

Although we may deplore Cicero's vanity and political vacillation, we must still accord him a sincere love for the Republic and a never-ceasing attempt to preserve an institution which was already too deeply rotted to survive. At the great moments of his life he showed courage—and he was, above all, as Caesar recognized, a genius with words.

Antony and Octavianus now moved to crush the two leading assassins of Caesar, Brutus and Cassius. After the battle of Philippi in Macedonia (42 B.C.), both Brutus and Cassius committed suicide. Antony took the East and Gaul and Octavianus took Italy and Spain. Lepidus was shifted to Africa, but he was soon written off. There was civil war in Italy and a naval struggle with the son of Pompey, Sextus Pompeius. Finally Octavianus added both Gaul and Africa to his share of the world. The eastern and the western halves of the Roman world were now arrayed against each other.

And, meanwhile, Antony had met Cleopatra. She fascinated him just as she had enthralled Caesar. It is probable that Cleopatra's every move was directed toward saving Egypt. Antony, a blunt, objective man, reckless, Herculean, a good soldier but intensely physical in his excesses, was no match for her subtleties. The final result was the naval battle of Actium (31 B.C.) off the coast of Greece. When Cleopatra's Egyptian contingent left the battle, Antony followed her.

Octavianus pursued them to Egypt. When they both committed suicide, he was, at last, sole master of the Roman world. After careful reorganization of the Near East, he returned to Rome. There, on January 13th, 27 B.C. he formally laid down his extraordinary powers and, just as formally, received them back again. Three days later, he was honored with the title of Augustus (one to be revered) from which the name of our month, August, comes. Although January 13th, 27 B.C. is the beginning of Augustus' formal principate, his rule really dates from the battle of Actium in 31 B.C.

Readings from Sources of the Period

(a) One of the most passionate and individualistic of the Roman poets was Catullus (84–54? B.C.) of Verona who, coming to Rome, fell in love with "Lesbia" who was almost certainly, Clodia, the sister of the politician and gang-leader, Clodius.

AN INVITATION TO DINNER

If the gods will, Fabullus mine,
With me right heartily you'll dine.
Bring but good cheer—that chance is thine
    Some days hereafter;
Mind, a fair girl too, wit, and wine,
    And merry laughter.

Bring these—you'll feast on kingly fare;
But bring them—for my purse—I swear
The spiders have been weaving there;
    But thee I'll favor
With a pure love, or what's more rare,
    More sweet of savor,

An unguent I'll before you lay
The Loves and Graces t'other day
Gave to my girl—smell it—you'll pray
    The gods, Fabullus,
To make you turn all nose straightway.
    Yours aye, Catullus.

(Guinagh and Dorjahn, *op. cit.,* pp. 288–289, translated by James Cranstoun.)

TO LESBIA

Equal to Jove that youth must be—
Greater than Jove he seems to me—
Who, free from Jealousy's alarms,
Securely views thy matchless charms.
That cheek, which ever dimpling glows,
That mouth, from whence such music flows.
To him, alike, are always known,
Reserved for him, and him alone.
Ah! Lesbia, though 'tis death to me,
I cannot choose but look on thee;
But, at the sight, my senses fly;
I needs must gaze, but, gazing die;
Whilst trembling with a thousand fears,
Parched to the throat my tongue adheres,
My pulse beats quick, my breath heaves short,
My limbs deny their slight support,
Cold dews my pallid face o'erspread,
With deadly languor droops my head,

My ears with tingling echoes ring,
And life itself is on the wing;
My eyes refuse the cheering light,
Their orbs are veiled in starless night;
Such pangs my nature sinks beneath,
And feels a temporary death.

(*Ibid.*, pp. 291–292 translated by Lord Byron.)

I LOATHE AND LOVE

I loathe and love, but why I cannot tell.
I simply feel that way and suffer hell.

(*Ibid.*, p. 305 translated by Kevin Guinagh.)

(b) Cicero in addition to his orations and his letters, wrote on Philosophy and Rhetoric. From his *De Officiis* (*Moral Duties*) to his son Marcus two extracts are taken to illustrate the thinking of an educated Roman of the 1st Century B.C.

I   The distinguishing property of man is to search for and to follow after truth. Therefore, when relaxed from our necessary cares and concerns, we then covet to see, to hear, and to learn somewhat; and we esteem knowledge of things either obscure or wonderful to be the indispensable means of living happily. From this we understand that truth, simplicity, and candor, are most agreeable to the nature of mankind. To this passion for discovering truth is added a desire to direct; for a mind well formed by nature is unwilling to obey any man but him who lays down rules and instructions to it or who, for the general advantage, exercises equitable and lawful government. From this proceeds loftiness of mind and contempt for worldly interests.

II   We ought, likewise, to take care that the punishment be proportioned to the offence, and that some be not punished for doing things for which others are not so much as called to account. Above all things, in punishing we ought to guard against passion, for the man who is to pronounce a sentence of punishment in a passion, never can preserve that mean between what is too much and too little, which is so justly recommended by the Peripatetics, did they not too much commend the passion of anger, by asserting it to be a useful property of our nature. For my part, I think that it ought to be checked under all circumstances; and it were to be wished that they who preside in government were like the laws, which in punishing are not directed by resentments but by equity. . .

(*Ibid.*, p. 258 and p. 271, translated by Cyrus Edmond.)

CHAPTER 9

The First Two Centuries of the Empire:
31 B.C.–180 A.D.

The Romans were fortunate. If, during the death-throes of the Republic, there had been any other civilized power capable of attacking Rome, or if the Germans had been advanced enough to pour across the frontiers, the Roman grip on the West and the Near East would probably have been shattered. As it was Rome had a second flowering. The Republic, except in theory, was finished. Now the Empire rose from its shattered trunk. The second founder of Rome was Octavianus, now known as Augustus Caesar.

The Rule of Augustus: 31 B.C.–14 A.D.

The portrait statues of Augustus show us a man with pinched lips and a calculating face. When battle came, Augustus was usually ill in his tent. But in handling the jealous nobles of Rome he was a better statesman than his uncle, Julius Caesar. He knew that after the terrible ordeal of civil wars from 49 to 31 B.C. Italy and the whole Roman world wanted peace at any price, yet he carefully avoided titles such as Dictator or King which might offend the Roman people. Instead, he maintained the fiction that he was not a king or dictator but simply the first citizen of the Republic, the *princeps civitatis*, usually shortened to *princeps* from which our words, "principate" and "prince" come.

The consuls and other magistrates were still elected, though Augustus presented a "slate" from which they were chosen. The powers of the Assemblies were carefully controlled but the Senate still met and debated. Everyone knew, however, who had the power.

In addition to *Augustus* and *Princeps*, the new ruler kept the titles of *Imperator* (from which is derived "emperor"), and Caesar (which now

The Roman Legion Under Augustus

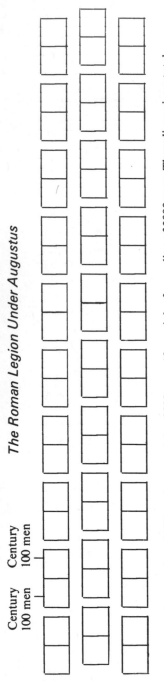

Century
100 men

Century
100 men

Century
100 men

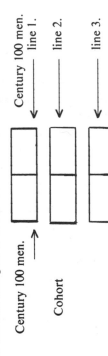

Century 100 men.

line 1.

line 2.

line 3.

Cohort

1. 2 centuries of 100 make a maniple of 200 men. 10 maniples form a line of 2000 men. Three lines give a total strength of 6000 infantry.

2. The legion also from the time of Marius was divided into 10 cohorts, vertically, that is each cohort was made up of a maniple from each of the three lines. The Augustan cohort, which could act independently, consisted, when it was full strength, of 600 men.

3. The defensive armour of the legionary consisted of a crested helmet, a leather corselet reinforced with plates of metal, a metal greave on his right leg from knee to ankle and an oblong shield about 4 feet by $2\frac{1}{2}$, of two thicknesses of wood, one of canvas and one of leather. A rim of iron edged the shield at top and bottom and there was a dome-like projection (a boss) at the centre.

   His offensive weapons were the *pilum* (a javelin for throwing with a long iron head) and a straight, two-edged sword, about three feet long, with which he was taught to thrust rather than cut.

4. The Romans by the time of Julius Caesar had developed "artillery", which used the torsion of heavy gut or cords as the propelling force. The *ballista* hurled a stone ball of 50 to 100 pounds weight from 500 to 1000 feet; the onager, a lighter piece, flung smaller stones; the *catapulta* fired either an immense arrow or flights of spears. In addition, there was the battering-ram for breaching walls.

became the regular designation of those who held the Empire). Meanwhile, the twin pillars of Augustus' dominance were the proconsular power (*imperium proconsulare*), which was in his case by law superior (*maius*) to that of all provincial governors and military commanders, and the tribunician power, which from 23 B.C. was made perpetual. The first of these pillars gave Augustus the supreme command over all the armed forces, the second the power to veto any legislation but also to bring in laws. Likewise he was the head of the Senate and after 12 B.C. Chief Pontiff.

All these powers, like those which Mussolini held in Italy, were technically constitutional, since they had been bestowed by vote of the Senate and the people. The control of the army, however, assured that no one could attack Augustus. In Rome itself he had 7000 police and just outside the city was his own personal bodyguard of 9000 Praetorian troops. The fiction of a double rule by the Senate and Augustus was carefully maintained. The "safe" provinces were under the control of the Senate, although the abuses of Republican days were corrected. Their revenues went into the republican treasury, called the *aerarium*. The provinces on the frontiers were governed by appointees of Augustus, and their revenues went into his treasury, called the *fiscus* (from which words like "fiscal" come).

During his reign, too, "Caesar-worship" began. Julius Caesar had been deified as the "Divine Julius" and one of Augustus' designations was "the Son of the deified Julius." In the Hellenistic East, where, as we have seen, Pompey and Flamininus, and other Roman generals, had received divine honors, and where the practice of deifying rulers was common, dating back to the Pharaohs of Egypt, Augustus was worshipped as a god during his lifetime. In Italy and the West, the *genius* of Augustus (the second self which, it will be recalled, was supposed to accompany a man throughout his life) was worshipped, and "colleges" of freedmen, the *Seviri* (six-men) *Augustales*, were formed to carry on this cult. After his death, Augustus was deified, a practice followed for many of the Caesars. In the Rome of today, one can sit at a restaurant and gaze at the huge mausoleum he built for himself and his family and descendants.

Augustan Policies

Augustus reorganized the whole empire. In Italy, he tried to get people back on the land and to reform morals by reviving the old Roman religion. When this attempt failed, he enacted laws to penalize bachelorhood, to encourage large families, and to punish adulterers. Augustus himself was married to a beautiful and strong-minded woman, Livia, whom he had taken from her husband while she was pregnant. A victim of his law about adultery was his own daughter, Julia, and later her daughter, another Julia.

In foreign affairs he extended the Roman frontier in the north to the Rhine and the Danube. An attempt to conquer Germany as far as the Elbe was frustrated when, in 9 A.D., the Germans annihilated 20,000 legionaries in the Teutoberg forest.

The greatest achievements of Augustus were to bring peace to the Roman world and to establish efficient administration in the provinces. Revenues poured in, trade boomed, and the whole empire became a paradise for the business-man. With a sigh of relief the Romans abandoned political freedom for security and prosperity. Yet the new government he founded possessed two inherent weaknesses: it depended ultimately on the control of the army and on the character of the rulers. A third problem was the determination of the succession to the purple (the distinguishing garment of the Caesars). Augustus himself had no sons and only one daughter, Julia, who was married first to Marcus Agrippa, Augustus' chief minister, and then after his death to Tiberius, his stepson, in the hope of providing heirs. But, by some unlucky fate, all possible heirs to the throne perished in one way or another (Roman writers hinted that Livia, Augustus' wife, was responsible, but this was probably a canard) until only Tiberius, Livia's son, was left. It was not, therefore, a Caesar but a Claudian (Livia had been married to Tiberius Claudius before Augustus took her from her husband) who succeeded to the rule of the empire. In this respect Augustus must have died as a somewhat disappointed man. But he was "the second founder of Rome."

It was during the reign of Augustus that another "king" was born who was to influence Western civilization more than all the Caesars. This was Jesus Christ. The year of his birth is uncertain, since the usually accepted date was not worked out until the 6th century A.D. by an abbot, Dionysius Exiguus. Today the data proves that Christ was born between 7 and 4 B.C. by our chronology.

Art and Literature in the Augustan Period

Architecture bloomed under Augustus. Temples and public buildings burgeoned in Rome, including the temples to the Divine Julius (in the Forum), to Apollo on the Palatine, in part to house a collection of Sibylline oracles, to Mars the Avenger, in a new Forum which Augustus built, and the Pantheon. Marble now became common building material and Augustus himself boasted that he "had found Rome of brick and left it of marble."

In sculpture the general trend was to imitate the Greeks except that the Romans were inclined to emphasize the vacuous and the colossal. In portrait sculpture, however, and in the representation of animals, the Romans were realistic and excellent, and the bas-reliefs in the panels of the Altar of Peace (*Ara Pacis*) are unexcelled.

Meanwhile, literature knew a Second Golden Age, in which poetry surpassed prose. The only outstanding prose writer was Livy (59 B.C.–17 A.D.) from Patavium (Padua) who wrote a monumental History of Rome in 142 books. His style is compact and epigrammatic and, like the Greek historian, Thucydides, he introduced many speeches so as to achieve telling dramatic effects. As a historian he made uncritical use of his sources and wrote with an ethical purpose, namely to prove that Roman greatness came from the old virtues of the early Republican period but had been vitiated by the luxuries and vices of his own day. As a result his account is often biased, but the parts of his work which remain are valuable as information.

Among the poets, Vergil (70–19 B.C.) from Andes near Mantua reigns supreme. His *Eclogues* are chiefly charming imitations of Theocritus, but his *Georgics*, though based partly on the Greek poet Hesiod, breathe a patriotic love of the Italian countryside. His great work was his national epic, the *Aeneid*. Although the first six books correspond to Homer's *Odyssey* and the last six to the *Iliad*, the chief objective is to show the fated and heroic destiny of Rome from the burning of Troy and the landing of Aeneas in Italy to its rise to a great world power and its second founding by Augustus. The poem is, from one point of view, a superb piece of propaganda for Augustus; from another it is a masterpiece of dramatic construction; and from a third it is superb poetry infused with a glowing patriotism.

Second only to Vergil as a poet was Horace (65–8 B.C.), the son of a freedman of Venusia in South Italy, who found the money to send his son to the best schools in Rome and then to Athens for a university education. Horace fought at Philippi on the side of Brutus and Cassius. On his return to Rome he was fortunate enough to be introduced by Vergil to Maecenas, the "home" minister of Augustus, who became the patron of both of them and gave Horace his "Sabine" farm.

Horace wrote charming *Satires* and *Epistles*, in which we get vivid glimpses of the daily life of Rome. His artistic masterpiece was his *Odes* in four books. Perfect in form, they preach the "Golden Mean", "Avoid Excess", and "Gather Ye Flowers While Ye May", although a few of them are strongly patriotic. Few authors have produced more quotable phrases.

A somewhat different strain appears in the Roman love elegy. The Romans claimed that the subjective love-elegy was, like satire, original with them but the metre is Greek and probably, too, the initial inspiration. The founder of the genre was said to be Cornelius Gallus, for whom Vergil

composed an artificial pastoral in Eclogue 10 and who as Augustus' first
prefect of Egypt in 27 B.C., on being reproved for assuming too much
adultation and power for himself, committed suicide. His elegies are
lost but we have those of Tibullus, Propertius, and Ovid. The love-elegies
are always addressed to some woman whose true name is concealed,
following the convention introduced by Catullus when he addressed
Clodia as Lesbia. The major theme is that love is the only important thing
in life. In the battles of love, every lover is a soldier. Sometimes, as in the
Greek epigram, the lover is locked out. Though at times there is the
ecstasy of fulfilment, storms of jealousy are frequent.

Although following the same general pattern, the three elegists differ.
Tibullus (54?–19 B.C.) presents us with a pervasive note of melancholy,
and he also wrote charmingly about the peace and joy of a rustic life.
His sixteen elegies in two books were addressed to two demi-mondaines,
named Delia and Nemesis by him. Propertius (c. 50–15 B.C.) a Roman
Knight from Assisi, was essentially an Alexandrine, wrapping his thoughts
in recondite allusions and using a compact, abrupt, yet brilliant style.
To judge from his three books of elegies to Cynthia, his feelings were
intense. In his fourth book he veers from the love elegy to Roman
antiquities and to vividly patriotic poetry in praise of Augustus. Ovid
(43 B.C.–17 A.D.), from Sulmo in the Abruzzi, in his love-elegies to
Corinna (three books of *Amores*) is sophisticated, witty, sportive, and
sensual. He uses the stock themes of Tibullus and Propertius but his
poems are exquisite miniatures in which he seems to be smiling at the
whole business of love.

Ovid's love elegies were only part of an enormous production. Well-
educated and widely travelled, he belonged to the smartest set of the
Roman court which included the two Julias (the daughter and grand-
daughter of Augustus). He wrote the *Art of Love*, a sophisticated and
explicit manual of seduction in three books, and the *Cure for Love* in one.
He composed a work on cosmetics. In his *Heroides* which purported to be
letters from famous women to their lovers, such as one from Dido to
Aeneas after his desertion of her, he exhibits a clever knowledge of
feminine psychology. More serious and entirely Roman in spirit are his
six books of *Fasti* which give us valuable information about Roman
religious festivals. Unfortunately the six other books of *Fasti* were not
completed because of his exile in 8 A.D. by Augustus for some unknown
reason (probably because of a scandal involving the younger Julia) to
barbarous Tomi (modern Costanza) on the Black Sea, where he lived until
his death. From this gloomy outpost of civilization he sent to Rome his
Tristia (sorrows) and *Epistles from Pontus*, complaining of his lot.

His crowning work was his fifteen books of *Metamorphoses*, completed before his exile and in chagrin flung into the fire by him but saved in copies. In the *Metamorphoses* (bodies transmuted into new forms) he transforms Greek myths such as the story of Apollo and Daphne into pretty stories which have no real depth of feeling but are charmingly done. Ovid was the last Roman imitator of Alexandrine models, but also in epigrammatic quality, polish, and poetic imagery he was the precursor of the Silver Latin of the First Century A.D. His impact on European literature was important, particularly through his *Metamorphoses*. To give one example only, in Shakespeare's *Midsummer Night's Dream*, the story of Pyramus and Thisbe is from the *Metamorphoses*.

The Julio-Claudians: 14–68 A.D.*

When Augustus was dying at Nola near Naples in 14 on August 19, he is said to have quoted from a Greek drama to the people around his death-bed "Have I played my part well? Then, applaud and take me off the stage." The transition to the rule of Tiberius (14–37) was accomplished smoothly, but Augustus' step-son began his reign with the murder of a posthumous son of Agrippa and Julia. A taciturn and embittered man (he had been forced to divorce a wife he loved to marry Julia when Agrippa died and had been in self-imposed exile at Rhodes for nine years) he strove at first to maintain the double rule of the Senate and the Emperor (known as the Dyarchy). Later in his life, when under the influence of Sejanus, an ambitious Knight, he retired to the island of Capri off Naples and let his favorite rule. Sejanus used his power cunningly to get heirs to the throne murdered or executed with the objective of securing the purple for himself. When at last Tiberius realized the designs of Sejanus, he took a vicious revenge on him and his family. Then, in a ferocity of despair, he resolved to eradicate certain suspicious persons. For this purpose he used the law of treason which included all offenses against the dignity of the state and, therefore, against the dignity of the emperor, and he employed informers (*delatores*), who were allowed to prosecute anyone they wished for a reward (customarily one-fourth of the property of an accused if he were convicted). The Roman historian, Tacitus, speaks of this period as a reign of terror, but the actual number of deaths (only twelve of those accused of treason were executed) suggests a somewhat vicious tyranny. It was enough, however, in the hands of Tacitus to blacken Tiberius' character.

In administration Tiberius was excellent. The treasury was filled, the empire governed efficiently, and the expansion into Germany was not allowed to be a danger. When he died in 37, however, there was a sigh of relief at the accession of his grand-nephew, Caligula (Little Boots), a young man of twenty-five.

* (All dates henceforward A.D. except when noted.)

Caligula (37–41 A.D.), although at first he seemed to rule wisely, turned out to be a madman. He claimed deification for himself, built a bridge between the Palatine and the Capitoline so that he could confer with "his brother, Jupiter", and lived in incest with his sisters. Among other excesses he had huge pleasure-boats built, equipped with baths, colonnades and banquet-halls. Two of these were dredged up in recent years at Lake Nemi near Rome but were, unfortunately, destroyed during World War II. His favorite horse, Incitatus ("Speedy"), was given a stall of marble, a manger of ivory and a jeweled collar. At long last Caligula proved to be too much, even for the Romans. In January of 41 he, his wife, and his daughter were struck down by praetorian officers.

The praetorians now elevated Claudius, uncle of Caligula and the supposed "dim-wit" of the Julio-Claudian family, to the purple (41–54). He was a man with a wobbly head, an ungainly form and a stuttering tongue, who had been kept in the background or laughed at as a buffoon but who, under the teaching of Livy and of Greek scientists and scholars, had become a philologist and antiquarian, his lost work on the Etruscans being highly regarded in his day. Curiously enough, or, perhaps not so strangely, once he donned the purple, he turned out to be a good administrator. The treasury was refilled, and the imperial civil service, which Augustus had instituted, was strengthened, although Greek freedmen now predominated instead of Knights.

These Greek freedmen, selected by Claudius himself just as the President of the United States appoints his advisers, in effect formed the cabinet. Narcissus, for example, was his Secretary of State, Callistus the head of the Justice Department, and Pallas the head of the Treasury Department. In consequence, although Claudius treated the Senate with deference, its powers were lessened and the government of the provinces was centralized. The increase in available revenue meant an extensive program of public works, including new highways throughout the empire, a canal between the Meuse and the Rhine, the eleven-year task of draining the Fucine Lake near Rome, using 30,000 men, and the development of Ostia as the port of Rome. In foreign affairs Claudius' chief accomplishment was the conquest of a large part of Britain, the emperor himself being present for the decisive battle north of the Thames.

All these accomplishments did not enable Claudius to manage his imperial consorts. The first of these, Messalina (his third wife), was notorious for her scandalous conduct. Finally, while Claudius was away at Ostia, she publicly married a handsome young noble, Gaius Silius. His freedmen persuaded Claudius to execute her, although it is reported by Suetonius that shortly afterward he wanted to know where she was. He next married his niece, Agrippina, whose influence on him brought her political power. When Claudius died suddenly, not without a suspicion of poison, Agrippina, aided by Burrus, Prefect of the Praetorian Guard, secured the throne for Nero, her son by a previous husband. Nero was sixteen years old at the time.

Nero (54–68) began his reign with the murder of Messalina's son, Britannicus. Until 61, however, the empire was well governed, chiefly because its administration was left to Burrus, to Nero's tutor, the Stoic philosopher and author, Seneca, and to the well-trained imperial civil service. Agrippina also had strong influence until Nero, weary of her domination, had her murdered in 59, after two earlier attempts failed. Shortly afterward, he had his wife killed so that he could marry the beautiful and ambitious Poppaea who had been wedded to his best friend.

These crimes did not affect the empire. But when in 62 Burrus died and Seneca went into retirement, Nero, whose own interests were in singing, acting, and pleasure (he fancied himself to be the "last word" in these pursuits), blossomed into a capricious despot. His mountebank antics on the stage alienated the upper classes, while his extravagances (such as his Golden House which had in it a triple colonnade a mile long and his thousand chariots drawn by horses shod with silver) emptied the treasury.

Meanwhile in 60 Queen Bouducca (usually Boadicea), angered at the rape of her daughters and at a flogging of herself by the arrogant Romans, led a fierce revolt in Britain which wiped out a legion, captured London, and massacred 70,000 Romans. The rebellion was suppressed.

Then, in 64, after an unusually hot and dry July, a great fire swept Rome, destroying most of ten of the fourteen regions of the city. According to the Roman historian, Tacitus, to dispel rumors that he himself had set the fire (he was said to have "fiddled while Rome burned") Nero put the blame on the Christians and inaugurated a fierce persecution of them. Actually Nero, who was at Antium on the coast, hurried into Rome and did everything possible to alleviate the lot of the homeless. Next in 65 there was the Conspiracy of Piso, involving Knights and Senators. Nero suppressed it savagely and the philosopher, Seneca, his nephew the poet, Lucan, and Nero's former "Arbiter of Elegance", the novelist Petronius, were among those who meekly opened their veins and committed suicide at the emperor's command.

Nero put to death a number of other leading figures and then, foolishly, made a concert tour of Greece, taking with him a host of musicians, a chorus of singers, and guardsmen. His performances before the Greeks as a singer, tragic actor, or charioteer at Olympia, Delphi, Corinth, and elsewhere further alienated the aristocracy of Rome although Nero was gleeful at winning 1808 prizes and trophies from the adulatory but secretly sneering Greeks.

While he was on his grand tour, feeling in the army, which had not been paid, mounted. In 68 there were revolts in Spain and Gaul. The Spanish legions hailed their commander, Galba, a man of 73, as Caesar, and he seduced the Praetorian Guard in Rome to declare for him by a bribe of 80,000 sesterces ($4000) per man. Once the Praetorian Guard had defected, the Senate declared Nero a public enemy. He fled from Rome and committed suicide with the help of a freedman. His last words are said to have been: "What an artist perishes in me!"

In this way ended the rule of the last of those who could claim some sort of descent, adoptive or otherwise, from Julius Caesar. Two evils were evident during their rule—the dependence of government on the character of the ruler and the power of the Praetorian Guard to make and unmake Caesars.

Flavian Absolutism: 69–96

68–69 was the year of the four emperors. Galba failed to pay the Praetorians the money he had promised and was murdered by them. They now proclaimed Otho emperor. Meanwhile, the armies on the Rhine had declared for Vitellius. Otho was defeated at Cremona in North Italy and Vitellius assumed the purple. During his reign of seven months he spent 900,000,000 sesterces ($45,000,000) on dinners alone and proved to be an inept ruler.

The armies in the East had not as yet had their say. They nominated their choice, Vespasian, who had been sent to Judea to crush a revolt of the Jews. Ever since Pompey had captured Jerusalem the Jews had been under various forms of government. Antony, for example, had set up Herod the Great, half-Jew and half-Idumean, as king, and he, ruling until 4 B.C., had rebuilt the temple. In 6 A.D. Judea had been placed under a Roman procurator but had been treated with tact and restraint by Augustus. Later, Claudius had given Judea to a friend, Herod Agrippa (grandson of Herod the Great), to govern as a client king. When this Herod died in 44, Judea was once more under the direct rule of Rome. Religious difficulties sprouted which were intensified by quarrels between different factions of Jews—the Sadducees, Pharisees, and Zealots. The last of these, the "Men of the Dagger", believing in a coming Messiah, engineered a revolt in 66. But by 68 Vespasian had reconquered Palestine and was besieging Jerusalem.

Leaving the siege of Jerusalem to his son Titus, who had as his mistress, Berenice, the sister of Herod Agrippa, Vespasian hurried to Alexandria to cut off Rome's grain supply. While he was still there, the armies on the Danube which had declared for him marched into Italy, defeated Vitellius' forces, again near Cremona, and broke into Rome. Vitellius in turn was killed.

It had now been proved that not only the Praetorian Guard of Rome but the armies on the frontiers could make and unmake emperors. Vespasian, however, (69–79), a shrewd down-to-earth man of almost 70 who had been born into an equestrian family in the Italian town of Reate, knew how to maintain order. Under his administration, revolts were suppressed and imperial finances rehabilitated. Meanwhile, in 70 his son, Titus, stormed Jerusalem after a desperate struggle, slew thousands of Jews, and sold many into slavery. This was another step in the dispersion of the Jewish people, although it must be remembered that by this time there were already large communities of them in Alexandria, Meso-potamia, Cyprus, and elsewhere. In today's Rome, the tourist can walk under the triumphal arch Titus erected to celebrate his victory and see on its inner side a relief showing the spoils from Jerusalem, including the seven-branched candlestick from the Temple.

Vespasian died in 79 with the wry remark: "I think I am turning into a god." As if to turn jest to earnest, he was deified after his death.

The brief reign of his son, Titus, (79–81) was marked by two events. The first of these was the great eruption of Vesuvius, which had been a quiescent volcano throughout the memory of the Romans. Spartacus had encamped on its crater. But in August of 79 its top blew off, and Pompeii was covered under a rain of volcanic ash and pumice-stone to a depth of some 16 feet, Herculaneum by a river of mud 60 feet deep. In this way two museums of Roman life were preserved. It is estimated that 2000 of the 20,000 inhabitants of Pompeii died.

The other event was the opening of the Colosseum which still stands as a massive remnant of ancient Rome. It held 50,000 spectators. There was a holiday for 100 days and 10,000 gladiators fought.

When Titus died suddenly at the age of 42, his brother, Domitian (81–96), had no trouble in securing the throne. As an administrator he was excellent, and it was during his reign that Britain was subjugated as far as the Solway, although campaigns, extending the Roman boundaries in the island, had been carried on under Vespasian and Titus. But in disposition he was autocratic, riding roughshod over the Senate, and later reviving the informers and executions of Tiberius. Opposition to him, as to his Flavian predecessors, was led by the Stoics. Domitian became a cruel and suspicious tyrant and met assassination, the usual fate.

The Five Good Emperors and Benevolent Despotism: 96–180 A.D.

The first emperor after Domitian, Nerva (96–98), was chosen by the Senate and was already aged and ill. Yet he showed initiative in alleviating a farm crisis in Italy by establishing a revolving loan fund to advance money to needy farmers at 5 per cent interest. As the money was repaid it was reloaned. The interest was used for the maintenance and education of orphans, 70 cents a day for boys to the age of 14 and 60 cents a day for girls to the age of 12. As his heir he adopted as his son and co-ruler, Trajan, the governor of Lower Germany.

Trajan (98–117) was to his contemporaries the ideal emperor. He was the first ruler to be born outside of Italy, his birthplace being Spain, although he was of Roman extraction. As a man he was tall, rugged, decisive, a product of the army, who was still in the prime of life. Popular with the Senate, the people, and the army and an excellent administrator who kept close check over finances, he is chiefly remembered for having pushed the empire to its widest extent, particularly by his conquest of the whole of Mesopotamia and of Dacia (modern Rumania). The thousands of Roman colonists who settled in Dacia produced a Latin-speaking people and as a result today's Rumanians use a language descended from Latin. The bas-reliefs on Trajan's column, which still stands in Rome, depict his exploits. In the last year of his life, there was a general revolt of the Jews in Mesopotamia, Cyrene, Egypt, Cyprus, and Palestine. In Cyrene and Cyprus, in particular, the Jews massacred men, women, and children, killing about one-fourth of the population. The final suppression of the revolt had to be left to Trajan's successor, Hadrian.

Hadrian (117–138) also appears to have been born in Spain. A man of refined and artistic tastes, he was likewise a good soldier and administrator. He abandoned Mesopotamia, however, and concentrated on peace. The most serious war in his reign was another revolt of the Palestinian Jews which was put down ruthlessly and resulted in their final dispersion. Hadrian's Wall in Britain is a memorial of him and so are the ruins of his tremendous villa at Tivoli near Rome, which covered 120 acres.

In administration, he is noted for taking over the finances of many of the cities by sending in his own officials, by magnificent donations to municipalities, towns, cities, and provinces, and by the use of Knights instead of Greek freedmen in his cabinet, a practice begun under Vespasian and intensified by Trajan. One great weakness in his policies was, as we shall see later, his putting a "defence mentality" into the army. He was succeeded by his adopted son, Aurelius Antoninus Pius (138–161). Handsome and eloquent, Antoninus received an empire that was at peace and kept it so, but he made the error of slackening military preparedness.

When Antoninus died, his heir, the "Philosopher-King" Marcus Aurelius, put on the purple. A practising Stoic of noble character and an author whose "Meditations", written in Greek, repay reading, he was a gentle lover of peace, who was compelled to spend most of his life in hard fighting to keep the frontiers intact against the Parthians and against the Germanic tribes along the Danube, who at one time broke through as far as Aquileia, situated near modern Venice. In addition a plague, brought from the East, ravaged the empire. Aurelius, whose column still stands in Rome and whose magnificent equestrian statue on the Capitoline Hill reminds the visitor of his kindliness and dignity, repaired the frontiers. But when he died at Vindobona (modern Vienna), the glorious age of the empire was over. It was of this period of benevolent despotism, from 96 to 180, that the historian, Gibbon, wrote:

"If a man were called upon to fix the period in the history of the world when the condition of the human race was most happy and prosperous, he would, without hesitation, name that which elapsed from the death of Domitian to the accession of Commodus," that is, from 96 to 180 A.D.

The Roman Empire of the First Two Centuries A.D.

In the first two centuries of our era the Roman Empire was an imposing structure. Augustus (*see map*) had added Egypt and had also extended the frontiers above the Alps to the Danube and across the Rhine into Germany, although Roman mastery of their provinces of Lower and Upper Germany was constantly disputed. Later emperors had added Britain, Mauritania, Thrace, Dacia, Cappadocia, and Lesser Armenia in Asia Minor, and had pushed the Arabian frontier to the fringes of the desert so that Palmyra, Trans-Jordania, and Arabia Petraea were included. Armenia, Assyria, and Mesopotamia may be omitted, since Hadrian withdrew from them in 117. Even so, in its heyday the empire, from north to south, stretched from the Great Wall in Britain, the North Sea and the Danube and Dacia and from an encirclement of the Black Sea to the Sahara desert and Nubia. In the West its frontier was the Atlantic Ocean, in the East the Arabian desert. In general, it was in extent about 2000 miles from north to south and 3000 from east to west. Its area was roughly two and a half million square miles and its peak population is estimated at 100,000,000.

This area, vast in ancient times and a sizeable unit today, was protected by the legions. The number of legionaries varied but the maximum force until the collapse was about 400,000. The general trend was to increase the pay, but even so it was ridiculously low by our standards. Under Domitian, to take a middle point in the two centuries, the ordinary soldiers received the equivalent of $60 a year and a grain allowance, and on discharge, after about twenty years' service, a bonus of about $600.

Communications

Within the ring of the legions a man or a woman could travel from York in Britain to Antioch in Syria or Memphis in Egypt with perfect

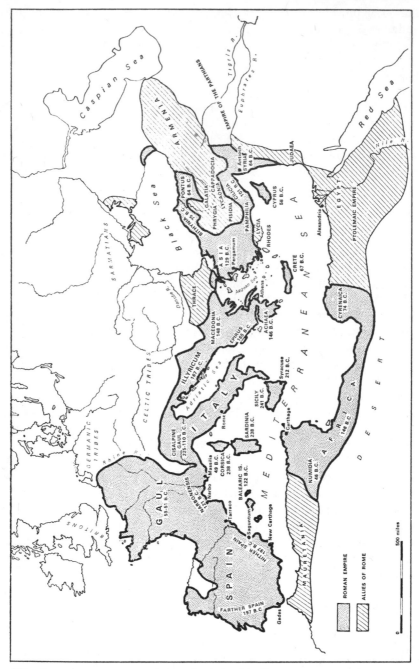

The Roman Empire at the End of the Republic

security. There was a network of roads, of which the total mileage is estimated at 47,000. All main roads were marked with distances in Roman miles (1000 paces from right foot to right foot) from the golden milestone set up in the Roman Forum. Under the later empire, in particular, a passenger, freight, and express service flowed along these roads. From the First Century A.D. there was even a sleeping carriage service. There were stations (called *mansiones*) where riders for the post-horses of the imperial mail and drivers, doctors, blacksmiths, and about 40 beasts were maintained to keep the coaches, carriages, and wagons moving. In addition, there were seaways. The Mediterranean was a great highway, crisscrossed by countless merchantmen carrying goods and passengers. We know of boats which carried as many as 1200 passengers.

The Roman "Common Market"

Along the roads and seaways flowed the tremendous internal trade of the empire. From Britain came lead, iron, oysters, and hunting-dogs. Gaul produced pottery, wines, hides, cheeses, and glass and had a big university at Lugdunum (Lyons). From Spain came base metals, gold, silver, dyes, linen-yarns, and olive oil. North Africa exported gold dust, slaves, yellow and green African marble, ebony, ivory, and wild animals for the shows. Asia Minor and Syria provided woollens, purple-dyed fabrics, carpets, tapestries, leather goods, and Damascene steel. From the Nile, the merchantmen bore to Italy linens, paper, cosmetics, glass, and a third of the wheat supply. Italy itself manufactured bricks, the Arretine pottery which has been mentioned, and the best of steel.

All this trade traveling back and forth explains how the Mediterranean world and beyond became welded into one economic, and, in spite of local differences, into one cultural unit—a Romanized unit. The spread of citizenship speeded the process. By the end of the 1st century B.C. all freemen south of the Alps were Roman citizens. Julius Caesar granted citizenship to whole towns and cities outside of Italy and to auxiliaries who had served in the army. During the reign of Augustus 900,000 were added to the citizen roll. Under Trajan and Hadrian the upper class in every city in the empire became citizens, except in Egypt. Finally, in 212 under Caracalla, every freeman in the empire was a citizen. This spread of citizenship was an achievement. It meant that there was no differentiation between Briton, Gaul, Italian, Spaniard, Greek, Syrian, and the rest. All could feel that they were citizens of the one empire, the Roman Empire.

Foreign Trade

Except for a permanent population on the dole, especially in Rome, the empire was prosperous. There was a humming small shop industry in most cities for domestic trade. In foreign trade, Romans found their way to Denmark, or along the old amber road from the Danube to the Baltic. They penetrated into the forests of Germany after furs and slaves. Romanized Greeks pushed their way into Somaliland and Abyssinia.

The most exotic trade was to *Arabia Felix*, and to India and China. There was a caravan route from Syria to Arabia for gold-dust and spices. Similar routes led to India for gems and cottons, and to China for silk. The Romans called the Chinese the "Silk People", and we know that in 97 a Chinese envoy traveled to Antioch in Syria to see the merchants there, proving a considerable intercommunication in the world of that day.

There was likewise the old Hellenistic route via the Red Sea to India. Each year a fleet of 120 ships set out. They carried gold and silver plate, metals, tools, weapons, trinkets, luxury goods, and Roman currency. Hoards of Roman coins are still dug up all over India. In the reign of Marcus Aurelius (161–180) Graeco-Roman traders even reached the coast of China by sea.

This eastern trade was a luxury trade. In India, for example, the Romans were after pearls, rubies, cottons, tortoise-shell, spices, teak, ebony, pepper, and Chinese silks. As early as the time of Nero, the philosopher Seneca, estimated that the luxury trade to the East cost Rome $5,000,000 a year. Part of the later shortage of gold and silver may be attributed to this fact.

An Appraisal of Imperial Government

In spite of the vagaries of Caesars such as Caligula, Nero, and Domitian, the life of the empire as a whole went on vigorously and prosperously. No matter what the Caesars were like, the civil service governed the empire well. From Augustus to Nerva, the cabinet-posts of the government, if we may so call them, were held by Knights and Greeks or Graeco-Oriental freedmen, with the freedmen predominating. From Trajan onward the chief men were Knights. These men gave to Italy and the provinces a government in which peace was maintained and, on the whole, an even-handed justice administered. Likewise, again thanks to Augustus, there was a vigorous local self-government in the cities, towns, and municipalities of the empire.

These local governments had an elected board of magistrates and a local senate, composed of the richest men of the community. Freedmen were not eligible; but they, as we have noted, formed the boards which carried on Caesar-worship. So keen was the competition for office that magistrates had to pay a fee when they began their term, just as if we made our mayors, aldermen, county councillors, and the like pay for the privilege of being aldermen and mayors. We ought to note, too, that rich men were supposed to make gifts to their communities. To give one example only, at Pompeii the rich family of the Holconii paid most of the cost for the reconstruction of the big theater there—and it held 5000 spectators.

This active municipal life lasted until Hadrian (121–138). Then, as a parallel to modern times, the cities, towns and municipalities found that they had over-spent and were hopelessly in debt. The emperor took over city after city and sent in his own men to take charge. Hadrian also scattered huge gifts across the empire—and cities, towns, and munici-palities began to expect "hand-outs". Even so, the affluence of the empire persisted. In 154 the rhetorian Aelius Aristides declared: "The whole inhabited world is one city-state." For by this time urbanization had reached into every sector of the empire. It was in fact a collection of cities to an extent not to be seen again until today. In Africa such ruins as those of Timgad and in the Near East, those at Baalbek and elsewhere prove that once there were cities where now there is only desert. Even the military camps were developing into cities. Along the northern frontiers, modern Bonn, Mainz, Cologne, and Strasbourg, as well as Vienna and Budapest, owe their origin to the Roman legions. So do many cities in Britain.

The Society of the Empire

The affluence reached to all except the slaves (though some of these were wealthy), those on the dole and the small farmers. For that matter, with the stopping of the wars, there were not so many slaves and, in addition, more and more slaves were freed. In this second process, Stoicism, Cynicism and Christianity had a hand.

Small farming did not prosper. The campaign of Augustus to get people back on the land in Italy was not successful. Although the revolving fund of rural credits with money loaned to farmers at 5%, established by Nerva, was continued and extended by Trajan, the Italian farmer remained in difficulties. In the provinces the trend was to large farms. Pliny the Elder, who was killed by the eruption of Vesuvius in 79, tells us that in his time all the land in North Africa was owned by six men. Sometimes these estates were worked by slaves. Quite often they were broken into small farms and leased to tenants, called *coloni*.

Guilds

Trade, industry and labor prospered. The inscriptions from all over the Roman world prove that there was a large number of occupations. Each occupation was organized into a *collegium*, to be translated not, as you might think, as "college", but as "guild." In Rome there were over a hundred guilds: carpenters, horn-blowers, bakers, ragmen, gladiators, pallbearers, physicians, porters, and so on. The guild of the silversmiths at Ephesus, it will be remembered, started a riot against St. Paul.

Most free workers, whether citizens or freedmen, and some slaves belonged to guilds. Guild members at times refused to allow non-guild workers to join in a job. Otherwise, they had more similarity to modern benevolent associations than to trade-unions. They had religious ceremonies and social meetings. The women of the workers were often organized into subsidiary associations. The members of each guild met in whatever cellar or tavern was available but, if possible, picked a rich patron to present them with a meeting-hall. They often called each other "brother" so and so. They paid dues. One association in Lanuvium, near Rome, charged $5 and an amphora of wine as an initiation fee, but the dues were only six cents a month. Fines were assessed. We read in the rules of one guild that: "If anyone shall have gone to fetch wine and shall have made away with it he shall give double the amount."

Many of the guilds paid the burial expenses of their members. Occasionally members left donations in their wills, as in the case of a man who provided money so that his "brothers" could have a free meal at his expense on each anniversary of his death.

There were high-sounding titles for the officers of the guilds. Once a year, in Rome, each guild was allowed a parade through the streets with horns, pipes, symbols and banners for "the most honorable and distinguished association" of the flask-makers or grocers or what have you. This was followed by the annual picnic. We are reminded of the Elks or the Oddfellows in our modern life. Even merchants, as, for example, those at Ostia, were joined in an association.

We might note in passing that professions and arts such as medicine, dentistry, sculpture, and the like were practised chiefly by slaves and freedmen. Medicine, in particular, was well advanced.

The Slaves

The inscriptions give us an insight into the "humble annals of the poor." Slaves, as has been mentioned, gradually became fewer in number, since the lack of war dried up a major source of supply, and since Stoicism, Cynicism, and Christianity promoted humanitarianism in the treatment of them. Further, it became a regular practice to free large numbers of slaves in one's will.

In the First Century A.D., however, they were still numerous. An ordinary man kept eight, the rich maintained hundreds. Pliny the Younger, who lived into the reign of Trajan, owned at least 500. A contemporary of his, the freedman Caelius Isidorus left behind him 4116 slaves (freedmen just emancipated liked to own slaves). Each emperor had at least 20,000 slaves. In Rome alone, it is estimated that there were 400,000 slaves.

One result is that "the slaves inherited the empire". It was they who had the large families, and their progeny took over. Furthermore, the freedmen became a very important element in the population of Rome and Italy. We have mentioned that under the Republic a freedman could not become a citizen, although his son could. In the early empire, especially under the emperor Claudius, freedmen were often made citizens and could become Knights. Claudius' freedmen, as has been noted, had great influence in running the empire.

The obvious consequence of this trend was that the Roman citizen, even in Rome, was, more often than not, whether commoner, Knight, or Senator, no longer of Roman or even of Italian stock. The emperors Trajan and Hadrian, although of Roman origin, came from Spain. Hadrian's successor, Antoninus Pius, was born in southern France.

The Society of the Freedmen

Another consequence was that wealthy freedmen ran much of the business of the empire, both in banking and in commerce. Their society and that of the Romans in general was as materialistic as many modern cultures. Our most vivid picture of these rich freedmen comes from the *Dinner of Trimalchio*, an excerpt from a novel by Petronius, the "arbiter of elegance" for Nero.

Trimalchio, the central figure in this part of the novel, is limned from life. He started his career in Italy as a Syrian slave. By ingratiating himself with his master he got his freedom. By the time of the dinner, he owns estates in Italy, Sicily, and Africa and is so rich he does not know how much he has. He has bees from Hymettus in Attica and has sent "to India for mushroom spawn." He wears a scarlet mantle and his slaves are in livery. Alexandrian boys sing as they wash the feet of the guests, and there is a blare of music throughout the dinner. Without a constant background of noise, as in many a cabaret today, and from many a television set in the home, the Roman of that day would have been uncomfortable.

The dinner itself is a gorge of bad taste—course after course *ad nauseam*. In every sentence Trimalchio shows his pretentious ignorance. He has his own poems recited. But what he really likes, he tells us, is rope-dancers and horn-blowing.

His friends, freedmen like himself, have only one god, money. They admire a man who, to quote one of them, "was ready to pick a copper from the dung-heap with his teeth". They tell stories of witches. They complain about high prices. They anticipate a gladiatorial show in a few days time with "no running away but butchery in full view of the amphi-theater." Their maxim is: "If you've got a nickel, that's what you're worth."

Roman Materialism and Luxury

This worship of possessions was particularly evident in the period from the battle of Actium to the death of Nero. According to the Roman historian, Tacitus, this was when Roman luxury reached its peak among the rich. But it continued throughout the first two centuries of our era. There was luxury in slaves. Thus Seneca, the Stoic philosopher and the tutor of Nero, tells of a rich man who owned one slave who knew all Homer by heart, another who had memorized Hesiod, and still another who could recite from memory all the lyric poets. At dinner these slaves stood behind the rich man and gave him apt quotations in Greek. Each of the three cost $5000.

There was luxury of the table. The Romans habitually over-ate and over-drank. The famous gourmand, Apicius, a contemporary of Tiberius, spent $4,000,000 on food and drink and committed suicide because he had only $500,000 left. Pliny tells of a man who served dishes of rare birds at a cost of $5000 a course. One of Nero's friends spent $200,000 on roses for a single banquet.

These were the very rich. At Pompeii, a middle-class town, there is more than one house in which a *vomitorium* is part of the equipment on the dining-couches. The Romans at elaborate meals used to induce vomiting so that they could start with a fresh appetite. Seneca once said of his fellow-countrymen: "They vomit so that they may eat and eat so that they may vomit."

Such grossness, unfortunately, described many of the Romans. They also went in for elaborate furnishings and equipment. There is at Pompeii a dining couch over which, when the ancient plumbing is turned on, a fine spray of water falls. There were Babylonian carpets, Corinthian bronzes, gold dishes, and crystal goblets, and silver was so common that even the lower middle-class had silver services. A slave of the Emperor Claudius owned one silver dish which weighed 500 pounds.

Gone, too, was simplicity of dress and adornment. Roman women spent fortunes on diaphanous Oriental silks, Tyrian purples, expensive perfumes, and jewels from the East. One of Caligula's wives, we are told, wore $2,000,000 worth of gems at a banquet. Similarly, hours were spent on makeup and hairdos. The coiffures of Roman women were as elaborate as any that Paris or New York can invent today.

Equal to the obsession for food and clothing was the obsession for building. An author of the period, Valerius Maximus, observes that a palace covering four acres is "cramped." Pliny the Younger was only moderately wealthy in an era when a freedman sneered that a man with $3,000,000 was "pitiably poor." Yet one of Pliny's villas included parks, ponds, fountains, temples, and libraries. In excavating Roman ruins the archeologist comes on floors of costly mosaics such as the mosaic in a Pompeian house which shows with marvelous artistry the charge of Alexander the Great at the Battle of Issus. He also finds pillars of costly and colored marbles shipped from Africa and Egypt.

Nero's Golden House, to which brief reference has been made, was the summit of this type of extravagance. It stretched from the Palatine to the Esquiline and Caelian Hills, where bits of it, now underground, can still be visited. Besides the triple colonnade a mile long, it had in its vestibule a statue of Nero, 120 feet high. On the site of one of its ponds Vespasian and Titus built the mighty Colosseum. There were rooms in it plated with gold or made entirely of pearls. There were vineyards, pastures, and woods filled with wild and domestic beasts. The main dining-room revolved on its axis day and night.

Even the good emperor, Hadrian, as already noted, had a great villa near modern Tivoli. We can wander for hours around its ruins today. It had a circumference of seven miles. Sheer size and extravagant decoration meant as much to the imperial Romans as it does to many moderns.

Architecture and Engineering

As another side to this passion for building we ought to observe that the Romans were the greatest engineers and architects until those of modern times. The Pantheon in Rome, built by Marcus Agrippa, one of Augustus' prime ministers, and rebuilt by Hadrian, is a massive dome in *concrete*, 142 feet in height and 142 feet in diameter. To do this without the use of steel was an achievement. Similarly, the great mausoleum of Hadrian, which still stands today on the Tiber's bank, was a castle in the Middle Ages.

With similar skill, Roman engineers constructed nine great aqueducts to bring water from the hills to Rome. The arches of the Claudian aqueduct still stride across the Roman plain. That aqueduct included a tunnel 3 miles long, 3 feet wide, and 7 feet high. We must remember that the arches of the aqueducts were simply to carry the water-channel over plains, valleys and rivers. Near Nimes in France is the Pont du Gard. This combined bridge and aqueduct, which has withstood the centuries, is 900 feet long and 160 feet high. In the water-channels, the Roman engineers achieved a drop of as little as *one* in 3000. They made traps to catch the sediment and had filters to stop debris. When the water reached

Rome, it was stored in reservoirs and distributed all over the city by underground pipes. The Roman author, Frontinus, tells us that before the ninth
aqueduct was opened, the other eight brought each day 222,237,000 gallons
of water to Rome. Rome then as now was a city of fountains.

The Roman Baths

Rome was also a city of huge bathing establishments. Today's traveler
stares in amazement at the huge arches of the Baths of Caracalla (211–217).
Those baths once covered 27 acres. The walls were lined with colored
marbles. The floors were of marble, and in the halls and porticoes were
famous sculptures. Still bigger were the Baths of Diocletian (285–305),
which covered 32 acres. In one small segment of them today is the National
Museum of Italy.

These baths were only two of over a dozen huge establishments, while
there were many smaller ones. The Romans regularly took a daily bath,
proceeding from warm bath to hot bath to cold bath. The heating system
was modern. The baths, however, were much more than baths. They had in
them promenades, gardens, libraries, restaurants, and concert and lecture
rooms. They were really civic centers.

This sort of building was spread all over the empire—roads, bridges,
aqueducts, fountains, baths and other massive public buildings. Today,
to give only one illustration, the villagers of Crete still drink from fountains
the Romans built.

The Proletariat

We have given a brief hint at the luxury and materialism of the upper
and middle classes of the Roman world. What of the poor? Our best
evidence comes from Rome. From Augustus onward those on the dole in
Rome numbered around 150,000, to which must be added women and
children. They lived in garrets and attics. Many of them were clients of
the rich. The poet Martial tells us how each day, before dawn, they hurried
to the halls of the rich for the *sportula* (hand-out). At first the rich gave
this in food, and Martial tells of clients who brought portable stoves with
them. By Trajan's time the *sportula* was passed out in money at 31 cents
a day. In return, the client was supposed to accompany his patron throughout the day. The rich man was also obligated to give a client a new toga
every now and then, and, at the Saturnalia, to present him with five or six
pounds of silverware.

Yet the presence of a huge mass of unemployed, not only in Rome,
but elsewhere, was a menace. To meet it, the policy of the emperors was
"bread and games." We have already mentioned the distribution once
each month of free grain. In addition, each emperor, from Julius Caesar

onward, passed out money gifts. Marcus Aurelius, altogether, dispensed $212.25 to each male citizen.

The Games

To amuse the unemployed there were the "games", the ancestors of today's great sports spectacles. The "games" (*ludi*) were originally religious celebrations. By the time of Marcus Aurelius, 135 days each year, or more than one day out of every three, were taken up with public spectacles to which there was no admission charge.

There were three sorts of games: theatrical, amphitheatrical, and the circus games. The theatrical shows were the least popular, though they emphasized the erotic, sensuous, and brutal. On occasion, criminals were killed or tortured on stage. The circus games never lost their popularity. There were other circuses in Rome, but the biggest was the Circus Maximus. In Rome today, if we look down from the southwestern rim of the Palatine Hill, we can see where it stood in the oval valley beneath. To get an idea of it as it was in the days of the Caesars, we must imagine a backbone of marble as the long axis of that oval. At both ends are gilded goal posts. Behind these at one end are seven huge eggs in cups on the tops of pillars; at the other seven bronze dolphins. In between are shrines, statues and an obelisk from Egypt. Around that backbone runs the race-track. To our right are the twelve stalls from which the chariots will break. The rest of the oval is tier on tier of marble seats, crowded with at least 250,000 spectators.

Then comes the first race. As the signal cloth is dropped, twelve chariots burst forth, each pulled by four plunging, galloping horses. Seven times, for a distance of almost three miles, those chariots careen around the backbone. As each lap is finished, one egg is taken down and one dolphin turned. There is, almost certainly, at least one collision at the turn and perhaps more. The remaining chariots, as the crowd rises to its feet, yelling and screaming to its favorites, dash for the winning chalk-mark. The people fall quiet until the winning color is announced. Then, as now, the bets will be paid.

There were also three-horse, two-horse, and one-horse races. Sometimes a man called a *saltator* (jumper) rode three to four horses, leaping from the back of one to the other. In between them were rope-dancers, acrobats, footraces, performing bears, horses that counted by pawing with one hoof, and the like.

In the chariot-races, the bet was on the color. Except for a short period there were four colors, or stables,—the whites, blues, greens, and reds, and riots broke out between their partisans. Great charioteers won fortunes. Diocles the Spaniard won 1462 victories in 4257 races and in 150 A.D. retired after winning $1,800,000 in prizes.

The circus-games provided excitement, color, betting, and the chance to meet a pretty girl or a handsome young man. The amphitheatrical games were even more popular. We have mentioned the Colosseum, which seated 50,000 people. Every city or town throughout the empire, except in the Greek world, had its amphitheater. You will see the remains of them today, at Nimes in France, at Verona in Italy, at Carnuntum in Austria, and elsewhere. The little town of Pompeii with 20,000 inhabitants had one which seated 20,000 spectators, probably to accomodate out of town visitors.

Why the popularity? Because the Romans liked the ultimate thrill of seeing men and beasts killed while they themselves sat in safety. The major events in the amphitheaters were beast-hunts and gladiatorial shows. One by-product of the beast-shows was a tremendous traffic in the capturing and shipping of wild beasts, and in consequence the scarcity of lions, bears, and the like in the Roman empire and beyond. For beast-hunts the Colosseum was decked with bushes and rocks. At one celebration in 202 its whole arena was transformed into a ship which suddenly broke open to pour out bears, lions, panthers, ostriches, and bison to attack each other. In one of Nero's games, the ground opened and a wood with fountains and wild beasts sprang into view. The Romans anticipated our modern stage-effects.

Sometimes, two beasts, such as a rhinoceros and an elephant, were set to fight each other. Sometimes, as often with the Christian martyrs, the beasts were let loose on human beings, armed or unarmed. Usually, the show was a massacre of animals such as those we have noted along with camels, crocodiles, hippopotamuses, and so on. The Emperor Trajan in his 123 days of continuous festivals to celebrate the conquest of Dacia (Rumania) had 11,000 animals killed.

The peak of this type of show, however, were the gladiatorial contests. Not all the gladiators were slaves or criminals. Many were free men who entered the ranks for fame and money. "How many idle men," says the Christian writer, Tertullian, "contract themselves out to the sword, for love of combat." Successful gladiators made fortunes and, if they survived a certain number of combats, were given a wooden sword as a sign of discharge.

Gladiatorial games were as varied as imagination could suggest. Gladiators often wore splendid armor of which you can see examples in our museums. They fought singly or in groups or even in cohorts, with the weapons of one country pitted against those of another. Trajan used 10,000 gladiators in the spectacle we have mentioned above.

One special variation was the sea-fight. On such occasions the arena of the Colosseum became a lake. The biggest affair of this kind was in

52 on the Fucine Lake, when two fleets with a total of 19,000 men on board fought. The emperor Claudius presided in a general's mantle. The signal to engage, as tens of thousands of spectators sat around the lake on the banks and hills, was given on a trumpet by a silver Triton diving up from the water. We can imagine the scene—the clash of warships, the blood staining the water, the shrieks of the dying, and the moans of the wounded, all to make a show for full-fed Romans. Today's bull-fights, vicious as they are, cannot compare to the Roman thirst for blood. We can also imagine the cost. In Rome alone, in 51 A.D. the official games cost the treasury over $85,000,000.

Morals and Manners

A lurid picture of Roman morals has been painted by Roman writers such as Tacitus and Juvenal. Besides the brutality of the Roman games, the grossness of eating habits, and the all-pervading search for money, sex and excitement, there were many instances of a decline in the old-fashioned virtues, particularly among the upper classes. The Roman satirist, Juvenal, for example, tells us of a woman who had had eight husbands in five years and he, Ovid, Tacitus, and Martial present us with a scathing account of a breakdown of morals in both men and women.

We must beware of taking this picture as being the whole picture. If we were to read certain modern magazines we would think that crime, divorce, and excesses of every sort characterized the whole of our society. We must remember, too, before we criticize the Romans too severely, that we of today exhibit a strong tendency toward materialism and the worship of money, and also toward spectator-sports.

There is likewise plenty of evidence in the inscriptions, in the letters of Pliny the Younger and in Tacitus himself, that there were devoted wives, loyal husbands and a middle-class which retained the old virtues. Particularly, we must recall that the Stoics, Cynics, and Christians of the first two centuries of the empire pursued the same moral ideals as we. The excesses were the excesses of a class with too much money and of a submerged group of poverty-stricken unemployed. In fact, if we were back in that world, we might not find the Romans too different from ourselves. The great defect of the Romans was that they had forgotten political freedom.

Religion

The state religion had by this time lost all its appeal. In a materialistic society, by a curious paradox, there seems always to be a strong desire to believe in something. This desire often leads the individual to superstitions or fanaticism.

In the Roman world there was a mingling of gods and cults from all over the empire. Oriental worships, in particular, had a strong vogue. Isis-Osiris worship is one example. The ruins of a temple of Isis still stand in Pompeii. Its shaven-skulled priests, as Juvenal tells us, imposed penances on high-born Roman women. Similarly, the worship of the Persian god, Mithras, spread widely, particularly among the legions. Mithraeums are found along Hadrian's Wall in Scotland, and one was recently uncovered in London, England. Both these cults promised immortality to their worshippers. Another very popular deity was *Tyche* or *Fortuna*, both of which words mean "good luck." And then, of course, the worship of the Genius of the reigning emperor was the official cult meaning almost as much or as little to the Romans as saluting the flag, or standing up with uncovered heads to sing "The Star-spangled Banner." It was, in a way, a test of patriotism.

One reason for so many deities was the tolerance of the Romans. On one occasion when a man was accused of impiety, the emperor Tiberius observed: "The gods, if they be gods, can avenge themselves."

For those to whom the worship of one or several of the multitude of gods did not appeal, there were the Hellenistic philosophical brotherhoods. Epicureanism had become unimportant. But in the First century A.D. the Stoics led the opposition to the absolutism of the Caesars. More than ever before the Stoics preached that God was within one and that all men were brothers. They emphasized the worth of the individual. So did the Cynics, who, like the early Christians, wandered all over the empire as missionaries, "having given up all," as they said, "for moral freedom." While the Stoics appealed to the upper classes, the Cynics, as the clever Greek writer, Lucian, tells us, preached to "the unlettered throngs." It is not surprising, then, that there were sometimes close connections between Cynics or Stoics and the early Christians. But Christianity was the religion which was to emerge as the final victor over all other cults and philosophies.

Christianity in the First Two Centuries of the Empire

It seemed at first that Christianity might become simply another division of Judaism. But the Jew, St. Paul, proceeded to carry its message to the Gentiles. Other disciples took up the task. In the process, churches were established at various points in the Graeco-Roman world, and a theology of Christianity began to be born. Christianity emphasized one God of Righteousness. It also promised redemption and a future life through a Savior-God. Another great strength was its intolerance. Christian believers could not worship pagan gods. Moreover, it imposed the idea of sin and a strict morality on its members, and emphasized the equality of all before God. It was a genuinely spiritual religion.

Its appeal, at first, was principally to the humble. But the world had been made ready for Christianity. In a way, Christianity was a merging and a summation of ideas which had been gradually developing in the Mediterranean complex since Alexander the Great. Almost every single detail of the ritual and beliefs of the early Christians can be paralleled in other beliefs and worships. But the intensity of the faith and the spiritual nature of the appeal made it reach all classes.

And then came the persecutions, first under Nero and then under Domitian and Marcus Aurelius. The faith of the survivors was intensified. By the end of the Second Century A.D. Christianity was almost a state within a state in its pervasiveness, organization, and separateness.

Literature

The First Century A.D. gives us what is known as the Silver Age of Latin Literature. There were two periods, the Neronian and the Flavian. In the first period lack of political freedom and of free speech produced a distinctly inferior literature. Vergil became the model for both prose and poetry. Oratory was limited to panegyrics of the reigning emperor, and history could not speak the truth. Poetry, much of it adulatory of the Caesars, poured out. We will only mention three authors, Seneca, whose philosophical works give us a statement of Stoicism, and whose fourth-rate tragedies influenced English literature, his nephew, Lucan, who wrote a historical epic with a strong Republican bias on the Civil War between Pompey and Caesar, and Petronius, the writer of the remarkable novel, the *Satyricon* which includes *The Dinner of Trimalchio*. This novel, although we only possess excerpts from the 16th and 17th books, is the spiritual ancestor of the romance of roguery or picaresque novel such as Fielding's *Tom Jones*, in which a rascal is the hero.

The Flavian period brought writers of genius. In history, Tacitus, in spite of a biased view, gives us a vivid narrative of the history of the First Century of the empire. His *Agricola* describes the final conquest of Britain and his *Germania* is the earliest account of the Germans except for references in Caesar's *Gallic Wars*. Tacitus gives our first Roman reference to Christ and the Christians when he describes the persecution under Nero, although the authenticity of the reference to the persecution is disputed.

A close friend of Tacitus was Pliny the Younger. His *belles-lettres* were written for publication and have neither the style nor the value of Cicero's letters. They do give us a picture of life under Domitian and Trajan. There is an eye-witness account of the eruption of Vesuvius in 79, and an inquiry into how to deal with Christians who refuse to sacrifice to the Genius of

Trajan, together with the answer of Trajan. Trajan's answer is tolerant and much in the tone of a British proconsul.

Satire was brilliantly written by Juvenal. A Stoic preacher, obsessed with the immorality of the day, he rips the Rome of his day apart. A more interesting picture of the life of the day is presented by the Spaniard, Martial. Life in its seamiest phases was his theme—and we see the gutters of Rome.

We have omitted Quintilian, who wrote about education in surprisingly modern terms and Pliny the Elder, who was an encyclopaedist. In the time of Hadrian, Suetonius composed his *Lives of the Twelve Caesars* in 8 books. Although completely uncritical and given to backstairs gossip, Suetonius does present us with intimate portraits somewhat in the style of modern biographers.

Somewhat later, we have the second Latin novel, the *Metamorphoses* of Apuleius, a native of Africa. In this fascinating story, a man who has been changed into an ass sees and overhears story after story until he is transformed back into a man by Isis. Some of these short stories found their way into later European literature. During about the same time, Aulus Gellius wrote a hodge-podge of literary criticism and antiquarianism in his *Attic Nights*.

In the same period there was a renaissance of Greek literature. Plutarch's (46–120) *Lives* have been popular for centuries. In the last half of the Second Century an extremely clever Greek, Lucian, traveled through the Roman empire and put down in amusing style his reactions to what he saw and heard. At about the same time another Greek, Pausanias, wrote a travel-book, *Tour of Greece*, which is very valuable to us. The "Meditations" of Marcus Aurelius in Greek have already been mentioned. Their real title is *To Himself* and they are touching dialogues between himself and the Supreme Power he worshipped.

In general, however, literature after Hadrian enters into a permanent decline, a sure indication of the decay of the empire.

Readings from Sources of the Period

(a) From the pen of the Emperor Augustus we have his own account of his deeds preserved in a copy cut in Greek and Latin at Ancyra in Asia Minor on the walls of a temple to Rome and Augustus. Extracts from it are given.

The Alps, from the district near the Adriatic to the Tuscan sea, I forced to remain peaceful without waging unprovoked war with any tribe. My fleet sailed through the Ocean from the mouth of the Rhine towards the rising sun, up to the territories of the Cimbri, to which point no Roman had penetrated, up to that time, either by land or sea. The Cimbri, and Charydes, and Semnones and other peoples of the Germans, belonging to the same tract of country, sent ambassadors to ask for the friendship of myself and the Roman people. By my command and under my auspices, two armies were marched into Aethiopia and Arabia, called Felix, nearly simultaneously, and large hostile forces of both these nations were cut to pieces in battle, and a large number of towns were captured. Aethiopia was penetrated as far as the town Nabata, next to Meroe. Into Arabia the army advanced into the territories of the Sabaei as far as the town of Mariba.

I added Egypt to the Empire of the Roman people. When I might have made the greater Armenia a province after the assassination of its king Artaxes, I preferred, on the precedent of our ancestors, to hand over the kingdom to Tigranes, son of King Artavasdes, grandson of King Tigranes, by the hands of Tiberius Nero, who was then my stepson. The same nation being afterwards in a state of revolt and rebellion, I handed over to the government of King Ariobarzanes, son of Artabazus, king of the Medes, after it had been reduced by my son Gaius; and after his death to his son Artavasdes, upon whose assassination I sent Tigranes, a member of the royal family of the Armenians, into that kingdom. I recovered all the provinces on the other side of the Adriatic towards the East and Cyrenae, which were by this time for the most part held by various kings, and before them Sicily and Sardinia which had been overrun by an army of slaves.

I settled colonies of soldiers in Africa, Sicily, Macedonia, both the Spains, Achaia, Asia, Syria, Gallia Narbonensis, Pisidia. Italy has twenty-eight colonies established under my auspices, which have in my lifetime become very densely inhabited and places of great resort.

A large number of military standards, which had been lost under other commanders, I recovered, after defeating the enemy, from Spain and Gaul and the Dalmatians. I compelled the Parthians to restore the spoils and standards of three Roman armies, and to seek as suppliants the friendship of the Roman people. These standards I laid up in the inner shrine belonging to the temple of Mars Ultor.

The tribes of the Pannonii, which before I was *princeps* an army of the Roman people never reached, having been subdued by Tiberius Nero, who was then my stepson and legate, I added to the Empire of the Roman people, and I extended the frontier of Illyricum to the bank of the river Danube. And when an army of the Daci crossed to the south of that river it was conquered and put to flight under my auspices; and subsequently my army being led across the Danube, forced the tribes of the Daci to submit to the orders of the Roman people.

To me there were often sent embassies of kings from India who had never been seen in the camp of any Roman general.

In my sixth consulship, I repaired eighty-two temples of the gods in the city in accordance with a decree of the Senate, none being omitted which at that time stood in need of repair. In my seventh consulship I constructed the Flaminian road from the city to Ariminum, and all the bridges except the Mulvian and Minucian.

On ground belonging to myself I built a temple to Mars Ultor and the Forum Augustum, with money arising from sale of spoils of war. I built a theatre adjoining the temple of Apollo, on ground for the most part purchased from private owners, to be under the name of my son-in-law Marcus Marcellus.

I three times gave a show of gladiators in my own name, and five times in the name of my sons and grandsons; in which shows about 10,000 men contended. I twice gave the people a show of athletes collected from all parts of the world in my own name, and a third time in the name of my grandson. I gave games in my own name four times, as representing other magistrates twenty-three times.

I gave the people the spectacle of a naval battle on the other side of the Tiber, in the spot where now is the grove of the Caesars, the ground having been hollowed out to a length of 1800 feet, and a breadth of 1200 feet, in which thirty beaked ships, triremes or biremes, and a still larger number of smaller vessels contended. In these fleets, besides the rowers, there fought about three thousand men.

While I was administering my thirteenth consulship, the Senate and equestrian order and the Roman people with one consent greeted me as FATHER OF MY COUNTRY, and decreed that it should be inscribed in the vestibule of my house, and in the Senate house, and in the Forum Augustum, and under the chariot which was there placed in my honour in accordance with a senatorial decree.

When I wrote this I was in my seventy-sixth year.

(Howe and Harrer, *op. cit.*, pp. 301–304, translated by E. S. Shuckburgh.)

(b) Vergil (70–19 B.C.) was the greatest of the Roman poets. In the sixth book of his epic on the founding of the Roman state by Aeneas, the Trojan, he set forth his vision of Imperial Rome.

> Let others better mould the running mass
> Of metals, and inform the breathing brass,
> And soften into flesh a marble face;
> Plead better at the bar; describe the skies,
> And when the stars ascend, and when they rise.
> But, Rome! 'tis thine alone, with awful sway,
> To rule mankind, and make the world obey.
> Disposing peace and war thy own majestic way;
> To tame the proud, the fetter'd slave to free:
> These are imperial arts, and worthy thee.

(*Ibid.*, p. 381, translated by John Dryden.)

(c) Second only to Vergil was the poet Horace (65–8 B.C.) who wrote charming satires and epistles as well as the *Odes* on which his fame chiefly rests. The Odes themselves vary from light love-poetry to nature lyrics and reflections on the whole range of life. As an Epicurean Horace, as the *Ode* below indicates, believed in "The Golden Mean".

> You better sure shall live, not evermore
>   Trying high seas; nor, while sea's rage you flee,
> Pressing too much upon ill-harboured shore.

> The golden mean who loves, lives safely free
> From filth of foreworn house, and quiet lives,
>   Releas'd from court, where envy needs must be.

> The wind most oft the hugest pine tree grieves:
>   The stately towers come down with greater fall:
> The highest hills the bolt of thunder cleaves

> Evil haps do fill with hope, good haps appal
> With fear of change, the courage well prepar'd:
> Foul winters, as they come, away they shall.

> Though present times, and past with evils be snar'd,
> They shall not last: with cithern silent muse
> Apollo wakes, and bow hath sometime spar'd.

> In hard estate, with stout shows, valour use,
> The same man still, in whom wisdom prevails;
> In too full wind draw in thy swelling sails.

(*Ibid.*, p. 406 translated by Philip Sidney.)

(d) The sophisticated poet, Ovid (43 B.C.–17 A.D.) produced a wide range of poetry. The selection below is taken from his *Art of Love*.

> I bid thee not to javelins bare thy heart;
> Soft are the cautions of thy master's art.
> Still stoop to conquer: when she thwarts thee, yield;
> Do all her bidding, thou shalt win the field.
> Thus, when she argues, argue on her side;
> What she approves approve; deny what she denied;
> Say and unsay; and, as her face appears,
> Smile on her smiles, and weep upon her tears.
> If with ill throw she cast the ivory die,
> Throw with ill luck; be hers the victory:
> Ne'er with good cast a lucky vengeance take;
> But throw ace-point: be thine the losing stake.
> Or, when the chessman moves in mock campaign,
> Thy pawn should by its glassy foe be slain.
> Her rod-distended parasol display;
> Make the rude crowd before her steps give way;
> Affix the footstool to her slight settee;
> Be the slid slipper placed, displaced, by thee.
> Oft, though thyself be shivering with the cold,
> Her hand within thy bosom, chafing, hold;
> Nor think it mean, such meanness charms, to bear,
> Though nobly bred, the mirror of the fair.
> When bidden to the square, obedient start
> At earlier hour, and, lingering, late depart.
> Run, to whatever place; all else defer;
> Not crowds should stay thee, when thou fliest to her.
> At night, the banquet o'er, she seeks her home,
> And calls her slave; do thou, obsequious, come.
> Or, should she bid thee from the rural shade,
> Love hates the slothful, be the call obeyed.
> If wheels be wanting, take on foot thy way;
> No lowering weather should thy haste delay;
> No parching dog-star heat; no whitening track,
> That leads through deepening snow-drifts, hold thee back.

Love is like war: ye faint of heart! begone!
No coward hands must bear our standards on.
In these soft camps are countless labors found;
Night, tempest, journeyings, many a grief, and wound.

(Guinagh and Dorjahn, *op. cit.*, p. 563, translated by Charles A. Elton.)

(e) Seneca (4 B.C.–65 A.D.), the tutor of Nero, was a Stoic philosopher. In the extract below he propounds the Stoic belief in a holy spirit within us.

SENECA TO HIS FRIEND LUCILIUS, GREETING
THE GOD IN US

You couldn't be better employed, or more for your own good, if, as your letter tells me, you're moving steadily towards the true sanity, for which it's foolish to pray, seeing that you have but your own consent to win. We needn't lift our hands to heaven, we need wheedle no sacristan into letting us approach the ear of some graven image, as if by so doing we made ourselves more audible. God's near you, with you, in you. Yes, Lucilius, within us a holy spirit has its seat, our watcher and guardian in evil and in good. As we treat him so he treats us. The good man, in fact, is never without God. Can any one rise superior to fortune without his aid? Isn't he the source of every generous and exalted inspiration? In every good man

'Dwells nameless, dimly seen, a god.'*

*Vergil, *Aeneid*, vii, 352.

(*Ibid.*, p. 591, translated by E. Phillips Barker.)

(f) Petronius (died 66 A.D.) was almost certainly the "arbiter of elegance" at Nero's court. Of the remains of his long novel, the *Satiricon*, the "Dinner of Trimalchio", is the most important excerpt. In it Petronius satirizes the conduct of the newly rich. The extract below is taken from the beginning of the dinner.

Just then some glass jars carefully fastened with gypsum were brought on, with labels tied to their necks, inscribed, "Falernian of Opimius's vintage, 100 years in the bottle." As we were poring over the labels Trimalchio clapped his hands and cried, "Ah me, so wine lives longer than miserable man. So let us be merry. Wine is life. I put on real wine of Opimius's year. I produced some inferior stuff yesterday, and there was a much finer set of people to dinner." As we drank and admired each luxury in detail, a slave brought in a silver skeleton, made so that its limbs and spine could be moved and bent in every direction. He put it down once or twice on the table so that the supple joints showed several attitudes, and Trimalchio said appropriately: "Alas for us poor mortals, all that poor man is is nothing. So we shall all be, after the world below takes us away. Let us live then while it goes well with us".

(Howe and Harrer, *op. cit.*, p. 573, translated by Michael Heseltine.)

(g) Quintilian (ca. 35–95 A.D.) was a professor of oratory in Rome. His Book on how to train an orator, tells us a good deal about Roman education. The extract below seems in some respects quite modern:

Some hold that boys should not be taught to read till they are seven years old, that being the earliest age at which they can derive profit from instruction and endure the strain of learning ... Those however who hold that a child's mind should not be allowed to lie fallow for a moment are wiser. Chrysippus, for instance, though he gives the nurses a three years' reign, still holds the formation of the child's mind on the best principles to be a part of their duties ...

I am not however so blind to differences of age as to think that the very young should be forced on prematurely or given real work to do. Above all things we must take care that the child, who is not yet old enough to love his studies, does not come to hate them and dread the bitterness which he has once tasted, even when the years of infancy are left behind. His studies must be made an amusement: he must be questioned and praised and taught to rejoice when he has done well: sometimes too, when he refuses instruction, it should be given to some other to excite his envy, at times also he must be engaged in competition and should be allowed to believe himself successful more often than not, while he should be encouraged to do his best by such rewards as may appeal to his tender years ...

As regards syllables, no short cut is possible: they must all be learnt, and there is no good in putting off learning the most difficult; this is the general practice but the sole result is bad spelling. Further we must beware of placing blind confidence in a child's memory. It is better to repeat syllables and impress them on the memory and, when he is reading, not to press him to read continuously or with greater speed, unless indeed the clear and obvious sequence of letters can suggest itself without its being necessary for the child to stop to think. The syllables once learnt, let him begin to construct words with them and sentences with the words. You will hardly believe how much reading is delayed by undue haste.

(*Ibid.*, pp. 599–600, translated by H. E. Butler.)

(h) Below are brief extracts from Pliny the Younger's (62 to c. 14 A.D.) description of the eruption of Vesuvius in 79 A.D., which was sent by him to his friend, the historian Tacitus. During the eruption, his uncle, who was in command of a fleet at Misenum, sailed out to try to bring aid but was forced to land at Stabiae and was then suffocated.

He was at that time with the fleet under his command at Misenum. On the 24th of August, about one in the afternoon, my mother desired him to observe a cloud of very unusual size and appearance. He had sunned himself, then taken a cold bath, and after a leisurely luncheon was engaged in study. He immediately called for his shoes and went up an eminence from whence he might best view this very uncommon appearance. It was not at that distance discernible from what mountain this cloud issued, but it was found afterwards to be Vesuvius. I cannot give you a more exact description of its figure, than by resembling it to that of a pine-tree, for it shot up a great height in the form of a trunk, which extended itself at the top into several branches; because, I imagine, a momentary gust of air blew it aloft, and then failing, forsook it; thus causing the cloud to expand laterally as it dissolved, or possibly the downward pressure of its own weight produced this effect. It was at one moment white, at another dark and spotted, as if it had carried up earth or cinders.

He ordered large galleys to be launched, and went himself on board one, with the intention of assisting not only Rectina, but many others; for the villas stand extremely thick upon that beautiful coast. Hastening to the place from whence others were flying, he steered his direct course to the point of danger, and with such freedom from fear, as to be able to make and dictate his observations upon the successive motions and figures of that terrific object.

And now cinders, which grew thicker and hotter the nearer he approached, fell into the ships, then pumice-stones too, with stones blackened, scorched, and cracked by fire, then the sea ebbed suddenly from under them, while the shore was blocked up by landslips from the mountains. After considering a moment whether he should retreat, he said to the captain who was urging that course, "Fortune befriends the brave; carry me to Pomponianus." Pomponianus was then at Stabiae, distant by half the width of the bay (for, as you know, the shore, insensibly curving in its sweep, forms here a receptacle for the sea).

In the meanwhile Mount Vesuvius was blazing in several places with spreading and towering flames, whose refulgent brightness the darkness of the night set in high relief. But my uncle, in order to soothe apprehensions, kept saying that some fires had been left alight by the terrified country people, and what they saw were only deserted villas on fire in the abandoned district. After this he retired to rest, and it is most certain that his rest was a most genuine slumber; for his breathing, which, as he was pretty fat, was somewhat heavy and sonorous, was heard by those who attended at his chamber-door. But the court which led to his apartment now lay so deep under a mixture of pumice-stones and ashes, that if he had continued longer in his bedroom, egress would have been impossible. On being aroused, he came out, and returned to Pomponianus and the others, who had sat up all night. They consulted together as to whether they should hold out in the house, or wander about in the open. For the house now tottered under repeated and violent concussions, and seemed to rock to and fro as if torn from its foundations. In the open air, on the other hand, they dreaded the falling pumice-stones, light and porous though they were; yet this, by comparison, seemed the lesser danger of the two; a conclusion which my uncle arrived at by balancing reasons, and the others by balancing fears. They tied pillows upon their heads with napkins; and this was their whole defence against the showers that fell round them.

When day dawned again (the third from that he last beheld) his body was found entire and uninjured, and still fully clothed as in life; its posture was that of a sleeping, rather than a dead man.

(*Ibid.*, pp. 622–623, translated by Melmoth-Hutchinson.)

(i) Suetonius (ca. 75–160 A.D.) wrote the *Lives of the Twelve Caesars* in a gossipy informal style. The extract below is from his biography of emperor Claudius (41–54 A.D.).

He gave frequent and grand dinner parties, as a rule in spacious places, where six hundred guests were often entertained at one time. He even gave a banquet close to the outlet of the Fucine Lake and was well-nigh drowned, when the water was let out with a rush and deluged the place. He always invited his own children to dinner along with the sons and daughters of distinguished men, having them sit at the arms of the couches as they ate, after the old time custom. When a guest was suspected of having stolen a golden bowl the day before, he invited him again the next day, but set before him an earthenware cup.

He was eager for food and drink at all times and in all places. Once when he was holding court in the forum of Augustus and had caught the savour of a meal which was preparing for the Salii in the temple of Mars hard by, he left the tribunal, went up where the priests were, and took his place at their table. He hardly ever left the dining-room until he was stuffed and soaked; then he went to sleep at once, lying on his back with his mouth open, and a feather was put down his throat to relieve his stomach. He slept but a little at a time, for he was usually awake before midnight; but he would sometimes drop off in the daytime while holding court and could hardly be roused when the advocates raised their voices for the purpose.

(*Ibid.*, p. 531, translated by J. C. Rolfe.)

CHAPTER 10

The Fall of the Empire: 181–476 A.D.

Within a century and five years after 180 the Empire collapsed. But, in spite of its fall, like a huge beast whose heart still keeps beating after the death-blow has been inflicted, the empire was reconstituted time after time. The Western half was "unconscionably long in dying"; while, amazingly, in the East the Byzantine Empire arose out of the carcass of imperial power: it was to last until 1453. From 754 B.C. to 476 A.D. was the span of Roman civilization in the western half—and will our modern civilization endure for as long a space?

The Decay of the Empire: Aurelius to Diocletian

When Marcus Aurelius assumed the purple in 161 the Roman world seemed on the lazy pinnacle of peace and prosperity. Yet Aurelius had to spend most of his nineteen years of rule on the northern frontiers fighting the pressure of the Germanic tribes, while in the East his colleague, Lucius Verus, was struggling against the Parthians. Equally as significant was the fact that in 167, to finance his wars, Aurelius had to sell the household furnishings of his palace. To add to the troubles, the troops from the east brought back a plague which carried off at least one-fourth of the population of the empire.

A virile state would have survived these blows. But within a little more than a century (181–285) the empire had crumbled. There were civil wars. Of 27 emperors, all but two met violent deaths. Meanwhile, the frontiers were broken. In the east, the Parthians were replaced by a Persian dynasty, that of the Sassanids. They raided as far as Antioch. In Europe, the Germans broke through the frontiers. When in 285 Diocletian pulled the empire together, there was little of careless ease or prosperity left.

Symptoms of Decay

It is clear, then, that the causes of the collapse must have been developing during the Second Century A.D. If we take a second look at the seemingly prosperous Roman world of that period we can perceive symptoms of decay. The lack of a vigorous literature is one. The decline of municipal life is another.

In the First Century, rich men had paid to become local magistrates and senators. Then the cities spent themselves into debt by expenditures on public buildings and civic sacrifices, religious processions, and the games. At the same time government taxes were repeatedly increased. The local rich men, who were what we would call the prosperous middle class, began to be squeezed too tightly. In some cases, force was used to compel them to serve in public office. In many cases, Hadrian (117–138) put in his own curators, as well as making huge gifts from the treasury. These gifts, in turn, meant more taxes. The Romans were giving up local freedom for government care. They could not seem to learn that, even in a welfare state, one still does not get "something for nothing."

Government control meant, as in our own day, a tremendous increase in the numbers of the civil service. By the time of Antonius Pius (138–161), there was a civil service bureaucracy as pervasive as that of modern times. By the Third Century A.D., to quote the historian, Trever, "the relentless system of taxation, requisition and compulsory labor was administered by an army of military bureaucrats . . . Everywhere . . . were the . . . agents of the emperors to spy out any remotest case of attempted strikes or evasion of taxes . . ."

To the cost of the civil service—for this had to be paid for out of taxes—must be added the expenses of the dole and the games. By the time of Marcus Aurelius, there was a daily distribution of pork, oil, and bread to the proletariat (which means "the child-producing group"), while it cost hundreds of millions of dollars to pay for the games. Army costs also doubled between 96 and 180.

To this overspending we may add an unfavorable balance of trade. As a result of all this, there was a creeping inflation. Marcus Aurelius had to debase the value of the currency by 25% which meant a 25% inflation. This inflation went on and on. In the time of Augustus, the Roman denarius had been worth twenty cents. By the time of Diocletian, it was stabilized at less than a cent.

The seemingly prosperous world of 150 was already sleep-walking toward catastrophe. Government paternalism, bureaucracy, over-taxation, inflation, and a mounting taste for the brutal spectacles of the amphitheater were symptoms of a spiritual *malaise* which had begun when the Romans tossed away political freedom for peace, security, and money. Slavery and a permanent mass of unemployed on government relief were cankers. At the top of the heap lolled a group of millionaires who thought chiefly of pleasure. Meanwhile, the middle-class, which the First Century had created, was slowly being squeezed out of existence. And nobody seemed to be able to do anything. The sense of futility may have been increased by the great plague during the reign of Marcus Aurelius, and by a similar fifteen years of plague in the middle of the Third Century.

Another symptom of the decay was the increase of Oriental religions and the pathetic dependence on astrology. The main mass turned their backs on reason and were willing to believe in anything. The Greek search for truth was forgotten. Instead, superstitions flourished and the miraculous and supernatural were expected and gaped at.

The historian, Gibbon, thinks that the spread of Christianity was one of the main causes of the decline of the Roman empire. Insofar as Christianity emphasized this world as a preparation for the next and regarded personal salvation as more important than the welfare of the state, it was, along with the other immortality cults of the day, a symptom, though not a cause, of the decline. In the First Century there had been Christian fanatics who, expecting the second coming of Christ in their own lifetime, had been a subversive and disrupting force. But by the end of the Second Century, the Christian Church was better organized than any other religion. There were congregations, bishops, and church officials. Except for their intolerance of the pagan gods, the Christian communities were a stabilizing force.

Last of all, we come to the army. During the principate of Augustus the legionaries had been Roman citizens or provincials who were given citizenship when they enlisted while the auxiliary troops were all provincials who, after twenty-five years of service, also received Roman citizenship. By the time of Hadrian the number of provincials in the legions had increased greatly, and Hadrian himself introduced the policy of recruiting soldiers for each legion from the province in which that legion served. Likewise, he began to form auxiliary troops from the barbarian border tribes, while Marcus Aurelius allowed throngs of Germans to settle in the Danubian provinces, with the proviso that they must serve in the army when called upon to do so.

As a result of these changes, by 180 the Roman army was composed chiefly of provincials from the more backward provinces of the Empire, of soldiers' sons, foreigners, and semi-civilized Germanic tribesmen. In outlook and culture the soldiers had little in common with the fat sheep they were supposed to protect in Italy and the more civilized provinces.

Hadrian, too, had introduced a defense mentality into the army. It was he who built the Great Wall in Britain between the Tyne and the Solway to keep back the Scottish highlanders. He also constructed a 340-mile-long palisade of split oak logs, nine feet high, along the frontier in Germany and Rhaetia. Behind this palisade were forts and the legions were now settled in permanent camps into which they were allowed to bring their families. Thus, they were immobilized.

Over-taxation, a sense of futility, a love of ease and security, government paternalism, a divorce between army and civilians—we can say that the empire rotted from within. The immediate causes of the collapse, however, were the two weaknesses implicit in the empire from Augustus onward—the fact that the Government was a despotism so that the weak, stupid, or debauched ruler could shake the empire, and the second fact that, in the final analysis, the despotism rested on the support of the army.

The Army Picks the Caesars

If we keep these two factors in mind we can see what happened. The son of Marcus Aurelius, the philosopher-Caesar, was Commodus. His excesses were such that he was assassinated (193). There came a struggle for power between rival generals, as in 68–69. In 197, after four years of turmoil, Septimius Severus won.

Severus, whose triumphal arch still stands in the Roman Forum, said frankly that he owed his power to the army and he catered to the soldiers at the expense of the civilians. He is the first "military monarch". When he died in Britain (211) his son, Caracalla, who gave the citizenship to all freemen in the empire, was assassinated (217) while on a campaign against the Parthians.

Macrinus, who was responsible for the assassination of Caracalla, ruled less than a year. Shortly after this the amazing Elagabalus, a grand-nephew of Julia Domna, the Syrian wife of Severus, attained the purple. He was put forward by the sister of Julia Domna, Julia Maesa, who on the death of Julia Domna had gone with her two daughters to Emesa, a Syrian town north of Damascus. Elagabalus was the son of one of her daughters, was only 14 years old at the time, and was the hereditary priest of the sun-god at Emesa. But the legions were induced to accept him by the fiction that he was the illegitimate son of Caracalla.

A year later Elagabulus (more properly in Latin Heliogabalus) arrived in Rome. One of his distinctions was that he was the handsomest of the Roman emperors, and was, to translate his appeal into modern terms, an idol of the teenagers. Only cushions of rabbit fur and partridge down, costly perfumes for his bath, golden coverlets and tunics of whole silk

woven with gold, and meals of cockscombs from living birds, peacocks'
and partridges' tongues, and birds' brains suited this Hollywood-like
prince. His debauched friends were raised to the highest positions in
the state. Meanwhile, his grandmother, Maesa, governed the empire along
with her other daughter, Mamaea. After four years, Maesa and Mamaea
realized that Elagabalus' excesses were pointing to downfall. Therefore
they had him and his mother assassinated (they were hiding in a latrine),
and put Alexander Severus (222–235), the son of Mamaea, on the throne.
He, too, was 14 years old when, he assumed the purple.

Then, for thirteen years, the empire was ruled, in effect, by Mamaea,
the first real empress of Rome. Meanwhile, in 227, the Parthian empire
was overturned in the east and the Sassanid dynasty of Persians came to
power. Finally Alexander and his mother were killed.

The record of the half century from 180 to 235 seems appalling enough.
In the next half century, from 235–285, the collapse was almost total.
Officially, eighteen Caesars (twenty-six if their colleagues are counted)
wore the purple. Only one escaped violent death. In addition there were
many who attempted to win the throne. 259 was called the "Year of the
Thirty Pretenders."

The army, then, made and unmade Caesars at will, and each Caesar
killed his predecessor and was then killed in his turn. It was in 235 that the
legions raised the first "barbarian" to the purple. Maximinus, a Thracian
peasant, began his career as a common soldier. According to the legends
about him, he was eight and a half feet tall, could crumble stones in his
hands, break a horse's leg with a kick of his heel, and each day could eat
forty pounds of meat and drink eight gallons of wine. Maximinus never
visited Rome. He lasted three years. Then the merry-go-round of assassi-
nations and civil wars began in earnest. At time sections of the empire
seceded. In Gaul, for example, Postumus and his successor, Albinus,
reigned for fifteen years.

The Breaking of the Frontiers

With the army busy with civil wars, the frontiers gave way. In the East
the Persians raided as far as Antioch and took the emperor Valerian
prisoner (259). At the same time the caravan-city of Palmyra, at an oasis
in the desert north of Damascus, rose to power. Palmyra lay across the
main routes from the Mediterranean to Mesopotamia and Central Asia,
and had become a rich and important city. Shortly after Valerian was
captured, the king of Palmyra, Odenathus, defeated and drove back the
Persians, and was rewarded by the Romans with the title of *Dux Orientis*
and the position of commander-in-chief of the Roman forces on the
Euphrates and in Egypt. On his assassination in 267, his beautiful and

energetic widow, Zenobia, took over the power and was able to occupy and hold the whole of the Near East, except for Asia Minor and Alexandria, from 267 to 272.

Meanwhile, in Europe the Germanic tribes had poured across the frontiers. In 257 the Goths overran Dacia, swept into Thrace and penetrated Greece. In 269 the Goths and another tribe, the Heruli, crossed the Danube again, 320,000 strong, with their families, and sailed into the Mediterranean with 2000 ships. Fortunately, one of the ephemeral Caesars, Claudius, cut to pieces both army and fleet.

Further west, as early as 254 the Marcomanni had penetrated Italy as far as Ravenna. A few years later the Alamanni ("the tribe of all-men") got as far as Milan. In Gaul, the Franks, from whom the French get their name, and allied tribes swept across the Rhine, and ravaged the country as far as Tarragona in Spain. Across the channel the Saxon and Jutish pirates were sailing against Britain.

To cap the disasters, starting in 252, the great plague already mentioned devastated the Roman world for fifteen years. Alexandria lost two-thirds of its population and in Rome, at the peak of the plague, 5000 died each day.

The emperor Aurelian (270–275) checked the disintegration briefly. He captured Palmyra and Zenobia and brought Gaul, Britain, and Spain back into the empire. As a necessary move he abandoned Dacia. He likewise built around Rome the Great Wall, twelve feet thick and twenty high, of which sections still stand today. Aurelian in his turn was assassinated. Chaos returned until 285 when the Illyrian, Diocletian, seized the throne.

Effects of the Collapse

Such was the collapse in one century of the ordered, peaceful, and secure Roman world. To understand what that collapse meant, we must imagine ourselves as peaceful Romans of the time of Marcus Aurelius. We know that the emperor is off across the Alps near a place called Vindobona (modern Vienna) fighting against two German tribes, the Quadi and the Marcomanni. What has that to do with us? We have plenty of money, although prices do seem to be going up and up. The plague is almost over, and at least it has got rid of over-population. True, there seems to be little to do except eat, sleep, go to the bath, and gossip. But next week there is to be a big show at the Colosseum and after that we will go to our villa at Baiae to swim, stroll on the beach, and look at the new hair-dos. If, on the other hand, we are farmers in Gaul, there is leisure, comfort, and plenty to eat, and an amphitheater some twelve miles away for excitement. The skies are blue, the grapes are ripening, and the legions hold the Germans back across the Rhine as they have always done.

But in 256 a descendant of one of those same farmers goes about somewhat uneasily. There are rumors (which, of course, can't be true) that the Germans have burst across the Rhine. That night that farmer wakens to shouts and screams amid the light of his blazing barns. Before his throat is cut, he realizes, still almost in disbelief, that an era is over.

His compatriot in Rome has not as yet had so hard a lesson. But services are disrupted, prices are out of sight, food is hard to get, there are dead bodies lying in the street from the plague, and it is almost impossible to know who is Caesar. Besides, the Caesar of today will be the dead man of tomorrow. It is with a kind of wonder that he hears from an old man, who heard it from his father, what it used to be like when there was a stable rule and when the legions, instead of murdering one Caesar after another, stayed on the frontiers where they belonged. He has heard too, about a class of aristocrats. But there are no aristocrats any more. There is now a military class on top and you no sooner pay one tax then the collectors are around to pick up a new one.

Mere words cannot describe the agony of the collapse. There was murder, rape, and pillage. What the soldiers or the barbarians spared, the agents of the emperors took for taxes. All freedom was gone. A military caste ruled. It was they who were the new landed aristocrats. The middle-class and labor had both become serfs of the state. Paternalism had ended in regimentation.

Diocletian

This was the situation when Diocletian (285–305) took over. He drove back the barbarians and reconstructed the empire. It was a new kind of empire, one ruled by an Oriental despot. The only approach to Diocletian, who called himself Jovius, was by prostration on the ground. To run the empire, he appointed three other Caesars and divided among them the 101 provinces he created. Hence there were four "prefectures." Rome was no longer even a capital, and Diocletian's own capital was at Nicomedia in Asia Minor.

In an attempt to straighten out inflation, he devalued the denarius and issued a new currency. In 301 he tried a price-fixing code. Death was the penalty for breaking it. But prices kept rising, all the same.

It is a measure of the collapse that taxes were now often paid "in kind", that is by actual grain, sheep, cattle, and the like, just as if there were no coinage. Because it was difficult to collect the taxes, the local senatorial class—that is, the middle class—in each community was made responsible. Whatever these men failed to collect from their fellows, they had to make up from their own pockets. This local senatorial class, by the way, was composed by law of all who owned fifteen acres or its equivalent. These men served as tax-collectors without pay. If they tried to enlist in the army or join the clergy so as to evade responsibility, they were forced to return to their job. Finally, they were forbidden to change their residences or to dispose of their own property. The middle class was taxed out of existence.

The same regimentation was applied to farmers and free labor. By law, the son of a farmer had to be a farmer, and the son of a baker or a metal-worker and so on had to be a metal-worker, or a baker, or whatever his father's occupation had been. All artisans, traders, shop-owners, and the like, again by law, had to furnish each year a fixed proportion of their produce at a price set by the state to their community and the state.

All this should make clear to us that we are now in a completely new world, even though that world is still called the Roman Empire. We might also reflect that in the change since 180 we have a sobering illustration of what can happen to any people who give up political freedom for the gift of security and the pursuit of money and pleasure.

Constantine the Great

After Diocletian there was a certain amount of trouble until in 324 Constantine the Great won the purple under the sign of the Cross. During his struggles in 313 an edict of toleration was issued for Christianity, which was finally to become the official religion.

Under Constantine, the capital was moved to the site of Byzantium and called Constantinople ("city of Constantine"). Eventually, in 395 A.D., an Empire of the East and an Empire of the West were set up.

The Last Act of the Drama

The eastern empire lasted until the capture of Constantinople by the Turks in 1453. Its culture, called Byzantine, had Greek for its official language but its spirit was that of an eastern despotism.

In the West, Visigoths, Ostrogoths, Vandals, Franks, and the Asian Huns burst over the frontiers. The Jutes, Angles, and Saxons planted themselves in Britain. In 410 A.D. Alaric and his Goths sacked Rome. The formal end of the Empire of the West is placed in 476, when the last Caesar, Romulus Augustulus, was dethroned. Out of the chaos in the West the Germanic Kingdoms gradually emerged.

The idea of the universal Roman Empire did not die. It lived on for centuries to influence, for example, such widely separated conquerors as Charlemagne and Napoleon. We must remember, in fact, that, just as today we are not always conscious of historical changes taking place in our own lifetime, so the people of the West in those days were not conscious of any separation from the past. There was no one to say: "At this point the

Roman empire has ended and the Middle Ages are beginning". Moreover, because the decline had been gradual, no one realized fully the tremendous drop in living standards and culture since the days of Hadrian or Augustus or Cicero. People lived from day to day, always hoping, as we do.

The Roman empire left behind it a great inheritor, the Christian Church. By 476 it was thoroughly organized in an efficient Roman way. It had overcome the great heresies. The Council of Nicaea in Asia Minor, held in 325 under the aegis of Constantine to settle the doctrinal dispute between the Athanasians and Arians, was one of the landmarks. The violent debate turned on one letter, the Greek *iota*. The Arians were *homoiousians*; that is, led by Bishop Arius, they held that Christ was not of the *same* substance as the Father but of *similar* substance (Greek *homoios*-similar), and that since he was the Son of the Father he must have been subsequent to Him. Bishop Athanasius and his followers were *homoousians* (Greek *homos*—same), who claimed that Christ was of the same substance as the Father, and that the Father, Son, and Holy Ghost were one in time, substance, and power. The Athanasians won and promulgated the Nicene creed, which is still the basic doctrine of Christianity. They then proceeded to persecute Arians with the same ferocity as Christians had been persecuted by the pagans.

Another landmark was St. Augustine's *City of God* in which he expounded the thesis of the universality of the Christian Church in place of the universality of Rome, a work which shaped the theology of medieval Europe. Well organized and vital in its missionary zeal, when the Western Empire fell the Church Christianized the pagans, and was the chief agent in preserving a certain amount of culture through the so-called Dark Ages of Europe. Later, through the concept of an over-riding Christian faith, it gave an over-all unity to the emerging nations of the West.

Summary

We have traced in far too brief a space the rise and fall of the Greeks and the Romans. In addition to the imprint left on the English we speak and write, in which one half our words are derived in one way or another from Greek and Latin, and apart from the Hebrew contribution, these two peoples provided the base on which our civilization is built. The Greek contribution, to repeat, is principally in art, literature and ideas, such as the idea of democracy. Even Christianity was, to a considerable degree, "hellenized", and also "romanized." To the Romans we owe order, organization, law, much of our architecture, and the idea of a universal empire to be ruled with an even-handed justice and to be welded, in spite of divergencies, into a basic unity.

It is a pity that so much of what the Greeks and Romans knew had to be rediscovered by a Europe which had relapsed into a near barbarism. Yet through the Christian Church and through the memories of the Roman empire, something of culture remained. Then, when the Greek spirit reached the West again, the Renaissance or "Rebirth" began. To understand our cultural heritage and, for that matter, to understand ourselves, it is vital to comprehend ancient Greece and Rome.

Readings from Sources of the Period

(a) The earliest of the four gospels of the New Testament was not composed until between 65–75 A.D. Between 50–65 A.D., however, St. Paul wrote a number of letters, which body forth his missionary fervour and the difficulties of organizing the first Christian communities.

The Epistle of Paul to the Galatians

Paul an apostle—not appointed by men nor commissioned by any man but by Jesus Christ and God the Father who raised him from the dead—with all the brothers who are beside me, to the churches of Galatia: grace and peace to you from God our Father and the Lord Jesus Christ who gave himself for our sins to rescue us from the present evil world—by the will of our God and Father, to whom be glory for ever and ever. Amen.

I am astonished that you are hastily shifting like this, deserting Him who called you by Christ's grace and going over to another gospel. It simply means that certain individuals are unsettling you; they want to distort the gospel of Christ. Now even though it were myself or some angel from heaven, whoever preaches a gospel that contradicts the gospel I preached to you, God's curse be on him! I have said it before and I now repeat it: whoever preaches a gospel to you that contradicts the gospel you have already received, God's curse be on him!

Now is that "appealing to the interests of men" or of God? Trying to "satisfy men"? Why, if I still tried to give satisfaction to human masters, I would be no servant of Christ. No, brothers, I tell you the gospel that I preach is not a human affair; no man put it into my hands, no man taught me what it meant, I had it by a revelation of Jesus Christ.

You know the story of my past career in Judaism; you know how furiously I persecuted the church of God and harried it, and how in Judaism I out-stripped many of my own age and race in special ardour for the ancestral traditions of my house. But the God who had set me apart *from my very birth called* me by his grace, and when he chose to reveal his Son to me, that I might preach him to the Gentiles, instead of consulting with any human being, instead of going up to Jerusalem to see those who had been apostles before me, I went off at once to Arabia, and on my return I came back to Damascus.

Then, after three years, I went up to Jerusalem to make the acquaintance of Cephas. I stayed a fortnight with him. I saw no other apostle, only James the brother of the Lord. (I am writing you the sheer truth, I swear it before God!) Then I went to the districts of Syria and of Cilicia. Personally I was quite unknown to the Christian churches of Judaea; they merely heard that 'our former persecutor is now preaching the faith he once harried,' which made them praise God for me.

Then, fourteen years later, I went up to Jerusalem again, accompanied by Barnabas; I took Titus with me also. (It was in consequence of a revelation that I went up at all.) I submitted the gospel I am in the habit of preaching to the Gentiles, submitting it privately to the authorities, to make sure that my course of action would be and had been sound.

(Moffatt, *op. cit.*, New Testament, p. 235.)

(b) During the collapse of the Roman Empire, literature declined. The best writing was produced by the Christian apologists. Below is an extract from *The Divine Institutes* of Lactantius, (250?–330? A.D.) a native of Numidia in Africa, who was invited by the emperor Diocletian to be professor of Latin Literature at his court but later suffered persecution for being a Christian. When Constantine the Great came to the throne his son, Crispus, was put under the tutorship of Lactantius.

And as there is but one founder and ruler of the world, God, and as truth is one; so wisdom must be one and simple, because, if anything is true and good, it cannot be perfect unless it is the only one of its kind. But if philosophy were able to form the life, no others but philosophers would be good, and all those who had not learned it would be always bad. But since there are, and always have been, innumerable persons who are or have been good without any learning, but of philosophers there has seldom been one who has done anything praiseworthy in his life; who is there, I pray, who does not see that those men are not teachers of virtue, of which they themselves are destitute? For if any one should diligently inquire into their character, he will find that they are passionate, covetous, lustful, arrogant, wanton, and, concealing their vices under a show of wisdom, doing those things at home which they had censured in the schools.

(Guinagh and Dorjahn, *op. cit.*, p. 786—translated by William Fletcher.)

(c) Saint Augustine (354–430 A.D.) may be regarded as the greatest Latin father. Born like Lactantius in Numidia, he was at first a Manichaean (a heretical sect of Christianity) but was converted to the orthodox faith in 387 A.D. His *Confessions* from which the extract below is taken, shows the intensity of his faith.

Oh in what accents spake I unto Thee, my God, when I read the Psalms of David, those faithful songs, and sounds of devotion, which allow of no swelling spirit, as yet a Catechumen, and a novice in Thy real love, resting in that villa, with Alypius, a Catechumen, my mother cleaving to us, in female garb with masculine faith, with the tranquillity of age, motherly love, Christian piety. Oh, what accents did I utter unto Thee in those Psalms, and how was I by them kindled towards Thee, and on fire to rehearse them, if possible, through the whole world, against the pride of mankind. And yet they are sung through the whole world, nor can *any hide himself from Thy heat*. With what vehement and bitter sorrow was I angered at the Manichees! and again I pitied them, for that they knew not those Sacraments, those medicines, and were mad against the antidote, which might have recovered them of their madness. How I would they had then been somewhere near me, and without my knowing that they were there, could have beheld my countenance, and heard my words, when I read the fourth Psalm in that time of my rest, and how that Psalm wrought upon me, *When I called, the God of my righteousness heard me; in tribulation Thou enlargedst me. Have mercy upon me, O Lord, and hear my prayer.*

(*Ibid.*, pp. 798–799, translated by E. B. Pusey.)

(d) The historians of Rome from the 3rd to the 5th centuries A.D. are not too reliable. Below are extracts from writers of the *Historia Augusta*.

1. A description of the luxury of the emperor Elagabalus.

He had couches made of solid silver for use in his banqueting-rooms and his bed-chambers. In imitation of Apicius he frequently ate camels-heels and also cocks-combs taken from the living birds, and the tongues of peacocks and nightingales, because he was told that one who ate them was immune from the plague. He served to the palace-attendants, moreover, huge platters heaped up with the viscera of mullets, and flamingo-brains, partridge-eggs, thrush-brains, and the heads of parrots, pheasants, and peacocks. And the beards of the mullets that he ordered served were so large that they were brought on, like cress or parsley or pickled beans or fenugreek, in well filled bowls and disk-shaped platters—a particularly amazing performance.

2. In the *Historia Augusta* a letter from the emperor Claudius (268–270 A.D.) to the governor of Illyricum describes his defeat of the Goths who had invaded Macedonia, Thrace and Greece, in 269 A.D.

"From Claudius to Brocchus. We have destroyed three hundred and twenty thousand Goths, we have sunk two thousand ships. The rivers are covered over with their shields, all the banks are buried under their swords and their spears. The fields are hidden beneath their bones, no road is clear, their mighty waggon-train has been abandoned. We have captured so many women that the victorious soldiers can take for themselves two or three apiece.

IX. And would that the commonwealth had not had to endure Gallienus! Would that it had not had to bear six hundred pretenders! Had but those soldiers been saved who fell in divers battles, those legions saved which Gallienus destroyed, disastrously victorious, how much strength would the state have gained! Now, indeed, my diligence has but gathered together for the preservation of the Roman commonwealth the scattered remains of the shipwrecked state."

3. Aurelian (270–275 A.D.) asked Zenobia to surrender but was refused. The extract tells how he captured her and Palmyra.

XXVIII. On receiving this letter Aurelian felt no shame, but rather was angered, and at once he gathered together from every side his soldiers and leaders and laid siege to Palmyra; and that brave man gave his attention to everything that seemed incomplete or neglected. For he cut off the reinforcements which the Persians had sent, and he tampered with the squadrons of Saracens and Armenians, bringing them over to his own side, some by forcible means and some by cunning.

(David Magie, *Translation of the Scriptores Historiae Augustae*, Vol. II. Loeb Classical Library, New York: G. P. Putnam's Sons, 1924.)

(e) In 301 A.D. the emperor, Diocletian, worried by the high cost of living, issued an edict setting a list of maximum prices. Below are extracts from this code, although it should be noted that the equivalents to Roman prices were set in 1911, and should, therefore, be quintupled to represent today's prices.

Diocletian's Edict and the Cost of Living

(Unit of measure, the bushel)

1 Wheat		
2 Barley	. . . .	74.5 cents
3 Rye	. . . .	45 "
4 Millet, ground	. . . .	74.5 "
5 Millet, whole	. . . .	37 "
7 Spelt, hulled	. . . .	74.5 "
8 Spelt, not hulled	. . . .	22.5 "
9 Beans, ground	. . . .	74.5 "
10 Beans, not ground	. . . .	45 "
11 Lentils	. . . .	74.5 "
12–16 Peas, various sorts	. . . .	45–74.5 "
17 Oats	. . . .	22.5 "
31 Poppy seeds	. . . .	$1.12
34 Mustard	. . . .	$1.12
35 Prepared mustard, quart	. . . .	6 cents

II *(Unit of measure, the quart)*

1a Wine from Picenum	. . . .	22.5 cents
2 Wine from Tibur	. . . .	22.5 "
7 Wine from Falernum	. . . .	22.5 "
10 Wine of the country	. . . .	6 "
11–12 Beer	. . . .	1.5–3 "

III *(Unit of measure, the quart)*

1a Oil, first quality	. . . .	30.3 cents
2 Oil, second quality	. . . .	18 "
5 Vinegar	. . . .	4.3 "
8 Salt, bushel	. . . .	74.5 "
10 Honey, best	. . . .	30.3 "
11 Honey, second quality	. . . .	15 "

IV *(Unit, unless otherwise noted, pound avoirdupois)*

1a Pork	. . . .	7.3 cents
2 Beef	. . . .	4.9 "
3 Goat's flesh or mutton	. . . .	4.9 "
6 Pig's liver	. . . .	9.8 "
8 Ham, best	. . . .	12 "
21 Goose, artificially fed (1)	. . . .	87 "
22 Goose, not artificially fed (1)	. . . .	43.5 "
23 Pair of fowls	. . . .	26 "
29 Pair of pigeons	. . . .	10.5 "

47 Lamb . . . . 7.3 cents
48 Kid . . . . .7.3 ”
50 Butter . . . . .9.8 ”

V *(Unit, the pound)*

1*a* Sea fish with sharp spines . . . . 14.6 cents
 2 Fish, second quality . . . . 9.7 ”
 3 River fish, best quality . . . . 7.3 ”
 4 Fish, second quality . . . . 4.8 ”
 5 Salt fish . . . . 8.3 ”
 6 Oysters (by the hundred) . . . . 43.5 ”
11 Dry cheese . . . . 7.3 ”
12 Sardines . . . . .9.7 ”

VI

 1 Artichokes, large (5) . . . . 4.3 cents
 7 Lettuce, best (5) . . . . .1.7 ”
 9 Cabbages, best (5) . . . . 1.7 ”
10 Cabbages, small (10) . . . . 1.7 ”
18 Turnips, large (10) . . . . 1.7 ”
24 Watercress, per bunch of 20 . . . . .4.3 ”
28 Cucumbers, first quality (10) . . . . .1.7 ”
29 Cucumbers, small (20) . . . . .1.7 ”
34 Garden asparagus, per bunch (25) . . . . . . .2.6 ”
35 Wild asparagus (50) . . . . .1.7 ”
38 Shelled green beans, quart . . . . .3 ”
43 Eggs (4) . . . . .1.7 ”
46 Snails, large (20) . . . . .1.7 ”
65 Apples, best (10) . . . . .1.7 ”
67 Apples, small (40) . . . . .1.7 ”
78 Figs, best (25) . . . . .1.7 ”
80 Table grapes (2.8 pound) . . . . .1.7 ”
95 Sheep's milk, quart . . . . .6 ”
96 Cheese, fresh, quart . . . . 6 ”

VII *(Where (k) is set down the workman receives his "keep" also)*

1*a* Manual laborer (k) . . . . 10.8 cents
 2 Bricklayer (k) . . . . 21.6 ”
 3 Joiner (interior work) (k) . . . . 21.6 ”
3*a* Carpenter (k) . . . . 21.6 ”
 4 Lime-burner (k) . . . . .21.6 ”
 5 Marble-worker (k) . . . . 26 ”
 6 Mosaic-worker (fine work) (k) . . . . 26 ”
 7 Stone-mason (k) . . . . .21.6 ”
 8 Wall-painter (k) . . . . .32.4 ”
 9 Figure-painter (k) . . . . .64.8 ”
10 Wagon-maker (k) . . . . 21.6 ”
11 Smith (k) . . . . 21.6 ”

12 Baker (k) . . . . .21.6 cents
13 Ship-builder, for sea-going ships (k) . . . . .26 ”
14 Ship-builder, for river boats (k) . . . . . .21.6 ”
17 Driver, for camel, ass, or mule (k) . . . . .10.8 ”
18 Shepherd (k) . . . . 8.7 ”
20 Veterinary, for cutting, and straightening hoofs,
      per animal . . . . 2.6 ”
22 Barber, for each man . . . . .9 cent
23 Sheep-shearer, for each sheep (k) . . . . . . .9 ”
24a Coppersmith, for work in brass, per pound   3.5 cents
25 Coppersmith, for work in copper,
      per pound . . . . 2.6 ”
26 Coppersmith for finishing vessels, per pound   2.6 ”
27 Coppersmith, for finishing figures and statues,
      per pound . . . . .1.7 ”
29 Maker of statues, etc., per day (k) . . . . . .32.4 ”
31 Water-carrier, per day (k) . . . . .10.9 ”
32 Sewer-cleaner, per day (k) . . . . .10.9 ”
33 Knife-grinder, for old sabre . . . . .10.9 ”
36 Knife-grinder, for double axe . . . . 3.5 ”
39 Writer, 100 lines best writing . . . . .10.9 ”
40 Writer, 100 lines ordinary writing . . . . . 8.7 ”
41 Document writer for record of 100 lines . . . 4.3 ”
42 Tailor, for cutting out and finishing overgarment
      of first quality . . . . .26.1 ”
43 Tailor, for cutting out and finishing overgarment
      of second quality . . . . .17.4 ”
44 For a large cowl . . . . .10.9 ”
45 For a small cowl . . . . 8.7 ”
46 For trousers . . . . 8.7 ”
52 Felt horse-blanket, black or white, 3 pounds
      weight . . . . .43.5 ”
53 Cover, first quality, with embroidery, 3 pounds
      weight $1.09
64 Gymnastic teacher, per pupil, per month   . .21.6 cents
65 Employee to watch children, per child, per
      month . . . . .21.6 ”
66 Elementary teacher, per pupil, per month   . .21.6 ”
67 Teacher of arithmetic, per pupil, per month   32.6 ”
68 Teacher of stenography, per pupil, per
      month . . . . .32.6 ”
69 Writing-teacher, per pupil, per month . . . .21.6 ”
70 Teacher of Greek, Latin, geometry, per pupil,
      per month . . . . .87 ”
71 Teacher of rhetoric, per pupil, per month $1.09
72 Advocate or counsel for presenting a case $1.09
73 For finishing a case $4.35
74 Teacher of architecture, per pupil, per month   43.5 cents
75 Watcher of clothes in public bath, for each
      patron . . . . .9 cent

VIII

1*a* Hide, Babylonian, first quality $2.17
2 Hide, Babylonian, second quality $1.74
4 Hide, Phoenician (?) . . . . 43 cents
6*a* Cowhide, unworked, first quality $2.17
7 Cowhide, prepared for shoe soles $3.26
9 Hide, second quality, unworked $1.31
10 Hide, second quality, worked $2.17
11 Goatskin, large, unworked . . . . 17 cents
12 Goatskin, large, worked . . . . 22 ”
13 Sheepskin, large, unworked . . . . 8.7 ”
14 Sheepskin, large, worked . . . . 13 ”
17 Kidskin, unworked . . . . 4.3 ”
18 Kidskin, worked . . . . 7 ”
27 Wolfskin, unworked . . . . 10.8 ”
28 Wolfskin, worked . . . . 17.4 ”
33 Bearskin, large, unworked . . . . 43 ”
39 Leopardskin, unworked $4.35
41 Lionskin, worked $4.35

IX

5*a* Boots, first quality, for mule-drivers and
  peasants, per pair, without nails . . . . . . 52 cents
6 Soldiers' boots, without nails . . . . 43 ”
7 Patricians' shoes . . . . 65 ”
8 Senatorial shoes . . . . 43 ”
9 Knights' shoes . . . . 30.5 ”
10 Women's boots . . . . 26 ”
11 Soldiers' shoes . . . . 32.6 ”
15 Cowhide shoes for women, double soles . . 21.7 ”
16 Cowhide shoes for women, single soles . . . 13 ”
20 Men's slippers . . . . 26 ”
21 Women's slippers . . . . 21.7 ”

XVI

8*a* Sewing-needle, finest quality . . . . 1.7 cents
9 Sewing-needle, second quality . . . . .9 cent

XVII

1 Transportation, 1 person, 1 mile . . . . .9 cent
2 Rent for wagon, 1 mile . . . . 5 cents
3 Freight charges for wagon containing up to
  1200 pounds, per mile . . . . 8.7 ”
4 Freight charges for camel load of 600 pounds,
  per mile . . . . .3.5 ”
5 Rent for laden ass, per mile . . . . 1.8 ”
7 Hay and straw, 3 pounds . . . . .9 cent

XVIII

   1*a* Goose-quills, per pound   . . . . .43.5 cents
11*a* Ink, per pound   5   "
 12 Reed pens from Paphos (10)   . . . . .1.7 "
 13 Reed pens, second quality (20)   . . . . .1.7 "

(F. F. Abbott: *Common People of Ancient Rome*, New York, Charles Scribner's Sons, 1911.)

APPENDIX OF SELECTED PRINTS

Cultural Evolution Represented By Art Prints

These prints illustrate the story of our cultural ancestors from the upper Palaeolithic to the fall of the Western Roman Empire. They begin with the birth of art in the Magdalenian period.

The first savage who, hundreds of thousands of years ago, shaped a stick or stone into an implement for future use started humanity on its stumbling journey toward civilization. Yet in over half a million years Old Stone Age man had learned little beyond the manufacture of stone tools, the use of fire and of caves as shelters, some form of community life and a rudimentary religion. Then, art was born.

The Beginnings

It was in 1879 that the first palaeolithic cave paintings were found at Altamira in northwestern Spain. There was skepticism until, two decades later, the learned Abbé, Henri Breuil, came upon similar paintings in a cave at Font-de-Gaume in France. Since that time over fifty "picture-gallery" caves have been explored in France and Spain, the latest discovery being in 1940 at Lascaux.

The picture-gallery caves are difficult to enter. It is thought that the animals were painted as part of a religious rite to ensure success in the hunt. Yet the people of Magdalenian times, often called by the generic name of Cro-Magnons, also made excellent carvings of horses' heads, ibexes, grouse and so on in bone or ivory. They were hunters, but hunters with that compelling aesthetic sense which is one of the differentiations between man and the rest of of animate beings. Here, certainly, are some of our cultural ancestors. In the Neolithic, or New Stone Age, the invention of farming and the taming of animals made men food-producers. Settled life began along with the discovery of new techniques, such as weaving and the making of pottery. This "neolithic revolution" occurred first in the Near and Middle East. In this same area, before the close of the 5th millenium B.C. copper was being smelted and the Age of Metals began. Bronze was invented about 2500 B.C. and iron came into use about a thousand years later. Furthermore, during the 4th millenium B.C. the first civilizations began in Egypt and Mesopotamia.

RUNNING BOAR
ALTAMIRA, SPAIN

MIDDLE MAGDALENIAN

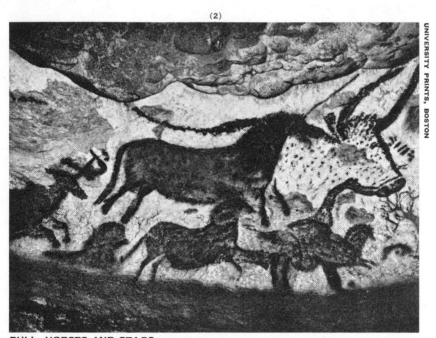

BULL, HORSES AND STAGS
LASCAUX CAVE, FRANCE

UPPER PALEOLITHIC (MAGDALENIAN)

Egypt

The pyramids of 4th dynasty Egypt (c. 2700 B.C.) still inspire wonder. Prints 6 and 7 present the culmination of the early mastaba tombs in the pyramids of Khufu, Khafre and Menkaure.

The pyramids, erected as tombs for the Pharaohs, prove the tremendous architectural skill of the ancient Egyptians. Their sculpture is equally indicative of the high level of their civilization. In the portrait of Khafre (8, 9) you will observe complete technical mastery of the stone. The rigidity is intentional. Egyptian sculptors aimed at producing an impression of majesty and timelessness. They achieved this by frontality, by centrality (each statue could be divided into two equal halves) and by planting both feet of the statue firmly on the ground and keeping the arms stiff. These conventions were carried over into both bas-relief and painting (10, 11).

The representation of daily occupations such as 12, a harvest scene, and 13, the force-feeding of geese as is still done to prepare for pâté de foie gras, are two examples from the tombs to remind us how the whole of life in the Old Kingdom, high and low, can be reconstructed from the tomb paintings and bas-relief. You

(3)

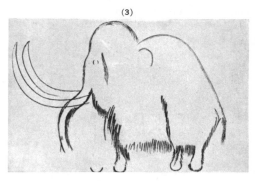

(5)

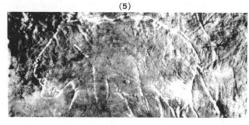

(3) **WOOLLY MAMMOTH (PAINTING)**
FONT DE GAUME CAVE, FRANCE

LATE AURIGNACIAN ?

(4)

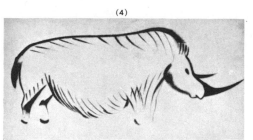

(4) **WOOLLY RHINOCEROS (PAINTING)**
FONT DE GAUME CAVE, FRANCE

LATE AURIGNACIAN ?

(5) **CAVE BEAR (INCISED)**
COMBARELLES CAVE, FRANCE

EARLY MAGDALENIAN?

UNIVERSITY PRINTS, BOSTON

might note, too, the developed hieroglyphic script.

You will recall that the Old Kingdom dissolved into chaos but that the 11th and 12th Theban dynasties re-united Egypt. A high period of peace and luxury was reached under Amenhemet III. From the rock-cut tombs of this Middle Kingdom come beautifully finished models of villas, the counting of cattle, the brewing of beer and so on. It was believed that these models would be reanimated in life size in the Egyptian paradise to serve the dead person. For by this time (2000 B.C.) the Egyptians had developed a definite theory of immortality, including mummification and elaborate instructions for the attainment of Paradise, which depended on living a good life (14). The "Book of the Dead," the manuscript of which reached the British Museum in 1888, is based on a Middle Kingdom original.

The Middle Kingdom was ended in 1788 B.C. by the Kyksos invasion. When in 1580 B.C. the intruders were expelled, the Egyptians began to build an empire.

Thutmose III (15) was the Napoleon of Egypt. At his death, an Egyptian empire stretched from the great bend of the Euphrates to the 4th cataract of the Nile. Wealth poured into Egypt. One of his descendants, Amenhotep (or Amenophis) III, erected the Colossi near Thebes (16) as the gateway (pylon) to a temple.

The most important Egyptian god of this period was Amon, or Amen, the ram-god of Thebes. Ikhnaton (17), the son of Amenhotep III, tried to replace Amon and all other gods by the worship of one universal god, symbolized by the Aten, the shining disc of the sun (18). He built a new capital, Tell-el-Amarna, and introduced a realistic style in art. The masterpiece of his reign is the bust of his beautiful wife, Nofretete (or Nefertiti) (19). This bust was found in the corner of a room in what had been a sculptor's house in Tell-el-Amarna. It glows with color—and one has only to look at it to realize that it is the portrait of a sensitive and sophisticated woman.

Ikhnaton's son-in-law, Tutankamon, was forced to restore the worship of Amon. It was his tomb which in November, 1922, was discovered by Carter in the cliffs behind Thebes. The richness and artistry of the objects found (20) amazed the world. Marvelous inlay work, gilded couches and chairs and three coffins of which the inmost was of solid gold and worth at least $175,000—such were the treasures buried with a minor Pharaoh.

While during Ikhnaton's reign much of the Egyptian empire was lost, later it was in part recovered. The most important Pharaoh of the period was Rameses II, who ruled for 67 years. Far up the Nile, Rameses built the underground temple at Abu Simbel (21, 22), which is tunneled 192 feet into the rock; this will soon be submerged under the waters of the new Aswan dam. He also erected the hypostyle hall of the Temple of Amon at Karnak near Thebes. This example of Egyptian monumental architecture measures 170 by 338 feet and could easily contain the whole of the Notre Dame cathedral in Paris. Tomb-paintings such as 23 further illustrate the luxury of the life of the period.

The empire was lost about 1190 B.C. because of folk-movements from the north. Thenceforward, Egypt was comparatively unimportant politically. But its way of life influenced the Hebrews and the Greeks and Romans, and through them, us, particularly in the fields of philosophy and religion.

PYRAMIDS FROM THE SOUTH, GIZEH
LEFT, MYCERINUS; CENTER, KHAFRA (CHEFREN); RIGHT, KHUFU (CHEOPS)

EGYPTIAN. IV DYNASTY

SPHINX OF KHAFRE AND PYRAMID OF KHUFU, GIZEH

IV DYNASTY

The great pyramid of Khufu (7) is estimated to contain 2,300,000 blocks of stone of an average weight of $2\frac{1}{2}$ tons each. It covers 13 acres and was built with mathematical exactitude.

(8)

KHAFRE
MUSEUM, CAIRO
IV DYNASTY

(9)

KHAFRE (CHEFREN)
MUSEUM, CAIRO

IV DYNASTY

(10)

WOODEN PANELS OF HESIRE
MUSEUM, CAIRO

III DYNASTY

(11)

PAINTED WALL DECORATION
MUSEUM, BERLIN

IV DYNASTY   The Egyptian sculptural conventions of rigidity and centrality were transferred to both bas-relief (10) and painting (11); notice that both shoulders and the full eye are shown in profile.

(12)

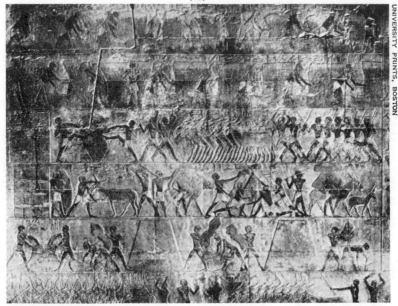

HARVEST SCENE
TOMB OF TI, SAKKARA

V DYNASTY

(13)

FATTENING GEESE
MUSEUM, BERLIN

OLD KINGDOM

UNIVERSITY PRINTS, BOSTON

WEIGHING OF THE HEART, FROM BOOK OF THE DEAD: PAPYRUS OF ANI
BRITISH MUSEUM, LONDON

XVIII DYNASTY

This reproduction from the "Book of the Dead" illustrates the weighing of the heart of the dead person against the "feather of truth." The Egyptians believed that after death the soul traveled to the realm of the god Osiris to be judged for its earthly deeds. Here the dead person would make a "negative confession," claiming that he had harmed no one during his life; in the presence of the feather of truth, the heart would cry out if a lie was told. If the dead person passed this test, he was admitted to Paradise, but if not, his soul was cast out to be devoured by demons.

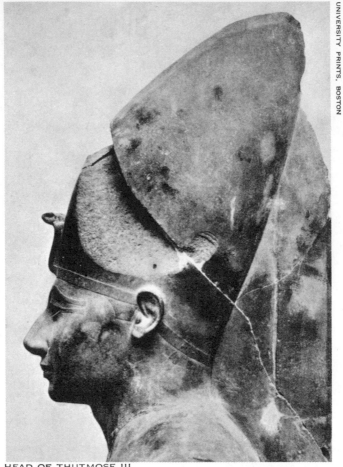

HEAD OF THUTMOSE III
MUSEUM, CAIRO

XVIII DYNASTY

COLOSSAL STATUES OF AMENOPHIS III (MEMNON COLOSSI), THEBES

EGYPTIAN. XVIII DYNASTY

Each of these Colossi was originally carved from a single block of stone and is still 52 feet in height, standing on a pedestal of 13 feet.

TWO COLOSSAL STATUES OF AMENHOTEP IV (IKHNATON)

MUSEUM, CAIRO

XVIII DYNASTY

(18)

IKHNATON WORSHIPING THE SUN

MUSEUM, CAIRO

XVIII DYNASTY

(19)

UNIVERSITY PRINTS, BOSTON

HEAD OF QUEEN NOFRETETE
MUSEUM, BERLIN

XVIII DYNASTY

(20)

UNIVERSITY PRINTS, BOSTON

RELIEF ON BACK OF THRONE OF KING TUTANKHAMON
MUSEUM, CAIRO

XVIII DYNASTY

UNIVERSITY PRINTS, BOSTON

GENERAL VIEW OF ROCK-CUT TEMPLES, ABU SIMBEL

EGYPTIAN. XIX DYNASTY

UNIVERSITY PRINTS, BOSTON

FAÇADE. TEMPLE OF AMON-RE, ABU SIMBEL

EGYPTIAN. XIX DYNASTY

GUESTS AT AN ENTERTAINMENT
TOMB OF NAKHT, THEBES

XVIII DYNASTY

The luxurious life of the Eighteenth Dynasty is reflected in this tomb-painting, where you will notice the piles of food, the airy costumes and the cakes of perfume which the banqueters have on their heads to melt gradually as the feast continues; meanwhile a musician plays and the guests sniff daintily at lotus flowers.

Near Eastern Cultures

Mesopotamia was the scene of the other of the two earliest civilizations. Here we find a mystery people, the Sumerians, an extremely religious culture. The focal point of each of their cities was a stepped pyramid of brick on which sat the temple of the city's patron deity.

In 1928-29, Sir Leonard Woolley uncovered the Royal Graves of the 1st dynasty of Ur, the Sumerian city from which Abraham of the Bible came. Because of the lack of stone the Sumerians built in brick. They also wrote on tablets of clay in a script called cuneiform. Their far-reaching trade included contacts with a recently discovered civilization in the Indus valley in India. Though later in date, this was a "riverine" civilization like those of Egypt and Mesopotamia.

The Sumerians exhausted themselves by civil wars. About 2350 B.C. they were conquered by the Semitic Akkadians under Sargon I. He and his successor, Naram-Sin, built an empire. The bas-relief of Naram-Sin conquering the Lulubu, a mountain-tribe (24), is full of vigor. In general, however, the sculpture of Mesopotamia does not equal the sculpture of Egypt.

When the Akkadian empire collapsed, the 3rd dynasty of Ur gave the Sumerians a century of glory. Then came the First Babylonian Empire of the Semite Hammurabi (c. 1750 B.C.). Sumerian culture was taken over, but the Sumerian language gradually ceased to be spoken.

Hammurabi had his famous code of laws carved on a pillar of basalt, which was found in modern times at Susa. These laws, of which 282 remain, are based on the principle of an eye for an eye. As you will note, Hammurabi claimed he received his laws from the sun-god (25).

This is one of many parallels between the religious attitudes of the peoples of Mesopotamia and the Hebrews. The Sumerian cities were holy cities. The Sumerians also had stories of creation and of the flood which are similar to the account in the first chapters of Genesis in the Bible. Above all they believed that the gods were everything and that man owed everything he had and was to them.

The First Babylonian Empire succumbed to the attack of a mountain people, the Kassites (c. 1600 B.C.). Centuries later the Assyrians welded Mesopotamia, Syria, Phoenicia, Palestine and Egypt into one empire. The black obelisk of Shalmaneser III (26), who ruled from 859 to 824 B.C., relates his conquests. In the second row of figures on it, the Jews are shown, bringing tribute.

Assyrian culture was derivative; they preserved much of Mesopotamian civilization and they built great cities and palaces. Their gateways were flanked by enormous winged and human-headed lions and bulls (27). In animal sculpture, however, Assyrian realism is unsurpassed. Their love of cruelty is shown here and in their representations of how, after capturing cities, they impaled people or flayed them alive.

Assyria was overthrown by the combined forces of Babylonia and the Medes. For a brief period the Second Babylonian Empire blazed in splendor. The procession-way for the god, Marduk, began outside the city and ran through the Ishtar Gate. The walls on either side were decorated by more than 500 reliefs in glazed tile, chiefly in blues and yellows, of animals and mythological creatures.

In 538 B.C. Babylon fell to Cyrus the Great, the King of the Medes and Persians. The Persian empire under Darius the Great (521–485 B.C.) reached from
the Danube in Europe to the first cataract of the Nile and westward to India and
deep into central Asia.

Persian culture was again inherited from Mesopotamia (28). They adapted the
cuneiform script to their language, which was a cousin-tongue to Greek and to
Old Anglo-Saxon. They followed the Assyrians in the division of their empire
into provinces, although their rule was much more humane. Their wealth was
prodigious.

Like that of Egypt, Mesopotamian culture had a considerable influence on the
Greeks and even more on the Hebrews. But the Hebrews did finally develop the
concept of one God of Righteousness for all mankind.

The far-off sources of our western culture spring from the soil of the Near and
Middle East. There are some definite contributions, such as the use of 60 as a
unit of the Phoenician alphabet and of the Hebrew Jehovah and Old Testament.
But most of what we have received from the Near and Middle East, including
Christianity, was transformed into what we call "Western" civilization by the
Greeks and Romans.

STELE OF NARAMSIN, FROM SUSA
LOUVRE, PARIS

AKKADIAN. SECOND HALF III MILLENNIUM B.C.

(25)

STELA OF HAMMURABI RECEIVING LAW CODE FROM THE SUN GOD, FROM SUSA
LOUVRE, PARIS

BABYLONIAN. XIX CENTURY B.C.

(26)

BLACK OBELISK OF SHALMANESER III
BRITISH MUSEUM, LONDON

858—824 B.C.

WINGED MYTHOLOGICAL FIGURES OF THE TIME OF SARGON II
LOUVRE, PARIS
721—705 B.C.

MAN-BULL CAPITAL (DETAIL) FROM TRIPYLON, PERSEPOLIS

ACHAEMENIAN.   STARTED BY DARIUS, 521—485 B.C.
COMPLETED BY XERXES, 485—465 B.C.

This print reflects traces of Oriental influences upon the Persian culture.

The Evolution of Greek Culture

The Greeks began to infiltrate southern Greece about 1750 B.C. They found a culture already spread throughout the Aegean. The chief center of this culture was Crete.

The Cretan culture is called Minoan and its apogée was from 1600–1400 B.C. There were great palaces, such as those at Phaistos and Knossos, and a wide-ranging trade. Life was gay and luxurious. The men wore gaily colored kilts (29), the women flounced skirts and open bodices as in 30. This fayence figurine is about 14 inches high. It and other figurines show women holding snakes as part of the worship of the Earth-Mother. Bull-grappling, probably a ritual connected with the fertility god, the Bull, of which Minos, the ruler of Knossos, was thought to be the incarnation, was an exciting and popular sport (31, 32).

In Minoan artistic expression there was, in general, movement and grace. The bull's head rhyton (33), about 14 inches high from nose to the top of the head, was fitted with golden horns and frontlet.

While the Minoans, a dark, lithe Mediterranean people, were civilizing the island of Crete, the blond Achaean Greeks established fortress-cities in the Greek peninsula, and about 1400 B.C. power and trade passed to them.

The principal city of the Achaeans was Mycenae. It is crouched on its hill like a lioness gazing down the gorge between Mount Zara and the Hill of Tombs over the red-earthed plain of Argos to the Bay of Nauplion. In print 34 you are looking southwest at its principal entrance, though the iron gates have now been removed and the great walls repaired. The wall to the right is a sally wall. From it the defenders could shoot at the unshielded sides of the attackers. To the left is the inner wall of the citadel. The lintel stone of the entrance is estimated to weigh 56 tons in one solid block. Above it two lions guard a Mycenean (really a Minoan) table-leg pillar.

Directly inside the entrance a ramp leads up under the inner wall to the palace in which, according to Greek legend, Klytemnestra murdered her husband, Agamemnon, leader of the Greeks against Troy, when he returned home victorious. To the right are the rock-cut tombs from which in 1876 Schliemann removed a treasure of bronze swords and daggers, jewelry, gold cups and golden death-masks. Print 35 is the death-mask of a bearded Achaean king.

Another and still earlier circle of tombs was found outside the walls in 1952 along with the remains of houses. In the Mycenean Age (1400–1200 B.C.) Mycenae was a powerful and populous city, although now the earth has covered its streets and houses.

The Dorian invasions of the 12th century B.C. destroyed the Achaeo-Mycenean culture and Greece relapsed into a "Dark Age." Into this primitive world came Phoenician traders, bringing with them such objects as the silver-gilt bowl seen in 36. The electrum earring from Rhodes (37) may well be reminiscent of Phoenician influence. In the 8th century B.C. Homer's epics began the world of the classical Greeks. During the next three centuries (800–500 B.C.) the Greeks spread themselves along the coasts of the Black and Mediterranean Seas. During those same centuries they developed lyric poetry and philosophy and made a beginning in architecture, vase-painting and sculpture.

Sculpture, like literature, can mirror the development of a people. In the archaic period of Greek sculpture (c. 620–500 B.C.) sculptors followed the stiffness of the Egyptian canons. The bronze statuette, 38, presents this archaic stiffness as expressed by what is called the Dorian School. Meanwhile, what we may term the Ionian School (although there were subdivisions) went in for decorative draped figures and an attempt to approximate movement (39).

In pottery, the Greeks used first a protogeometric and then a geometric style. This second style is exemplified by the oinochoe or wine-pourer (40) from Rhodes. There were also many pottery figurines. The horseman from Cyprus (41) is a prefiguration of certain styles of today.

The 7th century B.C. saw Corinthian potters invent the Orientalizing style with its profusion of animal, plant and human motifs. In the next century, Athenian potters came to the fore, when the black-figured style was invented. Here, the figures were painted in black on the natural reddish color of the clay, as in the amphorae (42, 43) signed by the famous vase-painters, Eskiar and Amasis. In 44 in the same style we see a picture of a blacksmith's shop in ancient Athens.

Toward the close of the 6th century B.C. the red-figured style began in which the background was painted black and the figures were left in the reddish clay color. The work in this style, together with the black-figured pots, present us with the best of the vase-paintings. There is a marvelous posing of the figures to suit the available space (45, 46); and all lines lead to a centre of interest but with enough variety to avoid a monotonous symmetry. Stories are told, and there is some of the finest freehand drawing in the history of art.

As already indicated, vase-painters signed their work. Excellent examples of artistry and command of detail are seen in the amphorae attributed to the Andokides painter (47) and the Lysippides painter (48). A skyphos signed by Hieron and Makron (49) and the rhyton by the Brygos painter are particularly good (50a and b).

We should not forget that most of the Greek vases were manufactured for household use. Even so, in general, they are works of art.

The excellence of the vase-painting continued through the 5th century B.C., which saw the peak of the Greek achievement, sparked, apparently, by the defeat of the Persians in Greece and of the Carthaginians in Sicily. In Athens, drama reached its zenith in the plays of Aeschylus, Sophocles, Euripides (51) and Aristophanes. Their plays were performed in the great outdoor theatre of Dionysus (52) on the south slope of the Acropolis. On the Acropolis itself, seen from the west in 53, gleamed the gem of the Doric order of architecture, the Parthenon (54). It faces east and in its outer *cella* stood the magnificent gold and ivory statue, 30 feet high, of Athena (*Cf.* other representations of Athena in 55, 56).

The Parthenon achieves its perfection by subtle deviations from the straight line. The Hephaestion (57) is another jewel of Doric architecture and so is the temple at Bassae in the heart of southern Greece, done by the same architect who designed the Parthenon.

The Erectheum, also on the Acropolis, is a beautiful building in the graceful and ornate Ionic order. The more pretentious Corinthian order is illustrated by print (58).

It was in the 5th century B.C., too, that Greek sculpture reached its ultimate. The years from 500–460 B.C. were transitional. During them sculptors learned complete mastery of stone and bronze and broke away from the rigidity of the archaic period. The Dorian transitional school is illustrated by the Charioteer of Delphi, one of the comparatively few hollow-cast bronze Greek statues which were not melted down during the Dark Age of Europe. The face is the Doric "mask" face, and the folds of the robe are like the flutings of a Doric column but the confidence in man is present and there is a strong twist to the torso.

In the same period the Argive school did the pediment sculptures for the temple of Aegine (59). The figures are a little less than life-size and there are traces of paint on them. The musculature and movement are excellent and all lines lead to the center of the pediment, although the treatment of the hair and eyes tends to be archaic.

This group of figures may well illustrate how sculpture to fill the pediments and metopes of temples (60) forced movement and composition upon the Greeks. Meanwhile, the Ionian school, as seen on the bas-relief on the back of the Ludovisi throne (61) was learning movement, a center of interest, a more skillful treatment of drapery and a progression toward the nude female figure. There is evidence of archaism in the handling of the eye, nose and hair and in the fall of the drapery. We have here the same theme as in Botticelli's famous painting of the Birth of Venus.

The same traces of archaism are to be seen in the Mourning Athena (62), a war memorial in which Athena leans on her spear before a stele commemorating the dead. But with the bronze Zeus from the Sea, dredged up fairly recently, we step into the full glory of the 5th century B.C. Here is Aeschylean grandeur at its best.

It is conjectured that this statue was done by Ageladas of Argos, the sculptor who taught the three 5th century B.C. masters, Myron, Phidias, and Polycleitus. Myron's Discobolus, though a Roman copy in stone of a bronze original, still shows movement. His contemporary, Phidias, is regarded as the master sculptor of all time. The three Fates (more probably the goddesses Artemis, Dione and Aphrodite) from the east pediment of the Parthenon illustrate his massive dignity combined with grace and his superb handling of drapery. Phidias makes one think of another giant of sculpture and painting, Michelangelo.

It is unfortunate that Phidias' supreme works, the Athena Parthenos and the Zeus of Olympia, are lost. The continuous frieze of the Parthenon, however, (63, 64) was done under his direction and ran high up, around the outer wall of the two *cellae*. This is the equal of any bas-relief.

Polycleitus, the last of the three, was famous for his statues of nude athletes with their weight resting on one leg and for his wounded Amazon. Restraint of emotion, dignity, and idealized representation of humanity, perfection of workmanship, and the thought behind the face—these are among the qualities which inform 5th century B.C. sculpture and literature (*cf.* 65).

The great sculptors of the 4th century B.C., Scopas, Praxiteles and Lysippus, kept these qualities but tended to choose more sensuous subjects. The Niobe and her daughter (66) is thought to be a Roman copy of an original group by Scopas. It exhibits his particular type of face—short nose, parted lips and wide-open, upward-looking Scopasian eye, an effect achieved by making the width of the eye one-half its length, by representing a bar of flesh over its outer edge and by sinking deep the part next to the nose. The same characteristics are shown in a Head of Heracles (67), thought to be a Roman copy of a work done by a follower of Scopas.

Scopas' contemporary, Praxiteles, achieved his sensuous effects by a narrow eye (width one-third the length), by the "Praxitelean slump" and the contrast between the smoothness of the body and the roughness of the drapery. The famous Venus di Milo (Aphrodite of Melo—68) is in the Praxitelean style.

These sculptures reflect the trend toward individualism and sensuousness in the 4th century B.C. Greek world after the Peloponnesian War had put a stop to the Great Age. So does a plastic lekythos representing the birth of Aphrodite (69). Gold earrings such as 70, 71, 72 remind us that styles in feminine adornment recur over the centuries.

Along with the change in sculpture went the trend to philosophic thought in Socrates (73), Plato (74), and Aristotle. In the second half of the century, sculpture began to move in new directions.

After Alexander the Great conquered the Persian empire, the fusion of Greek and Oriental culture which is called Hellenistic began. Once again sculpture, as well as literature, mirrored the trends of the new age. Realism, as seen in the bust of Socrates (75) and Art for Art's sake, as illustrated by the somewhat theatrical portrait of Homer (76), are among the new objectives.

Yet the sculpture is still magnificent. The Greek war-dance (77) and the Alexander Sarcophagus (78) are vivified with movement.

In the prints to illustrate the Greeks, sculpture in particular is used to embody the essential qualities of the Greek genius—its directness, dignity, perfection of workmanship, restraint of emotion, sense of proportion and emphasis on man. We must remember, however, that the Greeks also contributed democracy and an instinct for freedom to us as well as the standards by which western literature and architecture have lived. Furthermore, in philosophy, science, and almost every field of thought they blazed the paths we follow.

(29)

CUP BEARER (REPLICA)

MUSEUM, CANDIA

LATE MINOAN II

(30)

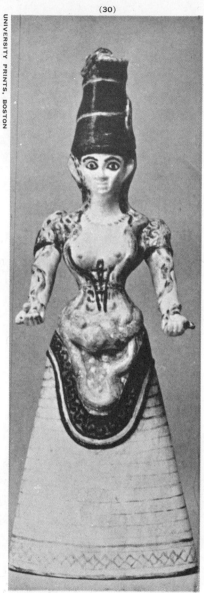

FAYENCE SNAKE GODDESS (REPLICA)

MUSEUM, CANDIA

MIDDLE MINOAN

(31)

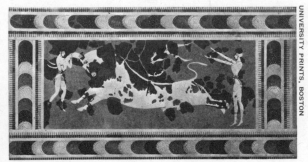

SCENE FROM A BULL FIGHT (REPLICA)
MUSEUM, CANDIA

LATE MINOAN II

(32)

IVORY BULL-JUMPER,
FROM PALACE OF KNOSSOS
MUSEUM, CANDIA

LATE MINOAN, c. 1550 B.C.

(33)

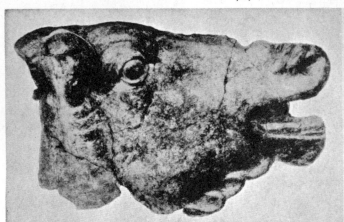

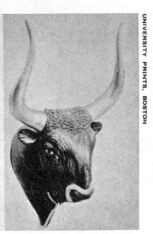

HEAD OF A BULL RELIEF
MUSEUM, CANDIA

LATE MINOAN II

BULL'S HEAD. STEATITE
MUSEUM, CANDIA

MIDDLE MINOAN

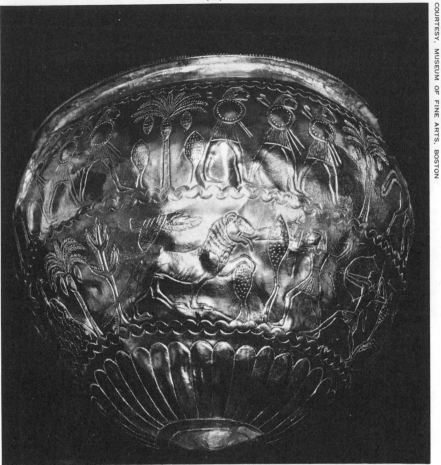

PHOENICIAN SILVER-GILT BOWL
7TH C. B.C.

ELECTRUM EARRING FROM RHODES
7TH C. B.C.

GATE OF LIONESSES, MYCENAE

GOLD FUNERAL MASK OF BEARDED WARRIOR (AGAMEMNON?), FROM MYCENAE
NATIONAL MUSEUM, ATHENS

ABOUT 1500 B.C.

HERMES HOLDING A RAM
BRONZE STATUETTE
6TH C. B.C.

BRONZE ATHENA PROMACHOS STATUETTE
NATIONAL MUSEUM, ATHENS

ABOUT 500 B.C.

RHODIAN OINOCHOE
7TH C. B.C.

GEOMETRIC HORSEMAN FROM CYPRUS
TERRACOTTA

AMPHORA BY ESKIAR
6TH C B.C.

AMPHORA WITH SIGNATURE OF AMASIS
6TH C. B.C.

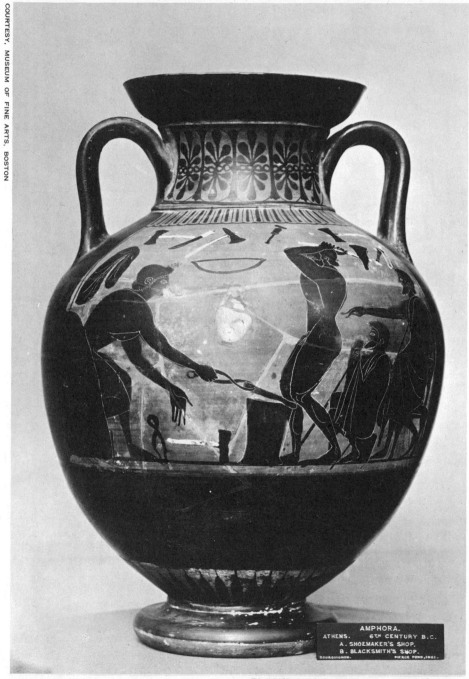

AMPHORA.
ATHENS.   6TH CENTURY B.C.
A. SHOEMAKER'S SHOP.
B. BLACKSMITH'S SHOP.
BOURGUIGNON.   PIERCE FUND, 1901.

BLACKSMITH'S SHOP
AMPHORA, LATE BLACK-FIGURED STYLE

RED-FIGURED AMPHORA: THESEUS CARRYING OFF KORONE
ALTE PINAKOTHEK, MUNICH

EUTHYMIDES.   END OF VI CENT. B.C.

RED-FIGURED KYLIX (EXTERIOR): SACK OF TROY
LOUVRE, PARIS

BRYGOS PAINTER.   FIRST QUARTER OF V CENT. B.C.

**AMPHORA ATTRIBUTED TO THE
ANDOKIDES PAINTER**

(48)

**AMPHORA ATTRIBUTED TO THE
LYSIPPIDES PAINTER**

(49)

SKYPHOS SIGNED BY HIERON
AND MAKRON
C. 480 B.C.

(50)

RHYTON BY THE BRYGOS PAINTER
C. 480 B.C.

DETAIL — RHYTON BY THE BRYGOS PAINTER

EURIPIDES
MUSEUM, NAPLES

EURIPIDES
MUSEUM, BERLIN

ABOUT 340 B.C., ROMAN COPIES

(52)

THEATRE OF DIONYSUS, ATHENS
GREEK. ROMAN RECONSTRUCTION.
LARGELY C. 330 B.C. REBUILT I—III CENT. A.D.

DRAWING BY RICHARD BOHN

THE ACROPOLIS OF ATHENS, RESTORED

GREEK.   GREAT BUILDINGS 447—409 B.C.

ACROPOLIS FROM THE HILL OF THE MUSES.   ATHENS

GREEK.   GREAT BUILDINGS 447—409 B.C.

(55)

ATHENA GIUSTINIANI
VATICAN, ROME

**HELLENISTIC ADAPTATION OF V CENT. B.C.
TYPE, ROMAN COPY**

(56)

ATHENA PARTHENOS
PRADO, MADRID

AFTER PHEIDIAS, c. 447—439 B.C., ROMAN COPY

THE "THESEUM" (TEMPLE OF HEPHAESTUS AND ATHENA), ATHENS
GREEK. 450—440 B.C.

TEMPLE OF THE OLYMPIAN ZEUS, ATHENS

GREEK AND ROMAN. C. 175 B.C.—140 A.D.

WARRIORS. NORTH CORNER OF WEST PEDIMENT, TEMPLE OF AIGINA
GLYPTOTHEK, MUNICH

490—480 B.C.

ATLAS BRINGS THE APPLES OF THE HESPERIDES TO HERACLES,
SHOULDERING THE WORLD WITH ATHENA
METOPE FROM TEMPLE OF ZEUS, OLYMPIA
MUSEUM, OLYMPIA

ABOUT 460 B.C.

(62)

"MOURNING" ATHENA

ACROPOLIS MUSEUM, ATHENS

ABOUT 470 B.C.

UNIVERSITY PRINTS, BOSTON

MAIDENS FROM EAST FRIEZE OF PARTHENON
LOUVRE, PARIS

442—438 B.C.

This continuous frieze, constructed under the direction of Phidias, is 523 feet $7^{1}/_{4}$ inches long. The undercutting at its deepest is $2^{1}/_{2}$ inches, yet at times five planes are shown. (63) is imbued with movement, while at the corners there is quiet (64)

(64)

UNIVERSITY PRINTS, BOSTON

SLAB FROM WEST FRIEZE OF PARTHENON
BRITISH MUSEUM, LONDON

442—438 B.C.

ATHLETE
LOUVRE, PARIS

Note the turn of the head and the treatment of the eyes and lips.

NIOBE AND YOUNGEST DAUGHTER
UFFIZI, FLORENCE

ABOUT 320—280 B.C., ROMAN COPY

HEAD OF HERACLES
ROMAN COPY OF A WORK BY
A FOLLOWER OF SCOPAS

(68)

APHRODITE OF MELOS
LOUVRE, PARIS

ABOUT 200 B.C.

(69)

BIRTH OF APHRODITE
PLASTIC LEKYTHOS
ATTIC — 4TH C. B.C.

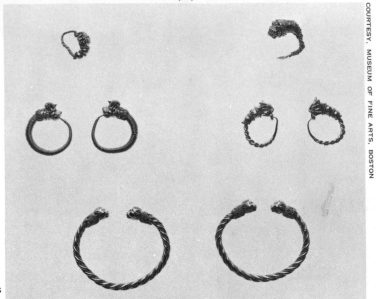

**GOLD EARRINGS
4TH C. B.C.**

**GOLD EARRING WITH NIKE
DRIVING HER CHARIOT
LATE 4TH C. B.C.**

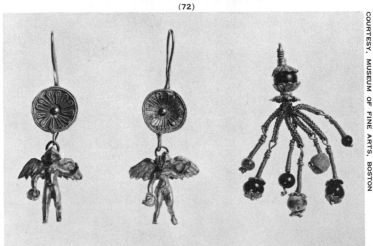

**GOLD EARRING
WITH DISC
AND PENDANT
4TH C. B.C.**

(73)

SOKRATES
CAPITOLINE MUSEUM, ROME

(74)

ΠΛΑΤΩΝ

PLATO
MUSEUM, BERLIN

POSSIBLY AFTER SILANION, c. 335—330 B.C., ROMAN COPY

PORTRAIT OF SOCRATES
GRAECO-ROMAN PERIOD

PORTRAIT OF HOMER
HELLENISTIC PERIOD

(77)

GREEK WAR DANCE
VATICAN, ROME

FIRST CENTURY B.C.

(78)

ALEXANDER SARCOPHAGUS
MUSEUM, ISTANBUL

320—300 B.C.

The Age of Rome

The Romans passed on Greek culture to us. They also made important contributions in their own right.

The grandfathers of early Roman culture were the Etruscans. Although strongly influenced by Greek artists, the Etruscans stamped their own individuality on their work. This fact is illustrated by 79 and by the cover of a sarcophagus (80) as well as by the scarab of a dead warrior with two winged figures (81) and another scarab of a warrior in the jaws of a dragon (82). The paintings in the rock-cut tombs (83) remind us that these tombs were "Houses of Eternity." Yet the Etruscans were also vigorously in love with life.

The Greek alphabet was passed on to the Romans by the Etruscans. They also taught their successors enduring masonry, the use of the arch and the practice of divination.

After the expulsion of the Etruscans in 509 B.C., the Roman Republic struggled for survival until the defeat of Carthage in 202 B.C. These three centuries of desperate conflict forged the Romans into a ruthless, practical, disciplined and materialistic people (84). They were taken captive by Greek culture but were never entirely at home in art or speculative thought. Their triumphs were in law, order, engineering and architecture.

The conquest of Greece, Macedon, and the Near East (200–133 B.C.) poured wealth, slaves and Hellenistic and Oriental influences into Rome and Italy. The society of "beggars and millionaires" which ensued, the failure to change institutions which had governed a small city-state to meet the administration of an empire and the ambitions of men such as Pompey led to the downfall of the Republic. You might note that the portrait-busts of Caesar (85) present the Roman genius in this field of sculpture. Pompey in late middle age is evidently pompous, sincere and fatuous while Caesar is ruthless and decisive.

The collapse of the Republic led not to chaos, but to the principate of Augustus. Then, for two centuries (31 B.C.–180 A.D.) the Romans, though political freedom was gone, enjoyed an almost unparalleled period of peace (*cf. Ara Pacis,* 86). The empire was extended to reach from Hadrian's wall in Britain to the frontiers of Mesopotamia and from the Rhine and the Danube to the Sahara Desert and the first cataract of the Nile. Under the emperor Trajan, it included Mesopotamia and Dacia (modern Rumania), but these were abandoned. Print 87 is a portrait of Trajan's sister, Marciana. Meanwhile trade and commerce flourished. The whole world, to quote a Greek rhetorician, became one inhabited city-state. There was one universal language—Latin—and one law, the Roman law. The triumph of the Roman genius was to weld diverse nationalities into a unit in which there was a common interest in the welfare of the whole. To a considerable extent there was also a uniformity of culture, as illustrated by the bust of Zeus from Lycia in Asia Minor (88).

It was in this period that Roman achievement flowered. In engineering and in monumental building they were unexcelled, except for the Ancient Egyptians, until modern times. The Pont du Gard has stood for almost 2000 years near Nimes in France. Most of the aqueduct it carries is underground. But the bridge itself is 880 feet long and 160 feet high. Another lasting engineering feat is the "Devil's Bridge" at Segovia in Spain (89). The remnants of approximately 47,000 miles of roads, and the remains of aqueducts, theaters, and amphitheaters attest to the Roman genius for construction in enduring stone and concrete. The fragments of cities where now is desert, such as the ruins of Timgad in North Africa and Baalbek in Syria remind us of the security and prosperity of the empire within the ring of the Roman legions.

All roads in those days led to the golden mile-post in the Forum of Rome. That Forum, once the thronged hub of an empire, now exhibits only fragments of its former grandeur. If we walk past that arch and leave the Forum, immediately to our right stands the Arch of Constantine, and to our left is the Colosseum. The Colosseum opened in 80 A.D., its might in its enduring structure, though it was used as a quarry for centuries. It seated about 50,000 spectators for the blood-drenched spectacles of the amphitheater.

If we leave the environs of the Forum and move to the left bank of the Tiber, at a point to the northwest of the Palatine Hill we come to a round temple. Like the Temple of Vesta this shrine preserves the earliest shape of the Roman temple, in imitation, probably, of the earliest huts of Italy.

To follow the Tiber northward into the former *Campus Martius* (Field of Mars) is to discover one of Rome's most magnificent monuments, the Pantheon. Built originally by Marcus Agrippa, chief minister of Augustus, and reconstructed by the Emperor Hadrian, this vast dome of concrete is 142 feet in both height and diameter. The obelisk in front of it was brought from Egypt by the Romans to stand in those days beside a temple of Isis.

Another example of the colossal in Roman architecture is the Baths of Caracalla, amid the ruins of which today, in summer, opera is presented. The Baths are just outside of Rome. Originally they covered 25 acres. Much of this space was taken up by colonnades, porticoes, exercise grounds, a race course and the like. The main building, of which the reconstructed central hall is shown had 1600 marble seats for bathers, libraries, rooms for games and lectures and so on. The floors were tesselated, the pillars were of colored and ornate marbles and the whole structure was replete with costly mosaics and works of art. Of these the Farnese Bull and the Farnese Hercules are today in the Naples Museum. Such baths were really clubs, although Romans normally took an elaborate bath each day. Even a small place such as Pompeii (20,000 inhabitants) boasted two public bathing establishments.

Pompeii, buried in 79 A.D. by an eruption of Mount Vesuvius, is one of our museums of Roman life. It proves to us the affluence of the empire in the first two centuries of our era. The houses are comparatively spacious and normally have a garden. In some of them priceless works of art were found, such as the sculpture of The Dancing Faun and the mosaic of the Battle of Issus.

The Romans were masters of mosaic painting. Pompeian houses also present us with murals done by unknown hands al fresco on wet plaster. The colors are vivid and brightened the rooms. Glass had also been invented, although it was mainly used for small pieces such as receptacles for unguents.

The discoveries at Pompeii, Herculaneum, Stabiae and elsewhere are evidence that in the first two centuries of our era an affluent society produced a prosperous and numerous middle class. These discoveries also suggest that the Romans were more appreciative of works of art than we. Their literature, even though it is often imitative of the Greeks, does present strong currents of Roman originality. Similarly, though much of their sculpture is copied from the Greeks and although some of it is tastelessly colossal under Hellenistic influence, in certain fields their work was excellent.

In these prints the emphasis is placed on the Roman achievement in engineering, monumental building, painting and sculpture. We must not forget, however, the Roman contribution in law. Apart from those countries of the modern world, such as France, in which Roman law lies at the basis of the legal system, Romans were the first to develop the "law of nations" and the idea of natural law. We should not forget either that the imperial structure they framed was so firm that it survived a century of military anarchy to re-emerge into a new type of empire under Diocletian and Constantine the Great. Even when the empire in the west fell, it became the foundation on which the Germanic kingdoms were built, while the eastern half survived until 1453 A.D. as Christendom's bulwark against the Turks. Above all, the Romans ensured that the Greek genius would be passed on to us.

A study of these prints brings it home to us that our cultural heritage reaches back to the Old Stone Age and received important contributions from the civilizations of the Near and Middle East. But the prints also make it clear that, while the genius of the Hebrews for religion still influences our life of today, the genius of the Greeks and Romans put into our way of life those elements which have distinguished it from any other civilization, past or present. Our instinct for freedom, our standards of beauty, our desire for law and order, our constant desire to know, these are qualities imprinted on the Western world by Greece and Rome.

RECLINING LEOPARD
STONE, ETRUSCAN

ETRUSCAN SARCOPHAGUS
DETAIL OF COVER

ETRUSCAN SCARAB — DEAD WARRIOR
AND TWO WINGED FIGURES
EARLY 5TH C.

ETRUSCAN SCARAB — WARRIOR IN
JAWS OF A DRAGON

WRESTLERS (FRESCO)
TOMB OF THE AUGURS, TARQUINIA

ETRUSCAN PAINTING. VI CENT. B.C.

TERRACOTTA PORTRAIT HEAD
LATE REPUBLICAN

JULIUS CAESAR: BUSTS IN GREEN BASALT AND MARBLE
MUSEUM, BERLIN; MUSEUM, NAPLES

ABOUT 50 B.C.; ABOUT 98—117 A.D.

PROCESSION, FROM THE ARA PACIS

TERME, ROME

13—9 B.C.

(87)

MARCIANA, SISTER OF TRAJAN

(88)

BUST OF ZEUS
SILVER PLAQUE FROM LYCIA
2ND C. A.D.

AQUEDUCT. SEGOVIA, SPAIN

ROMAN. I CENT. A.D. (?)

This "Devil's Bridge" at Segovia in Spain is 2,541 feet long and 132 feet high; its arches are built of unmortared stone.

INDEX OF PRINTS

1. Running Boar (Courtesy of University Prints, Boston)
2. Bull, Horses, and Stags (Courtesy of University Prints, Boston)
3. Wooly Mammoth (Painting) (Courtesy of University Prints, Boston)
4. Wooly Rhinoceros (Painting) (Courtesy of University Prints, Boston)
5. Cave Bear (Incised) (Courtesy of University Prints, Boston)
6. Pyramids from the South (Courtesy of University Prints, Boston)
7. Sphinx of Khafre and Pyramid of Khufu (Courtesy of University Prints, Boston)
8. Khafre (Courtesy of University Prints, Boston)
9. Khafre (Chefren) (Courtesy of University Prints, Boston)
10. Wooden Panels of Hesire (Courtesy of University Prints, Boston)
11. Painted Wall Decoration (Courtesy of University Prints, Boston)
12. Harvest Scene (Courtesy of University Prints, Boston)
13. Fattening Geese (Courtesy of University Prints, Boston)
14. Weighing of the Heart, From the Book of the Dead: Papyrus of Ani (Courtesy of University Prints, Boston)
15. Head of Thutmose III (Courtesy of University Prints, Boston)
16. Colossal Statues of Amenophis III, Thebes (Courtesy of University Prints, Boston)
17. Two Colossal Statues of Amenhotep IV (Ikhnaton) (Courtesy of University Prints, Boston)
18. Ikhnaton Worshipping the Sun (Courtesy of University Prints, Boston)
19. Head of Queen Nofretete (Courtesy of University Prints, Boston)
20. Relief on Back of Throne of King Tutankhamon: The King and Queen (Courtesy of University Prints, Boston)
21. General View of Rock-Cut Temples, Abu Simbel (Courtesy of University Prints, Boston)
22. Façade, Temple of Amon-Re, Abu Simbel (Courtesy of University Prints, Boston)
23. Guests at an Entertainment (Courtesy of University Prints, Boston)
24. Stele of Naram-Sin, from Susa (Courtesy of University Prints, Boston)
25. Stele of Hammurabi Receiving Law Code from the Sun God, From Susa (Courtesy of University Prints, Boston)
26. Black Obelisk of Shalmaneser III (Courtesy of University Prints, Boston)
27. Winged Mythological Figures of the Time of Sargon II (Courtesy of University Prints, Boston)
28. Man-Bull Capital (Detail) from Tripylon, Persepolis (Courtesy of University Prints, Boston)
29. Cup Bearer (Replica) (Courtesy of University Prints, Boston)
30. Fayence Snake Goddess (Replica) (Courtesy of University Prints, Boston)
31. Scene From a Bull Fight (Replica) (Courtesy of University Prints, Boston)
32. Ivory Bull Jumper (Courtesy of University Prints, Boston)
33. Head of a Bull (Courtesy of University Prints, Boston)

Selected Bibliography

*(Those titles marked with one asterisk are paperbacks,
with two, historical fiction.)*

A. Books for General Reference.

J. H. Breasted, *Ancient Times*, 2nd ed., Boston: Ginn & Co., 1944.

Cambridge Ancient History, 12 vols. Cambridge: Cambridge University Press, 1922–39.

A. A. van der Heyden and H. H. Scullard, *Atlas of the Classical World*, London: Nelson, 1960.

Osgood Hughes and C. H. W. Pullen, *The Making of Today's World*, revised by James H. McCrocklin, Rockleigh, N.J.: Allyn and Bacon, 1962.

Eilsworth Huntington, *Civilization and Climate*, 3rd ed., New Haven, Yale University Press, 1953.

T. B. Jones, *Ancient Civilization*, Chicago: Rand-McNally, 1960.

Ralph Linton, *The Tree of Culture,* New York: Knopf, 4th printing, 1961.

F. B. Marsh, *Modern Problems in the Ancient World*, Austin: University of Texas Press, 1943.

C. A. Robinson, Jr. *Ancient History*, New York: Macmillan, 1951.

Chester G. Starr, *A History of the Ancient World*, New York: Oxford University Press, 1965.

J. W. Swain, *The Ancient World*, 2 vols., New York: Harper, 1950.

Mary H. Swindler, *Ancient Painting*, New Haven: Yale University Press, 1929.

A. J. Toynbee, *A Study of History*, abridgment by D. C. Somervell, 2 vols., Oxford, 1948–57.

A. A. Trever, *The History of Ancient Civilization*, 2 vols. New York: Harcourt, Brace, 1950.

Thomas W. Wallbank, *Man's Story*, New York: Scott, 1961.

Sir Leonard Woolley, *Digging up the Past*, London: Penguin Books, 1940.*

B. Books about Primitive Man.

Robert Ardrey, *African Genesis*, London: Collins, 1961.

R. J. Braidwood, *Prehistoric Men*, Chicago: Chicago Natural History Museum, Popular Series, Anthropology, 1948.*

Georges Bataille, *Lascaux or the Birth of Art*, Lausanne: Skira, 1955.

Carleton S. Coon, *The Origin of Races*, New York: Knopf, 1962.

R. A. Dart, *Adventures with the Missing Link*, New York: Harper, 1959.

Jacquetta Hawkes and Leonard Woolley, *Prehistory and the Beginnings of Civilization*, London: Allen and Unwin, 1963.

W. Howells, *Mankind in the Making*, New York: Doubleday, 1959.

K. Kenyon, *Digging up Jericho*, New York: Praeger, 1957.

W. E. Le Gros Clark, *History of the Primates*, 6th Ed. London: British Museum (Natural History).*

Ashley Montagu, *Man, his first Million Years*, New York: Mentor Books, New American Library, 3rd printing, 1960.*

K. P. Oakley, *Man the Toolmaker*, 2nd Ed. London: British Museum, (Natural History) 1950.*

Marjorie and C. H. B. Quennell, *Everyday Life in the Old Stone Age*, London: B. T. Batsford, 1921.

Marjorie and C. H. B. Quennell, *Everyday Life in the New Stone, Bronze and Early Iron Ages*, London: B. T. Batsford, 1922.

Herbert Wendt, *I Looked for Adam*, translated from the German by James Cleugh, London: Weidenfeld and Nicholson, 1955.

F. E. Zeuner, *Dating the Past*, London: Methuen, 1950.

C. The Near East and Early Mesopotamia.

M. Burrows, *What Mean These Stones?*, New York: Living Age Books, 1957.*

Edward Chiera: *They Wrote on Clay*, Chicago: University of Chicago Press (Phoenix Books), 1955.*

V. G. Childe, *What Happened in History*, London: Penguin Books, 1954.*

V. G. Childe, *New Light on the Most Ancient Near East*, New York: Evergreen Books, 1957.*

H. Frankfort, *The Birth of Civilization in the Near East*, New York: Doubleday (Anchor Books) 1956.*

S. N. Kramer, *Sumerian Mythology*, Philadelphia: American Philosophical Association, 1944.

S. Piggott, *Prehistoric India*, Harmondsworth: Pelican Books,   *

Sir Leonard Woolley, *The Development of Sumerian Art*, London: Faber, 1935.

Sir Leonard Woolley, *Ur of the Chaldees*, London: Penguin Books, 1940.*

Sir Leonard Woolley, *Excavations at Ur*, London: Benn, 1954.

D. Egypt.

J. H. Breasted, *History of Egypt*, 2nd Ed. New York: Scribner, 1909.

J. Capart, *Egyptian Art*, translated by W. R. Dawson, London: Allen and Unwin, 1923.

L. Cottrell, *The Anvil of Civilization*, New York: New American Library (Mentor Books), 1957.*

L. Cottrell, *The Lost Pharaohs*, London: Pan Books, 3rd printing, 1956.*

E. S. Edwards, *The Pyramids of Egypt*, London: Penguin Books, 1947.*

S. R. K. Glanville (editor), *The Legacy of Egypt*, Oxford: Clarendon Press, 1942.

Margaret Murray, *The Splendour that was Egypt*, London: Sidgwick and Jackson, 1949.

J. H. Wilson, *The Culture of Ancient Egypt*, Chicago: University of Chicago Press (Phoenix Books) 1956.*

H. E. Winlock, *The Rise and Fall of the Middle Kingdom in Thebes*, New York: 1947.

E. Palestine, Phoenicia, Assyria and Persia.

Emmanual Anati, *Palestine before the Hebrews*, New York: Knopf.

J. A. Bewer, *The Literature of the Old Testament in its Historical Development*, rev. Ed., New York: Columbia University Press, 1933.

G. Contenau, *Everyday Life in Babylon and Assyria*, translated by K. R. and A. R. Maxwell-Hyslop, New York: St. Martins, 1954.

D. Diringer, *The Alphabet*, New York: Philosophical Library, 1947.*

O. R. Gurney, *The Hittites*, Harmondsworth: Pelican Books (A259), 1952.*

Werner Keller, *The Bible as History*, New York: Morrow, 1956.

W. O. Oesterley and T. H. Robinson, *A History of Israel*, 2 vols., Oxford: Clarendon Press, 1932.

A. T. Olmstead, *History of Assyria*, New York: Scribner, 1923.

A. T. Olmstead, *History of Palestine and Syria*, New York: Scribner, 1931.

A. T. Olmstead, *History of the Persian Empire*, New York: Scribner, 1948.
B. L. Ullman, *Ancient Writing and its Influence*, New York: Longmans-Green 1932.

F. Greece to the Hellenistic Age.

F. E. Adcock, *Greek and Macedonian Art of War*, Berkeley: University of California Paperback, 1957.*
W. R. Agard, *The Greek Mind*, Toronto: Van Nostrand (Anvil Books), 1957.*
A. Andrewes, *The Greek Tyrants*, London: Hutchinson, 1956.
Stringfellow Barr, *The Will of Zeus*, New York: Lippincott, 1961.
G. W. Botsford, *Hellenic History*, rev. by C. A. Robinson, Jr., New York: Macmillan, 1939.
G. M. Calhoun, *The Business Life of Ancient Athens*, Chicago, University of Chicago Press, 1926.
Cottrell, *The Bull of Minos*: London: Pan Books,   *
W. S. Davis, *A Day in Old Athens*, New York: Biblo and Tannen, 1956.
B. Farrington, *Greek Science*, Harmondsworth: Pelican Books, 1949.*
Ray C. Flickinger, *The Greek Theatre and its Drama*, 4th Ed., Chicago: University of Chicago Press, 1946.
W. S. Ferguson, *Greek Imperialism*, New York: Houghton, 1913.
E. J. Forsdyke, *Greece Before Homer*, London: Max Parrish, 1956.
E. N. Gardiner, *Athletics in the Ancient World*, Oxford: Oxford University Press, 1930.
Moses Hadas, *A History of Greek Literature*, New York: Columbia University Press, 1950.
H. D. F. Kitto, *The Greeks*, Harmondsworth: Pelican Books, 1951.*
H. D. F. Kitto, *Greek Tragedy*, New York: Doubleday, Anchor Books, 1954.*
Sir Richard Livingston, *The Greek Genius*, 2nd Ed. London: 1915.
P. L. MacKendrick and H. M. Howe, Classics in Translation, Vol. I, *Greek Literature*, Madison: University of Wisconsin Press, 1952.
Naomi Mitchison, *Black Sparta*, London: Cape, 1931.**
Naomi Mitchison, *Cloud Cuckoo Land*: London.**
G. Mylonas, *Ancient Mycenae*, Princeton: Princeton, University Press, 1957.
M. P. Nilsson, *Homer and Mycenae*, London: Methuen, 1933.
J. D. S. Pendlebury, *The Archaeology of Crete*, London: Methuen, 1939.
J. D. S. Pendlebury, *A Handbook to the Palace of Minos at Cnossos*, London: Max Parrish, 1954.
Marjorie and C. H. B. Quennell, *Everyday Things in Ancient Greece*, rev. ed. London: B. T. Batsford, 1957.
Marie Renault: *The King Must Die*, New York: Pantheon, 1958.**
G. M. Richter, *The Sculpture and Sculptors of the Greeks*, New Haven: Yale University Press, 1950.
C. Seltman: *Women in Antiquity*, London: Pan Books.*
M. H. Swindler, *Ancient Painting*, New Haven: Yale University Press, 1929.
A. E. Taylor, *Socrates*, New York: Doubleday, Anchor Books, 1953.*
T. B. L. Webster, *From Mycenae to Homer*, New York: Barnes and Noble, 1959.
L. Whibley, *Companion to Greek Studies*, 3rd Ed. rev., Cambridge: Cambridge University Press, 1916.
A. G. Woodhead, *The Greeks in the West*, London: Thames and Hudson, 1962.
E. Zeller, *Outlines of the History of Greek Philosophy*, New York: Meridian Books, 1955.*

A. E. Zimmern, *The Greek Commonwealth*, 5th ed. rev. Oxford: Oxford University Press, 1931.

G. Hellenistic Greece.

M. Bieber, *The Sculpture of the Hellenistic Age*, New York: Columbia University Press, 1955.

J. B. Bury, (editor), *The Hellenistic Age*, London: Cambridge, 1923.

Max Cary, *The Legacy of Alexander*: A History of the Greek World from 323 to 146 B.C., London: Methuen, 1932.

L. Sprague De Camp, *An Elephant for Aristotle*, New York: Doubleday, 1958.**

A. Körte, *Hellenistic Poetry*, Translated by J. Hammer and Moses Hadas, New York: Knopf, 1929.

J. H. Macurdy, *Hellenistic Queens*, Baltimore: John Hopkins University Press, 1932.

C. A. Robinson, *Alexander the Great*, New York: Dutton, 1947.

W. W. Tarn and G. T. Griffith, *Hellenistic Civilization*, 3rd ed. rev., London: Edward Arnold, 1959; also New York, Meridian Books, 1961.*

H. Rome and Italy to the End of the Roman Republic.

F. F. Abbott, *History and Description of Roman Political Institutions*, New York: Ginn, 1911.

F. E. Adcock, *The Roman Art of War Under the Republic*, New York: Barnes and Noble, 1960.

F. Altheim, *A History of Roman Religion*, New York: Dutton, 1938.

C. Bailey, *The Legacy of Rome*, London: Milford, 1923.

C. Bailey, *Phases in the Religion of Ancient Rome*, Berkeley: University of California Press, 1932.

G. P. Baker, *Hannibal*, New York: Dodd-Mead, 1936.

R. H. Barrow, *The Romans*, Harmondsworth: Pelican Books, 1949.*

Phyllis Bentley, *Freedom Farewell*, Toronto: Macmillan, 1936.**

S. F. Bonner, Education of a Roman, Liverpool: 1950.

John Buchan, *Julius Caesar*, London: Peter Davies, 1932.

Max Cary, *A History of Rome*, London: Methuen, 1954.

J. W. Duff, *A Literary History of Rome*, 2 vols. London: Benn: 1927.

A. L. Duggan, *Founding Fathers*, London: Faber and Faber, 1959.**

Jerome Carcopino, *Daily Life in Ancient Rome*, London: Penguin Books, 1956.*

F. R. Cowell, *Cicero and the Roman Republic*, Harmondsworth: Pelican Books, 1956.*

W. S. Davis, *A Day in old Rome*, New York: Biblo and Tannen, 1959.

W. Warde Fowler, *The Roman Festivals of the Period of the Republic*, London: Macmillan, 1908.

W. Warde Fowler, *Rome*, 2nd ed. rev. by M. P. Charlesworth, New York: 1947.

H. Grose-Hodge, *Roman Panorama*, Cambridge: Cambridge University Press, 1946.

Moses Hadas, *History of Roman Literature*, New York: Columbia University Press, 1952.

Edith Hamilton, *The Roman Way*, New York: W. W. Norton, 1932.

W. G. Hardy, *The City of Libertines*, Toronto: McClelland and Stewart, 1957.**

F. M. Hechelheim and C. A. Yeo, *A History of the Roman People*, Englewood Cliffs: Prentice-Hall, 1962.

H. Hill, *The Roman Middle Class in the Republican Period*, New York: Macmillan, 1952.

L. Homo, *Primitive Italy and the Beginnings of Roman Imperialism*, Translated by V. G. Childe, New York: Knopf, 1926.

H. S. Jones, *Companion to Roman History*, Oxford: Oxford University Press: 1912.

P. L. MacKendrick, *The Roman Mind at Work* (selections in translation from Roman authors), Toronto: Van Nostrand (Anvil Books), 1958.*

P. L. MacKendrick and H. M. Howe, *Classics in Translation*, vol. II, Madison: University of Wisconsin, 1952.

F. B. Marsh, *A History of the Roman World from 146 to 30 B.C.,* London: Methuen, 1935.

Naomi Mitchison, *The Conquered*, New York: Harcourt, Brace, 1923.**

Massimo Pallotino, *Etruscan Painting*, Lausanne: 1952.

Massimo Pallotino, *The Etruscans*, London: Penguin Books, 1955.*

G. M. A. Richter, *Roman Portraits*, New York: Metropolitan Museum of Art, 1948.

M. I. Rostovtzeff. *Rome*, London: Oxford University Press, 1960.*

Grant Showerman, *Rome and the Romans*, New York: Macmillan, 1931.

Sir John E. Sandys, *Companion to Latin Studies*, Cambridge: University of Cambridge Press, 1921.

W. A. Smith, *Ancient Education*, New York: Philosophical Library, 1956.

G. Walter, *Caesar*, translated by Emma Crauford, New York: Scribner, 1952.

I. The Roman Empire.

R. H. Barrow, *Slavery in the Roman Empire*, London: 1928.

John Buchan, *Augustus*, Boston: Houghton, Mifflin, 1937.

M. P. Charlesworth, *Trade Routes and Commerce of the Roman Empire*, Cambridge: Cambridge University Press, 1926.

M. P. Charlesworth, *The Roman Empire*, Oxford: Oxford University Press, 1951.

R. G. Collingwood and N. Myers, *Roman Britain*, New York: Oxford University Press, 1937.

S. Dill, *Roman Society from Nero to Marcus Aurelius*, New York: Meridian Books, 1956.*

S. Dill, *Roman Society in the Last Century of the Roman Empire*, New York: Meridian Books, 1958.*

T. Frank, *An Economic History of Rome*, 2nd ed. Baltimore: John Hopkins Press, 1940.

T. R. Glover, *The Conflict of Religions in the Early Roman Empire*, 10th ed. New York and London: Charles Scribner's Sons, 1923.

Ralph Graves, *The Lost Eagles*, New York: Knopf, 1955.**

W. S. Halliday, *The Pagan Background of Early Christianity*, Liverpool: University of Liverpool Press, 1925.

G. Highet, *Poets in a Landscape*, New York: Knopf, 1957.

S. Katz, *The Decline of Rome and the Rise of Mediaeval Europe*, Ithaca, N.Y.: Cornell University Press, 1955.

P. Louis, *Ancient Rome at Work*, translated by E. B. F. Waring, New York: 1927.

Amedeo Maiuri, *Pompeii*, 5th ed. Rome: La libreria dello stato, 1949.*

Amedeo Maiuri, *Roman Painting*, Lausanne: Skira, 1953.

Naomi Mitchison, *When the Bough Breaks*, London: Cape, 1924.**

A. M. D. Parker, *The Roman Legions*, 2nd ed. New York: Oxford University Press, 1958.

I. A. Richmond, *Roman Britain*, Harmondsworth: Pelican Books, 1955.*

M. I. Rostovskeff, *The Social and Economic History of the Roman Empire*, 4th ed. rev. by P. M. Fraser. New York: Oxford University Press, 1959.

E. T. Salmon, *A History of the Roman World from 30 B.C. to 138 A.D.* 3rd ed. London: Methuen, 1957.

F. W. Walbank, *The Decline of the Roman Empire in the West*, London: Cobbett Press, 1946.*

Marguerite Yourcenar, *Memoirs of Hadrian*, translated from the French by Grace Frick in collaboration with the author, London: Secker and Warburg, 1955.* *

INDEX